CRIME, JUSTICE,
AND SOCIETY

CRIME, JUSTICE, AND SOCIETY

SECOND EDITION

An Introduction to Criminology

Ronald J. Berger
Marvin D. Free Jr.
Patricia Searles

LYNNE
RIENNER
PUBLISHERS

BOULDER
LONDON

Published in the United States of America in 2005 by
Lynne Rienner Publishers, Inc.
1800 30th Street, Boulder, Colorado 80301
www.rienner.com

and in the United Kingdom by
Lynne Rienner Publishers, Inc.
3 Henrietta Street, Covent Garden, London WC2E 8LU

Library of Congress Cataloging-in-Publication Data
Berger, Ronald J.
  Crime, justice, and society : an introduction to criminology / Ronald
J. Berger, Marvin D. Free, Jr., and Patricia Searles.—2nd ed.
    p.   cm.
  Includes bibliographical references and index.
  ISBN 1-58826-258-8 (pbk. : alk. paper)
    1. Crime—Sociological aspects—United States.   2. Criminal
behavior—United States.   3. Criminal justice, Administration of—United
States.   I. Free, Marvin D.   II. Searles, Patricia.   III. Title.
  HV6789.B465   2004
  364.973—dc22
                                                              2004007791

British Cataloguing in Publication Data
A Cataloguing in Publication record for this book
is available from the British Library.

Photos on pages 2, 31, 47, 290, 425, and 479 © Brand X Pictures; photos on
pages 120, 163, 174, 211, 326, 352, 372, 438, 469, and 487 © PhotoDisc;
photos on pages 86, 237, 250, and 300 © Stockbyte.

Printed and bound in the United States of America

∞   The paper used in this publication meets the requirements
     of the American National Standard for Permanence of
     Paper for Printed Library Materials Z39.48-1984.

5   4   3   2   1

Contents

Tables and Figures

■ Tables

■ Figures

Preface

Most criminology textbooks are rather similar in their organization and content. They have an encyclopedic quality and lack a unified storyline or central theme. As sociologists, we've often been disappointed with these texts because the sociological perspective tends to get lost in all the detail. In contrast, *Crime, Justice, and Society* is explicitly *sociological* in orientation and is designed to help students cultivate a sociological imagination that can guide their thinking about crime and criminal justice. As C. Wright Mills (1959) noted, a sociological imagination allows us to see how personal or private troubles are related to public issues. It helps us understand the social forces that shape our lives, that define and constrain our choices and opportunities, our sense of the possible, our very sense of ourselves. A sociological imagination helps us recognize how personal biographies intersect with both broader historical and social conditions and the relationships we have with one another.

In developing this book we have been inspired by the innovative thinking about crime that has emerged from what has been loosely described as critical criminology. Although we do not think it is necessary to expose students to all the nuances of critical social theory and political thought, we do believe that sophisticated sociological thinking about crime requires us to step outside of conventional understandings and analyze issues from a critical standpoint.

A critical perspective places questions of social inequality and power at the center of criminological inquiry. It views *class, race/ethnicity,* and *gender* as pivotal organizing principles of social life—as prisms through which we come to know ourselves and our social world and as central mechanisms by which social relationships are patterned. Our class background, for example, affects not only our income and wealth but our entire experience of life—from the neighborhood we grow up in and the quality of schools we attend to our occupational choices and career paths. Class affects our incentives and disincentives to engage in criminal behavior, as well as the resources we have for committing certain types of crime and avoiding official sanctions for our actions.

Race and ethnicity also define our position in society, as social resources and privileges are unequally distributed on the basis of these characteristics. Racial and ethnic status, like class, creates incentives and disincentives for crime and affects our experiences with the criminal justice system. Gender, too, reflects social relations of inequality and power, and gender norms and expectations influence patterns of criminality and victimization. Males, for instance, commit the overwhelming majority of crimes, particularly crimes of violence, and they are the primary victims of crime by men. Women, on the other hand, disproportionately experience *sexual* victimization, especially by males they know.

■ Organization of the Book

Crime, Justice, and Society is appropriate for use as an undergraduate text in criminology courses taught in both sociology and criminal justice programs. It offers instructors and students an approach that is interesting and innovative yet organized to fit into conventional course formats.

Given our desire to avoid an encyclopedic style, we do not cover every theory that has ever been formulated, but examine the perspectives that we consider most central to criminology. We also avoid the tendency to proliferate chapter after chapter, cataloging every type of crime imaginable. Rather, we present a comprehensive range of topics in a way that facilitates critical and analytical thinking and helps students develop their sociological imaginations.

In this second edition of the book, we have revised and updated material to reflect the changing economic and political realities of the new millennium, from the multibillion-dollar scandals of Enron and other corrupt corporations to the problem of terrorism and the U.S. government's response to it in the aftermath of September 11, 2001. We have also added a new chapter on conflict theory and critical criminology that better integrates the perspectives associated with this line of criminological thought.

Chapter 1, "Perspectives on the Problem of Crime," begins the book by encouraging students to reflect on popular media and political constructions that may have influenced their own thinking about crime. Here we review, among other things, constructionist accounts of the gang, drug, and serial-murder problems. We then make the case for the value of a sociological perspective and introduce students to the central themes of the book.

Part 1: Methods and Theories, opens with Chapter 2, "Crime Data and Methods of Research," where we critically examine official and unofficial sources of quantitative crime data. We also look at other methodological approaches, including experimental and evaluation research, observational methods, and historical and comparative criminology. In Chapters 3, 4, and 5—"Individualistic Explanations of Criminal Behavior," "Sociological Explanations of Criminal Behavior," and "Conflict Theory and Critical Criminology"—we avoid the tediousness that is typical of theory chapters and make the material more relevant by interweaving the voices of offenders and by highlighting the practical applications of various theoretical perspectives.

Part 2: Patterns of Criminality and Victimization, begins with Chapter 6, "Corporate and Organized Crime," where we address the crimes of the powerful and highlight the interconnections between legal and illegal enterprise. Here we consider the historical development and contemporary manifestations of corporate law violation, the link between corporate and organized crime, and the structure of organized crime networks.

Chapter 7, "Street Crime," focuses on the class and racial/ethnic dimensions of conventional crimes of violence, crimes against property, drug crimes, gangs, and the like. We illuminate the economic context of urban street crime and examine the questions of criminal justice bias and differential involvement by race and ethnicity. We also discuss the problem of law-violating youth groups and gangs in both urban and suburban communities.

While issues of gender are integrated throughout the book, we believe that the experiences of women and girls warrant special attention. In Chapter 8, "Gender and Crime," we explore how social constructions of femininity and masculinity influence the nature of both female and male criminality. Focusing especially on female offenders, we consider the question of continuity versus change in traditional gender patterns of crime and discuss how offenders "do gender" in urban gangs, street robbery, the drug trade, prostitution, and murder. We also examine the ongoing controversy regarding the criminalization of women as "fetal abusers."

Chapter 9, "Sexual Violence," opens with a discussion of sexual violence as a continuum of violations ranging from nonviolent sexual intimidation to acts of severe brutality. We take a critical look at the role that pornography plays in promoting a cultural climate that sanctions and promotes such violence, and we explore in detail the problems of rape and sexual assault, child sexual abuse, and the battering of women. Although we present two separate chapters that focus on females, we recognize that women and girls do not always fit neatly into the categories of offender *or* victim/survivor. Our analysis thus reflects and elucidates these blurred boundaries.

Part 2 concludes with Chapter 10, "Political and Governmental Crime," where we cover often-neglected criminological topics such as collective violence, civil disobedience, terrorism, and hate crimes. We also discuss, among other subjects, the major presidential scandals from Watergate to the controversial George W. Bush administration.

Part 3: Criminal Justice and the Search for Solutions, includes two chapters that critically analyze the operation of the criminal justice system in the United States: Chapter 11, "The Police and the Courts," and Chapter 12, "Punishment and Prisons." Chapter 13, "Community Corrections and Alternative Solutions," examines community alternatives to prison and various preventative measures that chart a more progressive course for dealing with the problem of crime.

*   *   *

We would like to thank Lynne Rienner for her helpful suggestions, as well as Lesli Athanasoulis, Lisa Tulchin, Jason Cook, and the rest of the staff at Lynne Rienner Publishers for their support and assistance with this project.

CRIME, JUSTICE, AND SOCIETY

1

Perspectives on the Problem of Crime

One warm spring afternoon, Susan Resnick was riding her bike along the Charles River. Susan, a new arrival in Boston, was delighted to be sharing this glorious day with the many people pushing baby carriages, roller-blading, and sunning themselves. But as she wove along the bike path, Susan began to feel uncomfortable. A teenage boy was riding his bike suspiciously close to hers. She decided to veer off in a different direction, just to be safe, hoping he'd stay on his original path. The next thing Susan heard, however, was the boy barking out an order: "Get off the bike and you won't get hurt!" He had followed her, waiting for the right time to strike. Having reached a spot without a soul nearby, the teen slammed his bike into Susan's, forcing her off the path. Susan screamed loudly for help, somehow managing to remain upright, pedaling with all her might. Although no one responded to her cries of distress, they succeeded in scaring the boy away. "I escaped physically unharmed," Susan says, "but I may never be the same again. Because it happened in the middle of the afternoon in a crowded public place, I realize that I'm not safe anywhere in the city. Suddenly I'm jumpy whenever I'm traveling alone. My stomach flips when I hear footsteps behind me as I walk to work; my entire body tenses when I have to ride the elevator in my apartment building with a strange man" (Resnick 1993:64).

A few weeks later, Susan was again riding along the river when suddenly she heard brakes squeaking behind her. "Before I even turned my head," she recalls, "my heart was beating hard and panic was coursing through my veins." She raced ahead, only to realize that it was just another biker who had braked to avoid colliding with her: "I pulled to the grass and froze for a second. My arms and legs went from shaking to numb. . . . I wondered how many years the fright had taken off my life" (p. 65).

As this brief account poignantly illustrates, fear of crime can grip a

victim—take hold, hang on, become part of the fabric of life, even when one has managed to escape harm's way. And the more violent or traumatic the crime, the easier it is for us to understand the suffering of the survivors, the turmoil for their families.

Fear of crime, however, is a complex issue. It grows out of more than just firsthand experience. Studies find that being victimized by crime, or knowing someone who has been victimized, are not necessarily related to fear of crime or to attitudes about the punishment of criminals (Barkan 2001; Warr 2000). Survey research, for example, indicates that the elderly tend to be more fearful of crime than the young, even though they are less likely to be victims. Women are more likely than men to experience sexual assault and domestic violence, yet they express greater fear of other crimes as well, in spite of being less likely than men to be victims of crime overall (Ferraro 1996; Madriz 1997). African American and inner-city residents experience higher rates of victimization than white, middle-class suburbanites, and they are more fearful. But they are also more distrustful of the criminal justice system, less supportive of strictly punitive crime control policies, and more supportive of rehabilitative programs for offenders (Browning & Cao 1992; Hagan & Albonetti 1982; McCorkle 1993). Moreover, a large portion of the public believes that crime in their community has been rising, even at times when it has actually been on the decline (Kappeler et al. 2000; Roberts & Stalans 2000).

We think it is important, therefore, to begin our inquiry into the problem of crime by examining the roots of our attitudes and opinions. Our view of reality is drawn not just from personal experience but also from representations of events that we have not experienced directly. Research indicates that the mass media, politicians, and law enforcement officials are major sources of our knowledge about crime. They play a crucial role in generating, shaping, and reinforcing public opinion about crime and mobilizing support for particular crime control policies. They provide us with a taken-for-granted conceptual framework that helps us identify particular issues as crime-related, interpret the causes of criminal behaviors, and apply ready-made solutions (Beckett 1994; Kappeler et al. 2000; Surette 1998).

Unfortunately, the picture we get from these sources of information is in many ways misleading. Take, for instance, the simplistic distinction we often make between "good guys" and "bad guys," between the forces of good and the forces of evil. Typically we think of criminals as persons who are fundamentally different from the rest of us. Few of us, however, are paragons of virtue. Most of us have committed some crime for which we could have been incarcerated (Bohm 1986; Poveda 1994b). How many of us have consumed alcohol illegally, driven under the influence, or taken illegal drugs? How many of us have engaged in vandalism or shoplifting? How many have stolen something of value from an employer? Perhaps we did not think that what we did was serious or even criminal. But ask our employers about this and they'll likely disagree, for they lose more money annually from the "good guys"—us—than they do from theft by nonemployees. In his book *The Rich Get Richer and the Poor Get Prison,* Jeffrey Reiman (2004) estimates that employee embezzlement and pilferage cost businesses nearly $34 billion annually. Other criminologists suggest that this figure may be considerably higher (Barkan 2001). The costs of "white-collar" offenses more generally, including fraud and illegal price-fixing by corporations and other businesses, exceed $250 billion annually (Rosoff et al. 2002). Add to these costs the vast array of physical injuries, illnesses, and deaths caused by illegal business activity (through dangerous work conditions, defective consumer products, and environmental pollution), and our simplistic assumptions about crime and criminals quickly break down (see Chapter 6).

■ Media Constructions of Crime and Crime Fighting

The News and Entertainment Media

The mass media is an institutionalized system of communication that conveys messages to audiences through print and technology. The media are not simply neutral, unobtrusive observers providing news and entertainment. Their influence is pervasive. On average, for example, Americans watch in excess of four hours of television each day. About 20 to 25 percent of prime-time programming deals directly with crime and crime fighting, and about 70 percent of prime-time programs (crime and noncrime) depict incidents of violence. Most people report relying on the news media to learn about crime and criminals, and readers of newspapers are more likely to read crime items than any other subject matter (Surette 1998).

In the late 1980s a new genre of television crime programming appeared on the scene: the tabloid-style **infotainment**[*] shows such as *Cops, America's Most Wanted,* and *Unsolved Mysteries.* These programs present "true crime" stories (sometimes in documentary-style or as drama-tized reenactments) that blur the traditional distinction between news and entertainment. They promote a "shared disgust for anyone alleged to be a criminal" and serve to heighten our fear by suggesting that crime is all-per-vasive (Bond-Maupin 1998:33; Fishman & Cavender 1998).

Today, in all sources of news reporting, the distinction between news and entertainment is becoming less clear. Television news emphasizes the details of individual crimes, packaged in thirty- to sixty-second spots, and rarely discusses crime as a social issue. There is a heavy reliance on law enforcement officials as convenient sources of information, and deadlines leave little time for independent investigation or follow-up. The novelty or sensational quality of the crime increases its news value, although through repetition the extraordinary becomes ordinary. In both television news and entertainment, the crimes portrayed are the ones less likely to occur in real life: violent crimes are overrepresented, while property crimes and white-collar crimes are underrepresented (Chermak 1994; Sanchez Jankowitz 1991; Surette 1998; Zatz 1987).

Another problem with TV news and entertainment is the disproportion-ate representation of African Americans as criminals, especially as violent offenders (Eschholz 2003). In the infotainment programs, for instance, the majority of blacks are portrayed as "bad guys" while the majority of whites are portrayed as "good guys" (Oliver 1994). One study found that televi-sion news stories about drugs depicted blacks 50 percent of the time and whites 32 percent of the time (Reed 1991), even though surveys indicate that blacks constitute about 15 percent of illegal drug users in the United States while whites constitute about 75 percent (Chambliss 1995).

The criminal trial of O.J. Simpson, dubbed the trial of the century, highlighted the issue of race in media representations of crime. The Simpson trial was the most well-known case of high-profile media trials or "court news as miniseries" (Surette 1998:72). Such cases include elements of "human interest laced with mystery, sex, bizarre circumstances, and

---

[*] Key terms are indicated in boldface the first time they appear in the book.

famous or powerful people" (p. 74). The Simpson saga was especially appealing for these reasons. It was not just a case involving violence; it was a double murder—of Simpson's ex-wife Nicole Brown and her friend Ronald Goldman. Insofar as Simpson claimed to be innocent, it was a "whodunnit" murder mystery as well. Then there was the infamous slow-speed car chase, with onlookers cheering Simpson on, something "even Hollywood would have had trouble dreaming up" (Chancer 1996:82). There was the specter of domestic violence, of Simpson's battery and voyeuristic stalking of Nicole (see Chapter 9). There was, of course, Simpson's status as a sports icon and Hollywood celebrity. He and Nicole were among the "beautiful people" who enjoyed the lifestyle of the rich and

---

Further Exploration

Box 1.1   Race and Perceptions of the O.J. Simpson Case

On October 3, 1995, an estimated 100 million people worldwide witnessed the O.J. Simpson jury verdict, announced live on television or radio (Dershowitz 1996). This moment ranks with the 1963 assassination of John F. Kennedy and the 1986 *Challenger* space shuttle disaster as moments in history when people remember exactly where they were when the news broke. However, Jeffrey Toobin, whose July 1994 article in the *New Yorker* disclosed the Simpson defense team's intent to paint Mark Fuhrman as a racist cop, believes that years from now one of the main reasons "anyone will care about this case . . . is because of what it illuminates about race in America" (quoted in Dershowitz 1996:118).

Many people remember the media images of black college students cheering jubilantly over the "not guilty" verdict, while whites stood stunned in disbelief. Indeed there was a racial divide over the case (Elias & Schatzman 1996). Early on, national polls indicated that 60 percent of blacks thought that Simpson was framed or set up by the police (*Newsweek,* August 1, 1994). Only 23 percent of whites agreed. Just following the jury verdict, 66 percent of blacks but only 26 percent of whites believed that Simpson had probably *not* committed the murders; and 85 percent of blacks but only 32 percent of whites agreed with the "not guilty" verdict (*Newsweek,* October 16, 1995).

These poll numbers reflect attitudes that stem from the different experiences blacks and whites have had in the United States, experiences that have not surprisingly led African Americans to be more distrustful of the criminal justice system, experiences that we will explore more fully in this book. It is important to point out, however, that since there are more whites in the population than blacks, the number of whites who agree with the verdict or who think Simpson did not commit the murders may actually be larger than the number of blacks who hold these sentiments (Russell 1998).

famous. Accounts of their sexual exploits appealed to the public's prurient interest. And there was race: not just because of Mark Fuhrman, the Los Angeles police detective whose racist comments made him vulnerable to allegations that he planted evidence against Simpson, but also because of interracial sex and marriage, which Earl Hutchinson describes as "the last taboo for whites and blacks" in the United States (1996:4). According to Hutchinson, Simpson "became an instant metaphor and warning . . . of the menace posed by the abusive and sexually plundering black male" (p. 7).

Indeed, the image of the black man preying upon the white woman has been one of the most enduring myths of American society, although most rapes are in fact *intraracial,* committed against persons of the same race (Wriggens 1995). In the 1915 epic film *Birth of a Nation,* director D. W. Griffith portrayed African American men as either docile "faithful souls" or "brutal bucks" (Bogle 1994). This film, one of the most influential of the early twentieth century, conveyed an insidious stereotype: "Bucks are always big, baadddd niggers, over-sexed and savage, violent and frenzied as they lust for white flesh" (p. 13).

To those who believe Simpson is guilty, the criminal trial epitomized the failures of the criminal justice system in the United States, a common theme in crime news and entertainment. While the media tend to portray the police more favorably than the courts and corrections system, the message often conveyed is one of a criminal justice system unable to apprehend, convict, and punish criminals (Surette 1998).

The heroes in crime entertainment—literature, television, and motion picture films—are the crime fighters working either within the system or outside of it. Take, for example, the genre of the private eye or private detective, popularized originally in nineteenth-century print media. Here the "good guy" oddly resembles the criminals he is pursuing—a highly individualistic loner who may be on the side of justice, but who is not bound by the conventional rules of society. And the heroics of fictional super crime fighters like Batman, Superman, Spiderman, and the Lone Ranger also underscore the failures of the official legal order (Newman 1993; Surette 1998).

Dirty Harry, the 1971 film that spawned several sequels, best illustrates the popular media image of the crime fighter. Harry, who was played by (now octogenarian) film star Clint Eastwood, is a maverick police officer who feels little obligation to abide by "due process" formalities. Harry is a man of action who has no patience for the Bill of Rights, the constitutionally protected liberties that he holds responsible for allowing scores of dangerous criminals to go free. In the "Dirty Harry" films, the qualities that made Eastwood a Hollywood icon—"the quiet one with the painfully bottled-up capacity for violence"—break loose, as Harry challenges criminals to resist and "make my day" (Ebert 1986:193). The Andy Sipowitz character in the *NYPD Blue* television series exhibits a similar mentality, always on the edge, ready to bust a criminal upside his face.

On the other side of the battle of good against evil, the media passion for the sensational and bizarre is best exemplified by the proliferation of the increasingly graphic R-rated "slasher" movies such as *Texas Chainsaw Massacre, Child's Play, I Saw What You Did Last Summer, Scream,* and the popular series of *Halloween* and *Friday the 13th* films, including the recent movie *Jason vs. Freddy.* In this genre, "psychotic supermales . . . [who] possess an evil, cunning intelligence, and superior strength, endurance, and stealth" engage in acts of "twisted, lustful revenge or random . . . meaningless violence" (Surette 1998:41). Jason, Freddy, and the other killers in these films often become mythic figures of sorts, evoking amusement if not admiration in young viewers. And "once you kill the monster, he is never really dead" (Ebert 1986:126). Like the "Energizer bunny," he keeps coming back for more and more (sequels).

In her book *The Age of Sex Crime,* Jane Caputi (1987) argues that the targeting of female victims is a common theme in this genre of films and that the killers believe their victims deserve punishment for their assertiveness or display of sexuality. This genre has been dubbed **gorenography** due to its tendency to eroticize violence against women, juxtaposing images of nudity or sex with violence. These films effectively utilize the "point of view shot," whereby the camera "is used to encourage audience identification with the sex murderer" (p. 84). Take *Halloween,* for instance:

> The sex killer is first introduced as a five-year-old boy who is, nevertheless, man enough to slaughter his teenage sister for having sex with her boyfriend while their parents are out. It is Halloween night and the boy is wearing a clown costume and mask. The murder scene is shot through the mask; members of the audience see the action through two eyeholes, as if they were behind the mask too. (p. 84)

Experimental media research suggests that repeated exposure to such films can desensitize viewers to the problem of violence against women (Donnerstein et al. 1987; Strasburger & Wilson 2002; see Chapter 2).

Since the mid-1980s, pathological female murderers or "deadly dolls" have also been getting into the act in movies like *Fatal Attraction, Basic Instinct, The Hand That Rocks the Cradle,* and *Single White Female* (Holmlund 1994). In these films, the spectacle of protracted, bloody murders often takes a back seat to the erotic aura and dangerously alluring quality of the sensual female killer, "white, lithe and lovely" (p. 128). There is a decidedly antifeminist theme in this genre, as the protagonist is portrayed as obsessively driven to "take what she wants at any cost" (Faith 1993:265). The message that is often "embedded within the narrative is that a woman without a home and family is desperate and deviant" (Thompson 1998:69).

In the genre of organized crime films like *Goodfellas* and the *Godfather* trilogy, as well as *The Sopranos* television series, the glamorization of violence is reserved for those who employ it for economic ends. The hothead is portrayed negatively, as prone to irrational violent outbursts that disrupt the orderly business of crime. Better to carefully plan and choose "the appropriate level and timing of violence" so as to maximize its effect on one's enemies. Yet violence, when juxtaposed with scenes of camaraderie or the family dinner table, is made to seem like a positive force and "a natural part of everyday life" (Newman 1998:43).

The world of the ruthless, even predatory, white-collar businessman or professional has also found its way into the media through movies like *Wall Street, A Civil Action, Erin Brokovich, The Insider,* and *Enemy of the State,* and films based on John Grisham novels. It is clear, however, that media images of white-collar criminals are not as pervasive as the more common images of "street criminals" from the lower (especially minority) strata of society, nor have they "produced a fundamental change in popular understandings of crime" (Boyd 1997; Nichols 1999:61).

▓ *Crime Waves and Moral Panics*

The concept of a **crime wave** is used by criminologists to refer to a sudden rise (and eventual fall) of a particular type of crime. Crime waves may or may not be related to actual fluctuations in criminal behavior. Typically, media-reported crime waves are not. In a classic study of crime waves, Mark Fishman (1978) examined a seven-week media-reported crime wave in New York City in 1976 involving an alleged surge in what was labeled "crimes against the elderly." Police statistics, however, did not indicate any particular singling out of the elderly. Crimes increased for people of *all ages* during this period; for some crimes the increases were greater for the elderly and for some they were not. While the media began their coverage of crimes against the elderly with reports of several gruesome murders, and 28 percent of the news stories were about homicides, homicides actually made up less than 1 percent of crimes against the elderly. Crimes against the elderly was a convenient theme that allowed journalists to cast a particular incident as an instance of something threatening and pervasive, something with greater news value.

Fishman also found that the New York City Police Department (NYPD) was receptive to the media's claims about crimes against the elderly. In fact, the NYPD used the purported crime wave to justify expansion of its Senior Citizens Robbery Unit (SCRU), and SCRU officers dressed as old people arresting muggers provided attractive subjects for news-camera crews. One newspaper reporter, whose feature articles broke the crimes-against-the-elderly story, acknowledged that SCRU officers contacted him with information about muggings or murders of elderly persons and repeatedly complained that the SCRU unit was unappreciated, understaffed, and in need of more resources.

Importantly, the New York City crime wave had a nationwide impact on the public's perception of the crime problem, as the story was disseminated through the wire services and nationally read newspapers like the *New York Times* and *Washington Post*. The Harris polling organization also began to include a new category—crimes against the elderly—in its survey questionnaire, and the majority of polled respondents in a national sample indicated that they believed that such crimes had been increasing in their communities when, in fact, they had not.

Marjorie Zatz's study (1987) of the "gang problem" in the city of Phoenix yielded results that paralleled Fishman's research. In the late 1970s and early 1980s, newspaper accounts relying primarily on information provided by the Phoenix Police Department suggested that the city had experienced a dramatic rise in Chicano (Mexican American) youth gang activity. Police claims that the problem might escalate even further were coupled with well-publicized requests for additional local and federal funding for specialized gang-related law enforcement. The reality was, in fact, more complicated.

The term "gang" evokes a threatening social imagery that has the symbolic power to transform occasional or sporadic acts of delinquency into more purposeful systematic activity. In Phoenix, the police department provided its officers with the *Latin Gang Member Recognition Guide,* which included cartoon caricatures of youths in gang attire, a glossary of relevant Spanish words and expressions, and other criteria that could be used to identify gang members. Increased police surveillance of the Chicano community then yielded an identifiable population of offenders who provided the raw material for media reporting on the gang problem. Zatz found, however, that the police and media claims were disputed by some knowledgeable social service workers and counselors who worked with Chicano youths, as well as by representatives of the Chicano community. As one juvenile probation officer noted, "It's fair to say there is some violence and destruction going on. But maybe there is also a bit of an injustice when kids in cowboy hats and pickups, drinking beer and cruising . . . aren't thought of as a gang. But when you have Chicano kids driving lowriders, wearing bandannas, and smoking marijuana they are singled out as being gangs" (p. 136).

In addition, Zatz analyzed juvenile court records and found that while youths who were officially labeled as gang members were *more likely* than nongang youths to have been arrested in larger groups and for fighting offenses, they were *less likely* than nongang youths to have had prior court referrals and to have been referred for drug offenses. Zatz concluded that gang members "typically engaged in relatively minor squabbles, and not in . . . serious violent crimes that would be dangerous to . . . anyone outside of the gang world" (pp. 140, 143).

Zatz characterized claims about the Phoenix gang problem as a **moral panic**, that is, a discrepancy or disjuncture between a perceived and an actual threat that, when reported in the media, generates public support for doing something dramatic about a particular problem (Cohen 1980; McCorkle & Miethe 2002). In Phoenix, she suggests, the more ordinary inclinations of adolescents to congregate took on a more ominous appearance and fueled unwarranted fears about Chicano youths as an inherently lawless population. Zatz does not deny that youth gangs exist or that they can pose a serious problem for communities. Nor does she claim that the media are handmaidens of the police or that they always portray law enforcement in a positive light. Rather, she cautions us against uncritically accepting police and media accounts of social problems.

However, Fishman (1978) found that there are times in which public officials downplay media stories about crime, being concerned that media reporting will cause the public to panic unnecessarily or to believe that the police are ineffective. Thus, for instance, officials from the New York City Transit Authority (NYTA) stopped an emergent theme involving "crimes on the subways" from becoming a media-reported crime wave. In this case, the NYTA police chief told one reporter that there was no such crime wave, and three senior NYTA officials called a news conference to assure the public that "the subways were safer than the city streets" (Fishman 1978:541). (Business interests also fear that publicity about crime will hurt tourism and make it difficult to attract new commerce [Hagedorn 1988].)

Yet more often than not it seems that media and law enforcement interests converge in finding mutual benefit from portrayals of escalating crime. Philip Jenkins's study (1994) of the serial murder problem is a case in point. The media, as noted earlier, are attracted to the unusual. During the 1980s media accounts began to describe serial murder as having reached epidemic proportions. In 1984 the serial murderer—usually described as a psychotically compulsive offender capable of extreme violence who selects multiple victims at random, often while traveling from state to state—was featured in a front-page *New York Times* article that suggested that serial murders accounted for about 20 percent (about 4,000) of all the homicides committed in the United States each year. During the next two years this estimate was repeated in numerous other news reports. The data in these reports were based on Federal Bureau of Investigation (FBI) statistics on "motiveless" and "unsolved" murders and on interviews with law enforcement officials.

In his research, Jenkins was interested in ascertaining whether these numerical estimates were accurate and whether serial murders had, in fact, been on the rise. Jenkins compiled a list of cases that were reported between 1940 and 1990 in three well-indexed and highly regarded newspapers (the *New York Times, Los Angeles Times,* and *Chicago Tribune*), and he supplemented this data with other sources. Jenkins concluded that there had been a significant increase in this type of offense since the late 1960s, but that serial murders accounted for *no more than 2 to 3 percent* of all homicides.

Jenkins observes that officials in the U.S. Justice Department and in particular the FBI's Behavioral Sciences Unit (BSU) were the primary sources of information for the exaggerated media claims about the serial murder problem. He also notes that in 1983 concerns about serial murder became a central justification for the development of a new program, the Violent Criminal Apprehension Program (VICAP), at the FBI Academy in Quantico, Virginia, and for an expanded federal role in law enforcement regarding repeat killers as well as rapists, child molesters, arsonists, and bombers. According to BSU agent Robert Ressler:

> There was somewhat of a media feeding frenzy, if not a panic, over [the serial murder] issue in the mid-1980s, and we at the FBI and other people involved in urging the formation of VICAP did add to the general impression that there was a big problem and that something needed to be done about it. We didn't exactly go out seeking publicity, but when a reporter called, and we had a choice whether or not to cooperate on a story about violent crime, we gave the reporter good copy. In feeding the frenzy, we were using an old tactic in Washington, playing up the problem as a way of getting Congress and the higher-ups in the executive branch to pay attention to it. (Ressler & Schachtman 1992:203)

■ Drug Scares

Craig Reinarman and Harry Levine (1989) identify **drug scares** as a perennial type of crime wave and moral panic that in the United States goes back at least to the early part of the twentieth century. Drug scares typically involve an association between an allegedly "dangerous drug" and a "dangerous class" of individuals—working-class immigrants, nonwhite racial/ethnic groups, youths, or some combination thereof. This has been true, for example, of the Chinese and opium, African Americans and cocaine, and Mexicans and marijuana (Helmer 1975; Musto 1987). During drug scares, antidrug crusaders often receive extended media coverage, which helps to mobilize public opinion in support of new drug laws and to increase law enforcement against drug offenders. In the 1930s, for instance, Harry Anslinger, commissioner of the Federal Department of Treasury's Bureau of Narcotics, led a national campaign against the sale and use of marijuana (Becker 1963; Gray 1998). Under Anslinger's leadership the bureau prepared a number of "educational" articles for distribution to magazines and newspapers. These articles included a number of outrageous atrocity stories such as the following incident reported in *American Magazine* in 1937:

> An entire family was murdered by a youthful [marijuana] addict in Florida. When officers arrived at the home they found the youth staggering about in a human slaughterhouse. With an ax he had killed his father, mother, two brothers, and a sister. He seemed to be in a daze. . . . He had no recollection of having committed the multiple crime. The officers knew him ordinarily as a sane, rather quiet young man; now he was pitifully crazed. They sought the reason. The boy said he had been in the habit of smoking something which youthful friends called "muggles," a childish name for marijuana. (cited in Becker 1963:142)

In the 1980s crack cocaine emerged in the media as the preeminent dangerous drug (Reeves & Campbell 1994). Crack is a smokable form of cocaine that can be easily manufactured by boiling powdered cocaine (cocaine hydrochloride) with additives like novocaine and baking soda and placing the boiled mixture in ice water until it hardens. In his book *The Rise and Fall of a Violent Crime Wave: Crack Cocaine and the Social Construction of a Crime Problem,* Henry Brownstein (1996) attributes the rise of crack cocaine to the overproduction of coca leaves (the source of powdered cocaine) in the three countries that are the greatest source of cocaine imported into the United States (Bolivia, Columbia, and Peru) and to the consequent opportunity for drug traffickers to expand the cocaine market. Whereas powder cocaine had been consumed primarily by middle-class and more affluent individuals, crack can be sold in small, inexpensive quantities to low-income segments of the population. (Four ounces of powdered cocaine can serve 1,000.)

Media stories about crack cocaine first appeared in a November 1984 *Los Angeles Times* article and in the *New York Times* a year later. At that time crack was known to have appeared only in the impoverished neighborhoods of a few large cities. But by the spring of 1986, drug coverage reached a virtual feeding frenzy in the national media, which claimed that crack cocaine and a "coke plague" had spread to the suburbs and America's heartland and now constituted a "national crisis." Existing crime data, however, suggested that this simply was not true (see Chapter 2). Even the federal Drug Enforcement Administration (DEA) announced in 1986 that "crack was not a major problem in most areas of the country" (Brownstein 1996:41; Orcutt & Turner 1993; Reinarman & Levine 1989).

In his research, Brownstein (1996) was especially concerned with media claims, echoed by politicians and law enforcement, that crack cocaine was linked with an epidemic of violent criminal behavior.

According to Brownstein, when crack was first introduced the market was in fact "dominated by young . . . well-armed . . . entrepreneurs who operated independently of established drug trafficking organizations . . . [and who] turned to violence over such things as market share and product quality." But over time this disorganized and rather violent market evolved into "confederations of independent dealers . . . [and] a more highly structured and less violent business-like industry" (p. 40). Moreover, research indicated that while almost all crack users had previously used other illegal drugs, their involvement with crack was for the most part unrelated to increased nondrug or violent criminality (Johnson et al. 1995). Nevertheless, the media constructed a moral panic that suggested that crack-related violence could affect anyone anywhere. According to *Time* magazine, "A growing sense of vulnerability has been deepened by the belief that deadly violence, once mostly confined to crime-ridden ghetto neighborhoods that the police once wrote off as free-fire zones, is now lashing out randomly at anyone, even in areas once considered relatively safe" (Attinger 1989:38).

Reinarman and Levine (1989) acknowledge that crack is a very dangerous drug. They believe, however, that exaggerated drug scares are an ineffective way to solve the drug problem and may even increase interest in drug use.

■ The Politics of Crime Control

In 1905 William Taft, who was elected president in 1908, warned the American public:

> As murder is on the increase so are all offenses of the felony class, and there can be no doubt that they will continue to increase unless the criminal laws are enforced with more certainty, more uniformity, more severity than they now are. I presume it is useless to expect that courts will turn from their present tendency to amplify technicalities [on] behalf of defendants until legislatures shall initiate the change. (quoted in Sheley 1985:21)

Nearly eight decades later President Ronald Reagan reiterated this perennial message:

> It's time for honest talk, for plain talk. There has been a breakdown in the criminal justice system. . . . It just isn't working. All too often repeat offenders, habitual lawbreakers, career criminals, call them what you will, are robbing, raping, and beating with impunity and . . . quite literally getting away with murder. The people are sickened and outraged. They demand that we put a stop to it. (p. 21)

There seems to be an apparent consensus among politicians in the United States. We need to take tough measures to reduce crime. We need to declare war on criminals. Drugs are a heinous scourge. Three strikes and you're out! But underneath this apparent consensus lie the seeds of dispute: Has this tough talk been leading us in the desired direction? Have our lives become safer and our quality of life enhanced by the policies that derive from this stance?

Liberals and Conservatives

In many ways the 1960s defined the terms of the contemporary political debate over what to do about crime (Miller 1973). **Liberals** of that period claimed, as they do today, that crime could be prevented through social policies aimed at ameliorating the underlying "root causes" of crime associated with poverty and unequal opportunities, especially for racial and ethnic minorities, for whom discrimination is a persistent problem. Government-supported social programs that promote economic and educational opportunities and that provide needed social services are the prescribed cure. For those already caught up in the cycle of crime, rehabilitation rather than punishment per se is the preferred objective, with those accused and convicted of crimes being guaranteed rights of due process while under the control of the criminal justice system.

Conservatives, on the other hand, emphasized personal responsibility to refrain from criminal behavior. Unfavorable life conditions are no excuse. Criminal behavior is a choice; those who choose to commit crime must be held accountable. We must resign ourselves to the fact that "wicked people exist" and that we have no recourse but to set them apart from the rest of us (Wilson 1975:235). To the extent that there are root causes of crime, these reside in the decay of moral values, not in the absence of economic opportunities. The government can do little to solve these problems and should get out of people's lives. We need to liberate our criminal justice system from undue restraint so that punishment can be more certain, swift, and severe.

In 1965 President Lyndon Johnson, a Democrat, established the President's Commission on Law Enforcement and Administration of Justice (PCLEAJ). Johnson asked the commission to "deepen our understanding of the causes of crime and of how society should respond to the challenge of the present levels of crime" (PCLEAJ 1967:2). The commission acknowledged the liberal agenda when it wrote: "Crime flourishes where the conditions of life are the worst. . . . Reducing poverty, discrimination, ignorance, disease and urban blight, and the anger, cynicism or despair those conditions can inspire, is . . . essential to crime prevention" (p. 279). This apparent statement of liberal principles was a mere footnote, however, to the more conservative-oriented criminal justice strategies that dominated the commission's seventeen-volume report, that is, strategies that involved "policemen, prosecutors, judges, correctional authorities." Even so, in the 1968 presidential election Republican candidate Richard Nixon and ultraconservative American Independent candidate George Wallace accused the Democrats of being soft on crime (Conklin 2001).

▉ The Reagan-Bush Years

In 1974, less than two years after he was reelected, President Nixon was forced to resign for his involvement in a cover-up of a burglary on behalf of his reelection campaign at the Democratic National Committee headquarters in the Watergate hotel/office complex. The Watergate affair focused public attention on the problem of political corruption and encouraged the pursuit of white-collar crime as an investigative priority of the U.S. Justice Department during the Democratic presidency of Jimmy Carter (Katz 1980).

But in the 1980s President Reagan, a Republican, shifted federal law enforcement priorities by moving the drug problem to center stage in the political debate about crime. Reagan declared a "war on drugs," a war that would require not just a redoubling of conventional law enforcement efforts, but also an unprecedented involvement of the military in international drug interdiction (Gordon 1994a). On the home front, the slogan "zero tolerance" emphasized "the culpability of casual users and . . . [the belief] that . . . the present problem is [due] to past tolerance . . . [and] that nothing short of wiping out all illicit drug use will do" (p. 33). The war on drugs was, in Reagan's words, "our national crusade" (quoted in Gordon 1994a:34). To accomplish this goal, the Reagan administration diverted over $700 million dollars from drug education, treatment, and research to law enforcement (Kraska 1990).

Crime was a central issue in the 1988 presidential campaign between then–vice president George Bush, the Republican candidate, and Massachusetts governor Michael Dukakis, the Democratic candidate. This campaign has gone down in the annals of campaign history for the Willie Horton television commercials that were aired by Bush supporters. Horton, an African American, had been sentenced to life in prison for his involvement in an armed robbery that resulted in the death of a teenage gas station attendant in Massachusetts. After serving ten years in prison, he was released for the first of three furloughs (temporary home leaves or community releases). Furlough programs are used by more than half the prison systems in the United States as part of a risk-management policy aimed at the gradual reintegration of convicted felons back into the community. To be sure, furloughs are not without risk. But research on furlough programs in the 1970s and 1980s indicates that, on the whole, these programs actually reduced recidivism (return to crime). Horton, however, was not a good candidate for a fourth release. Although prison officials had received complaints about his behavior during his previous furloughs, they released him once again. This time he escaped and remained free for almost a year until he burglarized the home of a white suburban couple, Angela Miller and Clifford Barnes, and brutally assaulted them. While Horton was raping Miller, Barnes managed to escape and get help. If he had not, they would have likely been killed (Anderson 1995; Skolnick 1996).

The Horton incident was a tragedy. But Bush supporters used this tragedy to portray Governor Dukakis as responsible for the release of convicted violent felons. Because Dukakis also opposed the death penalty, Bush was able to portray him as soft on crime. The Democrats, in turn, accused the Bush campaign of exploiting racial stereotypes in an unconscionable way. Nevertheless, the ad was extremely effective.

As president, Bush continued his predecessor's focus on drugs. During his first year in office Bush addressed the nation in a televised Labor Day speech that illustrates how politicians exploit the crime issue. In a dramatic gesture Bush held up a bag of crack cocaine that had been purchased by DEA agents at a park across the street from the White House. We learned later that the arrest had actually been arranged to help dramatize the speech! The Bush administration had asked the DEA to make an illegal drug-buy at the park, but since agents could not find anyone who was selling crack at that location, they lured a dealer to the park in order to make the arrest (Kappeler et al. 2000).

▥ The Clinton Years

During the 1992 presidential campaign between President Bush and Arkansas governor Bill Clinton, it was difficult for Bush to characterize Clinton as a traditional soft-on-crime Democrat. As governor, Clinton had demonstrated his support for the death penalty by signing four execution orders, including the order to execute a brain-impaired African American felon (Kramer & Michalowski 1995). Clinton also favored the expansion of the nation's police forces, a cornerstone of his crime control policy. Clinton did, however, differ from Bush in his support of federal gun control legislation, particularly the Brady Handgun Violence Prevention Act (the Brady Bill), which would require a five-day waiting period for the purchase of a handgun. The Brady Bill was named for James Brady, the press secretary for President Reagan, who was shot and seriously disabled in 1981 during John Hinckley's attempted assassination of the president (see Chapter 3).

Politically, gun control has received more support from liberals than from conservatives. Many conservatives feel very strongly that the Second Amendment to the U.S. Constitution preserves their right to own any gun of their choice without government interference. (This amendment states: "A well regulated militia being necessary to the security of a free state, the right of the people to keep and bear arms, shall not be infringed.") Current federal court decisions, however, have not recognized an "application of the Second Amendment to an individual's right to possess, carry, or use firearms," making gun policy (rights or limitations) less a matter of constitutional law than of the legislative will to enact it (Vizzard 2000:53). President Reagan had opposed the Brady Bill, only to endorse it after he left office, perhaps because he no longer needed to worry about incurring the wrath of the National Rifle Association (NRA), a well-funded and influential organization that supports conservative anti–gun control political candidates. Unlike Reagan, Bush continued to oppose the bill. But since it was difficult to characterize Clinton's advocacy of gun control as soft on crime, Bush was unable to use the crime issue to his advantage. After Clinton became president, he signed the Brady Bill into law in December 1993. (The Brady Bill expired in 1998 and was replaced by a national computerized system of background checks operated by the FBI. For more on gun control see Chapter 5.)

During the campaign and the first year of his presidency, Clinton gave indications that he might also be more liberal than his predecessors on other crime issues. For example, Clinton appointed Lee Brown, a former New York City police commissioner, as director of the Office of National Drug Control Policy. Brown, an advocate of prevention and rehabilitation approaches to drug abuse, defined "drug abuse as a public health problem" that should be addressed through "efforts to grow the economy, to empower communities, to curb youth violence, to preserve families, and to reform health care" (quoted in Gordon 1994a:35). However, when Republicans accused Clinton of "slipping into the old permissiveness," he downplayed this view and Brown eventually resigned in frustration (p. 35). Brown was replaced by Barry McCaffrey, a retired four-star general. Similarly, when Attorney General Janet Reno questioned the existing federal policy of lengthy mandatory sentences for even minor drug offenders (which might necessitate shorter sentences for violent offenders to reduce prison overcrowding), she was removed from the White House policymaking loop. And when Jocelyn Elders, Clinton's surgeon general, expressed interest in examining the experiences of other countries that had decriminalized drugs (and made other controversial statements as well), she was forced to resign (Mauer 1994; Poveda 1994a; Reid 1997).

The most significant piece of crime legislation passed during the Clinton administration was the 1994 Federal Crime Bill. The provisions of the bill indicate that the conservative position on crime had at least temporarily prevailed, for law enforcement and punitive measures far outweighed crime prevention and rehabilitation strategies. The bill authorized the spending of over $30 billion dollars and allocated over three-quarters of this amount to the hiring of more police officers (45 percent) and the building of new prisons (33 percent). The bill also included a "three strikes and you're out" provision (life in prison for violent and drug felons if the third conviction is in federal court), and it expanded the death penalty to more than fifty federal crimes (*Milwaukee Journal* 1994b).

The bill was passed in August 1994, while the Democrats were still in control of Congress, and included three provisions that were generally opposed by Republicans. The policing provisions favored by the Clinton administration earmarked federal monies to local police departments willing to implement "community policing." Community policing is a rather general term used to describe law enforcement strategies aimed at putting police in closer touch with the community (e.g., foot patrols, meetings with residents, and an emphasis on solving community problems rather than just making arrests) (Cordner 1999; Stevens 2003; see Chapter 11). Republicans would have liked to allow police departments to define their own priorities—for instance, to use the money to buy more equipment (e.g., squad cars, high-powered weapons) or to expand other law enforcement activities (e.g., specialized crime units).

Republicans also opposed a provision of the bill that banned the manufacture of nineteen specific types of "military-style" assault weapons and other firearms having similar characteristics. (Guns and cartridges already owned would continue to be legal.) In addition, they opposed that portion of the bill that earmarked money (17 percent of the spending) for social programs aimed at crime prevention, such as youth clubs in housing projects, midnight sports leagues, and drug treatment programs. One Republican congressman characterized the bill as "riddled with social welfare spending that is pork and a cops-on-the-streets program that is a sham" (quoted in *Milwaukee Journal* 1994a:3A).

By supporting crime policies favored by both conservatives and liberals, Clinton hoped to have it both ways. But by attempting to appease everyone he ran the risk of alienating both sides. Politically his position was safe, however. He may not have been reelected because of his stance on crime, but neither was he defeated because of it.

Bush II

President Clinton was embroiled in a well-publicized scandal of his own that focused on his sexual relations with White House intern Monica Lewinsky and allegations that he lied about this relationship under oath. In 1998 he was impeached by the House of Representatives, and although he was acquitted in the Senate, he left office with a cloud hanging over his administration. In turn, George W. Bush, son of the former president, assumed his presidency amid controversy in the 2000 election over disputed ballots in the state of Florida. The U.S. Supreme Court, in a highly controversial decision, stopped a recount vote in Florida, giving Bush a narrow victory in the electoral college, in spite of the fact that Vice President Al Gore had won the popular vote nationwide (Conason & Lyons 2000; Corn 2003; Dershowitz 2001; see Chapter 10).

During the first year of his administration, President George W. Bush and Vice President Dick Cheney's financial and political connections to Enron, a multibillion-dollar energy corporation that went bankrupt due to fraudulent financial practices, were starting to draw attention in the media (Baker 2002; Corn 2003; Sloan 2001; see Chapter 6). What seemed to be emerging as an ongoing story was moved off the front pages, however, following the September 11, 2001, terrorist attacks on the World Trade Center and the Pentagon, which cost the lives of over 3,000 people and spurred the subsequent antiterrorism campaign against Al-Qaida and Iraq. Six weeks later, the president signed the USA Patriot Act into law, amid complaints by civil libertarians that the law went too far in undermining constitutional freedoms. ("Patriot" is an acronym for "Providing Appropriate Tools Required to Intercept and Obstruct Terrorism.")

The most controversial elements of the Patriot Act included provisions that allowed for "secret" (without notification) residential searches of individuals deemed a risk to national security, searches of computer files and tracing of Internet communications and library transactions, and detainment of noncitizens without charge for up to six months prior to deportation (Anderson 2003; McCaffrey 2003; Williams 2003). Equally controversial was the fact that the law did not contain any "new provisions for the monitoring or control of firearms" (Bergman & Reynolds 2002:21). In fact, Attorney General John Ashcroft did not even allow federal law enforcement investigators to use the national background-check system to track potential terrorists. Prior to his appointment as attorney general, as a senator from Missouri, Ashcroft had received thousands of dollars of political campaign contributions from the NRA.

The following year the Department of Homeland Security Act was also passed, creating a large, cabinet-level department to oversee homeland security. Although the purpose of the department was to centralize intelligence and security operations and to reduce duplication of functions among agencies, two key organizations (the Federal Bureau of Investigation and the Central Intelligence Agency) were excluded from this reorganization scheme (Martin 2003).

Whether or not we are any safer because of these efforts remains to be seen. More will be said of the terrorism threat later in this book (see Chapter 10). For now, we simply note that some provisions of the Patriot Act were set to expire in 2005 and that there has been growing opposition throughout the country to its continuance. Over 140 local governments have passed resolutions objecting to the act's infringement on civil liberties, indicating a growing rift between local and federal authorities (Isikoff & Klaidman 2003).

■ Criminology and the Sociological Imagination

In this book we aim to provide you with an alternative to the media and political constructions of crime that have been discussed in this chapter. By exploring the exciting field of criminology, we hope to encourage you to step outside of such conventional understandings and learn to exercise your sociological imagination.

Criminology is an interdisciplinary field of study that involves theoretical explanation and empirical research regarding the process of law making, law breaking, and the societal reaction to law breaking (Sutherland 1947). The discipline of sociology has occupied a special place among the interdisciplinary components of criminology (e.g., anthropology, biology, economics, political science, psychology), and according to Ronald Akers, still constitutes its "intellectual center of gravity" (1992:4). For much of the twentieth century, criminology in the United States was most often taught in departments of sociology and its most widely used textbooks were written by sociologists. Hence the study of criminology came to be defined as an attempt to understand crime as a social rather than an individual phenomenon, that is, as a consequence of social relationships and the organization of society.

In the late 1960s, however, sociology began to lose its hold on the field. The federal government provided funds that enabled law enforcement agencies to upgrade their educational requirements and encourage their personnel to obtain postsecondary education degrees. This resulted in an expansion of college and university criminal justice programs outside of sociology departments that was readily apparent by the 1980s. By 1990 there were over 1,000 such programs in the United States offering undergraduate degrees and nearly 100 offering graduate degrees (Akers 1992; Sorensen et al. 1994).

The terms **criminology** and **criminal justice** suggest different orientations. Criminology tends to focus on the phenomena of crime and criminals, while criminal justice tends to focus on the agencies that respond to criminal law violation—the police, courts, and corrections systems. Criminology tends to be more theoretical and research oriented, while criminal justice is more practical or applied. But in many respects the division between criminology and criminal justice is artificial, and the two are so closely interwoven that a convergence is said to be under way. As Jonathan Sorensen and colleagues note, "criminal justice programs often include criminology in the curriculum . . . [and] criminologists often teach in criminal justice programs . . . and conduct research on the criminal justice system. . . . As criminal justice develops further as a discipline, the methodology employed in criminal justice research will become comparable to that used in criminology" (1994:152–153).

■ Cultivating a Sociological Imagination
Whether you are reading this book as part of a course in sociology, criminal justice, or another related curriculum, you now have the opportunity to cultivate a **sociological imagination** for thinking about crime. According to C. Wright Mills (1959), a sociological imagination helps us see the ways in which personal or private troubles are related to public issues. It helps us understand how our lives are impacted by social forces that define and constrain our choices and opportunities, our sense of the possible, our very sense of ourselves. It helps us understand how our individual biographies and the biographies of others intersect with both broader historical and social conditions and the relationships we have with one another.

Victimization from crime, for example, is an unfortunate and often traumatic private experience. But when victimization falls disproportionately on a certain group or groups, such as the poor or economically disadvantaged, there is a nonrandom patterning to this problem that requires sociological explanation (Elias 1986; Maguire & Pastore 2001). Or when large numbers of women experience some form of sexual violence or abuse, mostly from nonstrangers, this cannot be understood without sociological insight (Belknap 2001; Russell 1984; Searles & Berger 1995).

This perspective is also well illustrated in the following accounts of the lives of African American gang members. In his book *A Nation of Lords: The Autobiography of the Vice Lords,* David Dawley (1992) gives voice to the experiences of Chicago youths growing up in the late 1950s and 1960s:

> When we got here, *the pattern was already laid out for us.* We weren't aware of what was going on and what we thought, but we were living in the years when you couldn't walk the streets without somebody telling you they were gonna down you. Much of what we did was bad, but we didn't know why, and there just wasn't anybody who could help us. Now we know something about what made us kill each other, but in 1958 we were crammed so close together that the least little thing could touch something off. (p. 3; emphasis added)

Similarly, in *Monster: The Autobiography of an L.A. Gang Member,* Sanyika Shakur (1993), aka Monster Kody Scott, writes about his life as a member of the Crips in South Central Los Angeles in the 1970s:

> My mind-set was narrowed by the *conditions and circumstances prevailing around me.* Certainly I had little respect for life when practically all

my life I had seen people assaulted, maimed, and blown away at very young ages, and no one seemed to care. I recognized early that where I lived, we grew and died in dog years. . . . Where I lived, stepping on someone's toe was a capital offense punishable by death. . . . *I did not start this cycle,* nor did I conspire to create conditions so that this type of self-murder could take place. . . . To be in a gang in South Central when I joined—and it is still the case today—is the equivalent of growing up in Grosse Pointe, Michigan, and going to college: everyone does it. (pp. 102, 138; emphasis added)

When Dawley and Shakur speak of "the pattern [that] was already laid out" or the prevailing "conditions and circumstances" that they "did not start," they are speaking of the influence of **social structure** on their lives. Social structure is a concept used by sociologists to refer to the patterns of social interaction and relations that endure over time and that constitute the expected taken-for-granted routines of our lives. As we shall see, social relations of inequality and power—particularly those based on class, race and ethnicity, and gender—are among the most significant elements of social structure. Social structure, however, does not exist independently of **social action**. Rather, it is an ongoing accomplishment that is reproduced by individuals acting in particular ways in specific situations (Giddens 1981; Messerschmidt 1997). The members of the Vice Lords and the Crips did not create the social structures that they confronted in their lives, but through their actions they recreated or reproduced the conditions that were already there.

A sociological imagination does not imply a view of individuals as mere dupes or passive recipients of social structures. Individuals are thinking, feeling beings potentially capable of exercising **personal agency**, that is, capable of making choices and exerting control over their lives and, in some instances, even transforming or reconfiguring the social relationships in which they are enmeshed (Emirbayer & Mische 1998; Sewell 1992). To illustrate this point we need only recall the actions of Rosa Parks, an African American seamstress who on a December day in 1955 refused to relinquish her seat to a white man on a bus in Montgomery, Alabama, as she was *required by law to do*. Parks had already been actively challenging bus segregation laws, and this "incident sparked a year-long citywide boycott of the public transit system and galvanized the entire civil rights movement of the 1950s and 1960s," dramatically changing the nature of race relations in the United States (Newman 2002:19).

▓ Challenges to the Legalistic Definition of Crime

Cultivating your sociological imagination also requires reconsidering the **legalistic definition** of crime. Paul Tappan was a prominent proponent of the legalistic definition: "Crime is an intentional action in violation of criminal law . . . committed without defense or justification, and sanctioned by the state as a felony or misdemeanor" (1947:100). Tappan believed that criminologists should narrowly confine their subject matter to behaviors that met this definition. It was inappropriate, he maintained, for criminologists to assert their own values by defining what should or should not be included in the criminal law as crimes.

Edwin Sutherland, one of the most important criminologists of the twentieth century, rejected this approach when he introduced the term "white-collar crime" at his 1939 presidential address to the American Sociological Society (Geis & Meier 1977). Although Sutherland had been interested in documenting the extent of law violation among the largest corporations in the United States, he did not wish his study to be constrained by the criminal code. It was Sutherland's contention that noncriminal *civil* and *regulatory* (or administrative) law violations should also be considered.

All three systems of law—**criminal, civil,** and **regulatory**—are concerned with the social control of what has been deemed harmful or injurious conduct by a governmental body. These systems of law all involve procedures set up to adjudicate competing claims and to ascertain responsibility regarding such conduct. Technically speaking, criminal law defines harmful conduct as a public matter and mandates the intervention of traditional law enforcement authorities (i.e., police and prosecutors). Civil law defines harm as a private matter to be settled by individuals (and their attorneys) as private parties in the courts. Regulatory law is concerned with the imposition of rules and standards for business-related activity, and at the federal level involves agencies like the Environmental Protection Agency, the Occupational Safety and Health Administration, and the Securities and Exchange Commission. While the lines of demarcation between these three systems are not always clear, only criminal law allows for the imposition of jail or prison sanctions instead of or in addition to financial penalties, although failure to comply with civil or regulatory rulings may lead to such sanctions. Violation of criminal law carries the greatest moral condemnation because of the stigma associated with crime (Friedrichs 2004).

In his research, Sutherland (1949) uncovered extensive law violations on the part of corporations in areas such as antitrust (price-fixing and restraint of trade), misrepresentation in advertising, copyright infringement, and unfair labor practices, although only 16 percent of these violations were prosecuted under criminal law. Nevertheless, Sutherland felt justified in calling these violations crimes. In his view, corporations that engaged in harmful conduct were able to avoid the application of criminal law and the consequent stigma associated with such application because of their economic and political clout. Sutherland was unwilling to also allow corporations to exert such influence on criminological research.

The legalistic view expressed by Tappan is often associated with the **consensus perspective** on crime. The consensus approach takes the existing criminal law for granted and assumes there is general agreement in society regarding what is right and what is wrong, regarding those behaviors that should be criminalized and those that should not. In contrast, many of Sutherland's followers prefer a **conflict perspective** on crime, viewing definitions of crimes as matters of disagreement, the assertion of economic and political power, and the struggles of competing groups to use the law to their advantage (Chambliss & Seidman 1971; Quinney 1970; Turk 1969; see Chapter 5).

The labeling approach. Thinking about crime with a sociological imagination requires us to move beyond the legalistic-consensus view. **Labeling theory** is a perspective in criminology that does just this. It encourages us to think about crime as "a label that is attached to behavior and events by those who create and administer the criminal law" (Barlow 1996:10). Legislators, for instance, establish legal definitions that label some actions as crimes, and criminal justice officials apply these definitions to particular individuals.

The labeling approach assumes that many (if not most) of us have violated the law at one time or another. If we were never caught, however, we were never officially designated or stigmatized as a criminal. What matters most then is the societal reaction to our behavior. Recall the comment of the probation officer whom Zatz (1987) cited in her study of the moral panic over Chicano gang violence: "Kids in cowboy hats and pickups, drinking beer and cruising . . . aren't thought of as a gang. But . . . Chicano kids driving lowriders, wearing bandannas, and smoking marijuana . . . are." This type of bias is also documented by William Chambliss (1973) in his study "The Saints and the Roughnecks." Chambliss found that the delinquent acts of the lower-class Roughnecks brought forth legal sanctions and community condemnation, while the (quite extensive) delinquencies of the upper-middle-class Saints were treated lightly or ignored. From the perspective of labeling theory, being a criminal is an accorded social status that is relatively independent of actual involvement in law breaking (Becker 1963; see Chapter 4).

Critical criminology. Sociological thinking about crime encourages us to consider the ways in which social privilege and influence affect the process of **criminalization**, that is, the process by which the criminal law is selectively applied to social behavior, making some individuals and groups more or less vulnerable or immune from legal control (Hartjen 1974). **Critical criminologists** have been the most radical in their critique of the legal system's bias in the criminalization process, and they have searched for an alternative to the legal definition of crime to broaden the subject matter of criminology. Herman Schwendinger and Julia Schwendinger (1970), for example, have advanced a definition of crime as the violation of **human rights**. According to the Schwendingers, egalitarian principles of social justice mandate that all individuals be entitled to certain inalienable rights that are "the fundamental prerequisites for well-being, including food, shelter, clothing, medical services, challenging work and recreational experiences," as well as security from predatory individuals, corporate transgressions, and governmental repression (p. 145). From this perspective, economic or political systems of injustice that deny these rights or that promote racism, sexism, economic exploitation, or environmental degradation, for instance, are proper topics of criminological inquiry.

This human rights definition of crime has been characterized as so broad as to entail the abandonment of criminology as a distinct field of study (Turk 1975). Hence Raymond Michalowski (1985) has proposed an alternative concept, that of **analogous social injury**, as a way to broaden our understanding of crime. Michalowski defines an analogous social injury as "legally permissible acts or sets of conditions whose consequences are similar to those of illegal acts" (p. 317).

The controversy over the marketing of infant formula (milk powder) by multinational corporations in less-developed countries is an example of the type of behavior that would fall within either the "human rights" or "analogous social injury" definition of crime. Problems associated with the use of infant formula in the poverty-stricken and rural areas of these countries have been reported since the late 1950s. Corporations aggressively marketed the product as a modern alternative to breast-feeding, but illiteracy, lack of clean water, and inadequate refrigeration made use of infant formula more dangerous than mother's milk. Moreover, the cost of infant formula unnecessarily consumed a large portion of a family's income, and parents often diluted the mixture to make it go further. Thus bottle-fed babies in these countries were more likely than breast-fed babies to experience malnutrition, disease, brain damage, and even death. In the late 1970s, public attention to this issue focused on the Swiss-based Nestlé corporation, one of the largest food processors in the world. By the early 1980s, a worldwide protest and boycott finally forced Nestlé to abandon its aggressive marketing techniques, which had included the oversupplying of hospitals with free samples and the bribing of hospital staff to encourage pregnant women to purchase the product (Ermann & Clements 1984; Gerber & Short 1986).

▪ Inequality, Power, and Crime

Sociological analysis of social structure and challenges to the legalistic definition of crime merge in efforts to place questions of **social inequality** and

power at the center of criminological inquiry. Inequality refers to the unequal distribution of valued social resources such as economic, educational, and cultural opportunities, while power involves the ability to impose one's will on others and to follow a course of action despite attempted resistance or interference from others (Gerth & Mills 1946). According to John Hagan (1989), social relations of power are of great interest to criminologists. "Perhaps this is because crime itself implies a power relationship. To perpetuate crime is often to impose one's power on others, while to be punished for a crime is to be subjected to the power of others. Of course, these power relations are subject to change. Therefore the study of social structure [and crime] often is concerned with changes in power relations . . . over time" (pp. 1–2).

Among the diverse elements of social structure, criminologists have increasingly emphasized the pivotal role that **class, race** and **ethnicity**, and **gender** play as predominant organizing principles of social life. We have already introduced a number of ways in which these three elements of social structure impact on crime. As you read further, their importance will become clearer still.

Class. Concern about the dangerous lower classes threatening the streets of cities can be traced to European social commentaries of the eighteenth and nineteenth centuries (Silver 1974). In 1880 Charles Loring Brace described U.S. cities as consisting of

> immigration . . . pouring in its multitudes of poor foreigners who leave . . . young outcasts everywhere in our midst. These boys and girls . . . will soon form the great lower class of our city. They will influence elections; they may shape the policy of the city; they will assuredly, if unreclaimed, poison society all around them. They will help to form the great multitude of robbers, thieves, and vagrants, who are now such a burden upon the law-respecting community. (cited in Platt 1974:373)

Likewise, to this very day, U.S. governmental crime control policy remains focused on the crimes of the lower class. As we have already suggested, however, this is only part of the story of crime, for criminal (or analogous) behavior is prevalent throughout the class structure of society, although the particular form of this criminality tends to vary from class to class (Hagan 1992).

Most people understand social class as a hierarchical relationship that designates individuals on a continuum of lower to middle to upper class based on monetary considerations such as wealth (total assets) or annual income. Viewed in this way, the class structure in the United States is marked by considerable inequality. For example, both the top 1 percent and the bottom 90 percent of American families each own about one-third of all wealth; while the top 20 percent earns about 40 to 45 percent of all income and the bottom 20 percent earns about 4 to 5 percent (Braun 1997; Messner & Rosenfeld 2001). Although economic inequality can be measured in various ways, numerous studies indicate that higher levels of inequality are associated with higher levels of predatory street crime among members of the lower stratum of society (e.g., Blau & Blau 1982; LaFree 1998; Messner 1989; Sampson 1985). On the other hand, crime among the affluent is facilitated by access to organizational resources that are "for white-collar criminals what the gun or knife is for the common criminal—a tool to obtain money from victims" (Hagan 1992:9). Access to these resources enable "individuals operating through formally organized associations and businesses [to] perpetrate larger-scale crimes than individuals acting alone" (Wheeler & Rothman 1982:1406). During the 1980s, for instance, looting by individuals within the savings and loan industry cost taxpayers (who had to bail out insured depositors) billions of dollars. More recently, fraudulent financial activities on the part of Enron and other major corporations cost investors countless billions of dollars as well (Reiman 2004; Rosoff et al. 2002).

In any case, Hagan suggests that classes should be viewed not simply as "'above' or 'below' one another . . . [but in] relation to one another, with each class representing a common structural position within the social organization of work" (1989:125). One of the earliest proponents of this relational concept of class was Karl Marx, a nineteenth-century German social theorist. Marx advanced a view of the class structure of **capitalism** as consisting of a division between the capitalist class and the working class. Capitalism is an economic system based on the principle of private rather than public ownership of the major means of production (i.e., factories, technology, raw materials). The viability of capitalism depends not merely on the vision, initiative, or risk-taking of capitalist entrepreneurs, but also on a supply of wage laborers who are dependent upon capitalists for employment. According to Marx, the relation between capitalists and workers is one in which capitalists remain dominant and enjoy a disproportionate amount of the economic benefit (and the consequent political power and social privilege) gained from the productive enterprise. David Newman aptly summarizes the advantages that accrue to the capitalist class:

> Capitalists have considerable sway over what will be produced, how much will be produced, and who will get how much of it. Such influence allows them to control other people's livelihoods, the communities in which people live, and the economic decisions that affect the entire society. In such a structure, the rich inevitably tend to get richer, to use their wealth to create more wealth for themselves, and to act in ways that will protect their interests and positions in society. (2002:288)

Estimates of the distribution of the population into discrete social classes are difficult to make. In fact, as Paul Sweezy has noted, "it would be a mistake to think of a class as perfectly homogenous internally and sharply marked off from other classes. . . . There is variety within the classes; and one class sometimes shades off very gradually and almost imperceptibly into another" (1953:24). Nevertheless, it is quite clear that, statistically speaking, the capitalist class is a minority class. U.S. survey data indicate that capitalists who own the large-scale means of production constitute about 1 to 2 percent of the adult population, with the employer/ownership class as a whole composing an additional 6 to 7 percent. Our contemporary class structure also includes a professional-managerial class (e.g., corporate managers, doctors, politicians) consisting of individuals who may be employed by others but who maintain a good deal of autonomy over their own work and who may exercise control over the work of others. This class comprises about 25 to 30 percent of the adult population. The working class (including the working poor and underemployed) is clearly the largest class, constituting about 55 to 60 percent of the adult population. In addition, another 5 to 6 percent are more or less permanently unemployed, composing what Marx characterized as a "surplus population." These data undoubtedly underestimate this latter group, as those who are homeless are often excluded from these surveys. In any case, U.S. census data indicate that the poor and near-poor constitute about 20 percent of the population (Hagan 1989; Newman 2002; Wright et al. 1982).

The precise statistical distribution of the population into social classes is less important than the observation that class matters. Your class background affects not only your income or wealth but also your entire experience of life—from your manner of speaking to your expectations about the future. As Michael Lynch observes, class "affects where you grow up, how you grow up, and the quality of the schools you attend. . . . It affects your occupational choices, your career path, whom you marry, and . . . even when you have children. It affects your ability to enter politics, and . . . to influence politics. . . . It affects everyday, mundane decisions, from where you shop, to where you eat, and sometimes, whether you eat at all" (1996:16). Class also affects your incentives and disincentives to engage in criminal behavior as well as the resources you have at your disposal for committing certain types of crimes and for avoiding official sanctions for your actions.

Race and ethnicity. In his book *Race Matters,* Cornel West, a distinguished professor of religion and Afro-American studies, recounts the following incidents:

Years ago, while driving . . . to teach at Williams College, I was stopped on fake charges of trafficking cocaine. When I told the police officer I was a professor of religion, he replied, "Yeah, and I'm the Flying Nun. Let's go nigger!" I was stopped three times in my first ten days in Princeton for driving too slowly on a residential street with a speed limit of twenty-five miles per hour. . . . [More recently] I left my car . . . in a safe parking lot . . . to catch a taxi. . . . I waited and waited and waited. After the ninth taxi refused me, my blood began to boil. The tenth taxi refused me and stopped for a kind, well-dressed, smiling fellow citizen of European decent. (1994:xv)

Inequality based on race and ethnicity remains an enduring fact of American life and has been a defining feature of our society since European colonization. This inequality has manifested itself in such phenomena as slavery, the forcible seizure of land from the indigenous populations, legalized segregation, political disenfranchisement, lack of economic and educational opportunities, and the like (Mann 1993; Newman 2002).

Biological typologies of race most often divide humans into three major groups—Caucasoid, Mongoloid, and Negroid—characterized by various physical traits transmitted through heredity. But distinct racial groups, if they ever did exist, do not exist today due to interracial mixing resulting from migration, exploration, invasions, and involuntary servitude. Speaking of whites and blacks in the United States, for example, Coramae Richy Mann observes:

Euro-Americans are a blend of many ethnic and tribal groups that originated in Africa and Europe, . . . [and] many millions of Africans were absorbed into the populations of Mediterranean countries such as Spain, Portugal, Italy, and Greece. . . . Furthermore, when we consider the rapes of African female slaves in the early years of this country, and the resultant millions of mulattoes who were the offspring of these forced alliances, . . . [as well as] those children born as a result . . . of interracial mixing, . . . [and] the millions of African Americans who have "passed for white" in this society, . . . the notion of a "black" race becomes somewhat ambiguous. (1993:5)

The concept of ethnicity further complicates the subject. Ethnicity refers to distinctions among groups according to cultural characteristics such as language, religion, customs, and family patterns. Often we speak of groups according to their country of origin, such as Irish Americans, Polish Americans, or Mexican Americans. Some use the term "minority" to refer to those racial and ethnic groups that experience discriminatory treatment from others in society. Today, the term "people of color" is increasingly used to describe nonwhite racial and ethnic groups. Sociologists, however, regard race and ethnicity as social rather than biological constructs that designate the structural position of a group within a society. A dominant group within a society may even impose a particular racial/ethnic label on another. In the United States, for instance, according to the "one-drop" rule, a person was classified as black if he or she had a single drop of "black blood" in their hereditary line (Newman 2002; Wright 1994).

For the purpose of data collection by federal agencies, the Office of Management and Budget has identified the following racial/ethnic categories: American Indian or Alaskan Native; Asian; Black or African American; Hispanic or Latino; Native Hawaiian or Other Pacific Islanders; and White. Census data indicate that non-Hispanic whites constitute about 69 percent of the population, followed by blacks (13 percent) and Hispanics (13 percent), Asian/Pacific Islanders (4 percent), and Native American Indian/Alaskan Natives (1 percent). The 2000 census was the first time the government gave respondents the option of checking more than one racial/ethnic category; just over 1 percent of the population, about 4 million people, identified themselves in this way (U.S. Department of Commerce 2002). Unfortunately, criminal justice system data are notoriously deficient in reflecting this racial/ethnic diversity. Most offenders are categorized only as black or white, and Hispanics are usually included as white. Moreover, "the criminal justice officials responsible for classifying persons may be poorly trained and may rely on their own stereotypes" about the appearance of different groups (Walker et al. 2004:14).

As we have already suggested, racial/ethnic stereotypes have influenced media representations, public opinion, and governmental policies regarding crime. The war on drugs in particular has unduly targeted African Americans, whose arrests and sentences for drug offenses, when compared to those of whites, have been disproportionate to their rates of law violation (Blumstein 1993; DiMascio 1997; Tonry 1995). Although less than 40 percent of crack users are African American, for example, nearly 90 percent of those sentenced for crack offenses are African American. Incarceration for drug offenses has constituted the largest component of the increase in the prison population. African Americans now constitute nearly one-half of persons who are incarcerated, and about one-third of African American men in their twenties are under the control of the criminal justice system (Mauer & Huling 1995; Pastore & Maguire 2002; see Chapters 7 and 12).

Michael Tonry (1995) argues that the racial impact of the war on drugs, broadly defined to include lower-level drug users, was deliberate and foreseeable. Even if justified by higher rates of law violation, a similar policy toward whites would not be tolerated; we would find another way to deal with the problem of crime. Diana Gordon (1994b) believes that the policy reflects a fear of racial minorities and is a smokescreen for our inability or unwillingness to address the problems of the inner city. No wonder African Americans are more distrustful than European Americans of the criminal justice system!

The war on drugs is but one example of the **institutional racism** that exists in the United States. Whereas the term "prejudice" refers to the unfavorable attitudes or beliefs held by individuals toward other groups in a society, institutional racism refers to the racial inequalities that are produced when persons in power act in discriminatory ways (Mann 1993; Newman 2002).

Gender. The position of women in both society and the field of criminology has undergone considerable change over the years. Before the 1970s criminologists either ignored or gave only passing notice to female offenders or victims. Albert Cohen (1955), well known for his research on male gang delinquency, dismissed females in this way:

> For the adolescent girl as well as for the adult woman, relationships with the opposite sex and those personal qualities which affect the ability to establish such relationships are central in importance. . . . "Boys collect

stamps, girls collect boys." . . . Dating, popularity with boys, pulchritude, "charm," clothes and dancing are preoccupations so central and so obvious that it would be useless pedantry to attempt to document them. (pp. 142, 147)

Travis Hirschi, in his influential book *The Causes of Delinquency,* relegated females to a footnote that said: "In the analysis that follows, the 'non-Negro' becomes 'white,' and the girls disappear" (1969:35). When female offenders were discussed in criminology, they were described in various disparaging ways, for instance, as childish, ugly, masculine, manipulative, sexually unsatisfied, plagued by penis envy, or inherently deceitful (because they could conceal lack of sexual arousal and fake orgasm) (see Balkan et al. 1980; Klein 1973). Similarly, women as victims of crime were either ignored or blamed for their victimization. According to Menachim Amir, the victim-precipitated rape victim "is the one who is acting out, initiating the interaction between her and the offender, and [who] by her behavior . . . generates the potentiality for criminal behavior of the offender or triggers this potentiality, if it existed before" (1971:259).

With these characterizations, criminologists were reflecting the attitudes and stereotypes of their day, attitudes and stereotypes that have historically existed in society at large. In the legal system, for example, women have experienced considerable **institutional sexism**, that is, discriminatory treatment by virtue of their sex. In the 1873 U.S. Supreme Court case of *Bradwell v. Illinois,* a woman was denied the right to practice law. One judge wrote: "Man is, or should be, woman's protector and defender. The natural and proper timidity and delicacy which belongs to the female sex evidently unfits it for many of the occupations of civil life" (cited in Lingren & Taub 1993:29). In an 1862 North Carolina Supreme Court case, a judge wrote: "The wife must be subject to the husband. Every man must govern his household . . . [and] there may be circumstances which will mitigate, excuse, and so far justify the husband in striking his wife" (cited in Bonsignore et al. 1994:10). More recently, in Wisconsin in 1977, a judge remarked, "Given the way women dress, rape is a normal reaction," and in 1982 another Wisconsin judge called a five-year-old sexual assault victim "an unusually sexually promiscuous young lady" (cited in Searles & Berger 1995:179).

The bias in these judicial proclamations is obvious to most of us today, although as we shall see, female *offenders* often receive more lenient treatment in the criminal justice system than their male counterparts. They may be the beneficiaries of paternalistic chivalry, simply be taken less seriously, or be deemed less blameworthy for their crimes (Daly 1994; see Chapters 11 and 12). Nonetheless, criminologists have critiqued outdated stereotypes and are now giving serious attention to women's experience from their point of view (Daly & Chesney-Lind 1988). Understanding this experience, however, will require familiarity with the concept of gender.

Gender refers to the "social statuses and meanings assigned to women and men" (Richardson et al. 1997:31). The social construction of gender begins at birth (or even before birth) when a child is designated as male or female on the basis of its genitalia. The child is named and dressed in such a way as to make this designation evident to observers, who respond to these gender markers by treating those labeled boys differently from those labeled girls. The children respond to this differential treatment by coming to feel and behave differently. As Judith Lorber observes:

> In social interaction throughout their lives, individuals learn what is expected, see what is expected, act and react in expected ways, and thus simultaneously construct and maintain the gender order. . . . Members of a social group neither make up gender as they go along nor exactly replicate in rote fashion what was done before. In almost every encounter human beings produce gender, behaving in the ways they learned were appropriate for their gender status, or resisting or rebelling against these norms. Resistance and rebellion have altered gender norms, but so far they have rarely eroded the statuses. (1997b:43)

A significant number of infants (1.7 percent) are actually born intersexed, with a mixture of male and female biological traits. Those with genitalia considered "ambiguous" are typically assigned at birth as male or female and treated with surgery and/or hormonal therapy. This practice has come under criticism by physicians, researchers, and the intersexed themselves (Fausto-Sterling 1993, 2000; Kessler 1998; see Boxes 2.1 and 5.1).

Traditionally, gender socialization has encouraged females more than males to be supportive, nurturant, and expressive of feelings. Girls have been more closely supervised by their families and given less freedom to "sow their wild oats." Boys, on the other hand, have been encouraged to be more aggressive and competitive and to take risks, both with each other and with females. These gendered norms and expectations are reflected in patterns of criminality and victimization. Males commit the overwhelming majority of crimes, particularly crimes of violence. Prostitution, shoplifting, and adolescent running away from home are the only crimes in which females have ever constituted a majority of arrests. In general, men are the primary victims of crimes by men, although women experience more sexual victimization—rape and sexual assault, child sexual abuse (including incest), domestic battery, and sexual harassment—especially from men they already know. This male predominance in criminal offending, previously glossed over by criminologists, has now become a central concern of criminological inquiry (Messerschmidt 1993).

According to Lorber, "Most societies rank genders according to prestige and power and construct them to be unequal" (1997b:40). Societies that ensure inequality between men and women—that grant men more power, prestige, and privilege—have been labeled **patriarchal**. In our society women continue, on average, to earn less than men, exercise less authority in the workplace, and exert less political and legal influence. Even sexual relationships have been wedded to power, for traditionally it has been assumed that "not only should a man be taller and stronger than a female in the perfect love-match, but he . . . [should] demonstrate his superior strength in gestures of dominance, which are perceived as amorous" (Griffin 1981:78). Traditional norms have encouraged men to adopt a "conquest mentality" toward women, to "act aggressively if they are to 'get' sex," and to regard women's protestations as efforts to appear respectable rather than as lack of interest in sex (Schur 1984:148). Hence it has been common and even socially acceptable for men to impose their sexual desires on women. Given the considerable resistance (especially by women) to traditional sexual scripts, notions of appropriate sexual expression are clearly in flux today. While sexuality has become "a domain of extensive exploration and pleasure for women," and one where many now feel entitled to pursue and initiate sex, "it remains simultaneously a site where gendered oppression may occur" (Messerschmidt 1993:76).

Clearly, many men do not feel more privileged than women. The pressures to be a breadwinner, to be economically successful, and to compete in the workplace with not only other men but now with women as well, suggest a complex relationship between men's subjective experience and the reality of their institutionalized advantage. It is also clear that not all men, or women, "do gender" according to traditional norms and expectations. Many feel, think, and behave in law-abiding and/or law-violating ways that defy gender stereotypes. But these variations do not deny the pervasiveness of gender. Rather, they speak to the need to recognize that masculinity and femininity are not homogeneous phenomena. There are a variety of masculinities and femininities that are socially constructed in interaction with class, race/ethnicity, sexual orientation, and other social experiences (Messerschmidt 1997).

PART 1

Methods and Theories

2

Crime Data and
Methods of Research

Susan Estrich (1987), professor of law and author of the book *Real Rape,*
received a phone call from a woman seeking advice. This woman had heard
that Estrich was an expert on rape. Estrich describes the conversation:

> She had been raped by the man she used to date. The relationship had
> gone sour. . . . He [had] followed her and raped her brutally. She felt vio-
> lated and betrayed. At first she did not know what to do. She talked to
> friends and relatives. She decided to report it to the police. She talked to
> the police and the assistant district attorney. . . . No one said she was a
> liar, exactly. No one laughed at her, or abused her. They just said that they
> would not arrest him, would not file charges. It was all explained thor-
> oughly, the way things are done these days by good district attorneys. She
> had not gone immediately to the doctor. By the time she did, some of the
> bruises had healed and the evidence of sperm had not been preserved. She
> had not complained to the police right away. She knew the man. They'd
> had a prior relationship of intimacy. He was a respected businessman. He
> had no criminal record. She couldn't believe their response. (p. 28)

The woman called Estrich to ask her what she could do to get the prosecutors to do something. Estrich, knowing how common this scenario is,
knowing how the system works, replied, "Nothing."

The story Estrich tells illustrates but one way in which our knowledge
of crime is limited, incomplete. It provides a striking example of how
crime—even reported crime—may fail to become part of the official
record. Not all crime is counted as crime. Not all crime seems to count,
seems to matter to law enforcement authorities.

Nevertheless, developing a sociological imagination, understanding
that personal troubles are also public issues, requires information about
what is occurring in the real world. In Chapter 1 we saw how information
presented by the media, politicians, and even law enforcement is sometimes misleading, can sometimes distort our knowledge of crime. So how

37

are we to proceed? Sociological thinking does not mean engaging in mere speculation or relying on faith alone. We want you to be able to ground your understanding of crime in empirical evidence, that is, in measurement and observation of crime phenomena. Some of the evidence used by criminologists comes from statistical data compiled by agencies of the government. Some of it (both statistical and nonstatistical) is generated independently by criminologists and other researchers. And some of it comes from testimonies by victims and offenders themselves.

Each method of data collection and analysis has inherent advantages and disadvantages. This chapter will familiarize you with the various sources of crime data, help you become critical consumers of this information, and show you how it can be used to enhance your understanding of crime.

Criminologists refer to the methods of measurement and observation that they use to gather information about crime as **social research**. It is this research component of criminology that underlies its claim to be a social science. Being scientific requires using particular procedures or techniques to gather and analyze data and being willing to subject your findings to the critical scrutiny of other researchers so that bias, error, and fraudulent claims can be detected (Neuman 2003). But being scientific does not, in our view, require you to be value-neutral, to abandon the moral compass that guides your understanding of the world. Indeed, the perspective from which apparently neutral data are analyzed "clearly makes a difference both in the conclusions to be drawn and in the policy implications that emerge from those conclusions" (Grant Bowman 1992:205). This is why theoretical explanation, the subject of later chapters, is so important to empirical research.

■ Counting Crime: The Uniform Crime Reports

The most widely used data on crime in the United States come from the official government statistics that have been published annually since 1930 in the Federal Bureau of Investigation's *Uniform Crime Reports (UCR)*. The *UCR* have their origins in the efforts of J. Edgar Hoover, director of the Bureau of Investigation (renamed the Federal Bureau of Investigation [FBI] in 1935), to expand his agency's role in federal law enforcement and in the collection of national crime statistics. Hoover received support from the International Association of Chiefs of Police (IACP), whose Committee on Uniform Crime Records published an elaborate guide in 1929 titled "Uniform Crime Reporting: A Complete Manual for Police." This manual proposed a standardized crime classification system to be used throughout the country. The IACP committee developed a schedule or form that all police departments were to voluntarily complete and submit to the federal government for compilation and publication of statistical information. In 1930 the U.S. Congress adopted the committee's recommendations and the FBI began publishing the *UCR*. Currently, most police departments around the country participate in the national reporting program (Balkan et al. 1980; Mosher et al. 2002; Poveda 1990).

The IACP committee's classification scheme was based on a distinction between "offenses which naturally and most inevitably are reported to police agencies and those which are less certain of becoming a matter of record" (cited in Balkan et al. 1980:108). This distinction is reflected in the *UCR* division between **Index crimes**, or *Part I offenses,* and **non-Index crimes**, or *Part II offenses.* In the original formulation, Part I offenses included four "crimes against persons," or violent crimes—homicide, forcible rape, robbery, and aggravated assault—and three "crimes against property"—burglary, larceny-theft, and motor vehicle theft. The Part II offenses include twenty-one additional (mostly nonviolent) categories of violations (see Table 2.4).

Annual data on arrests are published for both Part I and Part II offenses, but data on crimes reported by citizens to the police or those that are otherwise known to or observed directly by the police are published only for Part I offenses. Since most reported (or known) crimes do not result in an arrest, data on Part I offenses are the ones most often cited in media reports and public discussions about how much crime is occurring in society. (In 1979 arson was added to the list of Part I property crimes, although arson data remain inadequately collected by police departments and are not included in national estimates on crimes reported to the police. Arson is included in arrest data, however.)

The distinction between Index and non-Index crimes assumes that the former are more serious and thereby more reflective of the real crime problem. This assumption, however, is questionable. For example, Table 2.1 shows that 59 percent of reported Index crimes in 2002 were for the nonviolent crime of larceny-theft, which includes shoplifting and bicycle theft, offenses that do not rank high in the public's concern about crime (see Roberts & Stalans 2000; Warr 2000). Overall, 88 percent of Index crimes were property crimes, while just 12 percent were violent crimes. Homicide in particular constituted less than 1 percent. Moreover, the government's preoccupation with drugs is not reflected in the Index crime category, since drug offenses are classified as Part II offenses. Neither are white-collar crimes listed as Index crimes. To the extent that such crimes (e.g., fraud, embezzlement) are even included as Part II offenses, they generally consist of those committed by the less affluent rather than those committed by businesses or corporations.

Table 2.2 presents data on Index crime rates from 1960 to 2002. The crime rate provides a measure of the amount of crime relative to the size of

Table 2.1   *UCR* Reported Index Crimes (2002)

Type of Crime	Number	Percentage[a]
Violent crimes	1,426,325	12.0
Homicide[b]	16,204	0.1
Forcible rape	95,136	0.7
Robbery	420,637	3.5
Aggravated assault	894,348	7.5
Property crimes	10,450,893	88.0
Burglary	2,151,875	18.1
Larceny-theft	7,052,922	59.4
Motor vehicle theft	1,246,096	10.5
Total Index crimes	11,877,218	100.0

Source: FBI 2003, tab. 2.

Notes: a. It is possible for a single incident of criminality to include more than one crime; for example, a theft could involve both breaking and entering (burglary) and forceful action against an individual (robbery). In such cases, only the most serious of the offenses is recorded for the purpose of the *UCR* statistical record.

b. Homicide = murder and nonnegligent manslaughter.

Table 2.2   *UCR* Index Crime Rates (1960–2002)

Year	Total Index Crime Rate[a]	Violent Crime Rate	Property Crime Rate
1960	1,887.2	160.9	1,726.3
1965	2,449.0	200.2	2,248.8
1970	3,984.5	363.5	3,621.0
1975	5,298.5	487.8	4,810.7
1980	5,950.0	596.6	5,353.3
1985	5,224.5	558.1	4,666.4
1990	5,802.7	729.6	5,073.1
1995	5,274.9	684.5	4,590.5
2000	4,124.8	506.5	3,618.3
2002	4,118.8	494.6	3,624.1

Source: FBI 1976, tab. 2; 1986, tab. 1; 2003, tabs. 1–2.

Note: a. Rate = per 100,000 population.

the population. It is calculated by dividing the number of crimes by the size of the population and (according to convention) multiplying this quotient by 100,000. In 2002 the total Index crime rate was 4,118.8 per 100,000 persons in the United States.

Crime rates are the figures most often used to measure increases or decreases in crime over time. Between 1960 and 2002 the total Index crime rate increased by 118 percent. Overall, the most dramatic increases in the crime rate over the past four decades took place some time ago, in the

1960s and early 1970s. Since 1980 the total Index crime rate has actually decreased by 31 percent. The declining crime rate was especially apparent in the 1990s, as law enforcement, politicians, and the media orchestrated a good deal of fanfare over the apparent success of various crime control policies (Blumstein & Wallman 2000; Conklin 2003; Reiman 2004). While the decline seems to have tempered, this phenomenon begs for explanation. But first, we need to consider the fallibility of these figures. As critical consumers of crime data, especially government-generated data, you need to be familiar with their limitations.

▨   *Underreporting by Citizens*

Evidence from other sources of crime statistics (to be reviewed later) indicates that a large proportion of crime is not reported to the police and hence does not appear in these data. The reasons for citizen underreporting are numerous. People may believe that the crime was not serious enough to warrant police action or that the police could not or would not do anything about it. They may be uncertain that what they had witnessed or experienced was, in fact, an illegal act, or they may feel that what transpired (even if illegal) was a private matter. Some may be reluctant to inform on the individuals involved in the crime, may have something to hide themselves, may place a negative value on cooperating with the police, or may simply not want to get involved. Some may fear reprisal from the offender or be embarrassed about their own victimization (Sheley 1985).

Most of the reported crimes that are known to the police come to their attention because of citizen reports (Reiss 1971). Hence fluctuations in reported crime rates over time may be as much a function of changes in the likelihood of citizen reporting as a function of changes in the level of criminal activity itself. Take, for instance, the reporting of theft. Insurance companies generally require that thefts be reported before claims can be settled, making people with theft insurance more likely to report crimes than those who are uninsured. If, over time, the number of people who are insured increases, then the rate of reported thefts may increase as well. Similarly, it is likely that the introduction of the 911 emergency phone number across the country made it easier to call the police, thereby increasing the proportion of crime that is reported (Barkan 2001).

Historically, one of the most significant areas of unreported crime has involved violence against women, such as rape and domestic battery. Women have remained silent about their victimization for many reasons, for example, they may feel humiliated or embarrassed, fear further violence or retaliation by the offender, or fear hostile questioning or disbelief from the police or other criminal justice officials. Since the 1970s, however, the educational and law-reform efforts of the contemporary feminist movement have increased our sensitivity to these issues. The development of rape crisis centers and battered women's shelters, improvements in police training, the addition of female officers, and various legal reforms (e.g., "rape shield" laws that restrict courtroom questioning of victims' prior sexual conduct, mandatory arrest policies for domestic batterers) have encouraged women to come forward with complaints. These changes can increase the official rates of rape and aggravated assault (which may now include more domestic battery cases) even though they are relatively independent of the actual amount of crime that has occurred (Berger et al. 1994; Jensen & Karpos 1993; Merlo & Pollock 1995; Searles & Berger 1995).

■ The Organizational Production of Crime Data

Crime statistics need to be understood as outcomes of organizational processes that are conditioned by "the interpretations, decisions, and actions of law enforcement personnel" (Kitsuse & Cicourel 1963:167). Donald Black (1970), for instance, studied police decisionmaking in the cities of Boston, Chicago, and the District of Columbia. He found that the preference, attitude, and class status of the complainant (the person who calls the police) had a significant impact on police officers' decisions to record an incident as crime. Officers were *more likely* to record a crime when the complainant expressed a preference for formal rather than informal action, was deferential or respectful to the police, and was white-collar rather than blue-collar in status. Black also found that the relational distance between the complainant and suspect was a factor: the closer the relational distance (e.g., family member versus stranger), the *less likely* the incident was recorded.

Several studies have found that the relational distance between complainant and suspect is especially important in police responses to rape. The closer the relational distance, the more likely the police will label the complaint as "unfounded," as not a real rape (Estrich 1987). Often the veracity of a woman's complaint is judged according to the interpersonal context of the incident. Complaints by women whose moral character is questioned or whose perceived carelessness is thought to have made them vulnerable to attack are treated more skeptically (LaFree 1989; Sanders 1980). Among those least likely to have their complaints treated seriously are juvenile runaways, hitchhikers, and prostitutes; those who are raped in situations involving alcohol and drug use; those who willingly enter the offender's home or apartment; and those considered to be partiers, pleasure seekers, or sexually promiscuous. In addition, police officers may distinguish between "good victims" and "bad victims" on the basis of their perception of how well the case is likely to stand up in court. As one investigating officer remarked, "Generally speaking, I believe something happened. I believe what the lady is saying. . . . But I'm also aware that someone else looking at the incident may see it a little differently" (Beneke 1982:152). Another officer put it this way:

> I'm not going to lie to a woman and tell her she's got a case when she hasn't. She'll devote all her time and energy into putting this guy away and it'll be bearing on her mind and then the defense attorney tears her apart and the jury brings back a "not guilty" verdict. . . . Why give anybody false hopes? . . . I've had enough cases in front of juries so I can just about tell which way it's going to go. (pp. 145–146)

(Some of these thoughts probably ran through the minds of the police officers and the assistant district attorney who spoke to the woman whose rape was described at the beginning of this chapter.)

In another study, Barbara Warner (1997) examined the effects of community characteristics on police recording of burglary complaints (911 calls) in sixty-one neighborhoods in Boston. Warner found that overall only 40 percent of the burglary complaints were later verified and recorded by the police as burglaries. The majority of the incidents were downgraded to less serious Part II offenses or recorded as nonoffenses. The proportion of burglary complaints that were recorded as burglaries ranged across neighborhoods from 14 percent to 58 percent.

Warner found that burglary recording was *lower* in areas marked by more poverty. She offered several explanations for this finding. The poor generally receive few public services of all sorts, and police services are no exception. Police may view poor neighborhoods as inhabited by morally unworthy people who get what they deserve. Or police may simply feel that there is no reason to write an official burglary report when so many of the residents are without insurance and the likelihood of recovering the stolen goods is virtually nil. On the other hand, Warner found that police recording of burglaries was *higher* in neighborhoods that were more culturally diverse and that had more mobile residents. (Cultural diversity was measured by the percentage of residents who were foreign born; mobility was measured by the percentage of residents age five and older who had not lived in the same house for five years.) She reasoned that in more heterogeneous and residentially transient communities, police are less able to rely on informal methods of responding to citizens' complaints (e.g., mediation of disputes between neighbors).

Robert McCleary and colleagues (1982) also studied the organizational production of crime data. In one city McCleary and colleagues found that crime rates increased when police administrators removed supervisory sergeants from the radio dispatch bureau, the unit responsible for receiving citizen calls and setting priorities for officers' responses to calls. Requests for police assistance that were dispatched immediately were more likely than requests that were delayed to eventually yield an official crime report. When supervisory sergeants were present, dispatchers were relieved of the responsibility of setting priorities and filtering out less serious calls. But when sergeants were unavailable, dispatchers were more likely to order immediate responses to "play it safe" and "cover their asses." Under these conditions reported *UCR* crimes increased about 20 percent.

In addition, McCleary and colleagues found that the ways in which officers classified offenses could inflate or deflate *UCR* statistics. In one city, uniformed officers were more likely than detectives to classify a broad range of thefts as burglaries. Detectives employed a narrower (and technically accurate) definition of burglary as breaking and entering into a house or enclosed garage. Uniformed officers, on the other hand, recorded breaking through a fence and stealing from a yard as burglaries as well. Differences in such classification decisions increased the number of burglaries in this city by about 150 per month.

Henry Brownstein served more than two years as chief of the Bureau of Statistical Services for New York State's Division of Criminal Justice Services (DCJS), where he "was responsible for the collection, maintenance, and dissemination of official crime and criminal justice data" for the state of New York (1996:19–20). In New York, *UCR* data are voluntarily submitted by over 600 local police departments. *UCR* clerks in different locales have the responsibility of completing forms detailing information about crimes that have been reported in their jurisdiction. These clerks are poorly trained, overworked, and experience high turnover rates. They have difficulty completing the forms in ways that allow an understaffed DCJS to clearly differentiate Part I from Part II offenses. It is not always easy, for example, to distinguish murders and nonnegligent (willful) manslaughters, which are Part I offenses, from justifiable homicides, accidental deaths, suicides, and negligent manslaughters. Similarly, the line between Part I aggravated assaults and Part II simple assaults is not always clear-cut. Moreover, police departments in different jurisdictions often compete with each other "to show that they are responsible for a greater share of the problem that resources [they hope will be forthcoming] will be used to solve" (p. 23). This competition creates a problem of duplicate reporting, as departments try to get credit for the same crimes.

Each month the DCJS receives about 800 forms from the local police departments. Much discretionary decisionmaking is required to translate these forms into standardized *UCR* categories and to reconcile competing jurisdictional claims. The pressure of FBI deadlines for the submission of *UCR* statistics often means that this work is hastily performed. Brownstein found that it was not unusual for the DCJS to submit the New York State data before all the localities in New York City had submitted their forms. Hence the data eventually published in New York State's own *Crime and*

Justice Annual Report were at variance from those received by the FBI.

In Chapter 1 we noted that media and law enforcement interests often converge in finding mutual benefit from portrayals of escalating crime. At the same time we noted that there are occasions when public officials will downplay concerns about crime. The Philadelphia Police Department has been the focus of criticism over a number of years for reporting practices designed to minimize official recorded Index crime rates. An audit review of the department's 1998 data, for example, found that the department had failed to report some 37,000 Index crimes to the *UCR*. Similarly, a study of the Atlanta Police Department found that police officials downgraded the violent crime rate the year prior to both the 1996 Olympic Games and the mayoral election to make the city appear safer (Conklin 2003; Mosher et al. 2002).

Clearance Rates and Arrest Data

Crimes reported or known to the police are not the only statistical counts of crime included in the *UCR*. Clearance rates and arrest data are other important indicators. The **clearance rate** is essentially the rate of solved crimes. This rate is calculated by dividing the number of reports for each Index crime by the number of arrests for that crime, arriving at a percentage of each crime that is "cleared by arrest." Table 2.3 lists the Index crime clearance rates for 2002. The data show that violent crimes, especially murder, have higher clearance rates than property crimes. This means, of course, that the chance of the police recovering your stolen property is rather slim.

Like official reports, clearance rates are organizationally constructed. While there are times when police departments find lower clearance rates advantageous for requesting resources, a department's image is generally enhanced by a higher clearance rate. Hugh Barlow notes that police will "sometimes go to extraordinary lengths to 'clear' crimes" (1996:44). To

Table 2.3   Clearance Rates for *UCR* Index Crimes (2002)

Type of Crime	Percentage
Homicide[a]	64
Forcible rape	45
Robbery	26
Aggravated assault	57
Burglary	13
Larceny-theft	18
Motor vehicle theft	14
Arson	17

Source: FBI 2003, tab. 25.
Note: a. Homicide = murder and nonnegligent manslaughter.

illustrate his point, Barlow offers the case of Henry Lee Lucas. In 1983, law enforcement identified Lucas as a serial murderer who had confessed to nearly 100 murders across the country. Barlow writes:

> By 1984 it was reported that he had confessed to 360 murders, and by 1985 the figure stood at an incredible 600 killings in nearly 30 different states. In that same year, however, the *New York Times* reported that Lucas may actually have killed only one person, his mother! As the story unfolded, it became apparent that Lucas had been pressured by eager police into making confessions so that they could clear their books of unsolved murders. The truth will probably never be known, but most of the murders cleared by Lucas's arrest and "confessions" were not committed by him. (p. 44)

In addition to clearance rates, arrest data can be used to examine the proportion of police activity devoted to Part II offenses. In many respects the emphasis in the *UCR* on Index crimes misrepresents what the police actually do, since over 80 percent of arrests are for Part II offenses. Table 2.4 provides the percentage breakdown of the arrests for these crimes for

Table 2.4   Part II Offenses as a Percentage of All *UCR* Arrests (2002)

Type of Crime	Percentage of Arrests
Part II arrests	83.9
Other assaults	9.4
Forgery and counterfeiting	1.0
Fraud	2.4
Embezzlement	0.1
Stolen property[a]	1.0
Vandalism	2.0
Weapons[a]	1.2
Prostitution and commercialized vice	0.6
Sex offenses[a]	0.7
Drug abuse violations	11.2
Gambling	0.1
Offenses against family and children	1.0
Driving under the influence	10.4
Liquor laws	4.7
Drunkenness	4.2
Disorderly conduct	4.9
Vagrancy	0.2
All other offenses (except traffic)	26.6
Suspicion	0.1
Curfew and loitering	1.1
Runaways	1.0

Source: FBI 2003, tab. 30.
Note: a. Stolen property = buying, receiving, and possessing. Weapons = carrying, possessing, etc. Sex offenses = except forcible rape and prostitution.

2002. Taken together, drug and alcohol-related arrests constitute the largest group of offenses, nearly a third of all arrests (Part I and Part II). Arrests listed as "all other offenses (except traffic)," a catchall category reflecting a variety of minor state and local laws, constitute over a quarter of all arrests.

Finally, *UCR* arrest data also include information about the age, race, and gender of individuals who are arrested. Unfortunately, arrest data by class are not collected for the nation as a whole, although some studies have examined official records from particular localities and found an inverse relationship between class status and arrests, that is, lower-status people had higher arrest rates than higher-status people (Shaw & McKay 1942; Tracy et al. 1990; Wolfgang et al. 1972). Arrest data, however, may not reflect a group's actual rate of law violation, for persons who manage to avoid arrest may nevertheless be extensively involved in crime.

National *UCR* data can be used to construct age-specific, race-specific, and gender-specific arrest rates that allow for comparisons between age, race, and gender groups. Such rates are calculated by dividing the number of arrests for individuals in a particular group by the number of persons in that group. Age-, race-, and gender-specific Index crime arrest rates for 2002 are presented in Table 2.5. The data show that arrest rates are highest for adolescents and young adults, African Americans, and males.

As alluded to earlier, there are essentially two ways to interpret these arrest rates. They may represent "differential criminal involvement" or they may represent "differential likelihood of selection" (Sheley 1985). From this perspective we can ask whether higher arrest rates are indicative of a

Table 2.5   Age-, Race-, and Gender-Specific Arrest Rates for *UCR* Index Crimes (2002)

	Violent Arrest Rate[a]	Property Arrest Rate
Age		
10–14	99.1	594.4
15–19	419.3	1,770.5
20–24	451.4	981.5
25–29	321.7	579.2
30–34	261.3	504.4
35–39	222.4	447.6
Race		
White	115.8	343.5
Black	467.7	952.5
American Indian/Alaskan Native	179.6	498.6
Asian/Pacific Islander	45.9	155.1
Gender		
Male	264.0	579.8
Female	53.7	248.0

Source: FBI 2003, tabs. 38, 42–43; U.S. Department of Commerce 2002, tabs. 11–12, 14.
Note: a. Rate = arrests per 100,000 population of each group.

group's greater involvement in *these types of offenses,* or whether they are indicative of members' vulnerability to being apprehended by police. It is also possible that both differential involvement and differential selection account for these rates. Throughout this book we will present data that will allow us to assess these differing interpretations.

■ The Declining Crime Rate in the 1990s

Having considered the limitations of official crime data, we can now critically assess the declining crime rate in the 1990s. During that decade, national attention often focused on New York City, which previously had a reputation as one of the most dangerous locales in the country. Mayor Rudolph Giuliani, a former federal prosecutor, took the reins of city government, pledging to make New York safer. Giuliani appointed former New York City transit police chief William Bratton to head the city's police department. Under Bratton's leadership, New York police implemented a strategy of aggressive law enforcement against "quality of life" offenses such as jumping subway turnstiles, public drunkenness and underage drinking, truancy, prostitution, panhandling, graffiti writing, and playing loud music in public (Bratton 1998). The theory was that "zero tolerance" for these transgressions would have a trickle-down effect on reducing serious crimes. Bratton also initiated a computerized system of mapping city "hot spots" to improve police intelligence and deploy officers more effectively.

Some New York police officials, on the other hand, admitted that there was pressure on them to downgrade crimes to lower serious crime rates. In a review of the evidence for the nation as a whole, John Conklin (2003) concludes that police enforcement strategies like those adopted in New York may have had an impact on declining crime rates, but police alone did not exert an influence independent of other factors (also see Eck & Maguire 2000).

The age structure of society. Many criminologists attribute the previous dramatic rise in crime rates during the 1960s and early 1970s to the coming-of-age of the post–World War II baby boomers (Cohen & Land 1987; Steffensmeier et al. 1987). Darrell Steffensmeier and colleagues observed that the types of crime measured by the *UCR* seem to "peak in adolescence or early adulthood [and] then decline fairly steadily" (1989:806; see Table 2.5). This pattern, they believe, stems from

> the increased sources of criminogenic reinforcement experienced by young people . . . [and] the powerful institutional pressures for conformity that accompany adulthood. Juveniles have not as yet developed either a well-defined sense of self or strong stakes in conformity. . . . They are barred from many legitimate avenues for achieving socially valued goals; their dependent status insulates them from many of the social and legal costs of illegitimate activities; and their stage of cognitive development limits prudence concerning the consequences of their behavior. (pp. 806–807)

As the baby boom generation aged, and the size of the youthful population began to decline, property crime rates stabilized or declined (Cohen & Land 1987; Steffensmeier et al. 1987). The violent crime rate, however, has been more resilient to such demographic shifts, perhaps because of street gangs and the increased availability of guns among youths. As for the 1990s, Conklin (2003) estimates that age composition explains from 8 percent (for motor vehicle theft) to 20 percent (for homicide) of the declining crime rate, depending on the particular Index crime that is being assessed.

It is too early to tell whether the decline in both property and violent crime in the 1990s will be short-lived or long-term. Albert Blumstein (1993) warns that demographic data indicate an expected growth in the youthful population in the near future as the "baby boomerang" generation—the children of the baby boomers—continues to come of age. Steven Levitt, on the other hand, believes that "predictions of an impending demographically driven crime wave" are exaggerated (1999:581). His analysis of crime rate trends leads him to predict no more than a one percent change per year due to the age demographics through 2010. It is also important to note, however, that youths are not an undifferentiated mass, and broad generalizations about them mask critical distinctions. Later we will consider the ways in which the age structure of society intersects with class, race/ethnicity, and gender.

Additional influences. Most criminologists suggest that the declining crime rate can be explained by the confluence of a number of factors, although there is disagreement about which ones are more important for which types of crime. Blumstein (2002) believes that stabilization of the crack cocaine market, gun control measures (e.g., Brady Bill), and a vibrant economy have been the most significant factors. Conklin (2003) thinks that increasing incarceration rates may have been even more important (see Chapter 12). Jeffrey Reiman reminds us that the declining rate is not necessarily indicative of dramatic success in dealing with crime. While it may represent a reduction from the rather high crime rates of the past, crime rates remain "high nonetheless" (2004:18).

■ Other Counts of Crime

The FBI has recently developed a new system for collecting official crime data, the *National Incident-Based Reporting System (NIBRS)*. The *NIBRS* includes more extensive information on each crime incident and arrest, such as information about the relationship between offenders and victims and about the use of drugs and alcohol. (This type of data is already available for homicides in a supplement of the *UCR*.) The *NIBRS* is being phased in very gradually. As of 1999, law enforcement agencies that contributed to it represented just 6 percent of the U.S. population. Thus it will be a long time before the *NIBRS* will rival the *UCR* as the primary source of governmental crime statistics. Moreover, the *NIBRS* will likely suffer from many of the same validity problems as the *UCR*. Thus the *National Crime Victimization Survey,* conducted by the Department of Justice's Bureau of Justice Statistics (BJS), is likely to remain the major government-sponsored alternative to the *UCR*.

▨ *The National Crime Victimization Survey*

In the late 1960s the President's Commission on Law Enforcement and Administration of Justice recommended the implementation of a national survey of crime victimization to supplement the *UCR*. The commission hoped that this effort would provide information on criminal victimizations that remained unreported or unknown to the police. In 1972, after some pilot surveys, the BJS began conducting the *National Crime Survey,* now called the *National Crime Victimization Survey (NCVS),* to provide annual estimates of crime victimization. In the first few years the **victimization survey** included interviews with individuals in both households and businesses, but the business component was soon dropped. Although the size of the interviewing sample has varied over the years, in 2000 it involved 159,240 persons (age twelve years and older) from about 86,800 households. During the interview, which occurs in person or by phone, individuals are asked questions about victimizations they experienced over the previous six months. Follow-up interviews are then conducted every six months over a three-and-a-half-year period. The data gathered from these interviews are used to compute estimates of victimization rates for the nation as a whole (Maguire & Pastore 2001; Mosher et al. 2002; Sykes & Cullen 1992).

Until 1992 the BJS survey categorized victimizations as "personal crimes" or "household crimes." The former included an assortment of violent crimes and thefts; the latter included only thefts. (Questions about homicides are not included because homicide victims obviously cannot respond.) In 1992 the BJS redesigned the survey, reclassifying crimes as either "personal crimes" or "property crimes." The former include crimes of violence (rape/sexual assault, robbery, and assault) and purse snatching/pocket picking; and the latter include burglary, motor vehicle theft, and other household thefts (see Table 2.6). As with *UCR* data, *NCVS* data indicate that the majority of victimizations (74 percent) are for property crimes. Importantly, however, the *NCVS* also taps a domain of unreported crimes that is missing from the *UCR*. Only 43 percent of personal crimes and 34 percent of property crimes were reported to the police. Rape/sexual assault

Table 2.6 *NCVS:* **Number and Percentage of Victimizations Reported to Police (1999)**

Type of Crime	Number of Victimizations[a]	Percentage Reported to Police
Personal crimes	7,564,690	43.4
Crimes of violence	7,357,060	43.9
Rape/sexual assault	383,170	28.3
Robbery	810,220	61.2
Assault	6,163,670	42.6
Purse snatching/pocket picking	207,630	25.9
Property crimes	21,215,110	33.8
Household burglary	3,651,580	49.3
Motor vehicle theft	1,068,130	83.7
Theft[b]	16,495,400	27.1
Total crimes	28,779,800	36.3

Source: Maguire & Pastore 2001, tab. 3.38.
Notes: a. Completed and attempted crimes and threats are collapsed in this table.

b. Includes crimes previously classified as "personal larceny without contact" and "household larceny."

and purse snatching/pocket picking had the lowest rates of reporting (28 and 26 percent, respectively) and motor vehicle theft had the highest (84 percent). Overall, personal victimization rates have remained fairly stable since the 1970s, although they have experienced intervals of increase and decrease. (The 1990s was a period of decrease.) Property victimization rates, on the other hand, have undergone "a virtually uninterrupted decrease" (Maguire & Pastore 2001; Rand et al. 1997:1).

The *NCVS* suffers from some of the same problems as the *UCR*. There are no questions, for instance, about drug offenses or white-collar crimes. Homeless individuals are not sampled. Business victimizations, as indicated before, have been omitted since the early years of the survey. In addition, many respondents forget victimizations, are unaware of the victimizations of family members, or report crimes that occurred before the six-month period. And college-educated respondents, who have more experience with test-taking, may report a higher proportion of their victimizations than less-educated individuals (Sykes & Cullen 1992).

The survey is administered in a two-stage process. Respondents are first asked several screening questions pertaining to the number of times they have been victimized by each type of offense. If they answer in the affirmative, they are then asked a number of follow-up questions regarding details of the crime and characteristics of the offender(s). This mode of questioning has been particularly problematic when the information sought concerned rape.

Prior to a 1992 survey redesign, the first stage of the interview asked respondents "whether someone [had] tried to take something from them, rob them, beat them, attack them with a weapon, or steal things from them. *None of these questions ask[ed] whether someone ha[d] tried to rape them.* The question that [was] supposed to elicit rape [read]: 'Did anyone TRY to attack you in some other way?'" (Eigenberg 1990:657). Respondents were thus never specifically asked about rape victimizations. The BJS estimates that the survey redesign alone (which included more direct questioning about rape) more than doubled the reported rate of rape, although the rate has declined in recent years (Rand et al. 1997). Still problematic, however, is the fact that victims of rape and domestic violence may be asked about their experiences while the perpetrator (e.g., spouse or partner) is in the room with them.

Like *UCR* arrest data, the *NCVS* also provides information about the social characteristics of offenders. These data must be viewed with extreme caution, since respondents' perceptions of such characteristics can be inaccurate. Nevertheless, the data are consistent with the *UCR:* the offenders in these types of crimes are disproportionately young, nonwhite, and male.

Unlike *UCR* arrest data, the *NCVS* contains information on the social background of victims (see Table 2.7). To a large extent these data mirror

Table 2.7 *NCVS* **Victimization Rates by Age, Income, Race, Ethnicity, and Gender (1999)**

	Personal Rate[a]	Property Rate[a]
Age		
12–15	77.5	NA
16–19	78.9	NA
20–24	69.5	NA
25–34	37.4	NA
35–49	25.6	NA
50–64	15.0	NA
65 and older	4.4	NA
Income		
Under $7,500	59.5	220.8
$7,500–$14,999	45.6	200.1
$15,000–$24,999	36.1	214.9
$25,000–$34,999	39.1	199.1
$35,000–$49,999	30.8	207.6
$50,000–$74,999	33.7	213.6
$75,000 and over	24.1	220.4
Race[b]		
White	32.7	190.0
Black	42.9	249.9
Other	26.0	206.3
Ethnicity[b]		
Hispanic	35.3	232.5
Non-Hispanic	33.3	194.6
Gender		
Male	37.9	NA
Female	29.7	NA

Source: Maguire & Pastore 2001, tabs. 3.4–3.5, 3.7–3.8, 3.13, 3.24–3.26.
Notes: a. Personal rates = per 1,000 persons age 12 or older. Property rates = per 1,000 households.
b. Refers to head of household.
NA = not available.

the data on offenders: violent victimization rates are higher for adolescents and young adults, lower-income groups, African Americans and Hispanics, and males (except for rape). Property victimization rates (which are not categorized by age or gender) are higher for African Americans and Hispanics. The pattern of property victimization by income is less clear, with different income groups experiencing comparable rates of property crime. Although lower-income households in high-crime areas are more vulnerable to crime (especially burglary), higher-income households have more to steal and thus make attractive targets for theft.

■ Self-Report Surveys
Another source of quantitative crime data falls under the rubric of **self-report surveys**. Here respondents are asked to provide information on

offenses they have committed. The first known self-report survey was conducted by Austin Porterfield (1943) on a sample of adolescents and young adults in Fort Worth, Texas. Porterfield was interested in comparing the law-violation rates of youths who had juvenile court records with college students who did not. His survey results revealed comparable rates of crime among these two groups. Porterfield explained his findings in terms consistent with what later became known as "labeling theory," suggesting that the higher class status of college youth had insulated them from arrest (see Chapters 1 and 4).

Like victimization surveys, self-report studies tap into a domain of crime that is largely missing from the official record. Unfortunately, there have been few self-report studies conducted with adults (e.g., Dunaway et al. 2000; Evans et al. 1995; Thornberry & Farnworth 1982) and some of these have been limited to incarcerated offenders (e.g., Chaiken & Chaiken 1982; Tremblay & Morselli 2000; Wright & Rossi 1986). Most of the self-report research has been conducted with adolescents, often administered in high school settings. One of the most well-known self-report surveys (not administered in high schools) is the *National Youth Survey (NYS),* developed by the Behavioral Research Institute at the University of Colorado under the direction of Delbert Elliott. This national survey of about 1,700 youths born between 1959 and 1965 was administered annually from 1976 to 1980 and every two to three years until 1995 (Elliott & Ageton 1980; Mosher et al. 2002).

Like victimization surveys, self-report surveys suffer from memory problems of those who take them, both the forgetting of offenses and the reporting of offenses outside of a study's time frame (usually one year prior). Overall, self-report surveys have been found to contain relatively little distortion due to respondents' deception. But because some evidence suggests that African American youths may underreport the extent of their official police records, some researchers suspect that they may also underreport delinquency. Perhaps these youths are more distrustful of how the survey results will be used, or perhaps they dispute the validity of the official charges against them (Hindelang et al. 1981; Mosher et al. 2002; Walker et al. 2004).

These limitations notwithstanding, a large body of adolescent self-report research now exists that indicates that delinquent behavior is widespread among youths from all social backgrounds. However, the studies that suggest class and race parity in law violation are at variance with *UCR* arrest rates, and they have generated a great deal of controversy (Tittle & Meier 1990; Tittle et al. 1978). They not only raise the specter of discrimination but also call into question theories of delinquency based on economic and minority-group disadvantage. If delinquency is viewed primarily as a lower-class or racial minority-group problem, as liberals maintain, then the root causes of crime will be sought in the social conditions associated with lower-class and disadvantaged communities. If, on the other hand, there is little relationship between class, race, and delinquency, then the causes can be attributed to factors that affect all social groups (e.g., declining moral values, low family cohesion).

Michael Hindelang and colleagues were among the first to argue that the discrepancy between official (*UCR* arrests) and self-report measures of delinquency was "largely illusory," because the two sources of data did not "tap the same domain of behavior." Self-report surveys, they observed, generally ask about a wider range of behaviors than are reported in the *UCR,* and they are skewed toward less serious items that remain largely "outside the domain of behavior that elicits official attention" (1978:995–996). Thus Hindelang and colleagues argued that there is no relationship between class, race, and *less serious* delinquency, but that official data provide a valid measure of the *more serious* youthful offenses that are of primary concern to law enforcement authorities.

Delbert Elliott and Suzanne Ageton (1980) subsequently examined race and class differences for different categories of self-reported *NYS* offenses: *predatory crimes against persons* (e.g., assault, robbery), *predatory crimes against property* (e.g., burglary, auto theft), *illegal service crimes* (e.g., prostitution, selling drugs), *public disorder crimes* (e.g., carrying a weapon, disorderly conduct, marijuana use), *status offenses* (e.g., running away, truancy), and *hard drug use* (e.g., heroin, cocaine). They found statistically significant race differences for property crimes and class differences for violent crimes (i.e., higher rates for African American and lower-class youths) but not for the other offense categories. They also found that most of the race and class differences, to the extent they existed, stemmed from a small number of high-frequency or chronic offenders who inflated the overall rates of their respective groups (see Wolfgang et al. 1972; Tracy et al. 1990). Elliott and Ageton concluded that the differences between their findings and those of earlier self-report studies were "the result of differences in the specific [self-report] measures used" (p. 95).

In analyses of subsequent *NYS* samples, Delbert Elliott and David Huizinga confirmed the results regarding the class but not the race variations (Elliott & Huizinga 1983; Huizinga & Elliott 1987), although, as we noted above, African American youths may be more likely to underreport their delinquencies. In any case, Elliott and colleagues' self-report research points to an important distinction between the **prevalence of offending** and the **incidence of offending**. Prevalence refers to the proportion of a particular group that has engaged in law-violation, while incidence refers to the frequency of offending within the subgroup of offenders (Paternoster & Triplett 1988). The theoretical significance of this distinction has been noted by Alfred Blumstein and Elizabeth Grady: "It is reasonable to expect

. . . that one set of factors distinguishes between those persons who become involved in crimes the first time and those who do not, and that a different set of factors distinguishes those who persist in crime once involved, from those who discontinue criminality at an early age" (1982:265).

More recently, Bradley Wright and colleagues (1999) added a new twist to sorting out the class-delinquency relationship. Using data from New Zealand, they found that low social class promotes delinquency by "increasing individuals' alienation, financial strain, and aggression, and by decreasing [their] educational and occupational aspirations" (p. 176). High social class, on the other hand, promotes delinquency by increasing individuals' inclination toward risk-taking, insulating them from adverse social sanctions, and decreasing their commitment to conventional moral values.

Drug surveys and drug scares. Drug surveys are a special type of self-report research. Since 1975 the Monitoring the Future project at the University of Michigan's Institute for Social Research (ISR), under the direction of Lloyd Johnston, has been conducting annual surveys of drug use among high school seniors (Johnston et al. 1997). It is not unusual for data released from this and similar reports to become the source of media-generated crime waves or drug scares.

In one study, James Orcutt and J. Blake Turner (1993) analyzed how *Newsweek* magazine distorted statistical results from the annual ISR survey to make claims about an impending cocaine epidemic. In July 1986, the ISR had planned to release a study of 1975–1985 drug use trends among high school seniors. But as early as March 17, in a cover story titled "Kids and Cocaine," *Newsweek* scooped the other national media by publishing results from this report, along with an interview with Johnston, about a "coke plague" (Morganthau 1986:63).

The ISR data indicated that thirty-day prevalence and annual prevalence rates (the proportion of youths using illegal drugs) had risen dramatically from 1976 to 1979. Then drug use *overall* declined until 1985, when the downward trend abated (Johnston et al. 1986). The *Newsweek* story, however, focused on the cocaine statistics, which did reflect an increase that Johnston and colleagues characterized as "disturbing" (p. 48). But while Johnston and colleagues had emphasized the increase in "current use" of cocaine (thirty-day prevalence), current users constituted only 6.7 percent of high school seniors, a proportion that hardly substantiated *Newsweek*'s claims about a cocaine plague. *Newsweek* decided to focus instead on the 17.3 percent "lifetime" prevalence rate, that is, the proportion of seniors who had used cocaine at any time in their lives, even though the ISR data indicated that lifetime prevalence had, in fact, remained fairly stable since 1979.

The "Kids and Cocaine" article made the case for a "cocaine [plague] . . . seeping into the nation's schools" by contrasting the 1975 lifetime rate (9 percent) with the higher 1985 rate (17.3 percent), which, as *Newsweek* underscored, amounted to a near doubling of cocaine use (p. 63). They did *not* note, however, that the increase that had occurred prior to 1980 dwarfed the 1980–1985 rise. Including the 1975–1980 data would have shown that the real period of increased cocaine use occurred prior to the emergence of the so-called plague. Then *Newsweek* constructed a glossy, colored graph that accentuated the annual changes in the 1980–1985 period, which pictorially transformed "statistically nonsignificant fluctuations . . . into striking peaks and valleys" and an illusion of overall increased use (Orcutt & Turner 1993:194).

In the late 1980s and early 1990s, ISR data showed a decline in cocaine use, as well as use of other drugs, among high school seniors (see Table 2.8). The cocaine epidemic no longer seemed newsworthy and, ironically, *Newsweek* reported that "in their zeal to shield young people from the plague of drugs, the media and many drug educators have hyped the very real dangers of crack into a myth of instant and total addiction" (Martz 1990:74). Between 1990 and 2000 cocaine use remained fairly stable, although use of some other drugs (primarily marijuana) increased. The most significant decline in drug use occurred with alcohol.

Table 2.8   Self-Reported Drug Use of High School Seniors (1985–2000)

	Percentage Using over the Last 30 Days				Percentage Using over the Last Year			
	1985	1990	1995	2000	1985	1990	1995	2000
Marijuana/hashish	25.7	14.0	21.2	21.6	40.6	27.0	34.7	36.5
Inhalants	3.0	2.9	3.2	2.4	7.5	7.5	8.4	6.2
Hallucinogens	3.8	2.3	4.6	3.0	7.6	6.0	9.7	8.7
Cocaine	6.7	1.9	1.8	2.1	13.1	5.3	4.0	5.0
Heroin	0.3	0.2	0.6	0.7	0.6	0.5	1.1	1.5
Other narcotics	2.3	1.5	1.8	2.9	5.9	4.5	4.7	7.0
Stimulants	6.8	3.7	4.0	5.0	15.8	9.1	9.3	10.5
Sedatives	2.4	1.4	2.3	3.1	5.8	3.6	4.9	6.3
Tranquilizers	2.1	1.2	1.8	2.6	6.1	3.5	4.4	5.7
Alcohol	65.9	57.1	51.3	50.0	85.6	80.6	73.7	73.2
Steroids	NA	1.0	0.7	0.8	NA	1.7	1.5	1.7
Cigarettes	30.1	29.4	33.5	31.4	NA	NA	NA	NA

Source: Maguire & Pastore 2001, tabs. 3.73–3.74; Pastore & Maguire 1998, tabs. 3.72–3.73.

Note: NA = not available.

■ The Problem of White-Collar Crime

A major limitation of the three sources of statistical crime data we have discussed thus far—the *UCR,* the *NCVS,* and self-report surveys—is their lack of attention to white-collar crime. In this regard, Edwin Sutherland's and Marshall Clinard and Peter Yeager's groundbreaking works (1949 and 1980, respectively) on corporate crime remain the seminal pieces of research.

Sutherland compiled data on law violations of the seventy largest U.S. corporations. (The corporations had an average life-span of about forty-five years.) It is noteworthy that Dryden Press, the publisher of Sutherland's 1949 book, forced him to omit the actual names of the corporations for fear of lawsuits. It was not until 1983, three decades after Sutherland's death, that a new uncut edition that included the names of the companies was published.

As we noted earlier, Sutherland did not limit his research to violations of criminal law but included violations of civil and regulatory law as well (see Chapter 1). Sutherland believed it was appropriate to include the full range of offenses because, in his view, corporate law violations were *potentially* punishable by criminal law, contained the essential elements of criminal intent, and caused harm that was equivalent to or exceeded that caused by conventional crimes.

During the period covered by his research, Sutherland uncovered 980 legal decisions against these corporations. While only 16 percent of these were for violations of *criminal* law, about 60 percent of the corporations did have at least one criminal conviction, and among these, the average was four apiece. Overall, each of the seventy corporations had at least one decision against it. Two companies had as many as fifty decisions (Armour & Company, Swift & Company), one had forty (General Motors), and two had thirty-nine (Montgomery Ward, Sears Roebuck). Over 90 percent of the corporations had four or more violations, perhaps qualifying them for prosecution as habitual or repeat offenders. The largest proportion of violations was for *restraint of trade* (e.g., price-fixing, monopolistic practices) (31 percent), *infringement on patents, copyrights, and trademarks* (23 percent), *unfair labor practices* (16 percent), and *misrepresentation in advertising* (10 percent). Other violations included commercial and political bribery, tax fraud, manipulation of the stock exchange, short weights and measures, misrepresentation of financial statements, and fraudulent bankruptcies. Importantly, Sutherland noted that about half of the companies had engaged in law violations at their origin or in their early years of operation, making crime an essential part of their initial period of capital accumulation.

Marshall Clinard and Peter Yeager collected data on legal actions initiated against the 477 largest U.S. manufacturing corporations during 1975 and 1976. Clinard and Yeager found that about 60 percent of the companies had at least one action against them, 50 percent had two or more, and 18 percent had five or more. Over 75 percent of the cases involved what Clinard and Yeager classified as *manufacturing* violations (consumer health and safety), *labor* violations (worker health and safety, wage and hour violations, employment discrimination), and *environmental* violations (pollution). The largest corporations were the chief offenders, with just 13 percent of the companies accounting for over half of all violations. The most frequent offenders were in the motor vehicle, oil refinery, and pharmaceutical industries. Less than 3 percent of the imposed legal sanctions were for criminal offenses, however, and less than 1 percent involved nonmonetary criminal penalties against an officer of the corporation.

The task of collecting such data is daunting, and no criminologist has been able to surpass the scope of Sutherland's or Clinard and Yeager's work. Perhaps if there were a *UCR* or *NCVS* for corporate law violations we would hear more media reports about corporate crime waves or annual fluctuations in this serious form of criminality.

■ Other Research Methods

We have spent a good deal of time considering the ways in which criminologists acquire statistical counts of crime. But the various methods we have discussed represent only one element of the methodological diversity in criminology. The remainder of this chapter will expose you to other methods of research.

▪ Experimental and Evaluation Research

Practitioners of the hard sciences in disciplines like biology, chemistry, and physics, as well as applied fields such as medical research, are noted for their use of the **experimental method** (Neuman 2003). Researchers in the social sciences are less known for the experiments they conduct, but this work is rather extensive, particularly in the discipline of psychology. Many of these experiments have direct application to the field of criminology.

In an experiment the researcher exposes a group of *experimental* subjects to a particular stimulus and then monitors or observes the effects of this stimulus on the subjects' behavior or attitudes. The postexperimental condition is then compared to that of a *control* group, a group of subjects who are not exposed to the experimental stimulus. If the participants in the experiment have been randomly assigned to the experimental and control groups, ensuring that they did not differ significantly in their preexperimental condition, then the researcher may be able to attribute a change in the experimental group to exposure to the experimental stimulus.

Media experiments. One area of experimental research that is relevant to criminology deals with the effects of the media on aggressive behavior. In a classic series of experiments, Albert Bandura (1973) exposed groups of nursery school children, in person and through film, to an adult who hit and kicked an inflated Bobo doll. Bandura observed that these children, in comparison to a control group of children who did not witness the Bobo doll episode, played more aggressively for a short period following the exposure. Bandura reasoned that through imitation and modeling children will duplicate or copy the behavior of others. However, when Bandura introduced a number of additional variables the experimental results changed. For example, when the adult model was shown being scolded or spanked for striking the doll, the children did not respond in an aggressive manner. This study and other research suggest that appearance of the undesirable consequences will inhibit children's subsequent aggression (Goldstein 1986; Surette 1998).

Experimental research also indicates that some individuals may be more *predisposed* to the influence of the media than others. For instance, boys are more affected than girls, and children from families that emphasize nonaggression (e.g., where parents teach children to be kind to others) are less likely to be influenced (Goldstein 1986). Ray Surette notes that "whether or not a particular depiction will cause a particular viewer to act more aggressively is not a straightforward issue. An aggressive effect largely depends on the interaction between each individual viewer, the content of the portrayal, and the setting in which the portrayal is viewed" (1998:125). The following are among the many factors that appear to increase the violence-inducing impact of media exposure: the details of the media portrayal and the viewer's real-life circumstances are similar, the media aggression is portrayed as justifiable and in a way that does not stir distaste, and aggressive peer models are present during the viewing.

Experiments have also been conducted to measure attitudinal changes among subjects. Jeffrey Goldstein and colleagues (1975), for example, exposed adult males in four countries (Canada, England, Italy, and the United States) to a variety of full-length films. Following the experiment, subjects were asked to assign minimum prison sentences for persons convicted of a variety of crimes. Goldstein and colleagues found that the subjects who viewed films with aggressive conduct (e.g., *Clockwork Orange, Straw Dogs*) were more likely than those who had viewed nonaggressive films (e.g., *Fiddler on the Roof*) to assign more severe prison sentences.

Edward Donnerstein and colleagues (1987) used full-length, R-rated "slasher" films—*Texas Chainsaw Massacre, Maniac, I Spit on Your Grave, Toolbox Murders,* and *Vice Squad*—to measure attitudinal change among male college students. This type of film commonly includes female victims and explicitly violent scenes that are juxtaposed with erotic scenes. Donnerstein and colleagues found that over the course of viewing several films, the students became more desensitized to the violence (they reported seeing fewer violent and offensive scenes) and they rated the films as more enjoyable and less degrading to women. In the next stage of the experiment, the subjects viewed a videotaped reenactment of a rape trial that was based on the transcript of an actual trial. In comparison to control-group subjects who had not seen the films, these subjects expressed less sympathy for the rape victim and perceived her as a less worthy and attractive individual. They also judged the defendant to be less responsible for the rape and thought that the victim offered less resistance and received less injury. When female college students were included in a similar experiment, they experienced somewhat less desensitization but did have a negative reaction to the rape victim in the videotaped enactment (Krafka 1985). Other research found that male viewers enjoyed these types of films more when accompanied by female companions, while female viewers enjoyed them more (and found their male companions more attractive) when the male companion displayed a bravado attitude toward the violence (Zillman et al. 1986).

There is obviously a great deal of difference between the artificial climate of an experiment and the real world, and between behavioral aggression and attitudinal change on the one hand, and criminal violence on the other. It is also possible that the persons already predisposed to aggression and violence are the ones most likely to seek out these types of media and thus have the opportunity to be influenced by it (Surette 1998). Even the strongest proponents of the media violence-causes-aggression view acknowledge the reciprocal relationship over time between viewing aggression and acting aggressively (Huesman & Eron 1986). In other words, viewing violence increases behavioral aggression, but acting aggressively also increases violent viewing.

Moreover, surveys that have attempted to correlate youths' exposure to media violence with aggressive behavior and violent delinquency have yielded inconsistent results (Hartnagel et al. 1975; Surette 1998). Some longitudinal research has found that viewing media violence during childhood is positively correlated with aggressive behavior in both adolescence and adulthood (Strasburger & Wilson 2002). On the other hand, a study of 281 metropolitan areas found that communities' exposure to television violence (as measured by A. C. Nielsen Company estimates of local audience size for violent programs) was inversely related to *UCR* violent crime rates, perhaps because "high levels of television viewing imply that residents are spending large amounts of time within the relatively safe confines" of their homes (Messner 1986:230).

For some, however, the home may not represent safe confines. When Diana Russell (1982) asked 930 women whether they had "ever been upset by anyone trying to get you to do what they'd seen in pornographic pictures, movies, or books," about 10 percent responded yes. Among those women who reported being raped by their husbands or ex-husbands, nearly 25 percent responded yes. Russell argues that pornography is sometimes used "to try to persuade a woman or a child to engage in certain acts, to legitimize the acts, and to undermine resistance, refusal, or disclosure" (1988:63). We will discuss this issue further in Chapter 9.

The experimental media studies, however limited, do leave us with much food for thought. Surette (1998) observes an evolving consensus among experimental researchers that the media does play a causal role in behavioral aggression. Four prominent health associations—the American Medical Association, the American Academy of Pediatrics, the American Psychological Association, and the American Academy of Child and Adolescent Psychiatry—have issued a joint statement expressing their conviction that "prolonged viewing of media violence can lead to emotional desensitization toward violence in real life" as well as "increases in aggressive attitudes, values and behaviors, particularly in children" (cited in Holland 2000:1A; also see Strasburger & Wilson 2002).

Nonetheless, according to Surette, the issue for most researchers "comes down not to the existence of an effect but to the magnitude of the effect." The same levels of "explained variance" in aggression, that is, "the proportion of the changes in aggression that can be statistically associated with the media," have been interpreted by some researchers as important and by some researchers as trivial. Surette is persuaded, however, that the experimental research clearly shows that only the "unambiguous linking of violent behavior with undesirable consequences or motives appears capable of inhibiting subsequent aggression" in experimental subjects exposed to violent media (1998:128).

Policy evaluation: Mandatory arrest of women batterers. **Evaluation research** is a type of applied research concerned with assessing the impact of particular policies (Neuman 2003). In criminology there has been a plethora of proposals with diverse recommendations for reducing crime. Evaluation research helps us determine the extent to which our crime reduction strategies have had the desired effects, and it allows us to base our conclusions on more than hunch or intuition. While evaluation research can entail a variety of methods, one type utilizes experimental or quasi-experimental designs.

Traditionally, police have been reluctant to make arrests in cases of domestic violence involving battered women, viewing such incidents as private matters and as diversions from "real" police work (Miller 1993; Sherman & Berk 1984). Some departments have even had explicit policies against arrest. Feminists' critique of this hands-off approach led criminologists to experiment with different methods of intervention. In a landmark "field experiment" conducted in the early 1980s, Lawrence Sherman and

Richard Berk (1984) randomly assigned police officers in Minneapolis to three experimental groups. In one the officers merely advised the parties and attempted to mediate the dispute; in another they ordered the offender out of the house for a period of about eight hours; and in a third they made an arrest. To monitor occurrence of further violence, victims were contacted every two weeks for six months and official records were examined. The findings indicated that the arrest option resulted in significantly less violence during the follow-up period.

Encouraged by these findings, police departments around the country began to adopt mandatory arrest policies, and the National Institute of Justice funded several replication experiments in other cities (Mignon & Holmes 1995; Miller 1993). But since each study was conducted a little differently, the results were inconsistent. In all the cities studied, arrest appeared to deter batterers in the short run, that is, for at least thirty days (Jones 1994). In some cases, arrest appeared to deter batterers for a six-month period, as it had in Minneapolis, but in other instances arrest either had no impact or was associated with *increased* battering over the course of the study period (Berk et al. 1992; Dunford et al. 1990; Pate & Hamilton 1992; Sherman & Smith 1992). In a (nonexperimental) statistical analysis of victimization data, Lisa Dugan and colleagues (2003) found that victims in states with mandatory arrest laws were no more likely than victims in states without these laws to report incidents to the police, and third-party witnesses were less likely to report incidents when mandatory arrest policies were in place. Dugan (2003) also found that cities with mandatory arrest laws had higher rates of spousal homicides against wives.

Sherman (1992) and others have warned that mandatory arrest policies could backfire by making some offenders even more angry and hostile toward their accusers, and he recommended that these policies be repealed. Other researchers have disagreed, however, believing that an association between arrest and increased battering does not warrant a conclusion that arrest backfires and causes increased violence. According to Ann Jones, there is "a big difference between *failing to stop* violence and *causing* violence to escalate" (1994:159). J. David Hirschel and Ira Hutchinson add that even if arrest is not effective in deterring violence, it is "a more conscionable choice than nonarrest," since nonarrest legitimates abuse and leaves victims to fend for themselves (1992:73).

A number of explanations have been offered for the discrepant research findings. In some studies there was considerable subject attrition, with less than one-half of the victims remaining in the interview sample by the end of the study period (Miller 1993; Sherman & Smith 1992). In other instances police officers did not implement the mandatory arrest policy, believing that the women were not really in dangerous situations, or if they were, that they had chosen to remain in them (Ferraro 1989). When officers received more training regarding the problem of domestic violence, however, they were more likely to implement the policy (Mignon & Holmes 1995). Another variation in the studies involved the length of time arrested batterers were held in custody. This ranged from a couple of hours to over a week (Sherman et al. 1991). Moreover, those who were arrested were not necessarily prosecuted and convicted. One study found that those who were prosecuted and subsequently served jail time *and* a period of probation had lower battering rates than those who were prosecuted and subsequently received jail time *or* probation (Thistlethwaite et al. 1998).

Finally, there were sociodemographic variations in the experimental findings. Mandatory arrest was more effective in deterring offenders with a greater stake in conformity. Studies consistently showed that those who were employed were more likely to be deterred than those who were unemployed (Berk et al. 1992; Pate & Hamilton 1992; Sherman & Smith 1992). Some studies also found that married men, high school graduates, and whites were more likely to be deterred than unmarried men, high school dropouts, and blacks (Moore 1997; Sherman 1992).

Sherman argues that "even in cities where arrest reduces domestic violence overall, as an unintended side effect it may increase violence," especially against poor victims with few alternative resources (1992:19). Thus he believes that police confronting domestic violence should have options (offering to take the victim to a shelter, for example), rather than the shackle of mandatory arrest. Dugan's research (2003) suggests that strengthening civil protection and child custody provisions for women, and increasing penalties for men who violate these orders, may have a greater impact on reducing domestic violence than mandatory arrest.

Berk and his colleagues, on the other hand, believe that mandatory arrest studies do not offer any definitive policy implications other than "the general warning that a particular arrest will not necessarily lead to a beneficial outcome" (1992:706). The findings, they add, "do not provide a sound rationale for abandoning" mandatory arrest as a reasonable strategy for combating domestic violence. Other researchers are more certain in their support of the mandatory arrest approach, believing that women need *more* law enforcement not less (Grant Bowman 1992; Jones 1994). Many women, especially poor inner-city women who can't afford to leave public housing or women isolated in rural areas, are "sitting ducks" for further assault if there are no serious consequences for offenders. Clearly there is an urgent need for a comprehensive program of expanded community services for victims and offenders (e.g., shelters, counseling). These, in conjunction with effective law enforcement, will undoubtedly constitute the best strategy overall (Miller 1993; Sullivan 1997; Websdale 1995).

Observational Field Research and In-Depth Interviewing

Perhaps the most exciting area of criminological research entails researchers hitting the streets to meet, observe, and interact with people in their natural environments. This method, originally developed by cultural anthropologists, is known as **ethnography** (*ethno* meaning "people" or "folk" and *graphy* meaning "to describe") or **observational field research**. The earliest ethnographic studies of crime in the United States were conducted by sociologists at the University of Chicago in the first half of the twentieth century. Robert Park, influenced by his background as a journalist, encouraged his contemporaries to leave the confines of the libraries and get their hands dirty by hanging out on street corners or in barrooms, hotel lobbies, and the like, to see what was "really happening" in society (Neuman 2003).

Gaining access to and the confidence of subjects are key issues in field research. Occasionally opportunities present themselves by accident, as was the case for Patricia Adler and Peter Adler (1983), who became friendly with neighbors who turned out to be upper-echelon marijuana and cocaine traffickers (i.e., traffickers who earned upward of a half million dollars a year). Usually, however, a more concerted effort to locate subjects is required. Philippe Bourgois (1995), for instance, sought out people involved in the drug trade by moving to a tenement in an impoverished Puerto Rican neighborhood of East Harlem, New York. He lived there for five years in a community that was flooded with illegal drugs.

Over a ten-year period of research, Martin Sanchez Jankowski (1991) became intimately acquainted with the members of thirty-seven street gangs in Los Angeles, New York, and Boston. Sanchez Jankowski did "not simply show up on their streetcorners and say, 'I am a professor and I want to study you'" (p. 9). He first contacted knowledgeable persons—social workers, clergymen, community activists—who arranged for him to meet with gang leaders. When he explained to the gang leaders that he was a professor writing a book comparing gangs in different cities, most of them were intrigued by the idea and curious about how other gangs operated.

Sanchez Jankowski still had to surmount a number of obstacles before he was accepted by gang members. A criminologist's class, race/ethnicity, or gender, for example, may create barriers between researcher and subject. Sanchez Jankowski's ethnic background was both a plus and a minus. He is Latino; the Polish portion of his surname comes from his adopted father. Since he is not white, Sanchez Jankowski was more easily accepted by Latino and African American gang members. He had more difficulty, however, with white and Asian gangs. The Irish, on the other hand, were an exception to this rule. Because he was not Puerto Rican, the ethnicity of the

Irish group's rival gang, they didn't view him as a threat and allowed him access to their milieu.

Similarly, Bourgois (1995) comments on how gender posed a barrier to his research. "I faced the inescapable problem of how—as a male—I would develop the kinds of deep, personal relationships that would allow me to tape-record conversations with women at the same intimate level on which I accessed the worlds of men" (p. 215). Thus when Bourgois confronted the issue of pregnancy and drug addiction, he recruited a female African American colleague to help facilitate his discussions with pregnant addicts.

Both Sanchez Jankowski and Bourgois also had to overcome suspicions that they were working for the police or that they would betray their subjects in some way. In Sanchez Jankowski's case, he had to pass two tests that the gangs presented to him:

> The first test was designed to see if I was an informant. . . . What nearly every gang did was to undertake some illegal activities over a three- or four-week period in order to see if any of their members were arrested. During this time I was observed closely, and on those occasions that I did not stay with gang members, I was . . . followed to where I was staying. . . . On one occasion I did have some difficulty. It turned out that a member of the gang, for reasons no one ever discovered, had told the police about some crime that three other members had [committed]. . . . In order to protect himself, he told the leadership that he had heard that I was the one who had informed. The gang confronted and physically attacked me. Some time later, however, other gang members found out . . . who had really supplied the police with the information. The leaders contacted me, apologized, and gave me permission to study them.
>   The second test . . . had to do with determining how tough I was. . . . It involved a number of members starting a fight with me. This was done to see how good a fighter I was and to see if I had "heart." . . . Gang members wanted to know whether I had courage to stay and fight if we were all jumped by a rival gang, and whether I could handle myself and not jeopardize their flanks. In this test, it was considered acceptable to fight and lose, but it was unacceptable to refuse to fight. . . . The fact that I had training in karate did not eliminate the anxiety that such situations created, but it did help to reduce it. Although these tests often left bruises, I was never seriously hurt. Quite remarkably . . . in the more than ten years during which I conducted this research, I was only seriously injured twice. (1991:11–12)

Though Bourgois did not face such tests, he does report some initial difficulties accessing street-dealing scenes. As he writes, "I was painfully aware of my outsider status. . . . The first time . . . I went down a side street that happened to be a heroin 'copping corner' . . . I was greeted by a hail of whistles and echoing shouts of *'bajando'* (coming down)—the code alarms that lookouts posted on dealing corners use to announce the approach of a potential undercover agent" (1995:29). Bourgois actually experienced more problems from the New York City police, who "repeatedly stopped, searched, cursed, and humiliated" him because they thought he fit the profile of a "white drug addict" (p. 30). On one occasion, when Bourgois told the police that he "was an anthropologist studying poverty and marginalization," one of them exploded: "What kind of a fuckin' moron do you think I am. You think I don't know what you're doin'? . . . You're . . . [a] fuckin' drug addict. You're dirty white scum! Go buy your drugs in a white neighborhood! If you don't get the hell out of here right now, motherfucka', you're gonna hafta repeat your story in the precinct. You want me to take you in? . . . Answer me motherfucka'!" (p. 31).

Bourgois reports drinking beer with the dealers and addicts he met but not going so far as to use illegal drugs. Perhaps the **courtesy stigma** he had acquired from his encounters with the police helped him bond with his subjects. A courtesy stigma works somewhat like guilt by association. If you allow yourself to be seen and treated as a drug addict, gang member, prostitute, or the like, you may be accepted by your subjects as "one of them" without actually having to commit crimes (Anderson & Calhoun 1992).

Clearly, much of the skill involved in observational research is a matter of charm and the ability to build rapport and trust with others. Bourgois, who speaks Spanish, comes across in his book as a sociable and likable individual who was willing to take the time necessary to establish long-term relationships with the Puerto Rican subjects who became his friends. As he writes, "Only by establishing long-term relationships based on trust can one begin to ask provocative personal questions, and expect thoughtful, serious answers. . . . I spent hundreds of nights on the street and in crack-houses observing [and tape-recording] dealers and addicts. . . . I also visited their families, attending parties and intimate reunions—from Thanksgiving dinners to New Year's Eve celebrations" (p. 13).

Bourgois says that he was surprised to discover that the people whose confidence he was attempting to gain "were thrilled to be hanging out with someone who was 'such good people' that he did not even 'sniff'" (pp. 40–41). He found that he "became an exotic object of prestige." One of his new friends described him, affectionately, as "the white nigga' who always be hangin' with me."

One of the skills necessary in observational research and the building of rapport and trust is the ability to listen—to hear what people are saying, not what you want them to be saying, and to empathize with their "experience of pain and suffering" (p. 14). As Bourgois befriended two dozen street dealers and their families, he found that they "were not interested in talking primarily about drugs . . . [but] about their daily struggles for subsistence and dignity at the poverty line" (p. 2). At the same time, Bourgois hoped to avoid both "inferiorizing" his subjects, as we so often do with the poor in this country, and "sanitizing the . . . self-inflicted suffering" that is a consequence of their attempts "to escape or circumvent the structures of segregation and marginalization that entrap them" (pp. 12, 18).

Other researchers, unlike Sanchez Jankowski and Bourgois, may decide to conceal their identity (at least initially) from those they are observing in the field. This was the strategy adopted by William Chambliss (1988), who conducted research for over half a decade in the city of Seattle. Chambliss's research took him from the streets of skid row to the chambers of politicians. Starting from the bottom, Chambliss worked his way through an elaborate maze of social relationships that constituted what he later learned was a crime network:

> In an earlier time I had passed through skid rows in various cities while bumming around the country and working as a migratory laborer. I felt . . . that I could pass as a resident if I dressed and acted as I remembered others in those areas dressing and acting. With two days' growth of beard, a pair of khaki pants, and an old shirt, I drove down to the edge of that magical ring that circumscribes and, in fact, effectively hides skid row from the eyes of those who do not care to see it. I walked the two blocks between the commercial center and skid row, turned a corner, and found myself there. . . . It was raining this day. . . . So I looked for shelter and found a seat in Tip's Amusement Parlor, where I had a cup of coffee. I didn't like coffee and would have preferred tea, but coffee, I calculated, was essential for the image. (p. 14)

From that point on Chambliss observed and interviewed people associated with illegal gambling, prostitution, and other illicit enterprises (drugs, illegal liquor, loan-sharking, the buying and selling of stolen merchandise) that littered the community and were often appended to ostensibly legal businesses like restaurants and bars (see Lesieur & Sheley 1987). During the day, locals were the primary patrons, but at night a more "respectable" clientele arrived for activities "that may be found elsewhere but are concentrated here and brought conveniently together" (Chambliss 1988:23). Chambliss also discovered an elaborate payoff system to law enforcement and other governmental officials, which made tolerance of the illegal enterprises profitable for scores of other respectables as well.

While Chambliss maintained his clandestine identity, he did participate in illegal poker games to gain access to the crime scene. Eventually he decided to reveal himself to the manager of the cardroom where he played: "I told him of my 'purely scientific' interests and experience and, as best I could, why I had deceived him earlier" (p. 33). The manager agreed to help Chambliss and put him in touch with another knowledgeable person. From then on, Chambliss reports, "I let it be known to everyone I could that I was interested in studying the entire system of payoffs and political intrigue connected with the rackets. . . . Soon I began receiving . . . [a] surprisingly large number of telephone calls . . . [from] people 'in the know'" (pp. 47–48).

The **in-depth interviewing** that often accompanies field research is typically conducted in an unstructured manner, where the researcher and subject engage in an open-ended conversation-like exchange (Neuman 2003). At times, structured survey questionnaires may be administered as well. Mark Hamm (1993), for instance, used the observational method to locate skinheads for interviewing and completion of structured questionnaires. He began his research by visiting several cities to track "down skinheads in their natural habitat (street corners, coffee shops, record stores, survivalist outlets, rock concerts, and motorcycle shops)." These subjects, he notes, were easy to identify due to their shaved heads and white power and/or Nazi regalia. Often Hamm would have to wait for hours. When he spotted a skinhead he would approach him with a request to participate, presenting his "research as an attempt to set the record straight on the skinheads" (p. 101). He also offered them a $10 inducement. Later, Hamm was able to expand his interview sample by acquiring the names and addresses of individuals published in the underground teen press and the mailing roster of the White Aryan Resistance (WAR). He also used the WAR electronic bulletin board to solicit subjects, and he interviewed skinheads in prison.

To be sure, observational research is not a prerequisite for obtaining interesting interview subjects. Eleanor Miller (1986) began her study of female street prostitution and "hustling" (a variety of illegal economic activities) by locating women under criminal justice supervision who were living in halfway houses or more secure correctional facilities. She interviewed them about their life histories in crime, particularly about their initiation into street hustling and the development of their criminal careers. She expanded her contacts through a **snowball sampling** technique, where she asked one subject to refer her to another. Miller also interviewed other household members and was eventually able to observe situations in which street hustling actually occurred.

Sometimes **life history studies** can focus on one individual. These are more or less biographical pieces of research combined with criminological insight or analysis. Some of the most well-known criminology life histories have been conducted with "professional" thieves and fences (e.g., Sutherland 1937; King & Chambliss 1984; Steffensmeier 1986). **Professional criminals** are those who devote the greater portion of their "working day" to the rational planning and commission of crimes for profit. Professionals also possess specialized skills that are learned from and passed on to others, and they associate with people who share a common argot (manner of speech) and lifestyle and who provide each other with camaraderie and mutual respect.

In life history studies, in-depth interviewing, and observational research, one must be cautious about the accuracy of subjects' accounts—

whether they have faulty recollections or are reinterpreting events in a biased way, whether they are providing false or misleading information, whether they are omitting or failing to reveal important facts, or whether they have an ax to grind or other disingenuous motives for participating in the research (Neuman 2003). Miller (1986) reports that her subjects appeared more candid about their criminal activities than about their personal relationships. During the course of the interview she would sometimes bring up a topic again, in a different context, to see if the woman would change her story. Although it is important, whenever possible, to cross-check what you are told with other sources, a researcher who exhibits genuine empathy will often find that subjects enjoy talking about themselves, are flattered by someone who is interested in them, and want to provide accurate information to set the record straight. Miller found that some street hustlers who had heard about her research actually wanted "to be in the book" (p. 186).

Jeff Ferrell (1997) takes the issue of authenticity a bit further. He believes that only through "experiential immersion . . . in the dangers of criminality," only by participating in the very criminal activity under investigation, can researchers come to truly understand the social reality of crime (pp. 3, 16). Ferrell became involved with members of a Denver "hip hop graffiti underground." He describes one evening as follows:

> Settling into a narrow, half-lit alley between rows of warehouses . . . [we] begin the lengthy process of . . . painting a large, graffiti-style mural. Having brought along the usual supply of "forties" (40-ounce bottles of malt liquor), "shooters" (small bottles of Jack Daniels and Yukon Jack), cigarettes, and Krylon spray paint, we . . . anticipate a long night in the alley. . . . [The piece is] a vague commentary on a nearby nuclear weapons facility . . . [featuring] hooded laboratory workers and stenciled images of gaseous bubbles. In these hours . . . we share not only work on the mural but also an experience about which graffiti writers talk regularly: the tense excitement, the dangerous, almost intoxicating pleasure, of artistic production interwoven with illegality and adventure. (p. 5)

As part of this process, Ferrell exposed himself to possible arrests, court appearances, and criminal sanctions from legal authorities who take graffiti writing quite seriously. He argues, however, that a willingness to break the law may be the only genuine way to access the *experience* of criminality, the only way to acquire a level of intimacy with the pleasures and pains, meanings and emotions, excitement and adrenaline rush of engaging in illicit activity (see J. Katz 1988). The ethical issues involved in "going native" are significant, but according to Ferrell, failure to do so may cut researchers off from a variety of field contacts, social situations, and ways of understanding crime.

Artistic graffiti writing may be one thing. But what about rape, for example? Would Ferrell really advocate criminologists' participating in rape (as offender or victim) to gain an understanding of crime? Bourgois relates how unprepared he was for even hearing about the brutal gang rapes of adolescent females by the men who "had already become my friends. . . . I kept asking myself how it was possible that I had invested so much energy into taking these 'psychopaths' seriously. . . . I was confused because . . . with notable . . . exceptions, I had grown to like most of these veteran rapists. I was living with the enemy; it had become my social network. They had engulfed me in the common sense of street culture until their rape accounts forced me to draw the line" (1995:207).

Indeed, there are limits to Ferrell's logic, and to a researcher's toleration of the criminal experience. The sight of crack-craving mothers and pregnant women provoked this response in Bourgois: "On several occasions . . . I begged . . . [these] women to think through the potential consequences of their urge to get high. I repeatedly argued with . . . [the dealers], accusing them of having personal responsibility for the traumatized lives of the neonates whose mothers they regularly sold crack to" (p. 281). However much Bourgois wanted to debunk society's moralistic condemnation of the poor and dispossessed, his analytic stance could "not withstand the horror" of this plight. Although he had not begun his research intending to alter his subjects' drug-dependent lifestyle, he had not anticipated everything he would learn. Ferrell (1997) offers the advice of Ned Polsky (1969) for anyone contemplating observational research: "Before you can tell a criminal who you are and make it stick, you have to know yourself. . . . You need to decide beforehand, as much as possible, where you wish to draw the line" (cited in Ferrell 1997:19–20).

Historical and Comparative Criminology

A final set of research strategies employed by criminologists include **historical** and **comparative methods**. Historical studies provide information about the past that enables us to situate current circumstances in broader perspective. Historical data are derived from varied sources such as official documents, newspapers, magazines, personal letters, diaries, memoirs, and oral testimonies. Comparative data provide information about other societies that illuminates, by contrast, the ways of our own society, that helps us distinguish social relations we have in common from those that are dissimilar, and that contributes to our understanding of our place in the world (Neuman 2003).

Lessons of lynching. Studies of lynching in the United States illustrate how historical data can be used to achieve sociological insight by illuminating, in this case, the intersection of race and gender (Messerschmidt 1997). In the United States during the period of slavery, African Americans were treated as "property" for the purpose of economic transactions (i.e., they were inherited, traded, and sold) but as "persons" for the purpose of behavioral control. Slaves were not permitted to leave their plantations without their master/owner's permission, to resist their master's orders or administration of force, to congregate with other slaves, and above all, to have sexual relations with white women. Punishments for offenders ranged from whippings to castration or death (Noonan 1994).

During this time, the rape of black female slaves by their white masters was common and was a source of terror and humiliation for both women and men. One historical account notes a Louisiana slave owner who would tell the black husband "to go . . . and wait 'til he do what he want to do" (Jones 1986:37). Sexual assaults of female slaves even took place in the presence of their husbands and fathers. Rape served to simultaneously defile the women and emasculate the men.

Historical data on lynching indicate that in the two decades prior to the Civil War most of the persons lynched were not black slaves but white abolitionists; and most of the black lynchings were not for sexual violations but for political insurrections or perceived threats. Cases of alleged rape of white women by black men were even thrown out of court when unmarried women were perceived as impure and unchaste or when married women had not been observant of proper decorum. It was not until after the Civil War and the legal abolition of slavery (1865) that the control of black men's sexuality actually became more important than the control of white women's sexuality. And it was not until that time that black men became the archetypal victims of lynching (Messerschmidt 1997).

From the 1880s to the 1950s over 3,500 African Americans were lynched (Wriggens 1995). Though freed from slavery by the Thirteenth Amendment, African Americans continued to suffer the wrath of white society, including white male mob violence. The Ku Klux Klan established branches throughout the South and harassed, intimated, and killed black men who attempted to "act like white men." African American men who voted or joined political parties, who owned property or gained economic independence, or who refused to defer to whites in interpersonal interactions were the primary targets of violence: whippings, castration, and lynchings (Messerschmidt 1997).

James Messerschmidt (1997) connects this escalation of antiblack violence to Southern white men's collective attempt to defend their political and economic superiority, which defined the very nature of their masculinity. "If African American men were permitted to do what 'real men' (white men) did, the value of . . . masculinity was effectively compromised" (p. 30). Indeed, "white supremacist masculinity" was essentially defined in terms of "subordinate African American masculinity." For these white men interracial sexuality emerged as the terrain for the preservation of their manhood: "To be a man was to be a white man who had sole access to and the duty to protect white women" (p. 34). And some white women agreed; as the wife of a former congressman said in 1898, "If it needs lynching to protect woman's dearest possession from human beasts, then I say lynch a thousand times a week if necessary" (quoted in Wriggens 1995:216).

In the South the threat of white mob violence constantly loomed over judicial proceedings of African Americans accused of rape, and mobs often lynched defendants if they found the verdict unacceptable. Lynchings were also carried out to eliminate black leadership and intimidate the black population. Moreover, the lynching itself was a ceremonial ritual of torture and emasculation of the black male. The ordeal, which could last for several hours, included sexual mutilation and castration, and featured cheering spectators (men, women, and children) and scavengers who searched for souvenir body parts. The lynching was nothing less than a "white community celebration" (Messerschmidt 1997:32; Vandal 1991; Wriggens 1995).

One such mutilation-lynching involved a black man charged with rape of a white women who was not permitted to identify him because the shock, it was thought, might be too great for her (Ginzburg 1988). After the ordeal a placard was placed on a nearby tree that read, "We Must Protect Our Southern Women." These kinds of spectacles ensured white women they had nothing to fear, provided, that is, they submitted themselves to the chivalrous protection of white men. The message was clear: Do not be seduced by the suffragists and their image of the liberated "New Woman." It is men who will protect women, "in the name of the race," in the name of civilization itself (Messerschmidt 1997:34).

Law and lawlessness in international context. Comparative criminology enables us, among other things, to examine criminality and law from a global or international perspective. We often take for granted that the ways of our own society are the ways of all other social systems. However, behaviors that may be illegal in one society may be legal elsewhere (see Box 2.1). For instance, laws regulating the economic activities of corporations vary from one country to another. Less developed nations generally have weaker regulatory laws than developed nations like the United States when it comes to working conditions, environmental pollution, and consumer protection. Multinational and transnational corporations that are based in developed countries but that invest throughout the world thus find it advantageous to conduct business in places that tolerate practices that would be illegal in their own country. This situation has led to the practice of **corporate dumping** into foreign markets, that is, the selling of products

Box 2.1 Female Genital Mutilation

For more than 2,000 years, female genital mutilation (FGM) has been practiced around the world. Although FGM has been most extensive on the African continent and the Arabian peninsula, it has also occurred among some minority communities in Europe, North America, and Australia. Some nineteenth-century Western medical texts even considered removal of the clitoris appropriate treatment for masturbation, nymphomania, hysteria, depression, and epilepsy (Kiragu 1995; Morgan & Steinem 1983).

FGM is usually performed without anesthesia on girls between six and eight years of age. The most common forms involve "clitoridectomy," in which the clitoris and sometimes part or all of the labia minora are excised, and "infibulation," in which the clitoris, labia minora, and inner layers of the labia majora are removed and the scraped sides of the vulva are then sutured together with thread, catgut, or thorns to form a bridge of scar tissue over the vagina, leaving only a small opening for passage of urine and menstrual fluid. The girl's legs are then tied together and she is forced to remain immobile for several weeks until proper adhesion occurs. She undergoes additional cutting at marriage, when the wound is opened to permit intercourse, and at childbirth to allow passage of the fetal head without rupture of tissues. Those who are reinfibulated after each childbirth endure these procedures again and again. FGM is performed by tribal practitioners, midwives, family members, and increasingly by trained medical personnel (Crossette 1995; Lorber 1997a).

FGM is performed to ensure virginity, to prevent promiscuity or unfaithfulness, or to certify a girl as clean, proper, or marriageable. As "part of a code of modesty, fidelity, and women's obedience to fathers and husbands," it is often taken for granted culturally by women as well as men (Lorber 1997a:5). Female family members commonly assist in the procedure, holding the girl down and drowning out her screams by singing. Female practitioners receive social recognition and status and earn a living by performing the cycle of ritual cuttings and sewings.

It is estimated that as many as 140 million girls and women around the world have undergone genital mutilation, including over 160,000 in immigrant communities in the United States. The initial effects include not only pain and shock but also complications such as hemorrhage, infection, damage to adjacent organs, HIV transmission, and tetanus and blood poisoning from unsterile cutting instruments. Long-term consequences include greater susceptibility to problems in pregnancy and continued pain and infection, as well as reduced capacity for sexual pleasure (Heise 1989; Kiragu 1995; Lorber 1997a; *Ms.* 2002, 2003).

Growing condemnation and pressure from the United Nations, nonparticipating countries, and activists who have survived or escaped FGM have resulted in laws prohibiting the practice in an increasing number of countries. In 2002, for example, Kenya became the tenth African nation

continues

Box 2.1 continued

to outlaw FGM. Legal changes have not ended the tradition, however, as often no one involved notifies authorities and families who refuse to participate are commonly "shunned and excluded from the local marriage market" (Lorber 1997a:6). In some areas, alternative coming-of-age rituals are being initiated in hopes of creating new traditions and eliminating the stigma associated with not being circumcised. In Senegal, women have even taken to claiming, in an attempt to disrupt the practice, that it is those who *are* circumcised who will end up unmarried. In 800 villages they have made a pledge to their daughters: "We will no longer allow you to be cut" (Armstrong 2003:22; *Ms.* 2002; *Newsweek* 1999; Thomas 1998).

Educational campaigns emphasizing health issues and the rights of women and children have been an important component of reform efforts, but since it is commonly believed that clitoridectomy and infibulation promote cleanliness and even fertility, they have not always been successful. In Sierra Leone, however, a videotape of an eight-year-old Ethiopian being circumcised with a rusty razor has been quite effective in getting viewers to question FGM. The video documents the child's agony during and after the procedure and convincingly presents the negative long-term health consequences. Another important strategy has been the creation in more than two dozen countries of alternative employment programs for former practitioners in an attempt to undercut the resistance of those who have benefited financially from FGM (Armstrong 2003; Brandell 1998).

As the reform movement gathers strength, local successes spur new initiatives. In one dramatic and highly publicized case, an African teenager who fled her home to avoid FGM spent sixteen months in U.S. prisons trying to win the political asylum denied her. Her courage and perseverance paid off as her ordeal became the test case that forced the U.S. Immigration and Naturalization Service to consider FGM as a type of persecution worthy of asylum protection (Kassindja & Bashir 1998).

Due to the organized efforts of women's groups in Africa and elsewhere around the globe, the number of new FGM cases appears to be on the decline. At the same time, some defenders of the procedure have accused Western critics of cultural imperialism and have argued that the ritual must be understood as an integral part of the cultural transition to adulthood and initiation into female life in these societies. Consequently, we increasingly hear the procedure referred to as "female genital cutting" rather than female genital mutilation (*Ms.* 2002). On the other hand, the Intersex Society of North America (ISNA), an organization that seeks to reduce the number of genital surgeries performed on intersexed infants, has been trying to link their concerns about surgeries on infants not capable of giving consent with the international fight against FGM (see Chapter 1). To heighten the association with FGM, this group refers to intersex surgeries as intersex genital mutilation (IGM). The ISNA considers both IGM and FGM to be "culturally determined practices of harmful genital surgery" that are now being reconsidered (Kessler 1998:81).

and disposal of toxic wastes that cannot be sold or disposed of in the country of origin (Michalowski & Kramer 1987; Mokhiber 1988).

Government-sponsored **genocide**—which Frank Chalk and Kurt Jonassohn define as the one-sided mass killing of a group of people because of their race, ethnicity, religion, nationality, political beliefs, or any other quality "defined by the perpetrator"—is another practice that has for the most part eluded international legal control (1990:23). In fact, during the twentieth century more people were killed by their *own governments* than by war with opposing nations (Horowitz 1997).

Arguably the most infamous genocide in history occurred during the Hitler-Nazi period in Germany (1933–1945), when millions of European Jews, Gypsies, and other disenfranchised groups were incarcerated, enslaved, and exterminated (Berger 2002). The Holocaust was a matter of German law, part of the legal pursuit of governmental policy in Germany and German-occupied territories. But after World War II the victorious allied nations attempted to define these legalities as crimes. A number of criminal trials were conducted in Nuremberg, Germany. The most famous of these trials involved the prosecution of twenty-four German and Austrian "war criminals" who were tried under the auspices of the International Military Tribunal (IMT), with judges from the United States, Great Britain, France, and the Soviet Union. This was the first time in history that a country was held "internationally responsible for what it *did to its own people* . . . no matter what its own national laws . . . allowed" (Rosenbaum 1993:34, emphasis added).

In the aftermath of the Holocaust and the IMT Nuremberg trials, the United Nations established the Genocide Convention (GC), which declared genocide a crime (Chalk & Jonassohn 1990). The GC covered genocides perpetrated against a racial, ethnic, religious, or national group (but not genocides against groups targeted for their political beliefs). In 1948 the GC treaty was signed by thirty-three nations, not including the United States. The United States did not ratify the GC until 1986, when it became the ninety-seventh nation to do so. Leo Kuper (1990) has questioned the reluctance of the United States, especially in light of its dominant role in the early years of the United Nations and in the discussions, negotiations, and final compromises that led to the GC. He asks, did the United States "fear that it might be held responsible, retrospectively, for the annihilation of Indians in the United States or its role in the slave trade, or its contemporary support for tyrannical governments engaging in mass murder?" (pp. 422–423).

As symbolic moral statements, the IMT and GC made significant contributions to international law by asserting that nations do not have absolute sovereignty to pursue what they perceive as their national self-interest without being held accountable by the international community

(Rosenbaum 1993). At the same time, however, because international law has no teeth, it often appears to consist of little more than well-intentioned proclamations. In the late 1970s, for example, the Khmer Rouge, led by dictator Pol Pot, murdered 1–2 million Cambodians who were perceived to be politically hostile or socially incompatible with the government's goals. No international sanctions were imposed, and the Khmer Rouge was allowed to keep its seat at the United Nations. As Kuper notes, if the law "has been honored at all, it is in the breach, not the observance" (1990:423).

In the 1990s the most widely reported case of genocide occurred in the former republic of Yugoslavia (Bosnia-Herzegovina and Kosovo), where thousands of unarmed Muslims and Croats were massacred by Bosnian-Serb soldiers and women were subjected to systematic rape. In 1993 the United Nations established the International Criminal Tribunal for the former Yugoslavia (ICTY) to address these atrocities. About 100 individuals have been indicted, including Yugoslavian president Slobodan Milosevic, the first sitting president ever to be indicted for war crimes. In 1994 the United Nations also established the International Criminal Tribunal for Rwanda (ICTR) to prosecute the perpetrators of another 1990s genocide, the 1994 killing of an estimated 800,000 Rwandans. About sixty-five individuals have been indicted by this tribunal (Power 2002; www.un.org).

The ICTY and ICTR are temporary, set up for a specific purpose. More generally, it is the International Court of Justice, or World Court, established by UN Charter after World War II, that is charged with handling international legal disputes. This body, however, has been used primarily to adjudicate conflicts where the parties involved agree to abide by its decisions. For example, as part of the Reagan administration's efforts to topple the Central-American government of Nicaragua in the 1980s, the Central Intelligence Agency burned Nicaraguan oil facilities, mined harbors, and lent assistance to the Contras, the rebel forces that killed and terrorized the civilian population (see Chapter 10). When a 1986 World Court found the United States in violation of international law and ordered the payment of reparations, the United States simply ignored the ruling (Pfost 1987).

In 2003 the United Nations established the International Criminal Court, the world's first permanent court that will have jurisdiction over genocide, war crimes, and other human rights violations (Lederer 2003). It may be years before this court hears a case, however, because the United States remains opposed to it. As Christopher Simpson observes, major powers like the United States "continue to cynically exploit international law to support propaganda claims against their rivals. They call for strict enforcement of international sanctions when it suits their purpose, but they ignore rulings" when it is in their interest to do so (1993:286).

3

Individualistic Explanations of Criminal Behavior

In New Market, New Jersey, on February 25, 1867, the body of Mary Ellen Coriell, wife of the town doctor, was found gashed and bloody next to her smoldering bed. There were teeth marks on Coriell's face and dozens of stab wounds up and down her torso. Bridget Durgan, the twenty-two-year-old Irish servant, had grabbed Mamie, the Coriell baby, and run in her stocking feet through the snow to alert a neighbor that burglars were at the house and that, for all she knew, "they might be murdering Mrs. Coriell" (Jones 1980:198). The neighbor noticed a large patch of fresh blood on Durgan's skirt. Mamie's hair was singed and her clothes smelled of kerosene. Durgan was suspected right off the bat. But she'd be darned if she could get her story straight. She had never seen the men before and she wouldn't "recognize them again. . . . She would recognize one of them. She would recognize them both. . . . The killers were Barney Dole . . . and a man named Hunt. . . . It was her friend Anne Linen, another servant, who had done it. . . . [She knew] who killed Mrs. Coriell but her questioners made her so angry she wouldn't tell" (pp. 199–200).

Dr. Coriell reported that Durgan had always been peaceful, quiet, and respectful of his wife, but she had not been a satisfactory servant. She wasn't particularly neat and was often laid up with menstrual difficulties or wracked with seizures. When Mrs. Coriell discovered that Durgan had "filthy habits," it was the last straw. Durgan was dismissed. The night before she was to leave the Coriell home, she brutally murdered Mrs. Coriell, most likely "while suffering what modern medicine calls a seizure of psychomotor or temporal lobe epilepsy—a type of seizure often characterized by rage, physical violence, and amnesia" (p. 202). When the teeth marks were found on Mrs. Coriell, they were considered "absolute proof, according to the biases of the time, that the murderer was a woman" (p. 200). Linen was found to have an alibi, and Durgan, who had much circumstantial evidence against her, was charged.

Durgan's attorneys chose not to enter a plea that reflected diminished responsibility due to mental illness. After all, "coarse Irish girls like [her] . . . lacked the delicate sensibilities to go insane in a fashion picturesque enough to capture the heart of a jury" (p. 204). They claimed that Durgan was innocent and warned the jurors not to be affected by community prejudice. However, in the court of public opinion a beastly, seemingly motiveless crime such as this must have been committed by a "fiend." And "everyone was eager to believe that [Durgan] was indeed a fiend. After all, she was Irish" (p. 201). Even her physical appearance supported the diagnosis of subhuman character: "She is large in the base of the brain, and swells out over the ears, where destructiveness and secretiveness are located by [scientists of the day], . . . while the whole region of intellect, ideality and moral sentiment is small" (pp. 204–205). Durgan was convicted, and the courtroom audience burst into applause when the death sentence was pronounced. On the day of the hanging, 2,000 men and women crammed into the prison compound and perched on roofs to watch as the condemned fiend was "jerked into eternity" (pp. 206–207).

Few contemporary criminologists would find the nineteenth-century diagnosis of Bridget Durgan's subhuman character a persuasive explanation of her crime. Yet explaining why people commit crime is a central concern of criminology. It is without a doubt a complex task, especially given the diverse forms of criminality that exist in any society. Clearly no single explanation can account for all instances of murder (Durgan's included), let alone for crime in its infinite varieties—burglary, prostitution, sexual assault, state-sponsored genocide, and so forth.

The attempt to explain crime is sometimes characterized as a search for the causes of crime, where the analyst or researcher tries to locate some prior trait(s) or event(s) that determine or set in motion criminal behavior. Causal explanations rely on both theoretical formulations and empirical research. Although **theory** is often perceived as "a tangled maze of jargon . . . that [is] irrelevant to the real world," we all use theory—a set of "interconnected abstractions or ideas that condense and organize knowledge"— to help explain our lives and the world around us (Neuman 2003:41–42). If, for example, you believe that criminals commit crime because they do not face any credible punishment for their actions, you are invoking a particular theory about criminal motivation and the societal reaction (or lack thereof) to it. Moreover, theory has practical implications, for proposals to address the crime problem explicitly or implicitly assume a particular explanation or set of underlying causes. If the theory associated with a crime control or intervention program is inaccurate, then the program is likely to fail.

In criminology, and the social sciences more generally, theory and research are intertwined. In other words, theory guides empirical research, which in turn confirms or disconfirms theory. Unfortunately, it sometimes seems as if criminology is mired in competing theories and endless empirical tests that only produce mixed or inconsistent results. Nevertheless, sound and carefully tested theory offers a better guide to social policy than a hit-or-miss or purely ideological approach.

Much theoretical explanation in criminology is sociological, but some is not. In this chapter we hope to cultivate your sociological imagination through a critical assessment of **individualistic explanations** of criminal behavior, that is, theories that locate the central causes of crime within the individual rather than within the social environment. These theories assume that criminals are particular "kinds of persons" (e.g., fiends) who possess some flawed or defective trait or who think about themselves and the world in ways that make the "normal prohibitions against crime relatively ineffective" (Herrnstein 1995:40; Orcutt 1983). Such explanations are especially appealing to those with a conservative political ideology, for they minimize social-environmental influences and imply that we do not need to change society (and by implication ourselves or our way of life) to deal with the problem of crime.

■ Supernatural Explanations

Until the eighteenth century, before the emergence of criminology, **supernatural explanations** of crime were widely held to be true (Pfohl 1985; Vold et al. 1998). In ancient and medieval times, it was assumed that people who acted in deviant ways did so because God was testing their faith, punishing them, or using their behavior to warn others. Or else they were seen as sinners who had fallen from God's grace and were tempted or even possessed by the devil or other evil force. As outdated as this notion may seem to some, studies indicate that nowadays about half the U.S. public continues to believe in Satan and demonic possession (Turque & Chideya 1991).

In earlier times, witches (mostly women, but some men) were a major concern of religious authorities. Witches were viewed as individuals who had either entered into a compact with the devil or been taken by the devil against their will. For instance, the *Malleus Maleficarum (Hammer of Witches)*, a religious tract written in the late fifteenth century, described how the devil had sexual intercourse with sleeping women, often turning them into his prostitutes and the bearers of his children. Witches, it was believed, also engaged in sexual orgies with the devil, orgies that perverted and made a mockery of Christian rituals; and witches were sexually promiscuous with sleeping men, spiriting away their sexual organs and leaving them castrated and impotent. In reality, women accused of witchcraft were those who defied the social order of the day by their "deviant" sexuality (i.e., sex outside of marriage, homosexuality, even lustful desire), their political activities or religious beliefs, or their involvement in lay healing and midwifery. They were scapegoats upon whom the misfortunes of the time could be blamed (Balkan et al. 1980; Ehrenreich & English 1973; Einstader & Henry 1995).

Historical data indicate that millions of witches were tortured and executed for the alleged practice of witchcraft. The methods of torture were many. Victims were deprived of sleep, crushed by heavy weights, forced to bathe in boiling water, hoisted aloft and dropped, forced to eat salted herring and then denied water. Needles were driven into the quick of nails, hands and feet were cut off, flesh was torn from the breasts, eyes were gouged out. Burning was often deemed necessary to destroy the witch entirely and evoke the "image of hell as the final resting place for unpurged sinners" (Balkan et al. 1980; Daly 1978; Pfohl 1985:25).

The ritual application of pain was in general the standard mode of punishment during the Middle Ages (Phohl 1985). Torture was considered appropriate for both exorcising evil spirits and extracting confessions. In 1757, for example, the execution of Robert Francois Damiens for the murder of his father involved

> the flesh . . . torn from his breasts, arms, thighs and calves with red-hot pincers, his right hand, holding the knife with which he committed the said parricide, burnt with sulphur, and, on those places where the flesh [was to be] torn away, poured molten lead, boiling oil, burning resin, wax and sulphur melted together and then his body drawn and quartered by four horses and his limbs and body consumed by fire, reduced to ashes and . . . thrown to the winds. (Foucault 1979:3)

Sometimes the accused had the opportunity to be acquitted of the charges by undergoing a **trial by ordeal**, a process designed to elicit divine intervention for the innocent. In one ordeal the accused was required to dip his bare hand into a caldron of boiling water to find a small pebble. The hand was then wrapped in cloth, sealed with the signet of a judge, and unwrapped three days later. If the hand was healed, the individual would be declared innocent. In another ordeal the accused was forced to walk over red-hot iron ploughshares; if no injury occurred, acquittal would follow. In ordeals such as these it was assumed that God would intervene to protect the innocent (Einstader & Henry 1995; Tewksbury 1994).

■ Classical and Neoclassical Criminology

It is against this backdrop of superstition and cruelty that modern **classical criminology** emerged to offer new ways of thinking about and dealing with crime. The classical criminologists were part of the eighteenth-century European movement known as the **Enlightenment**, or Age of Reason.

Enlightenment philosophers believed that humanity need not rely on religious authority to govern its affairs. Rational thought or reason could be used instead to develop principles of morality and justice. Individuals could agree to enter into a social contract whereby they would surrender some of their individuality and submit themselves to governmental control in exchange for protection of the common good and the maintenance of natural liberties and rights (Barkan 2001; Beirne & Messerschmidt 1995).

Enlightenment thinkers and classical criminologists like Cesare Beccaria (1738–1794) and Jeremy Bentham (1748–1842) believed in the doctrine of "free will." In their view, individuals who break the law and violate the social contract are not driven by evil spirits. Rather, they *rationally choose* to commit crime because they believe that the pleasures or benefits of such actions outweigh the pains or costs. The role of government is to manipulate this rational calculation of benefits and costs by maintaining a level of punishment that exceeds the potential rewards of crime. In contemporary parlance this is known as the principle of **deterrence**.

▪ Deterrence and the Rational Criminal

The deterrence approach to crime control is often associated with those who believe that the criminal justice system is too lenient and that we should crack down on crime. Ironically, however, the classical criminologists were critics of the excessive punishments of their time—torture and the death penalty. As late as the early nineteenth century in England, for instance, the death penalty (or capital punishment) was available for about 200 offenses, most of them property crimes. The classical theorists argued that punishment should be sufficient to offset the benefits of crime, but no more extreme than that. The death penalty, they felt, should not be used as a public spectacle to satisfy the community's desire for revenge or retribution. Rather, punishment should be proportional to the nature of the offense it is designed to deter. As such, the classical criminologists believed that imprisonment should replace torture and the death penalty as the standard mode of punishment (Beirne & Messerschmidt 1995; Hay et al. 1975).

By the late nineteenth to early twentieth century, classical criminology was superseded by other theories of crime (to be discussed later). But in the 1960s it was revived by economist Gary Becker (1968). Becker argued that economists, who had expertise in cost-benefit analysis as applied to economic affairs, could apply the tools of their trade (i.e., assumptions about rational economic actors, complex statistical techniques) to the crime problem as well. This modern-day version of the classical school is generally referred to as **neoclassical criminology** or **rational-choice theory**.

Although deterrence remains a core objective of the neoclassical approach, it is not an undifferentiated concept. Even in his day, Beccaria (1764/1963) drew distinctions between the **certainty, celerity** (swiftness), and **severity of punishment**. Certainty refers to the likelihood of receiving punishment, celerity to the immediacy of punishment following the offense, and severity to the nature of the punishment itself. According to Beccaria:

> One of the greatest curbs on crime is not the cruelty of punishments, but their infallibility. . . . The certainty of punishment, even if it be moderate, will always make a stronger impression than the fear of another which is more terrible but combined with the hope of impunity. . . . [And] the more promptly and . . . closely punishment follows . . . the commission of a crime, the more just and useful it will be. . . . The criminal is spared the useless and cruel torments of uncertainty. . . . Privation of liberty, . . . itself a punishment, should not precede the sentence except when necessity requires. . . . Promptness of punishment is more useful because when the length of time that passes between the punishment and misdeed is less, [it is] so much the stronger and . . . lasting in the human mind. . . . The severity of punishment of itself emboldens men to commit the very wrongs it is supposed to prevent; they are driven to commit additional crimes to avoid the punishment for a single one. The countries and times most notorious for severity of penalties have always been those in which the bloodiest and most inhumane of deeds were committed. (1963:58–59)

Early classical theorists, critics of the punishment practices of their age, appear liberal in their call for moderation. However, use of prison, not reform of society, was their reform agenda. They were primarily concerned with designing a legal system that would discipline those who deviated from the established social order.

Contemporary Deterrence Research

A large body of contemporary deterrence research has examined the impact of punishment on criminal behavior. Much of this research has utilized official crime data for geographical areas like cities, counties, and especially states, and considers both certainty and severity of punishment. (Celerity of punishment is difficult to measure and has been omitted from most studies.) The findings have generally shown that while certainty of punishment (as measured by the proportion of reported crimes that result in arrest, conviction, and incarceration) is more highly associated with lower crime rates than severity of punishment (as measured by the average lengths of sentences), even the effect of certainty is weak (Krohn 2000; Paternoster 1987).

There are several factors that appear to mitigate the deterrent effect of punishment. Research indicates that individuals' *perceptions* of punishment may be more significant than the actual punishment itself. Perceptual deterrence studies, which typically use self-report data, have generally found that perceived certainty has a greater effect than perceived severity, and that perceived certainty has a greater effect on an individual's decision to *continue* breaking the law than it does on his or her decision to break the law in the first place (Paternoster 1987; Paternoster & Triplett 1988; Williams & Hawkins 1986).

A person's stake in conformity may also affect his or her responsiveness to deterrence. In a study of employee theft, for example, Richard Hollinger and John Clark (1983) found that older employees with more to lose were more deterred by their perceptions of punishment than were their younger coworkers. Similarly, David Matza (1964) observed that as juveniles grew older many underwent maturational reform and desisted from delinquency as they took on the responsibilities of work and family life. And Cheryl Carpenter and colleagues (1988) found that by age sixteen some juveniles reported being deterred by the fact that they would face greater consequences than they had so far if they continued to offend. These youths recognized that as they grew older they would end up not just in the juvenile justice system but in the more punitive adult criminal justice system (see Box 11.2).

Other criminologists argue that rational-choice models of deterrence have focused too narrowly on punishment, oversimplified the cognitive or thinking process underlying much criminality, and neglected a number of other factors that affect individuals' decisions to violate the law. For instance, much research suggests that labor market incentives (the relative economic rewards of legal and illegal work) affect decisions to commit crime more than the risks of punishment (Freeman 1996; Williams & Kornblum 1985). In a study of high-risk offenders (adults previously incarcerated, adult drug users, and seventeen- to twenty-year-old high school dropouts) involved in a federally funded work program, Irving Piliavan and colleagues found that while "risks of punishment [had] virtually no impact on criminal behavior . . . persons who perceive[d] greater opportunity to earn money illegally [were] more likely to violate the law" (1986:14).

Research also suggests that one's internalized or normative evaluation of right and wrong may be more central to the decision to violate the law than perceptions of punishment, and that informal sanctions or extralegal threats such as shame, embarrassment, and disapproval from family and peers may deter law violation more than formal punishment (Erickson et al. 1977; Paternoster 1989; Williams & Hawkins 1986). Harold Grasmick and colleagues (1993), for example, found that reductions in self-reported drunk driving (in Oklahoma City, 1982–1990) were more highly associated with increasing levels of shame and embarrassment than with changing perceptions of legal sanctions. They credited the social movement against drunk driving (e.g., Mothers Against Drunk Driving) with success in altering moral beliefs and community standards regarding this offense. Similarly, in interviews with corporate officials, Sally Simpson (1992) found that informal factors such as threats to personal reputation and future employment opportunities outweighed formal punishment in decisions to violate the law or engage in unethical business conduct.

In addition, the deterrent effect of punishment may not be substantial because many criminals are not the rational actors envisioned by classical and neoclassical theory. But this is not the same as saying they are irrational. It's just that drug addiction, crimes of passion, and crimes committed out of emotional or economic desperation, for instance, may not involve the kind of cost-benefit calculus that responds to traditional deterrence strategies. To a drug addict, the cost of not stealing the money to pay for one's next fix (inevitable suffering from withdrawal symptoms) probably seems greater than the cost of stealing the money (*possible* arrest, *possible* conviction). Consider also the comments of women who killed their battering husbands or lovers. Most of those whom Ann Jones (1980) interviewed expressed considerable remorse and sorrow. Some spoke of guilt and depression, "but

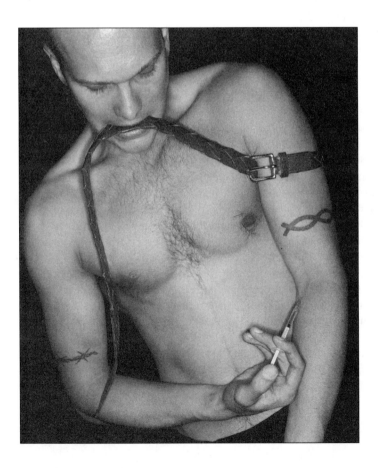

at the same time, many . . . experienced an exhilarating sense of release. 'Even when I knew I would have to go to prison,' said one woman, 'I felt as if a stone hand had been lifted off my head.' Another said, 'Suddenly I knew that I could take a walk, call my mother, laugh—and it would be all right. For the first time in eleven years, I wasn't afraid'" (p. 320).

We must remember that deprivations are relative, that they occur in a larger context. Yes, the poor, inner-city youth sent to prison is being deprived of his freedom to come and go. But maybe it's the first time in his life he's been cool in the summer, warm in the winter, or had three square meals a day. In some cases, the risk of getting caught may be part of the thrill motivating the offender, or the individual may be rather fatalistic about the prospects of getting caught (Ferrell 1997; J. Katz 1988). As former Los Angeles gang member Sanyika Shakur notes, "The total lawlessness [of gang life] was alluring, and . . . the sense of importance, self-worth, and raw power was exciting, stimulating, and intoxicating beyond any other high. . . . Prison loomed in my future like wisdom teeth. . . . [It] was like a stepping stone to manhood" (1993:70, 163).

To be sure, some offenders behave rationally insofar as they try to select targets that minimize the risk of apprehension and maximize the proceeds from crime. Interviews with burglars, for example, indicate that they prefer unoccupied single-family homes, homes that have fewer entry barriers (e.g., sophisticated locks, window bars, alarms), homes that appear affluent or that contain "good stuff," and neighborhoods where they fit in or look inconspicuous. And to the extent that thieves fear apprehension, they try to push it from their minds and focus instead on the stash awaiting them (Bennett & Wright 1984; Tunnell 1992; Walsh 1980; Wright & Decker 1994).

In his autobiography, Nathan McCall (1994) recalls his involvement in armed robbery:

> It gave me a rush to know that I'd taken all that money. . . . At the same time, there was this fear that had been nagging me. . . . Cats all around me were getting popped for one thing or another, and being sent to the penitentiary. . . . I figured that sooner or later I'd take a fall, too. Sometimes, when I thought about it, I didn't care. Sometimes I cared a whole lot more than I was willing to admit. . . . I was twenty, half burned out on drugs, depressed, and hopelessly lost. At some point in life . . . I had lost control. (pp. 136, 141)

On the night he was arrested for the robbery of a McDonald's restaurant that would send him to prison, McCall remembers, "My intuition . . . was telling me I shouldn't go. . . . Despite the wine I'd guzzled to numb my fear, I was nervous. It just didn't feel right. . . . I wished I could rewind . . . my fucked-up life and reset its course" (pp. 137–138, 140).

Some readers of McCall's autobiography will say that his life was simply a product of the choices he made. But others will recognize it is more complicated than that, for many factors impact on the course of one's life as it spins more and more out of control.

Deterrence and the death penalty. Although a majority of the U.S. population supports the death penalty, most criminologists have concluded that "the overwhelming weight of the evidence suggests that the death penalty cannot be shown to deter criminal homicide" (Smith 2000:628). Historically, those states that have used the death penalty most often have had the highest rates of homicide. Furthermore, states that have abolished the death penalty have not experienced a rise in homicide, nor have states that reinstated the death penalty experienced a reduction in homicide (Glaser & Ziegler 1974; Peterson & Bailey 1998).

In fact, some criminologists suggest that homicides may even increase as a result of executions due to what they call a **brutalization effect**. William Bowers and Glenn Pierce argue that executions "devalue life by the example of human sacrifice" and send a message that it is "appropriate to kill those who have gravely offended us" (1980:456). They examined the relationship between monthly executions in New York State between 1906 and 1963 and monthly homicides between 1907 and 1964 and found that, on average, two additional homicides occurred each month following an execution. Similarly, a study of California found that homicides were twice as high during the years (1952 to 1967) when California was executing an inmate every other month than during the period (1968 to 1991) when it carried out no executions (Godfrey & Schiraldi 1995). And research that examined the reinstatement of the death penalty in Arizona in 1992 after a thirty-year moratorium, and in Oklahoma in 1990 after a twenty-five-year moratorium, found evidence of a brutalization effect as well (Bailey 1998; Cochran et al. 1994; Thomson 1997).

Nevertheless, criminologists believe that further research is needed on the deterrence versus brutalization effect of the death penalty. Especially useful would be studies that examine the extent of publicity surrounding executions and the effects of executions on different types of homicides and homicides committed by different sociodemographic groups (Bailey 1998).

■ **Positivist Criminology:**
  Biological and Psychological Approaches

Earlier we noted that for many decades criminology's focus on the rational criminal was superseded by other theories of crime. These other theories entailed biological, psychological, and sociological perspectives and emerged from a school of thought called **positivism**. European positivists like Auguste Comte (1798–1857) and Adolphe Quetelet (1796–1874) advanced the proposition that human behavior could be studied as an empirical science. Scientific methods of inquiry were required to ascertain these forces ("positive" facts), diagnose the problem, and prescribe appropriate remedies. (While classical criminology predates positivism, neoclassical criminology is grounded in positivist science.) The remainder of this chapter examines *biological* and *psychological* approaches to crime. These theories depart from the classical/neoclassical assumption of the rational criminal and postulate that crime is caused by forces that are beyond an individual's control. As individualistic explanations, however, they assume that criminals are kinds of persons who are fundamentally different from the rest of us.

▨ *Social Darwinism and Early Biological Criminology*

Charles Darwin's (1809–1882) work on evolution was a major factor in the rise of positivism and biological thinking about crime. Darwin postulated that life had evolved through a process of natural selection or "survival of the fittest" among diverse species, including humans. Herbert Spencer (1820–1903) applied this notion to the social realm. He asserted that some people had natural qualities that made them more fit, more adaptable members of society, while others lacked such traits. This brand of **social Darwinism** justified social inequality, which it attributed to differences in people's ability to compete for scarce resources, with the most talented individuals ending up in positions of wealth, power, and responsibility (Balkan et al. 1980; Hofstader 1959).

It was in this context that Italian physician Cesare Lombroso (1835–1909) emerged in the late nineteenth century as the founder of criminological positivism and the biological approach to crime (Wolfgang 1972). Lombroso postulated that many criminals were born **atavists**, throwbacks to an earlier stage of human evolution. He believed that these criminals were less highly evolved than law-abiding citizens and that they could be recognized by distinctive physical traits that he considered common among "savages and apes" and "the coloured races" (e.g., hairy bodies, curly hair, receding foreheads, long arms, and large skulls, nostrils, jaws, and ears) (cited in Beirne & Messerschmidt 1995:350). According to Lombroso, these individuals were low in intelligence, excessively idle, and insensitive to pain; and they were lovers of orgies who had an "irresistible craving for evil for its own sake" (p. 350). Lombroso also believed that women were less evolved than men, and that they were inherently child-like, jealous, and vengeful. He thought that the "natural passivity" of women made them less inclined toward crime, but that when they did deviate they made exceptionally vile criminals whose "wickedness [was] enormous" (Lombroso & Ferrero 1895:152).

You may be surprised that someone who advanced such ideas could have become a central figure in criminology. Lombroso was a man of his time, when such race and gender prejudice was not uncommon. (Variants of such views continue to persist even today.) But it was Lombroso's attempt to prove his theory with the methods of science that brought him his fame. He measured and recorded in great detail the physical attributes of living and deceased Italian prisoners, compared these findings with data from nonprisoners, and claimed his hypothesis proven.

Nevertheless, Lombroso's research was methodologically flawed. The prisoner and nonprisoner samples were not pure types. The former may have included people who were innocent of the crimes they had been convicted of, and the latter likely included offenders who had not been caught and convicted. Moreover, the alleged physical differences found by Lombroso were rather trivial. And even if the alleged differences were noticeable, the fact that the prisoners were disproportionately Sicilian made the research problematic. For although Sicilians may have tended to have some of the physical traits Lombroso attributed to criminals, their low status in Italian society would have increased their chances of imprisonment (Barkan 2001).

The earliest scientific refutation of Lombroso's work was published by Charles Goring (1913). Goring compared the physical attributes of some 3,000 English prisoners with those of a large control group and found no differences along the lines postulated by Lombroso. He did claim, however, that the criminals in his sample were shorter in height and lighter in weight than noncriminals, leaving the door open for a hereditary or "born criminal" explanation. While Goring cautioned against equating physical difference with abnormality, and he acknowledged possible social-environmental influences, he was a social Darwinist at heart: "This physical inferiority, . . . originating in and fostered by selection, may tend with time to become an inbred characteristic of the criminal classes, just as, with the passage of generations, the upper classes of the noncriminal community have become differentiated in physique from those lower on the social scale" (p. 200).

Contemporary criminologist Nicole Rafter (1992) notes that in the United States **criminal anthropology**, as she calls it, even predated Lombroso and continued to have adherents into the twentieth century. Criminal anthropology refers to the practice of studying the criminal "as a physically anomalous human type" (p. 525). William Sheldon (1949), for instance, advanced a theory that body type was associated with personality and behavioral traits. He compared a group of official delinquent and nondelinquent boys according to three body types: the thin and introverted *ectomorph,* the rotund and easygoing *endomorph,* and the muscular and aggressive *mesomorph,* who, as you might suspect, was the criminal type in Sheldon's scheme. This theory occupied the attention of mainstream criminologists through the 1950s and is even taken seriously by some today (Glueck & Glueck 1950; Wilson & Herrnstein 1985).

Although these studies, like Lombroso's work, have been critiqued on methodological grounds, perhaps the strongest criticisms have concerned ideological issues. Social Darwinists in the United States had called for "eugenic" solutions to crime and other social problems since the 1870s. **Eugenics**, which means "well born" or "good genes," was a philosophy favoring social intervention to regulate the genetic composition of the population through methods such as compulsory sterilization and restrictions on the marriage and immigration of undesirable groups (i.e., those alleged to be biologically inferior). By the 1930s about thirty states had passed laws allowing for the involuntary sterilization of not only criminals but also the insane, feebleminded, and epileptic. Over 60,000 people were deprived of their choice to reproduce (Balkan et al. 1980; Katz & Chambliss 1995).

To be sure, many criminal anthropologists (including Lombroso) were not favorably inclined toward eugenics, but many others (including Goring) were. Some eugenicists even advocated death for the purpose of genetic engineering. In 1900 W. Duncan McKim proposed "a gentle, painless death . . . for the very weak and the very vicious who fall into the hands of the State. . . . [Execution by] carbonic acid gas . . . [is] the simplest, the kindest, and most humane means for preventing reproduction among those whom we deem unworthy of this high privilege" (cited in Rafter 1992:540–541).

The most well-known extermination program of this type was undertaken by Adolf Hitler's Nazi regime during the World War II period. The physicians in the Nazi program actually learned much from their U.S. counterparts and used the U.S. example to facilitate "a favorable reception for compulsory . . . sterilization in Germany" (Rubenstein & Roth 1987:142). Even prior to Hitler's rise to power, a prominent German medical director wrote to the Ministry of Interior: "What we racial hygienists promote is not at all new or unheard of. In a cultured nation of the first order, in the United States of America, that which we strive toward was introduced and tested long ago" (cited in Rubenstein & Roth 1987:141).

◼ Contemporary Biological Research

Late in his career, Lombroso actually retreated from a strictly biological position, acknowledging that crime was the product of a number of factors, some biological, some not (Beirne & Messerschmidt 1995). Similarly, most contemporary biocriminologists accept the proposition that there is an interaction between biology and social environment. This **biosocial theory** assumes the existence of biological factors that *predispose* some individuals toward crime (Ellis & Walsh 2000; Fishbein 1990; Wilson & Herrnstein 1985). This predisposition interacts with and is activated or triggered by particular environmental conditions that do not produce the same response in individuals with different biological traits. At the same time, according to this view, a person's biology will not produce a definitive or determinant outcome, nor will it prevent one from exerting any conscious control over their actions. Rather, biology operates in conjunction with other influences, each of which increases or decreases the probability or likelihood of criminal behavior. Unfortunately, much biological crime research does not concern itself with such nuances.

Family inheritance and crime. In the 1956 movie *The Bad Seed,* a precocious young girl, Rhoda Penmark, commits three murders without even the slightest expression of remorse. Yet she had been raised by two loving, law-abiding parents! How are we to explain her crimes? We are told that her biological grandmother (Rhoda's mother had been adopted) had also committed a number of murders, including the poisoning of her own father, whom she killed for inheritance money. Weren't criminals a product of their environment, queried Rhoda's mother? Some were, a knowledgeable friend replied, but some were simply "born with no capacity for remorse or guilt, no feeling of right or wrong—born with the kind of brain that may have been normal in humans 50,000 years ago. . . . [It was] as if they were born blind . . . and you just couldn't . . . teach them to see." Apparently, we are left to deduce, Rhoda's mother had passed on a gene for criminal behavior.

Perhaps the writers of this script had read Richard Dugdale's *The Jukes: A Study in Crime, Pauperism, Disease, and Heredity* (1877) or Henry Goddard's *The Kallikak Family: A Study in the Heredity of Feeblemindedness* (1912) for clues about the supposed genetic transmission of crime. Dugdale and Goddard had traced the criminal histories of family members across successive generations and claimed to have found a disproportionate amount of criminality. Although these particular studies do not stand up to scientific scrutiny, the role of genetic inheritance continues to be an issue in criminology. Contemporary research on this subject, which typically involves examination of twins and adopted children, has produced some intriguing findings.

Several studies of twins have found greater similarity in behavior (whether criminal or noncriminal) among identical or monozygotic twins (one ovum that divided after fertilization by one sperm) than among fraternal or dizygotic twins (two ova fertilized by two separate sperm). These findings suggest a genetic influence on criminality, since identical twins have the same biological makeup while fraternal twins do not. However, critics of these studies note that identical twins are more likely than fraternal twins to be treated similarly by others, and thus their common behavior patterns "could just as easily be due to environmental influences" (Bartol & Bartol 1989:144). Odd Dalgard and Einar Kringlen (1976), for example, found that any genetic influence on the criminality of twins was negligible when they controlled for such factors. Yet it is difficult to disentangle genetic characteristics from early childhood and family influences. Family experiences that are common to parents and children include diet, exposure to toxins, neighborhood conditions, and television-viewing habits (Ellis & Walsh 2000; Fishbein 1990; Katz & Chambliss 1995; Walters & White 1989).

Some adoption studies have also found greater similarity in criminal behavior between adoptees and their biological parents than would be expected by chance, especially for chronic or repeat offenders. When the biological parent is both criminal and alcoholic, the adoptee's behavior tends to be disproportionately violent. But since adoption agencies often match the class and racial background of adopted and natural parents, it is unclear whether the adoptee's behavior is attributable to genetics rather than environmental factors. In addition, the age at which an individual was adopted needs to be considered, for increased criminality among adoptees has been associated with amount of time spent with biological parents or in orphanages.

Both the twin and the adoption studies often beg the question of what precisely is being inherited that supposedly causes crime. Clearly no one today seriously believes there is a bad seed or crime gene that is inherited. What, then, do biocriminologists propose? They argue that there are genetic predispositions for alcoholism, mental disorders, or temperamental traits such as impulsivity, extroversion, hyperemotionality, anger, and deceitfulness that make one more vulnerable to environmental strains that trigger criminality (Ellis & Walsh 2000; Fishbein 1990; Rowe 1986). Nevertheless, only 20 percent of criminologists give any credence to genetic hypotheses about crime (Ellis & Walsh 1997). Glen Walters, one skeptic, examined the results of thirty-eight gene-crime studies and concluded that the "better designed and more recently [since 1975] published studies provided less support for the gene-crime hypothesis" (1992:595).

Intelligence and crime. In 1904 Alfred Binet was commissioned by the French Ministry of Public Education to develop a test to measure children's cognitive (linguistic and mathematical) abilities at various age levels. From this was born the intelligence quotient (IQ) test. Binet did not consider one's score on this test to be genetic or impervious to accumulated experience. When the IQ test was introduced in the United States, however, a contrary attitude prevailed, even though tests administered to army recruits during World War I indicated that about half scored below the cognitive level expected of a thirteen-year-old (Katz & Chambliss 1995).

A number of studies have found that low IQ is correlated with higher rates of official and self-reported juvenile delinquency (Hirschi & Hindelang 1977; Wilson & Herrnstein 1985), though obviously not to those crimes that require a good deal of intelligence (e.g., white-collar computer and financial crimes). How should we interpret the apparent IQ-delinquency association? Is intelligence genetic, environmental, or a combination of the two? How much are we limited by our genes? How much does an enriching environment matter? Who would deny the significance of social influences such as parents and teachers who encourage children to read and enjoy learning? The belief that people with low IQs are simply feebleminded or unable to understand right and wrong has long been discredited (Binder et al. 1988). But since IQ is associated with the cognitive abilities that lead to academic success, youths with low IQs may be more likely to feel alienated from or dissatisfied with school, which in turn may weaken their stake in conformity and increase their attraction to delinquency.

Perhaps the greatest point of contention regarding the IQ test has been its alleged class and race bias. In their well-publicized book *The Bell Curve,* Richard Herrnstein and Charles Murray (1994) compiled data that indicated that African Americans, on average, scored lower on IQ tests than European Americans, while Asian Americans scored the highest. (The bell curve refers to the shape of the distribution of IQ scores in a population from low to middle to high.) Herrnstein and Murray also argued that low IQ or cognitive disadvantage was causally related to a variety of social ills, including out-of-wedlock births, welfare dependency, and crime. Moreover, they claimed that IQ is in large part genetic and that it is *immutable,* impervious to change. Hence government programs designed to improve the lives of the cognitively disadvantaged are bound to fail.

The Bell Curve has been subjected to numerous criticisms, many of which were previously advanced against earlier works. For example, critics contend that the content of IQ test questions advantages individuals familiar with the white, middle-class cultural experience. Moreover, the property tax–based system of school funding means that low-income communities will have fewer educational resources for students, who consequently do poorer in school. Schools also use test scores to track students into vertical (high to low) tracks, which in turn become self-fulfilling prophecies of educational attainment, denying some youths access to desirable social roles (Katz & Chambliss 1995; Cullen et al. 1997; Menard & Morse 1984).

Criticism of *The Bell Curve,* however, goes beyond these standard refrains. As Charles Lane notes, many of the book's most important assertions "are derived partially or totally from the *Mankind Quarterly*–Pioneer

Fund scholarly circle" (1994:15). The *Mankind Quarterly* is an anthropology journal published in Edinburgh, Scotland, that promotes the view that the white race is superior. It is financially supported by the Pioneer Fund, a New York foundation established in 1937 with the money of Wickliffe Draper, a textile magnate. Draper was "fascinated by eugenics, expressed early sympathy for Nazi Germany, and later advocated the 'repatriation' of blacks to Africa" (p. 15). As recently as 1989 the Pioneer Fund called for the abandonment of integration in the United States because, says the organization, the intelligence of African Americans cannot be enhanced (Free 1996).

In a compelling empirical critique of *The Bell Curve,* Francis Cullen and colleagues (1997) examined data from nearly 500 studies containing over 42,800 offenders. These studies contain measures not only of intelligence and crime but also of respondents' social background (e.g., socioeconomic status, urban versus rural residence, religious participation, living with mother and father). Cullen and colleagues concluded that the association between IQ and crime was at best small, if not insignificant, after taking into account other social influences. Moreover, these social influences are often *amenable to change* (unlike Herrnstein and Murray's claims about IQ).

Cullen and colleagues believe that having "knowledge of an offender's intellectual capacity and aptitude is advantageous in designing" rehabilitative treatment programs. They also advocate a broadened conception of IQ that includes not just the standard linguistic and mathematical criteria but practical intelligence as well, that is, "a person's ability to learn and profit from experience, to monitor effectively one's own and others' feelings and needs, and to solve everyday problems" (pp. 403–404). Nevertheless, they believe that Herrnstein and Murray's thesis and policy conclusions are based more on ideology than on empirical science.

Other biological factors. There are countless other biological conditions that have been linked to criminal behavior. Indeed, the list of potential maladies seems endless. One of the most researched is the **XYY syndrome**. Whereas the normal male has one X and one Y chromosome, about 1 in 1,000 have an extra Y chromosome. XYY males appear to be taller, to have longer arms, more severe acne, more mental retardation, and, on average, lower intelligence than XY males. In the 1960s researchers began to postulate that they also exhibited more criminal violence (Binder et al. 1988; Katz & Chambliss 1995; Jacobs et al. 1965; Jarvik et al. 1984).

Considerable attention was drawn to this theory when the attorney representing Richard Speck, the mass murderer who killed eight nursing students in Chicago in 1966, claimed that Speck suffered from this syndrome.

Speck, it turned out, did not have this chromosomal pattern. But initial studies did indicate that XYY males were disproportionately found in prisons and mental institutions (Katz & Chambliss 1995; Sanders 1983).

On closer examination it was discovered that the criminal histories of XYY males consisted primarily of property offenses, not violence. Their overrepresentation in prisons may have been related to their tendency to have lower intelligence and greater impulsivity, and perhaps to legal biases against individuals with this physical appearance. In any event, the trait is so rare that it could at best account for only a small fraction of criminal behavior. Alice Theilgaard concluded that "there is no ground for anticipating that a person with a certain [chromosomal] status will demonstrate a preordained, inflexible and irremediable personality or pathology" (1984:108).

Another line of biocriminological investigation has focused on the autonomic nervous system (ANS), which regulates automatic bodily processes like breathing and perspiring. Hans Eysenck (1977) postulated that some ANS disorders make individuals less responsive to external stimulation, thus impeding their ability to be socially conditioned. Sarnoff Mednick and colleagues (1982) argued that chronic delinquents suffer from a sluggish ANS that interferes with the way in which fear (toward a punishing adult, for instance) inhibits aggressive impulses. They found that delinquents displayed significantly slower electrodermal responses (usually measured through sweat gland activity) than those in a nondelinquent control group. Other studies have linked low levels of serotonin, a neurochemical transmitter that carries messages between the brain and the body, to violence. Low-serotonin individuals appear to respond more slowly to emotional stimuli and are less inhibited in their aggressive or impulsive behaviors (Ellis & Walsh 2000; Fishbein 1990).

Remember, however, that the sources of biological maladies—whether they are genetic or environmentally induced—are not always clear. Take nutritional deficiencies and lead exposure, for example, which have been linked to a variety of mental and physical problems that put one at risk for low IQ, memory loss, depression, and behavioral aggression. Poor nutrition and children's exposure to lead from paint chips in dilapidated buildings, for instance, are not genetic but are inversely related to social-class life situations. Similarly, inadequate diet and alcohol/drug use during pregnancy can seriously impair fetal development and have long-term effects on central nervous system (CNS) functioning. (The CNS is the main switchboard consisting of the brain and spinal cord that controls the entire nervous system.) Such effects are caused by parental behavior, not genetics. But one should not simply write these off as "lifestyle choices," since a mother's ability to eat a balanced diet during pregnancy or to obtain access to an alcohol or drug treatment program is clearly related to social class.

Moreover, unhealthy prenatal practices and ineffective postnatal child-rearing are so intertwined that it is often difficult to distinguish the effect of one from the other (Barkan 2001; Fishbein 1990; Kandel & Mednick 1991).

It is also important to consider that fathers as well as mothers can contribute to birth defects or deficiencies. Environmental exposure to lead or other toxins can damage ova and sperm as well as fetuses. Toxins can even "be transmitted to a fetus during intercourse, *after* conception has occurred. Hence preconceptive and prenatal harm can result from *either* parent's exposure" to hazardous environmental substances (Narayan 1995:398). Clearly it makes little sense to blame parents for choosing to work in unhealthy conditions. The focus should be on the corporate and governmental policies that allow these conditions to persist (see Chapter 6).

At times, claims about biological causes of crime are simply taken too far. In 1978 Dan White, a city supervisor in San Francisco, shot and killed Mayor George Moscone and supervisor/gay activist Harvey Milk. (Apparently White did not like gays or politicians sympathetic to the gay rights movement.) During the murder trial White's attorney claimed that White had been under the influence of junk food (sugar and food additives) that had diminished his capacity to control his behavior. White's "Twinkie defense," as it has been called, helped convince the jury to convict him of the lesser charge of manslaughter rather than first-degree murder (Weiss 1984). (Perhaps the jurors did not like gays or gay sympathizers either.)

If junk food doesn't make you do it, perhaps your hormones will. Some research has linked higher testosterone levels in males to aggressive behavior. Overall, however, the research has produced inconsistent results, with some studies suggesting that at times higher testosterone levels may follow rather than precede aggression, and others finding that testosterone levels may drop after stressful events (Barkan 2001; Ellis & Walsh 2000; Katz & Chambliss 1995).

These inconsistent findings did not stop Ronnie Shelton from pleading not guilty to twenty-eight counts of rape in 1988, on the grounds that his high levels of testosterone left him a victim of "compulsive rape syndrome." But the Texas judge and jurors were unconvinced. *Female* offenders, on the other hand, have been somewhat more successful with hormonal defenses. That same year, Sheryl Lynn Massip was charged with murdering her infant son by driving her car over him. She pleaded diminished responsibility due to postpartum (after birth) depression. Although a California jury returned a guilty verdict, "the judge overruled their decision on the grounds that she was . . . 'bonkers'" (Tavris 1992:152).

Nevertheless, Robin Ogle and colleagues (1995) take seriously the notion of postpartum influences on female criminality. They argue, however, that postpartum inducements stem more from environmental factors

· than from hormonal ones. For example, after childbirth women experience a marked reduction in both sleep and personal space that can cause chronic levels of stress. Also, the birth of a child is often accompanied by "severe financial strains due to a host of new expenses and restrictions" on one's ability to earn a living (p. 183). According to Ogle and colleagues, these stresses can induce a state of intense physiological arousal, an autonomic nervous system response that energizes the organism to respond in ways that "reduce the state of arousal itself" (Bernard 1990:75). The arousal, which is experienced as a negative condition, is often associated with anger at the stress-inducing stimulus. Women who have little or no prior history of aggressive behavior do not know how to control this anger and may lash out at the most visible and vulnerable source of their arousal, that is, their child.

As a defense in criminal trials, premenstrual syndrome (PMS) has arguably received more media attention than postpartum depression. In Great Britain in 1981, Christine English drove a car over her lover and killed him after they had quarreled over his drinking and infidelity and he had threatened to end their relationship. During the widely reported criminal trial, physician Katharina Dalton testified that English had been suffering from an extremely aggravated premenstrual physical condition since 1966 that made "her irritable, aggressive, impatient, and confused, with loss of self control" (cited in Binder et al. 1988:494). Although originally charged with murder, English's plea of diminished responsibility resulted in a lesser conviction for manslaughter and a sentence of probation (Faith 1993).

In research that brought her notoriety, Dalton (1961) claimed that about half of the 156 women she studied in British prisons had committed their crimes during the eight-day premenstrual-menstrual period. She also claimed that about half of female drivers involved in motor-vehicle accidents were in this eight-day phase. PMS research such as this has been vulnerable to the same kinds of criticism as the testosterone studies. Julie Horney (1978), for instance, found that about half of female *passengers* in accidents were also in their eight-day phase. Moreover, most of Dalton's prisoner-subjects had been convicted of nonviolent crimes, particularly theft and prostitution (Katz & Chambliss 1995). It's also important to remember that crimes and accidents are stressful events, and stress can bring on early menstruation. So if any weak link does exist between menstruation and behavioral problems, it may be "not because the former causes the latter, but because the latter causes the former" (Tavris 1992:151).

Although they acknowledge multicausal interaction between biology and environment, most biocriminologists—whether they are considering family inheritance, intelligence, or other biological factors—give causal priority to biology and downplay social factors (Barkan 2001; Katz & Chambliss 1995). Studies generally rely on relatively small sample sizes and on officially labeled offenders, and the findings tend to be weak and inconsistent. Their focus is on violent criminality and juvenile delinquency to the exclusion of other types of crimes, especially white-collar crime. As David Friedrichs notes, "The pervasiveness of white-collar crime would seem to offer a powerful refutation of the proposition that criminality can be generally explained by biogenic explanations" (2004:194). This research also fails to account for group variations in crime, that is, it fails to explain why crime rates are higher among some groups than others. Thus we are left to assume that entire groups of people must be biologically flawed in some way. One case in point occurred in response to the urban race riots of the mid-1960s. Three neurosurgeons, well respected in their field, wrote a letter to the *Journal of the American Medical Association* claiming that "brain dysfunctions" not the "urgent social needs of the ghetto" underlaid much collective violence and looting, and that psychosurgical techniques might be appropriate to eliminate this "source of aggressive behavior" (cited in Chorover 1973:49).

We would be naive to deny that "biological conditions have a profound impact on the adaptive, cognitive, and emotional abilities" of individuals (Fishbein 1990:56). But we must be wary of premature and injudicious applications of biological thinking about crime. At its extreme we have noted the association of biological approaches with eugenics and the practice of compulsory sterilization and even extermination. Even when used with the best intentions, to prevent crime by diagnosing and delivering needed services to at-risk children, for example, biological interventions are fraught with ethical problems. Notice that here we are talking about *potential* offenders, children who might commit crimes some day. How will we avoid mistakenly diagnosing children or adversely stigmatizing them with a potentially harmful label or setting in motion a self-fulfilling prophecy? What type of treatment will we employ? Will it be physiological (e.g., drugs), psychological, or social? Or will we simply isolate or quarantine suspect populations (see Jeffery 1978)?

With convicted offenders as well, imposition of rehabilitative biological treatments is problematic. Diane Fishbein notes that "the appropriate administration of a medication or other treatment may . . . be warranted for some individuals with [an] identifiable pathology . . . [that] played a role in . . . [their] antisocial behavior" (1990:54, 56). She adds, however, that biological variables cannot be manipulated without attention to interacting factors. By the time individuals have entered the juvenile or criminal justice system, their behavior problems have been so substantially compounded that treating only one facet of their condition will be unlikely to yield the desired therapeutic results.

Box 3.1 DNA and the Criminal Justice System

DNA, or deoxyribonucleic acid, is found in the cells of the human body and contains an individual's genetic blueprint. Because only identical twins have the same DNA, it can be used to identify crime victims and to establish the statistical likelihood that a suspect was involved in a crime. In criminal investigations, DNA samples are derived from blood, saliva, skin tissue, bone, hair, earwax, sweat, mucus, urine, semen, and vaginal and rectal cells (Turman 2001).

Care must be exercised when gathering and analyzing DNA to avoid contamination and degradation. Contamination occurs when foreign matter comes into contact with the DNA sample. This can happen if someone sneezes or coughs in the vicinity of the DNA sample or if someone touches some part of his or her body and then touches the areas where the DNA will be extracted. Furthermore, exposure of the DNA to heat or humidity will accelerate the degradation process and make the sample unstable.

The use of DNA evidence in criminal investigations has increased dramatically in recent years. Between 1997 and 2000 publicly operated forensic crime laboratories reported annual increases of about 11,000 new criminal cases as well as over 103,000 cases of individuals already convicted of crimes. Given the burgeoning workload, many crime laboratories have been unable to accommodate requests from criminal justice agencies. Over 80 percent of crime laboratories reported backlogs totaling over 281,000 cases in 2001. Nevertheless, prosecutorial reliance on DNA evidence continues to proliferate. Whereas only about half of all state prosecutors used DNA evidence for plea negotiations or felony trials in 1996, over two-thirds used it in 2001. Use of DNA evidence was most pronounced in large, full-time prosecutor offices. In cities with populations of a million or more, 100 percent of the offices used DNA (DeFrances 2002; Steadman 2002).

While DNA evidence can and has been used to exonerate the innocent, some concerns about its use have emerged. One issue involves other ways the collected samples might be used. Because DNA samples can reveal genetic conditions such as sickle cell anemia and schizophrenia, the samples could be used to deny people health insurance or require them to pay higher premiums. Another concern is that the emergence of state and national DNA databases poses a threat to privacy rights and could also renew interest in discovering purported "crime genes" that would subject individuals to social control "regardless of whether or not they have violated the law" (Burns & Smith 1999:3).

The expansion of DNA databases has racial implications as well. African Americans are more likely than European Americans to come into contact with law enforcement agencies, a disparity that is especially

continues

Box 3.1   continued

evident among juveniles. Currently over half the states include DNA profiles of juveniles in their databanks, with no provisions for removing these profiles once the youths become adults (Kimmelman 2000).

Additionally, some critics have raised the specter of police tampering of evidence, especially in departments that have poor rapport with the residents in their communities. The Federal Bureau of Investigation itself has acknowledged that about 3,000 federal cases prior to 1997 may have been affected by skewed testimony, sloppy investigations, or tainted evidence (*New York Times* 2003). And several states have reported cases of evidence contamination, falsification of DNA data, inflation of the statistical likelihood of a DNA match, and questionable testimony by forensic experts and laboratory managers (Tanner 2003).

▓ *Freudian Psychology*

Like biological theories, psychological explanations assume that criminals are different kinds of persons. They postulate an assortment of defective mental, emotional, or personality traits that either cause criminal behavior or predispose one to the environmental triggers of crime. (Behaviorism, which we will discuss later, is an exception.) To a large extent, many of the biological theories we have reviewed identify such traits as intervening between biology and crime, and individual traits such as intelligence are sometimes elements of psychological (as well as biological) theories of crime.

One of the earliest psychological formulations was advanced by Austrian physician Sigmund Freud (1856–1939), whose **psychoanalytic theory** was quite influential in early explanations of juvenile delinquency (Aichorn 1935; Friedlander 1947; Healy & Bronner 1936). Freud and his followers believed that the human personality consists of three interdependent yet often conflicting elements: the id, ego, and superego.

> The *id* is the unrestrained, primitive, pleasure-seeking component with which each child is born. The *ego* develops through the reality of living in the world and helps manage and restrain the id's need for immediate gratification. The *superego* develops through interactions with parents and other significant people and represents the development of conscience and the moral rules that are shared by most adults. . . . All three segments of the personality operate simultaneously. The id dictates needs and desires, the superego counteracts the id by fostering feelings of morality and righteousness, and the ego evaluates the reality of a position between the two extremes. (Siegel et al. 2003:84)

According to Freudian theory, basic personality formation is completed in early childhood, and thus early parent-child interaction is of paramount importance. If parents are neglectful or abusive, or exert too little or too much discipline, imbalances may develop among the id, ego, and superego, creating unconscious psychological conflicts within individuals. Later-life juvenile delinquency and adult criminality may represent a symbolic expression or acting out of such conflicts. If parental socialization is weak or inadequate, for instance, the child's superego will be underdeveloped and the id will predominate the personality. Later in life this may lead the person to insist on the immediate gratification of selfish needs, to lack compassion or sensitivity to others, or to behave impulsively and aggressively. If, on the other hand, parental discipline is overbearing and punitive, the individual may become overly rebellious and defiant of authority.

Critics of Freudian psychology contend that it is too speculative. The postulated personality components are neither observable nor measurable, requiring one to rely on a psychoanalyst's retrospective "interpretation of a patient's interpretation of what is occurring in the [un]conscious" (Sheley 1985:202). Moreover, the influence of early-life events can be significantly altered by later experiences (Quay 1983). Robert Sampson and John Laub (1993), for example, found that earlier involvement in crime could be substantially reduced with the acquisition of adult commitments conducive to conformity, particularly marriage and stable employment (see Chapter 4).

Freud, nevertheless, was one of the first to draw attention to the important influence of family socialization. Contemporary family research suggests that parental affection and support of children, effective parental-child communication, absence of conflict in the home, and positive marital adjustment of parents mitigate antisocial conduct and increase prosocial behavior among youths (Cernkovich & Giordano 1987; Wright & Cullen 2001). Criminologists Michael Gottfredson and Travis Hirschi (1990) contend that effective parenting is the key to individuals' ability to control their impulses and delay short-term gratifications. Family studies also show that children raised with inconsistent discipline or with overly permissive or overly harsh discipline, particularly child abuse or neglect, are more likely to engage in later-life criminality (Capaldi et al. 1997; Kruttschnitt et al. 1986; Patterson & Stouthamer-Loeber 1984; Widom 1989; Zingraff et al. 1993).

Freud, women, and abuse. The treatment of women in Freudian theory has been particularly controversial. Freud believed that women were anatomically inferior to men and that they suffered from "penis envy" (Klein 1973). Women who were unable to adjust to their "natural" child-rearing role compensated for the absent penis by attempting to act like men (e.g., by pursuing careers). Other theorists working within the Freudian tradition attributed females' law violation to their inherent emotional dependency and intense need for love (Konopka 1966). To satisfy this need "good" women traded monogamous sex for marriage, while "bad" women traded sexual promiscuity and prostitution for excitement and novel experiences (Thomas 1923). The remedy for wayward girls and women (i.e., those who craved adventure, distinction, and "freedom in the larger world") required psychological adjustment to their traditional feminine role.

A number of female patients in Freud's psychoanalytic practice spoke to him of having had childhood sexual encounters with their fathers or other adult males. Initially Freud believed that these accounts were factual for "the memory must be extracted from . . . [the patients] piece by piece, and while it is being awakened in their consciousness they become the prey to an emotion which . . . would be hard to counterfeit" (cited in Masson 1984:47). Freud hypothesized that hysteria in adult women was the result of such childhood sexual abuse. But in 1895, when Freud and Josef Breuer published *Studies in Hysteria,* Breuer would not agree to include Freud's "seduction theory" in the book, "probably believing quite correctly that the world was not ready to hear of [such] . . . brutalizing of girls" (Williams 1987:48). After much disapproval and even downright hostility from his professional colleagues, Freud retracted his seduction theory and asserted that the "scenes of seduction" described to him were mere fantasies made up by his patients. Such widespread abuse of children, Freud now concluded, was not very likely (Masson 1984).

The sexual abuse of females by family members and others, however, is now widely documented (Belknap 2001; Russell 1984; Searles & Berger 1995). Within the home many girls are emotionally and physically exploited by fathers and stepfathers (or other relatives) who treat them as sexual property. The psychological trauma associated with such abuse is often (though not always) extensive, and can include both short- and long-term effects, such as "fear, anxiety, depression, anger and hostility, inappropriate sexual behavior, . . . difficulties in school, truancy, and early marriage" (Chesney-Lind 1989:21–22). Often girls run away from home to avoid further victimization, only to find that life on the streets involves additional exploitation, as some are forced to turn to crime and prostitution in order to survive. Eventually many of these young women are arrested and incarcerated, or they are returned to their homes and forced to remain "where their abusers have access to them" (p. 24; Schaffner 1999; Silbert & Pines 1981; Widom & Ames 1984).

■ Personality and Crime

There are other psychological perspectives that reject Freudian theory (in whole or in part) but that still postulate the existence of developmental personality types or ways of thinking that distinguish criminals from noncriminals. Criminals and delinquents have been variously described as emotionally unstable, mentally disordered, paranoid, schizophrenic, neurotic, egocentric, narcissistic, hedonistic, extroverted, aggressive, impulsive, hostile, defiant, attention-deficit disordered, learning disabled, insecure, low in self-esteem, shortsighted, and so forth—the list goes on and on. Among the most extreme of personality types is the **psychopath** or **sociopath**, an individual who is said to lack not only self-control but also the capacity to experience guilt or a sense of caring, responsibility, or obligation to others (Einstader & Henry 1995).

Critics of personality theory point to the ambiguity of psychological labeling. One study, for instance, found over 200 terms that were used to describe individuals with psychopathic or sociopathic symptoms (Carson 1943). William Sanders argues that "such multiple definitions of a concept render it so vague that it could mean almost anything" (1983:21). The majority of personality inventories (studies utilizing questions or true-false statements that attempt to ascertain personality types) examined in an early review failed to confirm the hypothesis that criminals have different personalities than noncriminals (Schuessler & Cressey 1950). Although later assessments suggested a more positive reading of the post-1950s research, with the Minnesota Multiphasic Personality Inventory (MMPI), an instrument developed by Starke Hathaway and Elio Monachesi (1963), given the most favorable review, methodological problems have led many criminologists to downplay the significance of this line of research (Tennenbaum 1977; Waldo & Dinitz 1967).

Some personality inventories have been faulted for containing similar items in both the personality and the criminality sections of the questionnaire, thereby biasing findings in favor of an association between the two (Caspi et al. 1994). For example, one section might include an item such as "Sometimes when I was young I stole things" while the other section includes "I have never been in trouble with the law." Sometimes the criminal behavior itself is used as a criterion for the classification of the aberrant personality type. And like the biological research on crime, personality studies tend to rely on relatively small samples and focus on officially labeled criminals and delinquents. Moreover, the research finds that personality differences *between law violators* is at times greater than the differences *between offenders and nonoffenders*. The research also finds that the amount of mental disorder among offenders or the amount of crime among the disordered is no more than is found among the general population (Akers 2000; Monahan & Steadman 1983).

What about the question of white-collar crime? There are a handful of personality studies that address this issue. For the most part the research indicates that white-collar offenders "fall within the range of normal personality types." A few studies suggest that these offenders are more likely than nonoffenders to display "a tendency toward risk taking and reckless-ness, ambitiousness and drive, and egocentricity and a hunger for power" (Friedrichs 2004:195). These traits, however, are also associated with legit-imate business success. Other characteristics noted in the literature include a tendency toward irresponsibility, lack of dependability, fear of failure, and an inability to defer gratification and exercise self-control (Coleman 1998; Wheeler 1992).

Psychologists D. A. Andrews and J. Stephen Wormith (1989) complain that sociologists who have advanced criticisms of personality theory have been biased against individualistic explanations of crime and have unfairly represented the evidence. To be sure, one can point to reputable studies that have found personality differences between offenders and nonoffenders (Calsyn et al. 1989; Caspi et al. 1994; Miller & Lynam 2001). And it is also important that the criminal justice system address the mental health needs of those who come under its jurisdiction (Slate 2003; U.S. Department of Justice 2000). However, a critical task of theory and research is to explain why these psychological differences occur in the first place. Does the cause of crime reside within the individual, in the developmental influences of the formative childhood years, or in broader social factors that we have yet to explore?

Finally, psychological **behaviorism**, also called "operant conditioning" or "learning-reinforcement" theory, offers another way of understanding individual behavior. Behaviorism, which is associated with the work of B. F. Skinner (1953), differs from Freudian and personality theories in that it focuses on observable behavior rather than on unconscious or personality factors. It postulates that "behavior is acquired or conditioned by the effects, outcomes, or *consequences* it has on a person's environment" (Akers 1985:43). Behavior that is reinforced by a reward or positive conse-quence will persist, while behavior that is unrewarded or punished will be discontinued. Individuals learn to favor particular courses of action, includ-ing the criminal variety, depending on the particular mix of rewards and punishments that is attached to their behavior. Rewards and punishments may be *social* or *nonsocial* in nature. The social include favorable or unfa-vorable reactions from other individuals (e.g., you receive approval or dis-approval from parents or friends); the nonsocial include the pleasurable or unpleasurable physical sensations associated with behavior (e.g., you feel euphoric or ill after consuming alcohol or drugs). Learning also takes place through the imitation or modeling of others' behavior (Akers 2000; Wood et al. 1997).

Since behaviorist explanations necessarily implicate social relation-ships, we will defer discussion of the behaviorist approach called "social learning" theory until we consider sociological explanations of crime in Chapter 4. For now it suffices to say that behaviorism postulates that the psychological mechanisms underlying criminal behavior are essentially the same as those underlying law-abiding behavior. Psychologically speaking, most criminals are actually *not so different* from the rest of us.

■ Applications of Psychological Theories

Psychological theories have been very influential in establishing the rehabilitative approach to crime control. These theories suggest therapeutic interventions designed to transform the offender from an individual with an abnormal or maladaptive personality to an individual with a normal personality. Such interventions typically employ professional therapists (e.g., psychiatrists, psychologists, social workers) who attempt to (1) help offenders uncover the childhood root causes of their behavior or gain insight more generally into why they behave as they do, and (2) train individuals to monitor and control their actions more effectively (Einstader & Henry 1995). These strategies have also been applied to at-risk youths with the goal of *prevention,* and as such pose some of the same ethical dilemmas that biological treatments pose: issues regarding accurate diagnosis, stigmatizing labels, and unwarranted intrusion into the lives of youths who have not yet committed crimes. On the other hand, failure to intervene to help individuals in need has its potential costs as well.

Samuel Yochelson and Stanton Samenow (1976, 1977) reject the "couch therapy" approach to psychology and focus instead on the criminal's current way of thinking. They are not interested in past environmental influences or the emotional burdens of childhood. Rather, they want to confront the individual's calculating, narcissistic personality. Offenders must acknowledge they are responsible and accountable for their own behavior, and they must reject "errors-in-thinking" that rationalize or blame others for their actions. According to Yochelson and Samenow, only through the development of such "internal deterrents" will the likelihood of future criminality be reduced.

Overall, the rehabilitative record of conventional psychotherapies is weak (Lundman 2001; Whitehead & Lab 1989). Behavioristic interventions that manipulate the distribution of rewards and punishments (e.g., a token economy or point system that grants or denies privileges based on the person's behavior) appear somewhat effective in inducing conformity within correctional settings, but they have negligible impact upon release (Trojanowicz et al. 2001). Successful programs generally require a more comprehensive approach than is typically available. Andrews and colleagues (1990) believe that the most effective correctional interventions utilize behavioristic and social learning principles, are carefully matched to offenders' particular learning styles and psychological needs, enhance aggression management and stress management as well as academic and vocational skills, change antisocial attitudes and ways of thinking, reduce chemical dependencies, foster familial bonds, modify peer associations and role models, and help access appropriate service agencies (Cullen & Applegate 1997; Gibbons 1999; Pearson et al. 2002).

Wayne Wooden and Randy Blazak (2001), however, are concerned about the mental hospitalization of youths, which has increased over the last two decades. Many of these hospital commitments, they believe, are unnecessary and may involve "rebellious teenagers struggling with their parents" over clothing, hairstyles, music preferences, sexuality, dating, and "other issues once thought of as typical 'growing pains.'" Wooden and Blazak note that "adolescent treatment hospitals have become big business" (p. 194). Since insurance companies tend to reimburse a higher percentage of inpatient expenses than outpatient expenses, parents may find it more cost-effective and convenient to commit their children than to find affordable, quality outpatient counseling.

Jill Rosenbaum and Lorraine Prinsky (1991) asked representatives of twelve inpatient treatment facilities in southern California whether a hypothetical fifteen-year-old boy needed hospitalization. The hypothetical scenario described parents who were concerned about their son's listening to heavy metal music, his spiked and color-dyed hair, his unconventional clothing, and the posters he put on his bedroom wall. Although the parents were not sure whether their son was drinking or using drugs, he was doing well in school and was not violent, suicidal, or depressed. Nevertheless, ten of the hospital representatives recommended placing the youth in an inpatient facility.

The insanity defense. Another controversial application of psychological thinking involves the insanity defense to crime. In our system of law the insanity defense is tied to the notion that "illegality alone does not make . . . a crime" (Sykes & Cullen 1992:37). Rather, the illegal act must be accompanied by *mens rea* (guilty mind), that is, criminal intent. According to this view, the individual must possess criminal intent at the time of the crime for punishment to be morally justified (Bonnie 1997). (Our law does expect that persons will exercise reasonable care to avoid the unintentional harm of others. If one behaves recklessly—for example, kills someone in a drunk-driving accident—they can be held criminally liable for such conduct.)

The insanity defense in the United States derives from English law and the 1843 case of Daniel M'Naghten. M'Naghten was tried for the murder of Edward Drummond, the secretary to Prime Minister Robert Peel. M'Naghten had intended to shoot the prime minister but killed Drummond by mistake. Apparently M'Naghten suffered from the paranoid delusion that the government was a deadly enemy out to get him. His attorneys claimed that he was insane and hence not legally responsible for his actions. M'Naghten was found not guilty by reason of insanity. This case established the **M'Naghten Rule**, whereby a defendant could be found not guilty by reason of insanity if it could "be clearly proved that, at the time of the committing of the act, the party accused was laboring under such a defect of reason, from disease of the mind, as not to know the nature and quality of the act he was doing; or if he did know it, that he did not know that he was doing what was wrong" (cited in Sykes & Cullen 1992:48).

By the middle of the twentieth century about two-thirds of the states in the United States had adopted this rule. In addition to recognizing defect of *reason,* U.S. law also recognizes defect of *will*. Here the will is considered to be so impaired that individuals cannot refrain from doing what their reason and emotion tell them to be wrong. Hence the doctrine of **irresistible impulse**, whereby defendants can be found not guilty by reason of insanity if mental illness prevented them from being able to control their behavior. (This doctrine covers what some refer to as temporary insanity.) Essentially the irresistible impulse defense makes the cognitive awareness of right and wrong less significant than the volitional control of one's actions (Reid 1997; Sykes & Cullen 1992).

The American Law Institute (ALI), an organization that proposes model penal codes to encourage legal uniformity throughout the nation, developed a model insanity defense that incorporates elements of the M'Naghten Rule and the irresistible impulse doctrine: "A person is not responsible for criminal conduct if at the time of such conduct as a result of mental disease or defect he lacks substantial capacity either to appreciate the criminality [wrongfulness] of his conduct or to conform to the requirements of law" (cited in Sykes & Cullen 1992:49–50). Moreover, the ALI model placed the burden of proof on the prosecution to establish the defendant's sanity; failing that, a defendant can be found insane. By the early 1980s this definition was adopted by more than half the states as well as the federal government.

Then came John Hinckley Jr. in a case that bears an uncanny resemblance to that of M'Naghten. During an attempted assassination of President Ronald Reagan in 1981, Hinckley shot and seriously disabled press secretary James Brady (see Chapter 1). At his criminal trial Hinckley pled not guilty by reason of insanity. He was apparently fascinated with the movie *Taxi Driver* and obsessed with Jodie Foster, an actress who was featured in that film. Hinckley was trying to impress Foster or at least attract her attention. Sue Titus Reid summarizes the testimony of the defense psychiatrists who took the witness stand on Hinckley's behalf:

> Hinckley was psychotic, was consumed by paradoxical thoughts, was depressed, had hypochondriacal tendencies, hated himself, suffered from schizophrenia spectrum disorder, had an abnormal thought process, thought of himself as a little boy who had done something terrible, and

was torn between childish love and dependence on his father and subconscious fantasies about killing him. (1997:128)

The prosecution countered that Hinckley had planned the crime in a cold and calculating manner, and it offered its own psychiatric witnesses who testified that Hinckley was legally sane. With the burden of proof on the prosecution, however, the jury ruled in Hinckley's favor.

The insanity defense has always had critics who argue that dangerous criminals will be allowed to avoid prison and will be free to commit more crimes. Successful insanity defendants are not set free, however. Like Hinckley, they are remanded to mental hospitals under civil commitment. Release from civil commitment requires the approval of the psychiatric authorities responsible for treating such individuals. Hinckley has not yet (and may never) receive a full discharge, although in December 2003 a federal judge ruled that he could have unsupervised visits with his parents outside the District of Columbia mental hospital where he was committed, provided these visits are restricted to the Washington area (Janofsky 2003).

The Hinckley case fueled a public backlash against the insanity defense and spawned the development of legal reforms to curtail its use. One reform, adopted by the federal government and several states, essentially returned the defense to its narrower M'Naghten definition regarding cognitive knowledge of right and wrong, and placed the burden to prove insanity on the defendant. A more controversial reform adopted by some states involves the development of a new legal category: **guilty but mentally ill** (GBMI). Under GBMI guidelines defendants may be held criminally responsible for their crimes, but they are first sent to a mental health facility for treatment; afterward they are transferred to a prison to serve the remainder of their sentence.

John Klofas and Ralph Weisheit (1987) conducted an evaluation of the GBMI reform in the state of Illinois, where GBMI was instituted as an option to the traditional insanity defense. Klofas and Weisheit found that use of GBMI did not reduce the number of insanity defense verdicts because it was used as an addition to, not as a substitute for, the traditional defense. Moreover, GBMI offenders were not sent to mental health facilities, and most did not even receive psychiatric treatment in prison.

Clearly the public fears that dangerous offenders will be deemed fit to reenter society before they are really cured or rehabilitated. We have all heard of cases where correctional officials concluded that an offender was ready to be released from custody when in fact he was not. The insanity defense is not the culprit in most of these cases, however, for there are more dangerous offenders who are released from prisons than from mental hospitals. Moreover, the insanity defense is attempted by less than 1 percent of felony defendants. Only one-quarter of these defendants are successful, and relatively few are ever released from custody (Reid 1997).

Box 3.2   Jeffrey Dahmer: Murderer Among Us

Between 1987 and 1991 Jeffrey Dahmer committed sixteen murders in Milwaukee, Wisconsin. Dahmer targeted gay males, people who often expect harassment from the police and who thus try to avoid contact with them. When stalking his victims, Dahmer chose venues such as shopping malls and gay bathhouses, where anonymity was assured or where he could at least blend into the crowd. He would invite his victims to his apartment for a drink or to watch pornographic movies, or he would offer them money to pose for pictures. At his apartment he would immobilize them with the sedative Halcion or hit them with a rubber mallet. Sometimes Dahmer would sexually assault his victims before he killed them, but more often he killed them and then sexually assaulted the corpse. He also cut up his victims, stored body parts in his freezer, and even ate them (Fisher 1997).

Unlike John Hinckley, Dahmer was unsuccessful in his attempt to use the insanity defense. He was convicted and sentenced to life in prison; he was beaten to death by another inmate in 1994. What some analysts consider to be the real story of the Dahmer case, however, is how he was able "to move about the city . . . with relative impunity, escaping detection" for such a long period of time (Fisher 1997:164; Williams 1999b). Countless individuals, in both official and unofficial capacities, were in positions to realize what he was doing and take action to stop him.

In 1987, around the time of his second Milwaukee murder, Dahmer was "kicked out of [a] gay bathhouse for drugging another patron to the point [that he] . . . had to be taken to a hospital. . . . On another occasion, Dahmer drugged and sexually assaulted two men" at a hotel (Fisher 1997:179). Yet when the police were called to investigate, the victims, fearful of being publicly outed as gay, failed to press charges. The police dropped the matter.

In 1988 after Keison Sinthasomphone, a thirteen-year-old Laotian boy, managed to escape Dahmer's apartment and alert the police, "Dahmer was arrested for sexual assault and enticing a child for immoral purposes" (Fisher 1997:181). Though he pled guilty to the charges, he served only ten months in jail. While under probation, Dahmer was required to see several psychiatric professionals, whom he used as a source of Halcion. And social workers who were assigned to do home visits missed the "shrine of bones in his living room because they were afraid—not of him but of visiting the inner-city neighborhood where he lived" (Williams 1999b:10).

Overall, during his murder spree Dahmer "had at least seven contacts with police, was arrested three times, was put on probation twice, and was jailed once" (Fisher 1997:182). Repeated and urgent calls to the

continues

Box 3.2   continued

police from women of the mostly black neighborhood were seemingly discounted—calls complaining of a stench emanating from Dahmer's apartment and of his public drunkenness. And with more than a dozen gay men missing in one city alone, no one alerted the community that "a serial killer might be on the loose" (Williams 1999b:10).

In 1991 fourteen-year-old Konerac Sinthasomphone, brother of Keison, escaped from Dahmer's apartment, drugged and naked. Five African Americans, aged eleven to twenty, came upon him and observed "blood around his buttocks, testicles, and pubic hair." One of them called the police as Dahmer appeared at the scene to retrieve Konerac. When the police arrived, Dahmer explained that "Konerac was his roommate, and he was taking him home" (Fisher 1997:184). The black witnesses, emotional and shouting, urged the police to look at Konerac's "butt," but the officers wouldn't listen and told them to "shut the hell up" and "get lost." Apparently the police preferred to take the word of a murderer, "polite, calm, and white," over a group of exuberant black youths (p. 186).

Dahmer even invited the officers back to his apartment to see photos of Konerac, who Dahmer said was nineteen or twenty years old, posing in black bikini underwear. The officers, who did in fact go to the apartment, later acknowledged detecting an unpleasant odor (which turned out to be a decomposing body). They did nothing, however, leaving Konerac to become Dahmer's twelfth victim. Back at their car, the officers "radioed the police dispatcher and between audible laughs said they had returned 'the intoxicated Asian naked male to his sober boyfriend'" (Fisher 1997:187). One added, amid more laughter, "my partner's gonna get deloused at the station." Even though follow-up calls from worried neighbors continued, the police dismissed the concerns with casual assurances that the fourteen-year-old was an adult (Williams 1999b).

Patricia Williams believes that the Dahmer case says a lot about the attitudes of those in power toward those without power. Dahmer's ability to escape suspicion rested on the official devaluing of gay lives and on a presumption of "adult Asian men as soft, effeminate, exotic, sexualized and perpetually childlike; of blacks as dangerous; and of women, particularly black women, as hysterical and unbelievable" (1999b:10).

4

Sociological Explanations of Criminal Behavior

Elijah Anderson (1999) begins his ethnography of Philadelphia street life with a tour down Germantown Avenue, an eight-and-a-half-mile thorough-fare that connects the northwest suburbs with the heart of the inner city. The shopping district at the northwest end attracts a diverse population of customers from all over the city. He writes: "Although most of the people are white, virtually every ethnic group is represented. . . . The community appears to be racially integrated in its public relationships, perhaps self-consciously so. . . . There are biracial groups of friends. . . . Street violence is the farthest thing from anyone's mind" (pp. 16, 18). There is a Borders bookstore as well as many small, upscale businesses—gourmet food shops, a camera shop, jewelry stores, clothing boutiques.

Further down the avenue, one reaches a neighborhood boundary: "There is more black street traffic. . . . Exterior bars begin to appear on the store windows . . . and doors. . . . The place isn't crime ridden . . . [but] it is prudent to be wary" (p. 20). Continuing on, the buildings become less well maintained. More graffiti is evident. More check-cashing and discount stores, and beeper and pawn shops. More vacant lots and abandoned, boarded-up buildings. Many of the people here are extremely poor. Swaggering youth "loiter on street corners . . . [and] men drink alcoholic beverages out of paper sacks" (p. 22). Off the main boulevard "open-air drug deals occur, prostitutes ply their trade, and boys shoot craps. . . . The neighborhood is sprinkled with crack dens. . . . Morning is generally the safest time of day. As evening approaches, the possibility of violence increases, and after nightfall the code of the street holds sway. . . . Under that rule the toughest, the biggest, and the boldest individual prevails. . . . People watch their backs. . . . [They] understand that you are not always tested, but you have to be ready . . . when it comes" (pp. 21–23, 25–26, 29–30).

This brief account illustrates what sociologists refer to as **social ecolo-**

gy (or human ecology), a concept adapted from the discipline of biology that refers to the relationship between human populations and the physical environment. The social ecology of a community influences its patterns of social interaction in ways that cannot be adequately understood by the sorts of individualistic explanations we discussed in the previous chapter. As we move into this terrain, we will need to use our sociological imagination and look beyond the individual to the social environment.

Sociological theories of criminal behavior are as diverse as the individualistic theories we explored in Chapter 3. We begin by distinguishing between macrosociological (*macro* meaning "large") and microsociological (*micro* meaning "small") levels of analysis. Typically, **macrosociological theories** focus on elements of social structure or entire societies or communities that account for group variations in criminal behavior. They look at the big picture, asking why certain groups of people living under particular circumstances commit more crime than other groups of people living under different circumstances. Macrosociological theories do not deny the autonomy or independence of the individual. They do not claim that everyone exposed to the same structural constraints and opportunities will respond in the same way. But they do examine the circumstances that increase the probability or likelihood that people will act one way rather than another.

As we noted in Chapter 1, social structure does not exist independently of social action. Rather, social structures are enacted by individuals in specific situations. **Microsociological theories** examine the link between the individual and society by focusing on the processes by which "individuals acquire social attributes through interaction with others" (Barlow 1996:468). These theories acknowledge that people exposed to the same social structure do not always behave in the same way, and people from dissimilar circumstances don't necessarily behave differently. Microsociological theories may be conceptualized as **social psychological theories** insofar as they consider how individuals learn to favor or disfavor criminal courses of action, how they interpret or account for the meaning of their actions, and how they are socialized or controlled through social relationships. In contrast to biological and psychological approaches that view individuals as deviant kinds of persons, microsociological theories emphasize the common ways in which normal people respond to varying social environments (Orcutt 1983).

■ Early European Contributions

Like the biological and psychological theories we discussed earlier, most sociological theories partake of the scientific-positivist tradition. Some sociological theories, however, are more akin to social criticism in that they serve as analyses of the social problems of the day and as visions of a more ideal future. We begin our inquiry by briefly examining the contributions of a few early European thinkers who either anticipated, influenced, or set the terms of the debate for the competing theoretical perspectives that were to constitute sociological criminology in the United States.

In many respects the roots of **sociological positivism** can be traced to the work of Belgian astronomer Adolphe Quetelet (1796–1874). Quetelet believed that social behavior could be studied scientifically in a manner similar to the study of nature, of the heavens and earth. He was a pioneer in his use of official statistics to make observations about crime, and was one of the first cartographers (mapmakers) to examine territorial or geographic variations in crime. Quetelet analyzed French crime rates and was impressed with their relative constancy over time. He concluded that there must be lawlike regularities that governed criminal behavior, just as there were laws that governed the physical universe (like the law of gravity), for individuals placed in similar circumstances were prone to act in similar ways. Those with the greatest propensity toward crime were people in the lower classes and young males. But, said Quetelet, it was not poverty per se but the unequal distribution of wealth and sudden fluctuations in the economy that were most highly associated with crime. Women, he believed, committed fewer crimes because they were physically weaker, led more restricted lives, and drank less alcohol than men. Quetelet maintained, however, that women were more likely to benefit from lenient or chivalrous legal treatment, but only if they conformed to traditional, patriarchal gender roles and were married and economically dependent upon men (Beirne & Messerschmidt 1995).

Like Quetelet, French sociologist Émile Durkheim (1858–1917) used statistical data to study social behavior. In his classic book *Suicide* (1897/1952), Durkheim noted that suicide rates varied between groups and regions and fluctuated over time. He argued that these patterns could be explained not by individualistic factors but by structural features of society.

Like many thinkers of his day, Durkheim assumed that humans were basically selfish or egoistic beings with potentially insatiable desires. It was the role of society to hold these desires in check lest chaos or social anarchy prevail. Durkheim developed the concept of the **collective conscience**, the sociological equivalent of Freud's superego. The collective conscience was the "totality of beliefs and sentiments common to average citizens of the same society" that provided the moral glue that held the society together (1893/1964:79). Durkheim believed that religion was a powerful source of social solidarity (moral glue), but that some religions were more controlling than others. He argued, for example, that suicide rates were higher among Protestants than Catholics because Protestantism was less doctrinaire and more tolerant of moral individualism.

Durkheim observed that the collective conscience was strongest and social control greatest in simpler societies—where people were less specialized in their social roles and the type of labor they performed—than in more diverse and complex societies such as our own. He coined the term **anomie** to refer to a state of normlessness whereby individuals were isolated, cut adrift from others, and lacked a common bond to bring them into sympathetic relationships with others. Anomie, Durkheim argued, was most likely to occur during periods of social upheaval, such as the transition from traditional-agrarian to modern-industrial societies. During these times, individuals were forced into unfamiliar surroundings or circumstances (i.e., cities) where old rules governing social interactions no longer applied and new ones had yet to develop. Such conditions could lead to suicide and other forms of deviant behavior.

Durkheim was also influential in establishing the school of sociology known as **functionalism**. He viewed society much like a biological organism that consisted of a number of interdependent parts that contributed to the overall functioning of the whole. In a functionally integrated society, social institutions such as the family, schools, economy, and government help satisfy basic human needs and socialize individuals to adopt their appropriate roles in society (Parsons 1951). In a dysfunctional society, these institutions break down or become out of balance, straining the relationship between individuals and society and weakening commitment to the law. Durkheim believed that a certain level of crime in society was normal, inevitable, and even functional, for criminals provided a negative example that helped clarify the norms of acceptable behavior and integrated law-abiding members vis-à-vis a common internal enemy. Crime thus reinforced social solidarity by "drawing people together in a common posture of . . . [moral] indignation" (Erikson 1966:4).

German social theorists Karl Marx (1818–1883) and Friedrich Engels (1820–1895) differed with Durkheim on a number of counts, rejecting the assumption of societal consensus that was implicit in the notion of the collective conscience. They believed that "class conflict" between capitalists and workers was inherent to capitalist societies. Marx and Engels were, in essence, "conflict theorists" who argued that the very definition of crime and the enforcement of laws were matters of economic and political power that, under capitalism, disadvantaged the working class (see Chapter 1).

Marx and Engels were politically active on behalf of the laboring masses and worked for the abolition of capitalism. Writing before the advent of Soviet-style communism, which lasted from 1922 to 1991, they envisioned a classless, socialist society as the solution to the woes of humankind—a society "where everyone receives what he needs to satisfy his natural and spiritual urges, where social gradations and distinctions cease to exist" (Engels cited in Greenberg 1993:51). Marx and Engels assumed that humans were fundamentally prosocial beings, but thought that the working class was simply ground down by a system it either did not understand or was unable to effectively challenge. In his book *The Conditions of the Working Class in England in 1844,* Engels wrote:

> Immorality is fostered in every possible way by the conditions of working class life. The worker is poor; life has nothing to offer him; he is deprived of virtually all pleasures. Consequently he does not fear the penalties of the law. Why should he restrain his wicked impulses? . . . Everyone looks after his own interests and fights only for himself. . . . Everyone sees in his neighbour a rival to be elbowed aside, or . . . [a] victim to be exploited for his own ends. (cited in Greenberg 1993:48–49)

To be sure, the practical attempts at nation building in the name of Marx and Engels have had a checkered history marked by undemocratic regimes and human rights violations. At the same time, many commonly accepted reforms that have occurred in capitalist societies—such as the eight-hour day, unemployment insurance, workers' (injury) compensation, and social security—have their roots in social movements that were inspired by socialist ideals. There is also a historical tradition of democratic socialism that believes in the expansion rather than in the denial of civil liberties and individual freedoms (Greenberg 1993).

Whereas Quetelet, Durkheim, and Marx and Engels worked primarily in the macrosociological tradition, the most influential early European microsocial theorist was French judge and sociologist Gabriel Tarde (1843–1904). Tarde noted the limitations of structural theorizing that made broad generalizations about criminal propensities but that could not explain why particular individuals commit crime. Tarde used the concept of "imitation" to advance an early form of social psychology, arguing that "individuals imitate each other in proportion to the amount of close contact they have" (Barkan 2001:176). Tarde did not conceptualize imitation as more contemporary learning or behavioristic theorists do, however. For Tarde, imitation was a "generally unconscious . . . partly mysterious action" analogous to sleepwalking or being in a trance (cited in Beirne & Messerschmidt 1995:367).

Nevertheless, Tarde believed that the impulse toward crime derived not from the lower classes but from the higher stratum of society. According to Tarde, as Piers Beirne and James Messerschmidt observe, "The masses are . . . tied to the ideas and fancies of their social superiors. Drunkenness, smoking, moral offenses, political assassination, arson, and even vagabondage are . . . crimes that originated with the feudal nobility and [that] were transmitted, through imitation, to the masses. Criminal propensities . . . typically travel downward and outward—from the powerful to the powerless, from urban centers to rural areas" (1995:367).

■ Social Disorganization and the Social Ecology of Crime

In the late nineteenth and early twentieth centuries, social theorists like Durkheim were concerned with the transition of societies from rural and small-town life to the larger urban milieu. Social commentators in the United States characterized the former as consisting of close-knit, extended families and strong communities that were bonded by a voluntaristic spirit and a common religious faith that enabled adults to "keep a firm grip on the process of socializing the young" (Sykes & Cullen 1992:291). But as families immigrated to the United States or emigrated from rural areas to the cities, they were often isolated from their larger kinship group and enmeshed in a set of fleeting, impersonal neighborhood and workplace relationships. The families of most newcomers and others at the bottom of the class hierarchy were not able to reap the benefits of the new industrial economy and often had to endure the additional stress of overworked parents or prolonged unemployment. Immigrant families in particular, who were unfamiliar with the culture of the new world, had difficulty inculcating in the young the values and skills necessary to successfully compete. Hence the city became filled with criminals and delinquents and a host of "maladjusted" inhabitants (Park & Burgess 1924).

To a large extent the contrast between the old and new way of life was a caricature, a romanticization of the old that reflected a nostalgic view of days gone by. As statements about crime, however, such commentaries were part of an effort to supplant individualistic (kinds of persons) explanations with sociological (kinds of places) ones. Liberal social reformers, social workers, sociological academicians, and the like adopted a paternalistic concern with the plight of the city dweller and hoped to use social science as a guide to the amelioration of their plight (Schwendinger & Schwendinger 1974).

■ The Contributions of Shaw and McKay

It is in this context that sociologists Clifford Shaw and Henry McKay made the most significant contribution to what has been termed **social disorganization theory** (Shaw et al. 1929; Shaw & McKay 1942). Shaw and McKay were part of the University of Chicago school of sociology that pioneered the use of ethnographic field methods (see Chapter 2). They also worked in the tradition of cartographers like Quetelet, mapping out the territorial or ecological distribution of crime and other social conditions. The Chicago school was known for its contribution to the study of social ecology.

According to Shaw and McKay, the problem of crime was tied to the social ecology of communities that were socially disorganized. Their cartographic research indicated that crime and delinquency were highest in areas marked by concentrated poverty and unemployment, physical dilapidation of buildings, residential overcrowding, absence of home ownership, high residential mobility, influx of immigrant populations of diverse cultures, and lack of "constructive agencies intended to promote well-being and prevent maladjustment" (cited in Sykes & Cullen 1992:292). Importantly, Shaw and McKay did not view economic issues per se as the key to the problem:

> [Rather] children who grow up in these deteriorated and disorganized neighborhoods . . . are not subject to the same constructive and restraining influences that surround those in the more homogenous communities further removed from the industrial and commercial centers. These disorganized neighborhoods fail to provide a consistent set of cultural standards and a wholesome social life for the development of a stable and socially acceptable form of behavior in the child . . . [whose] most vital and intimate social contacts are often limited to the spontaneous and undirected neighborhood play groups and gangs whose activities and standards may vary widely from those of . . . parents and the larger social order. (p. 293)

Moreover, the traditions of these delinquent groups are self-sustaining, transmitted through successive generations. Youths "in these areas have contact not only with other delinquents who are their contemporaries but also with older offenders, who in turn had contact with delinquents preceding them, and so on back to the earliest history of the neighborhood" (Shaw & McKay 1942:168).

The Chicago area project. In 1934 Shaw established the **Chicago Area Project** (CAP), which has been described as "the first systematic challenge to the dominance of psychology and psychiatry in public and private programs for the prevention and treatment of . . . delinquency" (Schlossman et al. 1984:2). The CAP pioneered the practice of community-level approaches to delinquency prevention that used community organizers to help residents exercise more control over their youths and to facilitate cooperative activities among community groups for the solution of common problems (Berger 1996).

The underlying philosophy of the CAP was that only through the collective mobilization and active participation of the entire community was it possible to impact significantly on the problem of delinquency. The CAP was overseen by a board of directors that raised and distributed money and assisted community groups in obtaining grants to match local government funds. Various committees that operated as independent, self-governing bodies with their own names and charters were formed. CAP staff organizers functioned in an advisory role, but decisions about policies and programs were made by resident members. The task for organizers was to convince local residents to assume responsibility and work together with the

churches, schools, criminal justice system, businesses, and other community groups.

The CAP pioneered a number of activities that were later employed in other prevention programs, including the development of recreation and camping programs, youth clubs, and hobby and rap (discussion) groups. The goal of these activities was to provide youths with structured, supervised alternatives to crime. In addition, they served as springboards for bringing people together, counseling delinquent youths, and providing minimal employment for youth leaders. The CAP also sent organizers called "detached street workers" out into the streets to provide "curbside counseling" for troubled youths and to identify indigenous gang leaders who might be encouraged to commit themselves to the project's goals.

The CAP also interceded in school-related matters by helping to reform curricula, mainstream students who had been incorrectly placed in classes for deficient or incorrigible youths (or conversely, place students who required special treatment into appropriate programs), transfer students to schools with more suitable programs or personnel, and reinstate students who had been expelled for minor delinquencies. Criminal justice interventions involved diverting youths to appropriate community agencies, reforming jails and prisons, and assisting parolees as they returned to community life.

The CAP was not without its problems and critics. It was often difficult to get residents to cooperate and to find common ground between them and various interest groups. For example, attempts to enlist the help of businesses in expanding employment opportunities for delinquent youths were not always successful. No effort was made to involve the absentee landlords who owned the rental properties and were interested only in speculative profits, not the quality of housing. The project was also forced to rely heavily on the volunteer services of the Polish Catholic Church, which was accused of using the recreational programs to proselytize. One of the strongest criticisms was levied by Saul Alinsky, the CAP's most well-known detached street worker. Alinsky faulted the CAP's inability to secure needed economic reforms. These, he believed, required more confrontational tactics to force concessions from the political and economic elites of the city. Alinsky was acutely aware of the difficulty of sustaining interest in the project when resources necessary to achieve goals came from sources outside of the residents' control. Eventually the CAP was absorbed by Illinois State's Division of Youth Services and transformed into yet another bureaucratic organization that has usurped local initiative. Nevertheless, the CAP serves as a prime example of the possibilities of engaging communities in problem-solving prevention efforts that do more than simply respond to crime on a one-to-one, after-the-fact basis (Berger 1996; Krisberg 1978; Schlossman et al. 1984).

■ The Decline and Revival of
Social Disorganization Theory

To criminologists of a liberal persuasion, the environmental focus of social disorganization theory was an improvement over individualistic approaches to crime prevention and control. By the 1960s, however, it fell into disfavor among liberals, who began looking to other theories for insight into the crime problem in the United States. Critics of social disorganization theory asked: Were not kinds-of-places theories simply the sociological analogue of kinds-of-persons theories, with entire communities now viewed as pathological, urban areas now seen as inherently criminogenic, and social disorganization now held responsible for breeding personal disorganization? Like most individualistic explanations, the focus was exclusively on lower-class crime (particularly among immigrant groups), and communities were blamed for a problem that was not entirely of their own making. It was as if these communities existed in a vacuum and capitalist investment decisions leading to uneven economic development did not exist (see Chapter 7). It was as if the poor had power comparable to the wealthy to resist economic and social policies that were not in their interest and that might even increase crime (e.g., the construction of public housing projects that concentrate poor people) (Balkan et al. 1980; Einstader & Henry 1995).

More recent work in the social disorganization tradition has attempted to resolve some of these deficiencies. Researchers have shown how the **deindustrialization** of the economy (the shift from manufacturing to low-paid service work) and the flight of the middle class (white and black) from the inner city to the suburbs have depleted the former of valuable economic and social resources and left behind an even greater concentration of what William Julius Wilson (1987) has described as the "truly disadvantaged," an urban underclass. Residential mobility and high population turnover have weakened informal neighborhood controls and decreased the number of residents who have a long-term stake in the community and who thus may be willing to intercede on each other's behalf to prevent victimization from crime. Impoverished, inner-city neighborhoods undergoing further economic decline have experienced higher crime rates. Even neighborhood **gentrification** (redevelopment to attract more affluent residents) has increased crime, perhaps because poor residents feel relatively more deprived and because it is difficult for a heterogeneous population lacking common interests to establish informal social controls over youths (Bursik 1988; Bursik & Grasmick 1993; Taylor & Covington 1988).

In support of Shaw and McKay's propositions about the noneconomic correlates of crime, Robert Sampson and W. Byron Groves (1989) found that the effect of economic disadvantage on crime was due to weak local friendship networks, low participation in voluntary organizations, and low supervision of teenage peer groups. They also found that crime was associated with the disproportionate number of (primarily female-headed) single-parent families in these communities, this for the most part a consequence of male joblessness (Sampson 1987; Wilson 1987). Similarly, Leann Tigges and colleagues (1998) found that poor blacks were more likely than non-poor blacks and nonpoor whites to be socially isolated; that is, they were less likely to live with another adult, less likely to have even one person outside of their household with whom they could discuss important matters, and less likely to be embedded in the types of social networks that provide access to social services and jobs.

Moreover, many poor women raising children alone in socially disorganized neighborhoods lack the parenting skills necessary to effectively discipline their children (Anderson 1999; Williams & Kornblum 1985). Often they have not had adequate parental models and may still be teenagers themselves. Some have succumbed to drugs and/or have become entrapped in abusive relationships. For poor, inner-city mothers faced with limited opportunities, insufficient social services and unsafe housing, life is a constant battle against forces threatening to engulf them. It is a daily struggle to maintain dignity, to keep one's head above the rising tide of hopelessness and despair. As one mother waiting for her son to return safely home from school said, "Mostly, you try to keep them away from the drugs and violence, but it's hard. I tell my oldest boy I don't want him hanging out with the boys who are getting in trouble, and he says, 'Aw, mama, ain't nobody else for me to be with'" (DeParle 1991:397).

Social disorganization theory assumes that frequent interaction among residents helps generate the informal community controls that reduce crime (Bellair 1997). However, there are conflicting effects of individuals' embeddedness in social relationships. Eleanor Miller (1986), for instance, found that females' involvement in extended "domestic networks"—households composed of immediate kin (parents, siblings), extended kin (grandparents, uncles, aunts, cousins), and non-kin (friends, lovers)—was a primary means by which they were recruited into "deviant networks" of street prostitution and hustling. And Mary Pattillo (1998) found that involvement of gang members and drug dealers in networks of law-abiding neighbors and kin at times impeded efforts to rid the neighborhood of its criminal elements. As one resident said, "I didn't wanna give this young man's name [to the police] because his mama is such a sweet lady" (p. 763).

Routine Activities and Crime

In the late 1970s Lawrence Cohen and Marcus Felson (1979) advanced a **routine activities theory** of crime that moved ecological thinking in a dramatically different direction from the traditional social disorganization approach. Cohen and Felson argued that it was possible, theoretically speaking, to bypass explanations of criminal motivation and simply assume there will always be a sufficient number of individuals willing to take advantage of the opportunity to commit crime. What criminologists needed to ascertain were the immediate situational circumstances that enabled such individuals to translate their criminal inclinations into action. The probability of crime increased, they observed, when there was a convergence in physical space and time of three basic elements: *motivated offenders, suitable targets,* and the *absence of capable guardians.*

According to Cohen and Felson, historical changes in the routine patterns of everyday life—such as the dispersion of work and leisure activities away from the home, the increased number of people who have become occupationally and residentially mobile, and the greater participation of women in the work force—have dissolved protective kinship and friendship networks, leaving homes unguarded and individuals vulnerable in the public sphere (Felson 1998; Neuman & Berger 1988). In addition, the ever-expanding production of commodities has increased the abundance and variety of goods available to be stolen. Before the advent of the automobile, for example, who could have imagined the crime of motor vehicle theft or car-jacking? Before the mass marketing of athletic clothing, who could have imagined being mugged for Nike shoes or a Starter jacket?

Like social disorganization theory, the routine activities approach focuses on the kinds of places that are associated with increased risk of crime. Research indicates that crime is not uniformly distributed across physical space and time. A disproportionate amount occurs along a relatively small number of streets or "hot spots," including areas in or around convenience and large discount department stores, high schools, public housing projects and high-rise buildings with easily accessible corridors and poorly monitored areas, drinking establishments, parties, and other places where people hang out in unstructured activities. People whose daily routines or lifestyles take them to these places, especially late at night, are more likely to be victimized by crime. Those who are themselves involved in crime are especially likely to be victimized (Felson 1998; Miethe & McCorkle 1998; Sherman et al. 1989).

Routine activities and violence against women. One criticism of the routine activities approach focuses on its inability to adequately account for the victimization of women. Kathleen Daly and Meda Chesney-Lind (1988) observe that many criminological theories ignore or misconstrue issues of gender and lack applicability to women. They argue that theories should have **gender generalizability**, that is, they should be able to explain the experiences of both males and females. Cohen and Felson (1979), for instance, argued that circumstances that take women outside of the home (e.g., employment, education) or reduce available guardians (e.g., being single) increase women's risk of rape and other predatory offenses. But as we have previously noted, women (and girls) are often victimized by persons they know, frequently in the privacy of their own homes. While women are vulnerable in both the public and the private spheres of life, the problems of domestic battery, nonstranger rape, intrafamilial sexual abuse, and the like, are not adequately explained by routine activities theory. In fact, efforts to reduce female dependency on male guardianship may actually decrease sexual violence against women by empowering women "to dictate the basic terms on which men must relate to them" (Schwendinger & Schwendinger 1983:217).

The routine activities approach has been more useful when the violence in question is gang rape. Nathan McCall (1994) describes how he and his cohorts would prey on vulnerable adolescent females who were lured under false pretenses to isolated places and then raped by a group of males hiding in wait. Although females attracted to the "bad boy" or "cool dude" image may be especially susceptible to this type of manipulation (Gaines 1993; Sikes 1997), these kinds of crimes are not perpetrated only by adolescent street gangs or youths from socially disadvantaged communities. They are a consequence of membership in proabuse, male peer groups that condone sexual aggression against women. Research suggests, for example, that fraternity gang rapes by white, middle-class college students are not uncommon. College campuses bring together in physical space and time the recipe for crime that is predicted by routine activities theory: a group of motivated offenders (male-bonded sexually predatory males) and suitable targets (Little Sisters and female partygoers) who are participating in particular activities (frequent partying and heavy drinking) in the absence of capable guardians (no parental or school supervisors) (Martin & Hummer 1989; Sanday 1990; Schwartz & DeKeseredy 1997; Schwartz et al. 2001).

Situational crime prevention. In contrast to conventional crime prevention strategies aimed at changing the behavior of offenders (like the CAP), the routine activities approach is directed at modifying the behavior of potential victims. Programs of this nature have been variously called victim prevention, opportunity reduction, target hardening, and **situational crime prevention** (SCP). Some of these programs entail measures that can be taken by individuals and businesses, and some involve entire communities. For instance, individuals and businesses can install locks, alarms, and window bars, and erect fences and gates. They can put identifying marks on property, hire security guards or private patrols, and acquire large dogs, mace spray, or guns for protection. Individuals can take and businesses can provide instruction in karate and other forms of personal defense. Bushes can be pruned and areas illuminated to prevent hiding places. Homes, buildings, apartment complexes, and even entire communities can be architecturally designed to ensure that public areas are highly visible, walkways are clearly delineated, and access to particular areas is reserved for legitimate users and activities and prohibited for use by others or for hanging out. Residents can organize themselves (often with assistance from police) into neighborhood or community-watch groups and even citizen patrols (Clarke 1992; Felson 1998; Newman 1972).

A potentially negative side effect of SCP is the problem of **crime displacement**, where motivated criminals simply decide to commit their crimes elsewhere or at other times. Research on this score is mixed, but it suggests that displacement is not an inevitable consequence of such measures (Felson 1998; Welsh & Farrington 1999). SCP can be costly, however, providing benefits primarily for those who can afford it, for those who live in communities already less troubled by crime. Evaluation studies indicate that SCP strategies have been "oversold as a stand-alone" approach (Rosenbaum 1988:363). Best results have been obtained when SCP is combined with offender-oriented prevention strategies (Curtis 1987; Bennett & Lavrakas 1989).

■ Crime and the American Dream: Anomie/Strain Theory

In general, ecological theories attribute causal significance to the physical and spatial features of urban crime. Social disorganization theory in particular views crime as a maladaptive response to the urban environment. But the theory's focus on communities overlooks a broader critique of life in the United States, one that locates the source of the crime problem in "the organization of the whole society" (Einstader & Henry 1995:145). This critique was advanced by Robert Merton in his seminal 1938 article "Social Structure and Anomie."

Merton (1938, 1968) drew upon Durkheim's work on functionalism and anomie and gave it a peculiarly American twist. For Merton, the structural condition of anomie was constituted not by normlessness but by a structural disjuncture or lack of integration between "cultural goals" and "institutionalized means." Merton believed that the predominant cultural goal of American society was the dream of financial success and bountiful material consumption. People who lacked access to the legitimate means to turn this dream into reality were structured into a relationship of "strain" with society and experienced a sense of frustration and injustice about their lot in life. In this sense, crime is endemic to a social system that dangles the enticements of materialism before everyone without being able to deliver the goods to all.

Given the pervasive social inequality in the United States, **anomie/strain theory** postulates that the greatest pressures for criminal behavior reside in the lower classes and among disadvantaged racial and ethnic minority groups. Families from these backgrounds often lack the economic and social resources to prepare their children well for school, provide them with enriching cultural experiences, bail them out if they get in trouble with the law, finance their college education, and set them up in businesses or professions. Minorities also face the additional problems of discrimination and lack of familiarity with the culture of white, middle-class institutional environments. Nevertheless, according to anomie/strain theory, those who turn to crime are not, at heart, different from the rest of us. They share the values that we all hold. They are not predisposed to crime. If given the chance, they would prefer to take a more conventional path to success (Cohen 1955; Hagan & McCarthy 1997; Williams & Kornblum 1985).

It is important to emphasize the **relative deprivation** component of Merton's insight. It is not poverty per se that is at issue, but *poverty amid affluence* in a society that values particular goals. Hence many studies have found that the level of economic inequality (the distribution of income or wealth) is more strongly related to crime than is the level of absolute poverty (the amount of income or wealth) (Blau & Blau 1982; LaFree 1998; Sampson 1985; Messner 1989). Indeed, there are societies around the world that suffer even worse poverty than our own without comparable levels of crime, in part because they have not (yet?) acquired our "fetishism" of money (Messner & Rosenfeld 2001:63). Money is for us the measure of all success, the currency of achievement. We pursue it relentlessly. There is "no final stopping point" (Merton 1968:190).

In this scheme of things, all else tends to be devalued or set aside. Many of us hold "neither the acquisition of knowledge [nor] learning for its own sake" in high regard (Messner & Rosenfeld 2001:70). We view education primarily as a vehicle for occupational attainment and economic rewards. Similarly, we see government as desirable to the degree that it aids us in our pursuit of economic goals, not for its potential to advance citizenship or improve the quality of our noneconomic lives. At the same time, however, the predominance of the economy makes it more difficult for other social institutions to exert countervailing prosocial controls. Family life, for example, is "dominated by the schedules, rewards, and penalties of the labor market. Whereas parents worry about 'finding time' for their families, few workers must 'find time' for their jobs. On the contrary, many feel fortunate that the economy has found time for them" (p. 72).

◼ Adaptations to Strain

Merton postulated that individuals adapt to structurally induced anomie or strain in a variety of ways. Table 4.1. presents his typology of five general

Table 4.1   Merton's Typology of Individual Adaptations to Strain

Modes of Adaptation	Cultural Goals	Institutionalized Means
Conformity	+	+
Ritualism	–	+
Innovation	+	–
Retreatism	–	–
Rebellion	–/+	–/+

Notes: + = acceptance; – = rejection; –/+ = rejection and substitution.

modes of adaptation: conformity, ritualism, innovation, retreatism, and rebellion. These should be conceptualized not as personality types but as behavioral options that emerge out of the particular mix of legitimate and illegitimate opportunities available to individuals differentially positioned in the social structure (Cloward & Ohlin 1960). Merton had little to say about why some individuals pursue one adaptation or another. That, he acknowledged, would require consideration of individualistic or micro-level criteria.

While Merton offered his scheme as a typology of individual adaptations, others understood them as collective in nature, as a means by which individuals similarly situated in the social structure work out group solutions to common problems, as in urban street gangs or organized crime, for example (Cloward & Ohlin 1960; Cohen 1955). It is also important to note that Merton did not consider crime to be an automatic consequence of strain. People could pursue noncriminal *conformity* not only through financial success but by moderating their expectations at particular points in their lives to exact a more realistic fit between goals and means, for example, by delaying short-term gratification of needs to pursue long-term future rewards. *Ritualism,* on the other hand, is a noncriminal adaptation that involves a more permanent scaling down or relinquishment of unattainable success goals and an overemphasis on the institutionalized means in and of themselves (e.g., the bureaucrat who always follows the rules, however irrational they may seem). The ritualist response may entail resigning oneself to working in a dead-end job or to just getting by to make ends meet.

Innovation in Merton's scheme is arguably the most prevalent criminal adaptation to strain. Innovation occurs when people continue to embrace financial success goals but pursue them through illegitimate means. Such individuals are following the cultural ethos of "winning at all costs" or "anything goes" (Derber 1996). The predominance of property crimes in official statistics is but one indication that innovation is the criminal adaptation of choice. The innovative adaptation is also found in the experience of disadvantaged ethnic groups that have used organized crime as a vehicle for upward social mobility and a shortcut to the American dream. As Al Capone once said, "Don't get the idea that I'm one of those goddamn radicals . . . that I'm knocking the American system. . . . Capitalism . . . gives to each and every one of us a great opportunity, if we only seize it with both hands and make the most of it" (quoted in Cockburn 1967:118–119).

Although anomie/strain theory has focused on lower-class criminality, Merton (1968) acknowledged white-collar innovation as well. Take, for instance, the nineteenth-century capitalist "robber barons," who justified their unethical actions as the legitimate pursuit of property and wealth. As Gus Tyler notes:

Box 4.1 Ethnic Succession in Organized Crime

Since the middle of the nineteenth century, organized crime has provided an illegitimate opportunity structure for disadvantaged immigrant groups seeking a short-term route to the "American dream." The Irish were perhaps the first ethnic group to make the successful transition from urban gangs to organized crime, using their muscle to ensure electoral victories for local politicians, who in turn offered criminals protection for their illegal enterprises. By the end of the nineteenth century, Eastern European Jewish immigrants started to challenge Irish dominance of organized crime, and during the alcohol prohibition era of the 1920s, the Italians began to make their mark (Abadinsky 2003; McCaghy et al. 2003).

Italian American organized crime benefited from the established traditions of European Mafia groups. In nineteenth-century Sicily, the Mafia (which in Arabic means "place of refuge") constituted a nongovernmental system of organized power that operated through a network of "gangs" or "families." Mafioso served as middlemen or mediators between the Italian elite and the peasantry—delivering votes, arbitrating disputes, and offering protection in exchange for remuneration or immunity to do as they pleased. Such men were respected for their loyalty to family and kin and for the ability to maintain their authority, even if that required the use of violence (Abadinsky 2003; Hobsbawm 1959).

In the United States, each new wave of immigration brought new ethnic groups who imitated as well as fought with those who came before them. Intergroup competition was lessened somewhat by an expanding U.S. economy, which generated more legitimate opportunities for the offspring of earlier arrivals, thus reducing the group's involvement in organized crime. This pattern of entering into and exiting out of organized crime has been dubbed "ethnic succession in organized crime" (Abadinsky 2003; Ianni & Reuss-Ianni 1976).

In spite of Italian American dominance of organized crime in the United States, which lasted from the Prohibition era to the 1970s, non-Italians made substantial contributions. Meyer Lansky, for example, a man of Polish-Jewish descent, played a major role during Prohibition and in the post-Prohibition development of the heroin trade and the casino-hotel industry. And Chinese groups have operated in U.S. urban communities with significant Chinese populations since the beginning of the twentieth century (Abadinsky 2003; Chambliss 1988).

Frank Hagan observes that the Italian American Mafia, also known as La Cosa Nostra ("this thing of ours"), now consists of a "dwindling empire with . . . remaining strongholds" in limited areas such as the suburbs of New York and Chicago (1998:400). It has lost control of the heroin market and has been a marginal player in the cocaine trade. The federal

continues

Box 4.1   continued

government has successfully prosecuted a number of key leaders and has exerted greater supervisory authority over the distribution of Teamster Union pension funds that the Mafia once controlled and used to finance some of its operations. Members facing prison terms no longer observe the traditional "code of silence," trading concessions from the government for information about the criminal activities of others. Hence the solidarity considered central to the Mafia's successful reign has begun to crumble. Currently the Mafia's primary competition comes from African American, Latino, Asian, and Russian organizations, as well as white outlaw motorcycle gangs (Kleinknecht 1996; Reuter 1995; see Chapter 6).

Land grants, covering the acreage of full states, were gained by bribery of colonial legislators and governors. Original accumulations of capital were amassed in tripartite deals among pirates, governors, and brokers. Fur fortunes were piled up alongside the drunk and dead bodies of . . . Indians. Small settlers were driven from their lands or turned into tenants by big ranchers employing rustlers, guns, outlaws—and the law. In the great railroad and shipping wars, enterprising capitalists used extortion, blackmail, violence, bribery, and private armies with muskets and cannons to wreck a competitor and to become the sole boss of a trade. (1967:44–45)

More generally, and up to this very day, corporate innovators respond to competitive pressures, unpredictable economic markets, and government regulatory controls by adapting illegal means to meet the "bottom line," achieve a competitive edge, or quite simply, make as much money as possible (Friedrichs 2004; Passas 1990; see Chapter 6).

Not all economic crimes, however, are committed for financial success goals. Many are done for the challenge or thrills, out of peer pressure, or to "keep the party going" (Hagan et al. 1998; Jacobs & Wright 1999; Shover & Honaker 1992). Merton recognized that the discrepancy between cultural goals and institutionalized means could produce strain regardless of the nature of the particular goal. Thus David Greenberg (1977) observed that much male delinquency is not a strategy for long-term economic gain but an attempt to satisfy the immediate concerns of adolescence—for example, acquiring a masculine self-image (e.g., through sexual conquests and acts of defiance, including violence) and maintaining an adolescent lifestyle (e.g., purchasing fashionable clothes, cigarettes, alcohol/drugs, CDs, DVDs, concert tickets, motor vehicles).

Albert Cohen (1955) was one of the first to point out that for youths a great source of strain is not the job market per se but an educational system that was ostensibly designed to prepare them for economic success. Cohen argued that lower-class youths are deprived of the preschool cultural resources available to higher-class youths (e.g., books, educational toys, educated parents) that could help socialize them for school achievement, yet teachers judge them by the same standards as their more privileged peers. Hence they are more likely to experience the strain of school failure, lose their stake in conformity, and engage in delinquency. Research suggests, however, that school failure is associated with delinquency among youths of all social classes, and low-achieving, middle-class youths may even be more delinquent than their lower-class counterparts (Agnew 2001; Frease 1973; Kelly & Balch 1971; Maguin & Loeber 1996; Polk et al. 1974).

Greenberg (1977) noted that much of youths' experience of school strain derives from the rules and regimentation of the school itself, the boredom and perception that education is a waste of time, and the denial of adolescents' autonomy at a point when they are trying to establish their independence. Some students view school as a hostile territory and express resentment directly through vandalism of school property and assaults against teachers. Indeed, much juvenile crime is committed on school grounds and sometimes involves crime against other students. Proximity to high schools is also related to higher crime rates in adjacent residential areas (Agnew 2000; Lawrence 1998; Liazos 1978; Roncek & Gaggiani 1985; Roncek & LoBosco 1983).

In addition to innovation, Merton described two other deviant (often criminal) adaptations to strain: retreatism and rebellion. *Retreatism* involves withdrawing altogether from the pursuit of legitimate success goals, whether through legal or illegal means. Retreatists are individuals who have essentially dropped out of society and adopted escapist lifestyles such as alcoholism and drug addiction. Retreatists may also be homeless or suffer from mental disorders: "They are in society but not of it. . . . [They] piece out an existence by eating little, sleeping a lot, and abandoning the effort to create patterns of daily life they can respect. . . . Some finally succeed in annihilating the world by killing themselves" (Merton 1964:219).

This is how Kenny Hall remembers his addiction to drugs:

> There was no participation in this thing that we call life. . . . I woke up, I got my drugs, and I went to sleep. . . . I was sleeping in basements. . . . I was sleeping on rooftops. . . . I didn't want to be seen during the daylight hours . . . [so] I would catch the [subway] . . . and . . . just ride it all day long. . . . I felt that ashamed about myself. . . . I would come out at night when the sun went down. . . . I would walk on the side of the building in the shadows where no one could see me. . . . I would do what I had to do to satisfy my addiction. . . . When the sun would come up, I would go back underground again. (profiled in Moyers 1991)

Similarly, Margaret, a drug addict and prostitute, observes: "I think using drugs is like committing suicide. Only you doing it slower. . . . Instead of taking a gun and blowing your brains out. . . . It might take you a lotta years, but eventually it's gonna kill you. If it don't kill you, it's gonna lame you or something" (quoted in Pettiway 1997:38, 50).

The last of Merton's adaptive types is *rebellion,* the rejection of legitimate goals and means and the substitution of new ones. Cohen, for instance, characterized the delinquent adaptation as largely "nonutilitarian, malicious, and negativistic" (1955:25). Delinquent boys "not only reject the dominant values system, but [they] do so with a vengeance. They 'stand it on its head' . . . exalt its opposition . . . engage in malicious, spiteful, 'ornery' behavior of all sorts to demonstrate not only to others, but to themselves . . . their contempt for the game they have rejected" (Cohen 1966:66).

In his book, Sanyika Shakur (1993) describes the nonutilitarian nature of gang violence in the inner city, where groups fight over symbolic possession of "turf" that none of the combatants owns. As he says of his years with the Eight Tray (83rd Street) Crips: "I don't own a brick on 83rd. . . . I don't own a brick in this country. . . . You ain't fighting for nothing" ("Eight Tray Gangster" 1993). Later in life, however, Shakur strove for a different kind of rebellion. "Little did I know," he writes, "that I had been resisting all my life. By not being a good black American I was resisting. But my resistance was retarded because it had no political objective" (1993:330). In prison Shakur was exposed to the political ideology of the revolutionary New Afrikan Independence Movement, which has as one of its objectives the securing of separate land (even separate states) for African American people. "My personal belief is that separation is the solution. . . . This country's 130-year-old experiment of multiculturalism has failed. Perhaps it was never designed to work" (p. 332).

Shakur came to this conclusion in prison after being exposed to the ideas of Malcolm X, a man who had undergone a transformation in prison from street hustler to political activist with the Nation of Islam. Shakur was impressed with Malcolm X's words in *Message to the Oppressed:* "Out of frustration and hopelessness our young people have reached the point of no return. We no longer endorse patience and turning the other cheek. We assert the right of self-defense by whatever means necessary, and reserve the right of maximum retaliation against our racist oppressors, no matter what the odds against us are" (cited in Shakur 1993:214). Quite clearly, Shakur's goals are controversial and utopian. More than a few African Americans, however, would likely sympathize with his sentiments.

A Decade of Liberal Reform

One of the most exciting eras in the annals of crime prevention history was the 1960s, when federal programs predicated on anomie/strain theory provided the rationale for liberal crime prevention policies aimed at improving the economic and educational opportunities of low-income and minority youths. Along with the Chicago Area Project, they remain the preeminent models for contemporary offender-oriented prevention efforts. The 1960s programs, which were part of the Johnson administration's "War on Poverty," had two basic thrusts: (1) opportunity programs that were administered by social service professionals and (2) comprehensive community action projects that involved residents in local collective action (Berger 1996).

Opportunity programs. The Economic Opportunity Act (EOA) of 1964 authorized involvement of the U.S. Department of Labor in delinquency prevention through the Neighborhood Youth Corps and the Job Corps. The Neighborhood Youth Corps included both summer and year-round training and work programs for youths, some of whom were enrolled in school and some of whom were not. The Job Corps placed low-income urban youths in residential centers for job training and had both an urban and a rural component. The urban centers trained youths in skilled trades such as auto mechanics and carpentry. The rural centers often emphasized forest conservation skills but provided training for many other jobs as well (Quadagno & Fobes 1995).

In addition, the Department of Health, Education, and Welfare (HEW) and the Department of Housing and Urban Development (HUD) established a broad range of prevention initiatives. HEW's Upward Bound program aimed to facilitate educational achievement by increasing the motivation and skills of disadvantaged youths. HUD's Model Cities program provided inner-city youths with college prep courses, college scholarships, and job placements, as well as direct social services such as counseling, drug abuse treatment, assistance for unwed mothers, and recreation and teen clubs.

Although the aim of programs such as these was to provide equal opportunity for individuals to compete in the U.S. economy, they did not always fulfill their promise. At times they merely offered job training without a concomitant guarantee of employment upon completion of the program. African American trainees even experienced discrimination from some of the skilled trade unions (Quadagno & Fobes 1995). Evaluation studies measuring the effects of these efforts on the long-term labor status of youths and on rates of delinquency were mixed and often unimpressive (Berger 1996; McGahey 1986). The most favorable results came from the Job Corps. According to Elliott Currie:

> Those who completed the program got better jobs, earned more, were less dependent on welfare, and cut down their use of drugs, compared to simi-

larly deprived youth who hadn't participated. They also committed fewer crimes, measured both by their own reports and by arrests during and after the program. The biggest effect on crime came during their enrollment in the program itself . . . but it also continued, though at a less dramatic level, after they went back to city life. (1985:13)

Unfortunately, rather than reaching hard-core delinquent or at-risk youths, the programs tended to help those who were more motivated and upwardly mobile to begin with. They were important in strengthening the black middle class but left behind an intransigent underclass that remained living in urban squalor. Moreover, the success of some only increased the sense of relative deprivation and strain among those who remained behind (LaFree & Drass 1996; Wilson 1987).

Comprehensive community action projects. The Comprehensive Community Action Projects (CCAPs) began in 1961 under the auspices of John Kennedy's President's Committee on Juvenile Delinquency and Youth Crime and continued under the Office of Economic Opportunity. These were large-scale, multidimensional programs established under federal control but rooted in local communities. In many respects, CCAPs were direct descendants of the earlier Chicago Area Project. But in the 1960s, New York City's **Mobilization for Youth** (MFY) was the model for such efforts (Berger 1996; Empey & Stafford 1991). MFY aimed to achieve the following:

1. Create job opportunities through work subsidies, vocational training, and career guidance.
2. Improve educational opportunities through teacher training, the development of relevant curricula and teaching methods, increased parent-school contacts, and preschool programs.
3. Provide services to youths and families through detached street workers, recreation, rap groups, child care, and counseling.
4. Establish neighborhood councils and mobilize low-income residents for social action to redress grievances in areas such as housing, health care, and employment discrimination.

Inspired by MFY, the federal government offered funding and planning assistance to other communities to set up their own CCAPs, which expanded to over 1,000 by the mid-1960s. However, the social action component of CCAPs led to withdrawal of political support. In MFY, for instance, residents were encouraged to participate in strikes, protests, and confrontations with public officials. The intended goal was to make political leaders aware that the community was an organized interest group that demanded their attention.

MFY was thus a classic case of "biting the hand that feeds you," and it wasn't long before it was derailed by accusations that it had communist sympathies and had misused government funds. Community organizers favoring social action strategies were purged and funds curtailed. The remaining CCAPs were transformed into predominately counseling/treatment programs or ones stressing vocational, educational, or legal assistance (Berger 1996; Empey & Stafford 1991).

It is doubtful there was ever full political support for the dramatic changes attempted in the name of anomie/strain theory (Marris & Rein 1973). When put into practice the programs probably exceeded what Merton himself might have imagined. Steven Messner and Richard Rosenfeld also point out a fundamental flaw in the assumptions of anomie/strain theory and the way the theory was applied to increase opportunities: in a society that celebrates "the unrestrained, competitive pursuit of monetary success, . . . greater equality of opportunity and a redistribution of economic resources would not by themselves . . . eliminate the strong temptations to try to win by any means necessary" (2001:98). Nevertheless, many liberals and progressive advocates of social change continue to believe that the 1960s programs contained the essential ingredients of effective crime prevention.

■ Gender and Strain

Like other theoretical formulations, anomie/strain theory has been criticized for lacking gender generalizability. As Allison Morris points out, "one might expect women to commit more crime than men since their [economic] opportunities are more limited" (1987:76). But as we noted previously, female crime rates are lower than male crime rates. Anomie/strain theory explains this paradox by noting that females have been traditionally socialized to place greater emphasis on domestic or relationship goals than on financial success goals (Broidy & Agnew 1997; Leonard 1982).

On the other hand, the changing position of women in society over the past few decades has led some criminologists to believe that financial goals have now become more salient for women. Rising rates of divorce and out-of-wedlock births have increased the number of female-headed households. Women have expanded their participation in the labor force and girls have been increasingly socialized (by parents, schools, and media) to develop occupational or career ambitions. To the extent that actual opportunities for women have not kept pace with rising expectations, females may be experiencing greater strain (Berger 1996; Broidy & Agnew 1997).

These observations are consistent with the apparent rise in rates of female criminality observed by some criminologists in the mid-1970s (Adler 1975; Simon 1975). This increase occurred primarily in the area of nonviolent property offenses, such as shoplifting, passing bad checks, check and credit card forgery, and welfare fraud. Rise in these crimes was also facilitated by the opportunities afforded by the expansion of self-service retail outlets, consumer credit, and governmental welfare (Steffensmeier 1978; Steffensmeier & Cobb 1981).

Furthermore, evidence from self-report surveys indicates that female delinquents are more likely than nondelinquents to see themselves as having fewer opportunities (Datesman et al. 1975; Rankin 1980; Segrave & Hastad 1985). Delinquent girls are more likely to believe that they won't finish high school or find satisfactory employment, though they are not more likely to believe that females experience discrimination in the job market (Cernkovich & Giordano 1979b). While some studies have found the strain-delinquency association to be stronger for males, others have found it to be stronger for females (Belknap 2001; Berger 1996). The mixed results stem in part from the varied ways in which strain has been measured or operationalized. Moreover, Gary Hill and Elizabeth Crawford (1990) have found measures of blocked opportunities to be more highly associated with crime among young black women (ages eighteen to twenty-three) than among young white women.

We will explore the complexity of the gender-crime relationship more thoroughly in Chapter 8. For now we simply note that gender stereotyping and discrimination were apparent in the application of the reforms of the 1960s based on anomie/strain theory. In a study of the Job Corps, for example, Jill Quadagno and Catherine Fobes (1995) document the initial political opposition to including females in the group of eligible trainees. Eventually the EOA required that one-third of the trainees be female. Still, it was the young men who received the training for the better-paying skilled jobs, while the young women received training in "home and family life and the development of values, attitudes, and skills that [would] contribute to stable family relationships and a good child-rearing environment" (p. 176). The idea was to prepare men to become primary breadwinners and to prepare women to become homemakers.

▪ *General Strain Theory*

Criminologists who dispute anomie/strain theory's focus on lower-class criminality have revised the theory to account for delinquent behavior across all social classes. Robert Agnew (1992) advanced a social psychological or micro-level **general strain theory**, arguing that strain results not simply from the actual or perceived failure to achieve economic or educational goals, but more generally from a broader array of stressful or negative life experiences. These include the actual or anticipated *removal* of "positively valued stimuli" (e.g., death of a parent, end of a romantic relationship, moving from one's neighborhood) as well as the actual or anticipated *presentation* of "negatively valued stimuli" (e.g., an abusive parent, an unfair teacher, hostile peers). Agnew also proposes that the relationship between strain and delinquency is mediated by a youth's *emotional reactions* (e.g., frustration, depression, anger) and *coping strategies* (e.g., talking to others, cathartic physical exercise, revision of goals) that affect the behavioral outcomes of structurally induced experiences.

Empirical tests of general strain theory have lent support to Agnew's propositions (Agnew & White 1992; Broidy 2001; Hoffman & Cerbone 1999; Paternoster & Mazerolle 1994). The practical implications of the theory suggest the importance of remedial interventions that improve familial, peer, and school relationships and that provide youths with resources that improve their coping strategies (e.g., positive adult mentors, anger-management/conflict-resolution training) (Agnew 1995, 2001).

■ Social Learning and Symbolic Interaction

Outside of general strain theory, the theories we have reviewed in this chapter have entailed macrosociological approaches to crime. We now turn more directly to microsociological explanations. As we noted earlier, these theories address how individuals learn to favor or disfavor criminal courses of action, how they interpret or account for the meaning of their actions, and how they are socialized or controlled through social relationships. We begin with the important contribution of Edwin Sutherland.

Edwin Sutherland and the Theory of Differential Association

Sutherland stood heads above his contemporaries when it came to recognizing the problem of white-collar crime. He was acutely aware of the restrictive focus on lower-class crime in most criminological explanations (be they biological, psychological, or sociological), and he appreciated the need for a general theory that could explain the existence of criminality among all social strata.

Sutherland was drawn to a micro-level orientation from his exposure to Tarde's theory of imitation and to a body of thought known as **symbolic interactionism**. George Herbert Mead (1863–1931), arguably the most influential symbolic interactionist, was concerned with the symbolic meaning of social action for the individual. The very same experience, Mead (1934) noted, could mean different things to different people. Such meanings, and consequently a person's very sense of self or personal identity, were acquired through social interaction with others.

Sutherland's **differential association theory** (1947) has been classified as both symbolic interactionist and behaviorist in orientation (Einstader & Henry 1995; Empey & Stafford 1991). You will recall that behaviorism is at variance with much psychological theorizing about crime in that it assumes that criminal behavior is learned or conditioned in the same manner as law-abiding behavior—through the particular mix of rewards and punishments that are attached to a person's behavior (see Chapter 3). However, whether one situates Sutherland in the interactionist or behaviorist tradition, he clearly viewed crime as an outcome of normal social psychological processes.

According to differential association theory, "Criminal behavior is learned in interaction with other persons in a process of communication . . . within intimate personal groups" (cited in Akers 2000:72). The learning of crime includes not only "the techniques of committing the crime, which are sometimes very complicated and sometimes very simple," but also "the specific direction of motives, drives, rationalizations, and attitudes" under-lying the illegal behavior. A person becomes delinquent or criminal when he or she is exposed to "an excess of definitions favorable to violation of law over definitions unfavorable to violation of law." Since individuals are typically exposed to both crime-inducing and crime-inhibiting associations, what matters is the relative *frequency* (how often you spend time with par-ticular others), *duration* (how much time you spend with them on each occasion), *priority* (how early in life you began associating with them), and *intensity* (how much importance you attach to them) of each.

Perhaps the most obvious example of differential association is the adolescent peer group that provides social approval for participating with others in underage drinking, drug use, gangs, and other forms of crime. Participation in such activities is reinforced through the acquisition of friendship ties, while nonparticipation may lead to exclusion. McCall (1994) recalls how he was initially reluctant to participate in gang rapes: "I was in no great hurry to have sex in front of a bunch of other dudes. . . . [But] I wasn't about to let it be said that I was scared of pussy." The first time he participated he felt sorry for the thirteen-year-old girl he and his friends had raped, "knowing she would never be able to live [it] down. . . . But the guilt was short-lived. It was eclipsed in no time by the victory cele-bration we held after she left" (p. 48).

Sutherland was aware, as symbolic interactionists have noted, that individuals are malleable and subject to change over time in the course of ongoing interactions (Thornberry 1987). In his book *White Collar Crime,* he presented an account by a young man who underwent a redefinition of self upon entering the labor force after college:

> While I was a student in the school of business I learned the principles of accounting. After I had worked for a time for an accounting firm I found that I had failed to learn many important things. . . . An accounting firm gets its work from business firms and, within limits, must make the reports which those business firms desire. On my first assignment I dis-covered some irregularities in the books of the firm and these would lead

> anyone to question the financial policies of that firm. When I showed my
> report to the manager . . . he said that was not a part of my assignment and
> I should leave it out. Although I was confident that the business firm was
> dishonest, I had to conceal this information. Again and again I have been
> compelled to do the same thing in other assignments. I get so disgusted
> with things of this sort that I wish I could leave the profession . . . [but] it
> is the only occupation for which I have training. (1949:239)

Although this story is anecdotal, the criminological literature is replete with
studies that support the general thrust of Sutherland's theory. In particular,
self-report delinquency research has confirmed the theory's basic tenets.
Since these studies typically involve broader tests of social learning theory,
we will now turn to that theory.

■ Social Learning Theory

In a large body of theory and research, Ronald Akers and colleagues have
advanced a **social learning theory** of crime that merges principles of differential association theory with those from behaviorist psychology in
order to examine processes that both "motivate and control criminal behavior" and "promote and undermine conformity" (Akers 2000:75). From
Sutherland, Akers takes the concepts of *differential association* and *definitions* and adds the behaviorist concepts of *imitation* and *differential reinforcement*. Imitation refers to one's observation and replication of role
models' behavior in both actual and simulated environments (i.e., the
media). Akers's research finds that imitation is "more important in the initial acquisition and performance of novel behavior than in the maintenance
or cessation of behavioral patterns once established" (p. 79). Differential
reinforcement "refers to the *balance* of anticipated or actual rewards and
punishments that follow or are consequences of behavior" (p. 78, emphasis
added). As noted earlier, rewards and punishments can be both social and
nonsocial, and they can range from approval or disapproval of parents and
friends to the euphoric or unpleasant physical effects of drugs. You will
also recall that studies find anticipation of informal sanctions from others
to be a more salient deterrent to crime than anticipation of formal sanctions
from the law.

Akers (1998) acknowledges the macro-level social phenomena that
structure environments of social learning, although these are not his primary concern. He is interested in specifying the precise micro-level mechanisms by which learning takes places. On this score social learning theory
has fared rather well in empirical research, especially in studies of juvenile
delinquency. As Akers notes:

> There is abundant evidence to show the significant impact . . . of differen-
> tial association in primary groups such as family and peers. . . .

> [Delinquency] may be . . . directly affected by deviant parental models, ineffective and erratic supervision and discipline . . . and the endorsement of values and attitudes favorable to deviance. . . . In general, parental . . . criminality is predictive of . . . children's future [criminality]. . . . The role of the family, [however], is usually as a conventional socializer against delinquency. . . . It provides anti-criminal definitions, conforming models, and the reinforcement of conformity through parental discipline. . . . Other than one's own prior . . . behavior, the best single predictor of the onset, continuance, or desistance of . . . delinquency is differential association with conforming or law-violating peers. . . . It is in peer groups that the first availability and opportunity for delinquent acts are typically provided. Virtually every study that includes a peer association variable finds it to be significantly and usually most strongly related to delinquency . . . and other forms of deviant behavior. (2000:86–87)

Moreover, social learning theory does not lack gender generalizability. Several studies have found that female delinquents are at least as likely as male delinquents to have delinquent peers (Figueira-McDonough et al. 1981; Inciardi et al. 1993). Akers and colleagues (1979), for example, found that differential association and other social learning variables were effective predictors of alcohol and drug use among both male and female adolescents. Similarly, Peggy Giordano (1978) reported that peer-group involvement was central to females' acquisition of attitudes favorable to delinquent conduct. She and her colleagues also found that females were just as likely as males to indicate that they got drugs or alcohol from friends or that they hung out at friends' houses when parents were away (Giordano et al. 1986): "Females spend as much . . . time in the company of their friends as do males. . . . [Those] who . . . become involved in delinquent acts . . . adopt both a set of attitudes in which they [see] delinquency as appropriate, possible, or desirable . . . and a friendship style in which they . . . encourage each other as a group to act on these orientations" (p. 1194).

In terms of practical applications, both social learning and differential association theories suggest rehabilitative interventions that utilize group dynamics to reinforce conventional behavior. Such applications are referred to variously as guided group interaction, peer-group counseling, positive peer culture, and therapeutic communities (Gottfredson 1987). In juvenile correctional settings these approaches offer advantages over individual-oriented treatments. Insofar as offenders often manifest their law-violating behavior as part of a group, the group therapy situation is the natural vehicle for personal change or growth:

> The [beginning] stages of the group are used to vent hostility and aggression. Initially, the groups' members are self-centered and unable to realistically or meaningfully involve themselves or their peers in the problem-solving process. Later, as the group progresses and the . . . members see

> that their . . . peers have similar problems and backgrounds, empathy and group identification is facilitated, . . . ultimately produc[ing] insight and new patterns of adaptation. (Trojanowicz et al. 2001:363–364)

These groups are often staffed by ex-offenders and ex-addicts and "show remarkably consistent reductions" in criminal behavior for those who complete the programs (Lipton 1996:12).

◼ Techniques of Neutralization

Both social learning and differential association theories make use of the concept of "definitions" when describing the process by which individuals come to define or interpret law-violating behavior as acceptable or unacceptable. In some studies, definitions have been operationalized according to Gresham Sykes and David Matza's concept (1957) of **techniques of neutralization**. Sykes and Matza argued that most law violators have some appreciation or respect for conventional values and must therefore neutralize the hold these values have on them through various self-rationalizations or justifications.

In their research on delinquent youths, Sykes and Matza identified five general techniques of neutralization. *Denial of responsibility* involves the delinquent's assertion that his or her behavior is due to external forces such as "unloving parents, bad companions, or a slum neighborhood." Youths often view themselves "as helplessly propelled into" unlawful behavior, as "more acted upon than acting" (p. 667). For example, a youth may explain that "the alcohol made me do it" or "the other guy started the fight." *Denial of injury* describes the offender's view that no harm has been caused by his or her actions—for instance, by drinking alcohol, smoking marijuana, or "borrowing" someone's car for a joyride. *Denial of the victim* is used as a way to distinguish people who are deserving targets of crime, such as a black person who's gotten "out of his place," a teacher who's been unfair, or a store owner who's ripped off customers. *Condemnation of the condemners* shifts attention away from the youth and toward the disapproving others, who are viewed as "hypocrites, deviants in disguise, or impelled by personal spite" (p. 688). For example, a youth may resent police officers who are corrupt, teachers who show favoritism, or parents who abuse their children. Finally, *appeal to higher loyalties* involves the imperative to sacrifice the rules of the larger society for the demands of the smaller group, such as the friendship clique or gang.

Critics have faulted Sykes and Matza for failing to establish that techniques of neutralization actually *precede* rather than *follow* delinquent acts, arguing that techniques of neutralization are mechanisms that facilitate the "hardening" of youths already involved in crime (Hamlin 1988; Minor 1984). Others have observed that rationalizations are used not so much to neutralize moral commitments as to minimize "risks or other tactical considerations" (Schwendinger & Schwendinger 1985:139). For instance, delinquents often rationalize stealing from people they perceive as "careless victims," that is, as people whose "inefficiency in protecting their possessions makes them 'responsible' in part for their own victimization" (e.g., people who leave their keys in their car, who don't lock up their bicycles, or who leave their houses unlocked) (Carpenter et al. 1988:104).

These criticisms notwithstanding, the techniques-of-neutralization concept sensitizes us to the way in which offenders interpret or account for their actions. Rapists, for example, employ culturally available "rape myths" they have learned from the media and peers (Jackson 1978; Scully & Marolla 1984). These myths contain neutralization techniques that deny responsibility (e.g., the urge was uncontrollable), deny injury (e.g., she really liked it), and deny the victim (e.g., she was a cock-teaser so she had it coming). As one rapist, a married man, explains, "Sometimes you just get the urge to go out and fuck the living shit out of some broad. . . . It doesn't matter who they are or what they look like. . . . Most women like to get their box battered as much as a man likes to get his balls off. They want to be grabbed and taken hard. It makes them feel like a woman" (Skipper & McWhorter 1981:29).

White-collar criminals, as Sutherland observed, rely on comparable rationalizations for their crimes (Benson 1985). In a well-documented price-fixing case that came to light in the early 1960s, corporate personnel from General Electric (GE), Westinghouse, and other electrical-equipment manufacturers conspired to avoid the competition that would have kept prices down (Geis 1996). The conspirators all testified that this was an ongoing practice even before they had been hired by their respective companies and that they were expected to conform. They also denied they had caused any harm. One GE spokesmen rationalized his company's actions this way: "The prices which . . . purchasers . . . have paid during the past years were appropriate to value received and reasonable as compared with the general trends of prices in the economy" (p. 102). And a Westinghouse executive replied, when asked during a Senate Subcommittee inquiry whether he was aware that the meetings he had with competitors were illegal, "Illegal? Yes, but not criminal. . . . I assumed that criminal action meant damaging someone, and we did not do that. . . . I thought that we were more or less working on a survival basis in order to try to make enough to keep our plant and our employees" (p. 106). This conspiracy, however, went on for several years and netted the industry nearly $3 billion in illegal profits (Barlow 1996).

Labeling Theory

Previously we introduced you to the **labeling theory** challenge to the legalistic definition of crime (see Chapter 1). Crime, according to labeling theory, is not an objective condition but a process of social definition and the societal reaction to rule-violating behavior. Labeling theory is not concerned with explaining **primary deviation**, the initial impulse for rule violation, but with **secondary deviation**, how labeling transforms the initial behavior into a stable pattern. Drawing on symbolic interactionism, the theory is concerned with how individuals develop a sense of personal identity or self through interaction with others. It postulates that labeling of persons as criminal can become a self-fulfilling prophecy that promotes further involvement in crime. The offender internalizes the negative stigma and suffers a decline in self-esteem, while hostile reactions from others reduce opportunities to resume a conventional status (Becker 1963; Lemert 1951; Schur 1971).

Although results of delinquency research on the effects of labeling on juveniles' self-esteem have been mixed, they are not generally supportive of the proposition that youths experience a decline in self-esteem following arrest or juvenile court contact. Some studies have found that self-esteem was more likely to decline among youths who were less involved in or committed to delinquency (e.g., first-time, middle-class offenders) than among more involved or committed youths (e.g., high-frequency, lower-class offenders) who already possessed "a negative social status, . . . [who were] not highly integrated into society . . . [and who were] less sensitive to and less affected by the judgments of officialdom" (Waegel 1989:113). Labeling may be irrelevant for those already designated as social outsiders, as having delinquent peers and engaging in delinquency may (in the short run) actually increase their self-esteem (Jang & Thornberry 1998; Kaplan et al. 1986). Labeling theory, however, distinguishes between *relative* and *absolute* labeling effects. Relative labeling refers to the impact of varying degrees of sanction (e.g., probation versus incarceration), while absolute labeling refers to "the difference between those who are labeled and those who are not" (Paternoster & Iovanni 1989:385). Compared to the research on relative labeling, the research on absolute labeling has been more supportive of the theory's propositions regarding secondary deviation (Berger 1996; Shoemaker 1996).

Issues of self-esteem aside, ethnographic studies of gangs illustrate how excessive official intervention in the lives of youths may make matters worse, as conflict with the police solidifies youths' commitment to the gang (Hagedorn 1988). As one gang member recounts:

> The police . . . would pull me into their car and harass me. I kept telling them that I was not a banger. But they don't believe anything. . . . They asked me questions about . . . friends, guys from the hood who are gangbangers, and, since I wouldn't tell them what they wanted to hear, they would say things like, "Yes, you are one of those hoodlums from this street. We've been watching you for a long time, and now we got you, and you're going to pay." (Padilla 1992:85)

According to another youth:

> I was picked up on several occasions . . . because I was Puerto Rican and was walking down the street. I wasn't into gangbanging, but the cops kept asking me questions about my gang and shit. One time . . . [they] picked me up and dropped me off in a white neighborhood . . . [and] took my money so I couldn't catch the bus back to the hood. The white dudes from that neighborhood had a field day with me. . . . I tried protecting myself . . . but I did get the shit smashed out of me. So, what do you do after something like that happens to you? . . . I turned. I became an official member of the [gang]. (pp. 87–88)

The stigmatization associated with official labeling also makes it difficult to find employment after serving punishment for one's crime (Pager 2003; Schwartz & Skolnick 1962). After serving three years for armed robbery, McCall (1994) could not land a newspaper job even after receiving a college degree in journalism. As he writes, "Every time I filled out an application and ran across that section about felony convictions, it made me feel sick inside. . . . I knew what they were going to do. . . . A black man with a felony record didn't stand a chance" (p. 234). Through perseverance, however, McCall eventually became a successful journalist, but only after he decided to lie about his criminal record. He hoped that if he got his foot in the door and had a chance to prove himself, people might finally forgive him for his past.

John Braithwaite's observations (1989) about **disintegrative** and **reintegrative shaming** are helpful as we contemplate the obstacles faced by McCall and others like him as they attempt to reintegrate into conventional society. Shaming is social disapproval or condemnation designed to invoke remorse. In disintegrative shaming, the offender continues to be treated as an outsider, is not forgiven for past sins, and thus is more likely to relapse into crime after having difficulty reentering the community. In reintegrative shaming, on the other hand, the offender is shamed, but if remorseful, is forgiven, welcomed back into the fold, and enmeshed in supportive community relationships. The Japanese are more inclined to reintegrative shaming than we are in the United States, and they have been more successful at lowering rates of criminality (Vincentnathan 1995).

The fact that labeling itself may promote criminal identification has led some criminologists to favor a policy of "radical nonintervention" or use of less punitive measures when dealing with some offenders (Schur 1973). For instance, youths who commit minor crimes can be diverted from the juvenile justice system into community-based programs that offer various rehabilitative services. Other criminologists critical of the overreach of the law have favored the **decriminalization**—the removal of criminal sanctions—of so-called victimless crimes committed by adults (e.g., gambling, drug use) that for the most part lack the forced victimization of predatory crimes of theft and violence (Geis & Meier 1997; Morris & Hawkins 1970). Such noninterventionst strategies—especially decriminalization—remain controversial and raise complex issues that we will explore later in the book (see Chapters 5 and 8).

■ Social Control and the Life Course

The major micro-level alternative in criminology to social learning and symbolic interactionism is **social control theory**. The concept of social control can be found in the works of both early European and U.S. social theorists and has been considered to be the micro-level analogue of social disorganization theory (Bursik 1988). Whereas social disorganization theory attributes crime to communities marked by weakened social control, control theory focuses on individuals who are weakly controlled (Reiss 1951; Reckless 1967). Unlike social disorganization theory, however, control theory assumes that weakened social control may occur at any level of society, under conditions of economic deprivation or affluence.

▥ *Travis Hirschi's Social Control Theory*

In his book *The Causes of Delinquency,* Travis Hirschi (1969) advanced the most influential formulation of social control theory. Hirschi believed that most criminological theories ask the wrong question: Why *do* people engage in criminal behavior? Hirschi thought the more appropriate question to ask is: Why *don't* people engage in criminal behavior? He assumed that human self-interest provided sufficient motivation for crime, and hence what was in need of explanation—the key theoretical issue—was how these impulses are controlled.

According to Hirschi, most other macro- or micro-level sociological formulations are essentially "bad things happen to good people" theories, that is, they assume that people are largely benign and naturally prone to conformity, unless exposed to social strain, deviant associations, social stigmatization, and so forth. These theories, however, fail to address questions like: Why do so many (if not most) economically disadvantaged people not commit crime? Why would one be attracted to delinquent peers in the first place?

Following Durkheim, Hirschi argued that "the more weakened the groups to which [one] belongs, the less he depends on them, the more he consequently depends only on himself and recognizes no other rules of conduct than what are founded on his private interests" (Durkheim 1952:209). According to Hirschi, conformity arises only if, through the socialization process, a person establishes a bond with the conventional society. When this bond is weak, one is freed from social constraint and is more at risk for delinquency.

Hirschi conceptualized the social bond in terms of four key elements. *Attachment* refers to the ties of mutual affection and respect between children and their parents, teachers, and friends. People with such positive ties (with their parents especially) are reluctant to place those ties in jeopardy by engaging in law-violating behavior. *Commitment* suggests an individual's stake in conformity, as indicated by a youth's willingness to conform to the ideal requisites of childhood (e.g., getting an education; postponing smoking, drinking, and sex) and their assessment of anticipated losses associated with nonconformity. *Involvement* refers to participation in conventional activities that minimize idle and unsupervised time (e.g., chores, homework, organized sports, Scouts). *Belief* indicates acceptance of the moral validity of laws.

During childhood and adolescence, parents are the key agents of social control, since "the family is the most salient arena for social interaction" at this stage of life (Thornberry 1987:873). In Chapter 3 we noted elements of family life that are associated with delinquency, including (among other things) the degree of parental-child affection and communication. In his self-report survey research, Hirschi (1969) measured attachment to parents by asking youths various questions such as: "Do you share your thoughts and feelings with your parents?" "Do your parents know where you are when you are away from home?" Those who answered affirmatively to questions like these—as well as other measures of the social bond—were less likely to engage in delinquency. Importantly, Hirschi placed emphasis on the *quality* of the relationship between children and parents rather than on the *number* of parents in the home (e.g., single-parent versus two-parent families). All other things being equal, it may be desirable to have two parents in the home (Gallagher & Blankenhorn 1997; Rankin & Kern 1994). But research indicates that the quality of family interaction has similar effects on delinquency regardless of the number of parents (Cernkovich & Giordano 1987).

Although Hirschi's theory has received considerable empirical support through self-report studies, the evidence has appeared most compelling as an explanation of (1) minor rather than serious delinquency, (2) the onset of delinquency rather than the continuation of delinquency, and (3) delinquency in early rather than late adolescence (Agnew 1985; Krohn & Massey 1990; Paternoster & Triplett 1988). Moreover, as Terence Thornberry notes, "Attachment to parents is not . . . an immutable trait, impervious to the effects of other variables. Indeed, associating with delinquent peers, not being committed to school, and engaging in delinquent behavior are so contradictory to parental expectations that they tend to diminish the level of attachment between parents and child" (1987:874).

In a later work, Michael Gottfredson and Hirschi (1990) argue that an effective social bond leads to the development of *personal* self-control, which is important to establish early in the socialization process. Consistent with conservative proscriptions for preventing crime, Gottfredson and Hirschi maintain that informal family controls are the first line of defense in the fight against crime. If the family and then the schools fail in bonding the individual to society, the criminal justice system becomes the last line of defense. Contrary to labeling theory, Gottfredson and Hirschi suggest, law enforcement should be strictly applied to increase the certainty of apprehension, and punishment (not rehabilitative treatment) should be employed, since criminal justice intervention comes too late to effectively prevent crime (Einstader & Henry 1995).

While some social control theorists downplay the significance of class, Terry Williams and William Kornblum ask a question consistent with Hirschi's perspective: How is it that some lower-class youths "manage not only to survive in a community devastated by crime, drug addiction, and violence, but to be recognized as achievers and encouraged to realize their potential as fully as possible"? (1985:16). Their answer, for many youths, is family involvement:

> In every low-income community there are young people who work and go to school and fulfill family responsibilities. The largest proportion of these youths is from homes where parents have struggled for years to provide them with as many of the benefits of stability and education as possible, even at great sacrifice to themselves. The influence of family values . . . , the relative security of religious beliefs and practices, fortunate experiences with teachers and school—all of these factors are important in shaping the life chances of young achievers. (p. 17)

However, Williams and Kornblum also agree with the African proverb "It takes a village to raise a child." They believe that positive adult mentors who "spend time with . . . youth . . . are among the most precious resources a community can have" (p. 106). Mentors who can nurture self-esteem and foster aspirations—whether they are from schools, religious organizations, youth groups, or athletic associations—can make a world of difference in a young person's life. Williams and Kornblum thus take a different tack than Gottfredson and Hirschi, one more consistent with strain theory. They maintain that efforts to encourage adult mentoring of youths should be incorporated into governmental programs that promote "continual opportunities for growth" so as to provide disadvantaged youth "a constant supply of diverse opportunities for entry into the economic and social mainstream" (p. 113).

Box 4.2 Religion and Crime

Although the United States is one of the most churchgoing countries in the world, contemporary political discourse is filled with lamentations about America's moral decline (Fineman 1994; Hadaway et al. 1993). Conservative politicians and religious leaders often blame rising crime rates and immorality on the decline of religious beliefs and the growth of moral relativism. They assume that religiosity is associated with less crime because it promotes "goodness, morality, concern for the rights and welfare of others, righteousness, and rewards in the hereafter for proper behavior in life" (Binder et al. 1988:465). Within criminology, social control theory suggests an inverse relationship between religion and crime insofar as religion may increase the bond between individuals and society and promote moral beliefs that discourage deviancy.

Few studies of religion and crime have focused on *adult* criminality. T. David Evans and colleagues (1995) found that participation in religious activities (attending religious services and social events, reading religious material, listening to religious broadcasts) was inversely related to self-reported criminality among adults. And Harold Grasmick and colleagues (1991) found that respondents who identified themselves as religious and felt that religion was an important part of their life were less likely to say they would cheat on their income taxes.

Most criminological research, however, has focused on *juvenile delinquency,* and the results have often been mixed. In one of the first major studies that questioned the religion-delinquency (RD) relationship, Travis Hirschi and Rodney Stark (1969) discerned no association between delinquency and church attendance or belief in the supernatural. To explain their findings, they suggested that churches were unable to instill neighborly love in their members and that "belief in the possibility of pleasure and pain in another world cannot now, and perhaps never could, compete with the pleasures and pains of everyday life" (pp. 212–213).

Other research suggests that the RD relationship may vary by denomination and geographical context. Several studies have found the lowest rates of delinquency among Jews and persons from fundamentalist or highly ascetic Christian denominations (e.g., Baptist, Morman, Church of Christ) and that religion appeared to inhibit delinquency more in rural and southern communities than in urban and nonsouthern areas (Albrecht et al. 1977; Higgins & Albrecht 1977; Jensen & Erikson 1979; Rhodes & Reiss 1970). Other research indicates that the RD relationship is mediated by additional social factors such as association with peers. Stephen Burkett and Bruce Warren (1987), for example, found that youths with less religious commitment were more vulnerable to the influence of delinquent peers. Stark, however, argues that what is critical is not a

continues

Box 4.2   continued

youth's personal beliefs but the beliefs of most of his or her friends: "In communities where most young people do not attend church, religion will not inhibit the behavior even of those . . . who personally are religious. . . . In communities where most kids are religious, then those who are will be less delinquent than those who aren't" (1984:274–275).

Other criminologists conclude that the impact of religion is so "closely tied to the family and other influences" that it has little independent effect (Binder et al. 1988; Cochran et al. 1994; Elifson et al. 1983:521). Nevertheless, it seems unwise to dismiss religion as a factor in young people's behavior, for some studies have found significant effects, although the relationship appears strongest for behaviors, like alcohol/drug use and teenage sex, that are not universally condemned by secular society (Burkett & Ward 1993; Jang & Johnson 2001; Johnson et al. 2000, 2001; Sloane & Potvin 1986; Tittle & Welch 1983).

In recent years the work of activist (especially African American) clergy has been making the news, and we are hearing more about faith-based efforts to reach at-risk youths and convert them away from gangs, drugs, and violence. Reverend Eugene Dovers of Dorchester, Massachusetts, for instance, runs a "safe haven" center that combines religious and recreational activities for youths. He and others like him work with police to pull the hard-core kids off the streets—where they can hopefully be reached in a prison ministry—and get the "more winnable" ones into alternative community programs (Leland 1998:22). For these clergy, saving youths is "a calling, not a caseload" (Woodward 1998:28). As Reverend Rivers says, "There will be virtual apartheid in these cities if the black church doesn't step into the breach" (quoted in Leland 1998:23). While church activists cannot solve the problems of the inner city alone, many feel that their efforts are crucial in stemming the tide of violence and despair (Pattillo 1998).

▪ *Gender and Social Control*

Assessments of the gender generalizability of social control theory, like those of strain theory, are complicated by the various ways in which studies have measured or operationalized theoretical concepts. Some studies, for example, have found that the relationship between family-bonding and school-bonding variables and self-reported delinquency is stronger for males than females, while others have found it to be stronger for females (Belknap 2001; Berger 1996). Nevertheless, the literature on gender socialization, as we noted earlier, suggests that the lower rates of female delinquency may be explained, in part, by the greater family supervision traditionally imposed on females and the lesser degree of freedom girls have been given to take risks and "sow their wild oats" (Hagan et al. 1985; see Chapter 1).

In general, males are more likely than females to be socialized to regard aggressive behavior as a masculine way to exert control and authority over others (Campbell 1993). They are thus more likely to blame others for their problems and channel their frustrations toward external targets. Females, on the other hand, are more likely to be taught to regard aggression as a loss of self-control, as unfeminine, as something to avoid. They are also more likely to develop and value emotional ties and nurturing relationships. While this type of socialization may produce prosocial behavior, it may also lead females to blame themselves for their problems, internalize their frustrations, and suffer from depression (Broidy & Agnew 1997). In addition, as we have observed, family life is often more stressful for females than males. Females are more vulnerable to sexual victimization in the home, which sometimes leads them to run away and become caught in a spiraling web of criminality and victimization out on the streets (Chesney-Lind 1989; Hagan & McCarthy 1997; see Chapter 3).

Social Bonds Across the Life Course

Robert Sampson and John Laub (1993) have extended social control theory to help explain how the establishment of bonds in adulthood can attenuate and modify previous life-course experiences or patterns of behavior. A **life course** is a developmental pathway or "sequence of culturally defined age-graded roles and social transitions that are enacted over time" (Caspi et al. 1990:15). During childhood and adolescence, the family, school, and peer groups are the most significant sources of informal social control. During young adulthood, higher education and/or vocational training, work, and marriage are most important. During later adulthood, work, marriage, parenthood, and involvement in community are most important.

Sampson and Laub analyzed longitudinal data collected by Sheldon Glueck and Eleanor Glueck (1950, 1968) on 500 delinquent and 500 non-delinquent males born between 1924 and 1935 who were followed from childhood until they were thirty-two years of age. They found that childhood and adolescent delinquency were predictive of later-life criminality, but young men who married and found stable employment were more likely to desist from crime than those who did not. Their research supports a theory of "informal social control that recognizes both stability and change in antisocial behavior over the life course" (Sampson & Laub 1990:609; also see Horney et al. 1995).

Sampson and Laub argue that marriage per se does not increase social control, but that close emotional ties and a strong attachment to one's spouse increase the bond between individuals and society. Marriage also reduces time spent with law-violating peers, as other studies have found as well (Simons et al. 2002; Warr 1998). And while employment per se does not increase social control, it does so when accompanied by job stability, job commitment, and workplace ties. Under these conditions a person develops a social investment in institutions of conformity and becomes embedded in networks of relationships that "create interdependent systems of obligations and restraint that impose significant costs for translating criminal propensities into action" (Laub & Sampson 1993:311).

It is important to add, however, that the circumstances for personal reform are not entirely of one's own making. Structural features of the labor market, for instance, "have as much to do . . . with employment outcomes . . . as do individual predispositions to work." The subjects in Sampson and Laub's study "grew to young adulthood in a period of expanding economic opportunities during the 1950s and 1960s" (pp. 318–319). Some also experienced positive life-course changes as a result of military experience, which made them eligible for numerous benefits offered by the G.I. Bill.

At the same time, Sampson and Laub note that marriage and employment did not have the same impact on everyone in their study. Such experiences "only provide[d] the *possibility* for change to occur" (p. 318, emphasis added). At some point individuals who desisted from crime made a decision to change (see Anderson 1999; Giordano et al. 2003). Importantly, the faith and support that others had given them weighed heavily on their minds. Like many others, McCall (1994), for example, was tempted to return to crime after being released from prison:

> One night. . . . I stopped at a convenience store. . . . It was late and there was only one attendant. . . . I thought, I can take this place by myself. . . . I'd been doing that a lot lately. I'd enter stores, case them, and assess my chances of being able to pull off another job. . . . [That night] I sat there for a long while, struggling inside my head. . . . Then I thought about something . . . that I had . . . that most cats coming out of the joint did not: I had supportive parents. I thought about my mother and stepfather, who had suffered through three years of hell with me. . . . I thought about how hard they'd pulled for me since I'd gotten out. They gave me money. I had a place to lay my head. . . . They cared about me. . . . I couldn't let them down. (pp. 236–237)

Life-course research in criminology returns us to the tension between social structure and social action that is a central element of the sociological imagination (see Chapter 1). Individuals are influenced by external constraints but are at times capable of defying the odds. This capacity for personal agency, however, does not emerge spontaneously. It is an ability, like language, that is nurtured through social experience and acquired in varying degrees of proficiency. McCall's ability to eventually steer a successful life course from prison to the *Washington Post* newsroom was in no small part dependent on early family and school experiences that he could fall back on. (Before succumbing to prodelinquent peer influences, McCall had been "into honor rolls and spelling bees" [p. 27].) He did not create his life completely anew, but continually struggled to overcome social deficits that his involvement in crime had created (e.g., a prison record that limited employment opportunities).

People who desist from crime must overcome considerable adversity in their lives. It is regrettable that sociologists have invested so much time attempting to explain how individuals succumb to adversity but have paid relatively little attention to the process of change. Nevertheless, life-course research in criminology encourages us to reject static models of human behavior in favor of a model that recognizes both stability and change in criminal conduct over time.

5

Conflict Theory and Critical Criminology

Wissan Abyad, imprisoned for allegedly committing "habitual debauchery," has been serving a fifteen-month sentence in a dark and clammy prison cell in Cairo, Egypt. Since the cell has no toilet or running water, he and his five cellmates who share this eight-by-fourteen-foot cubicle are forced to urinate in a bathtub that has no drain. Prior to his incarceration, Abyad had agreed, after several online conversations, to meet a man named "Raoul" at a McDonald's restaurant in an upscale section of Cairo. Upon his arrival at McDonald's, Abyad was surrounded by four men who grabbed him and muscled him into a police car. He never even had sex with "Raoul" (Dahir 2002).

Abyad is just one of many recent victims of a growing "choreographed crackdown" on gay men in Egypt. Police there have been entrapping gay men like Abyad through Internet stings. They've also been raiding gay discos and private parties and "tapping phones of known gay men in order to trace their friends, and using threats, allegedly even torture, to turn" cornered men into informants (Dahir 2002:27).

At the time Abyad was imprisoned for his "crime," only thirteen states in the United States still outlawed **sodomy**, a term coined after the biblical story of the decadent ancient city of Sodom. Nine of these states had laws that criminalized sodomy—which includes oral and anal sex—for both same-sex and different-sex pairs, but in practice these laws have been used only against gay men and lesbians. Sodomy statutes have historically been used to deny gay and lesbian parents custody or visitation rights on the grounds that their children may be exposed to "criminal activity." Additionally, these laws have been used as the basis for discrimination in housing, employment, schools, health care, and immigration status. Their existence also increases the likelihood of police harassment and decreases the likelihood that gays and lesbians will report hate crimes or domestic violence or seek refuge at shelters for victims of battery (Graff 2003; see Chapters 9 and 10).

In a six-to-three decision in *Lawrence v. Texas* (2003), the U.S. Supreme Court struck down a Texas ban on same-sex sodomy that eviscerated sodomy laws in the thirteen states and effectively "carved out a zone of sexual freedom" for gays and lesbians (Kim 2003:6). This decision does not mean the end of discrimination, but the history of sodomy laws in the United States and elsewhere does illustrate the conflict perspective on crime that we introduced in Chapter 1. Understanding this perspective will constitute an essential part of your sociological imagination.

According to **conflict theory**, definitions of crime and the enforcement of criminal laws often lack societal consensus and are subject to the assertion of economic and political power and the struggles of competing groups in society. Such conflict, as we shall see, can take various forms. **Critical criminology**, an offshoot of conflict theory, emphasizes how social structures of inequality impact the criminalization process in ways that advance the interests of societal elites at the expense of those who are disadvantaged. Critical criminologists reject a legalistic definition of crime in favor of one that defines crime as a violation of human rights or as analogous social injuries, that is, as acts or conditions that may be legal but the harmful consequences of which are similar to those of illegal acts.

■ Group and Class Conflict

▨ Culture Conflict and Crime

Criminologists designate one type of group conflict that constructs crime as **culture conflict**. Culture conflict occurs "when persons acting according to the norms and violations of their own group violate those of another group that have been enacted into law" (Akers 2000:181; Sellin 1938). Foreign immigrants, for instance, "may violate the laws of a new country simply by behaving according to the customs of the old." During the era of alcohol prohibition (1919–1933), individuals wishing to drink violated the Eighteenth Amendment to the U.S. Constitution. The prohibitionist (or temperance) movement was composed mainly of pious, middle-class rural and small-town Protestants who believed that drinking was sinful. They were especially concerned about the cultural practices of working-class Catholic immigrants and other urban dwellers whose presence in the United States appeared to threaten their way of life (Gusfield 1963). Today, many people believe that the government's prohibitionist drug policy, especially laws against marijuana use, constitute an unfair and unnecessary overreach of the law, and that drug abuse should be treated as a medical rather than criminal problem. (We will explore the contemporary debate over drug policy later in this chapter.) Abortion law is another area where culture conflict emerges. Some people believe that abortion is murder, while others consider it a private matter that should be subject to a woman's right to choose what is done to her body.

A provocative contemporary example of culture conflict has involved Hmong refugees in the United States. Traditional Hmong marriages in native Laos often involved force. A man would take a girl of his choice (usually between fourteen and eighteen years of age) to his family home. He would dispatch a clan messenger to the girl's family to inform them "of her whereabouts and to deliver a token sum of money to start bride-price negotiations" (Titunik 1992:1). The girl would then be forced to have sex, at which point the man would be in a strong bargaining position, as the girl's loss of virginity rendered her unmarriageable to others. In the United States, however, young Hmong women may reject these traditional practices and have their "suitors" charged with kidnapping and sexual assault. According to a Hmong social worker in Wisconsin, the traditional Hmong view is that if "you are willing to go [in a car] with a guy, you are willing to marry him. The man may not understand that in this country if you get in someone's car, it might just mean you want a date" (p. 8).

Such culture-conflict crimes have prompted considerable debate. How severely should you punish a person for behavior that would be acceptable, even customary, in his or her home country? Is it fair to the victim to take cultural norms into account when charging and sentencing the offender? "There is no such thing as a 'cultural' legal defense—akin to . . . an insanity defense—to excuse a person from criminal acts," but in practice prosecutors and judges may consider cultural background a mitigating circumstance in these cases (p. 8). Although defense attorneys argue that it is naive to expect refugees who experience cultural and language barriers to absorb U.S. law on their own, absent a more formal mechanism to educate the foreign born, refugees often get a crash course courtesy of the prosecutor's office. As one district attorney said, "I saw it as an opportunity to send . . . [a] message to the community that sexual assault like this wouldn't be passed over simply as a culture issue. You've got 12-, 13-, and 14-year-old girls who are forced into motherhood and thereby deprived of all the opportunities that teenagers ought to have" (p. 9).

▓ *Racial Conflict, Social Protest, and Collective Violence*

In other types of group conflict dissident groups engage in protest to change existing political arrangements. Over the years, for example, protesters associated with the civil rights, women's, antiwar, and other social movements have engaged in **civil disobedience**—the deliberate yet nonviolent public refusal to obey a law that one thinks is unjust.

In 1955, as noted earlier, Rosa Parks refused to move to the back of the bus, sparking a movement of civil disobedience that challenged segregation laws and forever changed the social fabric of the United States (see Chapter

1). During the civil rights protests of the 1950s and 1960s, southern blacks were arrested countless times for "sitting-in at lunch counters, libraries, and movie theatres, . . . for 'kneeling-in' at segregated churches . . . [and] for peacefully marching after being unfairly denied parade permits" (Barkan 2001:388). In his famous 1963 "Letter from Birmingham Jail," Martin Luther King Jr. wrote:

> One has not only a legal but a moral responsibility to obey just laws. Conversely, one has a moral responsibility to disobey unjust laws. . . . Any law that uplifts the human personality is just. Any law that degrades human personality is unjust. All segregation statutes are unjust because segregation distorts the soul and damages the personality. . . . [But] in no sense do I advocate evading . . . the law. . . . One who breaks an unjust law must do so openly, lovingly, and with a willingness to accept the penalty. . . . [That person] is in reality expressing the highest respect for law. (King 1994:463)

Group conflict can also spill over into violence, as in the case of race riots. Urban African Americans, for instance, have at times rioted in response to real or perceived brutality by the police. Many readers are familiar with the 1992 riots that occurred in Los Angeles and other parts of the country after the acquittal of the police officers accused of beating Rodney King, an African American who had been stopped for speeding. According to some observers, such incidents represent "small-scale political revolts stemming from blacks' anger over their poverty and others aspects of racial oppression by white society" (Balbus 1977; Barkan 2001:381).

Arguably the most well-known period of urban race rioting in the United States occurred during the 1960s. During that era, some 500 riots involving an estimated 350,000 participants caused massive property damage and the deaths of nearly 250 people, most of whom were shot by police and National Guard troops. These riots were more common in cities with depressed economic conditions (Barkan & Snowden 2001; Downes 1968; Gurr 1989; Myers 1997). One study of the 1965 Watts riot in Los Angeles found that over half of the African Americans interviewed felt that the revolt had been "a purposeful event which had a positive effect on their lives" (Tomlinson & Sears 1967:73). Another post-Watts study concluded that "while the majority expressed disapproval of the violence and destruction," this disapproval "was often coupled with an expression of empathy with those who participated" and a sense of pride that African Americans had brought worldwide attention to their plight (Cohen 1967:4).

Some analysts believe that these riots helped stimulate governmental policies, such as the expansion of welfare and equal-employment opportunity legislation, which benefited the black community. Michael Betz

(1974), for example, found that cities that experienced riots during that era subsequently received more welfare funding than cities that did not. The riots, however, also provoked an antiblack white backlash and brought forth a more punitive response from police in the form of increased arrests and use of deadly force against African Americans (Barkan & Snowden 2001; Button 1989; Piven & Cloward 1971).

The struggles of Native Americans. The native peoples of North, Central, and South America have suffered greatly as a result of European conquest. Between the sixteenth and nineteenth centuries the indigenous population of these areas declined by about 90 percent, some 70 million people. Most of the deaths were due to exposure to disease for which the people had no resistance. Susceptibility to disease, however, was aggravated by depletion of the food supply, forced territorial displacement, and overall hardship that accompanied European domination (S. Katz 1988, 1996).

Between 1775 and 1890, in the United States alone, there was an estimated decline of 1.5 million Native Americans. While less than 4 percent of the people who died during these years were killed through military conflict or genocidal massacres sponsored or encouraged by governmental officials, the American principle of **manifest destiny**—the belief in the inevitable territorial expansion of the United States—legitimized the seizure of Indian land and the attempted annihilation of Indian culture (Katz 1996; Stannard 1992). During that period the federal government ratified some 370 treaties with individual tribes as sovereign nations, but most of these treaties were broken by the United States. There is a saying among Native Americans: "They made us many promises . . . but they never kept but one; they promised to take our land and they took it" (Balkan et al. 1980:198–199). In 1890, about 200 unarmed Native American men, women, and children were massacred by the U.S. Seventh Calvary at Wounded Knee, South Dakota. This battle "symbolizes the end of formal fighting and the destruction of Indian civilization as it . . . previously existed" (Hagan 1997:94). Since then many Native Americans have lived in abject poverty on government reservations around the country.

Over the years Native Americans, like other oppressed groups, have organized to protest their plight. In 1968 the American Indian Movement (AIM) was founded by Dennis Banks and other Native Americans to combat police harassment and brutality. AIM's goals quickly expanded to the restoration of traditional Native American culture and the pressuring of the U.S. government to honor its broken treaties (Hagan 1997; Messerschmidt 1983).

The village of Wounded Knee, on the Oglala Sioux Pine Ridge reservation, has been the site of further conflict. In 1973 about 200 armed AIM militants seized and occupied the village for seventy-one days, demanding

U.S. Senate investigations of Indian affairs (Hagan 1997). During a shoot-out with authorities, several people on both sides were injured and two Native Americans were killed. Another incident occurred in 1975 when two FBI agents entered the Pine Ridge Reservation in search of a Native American suspected of stealing a pair of boots. In a subsequent shoot-out, the two FBI agents and an AIM member were killed. Four AIM members were charged with murder and one, Leonard Peltier, was convicted and sentenced to life in prison. Many people familiar with the case believe that Peltier was convicted despite questionable evidence (including testimony of fabricated eyewitnesses and suppression of exculpatory evidence) and "apparent improper conduct by the prosecution and judge at his trial" (Barkan 2001:372). Amnesty International considers Peltier to be a "political prisoner," and over 14 million people around the world have "signed petitions demanding a new trial" for him (Beirne & Messerschmidt 1995:302; Messerschmidt 1983; Peltier 1989).

▓ *Class Conflict and Left Realism*

Some conflict theorists, following Karl Marx and Frederich Engels, view crime as a consequence of class conflict and the social inequalities and competitive forms of interaction endemic to capitalist societies, where property acquisition goals predominate and economic relations define people as objects to be exploited for personal gain (Balkan et al. 1980; Bonger 1916; see Chapter 4). According to this view, crime occurs in all classes of society, although the criminal law is unevenly enforced and most often directed at subordinate groups. Corporations commit "crimes of economic domination," which range from illegal price-fixing and fraudulent financial bookkeeping to the manufacture of harmful consumer products, the operation of dangerous workplace environments, and the proliferation of toxic pollution (Quinney 1977). Workers, in turn, commit "crimes of accommodation and resistance," which include stealing from employers, participating in illegal strikes, and joining dissident political groups. In addition, the government itself may commit "crimes of repression," which range from police brutality and the illegal surveillance of citizens to the undermining of foreign governments and the assassination of foreign leaders. Government officials engage in these activities in order to advance their own interests or the perceived interests of their country and/or to maintain conditions favorable to capitalist profit-making at home and abroad (see Chapters 6 and 10).

One of the central characteristics of a capitalist economic system is the creation of a **surplus population** of potential laborers who are more or less permanently unemployed (Quinney 1977; Spitzer 1975). This population provides a large pool of workers whom employers can hire when needed (e.g., when workers strike) and who keep wages down by increasing competition for jobs. Individuals in this group are the most vulnerable to involvement in "street crimes" (predatory theft, violence, drugs, and gangs), which are the primary concern of the criminal justice system. The surplus population is a volatile and potentially rebellious group, and some conflict theorists have seen in it the seeds of resistance that might lead to progressive social change. However, street crime for the most part only exacerbates the plight of the disadvantaged; it is primarily committed not against the affluent but against the most vulnerable people in society (Balkan et al. 1980; see Chapter 7).

Critical criminologists, as we have noted, have focused attention on the neglected criminality of the privileged class. However, a branch of critical criminology called **left realism** has emphasized the destructive nature of street crime as well. In doing so, left realists reject grand utopian schemes—such as Marx and Engels's vision of a classless society—and call instead for realistic solutions to the problem of street crime. They advocate more modest local-organizing and government-sponsored strategies that are generally consistent with the liberal agenda on crime prevention (see Chapters 1 and 4). They support efforts to improve police-community relations as well as the development of citizen protection patrols. They favor rehabilitative modes of punishment designed to reintegrate offenders back into society. Left realists also support government-funded social services and job creation programs, but would go further than most liberals in using the tax system to create disincentives for corporations to close plants or relocate jobs to lower-wage foreign countries. Finally, they advocate promotion of workplace democracy by including workers and community representatives on the boards of directors of large corporations (DeKeseredy & Schwartz 1996; Lea & Young 1984; Matthews & Young 1992; Michalowski 1983).

Some critical criminologists' emphasis on the criminogenic qualities of capitalism should not be misconstrued as an assertion that *only* capitalism causes crime (Greenberg 1993). While corporate crime ceased to exist in the former Soviet-bloc nations under communist rule and in noncapitalist societies like China, Cuba, and North Korea, government corruption as well as illegal markets in monetary currencies and other commodities have been common. There does appear to be less street crime in these countries than in capitalist nations like the United States, but this may result more from government repression than from the attempt to satisfy economic needs. Nevertheless, as Ronald Akers asks, "If there is something inherently criminogenic" about capitalism, why do different capitalist nations have dissimilar rates of crime (2000:202)? Clearly, sweeping generalizations about capitalism fail to account for such variations.

■ Feminist Criminology

Another branch of critical criminology is known as feminist criminology. **Feminism** is a social movement concerned with understanding and alleviating the oppressive conditions that women (and girls) experience as a group, and **feminist criminology** is the perspective taken by those who are dissatisfied with the neglect of gender in much sociological thinking about crime (conflict and critical thinking included). According to Meda Chesney-Lind, "gender stratification in patriarchal society is as powerful a system as is class. A feminist approach . . . requires explanations of . . . behavior that are sensitive to its patriarchal context" (1989:19; see Chapter 1).

▩ *Gender and Crime*

As you will recall from Chapter 1, gender refers to the "social statuses and meanings assigned to women and men" (Richardson et al. 1997:19). It involves institutionalized arrangements of power that, in patriarchal societies, entail men's dominance over women. Women are more likely than men to be employed in lower-paid service, retail, and clerical positions that offer fewer opportunities for advancement. They are often segregated in "gender appropriate" occupations such as nursing, child care, preschool and elementary school teaching, secretarial work, and waitressing. Even when women work outside the home, as the majority do today, they usually remain responsible for the bulk of child-rearing and daily home maintenance, and they are often expected to compromise their careers for their families. In the corporate world, women have made significant gains but are still more likely than men to be excluded from the upper ranks of managerial power. Likewise, women are substantially underrepresented in positions of political power (Coverman 1983; Hochschild & Machung 2003; Messerschmidt 1993).

Traditional gender roles are rooted in these structural arrangements. Males have been socialized to associate risk-taking, competitiveness, aggressiveness, and occupational ambition with masculinity. Females, in turn, have been given relatively less support and freedom to explore the world in these ways, and they have been encouraged to associate femininity with being sexually attractive to males and establishing nurturing relationships with others. Even in today's world of changing gender relations, parents often remain traditional in their socialization practices. They tend to trust sons at an earlier age when it comes to leaving them home alone or letting them go out on a date without a chaperone, although daughters are trusted more to be left at home with a same-sex friend. Even parents who are concerned about sexism and who favor gender equality hesitate to stray too far from traditional socialization practices for fear that their children might be perceived as or become "deviant." Parents continue to hope for and expect higher educational achievement for their sons than their daughters, and they are more likely to view sex as ruining daughters' but enhancing sons' maturation (Bursik et al. 1985; Morash & Chesney-Lind 1991; Orenstein 1994).

According to feminist criminologists, traditional criminology has marginalized women's experiences and ignored, neglected, or misrepresented female offenders and victims. Traditional criminology, for example, has tended to characterize females' relative disinclination to commit crime as a sign of inadequacy or inferiority (e.g., socialized passivity or dependency). Why not see it instead as a model for responsible prosocial behavior? Feminists believe that the problem of "gender generalizability" requires placing gender at the center of criminological analysis rather than merely applying traditional criminological theories to women (see Chapter 4). How ironic it is, they say, that traditional criminology has focused on male offenders without emphasizing that crime is a means by which men demonstrate their masculinity (Daly & Chesney-Lind 1988; Messerschmidt 1993; Morash & Chesney-Lind 1991; Simpson 1989).

Feminist criminologists focus on the intersections of gender, race/ethnicity, and class. They urge us to recognize the multiple inequalities or "intersectionalities" that arise from diverse and crosscutting social statuses and identities (Daly & Maher 1998). Recognizing intersectionality helps us, for instance, to avoid seeing "*women* as a unified category" or thinking of "race in ungendered terms" (pp. 3, 5). As we suggested earlier, not all women and men "do gender" according to traditional norms and expectations. Many, in fact, defy gender stereotypes to construct alternative femininities and masculinities. We will develop this idea further in Chapter 8.

Whereas traditional criminology has tended to distinguish "them" (the lawbreakers) from "us" (the law abiding), feminist criminology highlights what are often "blurred boundaries between victimization and criminalization"—for example, when girls flee abusive households and their "street survival strategies" result in their arrest and incarceration (Daly & Maher 1998:8; see Chapter 3). Walter DeKeseredy and Martin Schwartz (1996) also illuminate such interconnections when they note that the problem of male violence *against women* is related to the problem of male violence *against men*. Given the evidence that indicates that "children who grow up watching their mother being abused are more likely than other children to become delinquents and adult criminals both inside *and* outside the home," they suggest that "one way to reduce street crime against *men* is to reduce violence in the home against *women*" (pp. 478–480).

■ The Criminalization of Gay and Lesbian Sex

Feminist criminologists have been at the forefront of the gay and lesbian rights movement and of efforts to advance understanding of sexual diversity. Historically the laws that criminalized sodomy in every state in the United States were not "stand-alone statutes . . . [but] part of a much larger package of law that prohibited all forms of nonprocreative and nonmarital sex" (John D'Emilio, quoted in Graff 2003:A22). Sodomy was considered immoral, regardless of the sex of one's partner, because it allowed people to enjoy sex without the possibility of producing a child.

In 1969 a historic uprising occurred when police officers in New York City's Greenwich Village raided the Stonewall Inn gay bar. Although police raids were common and patrons "were expected to endure humiliation, slurs, and brutality in silence," one hot summer night the accumulated anger and frustration bubbled over and patrons of the bar as well as the throng of supporters that gathered "fought back against the police so valiantly that the cops were forced to retreat" (Feinberg 1996:7). The uprising, which has come to be known as the **Stonewall Rebellion**, continued for four nights and now marks the birth of the contemporary gay and lesbian movement in the United States.

In the past two decades, two cases involving prosecution for sodomy have resulted in landmark U.S. Supreme Court decisions. In the 1986 case of *Bowers v. Hardwick,* an Atlanta police officer came to the home of Michael Hardwick with a warrant to arrest him for failing to appear in court to face a charge of carrying an open bottle of beer outside a bar. The officer was let into the house by one of Hardwick's roommates and found Hardwick having consensual sex with a male friend in his bedroom. Both Hardwick and his friend were arrested for violating the state sodomy law. The U.S. Supreme Court, in a five-to-four decision, upheld Georgia's statute, ruling there was no constitutional right to privacy for homosexual conduct.

In 1998 a Texas county sheriff's office received a false tip about an armed man in a Houston apartment. When the investigating officer arrived on the scene, he drew his gun and pushed open the unlocked apartment door, only to find John Lawrence and Tyrone Garner locked in an embrace. Arrested for "deviate sexual intercourse," Lawrence and Garner were handcuffed and hauled off to jail in their underwear. The two were released the next day and fined for violating Texas's "Homosexual Conduct Law" (Graff 2003).

In *Lawrence v. Texas,* the Court struck down the Texas ban on same-sex sodomy, thereby correcting, in David Cole's words, "the wrong the Court committed in *Bowers v. Hardwick* . . . when it narrowly upheld a sodomy statute with the tortured reasoning that since gays and lesbians have been repressed and vilified from time immemorial, it cannot be unconstitutional to continue to do so" (2003:5). Justice Anthony Kennedy, writing the majority opinion, asserted that the law criminalizing consensual gay sex "demeans the lives of homosexual persons . . . [who] are entitled to respect for their private lives" (cited in Bull 2003:35).

Although the Court's decision was not unexpected, the far reach of its reasoning did stun many. Clearly the right to privacy now granted gays and lesbians will provide them some constitutional protection, but a "legitimate state interest" could still override these rights. As Evan Thomas observes, "National security could trump privacy in the military and preserve the Pentagon's 'don't ask, don't tell' policy on gays," a policy that results in about 1,250 dismissals a year from the armed forces (2003:42; *Wisconsin State Journal* 2002c). Or, "the state's interest in preserving 'traditional institutions'—like marriage between different-sex couples—might overcome a homosexual's right not to be 'demeaned,' as Justice Kennedy put it" (Thomas 2003:42). As recent history has shown, some national leaders persist in condemning homosexuality, as when Senator Trent Lott called same-sex love a disease like kleptomania and alcoholism, and Senator Rick Santorum compared homosexuality to incest, bigamy, polygamy, and adultery. This kind of rhetoric fuels the public's **homophobia**, the fear and disdain of anyone who is not heterosexual (gays, lesbians, and bisexuals), and it encourages ongoing discrimination, harassment, and hate crimes against those who are different (see Box 5.1 and Chapter 10). It also fuels "attacks on everything from sex education and condoms in schools to needle exchange" programs that benefit people of all sexual orientations (Ireland 1998:22).

Box 5.1   Gender Outlaw: A Transgendered Perspective

The intersections of gender, sexuality, and crime are complex and nuanced, given the diverse identities of "men" and "women" in society. And sometimes it is the very narrowness of what is deemed gender-appropriate that marks one as deviant. Leslie Feinberg "grew up a very masculine girl." She liked to keep her hair short and felt most comfortable in T-shirts, jeans, and sneakers. "When I was most at home with how I looked, adults did a double-take. . . . The question 'Is that a boy or girl?' hounded me. . . . The answer didn't matter much. The very fact that [they] had to *ask* . . . already marked me as a gender outlaw" (1996:3–4).

As a young woman in Buffalo, New York, in the 1960s and 1970s, Feinberg learned that if she wasn't wearing at least three pieces of "women's" clothing, as she was *required by law* to do, she was vulnerable to arrest. (Biological males had to wear at least three pieces of "men's" clothing.) And work was hard to come by, as Feinberg "was considered far too masculine a woman" to get a job in a restaurant, store, or office (p. 12). Desperate for employment, she put on earrings and a wig in preparation for one job interview:

> On the bus ride . . . people stood rather than sit next to me. They whispered and pointed and stared. "Is that a man?" one woman asked her friend, loud enough for us all to hear. The experience taught me an important lesson. The more I tried to wear clothing or styles considered appropriate for women, the more people believed I was a man trying to pass as a woman. I began to understand that I couldn't conceal my gender expression. (p. 12)

Feinberg decided to try a different tack. She glued on a pair of theatrical sideburns and drove to a nearby art gallery:

> As I walked around, nobody seemed to stare. That was an unusual experience and a relief. I allowed my voice to drop to a comfortably low register and chatted with one of the guards about the job situation. He told me there was an opening for a guard and suggested I apply. An hour later, the supervisor who interviewed me told me I seemed like a "good man" and hired me on the spot. I was suddenly acceptable as a human being. The same gender expression that made me hated as a woman made me seem like a good man. (p. 12)

Feinberg's life changed dramatically when she began working as a man. But although the daily harassment she had endured for years subsided, she lived in constant fear of being discovered. She took male hormone shots in order to grow a beard and had breast reduction surgery as well. These changes gave her a "greater sense of safety," but using public restrooms was still awkward, not to mention risky, and applying for jobs that required physical exams was out of the question (p. 13). Passing as a

continues

Box 5.1   continued

man took an emotional toll, as Feinberg "long[ed] to live openly and proudly," to let people knew her true identity (p. 15).

Feinberg is **transgendered**. Someone who is transgendered bridges, blurs, or traverses gender boundaries. In a society where men are assumed to be masculine and women feminine, a transgendered person's biological sex appears to be at odds with his or her gender expression. Feinberg is categorized as "male" on her driver's license. That she was issued such a license demonstrates, as she says, "that many strangers 'read me' as a man, rather than as a masculine woman." Each time Feinberg has been pulled over for a traffic violation the officer has requested, "'Your license and registration—sir.' Imagine the nightmare I'd face if I handed [him] a license that says I'm female. The alleged traffic infraction should be the issue, not my genitals" (p. 61).

To avoid this nightmare Feinberg broke the law by putting an "M" in the box marked sex on her driver's license application. If this was discovered she could be fined, have her license suspended, and be sentenced for up to six months in jail. Categorizing herself as "male" on a passport application could subject her to a felony violation. Not wanting to take that risk and not feeling safe traveling with a passport marked "female," her freedom of travel is restricted.

Feinberg could have her birth certificate amended to read "male" to avoid these legal problems. She has chosen not to do so, however, because she believes that the policy that mandates this categorization violates her rights as a human being. Feinberg reminds us that racial categorization used to be required on all legal documents, but protest against this practice resulted in the removal of that mandatory check-off box. She asks, "Why should I have to legally align my sex with my gender expression? . . . Why do we still have to check off *male* or *female* on all records? Why is the categorization of sex a legal question at all? Why are those categories policed?" (pp. 61–62).

Transgenders like Feinberg, who do not conform to the gender expression expected of them, can be distinguished from **transsexuals**, those who "traverse the boundary of the *sex* they were assigned at birth" (p. x). A female-to-male transsexual, for example, is one who believes himself to be male although he was born in a female body. Transsexuals usually cross-dress and commonly use hormones and/or surgery to alter their bodies. Although Feinberg cross-dressed and shaped her body hormonally and surgically to decrease the likelihood of harassment, she is not transsexual since she does not consider herself the "other sex." The word "transgender" is thus commonly used to distinguish someone like Feinberg, whose gender expression is not considered appropriate for his or her sex, from male-to-female or female-to-male transsexuals. Nevertheless, "transgender" is also used as an "umbrella term to include everyone who challenges the boundaries of sex and gender" (p. x).

Western culture is deeply committed to a binary (i.e., either/or) conceptualization of sex and gender. According to Anne Fausto-Sterling, this "two-party sexual system [stands] in defiance of nature. For biologically speaking, there are many gradations running from male to female" (1993:22; see Chapter 1). "People whose bodies or behavior unsettle" the clear division of "M" or "F," however, are often subjected to discrimination and a world of hurt (Graff 2001:20; Nanda 2000).

■ Peacemaking Criminology

Critical criminologists' concern for suffering in the world has led to a movement that Hal Pepinsky and Richard Quinney (1991) call **peacemaking criminology**. Whereas *peacemaking* involves attempts to weave and reweave ourselves "with others in a social fabric of mutual love, respect, and concern," *warmaking* entails the belief that threats to our personal and collective security can be traced to identifiably evil people who must be suppressed "by killing them, separating them from the social fabric in which they live, or intimidating them into remaining in their proper place and conforming to the social roles their betters prescribe for them" (Pepinsky 1999:56, 59).

■ *The Way of Peace*

Peacemaking criminology participates in a grand tradition of social prophecy consistent with Judeo-Christian teachings and other social philosophies (e.g., Marxism), including ideas of Mahatma Gandhi and Martin Luther King Jr. (Fuller 1998; Quinney 1999). In the prophetic tradition, human beings are seen as estranged from their fundamental state of goodness. Imagining the possibility of a better world is considered the first step toward its realization. According to Quinney, such an imagining requires recognition of the "interconnection between the inner peace of the individual and the outer peace of the world. The two develop and occur together. The struggle is to create a humane existence, and such an existence comes only as we act peacefully towards ourselves and one another" (2000:21). Beyond this, peacemaking criminologists argue, we must acknowledge that while "few are guilty . . . all are responsible. If we admit that the individual is in some measure conditioned or affected by the spirit of society, an individual's crime discloses society's corruption" and requires us all to take responsibility to think and act in ways that will make the world a better place in which to live (Heschel 1962:16).

The peacemaking approach, as we have suggested earlier in this book, encourages us to view crime as a social relationship of *power:* "To perpetuate a crime . . . is to impose one's power on others, while to be punished for . . . crime is to be subject to the power of others" (Hagan 1989:1; see Chapter 1). Thus, crime may be understood as an act of power that inflicts suffering and denies the humanity of another, and the most fundamental cause of crime may be seen as *any* social process that equates differences among people with evaluations of worth and that allows people the "delusion that they are unconnected to those with whom they interrelate" (Henry & Milovanovic 1994:124). From this point of view, the search for the causes of crime somehow misses the point. Crime is not something apart from ordinary social life but is an integral part of society, for the ability to subject one to the power of another is much of what passes for family life, business practice, and the exercise of governmental authority (Beirne & Messerschmidt 1995; Wozniak 2002).

According to peacemaking criminologists, the elimination of crime will require the elimination of suffering more generally. They believe that the strategy of waging war on crime through punitive policies is fundamentally flawed, for it participates in the very power dynamics that are constitutive of crime itself. They ask that we search for another way, the way of peace, which entails strategies of negotiation and conflict resolution, redemption and reconciliation, and nonviolent resistance to social injustice. Ultimately, peacemaking criminologists argue, it will be necessary to establish a more *just social order* before we can establish *law and order* (Fuller 1998; Pepinsky & Quinney 1991).

Peacemaking solutions to crime focus on the *prevention* rather than on the repression of crime. Although crime prevention often means different things to different people, practitioners in the public health community have delineated three general approaches: **primary, secondary,** and **tertiary prevention** (Moore 1995). Primary prevention attempts to keep criminal behavior from arising in the first place; it is directed at the entire community and not just at individuals who are seeking or need rehabilitative treatment. Secondary prevention concentrates on early identification and treatment of vulnerable or at-risk youths, and tertiary prevention entails interventions that protect society from offenders and that reduce the likelihood of recidivist behaviors. Clearly the most effective prevention strategy is one that combines all three modalities. In many respects, the 1930s Chicago Area Project and the 1960s opportunity and community action projects (e.g., Mobilization for Youth) anticipated the comprehensive strategy that is still needed (see Chapter 4).

In the concluding chapter of this book, we will review what we believe to be essential ingredients of effective crime prevention, and we will explore peacemaking approaches to criminal justice reform. In this chapter, we will focus on two areas of social policy where peacemaking criminologists advocate alternatives to the conventional war on crime: drug and gun regulation.

▪ *Deescalating the War on Drugs*

In addition to a focus on prevention, peacemaking criminology entails a policy of deescalating the war on drugs. According to Franklin Zimring and Gordon Hawkins (1992), the drug war has focused not on the *adverse consequences* of drug use but on *drug use itself*. Little distinction has been made between experimental use, casual use, regular use, and addictive use (see Office of National Drug Control Policy 1989). Drugs have been viewed as a moral problem, and the effort to control drugs has been characterized as a battle between the forces of good and the forces of evil.

Critics of this war-on-drugs approach believe that it has been both ineffective and destructive. Mike Gray (1998), for example, notes that roughly
2 million tons of cargo arrive at various ports of entry in the United States
each day:

> Los Angeles alone will land 130,000 containers [each] month. Customs
> inspectors will examine 400. The other 129,600 will pass through without
> so much as a tip of the hat. And as this tidal wave of . . . [cargo] moves off
> the wharf on endless lines of semitrailers and flatcars, it's worth remem-
> bering that the entire annual cocaine supply for the United States would
> fit in just 13 of those . . . [containers]. A year's supply of heroin could be
> shipped in [just one]. (p. 152)

Drug policy critics also argue that criminalization of drugs increases
theft and violence associated with drug use—crime that is unrelated to the
pharmacological properties of most illegal substances. Criminalization
heightens the risk of selling drugs and hence increases drug prices, making
it more difficult for users to obtain funds to support their habits. Since the
drug market is unregulated, entrepreneurs (including organized crime networks) use violence rather than advertising or the courts to gain advantage
over competitors and to resolve disputes with competitors, employees, and
customers. In addition, users lack safeguards to regulate the potency of the
drugs they take and the ingredients that are added to them. Criminalization
also creates disrespect for the law by making criminals out of some users
who are not involved in other crimes, and it forces users to associate with
more hardened offenders. Finally, criminalization of drugs is the primary
source of both corruption in law enforcement and the police's need to rely
on aggressive and controversial tactics (e.g., military-style policing, undercover surveillance, use of criminal informants) (Fuller 1998; Nadelmann
1989; see Chapter 11).

Some critics believe that drugs should be either decriminalized or
legalized. **Decriminalization** would reduce the penalties for possession of
small quantities of drugs to roughly the equivalent of a traffic offense,
while simultaneously maintaining stiff penalties for possession of larger
quantities as well as for growing, manufacturing, and selling drugs.
Legalization, on the other hand, would set up a government-regulated system that is comparable to the one that is used for alcohol (Goode 1999).

Zimring and Hawkins dispute the notion that drugs represent "a unitary
social problem" that compels a choice between criminalization or decrimi-
nalization/legalization (1992:110). Instead, they contend, the legal status of
each drug should be determined on a case-by-case basis. The harm caused
by a drug law should not be worse than the harm caused by the drug itself.
And drug policy should focus not on eradicating use per se but on the prevention of drug-related predatory crime, serious injury and death from drug

overdoses, drug-related HIV/AIDS cases, driving under the influence, harm to newborns, and drug use by children and adolescents.

Although Zimring and Hawkins believe that most of the current crop of illegal drugs are too dangerous to be legalized, they maintain that the war approach should be abandoned. The federal government alone spends about $18 billion a year on drug control, less than 30 percent of which is allocated to prevention and treatment (Lock et al. 2002). Drug treatment programs have been especially hurt by the war on drugs, as spending on these interventions has been cut in half since the early 1980s. This policy should be reversed in light of research that shows a substantial drop in criminality following drug treatment (Harrison 2001). Moreover, drug policy for minors "demands a definition of the drug problem . . . that includes tobacco and alcohol," two drugs that cause more harm than the illegal substances (Zimring & Hawkins 1992:135). And since society assumes that minors lack the maturity of judgment to use tobacco or alcohol responsibly, they should not be penalized as harshly as adults for violating drug laws.

Erich Goode (1999) also opposes the legalization of most illegal drugs. He does believe, however, that arrest of users and even petty dealers should be a last resort and that these offenders should be offered nonpenal alternatives such as rehabilitative treatment and community service, with arrest used if necessary to get them into these programs. Goode also favors the use of needle exchange programs for intravenous drug users and addicts to prevent the spread of disease, especially HIV/AIDS, as well as the expansion of methadone maintenance programs for heroin addicts. Methadone is a synthetic narcotic that can be administered to addicts in the hopes of regulating and gradually reducing their drug use, lowering their involvement in other crimes, and enabling them to hold steady jobs. Although the results of methadone maintenance programs have been mixed, methadone maintenance remains one of the most cost-effective treatments available for heroin addiction, often leaving the addict "much better off than on heroin—with respect to his well-being and ours" (Kaplan 1983:222).

The special case of marijuana. Many drug policy critics believe that marijuana is the illegal drug that is most suitable for decriminalization, if not legalization. In fact, in 1972 a bipartisan commission appointed by President Richard Nixon called for the nationwide decriminalization of marijuana. Although Nixon rejected this recommendation, eleven states passed decriminalization laws and experienced no increase in marijuana use that was attributable to the new policy (Goode 1999; Schlosser 2003). There has also been increasing recognition of the useful medicinal purposes of marijuana (e.g., to alleviate nausea or increase appetite in cancer and AIDS patients) (Gray 1998; Stein 2002). (Currently possession of at least small amounts of marijuana is decriminalized in California, Colorado,

Maine, Minnesota, Mississippi, Nebraska, New York, North Carolina, Ohio, and Oregon. Alaska had a decriminalization statute that was repealed [see www.norml.org].)

According to a 1998 report published in *The Lancet,* Great Britain's leading medical journal, people who smoke marijuana daily for many years risk developing psychological dependency, subtle impairments of memory, bronchitis, and cancers of the lung, throat, and mouth. These are certainly good reasons to avoid using the drug. *The Lancet* noted, however, that marijuana poses "less of a threat to health than alcohol or tobacco" and that "moderate indulgence . . . has little ill effect on health" (cited in Schlosser 1999:47).

Although President Jimmy Carter favored marijuana decriminalization, President Ronald Reagan opposed it, viewing marijuana as "probably the most dangerous drug in America" (quoted in Schlosser 1999:49). His first drug czar, Carlton Turner, blamed it for young people's involvement in antiestablishment demonstrations and even for turning people into homosexuals. Such claims notwithstanding, marijuana is the most widely used illicit drug in the United States. According to survey data, over a third of the U.S. population has used marijuana at some time in their life, about 9 percent in the past year, and about 5 percent in the past month (Pastore & Maguire 2002). Extrapolating these data to the population as a whole, this would amount to nearly 92 million lifetime users, 24 million yearly users, and 14 million monthly users. Most people who use marijuana do not use other illegal drugs, and many are successful students and workers in mainstream occupations (Goode 1999; Kleiman 1998; Zimring & Hawkins 1992). According to Gray, if you remove marijuana from the equation, the number of illegal drug users in the United States drops substantially to about 3 million people, shrinking the drug war "from a national crusade to a sideshow" (1998:174).

Nevertheless, there is currently bipartisan political support for strong enforcement of marijuana laws. Under the leadership of President Bill Clinton, the first president ever to admit using marijuana (though he claimed he did not inhale), marijuana arrests approached (and currently exceed) 700,000 a year, nearly 90 percent of which were for possession, a crime usually involving less than an ounce of the drug. Moreover, the hypocrisy of antimarijuana politics is striking. Two Republican congressmen who represent major tobacco-growing states, Kentucky senator Mitch McConnell and Georgia representative Bob Barr, tried (unsuccessfully) to make federal penalties for selling or possessing marijuana comparable to those for heroin and cocaine. And Representative Dan Burton, a Republican from Indiana, introduced legislation that, if passed, would have required the death penalty for drug dealers. But when Burton's son was arrested for growing thirty marijuana plants and for transporting nearly eight pounds of

Further Exploration

Box 5.2   Drug Policy in Comparative Perspective

Some Western European countries have had relatively more success with drug policies that are less restrictive than those used in the United States. During the 1920s, when U.S. Federal Bureau of Narcotics director Harry Anslinger was harassing the American Medical Association for its permissive approach to drug use, the British Royal College of Physicians remained steadfast in its belief that drug addiction was a medical, not a criminal, problem. At that time, "the Englishman with a habit could go to his family physician, get a prescription for heroin—or morphine, or cocaine . . . [etc.]—and pick it up at the corner pharmacy" (Gray 1998:155). In the 1960s, however, the addiction rate in Great Britain doubled, although the total number of addicts in the entire country (1,400) was still just 7 percent of the number in the city of Manhattan, New York, alone. (The population of Great Britain is twenty-six times greater than the population of Manhattan.) The increase provided the impetus for a change in British drug policy. Addicts were no longer allowed to obtain drugs from a general medical practitioner, and methadone maintenance programs were introduced. This shift in policy was followed by escalating heroin prices and increased violence in the drug trade.

In 1976 the Netherlands adopted a policy of nonenforcement for drug law violations involving thirty grams or less of cannabis (marijuana, hashish) in order "to erect a wall between the so-called soft drugs . . . and hard drugs like heroin and cocaine" (Gray 1998:166). As a result, "youth clubs" and "coffee shops" were permitted to sell cannabis. During the first seven years this new drug policy "had little if any effect on levels of [cannabis] use" (MacCoun & Reuter 1997:50). Although cannabis use did increase between 1984 and 1992, similar increases were reported in the United States between 1992 and 1996. Presently, with the more lenient policy, the rate of cannabis use is no higher in the Netherlands than in the United States. Furthermore, there is little evidence that cannabis use has been a gateway drug to hard-drug use in the Netherlands. In the city of Amsterdam, for instance, where use of cannabis is higher than in other parts of the Netherlands, about 22 percent of persons twelve years of age and older who have ever tried cannabis have also tried cocaine. In the United States this figure is 33 percent (Cohen & Sas 1996; MacCoun & Reuter 1997).

Nevertheless, in 1995, under pressure from other European countries, the Dutch parliament passed legislation reducing by half the number of shops where cannabis could be sold and limiting purchases to five grams (*U.S. News & World Report* 1996a). (The legislation did not restrict the number of shops a consumer could visit.) The parliament also authorized the courts to require hard-drug addicts with a history of (nondrug) criminal behavior to undergo two years of compulsory rehabilitation. Otherwise, "people holding small amounts of heroin or cocaine for personal use are ignored," as are lower-level street dealers (Gray 1998:168). The Dutch police, however, do aggressively pursue major drug distributors.

Other countries have also dealt with heroin addiction differently than the United States. In 1994 Switzerland began the first large-scale controlled experiment in *heroin maintenance*, a three-year program under the

continues

Box 5.2   continued

supervision of the World Health Organization and the Swiss Academy of Medical Sciences that provided heroin to a thousand regular users. Evaluation of the program indicated that crime among the addicted subjects declined by 60 percent. Half of the formerly unemployed users were now working, and a third who had been on welfare were self-supporting. Homelessness among these users was eliminated and improvements in their health were noted. About 8 percent of the users gave up heroin altogether (*The Economist* 1998; Killias et al. 2000).

Currently, hard-core heroin addicts in Switzerland (those using heroin for over two years who have been unsuccessful in previous attempts to stop) are provided drugs, medical advice, and assistance locating employment and housing. Needle exchange programs and self-injection rooms are also available. In the city of Bern, the nation's capital, this approach has stabilized the rate of HIV transmission, eliminated drug-related deaths, increased the number of addicts who are steadily employed, and reduced the amount of nondrug crime.

Italy, whose drug policy has vacillated over the years, has provided criminologists with a "natural experiment" on the effects of drug prohibition. Italy's first antidrug law, the Drug Act of 1923, included no criminal penalties for drug use or possession and provided a maximum sentence for trafficking of only six months incarceration. And though the maximum sentence for trafficking was increased to three years in 1930, no additional penalties for use or possession were implemented unless the offender was "in a state of serious psychic disorder" (MacCoun & Reuter 2001:231).

The Drug Act of 1954 was the first law in Italy to define drug use as a serious crime, increasing sanctions for both use and trafficking to up to eight years in prison. According to Robert MacCoun and Peter Reuter (2001), the law was passed to enable Italy to comply with various international treaties and not to address an upswing in the drug problem. The 1954 law, with its heightened sanctions, did not prevent the apparent escalation of soft-drug use in the late 1960s or heroin use in the early 1970s.

In 1975 Italy's law underwent further revision, lengthening the penalty for trafficking in hard drugs to eighteen years, in response to the rising use of opiates and increasing involvement of organized crime in heroin trafficking. At the same time, the maximum sentence for trafficking in cannabis was shortened, penalties associated with drug use were eliminated, and chronic use was reconceptualized as an illness. Social, psychiatric, and medical services for addicts were made available as well.

In 1990, following a decade of burgeoning drug deaths and the spread of AIDS among intravenous drug users, Italy once again expanded sanctions for drug trafficking and reestablished criminal penalties for possession of drug quantities that exceeded an "average daily dose" (p. 232). Three years later, however, a successful referendum led to the striking of the phrase "personal use of psychoactive drugs is forbidden," effectively eliminating the criminalization of drug use in the country.

MacCoun and Reuter evaluated the impact of Italy's vacillating drug policy on drug use and drug-induced deaths and concluded that the law has had little effect. They suggest that changing cultural trends in drug use and international patterns of drug trafficking influenced Italy's drug problem more than the laws that were in place at any particular point in time.

marijuana across state lines, the son served no prison time. Apparently, "what's good for the goose" is *not* "good for the gander" (Schlosser 1999, 2003).

■   *The Regulation of Guns*

In their book *Crime Is Not the Problem,* Zimring and Hawkins observe that people in the United States often "use the terms 'crime' and 'violence' interchangeably," as if they were one and the same thing. Many also believe "that there is much more of *all kinds* of crime in the United States than in other developed countries" (1997:3, emphasis added). This is not the case. The United States substantially exceeds other industrial nations not in its rate of nonviolent theft but in its rate of lethal violence. The United States also stands out in its greater availability of guns. As Zimring and Hawkins observe:

> Firearm use is so prominently associated with the high death rate from violence [in the United States] that starting with any other topic would rightly be characterized as an intentional evasion. . . . If crime is nominated as the problem, guns are involved in [only] one of every 25 cases; if lethal violence is nominated as the problem, then guns are implicated in seven of every 10 cases. . . . Guns alone account for more than twice as much homicide in the United States as all other means combined. . . . No program for the prevention of lethal violence can possess even superficial credibility without paying sustained attention to guns. (pp. 106, 108, 200)

Thus another peacemaking strategy of crime prevention involves increased regulation of guns.

Opponents of gun control often remind us that "guns don't kill people, people kill people." But the truth of the matter, says Tom Diaz, is that "people attack people, but people with guns kill people," and they kill people (including themselves) primarily with handguns (1999:196). Since 1960 over "three-quarter of a million Americans have died in firearm suicides, homicides, and unintentional injuries." Nearly three times as many have been "treated in emergency rooms each year for nonfatal firearm injuries. The United States leads the industrialized world in the rate at which children die from firearms: A 1997 study by the federal Centers for Disease Control analyzed firearms-related deaths for children under age 15 in 26 countries and found that *86 percent* . . . occurred in the United States" (p. 8; emphasis added).

To be sure, the small proportion of gun users who are responsible for these incidents is dwarfed by the much larger proportion of law-abiding citizens who safely use guns for legitimate purposes, and many of this latter group view guns as "venerated objects of craftsmanship and tangible symbols of such fundamental American values as independence, self-reliance, and freedom from governmental interference" (p. 3). Diaz, however, encourages us not to view guns as "a repository of American values" but as a business or industry that generates $2 to $3 billion in sales each year (Hays 1999). Unlike most other businesses though, the gun industry is exempt from government safety regulations aimed at ensuring that consumer products are "designed and manufactured in such a way as to minimize [their] threat to human life" (Diaz 1999:13). Whereas manufacturers of toys and power tools, for instance, "must meet minimum safety standards, gun makers are free to (and almost universally do) ignore even the most rudimentary improvements in firearms design that might help ensure the safety of users and those third parties, like children, who may happen upon a firearm" (p. 14).

Critics of the gun industry charge that gun makers have been slow to design and manufacture devices such as tamper-proof safety locks, devices that indicate that the gun is loaded, and other "smart gun" technologies (e.g., fingerprint scanners, radio wristband transponders) that prevent anyone but the owner from firing the weapon (Bai 1999). Instead, gun makers have been offering their customers ever-increasing lethality: "new guns that are specifically designed to be better at killing—guns with greater ammunition capacity, higher . . . caliber or power, [and] increased concealability" (Diaz 1999:15). And like the tobacco industry (see Chapter 6), gun makers have targeted children in order to increase their future market share. The National Shooting Sports Foundation, for example, has advised manufacturers to invest in school education programs that focus on hunting and wildlife management:

> There's a way to help ensure that new faces and pocketbooks will contin-
> ue to patronize your business: Use the schools . . . they can be a huge
> asset. . . . Schools collect, at one point, a large number of minds and bod-
> ies that are important to your future well-being. How else would you get
> these potential customers . . . together, to receive your message about
> guns and hunting. (cited in Diaz 1999:188)

Opponents of gun control argue that there is already enough regulation
on the books. Gun retailers are required to obtain a federal firearms license,
and handgun buyers at licensed retail establishments are subject to a background check to screen out unauthorized users (e.g., convicted felons).
According to Diaz, however, about 40 percent of all gun transfers in the
United States involve private transactions in secondary markets "such as
sales through classified advertising in newspapers or newsletters, contacts
made through the Internet, and sales or 'swaps' across backyard fences or
at . . . 'flea markets' or 'gun shows' . . . [that] in almost all states . . . are
entirely free of . . . regulatory oversight" (1999:4).

Gun industry critics observe that legal markets are a significant source
of guns that are used in crimes. They also believe that gun manufacturers
intentionally oversupply low-regulated "gun-friendly" areas with handguns, with full knowledge that the excess supply will flow into other areas
with more stringent antigun laws. A small percentage of licensed gun dealers even provide arms to those who are prohibited from owning guns. For
instance, a recent undercover investigation by the Chicago police found
that suburban gun dealers, who are exempt from Chicago's ban on handguns, actively pursued sales to city residents. Licensed dealers in the
United States even supply guns to criminals abroad. According to an
exposé by Jake Bergman and Julia Reynolds, "even after September 11,
America remains a global shopping center for terrorists, mercenaries, and
international criminals of all stripes" (2002:19; Butterfield 1999; McBride
1999; Shapiro 1999; Vizzard 2000).

Nevertheless, opponents of gun control argue that gun regulation does
not work, that it leaves law-abiding citizens unarmed and defenseless
against criminals who care little about antigun laws. While only about 1
percent of guns in private hands are used for self-protection in any given
year (Kleck & Gertz 1995), one study found that about a third of incarcerated felons said they had been "scared off, shot at, wounded or captured by
an armed victim" (Wright & Rossi 1986:155). Moreover, research by John
Lott (1998) has shown that official crime rates are lower in states that have
enacted "right to carry" (RTC) laws that license citizens to carry concealed
weapons (also see Lott & Mustard 1997). Lott's research, which is based on
the largest data set to date (over 3,000 counties), is impressive. Overall,
however, RTC research has been inconsistent, as some studies have identi-

fied communities where crime rates rose rather than declined as a result of easing restrictions on concealed weapon carrying (Black & Nagin 1998; Kovandzic & Marvell 2003; McDowall et al. 1995). Moreover, Diaz (1999) questions whether it is just law-abiding citizens who will be advantaged by RTC laws. He notes that hundreds of concealed weapons license holders have themselves "committed a wide variety of crimes." In Texas, for instance, "holders of concealed handgun licenses [have been] arrested for weapons-related offenses at a rate 22 percent higher than the general [adult] Texas population" (p. 171). Thus places that pass RTC laws may be playing "Russian roulette" with the citizenry.

Although most studies have found little evidence that gun control reduces crime (Kleck 1991; Walker 2001; Wright & Vail 2000), local anti-gun measures, as we have noted, are often muted by more lenient laws elsewhere. Moreover, evidence indicates that the current federal system of instant background checks is flawed, as "most states rely on outdated records and computer technology" that allow thousands of "felons and others legally barred from buying guns" to purchase them (*Wisconsin State Journal* 2002a:A3). Thus James Wright and Teri Vail conclude, "Has control reduced crime and violence in the United States? The answer, clearly, is no. Would stronger controls, enacted on a national level, do so? This has to be considered an open empirical question" (2000:580). Lawrence Sherman (2001) believes that research on the effects of programs that implement gun safety measures is especially needed. At this time, however, political ideology and not empirical research will likely be the ultimate adjudicator of the debate (Vizzard 2000).

The well-publicized 1999 Columbine High School shootings in Littleton, Colorado—in which Eric Harris and Dylan Kleibold (armed with semiautomatic weapons, sawed-off shotguns, and homemade bombs) went on a shooting rampage, murdering thirteen people and wounding twenty-three before killing themselves—created a political climate somewhat more favorable to gun law reform (Fineman 1999; Vizard 2000; see Box 8.1). Victims and families, city governments, and the National Organization for the Advancement of Colored People (NAACP) filed lawsuits alleging gun manufacturers' complicity in the illegal spread of firearms and liability for failure to install safety features on their products. These litigants sought a variety of remedies, including compensation for health care costs and mandated restrictions on gun sales. Although these lawsuits have not yet been successful (with one exception), they have caused concern among gun makers and enthusiasts. Hoping to insulate itself from legal liability, Smith & Wesson (S&W), one of the largest gun manufacturers in the world, was willing to enter into an agreement with the pro–gun control Clinton administration to advance safety innovations. The National Rifle Association (NRA) was outspoken in its objection to this arrangement, accusing S&W

of being unprincipled in abandoning its opposition to gun control. Gun advocates threatened a virtual boycott of S&W products and the deal fell through as the anti–gun control Bush administration came into power. The NRA has also been lobbying for legislation that would protect gun manufacturers from legal liability (Bai 2001; Hays 1999, 2003; Vizzard 2000).

Recently, the NAACP lost its lawsuit. The judge ruled that the organization had failed to demonstrate that its members were "uniquely harmed," leaving the door open for similar lawsuits elsewhere (Hays 2003:A3). The NAACP had highlighted the racial dimensions of the gun debate, charging that gun makers had engaged in practices that fueled gun violence in black and Hispanic neighborhoods. The NRA had been fanning the flames of controversy on this issue for some time. As NRA board member Jeff Cooper wrote:

> Los Angeles and Ho Chi Min City have declared themselves sister cities. . . . It makes sense—they are both Third World metropolises formerly occupied by Americans. . . . No more than five to ten people in a hundred who die by gunfire in Los Angeles are any loss to society. These people fight small wars amongst themselves. It would seem a valid social service to keep them well-supplied with ammunition. (cited in Diaz 1999:191)

And former NRA president Charlton Heston said in a 1997 speech before the right-wing Free Congress Foundation:

> Heaven help the God-fearing, law-abiding, Caucasian, middle class, Protestant, or—even worse—Evangelical Christian, Midwest, or Southern, or—even worse—rural, apparently straight, or—even worse— male working stiff, because not only don't you count, you're a downright obstacle to social progress. . . . The Constitution was handed down to guide us by a bunch of those wise old dead white guys who invented this country. . . . So why should I be ashamed of white guys? Why is "Hispanic pride" or "black pride' a good thing, while "white pride" conjures up shaved heads and white hoods? . . . I'll tell you why: Cultural warfare. (cited in Diaz 1999:192)

■ Postmodern Currents in Criminology

As we entered the new millennium, we often heard that the *postmodern* era had arrived. Postmodernism connotes a diverse and complex array of ideas that have recently engaged the discipline of criminology. While some criminologists dispute the value of exposing undergraduate students to all the nuances of postmodern criminology, we do think it useful for students to be familiar with some of the issues that have been raised by this body of critical thought (Arrigo 1999a, 1999b; Friedrichs 1999; Schwartz & Friedrichs 1994).

■ *Postmodernity as a Stage of Society*

It is important to distinguish between **postmodernity** as a stage of societal development and **postmodernism** as a mode of analysis or social criticism (Lemert 1997). The *modern* period of societal development is often associated with the industrial revolution of the eighteenth and nineteenth centuries and the growing mechanization and bureaucratization of social life. This period was characterized by faith in science as a means of gaining control over the forces of nature and of achieving progress for humankind. The postmodern period is associated with the technological revolution in mass communications and computerization (e.g., television, Internet) that began in the latter half of the twentieth century, with implications that we are only beginning to understand.

In postmodern society we increasingly experience life as "a media-generated 'virtual' reality," where we lose sight of the difference between what is symbolic or simulated and what is real (Schwartz & Friedrichs 1994:225). Mass advertising drives people to view consumption as the ultimate measure of self-worth, creating an insatiable appetite for "things" that are consumed not just for their practical function but for what we think the product says about us—that a car begets sex appeal, a toothpaste self-confidence, a soft drink popularity (Barak & Henry 1999). Or take the infotainment crime shows, for instance, which blur the distinction between news and entertainment (see Chapter 1). Although we are given the impression that we are "really there," we are in fact being subjected to a well-orchestrated form of legal theater that powerfully influences our perceptions of crime and criminal justice (Manning 1999). Moreover, local incidents such as the Rodney King beating, the O.J. Simpson trial, and the Columbine high school shootings are transformed into media events that take on broader national significance as they become embedded in the public's consciousness and become fodder for media "talking heads" seeking to exploit the incident for television ratings as well as for politicians vying for political gain.

At the same time, however, media-generated reality may have a democratizing influence, opening up the "backstage" of a criminal justice system that was previously private, beyond public scrutiny (Manning 1999). Now that we've seen police brutality on videotape, for example, everyone (not just racial/ethnic minorities) knows that such behaviors exist. And it's sometimes average citizens, armed with video camcorders, who are offering us this glimpse of the world. Indeed, we have George Holliday, a manager of a plumbing company, to thank for videotaping the Los Angeles police officers who beat Rodney King that March 1991 morning (Cowley 1991; Skolnick & Fyfe 1993). Nevertheless, one is left wondering if some zones of privacy should remain protected. Believing that they should, the U.S. Supreme Court issued a ruling in 1999 that prevents journalists and photographers from accompanying police into people's homes in order to observe searches or arrests. The Court argued that such practices violated citizens' Fourth Amendment right to privacy (Greenhouse 1999).

Crime in the computer age. The computerization of society is another characteristic of postmodern society. Crimes that were unheard of two decades ago have now become commonplace. In the world of computer crime, it is not even necessary for motivated offenders and suitable targets to meet in the same physical space and time (see "routine activities" theory in Chapter 4). A knowledgeable computer programmer, for instance, can access payroll or bank accounts from afar and program the computer for a crime that will take place at some future date. In one case, an employee of a big-city welfare department stole $2.75 million "by entering fraudulent data into the computerized payroll system and . . . creating a phantom workforce complete with fake social security numbers" (Rosoff et al. 2002:424). In a practice known as **salami slicing**, or "shaving," programmers siphon off small amounts of money from a large number of accounts to yield huge ill-gotten gains. In one case an employee of an investment firm stole $200,000 by creating fraudulent computer accounts and then filling them "by diverting three tenths of a cent interest [earned] from actual accounts" (p. 424). Some computer thieves are fairly adept at covering their crimes. "We only read about the failed computer criminals. The really successful ones are never detected in the first place" (Schuyten 1979:D2).

Increasingly computers are being used for a variety of illegal and disturbing purposes. For example, banks have used computers to electronically transfer (launder) illegal drug proceeds, and right-wing hate groups have used the Internet to communicate with sympathizers and potential recruits (see Chapters 6 and 10). Information about making bombs has become easily available on the Internet. In addition, **computer hackers**, individuals who gain access to an individual's or organization's computer system without authorization, have caused abundant damage. Hackers are primarily intelligent young men who are often "motivated by the challenge of figuring out how to beat a security system" and who exhibit a "high level of skill, knowledge, commitment, and creativity" (Barlow & Kauzlarich 2002:109). Hackers have spawned their own subculture, in which they exchange information on the Internet, communicate through a common argot, and develop a sense of camaraderie. They do not necessarily commit crimes but simply enjoy exploring a system to learn about its capabilities and vulnerabilities (Carter & Bannister 2002; McCaghy et al. 2003).

Some hackers implant **computer viruses** into other systems. Viruses are sets of instructions that cause a computer to perform unauthorized operations and that spread from one computer system to another as "the 'infected' program is copied or transmitted. . . . Viruses may be relatively benign, such as . . . [one] that merely displays an innocuous message on a computer screen," or they can create serious damage by erasing files, changing data, or forcing the system to crash (Barlow 1996:208). Hackers have forced businesses to shut down and caused millions of dollars in damage. They have broken into military computers and stolen sensitive information about weapons systems and battle simulations. Copyright infringement, through the illegal downloading of software, music, and business information, abounds. Computerized power grid systems and electronic voting machines are also susceptible to hacking (Dugger 2004; Krane 2003).

Recently, the problem of **identity theft** has become a growing concern. Here programmers access databases that contain information on individuals (e.g., social security numbers, credit reports, ATM and charge accounts) and use this information for fraud and theft. Corporations that sell private customer information to other companies make the public even more vulnerable to this type of crime (Carter & Bannister 2002; Court 2003; McCaghy et al. 2003; Rosoff et al. 2002).

In addition, computers have been used to facilitate sexual exploitation. Child pornographers and pedophiles use the Internet to buy and sell pornographic materials, exchange information, and "troll" for potential victims (McCaghy et al. 2003; Nordland & Bartholet 2001; Rosoff et al. 2002). These people share information and experiences, and their ability to communicate with each other validates their sense of normality, makes them think, "See, I'm not so weird. There's lots of people out there who like the same things I do" (Washington 2002:A5). Computers have even been used for **cyberstalking**. One victim described feeling terrified and confused when men started calling and even knocking on her door soliciting sadomasochistic sex. After the police told her they couldn't help, she started taping the creepy phone messages and returning the calls, explaining to the solicitors that she was being victimized and asking for help tracking the culprit. Eventually she discovered that "a stalker had assumed her identity in cyberspace and was posting ads on the Internet seeking men to fulfill kinky sexual desires" (Foote 1999:64). The cyberstalker had not only been giving out her address but also directions to her apartment, "details of her social plans and even advice on how to short-circuit her alarm system." The cyberstalker was eventually arrested and charged with solicitation for rape, computer fraud, and violating a law that criminalizes stalking and harassment on the Internet.

Cyberstalking and using the Internet to transmit child pornography or arrange sexual liaisons with juveniles are criminal offenses. But most of the sexually explicit interactions or transmissions via computer (from "hot chats" to digital videos) are not. In fact, there are some 300,000 Internet sites that offer cyberpornography, which U.S. courts have ruled is constitutionally protected "speech" (Schlosser 2003). Also available are interactive pornographic CD-ROMs. For instance, a *Penthouse* CD-ROM titled "Virtual Photo Shoot" features "video footage of models . . . [that] changes instantly in response to the viewer," who directs the actions by choosing from an array of commands such as "Take Bra Off," "Suck Finger," or "Touch Self" (Tierney 1994:18).

So-called **webcams** offer yet another computer-based virtual experience. Nowadays "there are hundreds, if not thousands of people" who have set up video cameras in their homes in order to bare "their lives 24 hours a day on the World Wide Web" (Reichard 1998:35). These webcams capture still images at specific intervals (from thirty seconds to three minutes), which are sent out on the Internet. Although most of what viewers see are people (predominately women) doing everyday things, some viewers spend hours watching, hoping to catch a glimpse of Jenny or Samantha or Tiffany stripping down to their underwear, toweling off after a shower, or entertaining a lover. One can't help wondering whether some viewers will conclude that women are natural exhibitionists or whether some real-life "Peeping Toms" will tell themselves, "My looking in windows can't really be so bad if these girls set up cameras in their bedrooms!" The question remains whether virtual realities like webcams and cyberpornography will play a role in desensitizing some portion of the public to the harms of sexual exploitation (see Chapter 9).

Finally, the computerization of society is also evident in postmodern methods of crime control, which range from computerized national systems of crime data, high-tech military hardware, metal detectors, and electronic surveillance of offenders and communities. The Compstat computer tracking system, first used by the New York City police and then adopted by other departments, "offers the police unprecedented power to track and analyze daily crime statistics block by block and deploy resources accordingly." Chicago police have established a website as part of their community policing program whereby "police and citizens can communicate easily, directly, and sometimes anonymously" (Laporte 1998:217). Through the site residents can send information about illegal activity in their communities and notify law enforcement of the whereabouts of wanted criminals or missing persons. Even a daily newspaper, the *San Antonio Express-News,* operates a subscription website that enables residents to access up-to-date information about crime in their neighborhoods. Some of these developments seem beneficial, but some may increase fear or raise concerns about privacy. Do we really want police patrolling our streets with closed-circuit cameras? Do we want our employers training cameras on us at work? Or department store personnel watching us in dressing rooms? Do we want the government or businesses sharing information about us with others? Have our lives become one big "electronic fishbowl"? Has "big brother" become our neighbor with a video camcorder? These are all serious questions that remain unanswered as we plummet forward into the future (Garfinkel 2000; Hill 1998; Stevens 1999).

To be sure, postmodernity is about more than computerization, electronic surveillance, media-generated reality, and the like. More generally, it "is about the extent to which our world has changed . . . in some . . . unmistakable . . . [and] meaningful way" (Lemert 1997:20, 53). For better or for worse, things are no longer as they once were.

◼ *Postmodernism as Social Criticism*

"Postmodernism" is a term used not only to describe a stage of society but also a mode of analysis or social criticism. In this regard, there are two general trends in postmodern thought: **skeptical postmodernism** and **affirmative postmodernism** (Friedrichs 1999). Skeptical postmodernists are deeply cynical about the modernist belief that science and technology can be used to achieve a better world, viewing notions of progress as an illusion. One of the primary impacts of modernization, they believe, has been the extension and amplification of the scale of violence throughout the world, not only in wars but in genocide as well. As Michael Dobkowski and Isidor Wallimann observe, "The 20th century can be characterized as the 'age of genocide.' The 'progress' of this century has been constant along its journey of horrors—from the massacre of the Armenians, to Stalin's planned famine in the Ukraine, to the Holocaust, to the killing fields of Cambodia, to the ethnic massacres in Burundi and Rwanda, to the ethnic cleansing in the former Yugoslavia" (1998:1). And Charles Lemert adds, "Postmodernism, if it is about anything, is about the prospect that the promises of the modern age are no longer believable because there is evidence that for the vast majority of people worldwide there is no realistic reason to vest hope in any version of the idea that the world is good and getting better" (1997:xii).

Some skeptical postmodernists also question whether it is possible to discover any central enduring "truths" about the human condition or the nature of social relationships. They believe there are multiple or different truths, each with its own undergirding of political interests aimed at domination of one group by another. Thus doubt is "the essential postmodern sensibility," compelling us to view calls for radical social change or even for reform as "self-indulgent fantasy and illusion" (Musolf 1993:233; Schwartz & Friedrichs 1994:237).

There is, on the other hand, an affirmative postmodern vision that celebrates the value of "differences" among people (e.g., race/ethnicity, gender, sexual orientation), that wants to give voice to those who have been marginalized by society, and that is optimistic about people's ability to change both themselves and the world in which they live (Schwartz & Friedrichs 1994). Unfortunately, differences in society are all too often "criminalized, stigmatized, or otherwise devalued" (Arrigo 1999b:259). And to these post-modernists this is the essential nature of crime: the use of "power to deny others their ability to *make a difference*" (Henry & Milovanovic 1996:116, emphasis added). Social justice in the good society would not require "that we do away with difference but that we think carefully about which differences . . . [should] matter and that we continually critique our own role in perpetuating differences that should not matter" (Wonders 1999:123).

In affirmative postmodernism, of which peacemaking criminology is a part, "social justice" is valued over "criminal justice" (Arrigo 1999b). Although what constitutes a just society and how it can be achieved are precisely the issues that divide many of us today, affirmative postmodernism provides us some food for thought. To reiterate a point we made earlier, the most fundamental cause of crime may be viewed as any social process that allows one "the delusion that they are unconnected to those with whom they interrelate" (Henry & Milovanovic 1994:124). Criminals, quite clearly, often feel unconnected to their victims. In this respect they are a reflection of ourselves, for many of us experience our world as a collection of "atomized individuals in crass pursuit of their own aggrandizement" (Cullen et al. 1999:197). How many of us long for a better world, one that fosters and sustains mutuality and community? As Michael Lerner writes in *The Politics of Meaning,* "Crime will be reduced [only] when people feel a social bond toward one another. That bond . . . is the cumulative product of a society that validates the spiritual and ethical dimensions of human reality, that embodies in all its actions a respect for every human being, and that encourages and rewards mutual recognition and caring among all" (1996:3, 146).

PART 2

Patterns of Criminality and Victimization

6

Corporate and
Organized Crime

In 1965 Ralph Nader published *Unsafe at Any Speed,* a book that exposed structural design defects in General Motor's Corvair that caused it "to become uncontrollable and to overturn at high speeds" (Cullen et al. 1987:152). Nader offered the Corvair not as an isolated case but as an example of all-too-common corporate misconduct that sacrifices "human well-being for profits" (1965:ix). A serious contemporary dilemma, Nader believed, was "how to control the power of economic interests which ignore the harmful effects of their applied science and technology." His exposé of the automobile industry established him as the leading spokesperson of the contemporary consumer rights movement. It also gave impetus to federal legislation that established the National Highway Traffic Safety Administration (NHTSA), a division of the Department of Transportation (DOT), to regulate the automobile industry in the United States.

Several years later, in 1971, Ford Motor Company chairman Henry Ford II and president Lee Iacocca met with President Richard Nixon in the White House Oval Office to express their concern about NHTSA safety standards. As excerpts from the infamous Watergate tapes reveal, Ford told the president, "What we're worried about . . . is the economy of the United States. . . . If the price of cars goes up because emission requirements is gonna be in there, . . . safety requirements are in there, bumpers are in there . . . it'll kick up the prices of cars . . . so high that people . . . [are] gonna buy more foreign cars" (Cullen et al. 1987:156–157). Iacocca added that he had repeatedly complained to DOT officials that the automotive industry couldn't withstand further regulation. He continued,

> And the Japs are in the wings ready to eat us up alive. So I'm saying . . . "Would you guys cool it a little bit? You're gonna break us." . . . And they

187

talk about Naderism, and . . . the great pressure on them [and that] "people want safety." . . . I say, "What do you mean they want safety? We get . . . letters. . . . We get thousands on customer service. . . . We don't get anything on safety!" (pp. 157–158)

President Nixon was quite sympathetic to Ford Motor Company's antiregulatory stance. "We can't have a completely safe society or safe highways or safe cars and pollution-free and so forth," he said. "Or we could . . . go back and live like a bunch of damned animals. . . . But . . . the environmentalists and . . . the consumerism people . . . aren't really one damn bit interested in safety or clean air. What they're interested in is destroying the [capitalist] system" (p. 156).

Between 1971 and 1976 Ford Motor Company manufactured Pinto automobiles that suffered massive fuel-tank leaks during rear-end collisions at low to moderate speeds (about thirty miles per hour). These leaks stemmed from a design problem involving the placement of the gas tank only six inches from the rear bumper. This placement was intended to reduce trunk space to make the car smaller, lighter, and cheaper in order to compete with Japanese and German automakers who had cornered the market on small-car sales. Upon impact, however, large quantities of gasoline could spill out of the Pinto if the tube leading from the tank to the gas cap was severed or if the bolts on the differential housing (the bulge in the middle of the rear axle) punctured the tank. "At that point, all that was needed to ignite the fuel and to create an inferno was a spark—from steel against steel or from steel against pavement" (Cullen et al. 1987:161).

At one time it was estimated that burning Pintos caused the deaths of at least 500 burn victims who otherwise would not have been seriously injured (Dowie 1977). This estimate is probably exaggerated. But a NHTSA report published in 1978 did verify thirty-eight Pinto fires involving twenty-seven fatalities (twenty-six due to burns and one due to impact injuries) and twenty-four nonfatal burn injuries (Birsch & Fielder 1994). As these figures are based on police accident reports that often fail to report fires or distinguish between deaths due to fires and deaths due to impact, some fire deaths were probably not recorded as such. Douglas Birsch and John Fielder conclude, "It is likely that the number of unnecessary deaths exceeded [the NHTSA estimates] . . . but it is impossible to determine accurately how many deaths there were" (p. 10).

Especially controversial was the fact that the design problem was known to Ford managers and engineers *before* the Pinto was put on the market! Ford had considered alterations that could have prevented the gas leakage (e.g., lining the gas tank with a rubber bladder, covering the bolts on the housing with a polyethylene shield). Ford officials, however, did not think these safety measures were worth the cost. As one high-ranking Ford engineer recalls, "Safety wasn't a popular subject around Ford in those days. With Lee [Iacocca] it was taboo" (Dowie 1977:21).

In spite of considerable resistance and delay by Ford, the NHTSA eventually forced the company to recall the Pinto and fix the problem. Ford also paid many millions of dollars as a result of civil lawsuits brought against it, and it was prosecuted in an Indiana criminal court for "reckless homicide" in the 1978 deaths of three teenagers. This was the first time in history that a homicide indictment had been brought against a corporation for manufacturing a defective product. (Corporations may be considered as "persons" for the purpose of criminal prosecution.) But the jury found reasonable doubt as to Ford's criminal intent and acquitted the company (Cullen et al. 1987).

Corporations in capitalist societies are set up for legitimate business purposes. Ford Motor Company, for example, did not manufacture the Pinto for the purpose of killing and maiming consumers. Yet in the course of ostensibly legitimate business activities, law violations all too often occur. Although these are usually civil and regulatory violations rather than criminal violations, they are violations nonetheless (see Chapter 1).

In this chapter we use our sociological imagination to examine the phenomenon of organizational crime perpetrated by businesses in the United States. We will not be constrained by a legalistic definition of crime but will also consider analogous social injuries. Most of the chapter focuses on **corporate crime** committed by corporate employees on behalf of the company in which they work. The principal driving force of such crime is to increase company profits. Individuals benefit indirectly, as they are often rewarded for the (illegal) profits they make for their organization. In the latter part of the chapter, we examine crimes committed by business organizations that are set up explicitly for criminal purposes. Commonly known as **organized crime**, these groups aim to profit from illegal enterprises in areas such as drugs, gambling, and loan-sharking (lending at exorbitant interest rates). As we shall see, however, the activities of organized crime often resemble and blur into the world of legitimate business.

Earlier we discussed how anomie/strain theory may be used to explain corporate and organized crime (see Chapter 4). You will recall that strain theory, most often applied to lower-class criminality, views crime as a response to blocked opportunities for the achievement of culturally valued financial success goals. Financial success goals are especially acute in business organizations, and an organization's prestige and status—as well as the prestige and status of its members—are dependent upon its ability to maintain and expand profits. Competition with other organizations, unpredictable economic markets, or the simple desire to make as much money as possible can exert sufficient pressure on organizations to engage in unlawful behavior.

Strain theory also suggests that crime occurs not only when legitimate opportunities are blocked but also when illegitimate opportunities are available. In this regard, organizations provide members with greater resources for committing crime on a large scale, and getting away with it, than individuals acting alone would have. The division of labor within the organization allows for the diffusion of tasks and responsibility, making it difficult to pinpoint the person (or persons) who actually committed the act. Importantly, individuals higher up in the organizational hierarchy are able to delegate tasks and responsibility to others in order to protect themselves. Organizations also provide members with means of protection through bribery or corruption of law enforcement. What is noteworthy about legal organizations, however, is that the same resources that are used for lawful behavior are the ones that are used for unlawful behavior (Cressey 1972; Jamieson 1994; Poveda 1994b; Vaughan 1983).

■ Business Concentration and Corporate Crime

The **industrial revolution**, which began in Great Britain and took hold in the United States in the nineteenth century, introduced both power-driven machinery and factory organization into the production process. In post–Civil War United States, industrialization dovetailed with westward expansion to fuel unprecedented economic growth. The business **corporation** emerged as the capitalist economic unit most capable of coordinating and rationalizing large-scale economic activity and of providing a vehicle for the concentration of investment capital. Through the legal chartering of corporations, the government (mostly state governments) granted these enterprises the right to own property, manufacture and buy and sell products, and bring lawsuits as if they were individual persons. Corporations now constitute about 15 percent of all businesses in the United States and account for over 75 percent of all business assets (Carson 2002; Inverarity et al. 1983).

In the latter part of the nineteenth century, the railroads played a key role in the initial expansion of corporations by providing a system of transportation that integrated the nation into a single marketplace. Thus companies like Montgomery Ward and Sears Roebuck were able to sell their products directly to consumers through mail-order catalogs. Similarly, national "chain" stores were able to integrate wholesaling, distributing, and retailing functions, to guarantee sufficient supply and uniform products, and to extend credit to subsidiaries.

The corporate mode of organization proved highly suitable to the national marketplace. Its militarylike, top-down organizational structure was capable of administering hundreds of subunits across a wide geographic territory. An expanded cadre of professional executives, middle-level managers, and functional and technical specialists worked together "to mobilize capital, equipment, technological talent, and labor over the extended periods associated with modern industrial production" (Inverarity et al. 1983:223).

One of the problems facing corporations, however, was their inability to rationalize or achieve predictability in the marketplace. Competition among firms threatened their profitability, even their survival. Businessmen came to realize that cooperation might serve them better than competition. Railroads, for example, entered into pools or trade associations that fixed rates of profit and allocated business among competing lines. Some corporations entered into cooperative trusts or holding companies whereby a board of trustees would "coordinate the economic activities of the various member corporations, who voluntarily surrendered their individual autonomy to a centralized authority" (p. 225).

At the same time, corporations remained unaccountable to the public, despite the fact that their concentrated wealth and cooperative arrangements seemed antithetical to many Americans' belief in a "free market" competitive economy. Small farmers in particular blamed the exploitative profit-making of railroad and grain-elevator operators for a series of agricultural depressions that occurred in the latter third of the nineteenth century. They attributed "falling prices, rising costs, increased debts, and massive foreclosures [to] the monopolistic control of corporations and trusts," and they organized opposition political groups and parties like the Grangers and Populists to press for regulatory reform (McCormick 1977:31).

▪ Antitrust Law and the Decline of Moral Indignation

As state laws proved inadequate to regulate corporations that were national in scope, the U.S. Supreme Court gave the federal government the exclusive right to regulate interstate commerce. In 1890 the U.S. Congress passed the landmark **Sherman Antitrust Act** (SAA), which contained both criminal and civil provisions. For the first time in history business combinations that resulted in a *restraint of trade* (including cooperative agreements to fix prices) or the *monopolization* of an industry became federal offenses that could be prosecuted as criminal misdemeanors. The SAA also "authorized injunctions to prevent further misconduct . . . [and] allowed any private person who was adversely affected . . . to bring a civil suit and to recover treble damages for any injury suffered" (Inverarity et al. 1983:230). Maximum criminal penalties were set at that time at one year's imprisonment and a $5,000 fine.

The SAA defined as crimes business activities that were previously legitimate. The moral stigma associated with these new crimes, however, was relatively weak, for though the large corporation was perceived as a threat to the traditional American way of life, it was also viewed as a source of economic efficiency, employment, and improved living standards. Some regulation of corporations was deemed necessary, but not regulation "so stringent as to curtail seriously the desirable" benefits of corporate capitalism (p. 227).

Albert McCormick (1977) has argued that the most critical period for establishing a new law as an effective mechanism of social control occurs immediately following the law's enactment. Failure to enforce the SAA was thus a key factor in the neutralization of the moral stigma associated with antitrust violations. McCormick notes that no extra funds were allocated by Congress for antitrust enforcement, and a separate antitrust division in the Department of Justice (DOJ) was not created for another thirteen years. Up until then the DOJ initiated just six criminal cases and sixteen civil cases. Among these, only one criminal case and three civil cases were successfully prosecuted, and no one was incarcerated.

Although the U.S. Supreme Court upheld the constitutionality of the SAA, laying the groundwork for future expansion of regulatory law, the Court narrowed the scope of the SAA's applicability. In a 1895 case the Court ruled that the law did not apply to companies that manufactured their products within a single state. Thus the American Sugar Refining Company, for instance, which accounted for 98 percent of the country's sugar manufacturing, was not considered an illegal monopoly. And in a 1911 case involving the Standard Oil and American Tobacco corporations the Court ruled that the SAA applied only to "unreasonable" and not "reasonable" business combinations. The SAA, therefore, had relatively little impact on the growth and consolidation of corporations in the United States (Inverarity et al. 1983; Neuman 1998).

McCormick (1977) examined data on the 1,551 antitrust cases that were brought by the DOJ between 1890 and 1969. Less than half of these cases (45 percent) were brought as criminal violations, and only a third (35 percent) resulted in conviction. Moreover, nearly three-quarters of the criminal cases (73 percent) were brought between 1940 and 1944, during a time when monopolistic practices were deemed threatening to the U.S. war effort. It was not until 1961, in the electrical equipment price-fixing case, that any corporate officials were actually imprisoned, and these men served just twenty-five days in jail (Geis 1996; see Chapter 4). In fact, the first eleven individuals to be imprisoned for antitrust violations were *labor* and *union* defendants.

James Inverarity and colleagues conclude that the SAA "symbolically affirmed a legal commitment to free competition while institutionalizing consolidation and regulation" (1983:231). For the most part, successful corporations could "have their cake and eat it, too." Some federal involvement would help stabilize the economy and achieve greater market predictability. And a centralized regulatory authority made it easier for corporations to lobby the government on their behalf. At the same time, failure to establish an identifiable group of corporate offenders (and victims) neutralized the already tenuous moral stigma associated with antitrust violations and gave rise to a dual or contradictory economic value system. As McCormick (1977:36) observes, our society "officially recognizes and pays lip service to the ideals of free competition but practices private . . . collectivism," what Edwin Sutherland (1983) described as "corporate socialism."

■ Criminogenic Market Structures

You will recall that Sutherland (1949) found that nearly half of the seventy largest U.S. corporations had engaged in law violations at their origin or in their early years of operation, making crime an essential part of their initial period of capital accumulation (see Chapter 2). He also observed that corporations within the same industry tended to have comparable rates of law violation, with companies in the meat-packing and mail-order businesses leading the way. Similarly, Marshall Clinard and Peter Yeager's study (1980) of the 477 largest manufacturing corporations found that the most frequent offenders in the 1975–1976 period were concentrated in three areas: the motor vehicle, oil refinery, and pharmaceutical industries. But while a majority of corporations had a record of law violation, 40 percent did not, and just 13 percent accounted for over half of the violations in the Clinard-Yeager study. What makes some corporations more prone to law violation than others? Are there conditions within particular industries or economic markets that are more or less conducive to law violation?

William Leonard and Marvin Weber (1970) introduced the term **criminogenic market structure** to identify elements of social structure that produce strain that generates crime. According to Leonard and Weber, criminogenic market structures consist of industries characterized by (1) a high concentration of producers who can easily get together to avoid unprofitable competition, and (2) products that retain an inelastic demand, that is, that remain in demand and continue to be purchased even if prices are increased.

The automobile industry, for example, is characterized by a high degree of seller concentration due to the formidable entry barriers inherent in a market that requires a high volume of sales in order to maintain a profitable business. Between the early 1900s and the late 1920s the number of U.S. automakers declined from 181 to 44. Currently there are only two U.S.-owned companies (General Motors and Ford), since Chrysler was acquired in 1998 by the German-based Daimler-Benz, the largest industrial corporation in Europe. There has not been a successful new domestic entrant into the U.S. market since Chrysler began in 1925, and in 1980 that company needed the federal government to guarantee a $1.5 billion loan to prop up its sagging profits (Simon 2002).

The automobile industry has a well-deserved reputation for emphasizing style over safety. Leonard and Weber (1970) focus on a less acknowledged problem: the pressure manufacturers exert that constrain dealers' ability to operate ethically or within the law. The franchise agreements that manufacturers offer dealers typically require dealers to sell a high volume of vehicles at a low per-unit cost. If dealers fail to comply they may lose their franchise or receive unfavorable treatment from the manufacturer (e.g., slow delivery or insufficient supply of popular models), thus forcing dealers to recoup profits elsewhere. For instance, dealers may order new cars with accessories that customers haven't ordered and require them to pay for these if they want to receive the car. Dealers also mark up used-car prices excessively and fail to disclose the mechanical problems with these vehicles.

In addition, dealers enjoy an excessively high profit margin in their service departments. An industrywide flat rate is generally charged for particular repairs, allowing dealers to charge customers for more time than is actually spent fixing the vehicle. Dealers also have a monopoly on new parts, which enables them to charge exorbitant prices for these products. And they may charge for unnecessary repairs and unnecessary replacement of parts, as well as for repairs that are not made and parts that are not used. (Dealers are not the only establishments that make unnecessary or fraudulent auto repairs. Overall, about a third of the money consumers spend on auto repairs involves unnecessary or fraudulent work [Coleman 1998].)

Other industrywide practices include dealers turning odometers back on cars—even on "executive" cars that have been used by the dealers themselves. Dealers also cut corners by not inspecting vehicles before they are delivered to customers, and they may fail to honor warranties, claiming that repairs that should be covered are not. But again, according to some criminologists, it is the criminogenic market structure in the automobile industry that pressures dealers to engage in such practices. As Harvey Farberman notes, a small number of "manufacturers who sit at the pinnacle of an economically concentrated industry" have established an economic policy that "causes lower level dependent industry participants to engage in patterns" of unethical and illegal activities (1975:456).

James Coleman (1998), however, finds the evidence regarding the effect of market structures on corporate crime more difficult to evaluate. Much corporate crime research, he observes, is based on official records and thus suffers from some of the same flaws as official rates of ordinary crimes (e.g., they do not include large numbers of unreported crimes). Coleman suggests, for example, that the high rates of law violation in the motor vehicle, oil refinery, and pharmaceutical industries studied by Clinard and Yeager (1980) may be due, in part, to the fact that "industries whose products cause serious and clearly identifiable harm to the public or the environment tend to be subject to more stringent regulation than those that do not" (p. 203).

Coleman also notes the inconsistent results of quantitative research on the association between market structure and official rates of antitrust violations by U.S. corporations. Some studies have found higher rates of antitrust violations among firms in highly concentrated industries (industries with few firms), some have found higher rates in moderately concentrated industries, and some have found no relationship at all between antitrust violations and degree of industry concentration. Coleman reasons that antitrust practices like price-fixing would appear easier in markets dominated by a few large firms, but more competitive markets, on the other hand, might exacerbate the economic strains that encourage crime. In addition, Coleman notes that these studies are methodologically flawed in that they tend not to consider the effect of international competition.

Inconsistent findings in studies of corporate bribery of government officials also suggest an ambiguous relationship between market structure and crime. Coleman concludes that in noncompetitive industries dominated by a few firms "political bribery aimed at influencing government policies and programs" may be more common. But intense competition in less concentrated industries "appears more likely to be associated with commercial bribery [of sales or purchasing agents] to promote the sale of a firm's products" (p. 201). In either case, it is clear that one cannot understand the behavior of organizations without examining the broader opportunity structure in which organizations do business (Vaughan 1983).

■ Corporate Culture and the (Mis)management of Power

Clinard (1983) interviewed sixty-four retired middle-level managers from fifty-one Fortune 500 Corporations and found that about a third of these executives disapproved of the ethical standards practiced in their respective industries. When explaining corporate crime they tended to downplay *external* factors such as "corporate financial problems, unfair practices of competitors, or the type of industry" and to emphasize the *internal* cultural environment of the organization (p. 70). These middle managers said, for example, that in many cases the ethical history or tradition of the corporation had been established long ago by the company founder and had been passed on to subsequent generations of managers. Over 90 percent of the middle managers felt that *top managers* were responsible for setting the ethical (or unethical) tone of corporations. Over 70 percent thought that top management was generally aware of all the violations that were occurring in their companies, and an additional 22 percent thought that top management knew about some of the violations. The middle managers believed that top managements' knowledge was especially likely in cases of product-safety design defects, illegal kickbacks and foreign bribery, and antitrust (including price-fixing), labor, environmental, and tax violations.

Clinard's middle managers also drew a distinction between top managers who are "professionally oriented" and those who are "financially oriented." The former are concerned with a corporation's responsibility to consumers, the community, and the society at large, while the latter are concerned only with company profits and their personal ambition and financial gain. One manager explained, "Corporations with many violations are being run primarily for the top and bottom line in order to make a buck." Another said, "Violations are likely if top management is seeking to advance their personal reputations and be 'hot shots'" (p. 57).

Top executives are more likely than middle managers to attribute law violations to financial strains facing the company. According to one top-management official, "Business executives . . . have no right to wrap themselves in the mantle of moral philosophers and judges—especially to the detriment of the interests of their shareholders whose money they are using" (Silk & Vogel 1976:229). Top management, however, "tends to 'signal' its expectations [to subordinates] rather than [issue] specific orders to break the law" (Friedrichs 2004:201). A high-ranking Ford Motor Company engineer recalls, "Whenever a problem was raised that meant a delay on the Pinto, Lee [Iacocca] would chomp on his cigar, look out the window and say, 'Read the product objectives and get back to work'" (Dowie 1977:21). As Christopher Stone observes, top management prefers "not to know" everything their organization is doing and "they arrange patterns of reporting so they cannot find out (or . . . if they do find out, they . . . [do so] only in such a way that it can never be proved)" (1975:53).

All types of organizations, including corporations, tend to "selectively recruit new members who in many respects match those already there" (Vaughan 1982:1389). New managers are led "through an initiation period designed to weaken their ties with external groups, including their own families, and encourage a feeling of dependence on and attachment" to the company (Clinard & Yeager 1980:63). Employees learn not to question standard operating procedures. We previously noted, for instance, that executives involved in the electrical equipment price-fixing conspiracy testified that price-fixing had been an ongoing practice before they joined their respective companies and that they were expected to conform (see Chapter 4). In another case involving the marketing of an anticholesterol drug that was known by company officials to have harmful side effects, "no one involved expressed any strong repugnance or even opposition to selling the unsafe drug. Rather they all seemed to drift into the activity without thinking a great deal about it" (Carey 1978:384). Dennis Gioia, who became Ford Motor Company's field recall coordinator in 1973, remembers that at the time he "perceived no strong obligation to recall [the Pinto] and [saw] . . . no strong ethical overtones to the case whatsoever" (1996:54).

Even when managers have ethical reservations about what they are doing, the pressure from superiors to meet production quotas and target dates can be immense. As one of Clinard's subjects relates, "You get the pressure so strong from top management that you will make judgmental efforts to make things come out right even if you use unethical practices such as lying about production or marketing progress . . . [or] cutting corners . . . on quality" (1983:142). Another middle-level manger said, "When we didn't meet our growth targets the top brass really came down on us. And everybody knew that if you missed the targets enough, you were out on your ear" (p. 143).

James Messerschmidt (1997) notes that corporate managers often conflate profit-making with masculinity. "Real man(agers)" take risks and are willing to "go to the limit" to bring the company success and prove themselves worthy combatants in the competitive struggle for corporate profits (p. 101). **Man(agerial) masculinity** requires one to set aside personal or emotional concerns and make decisions without regard to their effects on people. In this context a cost-benefit approach is the perfect vehicle for corporate decisionmaking. In the midst of the Pinto controversy, Mark Dowie (1977) published a chart from a Ford Motor Company memorandum that contained calculations regarding the costs and benefits of installing a special valve in all cars and light trucks to prevent carburetor and other fuel leakages during a rollover accident (see Figure 6.1). Ford reasoned that the costs ($137 million) of installing this valve far outweighed the benefits ($49.5 million). Notice that in this estimate the potential benefits ignored by Ford included saving human injuries and lives!

Figure 6.1 Ford Motor Company Cost-Benefit Memorandum

Costs
Sales: 11 million cars, 1.5 million light trucks
Unit cost: $11 per car and truck
Total cost: 11,000,000 × ($11) + 1,500,000 × ($11) = $137 million

Benefits
Savings: 180 burn deaths, 180 burn injuries, 2,100 burned vehicles
Unit cost: $200,000 per death,[a] $67,000 per injury, $700 per vehicle
Total benefits: 180 × ($200,000) + 180 × ($67,000) + 2,100 × ($700) = $49.5 million

---

Source: Adapted from Dowie 1977.
Note: a. Ford got the $200,000 figure from the NHTSA, which had given in to auto-industry pressure to institutionalize cost-benefit analysis in regulatory decisionmaking. The memorandum was intended to persuade regulators to not adopt a new safety standard (Lee & Freeman 1999).

▪ Regulatory Law and the Deregulation Movement

Federal regulatory agencies have the main responsibility for dealing with corporate law violations in the United States. These agencies have evolved primarily during three periods of regulatory enactment. The first wave of regulation came in the early twentieth century in the wake of the social movement that had led to antitrust reform. Upton Sinclair's *The Jungle* (1906), an exposé of the horribly unsanitary conditions in the meatpacking industry, was especially instrumental in generating public support for passage of the Pure Food and Drug Act and the Meat Inspection Act in 1906. And as Sinclair's book had triggered a dramatic drop in sales due to loss of public confidence in meat products, the larger corporations also supported this legislation, for government-inspected meat served to restore public confidence. Smaller companies, however, were unable to absorb the additional cost of regulatory compliance. Hence some regulatory reform actually helped larger corporations consolidate their control of the market (Friedrichs 2004).

A second wave of regulatory initiatives was associated with President Franklin Roosevelt's New Deal policies of the 1930s. This period of reform was motivated in large part by the 1929 stock market crash and the ensuing economic depression. Many people lost their life savings to failed banks. The government hoped that public confidence could be restored through greater regulatory protection afforded by newly established agencies such as the Federal Deposit Insurance Corporation, the Securities and Exchange Commission, and the National Labor Relations Board.

A third wave of regulatory reform occurred during a period of social protest and liberal reform in the 1960s and early 1970s. The Consumer Protection Agency, the Environmental Protection Agency, and the Occupational Safety and Health Administration are among the regulatory bodies that were created during this era. The Food and Drug Administration (FDA), established by the Pure Food and Drug Act in 1906, was also given expanded regulatory powers at this time. At the outset, FDA regulatory activity was limited to spot checks designed to detect adulterated or mislabeled food and drugs. But over the years, well-publicized scandals involving harmful products prompted legislation to broaden its role in consumer protection (Clinard & Yeager 1980).

The FDA now requires food, drugs, cosmetics, and medical devices to be tested to ensure that they are safe and effective before they are sold to the public. Coleman describes the current approval process this way: "Before permitting a drug to be put on the market, the FDA requires the manufacturer to conduct extensive tests (first on laboratory animals and then on small groups of patients under carefully controlled conditions) and finally, the drug is released to a limited number of physicians to see how safe it is in ordinary medical use." He also notes, however, that "although these procedures appear to be careful and cautious, they are seriously weakened by the fact that the manufacturer, not the FDA, conducts the tests. Because drug companies often have an enormous financial stake in the drugs they test, there is a strong motivation to bias the testing procedures or even falsify the data" (1998:129).

The Richardson-Merrell pharmaceutical company's marketing of the anticholesterol drug MER/29 in the early 1960s is a case in point. Before the drug was put on the market, top-management officials had been preparing a major marketing campaign in anticipation of sales worth millions of dollars. But animal laboratory tests revealed abnormal blood changes and cataracts (some causing blindness) associated with use of MER/29. Richardson-Merrell managers told company technicians to falsify the data that were submitted to the FDA. Once approved, MER/29 was given to over 400,000 people before it was withdrawn from the market in 1962. At least 5,000 people appear to have suffered serious side effects—most notably cataracts, severe skin problems, and hair loss. A company vice president and two laboratory supervisors pleaded "no contest" to criminal charges and received probationary sentences. Richardson-Merrell, a company that made nearly $18 million in profits that year, was fined $80,000 (Rosoff et al. 2002).

The fairly "high level of consensus on the desirability of government regulation" began to erode in the late 1970s (Friedrichs 2004:249). An economic downturn coupled with high inflation was crippling the economy. Corporate officials and their political supporters blamed federal government regulation (and high taxes) for much of the nation's economic woes, and they called for the **deregulation** of the economy.

The movement toward deregulation emerged full blown with the 1980 election of President Ronald Reagan. Coleman (1998) believes that the Reagan administration would have liked to dismantle the federal regulatory structure almost entirely, but the public did not support such a radical approach. Instead the administration began a three-pronged effort to debilitate regulatory agencies: (1) the Office of Management and Budget, a federal agency that assists the president in preparing the budget and evaluating government agencies and programs, was authorized to review all new regulatory proposals, subject them to cost-benefit analysis, and reject them if they deemed it appropriate; (2) the budgets and staff of regulatory agencies were dramatically cut; and (3) new administrators sympathetic to deregulation were appointed to head the regulatory agencies.

Kitty Calavita (1983) argues that curtailment of the Occupational Safety and Health Administration (OSHA) was an especially high priority of the Reagan administration, which was hoping to put the labor movement on the defensive. OSHA had been established in 1970, Calavita believes, as a symbolic concession to organized labor, whom President Nixon had been courting for support of his reelection. At that time it was estimated that harmful workplace conditions in the United States killed at least 100,000 workers and disabled 390,000 others each year. From the very beginning, however, OSHA was underfunded and understaffed. Although it was supposed to promulgate new standards, in its first four years of operation it adopted only one, a maximum legal level of asbestos exposure. In the meantime, workers were exposed to nearly 600 new toxic substances generated annually by corporate industrial production. By 1980 OSHA had established only about three protective standards a year (and even less since then) (Coleman 1998).

As OSHA is housed in the Department of Labor, it came under the supervision of Raymond Donovan, the first secretary of labor appointed by President Reagan. Prior to his appointment, Donovan was one of two principal owners of Shiavone Construction, a New Jersey firm that had been accused many times of making illegal payoffs and bribes to union officials and local politicians. Shiavone also had a lengthy history of OSHA violations. In the six years prior to Donovan's appointment, Shiavone had been cited for 135 violations, 57 of which were for workplace conditions involving "a substantial probability that death or physical harm could result." In addition, the National Labor Relations Board had filed six charges against Shiavone for unfair labor practices (i.e., violating federal wage standards), and the Department of Labor's Employment Standards Administration had investigated a dozen complaints of race and sex discrimination. In 1985 Donovan became the first cabinet officer in U.S. history to be criminally indicted while in office. Charged with criminal fraud associated with the operation of Shiavone, he was forced to resign, even though a jury eventually found him not guilty. Such was the record of the man President Reagan appointed to protect the workers of the United States (Brownstein & Easton 1982).

Because OSHA law enforcement relies primarily on workplace inspections, OSHA's record of controlling some of the more visible safety hazards that cause workplace accidents has been better than its record of controlling occupational-related diseases that take a long time to develop (Frank 1993; Gray & Scholz 1993). Even so, one OSHA inspector said, "The typical establishment will see an OSHA inspector about as often as we see Halley's Comet" (Coleman 1998:134). Moreover, in 1981 OSHA adopted a policy of first reviewing a company's log of occupational injuries. If the company had lower-than-average injury rates, it would be exempted from a "wall-to-wall" inspection. In response to this policy, many businesses falsified their records, prompting OSHA to bring legal charges in 1986 and 1987 against Ford, Chrysler, Caterpillar Tractor, General Dynamics, Shell, and Union Carbide, among others.

Anne Gorsuch, a conservative antiregulation state legislator from

Colorado, was President Reagan's choice to head the Environmental Protection Agency (EPA). During her term in office, the EPA was increasingly staffed with people who had once worked for the very companies it was supposed to be regulating. In 1982 the so-called **Sewergate** scandal erupted, involving the EPA's rather cozy relationship with regulated firms—assurances of nonenforcement of environmental laws, "sweetheart" deals allowing polluting industries to avoid full payment of environmental cleanup costs, and delays in waste-site cleanup timetables. The scandal forced Gorsuch to resign. And Rita Lavelle, who had been appointed to head the EPA's $1.6 billion Superfund environmental cleanup program, was convicted on criminal charges of perjury for lying about her antiregulatory activities. The negative publicity associated with Sewergate forced Reagan to appoint a more moderate EPA director (Barnett 1993; Szasz 1986b).

Coleman (1998) argues that the EPA has withstood the antiregulatory movement better than OSHA has. He credits this to the political strength and lobbying efforts of the environmental movement, which enjoys much public support. Organized labor, on the other hand, has focused more on wage and benefit issues than on health and safety concerns and has been losing public support. Over the years the EPA has been able to expand its original legislative mandate to regulate air and water pollution to also include regulation of pesticides, solid and toxic wastes, and noise pollution. By 1990 its budget had returned to 1980 levels and increased throughout the Clinton administration. Nevertheless, Coleman concludes, "Although the EPA has shown considerable strength in the face of determined and powerful opposition, it has . . . fallen short of the urgent task it was created to accomplish. Every year more wilderness is destroyed, more animals are driven to extinction, more pollutants are dumped into the environment, and the rate of environmentally induced cancers continues to go up" (p. 150).

Nearly 60 percent of the middle-level Fortune 500 managers interviewed by Clinard (1983) believed that corporations cannot be relied upon to police themselves and that some government regulation is therefore needed. Nearly all, however, felt that regulation has been carried too far. They believed that there are too many rules, that the rules are too costly, complex, unrealistic, and unfair, and that regulators lack familiarity with corporate problems.

David Friedrichs (2004) notes that it is difficult to accurately measure the costs and benefits of regulatory policies. Parties in the regulatory debate have an incentive to inflate or deflate costs and exaggerate or conceal benefits. In matters of environmental, health, and safety protection, it is especially hard to estimate long-term costs and benefits. The HIV/AIDS epidemic, for example, has generated public support for speedier approval of experimental drugs, since persons with incurable, fatal diseases such as HIV/AIDS and some cancers are obviously "willing to run the risks of . . .

unknown side effects from a drug that offers them some hope of survival"
(Coleman 1998:130). Approximately 80 percent of new drugs put on the
market, however, are not medical breakthroughs. They are "me too" drugs
that duplicate similar products (Neergaard 1998; Relman & Angell 2002).

Nevertheless, regulatory agencies for the most part enjoyed greater
support from the Clinton administration than from Republican predecessors
and the subsequent Bush administration. Whereas corporate price-fixing,
for instance, has been largely ignored during Republican administrations,
the ten largest fines ever given for price-fixing were handed down during
the Clinton years. In 1996 Archer Daniels Midland (ADM), a grain and
soybean processing conglomerate whose products are used in a wide range
of goods, led the way with a recording-breaking $100 million fine. ADM's
price-fixing violation involved the lysine used in animal feed and the citric
acid used in food and beverages. ADM agreed to the fine in order to avoid
an even more costly penalty (which the government agreed to waive) for
antitrust activity involving its high-fructose corn syrup. However, as ADM
had $2 billion in cash on hand, it was easily able to absorb the $100 million
fine (Coleman 1998; Rosoff et al. 2002).

The Clinton administration also pursued a controversial antitrust case
against Bill Gates's Microsoft Corporation. In 1999 a federal judge ruled
that the company had abused the virtual monopoly it had on its Windows
operating system to gain an unfair advantage over competitors on the sale
of other products. The most egregious case involved Microsoft exerting
pressure on retailers who sold Windows to sell Microsoft's Internet
Explorer browser rather than the Netscape Navigator browser. At one time
Netscape controlled a larger share of the Internet browser market, but
Microsoft now dominates that area. Similar accusations have been raised
over the process by which Microsoft's Word word-processing software
achieved market dominance over WordPerfect. Microsoft has also denied
competitors technical information about Windows, which caused problems
for consumers using other companies' products (Glass 1999; *New Republic*
2000; Phillips 2002).

The judge in the federal case suggested that severe sanctions might be
in order, including breaking Microsoft into two or more companies and
increasing governmental monitoring of its contracts with retailers and its
future corporate acquisitions. Microsoft appealed the ruling, and when the
Bush administration took office a modest settlement was proposed. This
settlement essentially limited sanctions to a requirement that Microsoft provide competitors with technical information that would allow them to run
their software more seamlessly with Windows.

Regardless of the regulatory policies of particular administrations,
larger corporations are always better able than smaller firms to withstand
the constraints of regulatory controls. Their greater financial resources and

market share enable them to absorb costs or pass them on to customers, and they are more likely to have the technical and legal expertise to challenge regulations effectively and negotiate favorable terms with regulators (Coleman 1998; Yeager 1987). Typically the regulatory response of first resort is for a federal agency to enter into negotiations with the corporation and/or issue an official warning that further action will be forthcoming unless the company takes measures to remedy the problematic activity. Successful negotiations between regulators and corporations may involve a consensual agreement to "cease and desist" from further violations and/or recall the product and make the necessary repairs. In doing so, the company admits to no legal culpability that can be used against it in subsequent civil or criminal cases. If a settlement cannot be reached, then the regulatory agency may decide to pursue further administrative, civil, or even criminal actions that carry heavier sanctions. Clinard and Yeager (1980), however, found that no penalties were issued in over three-quarters of the cases they documented in their study.

■ The Economic and Physical Costs of Corporate Crime

Criminologists often note that the economic costs of white-collar crime, including corporate crime, exceed the costs of ordinary street crime. In the their book *Profit Without Honor: White-Collar Crime and the Looting of America,* Stephen Rosoff and colleagues write, "Annual losses from white-collar crime are probably 50 times as great as the losses from ordinary property crime." The cost of the taxpayer bailout of a single corrupt, federally insured savings and loan in the late 1980s, for example, "surpassed the total losses of all the bank robberies" in U.S. history (2002:viii).

White-collar crime also entails enormous *physical* costs. Jeffrey Reiman (2004), for instance, argues that far more people are seriously harmed each year from occupational hazards than from ordinary street crime. After reviewing the available data on deaths and injuries due to occupation-related diseases and other workplace hazards, he concludes that over 55,000 workers die, and another 3 million get sick or are injured, as a result of dangerous occupational conditions each year. This toll greatly exceeds the approximate 16,000 homicides and 890,000 aggravated assaults that occur annually. Although Reiman acknowledges that not all occupational hazards involve crime or other law violations, he observes:

> What keeps a mine disaster from being [viewed as] a mass murder . . . is that it is not a one-on-one harm. What is important in one-on-one harm is . . . the *desire of someone (or ones) to harm someone (or ones) else.* An attack by a gang on one or more persons or an attack by one individual on several fits the model of one-on-one harm; that is, for each person harmed there is at least one individual who wanted to harm that person. Once he

selects his victim, the rapist, the mugger, the murderer all want this person they have selected to suffer. A mine executive, on the other hand, does not want his employees to be harmed. He would truly prefer that there be no accident, no injured or dead miners. What he does want is something legitimate. It is what he has been hired to get: maximum profits at minimum costs. . . . If ten men die because he cut corners on safety, we may think him crude or callous but not a murderer. He is, at most, responsible for an *indirect harm,* not a one-on-one harm. . . . The ten men are dead as an unwanted consequence of his (perhaps overzealous or undercautious) pursuit of a legitimate goal. (p. 67)

We believe it is important for students to be familiar with the pervasiveness of corporate crime, with how it impacts nearly every area of society. What follows is a review of some of the most notable instances of corporate crime that illustrate its historical and ongoing legacy, a legacy that has entailed significant costs to *workers, consumers, and the general public.* All told, these crimes constitute what conflict and critical criminologists refer to as "crimes of economic domination" (Quinney 1977), crimes that are imposed upon us from atop, crimes that underscore Gabriel Tarde's observation that "criminal propensities . . . travel downward and outward— from the powerful to the powerless" (quoted in Beirne & Messerschmidt 1995:367; see Chapters 4–5).

■ Costs to Workers

Many of the occupational harms experienced by workers are not immediately observable. They involve debilitating diseases that take years (often decades) to develop. Craig Calhoun and Henryk Hiller (1988) have labeled these types of diseases **insidious injuries.** Insidious injuries entail diseases where the link between the cause of the malady and its manifest symptoms is obscure. They have a long gestation period and "strike only a segment of the exposed population, either randomly or patterned by varying individual vulnerabilities." Moreover, insidious injuries "manifest themselves by raising . . . risk for diseases that also have other causes" (p. 163). Occupational exposure to workplace toxins, for example, may multiply the risk of cancer from other sources (e.g., cigarette smoking, air pollution).

Exposure to asbestos has been a significant source of insidious injuries for millions of workers in the United States. Asbestos is a fibrous mineral mined from rock that has been used mainly as a fire retardant in products such as textiles, brake linings, and especially construction materials (insulation, ceiling and floor tiles, pipe wrap, textured paint, cement). Asbestos fibers can crumble and become airborne. When inhaled over the long term these fibers can cause several debilitating if not fatal lung diseases, including cancer, as well as damage to other internal organs (Rosoff et al. 2002).

The Johns-Manville Corporation has been a major manufacturer of asbestos. Internal company documents going back to the 1930s and 1940s indicate that the company had full knowledge of its harmful effects. To protect itself from financial liability, Johns-Manville had a policy of negotiating settlements with sick workers if they agreed to drop all other claims against the company. In addition, a Johns-Manville medical director advised that workers who had contracted illnesses but who had not yet manifested debilitating symptoms should not be informed of their condition. It was not until 1964 that Johns-Manville finally warned workers of the dangers of asbestos exposure. By 1972 it was still refusing to install a dust-control system to protect them. Company executives had calculated that it was more profitable to pay worker compensation to disabled employees or to the families of the deceased than to install the system.

In 1973 the EPA began implementing various policies to ban some asbestos applications and to ensure that asbestos in schools would be replaced if it was not at safe levels. Currently the manufacture, processing, importation, and distribution of most asbestos products have been banned in the United States. Several asbestos manufacturers have lost civil lawsuits and have been forced to pay millions of dollars in damages to injured or deceased workers or their families. In 1982 Johns-Manville negotiated a bankruptcy settlement with the federal government and was allowed to reorganize. The settlement called for Johns-Manville to set up a trust fund of some $2.5 to $3 billion to settle claims with injured parties in exchange for immunity from further lawsuits (Calhoun & Hiller 1988; Rosoff et al. 2002).

Like asbestos, the textile industry has been a source of insidious injuries to thousands of workers. Exposure to cotton dust causes an irreversible lung disease called byssinosis, or brown lung. The industry's history of denying harm and suppressing information parallels that of the asbestos industry. Over the years the southern-based J. P. Stevens company, the second largest textile manufacturer in the United States, has become known as the greatest cotton dust violator (Rosoff et al. 2002).

The 1983 film *Silkwood,* based on a true story, highlighted the dangers of working in the nuclear power industry. In the early 1970s Karen Silkwood was employed by the Kerr-McGee Corporation in Oklahoma, a company that manufactured highly radioactive (and carcinogenic) plutonium fuel for nuclear reactors. Kerr-McGee had a history of careless handling of plutonium—for instance, storing the material in leaking drums and shipping it in improper containers. Inside the plant a number of workers, including Silkwood, had been contaminated. After Silkwood was elected to be a union representative, she decided to go public in an effort to pressure Kerr-McGee to take measures to protect its employees. She contacted a *New York Times* reporter, saying she had obtained internal company documents that indicated that Kerr-McGee had falsified records regarding levels of plutonium exposure in its plant. On her way to deliver the documents to the reporter, she was killed in a car accident. Investigative journalist Jack Anderson claimed there was evidence that Silkwood's car was run off the road and that the documents she was carrying were stolen. A 1977 congressional investigation, however, concluded that her death was an accident. The following year a civil jury ruled that Kerr-McGee was liable for having exposed Silkwood to plutonium and was ordered to pay $10.5 million in damages to her estate (Rashke 1981; Rosoff et al. 2002).

Earlier we noted that OSHA has had a better record of controlling the more obvious workplace safety hazards than of controlling health hazards that emerge over the long term (insidious injuries). Even so, countless employees have been injured and killed in workplace accidents (e.g., electrocutions, head injuries, falls, fires, asphyxiation) that often involved violations of OSHA safety standards. One well-known case involved the Chicago-area firm Film Recovery Systems (FRS), a multimillion-dollar company that salvages silver from used x-ray plates. Part of the silver extraction process involves soaking the plates in a cyanide solution. Most of the employees at the FRS plant were illegal workers from Mexico and Poland who could not speak or read English very well and who thus did not understand the labels on the 140 cyanide tanks. The employees were required to add and remove plates from the tanks manually, but they were not given proper protective gloves, boots, or aprons. And although inhaling cyanide fumes can be deadly, neither were the workers given respirator masks nor was the workplace properly ventilated. In 1983 Stefan Golab, a fifty-nine-year-old Polish immigrant, died from cyanide exposure. A week later the company was cited for seventeen OSHA violations. OSHA also learned that the company had not warned its workers about the dangers of cyanide and that other workers had suffered recurring bouts of vomiting, headaches, and dizziness. One employee had lost 80 percent of his eyesight from a splash at his tank (Rosoff et al. 2002).

In the wake of the Ford Pinto reckless homicide trial, the FRS president, plant manager, and foreman were convicted of murder and received twenty-five-year prison sentences. Due to a minor technicality, however, their convictions were overturned on appeal. While the three men had been convicted of murder, the corporation had been convicted of involuntary manslaughter, leading an appellate court to rule that the defendant and the company had been convicted of two mutually inconsistent offenses. Nevertheless, the FRS prosecution was a precedent-setting workplace injury case. While there had been prior corporate manslaughter cases, there had never before been an indictment for murder. Rosoff and colleagues (2002) favor more prosecutions of this nature, hoping they will deter work-related deaths. The stigma of criminal sanctions, they believe, may potentially be more effective than civil or regulatory penalties.

▣ Costs to Consumers

In many respects price-fixing, as in the case of ADM, is the perfect corporate crime against consumers. The higher cost of the product can be distributed across millions of customers so that each person only pays a small price for the crime. Moreover, at the time of the purchase consumers do not realize they are being victimized by crime. They may think they are being ripped off by greedy companies perhaps, but they don't consider themselves crime victims. Yet corporations make millions of dollars in illegal profits each year from price-fixing activities.

We have already noted some of the economic and physical costs to consumers associated with motor vehicle industry practices, including the Ford Pinto case. Less well known than the Pinto controversy was the problem with some of Ford's automatic transmissions, which malfunctioned by slipping from "park" to "reverse," causing the (often unattended) car to roll. The NHTSA has documented at least eighty deaths as a result of such accidents between 1980 and 1985 alone. Ford, of course, is not the only company whose vehicles suffer from dangerous design defects. The "sidesaddle" fuel tanks on General Motors pickups built between 1973 and 1987, for instance, are estimated to have caused some 150 deaths. And faulty rear-end latches on Chrysler minivans built between 1984 and 1995 allowed passengers (especially children) in moderate-speed rear-end collisions to be thrown out of the vehicle, killing an estimated thirty-seven people (Barkan 2001; Friedrichs 2004; Safetyforum.com 2003).

In 2000 problems with Bridgestone/Firestone tires, which were most commonly used on Ford's Explorer sports utility vehicle (SUV), surfaced in the news. The defective tires, which were prone to tread separation that caused blowouts at high speeds, are believed to have caused over 200 traffic deaths and 700 injuries. The tragedies are made even more egregious by the fact that both Bridgestone/Firestone and Ford knew about the problem but failed to do anything about it. The tire company's response to the scandal was to blame Ford, since the Explorer was dangerously prone to rollover accidents, even though Ford had advertised the SUV as handling like a car. Some 20 million tires were recalled as both companies settled lawsuits entailing millions of dollars (*Nation* 2000; Naughton 2000; *Wisconsin State Journal* 2002b)

Other corporate law violations have involved the pharmaceutical industry. In the early 1960s, for example, it was discovered that thousands of pregnant (mostly European) women who had taken thalidomide, a drug prescribed for morning sickness and sleeping disorders, had given birth to severely deformed infants. Although thalidomide was first developed in Europe, Richardson-Merrell, a U.S. corporation, purchased the rights to sell it in the United States even though it knew the drug had already been withdrawn from the German market because it was suspected of causing birth defects. The FDA did prohibit the sale of thalidomide in the United States, despite heavy lobbying from Richardson-Merrell, but not before the corporation had distributed free pills for doctors to pass on to patients (Dowie & Marshall 1980).

In the early 1970s another pharmaceutical corporation, the A. H. Robbins Company, distributed an intrauterine birth control device (IUD) called the Dalkon Shield to about 2.2 million women in the United States and another 2.3 million worldwide. Sold without adequate premarket testing, the Dalkon Shield turned out to be both ineffective and harmful. A design defect in the wick used to insert and remove the IUD allowed bacteria to travel up into the uterus, where it caused infection. Thousands of women who used the device were rendered sterile, suffered miscarriages, or gave birth to stillborn or premature babies with congenital birth defects. At least eighteen women in the United States alone died from its use before the FDA forced its withdrawal from the U.S. market in 1974. A. H. Robbins, however, continued to sell the Dalkon Shield abroad for at least another nine months. The company even persuaded the U.S. Agency for International Development (USAID) to distribute it in over forty countries overseas. One USAID official reported that the IUD was still being used in Pakistan, India, and possibly South Africa as late as 1979. In the late 1980s, after paying millions of dollars to settle thousands of lawsuits, A. H. Robbins agreed to a settlement and declared bankruptcy, reorganized, and established a $2.5 billion fund to compensate victims (Coleman 1998; Ehrenreich et al. 1979; Mintz 1985; Perry & Dawson 1985).

In 1980 women bore the costs of another harmful product when Procter & Gamble (P&G) sent 60 million sample packages of its superabsorbent Rely tampon to 80 percent of U.S. households. Unfortunately, Rely not only contained cancer-causing synthetics such as polyurethane, but it also allowed potentially deadly bacteria to grow and move from the vagina or cervix into the uterus and then the bloodstream, causing a possibly fatal condition known as **toxic shock syndrome**. Symptoms of this disease include high fever, vomiting, sunburnlike skin rash, peeling skin on hands and feet, and damage to internal organs, including the lungs, which fill with fluid until respiratory or cardiac failure ensues. At P&G complaints about such problems were considered routine (the company had been receiving over 100 complaints per month), and company officials first attributed them to allergies. In its first year on the market, however, the Centers for Disease Control documented 55 fatal and over 1,000 nonfatal cases of toxic shock syndrome. P&G did bow to FDA pressure to pull Rely off the market, and it agreed to pay for a massive advertising campaign to warn women to stop using the product. But the corporation never admitted that the product "was defective or that they had done anything wrong" (Riley 1986; Rosoff et al. 2002:116; Swasy 1993).

During the 1980s the Eli Lilly pharmaceutical corporation marketed Oraflex, a painkiller intended for arthritis patients. When the company asked the FDA to approve the sale of the drug in the United States, it did not inform the FDA of at least twenty-six deaths that had been linked to Oraflex overseas. The drug was sold in the United States for about six months, but it was withdrawn after reports of deaths began circulating in the news. The company and one executive were criminally prosecuted, entered guilty pleas, and were fined. (The company was fined $25,000 and the executive $15,000.) It is alleged that Oraflex caused the death of about 50 people overall as well as serious liver and kidney damage in more than 900 others (Coleman 1998; Rosoff et al. 2002).

Decades after Upton Sinclair exposed contaminated food products in the meatpacking industry, millions of Americans continue to get food poisoning and some 5,000 die each year from diseased meat and poultry products, some as a result of corporate law-violating behavior (Rosoff et al. 2002). In 1998 it was revealed that the Department of Agriculture (DOA) "permitted hundreds of meat and poultry plants to operate virtually uninterrupted even while federal inspectors [filed] tens of thousands of citations against them for unsanitary conditions and food contamination" (Jaspin & Montgomery 1998:7A). One Arkansas plant operated by Tyson Foods was cited for 1,753 "critical" violations in 1996 alone, yet it did not lose a single day of production. ("Critical" is defined by the DOA as a condition "certain" to cause contamination, "certain" to reach consumers, and "certain to have a detrimental effect upon the consumer" [cited on p. 7A].)

A highly significant case in the 1990s involved silicone-gel implants that have been used for breast enlargements. Although scientists working for the Dow Corning corporation, the leading implant manufacturer, had been concerned about implant leaks and ruptures since the 1970s, Dow falsified some of its quality control tests and continued to sell the product to some 150,000 women annually for three decades. Dow claims that its critics have not proven any adverse effects from the silicone implant. However, thousands of women have filed legal claims against Dow, alleging that silicone released into their bodies has caused tremors, extreme fatigue, and connective tissue diseases such as rheumatoid arthritis, scleroderma, and lupus. Plaintiffs also believe that children breast-fed by mothers with silicone in their system have suffered similar symptoms. Dow and other breast implant manufacturers have lost several multimillion-dollar civil lawsuits. In 1995 Dow went into bankruptcy after determining that an agreement it had made the year earlier to pay over $4 billion in liability costs would not cover the claims against it (Rosoff et al. 2002).

Another significant area of anticorporate litigation in the 1990s involved the insidious injuries caused by tobacco products. Smoking has been recognized for decades "as the primary preventable cause of death in the United States" (Rosoff et al. 2002:90). Its role in heart disease and lung cancer is incontrovertible. Even research conducted by the tobacco industry itself, dating back to the 1960s, recognized these adverse effects, although this information was not disclosed until it was leaked three decades later. It has also been recently revealed that the industry manipulated the level of nicotine beyond that which occurs naturally in tobacco in order to increase the addictive quality of the product. Internal corporate memos indicate that tobacco company officials viewed cigarettes as nothing more than "nicotine-delivery systems" and saw themselves as being "in the business of selling nicotine" (cited on p. 91). Yet they continued to deny that they manipulated nicotine levels, and they repeatedly suppressed research that demonstrated nicotine's addictive properties.

It is now also clear that tobacco corporations, in spite of their denials, intentionally marketed their products to teenagers. Internal documents of the Philip Morris corporation, for example, show that in the 1970s they commissioned a poll to ascertain the smoking habits of youths as young as fourteen years of age. Philip Morris wanted to know which competing brands were discouraging the use of its Marlboro cigarettes among the young. An R. J. Reynolds company memo indicates that company officials felt "unfairly constrained from directly promoting cigarettes to the youth market," but they believed it was imperative nevertheless to "offer . . . the '21 and under' group . . . an opportunity to use our brands" (cited on p. 94).

Much of our current knowledge of industry suppression of information comes from the Ligget Group, one of the smallest of the main tobacco corporations, which broke ranks with the industry by agreeing to settle claims against it and by releasing what it described as a "treasure trove of incriminating documents" from thirty years of meetings with other tobacco companies (cited on p. 93). Although most individual lawsuits against tobacco companies have been unsuccessful, in 1998 the attorneys general of all fifty states settled lawsuits totaling nearly $250 billion to recoup public funds that have been spent treating tobacco-related illnesses. In what seems like a violation of their agreement, however, tobacco companies continue to spend nearly $130 million a year advertising their products in magazines targeted at youths (Donn 2001).

▪ Costs to the General Public

One does not have to work under hazardous conditions or use dangerous products to be harmed by corporate law-violating behavior. Since World War II the production of hazardous synthetic chemicals in the United States has increased dramatically. Today about 125 billion pounds are added to the environment each year, and only 20 percent of this waste is disposed of safely. The public cost of exposure to toxic substances in our ground, water, and air is immense. The federal government, for instance, has estimated

that as much as 90 percent of cancers may be environmentally produced (Conrad 1997; Friedrichs 2004).

During the 1940s and early 1950s, the Hooker Chemical Corporation burned and stored millions of pounds of chemical waste containing carcinogenic substances such as dioxin and benzene in Love Canal, an abandoned waterway near Niagara Falls. The canal was subsequently covered up and turned into a housing development. By the late 1970s contaminated black sludge began seeping into the basements of homes, and residents reported an unusually high number of miscarriages and stillborn and deformed babies. A 1980 study found that over 900 Love Canal children were suffering from "seizures, learning problems, eye and skin irritations, incontinence, and severe abdominal pains" (Griffin 1988:27). Internal Hooker documents indicate that the company had known of the problem as early as 1958 but failed to notify the residents. In 1984 Hooker settled a lawsuit and agreed to pay $20 million to 1,300 families who were forced to evacuate their homes. In 1995, after sixteen years of resistance, Occidental Petroleum, the parent company of Hooker, agreed to reimburse the federal government $129 million for cleaning up the site (Rosoff et al. 2002).

Over the years other communities around the country have suffered problems similar to those in Love Canal, and residents have been forced to evacuate their homes because of leaks from hazardous waste sites or contamination of drinking water. As these problems disproportionately affect poor, minority residents, some have raised concerns about **environmental racism** (Bullard 1993). One study, for example, found that in 1987 about a third of the hazardous waste landfills in the contiguous United States were located in just five southern states and that 60 percent of the waste contained in these sites was located in three predominately African American zip code areas (Bullard & Wright 1989–1990). Another study of corporate industrial accidents in Florida in the 1990s found that black and Hispanic residents were more likely to be exposed to harmful chemicals than white residents (Stretesky & Lynch 1999).

For decades harbors, beaches, and waterways all around the country have been polluted with toxic waste. These materials enter the food chain with deleterious consequences that we may not fully recognize for many years. In 1988 the New York–New Jersey coast was inundated with medical waste that washed on to public beaches. "Among the debris were hypodermic needles, IV tubing, catheter bags, and vials of blood—some of which tested positive for AIDS" (Rosoff et al. 2002:135). Some of this debris was dumped by disreputable haulers who contracted with hospitals to dispose of the waste and then disposed of it illegally. Some of the waste, however, is suspected to have come from hospital personnel getting rid of it themselves.

In 1984 a deadly poisonous gas was leaked from a Union Carbide plant in Bhopal, an impoverished city in India. It is estimated that as many as 5,000 people died and 200,000 were injured (20,000 permanently) from this tragedy. The gas leak apparently occurred as a result of Union Carbide's decision to cut corners on safety, even after it had received warnings from its engineers about a potential problem at the plant. Civil actions were brought against the company by injured parties, but Union Carbide was never officially sanctioned (Friedrichs 2004; Rosoff et al. 2002).

In 1989 the oil tanker *Exxon Valdez* lost 11 million gallons of oil when it struck a reef off the coast of Alaska, devastating the wildlife, environment, and economy of the region. Questions regarding Exxon Corporation's responsibility for the disaster arose as evidence surfaced that the company had known of the ship captain's drinking problem but had failed to take appropriate action. In addition, Exxon had reduced the size of the crew, causing the remaining crew members to work while very fatigued. The company agreed to pay $100 million in criminal penalties and over $1 billion in civil damages. It was also discovered that year that the Colorado Rocky Flat nuclear weapons plant, which was operated by Rockwell International for the U.S. Department of Energy, was contaminated and that the plant had been dumping radioactive material into local rivers. At the same time that Rockwell was fined $18.5 million for its actions, however, it also received a $22.6 million performance bonus from the federal government (Friedrichs 2004; Rosoff et al. 2002).

More recently, twenty-five miles down the road from Love Canal, residents in the Hickory Woods neighborhood of Buffalo, New York, began complaining about "Love Canal symptoms" from toxic waste byproducts left over from the operation of a steel plant (Rosenberg 2003). Environmentalists cite delays and funding cuts in the federal government's Superfund cleanup program as part of the problem. They note that the Bush administration has been cutting deals with offending corporations, placing the brunt of the cleanup costs on taxpayers and not polluters. They also criticize the Bush administration for relaxing clean air and water regulations, removing millions of acres of wilderness land from government protection, and endangering fish and other wildlife (Daly 2003; Grunwald 2003; Heilprin 2002).

In addition to physical harms, the general public of taxpayers bears the economic costs of corporate misconduct through income tax evasion. The General Accounting Office (GAO), an independent agency of the U.S. Congress that audits federal government agencies, estimates that over 40 percent of U.S. corporations fail to report interest earnings that amount to about $7 billion of untaxed income a year (Coleman 1998). Many billions more are funneled though offshore banks or lost to the federal treasury through **corporate inversion**, the process by which U.S. corporations incorporate abroad and hence avoid paying U.S. taxes (Beinart 2002; Komisar 2001). In addition, over half of the nation's top defense contractors have been the subject of Department of Justice criminal investigations for practices such as "overbilling, bribery, kickbacks, and the deliberate provision of defective weapons components and other military equipment" (Barkan 2001:342; Friedrichs 2004; Simon 2002).

Another way in which taxpayers are bilked is through Medicare and Medicaid insurance fraud, which drains from 10 to 25 percent of the multibillion-dollar budget for these programs. (Private insurance companies and patients are also victimized by medical fraud.) Medicare and Medicaid are government programs that provide health care benefits to the aged and the poor, respectively. Fraudulent practices include overcharging for services rendered, billing for services not rendered, and conducting superfluous and unnecessary tests and other medical procedures. While some medical fraud involves individual physicians operating as independent businesspeople, much of it involves large-scale businesses, including hospitals, health maintenance organizations, home-care providers, and medical laboratories. In 1998, for example, Blue Cross and Blue Shield of Illinois pleaded guilty to having submitted fraudulent Medicare claims over a period of years. They agreed to pay $144 million in fines, the largest penalty ever assessed for Medicare fraud (Friedrichs 2004; Rosoff et al. 2002; *Wisconsin State Journal* 1998a).

The savings and loan scandal. Arguably the single most devastating area of corporate financial crime in the history of the United States involved the savings and loan (S&L) scandal of the 1980s. By the time the borrowed money for the entire taxpayer bailout is paid back some twenty years into the twenty-first century, the estimated bill may exceed an unfathomable $1 trillion. Moreover, it is no small matter that criminal activity was a major factor in 70 to 80 percent of the failed S&Ls and that as much as 25 percent of the total losses were due to crime (Rosoff et al. 2002).

What was this scandal all about? The federally insured S&L system was established in the early 1930s as a depression-era measure designed to ensure the availability of home loans, promote the construction of new homes, and protect depositors from the types of financial devastation that followed the 1929 stock market crash (i.e., massive investment losses and withdrawal of bank funds). Federal regulations prohibited S&Ls from making risky investments, essentially confining them "to the issuance of home loans within 50 miles of their home office" (Calavita & Pontell 1990:311). By the 1970s S&Ls could no longer compete with other financial institutions such as mortgage companies (for home loans) and money markets (for savings investments). They were locked into long-term, low-interest loans they had previously made and were prohibited by law from offering adjustable-rate mortgages or from paying more than 5.5 percent interest on deposits (even during a period of double-digit inflation).

During the 1970s the S&L industry's net worth declined dramatically, and by 1980, 85 percent of S&Ls were losing money. At that time a complete bailout of the industry utilizing taxpayer dollars might have cost about $15 billion. But instead of cutting losses at this level, President Reagan and the U.S. Congress opted for a strategy of deregulation. Federal legislation passed from 1980 to 1982 phased out restrictions on interest rates and opened up new areas of investment for S&Ls. S&Ls were now authorized to "make consumer loans up to 30 percent of their total assets; make commercial, corporate or business loans; and invest in non-residential real estate worth up to 40 percent of their assets" (Calavita & Pontell 1993:530; Jackson 1990; Pizzo et al. 1989).

The new (de)regulations also gave the S&Ls unprecedented access to funds by removing the 5 percent limit on brokered deposits. (Brokered deposits are "jumbo" or aggregated deposits placed by middlemen that yield high interest rates for investors and exorbitant commissions for brokers.) These funds were used to finance risky speculative investments that had the potential for either high payoffs or financial calamity. In addition, S&Ls were allowed to provide 100 percent financing to borrowers, essentially giving the borrower a risk-free loan. And the government dropped the requirement that S&Ls "have at least 400 stockholders with no one owning more than 25 percent of stock," thereby allowing a single entrepreneur to own and operate a federally insured S&L (Calavita & Pontell 1993:530). At the same time, the amount of federal depository insurance was raised from $40,000 to $100,000 per deposit.

Deregulation was "the cure that killed" (Calavita & Pontell 1993:312). S&Ls lost billions of dollars through legal investments that were previously illegal, and the deregulated climate opened the industry to insider abuse and criminality. Kitty Calavita and Henry Pontell (1990, 1993) identify three general categories of fraudulent activities that occurred: unlawful risk-taking, collective embezzlement, and illegal cover-ups.

Unlawful risk-taking involved S&Ls that extended their investment activities beyond the levels allowed by law—for example, by exceeding the 40 percent limit on commercial real estate loans. In addition, S&Ls failed to conduct adequate marketability studies required to insure the feasibility of their investments.

Unlike ordinary instances of embezzlement (which typically entail lone, relatively subordinate employees stealing from the company in which they work), **collective embezzlement** involved an organization's top management in the misuse and theft of S&L funds. During the 1980s some S&L owners and managers treated their institutions as personal slush funds, throwing elaborate parties and purchasing expensive luxury goods like artwork, antiques, yachts, airplanes, and vacation homes. They also violated the law by giving themselves and their associates excessive "salaries as well as bonuses, dividend payments, and perquisites" beyond what was "reasonable and commensurate with their duties and responsibilities" (GAO, cited in Calavita & Pontell 1990:323). In addition, S&L operators engaged in a number of fraudulent loan schemes. The practice of *nominee loans* involved "straw borrowers" outside of the S&L who obtained loans on behalf of individuals within the S&L. Such schemes were used to circumvent laws that limit the proportion of an institution's loans that can be made to insiders. *Reciprocal loan* arrangements entailed insiders from one S&L authorizing loans to insiders of another S&L in return for a similar loan. *Linked financing* involved one S&L depositing money in another S&L on the condition that a subsequent loan be made to a designated party. And in *land flips* a piece of property was transferred from one party to another in a short period of time, with each transaction artificially inflating the land value, which was then used as collateral for other loans.

Illegal cover-ups entailed the manipulation and misrepresentation of S&Ls' financial books and records to conceal fraudulent practices from regulators and to prevent regulators from learning of an S&L's pending financial insolvency, which might have forced the closing of the institution. Government officials were not always adversaries of the S&Ls, however. Some regulators, wooed with lucrative "job offers at salaries several times . . . their modest government wages," even collaborated with S&L operators to shield them from scrutiny and criminal prosecution (Calavita & Pontell 1993:535). Even more important were connections between S&L executives and elected officials. California representative Tony Coelho, for instance, as chair of the Democratic Congressional Campaign Committee (DCCC) in the mid-1980s, regularly solicited S&L industry money to fund the DCCC. Coelho admitted that "doing official favors for donors was permitted. The unforgivable sin was to make the connection explicit" (quoted in Jackson 1988:104).

Texas Democratic congressman Jim Wright, who served as Speaker of the House from 1987 to 1989, was a primary beneficiary of S&L industry campaign contributions. Wright intervened on the S&L industry's behalf and threatened to hold up a much-needed Federal S&L Insurance Corporation recapitalization bill if federal regulators did not back off from their investigations of Wright's S&L associates. In 1989 Wright was forced to resign from Congress when it was learned that he had accepted about $145,000 worth of gifts from a Texas real estate developer who stood to benefit from legislation over which Wright had control (Calavita & Pontell 1993).

In perhaps the most well-known case involving collusion of elected officials and the S&L industry, California S&L magnate Charles Keating received the support of the "Keating Five"—Senators Alan Cranston (D, California), Dennis DeConcini (D, Arizona), John Glenn (D, Ohio), John McCain (R, Arizona), and Don Riegle (D, Michigan)—in his efforts to thwart regulators investigating his California-based Lincoln S&L. Keating contributed a total of $1.4 million to these senators' campaigns (Cranston's especially). When Keating's S&L was finally closed in 1989, the taxpayers were left with a bill of over $3 billion (Rosoff et al. 2002).

Keating has been the subject of several government-initiated lawsuits and criminal investigations for a host of activities involving his Lincoln S&L. In a California state court in 1992, Keating was convicted on seventeen counts of fraud for a scheme involving the sale of millions of dollars of soon-to-be worthless bonds to thousands of customers, most of them elderly or poor, who were told that the bonds were government-insured when in fact they were not. Some of the victims lost their entire life savings. The following year he was convicted in federal court on seventy-three counts of fraud, conspiracy, and **racketeering**. (Under federal law, "racketeering" refers to a pattern of criminal activities that occur over a period of time and that are associated with a particular financial enterprise.) Keating received a maximum prison term of ten years for his state convictions and nearly thirteen years for his federal convictions. In 1996 his convictions were overturned due to legal technicalities (e.g., improper jury instructions) (Rosoff et al. 2002).

By 1990 over 300 S&L executives, accountants, and lawyers had been convicted of criminal law violations related to the S&L scandal. The average prison term they received was just over two years. The average sentence for ordinary bank robbery is nearly eight years (Simon 2002).

Insider trading and corporate fraud. Some observers have referred to capitalism in the United States today as a "casino economy," whereby money is "made from speculative ventures designed to bring windfall profits from having placed a clever bet. . . . In contrast to *industrial capitalism,* where profits are dependent on the production and sale of goods and services, profits in *finance capitalism* increasingly come . . . from . . . [buying and selling stock]. . . . Nothing is . . . produced but capital gains" (Calavita & Pontell 1990:335–336, emphasis added).

Who benefits from this type of economy and is the game fair? Corporate profits have risen as companies have downsized and put countless employees out of work. As Rosoff and colleagues note, "It has become an economic fact of life that stock prices generally jump when companies terminate workers" (2002:235). In addition, many investors do not play by the rules. In 1934 the Securities Exchange Act criminalized **insider trading**. Insider trading occurs when "stockholders, directors, officers, or any recipients of information not publicly available . . . take advantage of such limited disclosure for their own benefit" (p. 218). The logic behind the prohibition of insider trading is that the legitimacy of capitalism depends upon the expectation of a positive association between the economic risk taken by an investor and the potential return to that investor. But "the insider trader collects the highest returns with little risk at all, while the ordinary investor, who assumes most of the risk, is exploited like some naive bumpkin lured into a rigged game of chance" (p. 234).

Between 1934 and 1979 the Securities and Exchange Commission took just 53 actions against insider trading (Friedrichs 2004). Between 1980 and 1987 it took 177. Indeed, the 1980s was a period in which the names of such high-flying insider traders as Ivan Boesky and Michael Milken dominated the news. Although some of these traders were prosecuted, they still profited in the long run. For example, in 1987 Boesky was fined $100 million dollars and sentenced to three years in prison. It is estimated, however, that he made about $200 million in illegal trades alone. And in 1989 Milken was fined a record-breaking $600 million and sentenced to two years in prison; his financial dealings had earned him over $1 billion (Rosoff et al. 2002; Stewart 1991).

Perhaps because insider trading continues to be profitable, the practice has not declined. According to a 1994 report in *Business Week* magazine, "insider trading is alive and well—and growing" (Barrett 1994:70). More recently, homemaking diva and corporate entrepreneur Martha Stewart received a great deal of attention for her involvement in insider trading. Stewart apparently received privileged information from her stockbroker that caused her to sell some 4,000 shares of ImClone Systems Inc. stock the day before "a negative government report on the ImClone cancer drug Erbitux sent its share price falling" (McClam 2003b:D10). Stewart profited about $45,000 from the deal but was subsequently indicted and convicted on criminal charges (Thottam 2003).

In spite of the publicity Stewart received, her actions pale in comparison to the devastating acts of financial fraud perpetrated by corporate executives at scores of companies that were enabled by numerous other corrupt accounting, stockbrokerage, and investment-banking firms. Enron is arguably the "poster child" company that has come to represent this multi-billion-dollar scandal. Under the leadership of Kenneth Lay, Enron was transformed from a "small pipeline operation" into a powerful energy-trading business that was at one time "nominally" the country's eighth largest corporation (Kuttner 2003a:48). Enron capitalized on its dominant market position to create an artificial energy shortage that enabled it to raise prices, most notably in California. As that state was experiencing energy blackouts and escalating prices, Enron's stock price soared. But Enron was not really making as much money as it appeared—it was "cooking the books." It did this by creating a myriad of corporate subsidiaries and using these subsidiaries and other accounting gimmicks to disguise financial losses. When the bubble finally burst, Enron investors lost some $60 billion, which included the pensions and retirement savings of thousands of people, among them Enron employees who were prohibited by the company from selling their stock. In the meantime, just before the stock price collapsed, Enron executives including Lay collectively unloaded nearly $1 billion worth of stock for themselves (Bryce 2002; Greider 2001; Reiman 2004).

Global Crossing (an optical fiber company), WorldCom (a telecommunications company), Adelphia (a cable company), and Quest Communications (a telephone company) were among the most well known of the other corporations that lost billions of dollars through fraud. Prestigious accounting firms like Arthur Andersen helped these companies manipulate their books and investment-banking firms like Citigroup and J. P. Morgan Chase & Company lent money and touted their clients' stocks to line their own pockets at the expense of naive investors. Even Dick Cheney, before being elected vice president, got into the act. As chief executive officer of Halliburton (a company that sells products and services to the petroleum and energy industry) from 1995 to 2000, Cheney cashed out stock worth about $30 million before he resigned and before Halliburton's stock plummeted amid allegations that the company engaged in the types of schemes that brought Enron and others down (Bussey 2002; Gordon 2002; Reiman 2004; Sloan 2002; Toffler 2003)

Financial corruption also rocked the formerly venerable mutual fund industry. In practices known as **late trading** and **market timing**, a few favored, big-money shareholders were allowed to profit at the expense of smaller investors (Sloan 2003). Financial adviser Humberto Cruz explains the problems associated with these practices:

> Late trading, which is illegal, involves the placing of buy or sell orders for mutual fund shares after the stock market has closed for the day at 4 p.m., but using that day's closing price. By law, those orders should receive the next day's price. Shareholders allowed to engage in late trading profit illegally from knowledge of events that occur after the market has closed when those events can be expected to affect the next day's share price a certain way. These illegal profits in turn dilute the returns that shareholders like you and I would get. Market timing, which is the rapid-fire trading of fund shares to profit from short-term market swings, is not in itself illegal. But most funds have policies against it because it drives up fund transaction costs and can disrupt management of the portfolio. (2003:C1, C4)

The full legal implications of these financial fiascos are yet to be resolved, and may never be. But a lawyer for one of the indicted executives at WorldCom indicated what a typical defense might entail: "Everyone's doing it" (McClam 2003a:C10). How true indeed!

■ The Business of Organized Crime

Corporations, as we have noted, are set up for legitimate business purposes, yet in the course of ostensibly legitimate activities, law violations all too often occur. Moreover, the same organizational resources that are used for lawful behavior are the ones that are used for unlawful behavior. The essential difference between corporate crime and organized crime is that the latter sets up its enterprise explicitly for illegal gain. Nevertheless, organized crime often resembles and blurs into legitimate business. Organized crime also obeys what Sheila Balkan and colleagues describe as "the general law of capitalist accumulation," that is, the reinvestment of profits to ensure expansion of the enterprise (1980:151)

The mainstay of organized crime as a distinct form of criminality is its systematic involvement in illegal goods and services. It is a multibillion-dollar industry that derives its largest source of revenues from drugs, followed by illegal gambling and then loan-sharking. Organized crime is also involved in high-stakes thievery: hijacking cargo from trucks, warehouses, docksides, and airports; stealing stocks and bonds from brokerage houses; and fencing valuable property (including cars). Other areas of criminality include prostitution and pornography, cigarette and alcohol bootlegging, arms trafficking, and arson-for-profit. Since the late 1970s illegal disposal of hazardous waste has been a growing area of activity. Such enterprises may be run as clandestine operations or as legitimate businesses that are operated illegally (McCaghy et al. 2003).

In addition, organized crime has significant holdings in legal businesses in such areas as the building trades and construction, the garment, fish, meat, and liquor industries, stevedoring (loading and unloading of ships), garbage collection, vending machines, casinos and hotels, restaurants and bars, entertainment, real estate, and securities/investment businesses. While these businesses allow organized crime to earn profits legally, they also generate substantial untaxed income that is skimmed off the top. Legitimate businesses also provide organized crime with a front for operating their illicit activities, with a tax cover to report earnings to the Internal Revenue Service, and with a facade of respectability that allows them to circulate among the social and political elite. Sometimes organized crime will buy into or infiltrate another business and draw on its established line of credit to order products (which are sold like "stolen property") until the business is bled dry and forced into bankruptcy. At other times organized crime will use its readiness to engage in violence to muscle out competitors who operate their businesses "by the book" (Cressey 1969; McCaghy et al. 2003).

Extortion is another area of organized crime profit-making. Extortion includes the sale of "insurance" to proprietors to ensure that their businesses "remain free of unusual 'accidents,' such as delivery people being beaten up, store windows being broken, merchandise being vandalized," and so forth (McCaghy et al. 2003:272). It may also entail intimidation of either employees or employers/managers in labor negotiations. Workers can be kept in line (e.g., deterred from organizing unions and striking) through threats of violence. Employers/managers, in turn, can be forced to grant concessions to workers through threats of strikes or walkouts.

Over the years, organized crime (or individuals affiliated with organized crime) have infiltrated the leadership of some labor unions, most notably the International Brotherhood of Teamsters. Although organized crime has at times used its clout to negotiate favorable contracts for workers, it has also used its position of power to plunder union benefit and pension funds and to invest these funds in other organized crime enterprises. On other occasions organized crime has used its influence in unions to negotiate **sweetheart contracts** with employers. A sweetheart contract is an agreement between union leaders and employers/managers that includes terms unfavorable to rank-and-file workers or permits employers/managers to violate collective bargaining agreements (e.g., using nonunion labor) in return for payoffs to the corrupt union leadership (Beirne & Messerschmidt 1995; Block & Chambliss 1981).

■ The Interdependence of Organized and Corporate Crime

Several criminological studies have explored the blurred boundaries or interdependence of organized crime and corporate crime. We have already noted organized crime's involvement in the illegal disposal of hazardous waste. Disreputable haulers dump hazardous materials in landfills, sewers, and waterways, along roadways, or just about anywhere they wish. This illegal service saves millions of dollars for corporate manufacturers of waste, for they would incur far greater costs if they had to dispose of the waste safely themselves (Szasz 1986a).

Corporations are indeed fortunate that the **Resource Conservation and Recovery Act** (RCRA) of 1976 protected them from legal liability for what happens to the waste they turn over to haulers. In his research on the creation of the RCRA, Andrew Szasz (1986a) documented how corporations lobbied heavily for a regulatory structure that would place the burden of responsibility on those involved in the final stage of disposal. He notes that the federal government could have mandated "generators to treat all of their wastes themselves, or legislated that generators retain full responsibility for their wastes even if they assign them to other parties for shipping and disposal" (p. 12).

Corporate generators of hazardous waste argue that "they do not know they are dealing with organized crime" and that "they are in fact being cheated because they pay large amounts for treatment and disposal that are not performed." But since corporations "explicitly fought for RCRA language that entitled them to a state of ignorance," Szasz finds their claims unconvincing. He observes, for instance, that "organized crime control of garbage hauling and disposal had been considered a fact of life in New Jersey for decades" and that rational industrial managers "would have had ample reason to distrust the identity of their contractual partners" (p. 17). On the other hand, Szasz does not think that corporations consciously wished to create a regulatory structure that encouraged organized crime involvement in hazardous waste disposal. Rather, they simply acted out of a general tendency to be indifferent to and to "resist full social responsibility for . . . the environmental and public health consequences" of their operations (p. 19).

The tobacco industry is another area of commerce that illustrates the blurred boundaries between organized and corporate crime. As a result of the $250 billion settlement and declining cigarette sales in the United States, tobacco companies have increasingly looked to foreign markets to sustain their profits. Evidence indicates that illegal (tax-free) smuggling is a significant way that tobacco products make their way into these markets. This occurs through criminal organizations that are sometimes aided and abetted by tobacco companies themselves (Dickey & Nordland 2000; Schapiro 2002).

Take the case of British American Tobacco (BAT), the parent company of Brown & Williamson (B&W), for example. One BAT salesman responsible for marketing BAT products in Colombia estimates that at one time 95 percent of BAT's cigarettes in that country were contraband. He says that BAT encouraged and benefited from smuggling as a way to establish market dominance for BAT and B&W products. Evidence suggests that the Philip Morris company did the same—for instance, by heavily advertising its cigarettes in Colombia at a time when its legal imports were next to zero. Both BAT and Philip Morris also initiated mass advertising campaigns and provided local distributors with favorable wholesale prices at a time "when their sales were almost entirely illegal" (Schapiro 2002:13). Additionally, the companies launched a rather cynical ploy, pressuring and bribing Colombian government officials to "lower taxes as a means of reducing the incentive for smuggling" (p. 15). With the lower tax rates in place, the companies gradually increased their legal imports. On top of all this, evidence suggests that criminal organizations within Colombia used drug profits from their U.S. sales to purchase the contraband tobacco, making the tobacco companies complicit in the laundering of drug proceeds.

This is a global problem and in 1999 and 2000 several countries in Latin America, Europe, and Canada filed racketeering lawsuits against tobacco corporations. Most of the suits have been dismissed on technical grounds, but some are still ongoing. Recently, Les Thompson, the former president of Northern Brands, a Canadian affiliate of the U.S.-based R. J. Reynolds company, pled guilty to criminal charges. According to Thompson, Northern Brands "shipped five billion cigarettes per year to the U.S. side of a small . . . Indian reservation" on the Canadian-U.S. border with the intention of having the tax-free cigarettes shipped "back into Canada for illegal resale." Thompson also said that R. J. Reynolds set up Northern Brands "expressly for the purpose of smuggling cigarettes back into Canada and was fully aware of the affiliate's efforts to encourage and support smuggling" ("Smoking Gun" 2003:3).

Arson-for-profit is another area where organized crime interfaces with legitimate business. In his research in the city of Boston, James Brady (1983) documented the collaboration between bankers and organized crime businessmen (whom Brady calls racketeers) in arson-for-profit schemes. Brady found that arson in Boston was not randomly distributed. For the most part it occurred in poor neighborhoods (primarily minority) and in buildings in these neighborhoods owned by absentee landlords (primarily white). There was curiously little arson in government-owned housing projects occupied by the poor. Brady connects this pattern to declining property values in neighborhoods where most of the arsons occurred. Some landlords, no longer finding their investments worthwhile, stopped paying their mortgages, essentially abandoning their properties. Some tried to recoup their losses by burning their properties and collecting insurance money. But this is not, argues Brady, the crux of the arson problem.

The incentive for banks to be complicit in arson-for-profit stems from the practice of **redlining**. Redlining is a discriminatory lending practice that denies residents and small businesses in some communities loans for home and business purchases and improvements. Although redlining is illegal, banks prefer to lend money to people investing in more profitable suburban areas. Redlining, according to Brady, is a principle cause of depreciating property values in the inner city, for as property values decline, landlords lose their incentive to repair their buildings and may even abandon them altogether.

Banks that foreclose on properties with unpaid mortgages are left holding an investment with little market value. Their association with racketeers, however, helps them recover their profits. In Boston, Brady found that racketeers were willing to purchase these properties from banks, provided they were required to pay little or no down payment. Banks not only agreed to this arrangement but were willing to write mortgage loans for property values that far exceeded actual market values.

With the artificial purchase price in hand, racketeers obtained additional second, third, and fourth mortgage loans and used this money to make other profitable investments. They also used the purchase price to acquire inflated insurance coverage. Then the racketeers hired professional arsonists to burn their buildings: "Often a series of fires of escalating scale [were] set to net the owner several partial insurance payments before the building [was] totally destroyed in one final blaze." Phony contractors were hired to "repair" the damage, and corrupt building inspectors were paid to file false reports, "concealing the fact that repairs were never made" (Brady 1983:11). The banks profited from this ruse as well, often more than the racketeers themselves. As Brady notes:

> Since . . . the insurance company must pay the holder of the mortgage first in the event of a fire which destroys the building, . . . the potential losses represented by foreclosed properties are converted into a substantial profit for the bank because the new mortgage paid by the insurance company greatly exceeds the old bad debt assumed under foreclosure. . . . The relationship between banks and racketeers can become quite cozy as the racketeers return again and again to the same bank and often the same loan officer. (p. 11)

Why didn't insurance companies do anything about this? Brady found that companies seeking to expand their businesses did not want to develop a reputation as tough on claims, and they were afraid of losing lawsuits if claimants who were denied payment took them to court. Neither did companies want to draw government attention to themselves, for fear it might lead to more regulation of the insurance industry itself. And some of the companies were owned by "foreign investors eager to break into the U.S. insurance market . . . [who] were unaware of the scale of arson fraud in the United States" (p. 14). Brady describes one case where four insurance adjusters were convicted along with twenty-eight other individuals for their participation in an elaborate arson-for-profit ring that included two finance company officers, four real estate agents, six lawyers, two housing contractors, a city housing inspector, the captain of the Boston arson squad, and the commander of the state fire marshal's arson squad, among others.

Another way in which banks benefit organized crime is through **money laundering**, the process by which illegal "dirty" money is made "clean" and recycled into the legitimate economy. Under U.S. law, money laundering entails engaging in a financial transaction that the person knows to involve illegal proceeds, as well as attempts to conceal or disguise information about those proceeds or failing to comply with transaction-reporting requirements (Abadinsky 2003).

Much of the money earned by organized crime is taken in as cash, most often in bills no larger than $20. When somebody shows up with a suitcase of small bills, bankers are surely aware that something is awry. Banks may even charge a percentage for accepting such deposits or for electronically transferring funds from one bank to another. In the United States, banks are required to report currency transactions of $10,000 or more. But this is not the case in many places abroad. Countries such as Switzerland, Austria, Panama, and the Cayman Islands, among others, "allow numbered bank accounts without identification of names" (Adler et al. 2001:415). Moreover, the sheer volume and speed of bank-to-bank electronic transfers make it "extremely difficult to trace . . . funds or document their illegal nature" (Webster & McCampbell 1992:5). And complicit bank officials often accommodate organized crime by wiring the money between their bank's own account (rather than their customer's account) and the account of another bank, making the laundering of illegal funds nearly indistinguishable from legal banking transactions.

The Bank of Credit and Commerce International (BCCI) illustrates a case where a bank's *primary* function was to provide financial services (including money laundering) to an assortment of drug and arms traffickers, smugglers, tax evaders, political dictators, and intelligence agencies around the globe. Established in 1972 by a Pakistani financier, the BCCI became one of the largest financial institutions in the world, with over 400 branches operating in 75 countries, including the United States. The BCCI's more infamous clients included the Colombian Medellin cocaine cartel, former Iraqi president Saddam Hussein, former Panamanian dictator Manuel Noriega, the terrorist organization Abu Nidal, and the U.S. Central Intelligence Agency. Between 1988 and 1992 the BCCI twice pled guilty to money laundering and once to racketeering, and it was forced to pay several million dollars in fines. Some bank officials were sentenced to prison as the bank was closed down and its assets were frozen (Passas 1995; Simon 2002).

■ The Structure of Organized Crime Networks

In the early 1950s, Senator Estes Kefauver headed a special congressional committee that revealed the existence of the Mafia in the United States (Albanese 1985). Kefauver's committee described organized crime as a transplant of criminal organizations originating in Italy, most notably the Italian island of Sicily. Joseph Valachi, testifying a decade later before another congressional committee, became the first person in the United States to admit publicly that he was a member of the Mafia or, as he called it, **La Cosa Nostra** (LCN) ("this thing of ours"). Valachi's characterization of organized crime was shared by criminologist Donald Cressey (1969), an adviser to the President's Commission on Law Enforcement and Administration of Justice. Both Valachi and Cressey described the Mafia or LCN as consisting exclusively of men of Italian descent who are organized into at least twenty-four tightly-knit "families" throughout the United States. Each family has an internal, militarylike hierarchical structure headed by a boss (who is advised by a *consigliere*), who serves over an underboss and a number of captains (*caporegime*) and soldiers (*soldato*) (see Figure 6.2). These families are regulated by a national alliance known as "The Commission" that oversees the different groups.

In 1980 the Federal Bureau of Investigation published data indicating that LCN organizations were concentrated in the eastern half of the United States. Only seven of twenty-seven LCN groups were located west of the Mississippi River, and about half were located in the north-central and northeastern part of the country. Thus there were (and are) many parts of the country where the criminal activities known as organized crime do not involve the LCN (Albanese 1985).

Moreover, the Valachi/Cressey portrait of organized crime "overstates the degree of structural rigidity and militaristic hierarchies of command that characterize organized crime" (Calavita & Pontell 1993:524; Chambliss 1988). Members of LCN families have considerable autonomy to conduct illegal business on their own. The main function of the organization is mutual protection, including negation of law enforcement through corruption. Otherwise, by Valachi's own account, everyone operates on his

Figure 6.2   La Cosa Nostra Crime Family

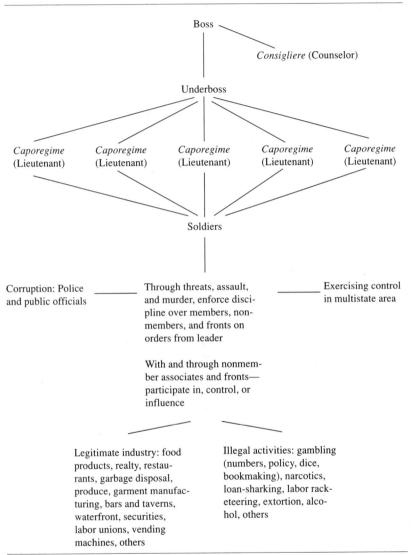

Source: Task Force on Organized Crime 1967:9.

own. Although LCN bosses around the country may occasionally get together to discuss matters of mutual concern or to engage in joint business ventures, this is far from a centralized commission that coordinates organized crime activities nationwide. Additionally, as we pointed out earlier, members of organized crime networks in the United States are by no means exclusively Italian, nor were they ever, and the influence of Italian groups has declined in recent years (see Box 4.1). Currently there are a variety of racial/ethnic groups that are playing a significant role in organized crime in the United States and throughout the world (Ryan & Rush 1997).

Joseph Albini (1971) offers an alternative view of the structure of organized crime, arguing that it consists of a series or network of **patron-client relationships**. A patron is an individual (like an LCN boss) who maintains a dominant position in a criminal network by virtue of his ability to offer practical assistance to others (e.g., financing, political protection). Clients, in turn, offer patrons something in return (e.g., a share of their illegal proceeds). A patron in one relationship may also be a client in another. Such networks consist of flexible, loosely structured associations that are held together primarily by members' mutual self-interest in illegal profit-making. Influence within a network depends on the number of significant patron-client relationships a person is able to establish and his ability to wield informal power. William Chambliss (1988) adds that the members of these networks are not simply conventional criminals. They include corrupt businessmen, politicians, and law enforcement officials who help finance and coordinate illegal activities and protect members from legal sanctions.

Finally, our theme of blurred boundaries between organized and corporate crime is highlighted by Dwight Smith's notion (1976) of **illicit enterprise**. The term "enterprise" refers to an activity that is entrepreneurial in nature, one that entails risk-taking in the operation of a business. Although "illicit" may connote criminal activity, it also suggests something more vague, something that is secret, underhanded, or unauthorized. Smith believes that conventional ways of understanding organized crime make a simplistic distinction between what is illicit and what poses as shrewd business practice. Is it really feasible, Smith asks, to "assume that loan-sharking bears no relationship to banking, or that fencing bears no relationship to retailing, or that narcotics importation and the wholesale trade have nothing in common" (1980:370)?

Take, for example, Calavita and Pontell's observation regarding elements of the S&L scandal that "more closely approximate organized crime than corporate crime" (1993:519). They cite a GAO study of twenty-six failed S&Ls that found that 62 percent of the S&Ls had undergone a change of ownership in the period just preceding their financial insolvency. Typically the new owners were individuals who had never been in banking before but who were attracted to the opportunities afforded by the deregulated environment. Calavita and Pontell argue that these cases indicate that the primary purpose of the S&L, like organized crime, "was to serve as a vehicle for illegal transactions" (p. 534). Or take the case of Adelphia, a large cable company that recently went bankrupt, costing investors billions in stock loses. Evidence indicates that members of the Rigas family, which founded Adelphia, "used the company as their personal bank" and improperly took "off-balance-sheet loans" and other pay-outs amounting to $2.3 billion (Reiman 2004:124).

In his study of the hazardous waste industry that we cited earlier, Szasz (1986a) introduced the notion of a **criminogenic regulatory structure** to explain the structural conditions that facilitated illicit activities in that area of commerce. Just as Leonard and Weber (1970) observe that there are criminogenic market structures that generate crime, Szasz notes that there are regulatory frameworks that generate crime as well. Certainly the absence of regulation, as we saw in the S&L scandal, can exert criminogenic influence, allowing people's inclination toward greed and opportunism to move into outright criminality. We seem to be under the mistaken impression that because someone says he's a businessman he will act appropriately. Perhaps the recent Enron-like scandals have caused people to reconsider. Polls show that the public's confidence in big business and belief in executives' honesty is lower than it has been in years (Teixeira 2002). Conversely, public support for government regulations has risen. The question remains, however, whether we will be sufficiently distracted by political double-talk, the war on terrorism, and the lure of consumerism—the "toys that make us think we [have] power—cell phones, big-screen TVs, PCs, DVDs and SUVs"—to demand change in the way the United States does business (Jackson 2002:F3).

7

Street Crime

During his research on gang life in Detroit, Michigan, criminologist William Brown befriended a fifteen-year-old African American youth named Jimmy. Jimmy was living with his sister, for his mother was in prison and he had never met his father. Brown recounts the day he and his wife took Jimmy out for a birthday celebration:

Where does a white, middle-class couple take a black [inner-city] soon-to-be-15 gang member for his birthday? . . . We decided that the Detroit Zoo, followed by a movie, and perhaps dinner, would be both appropriate and appreciated. . . . It had never occurred to [us that Jimmy] had never visited a city zoo. The day was absolutely perfect. . . . Jimmy was "hanging" outside his apartment . . . in . . . "the projects." Although attempting to maintain the . . . attitude of a streetwise kid, there was a hint of excitement in Jimmy's voice as we exchanged greetings. . . .

I knew that Jimmy had been involved in illegal drug sales . . . [but] he was, as usual, broke. . . . I gave [him] $20 so that he could have some sense of independence. . . . We walked around the zoo for nearly six hours. It was interesting . . . to watch Jimmy eat cotton candy, ice cream bars, popcorn, and so on like a normal kid on an outing. I had seen him navigate around a crack house and . . . he had been taking care of himself on the streets of Detroit for several years now. . . .

Following the zoo . . . we went to a movie. . . . Jimmy ate two more boxes of popcorn and one ice cream sandwich and drank an extra-large drink. . . . After the movie we went to a preselected restaurant. At the restaurant we encountered many stares and subtle examples of disapproval from many of the [white] occupants. There were instances during our visit to this restaurant when I wanted to respond to some of the rude onlookers, but this was Jimmy's Day. . . .

My wife and I will never forget Jimmy's 15th birthday. It was a day filled with good intentions. . . . [But it] was also filled with cruelty. We removed Jimmy, for a day, from "the projects." . . . We gave him a glimpse of life outside his . . . environment . . . [of] poverty. . . . The probability of escape for Jimmy, and for the thousands . . . like him, is very

229

low—despite all the political rhetoric of "American opportunity." (quoted in Shelden et al. 2001:268–270)

This chapter is about the social inequality that, for some, makes the experience of street crime commonplace and a rather ordinary day at the zoo an unusual life event. Although criminal behavior, as we have seen, is pervasive among all groups in society, it is largely the crimes of the under-privileged and powerless that command the attention of law enforcement, politicians, the media, and the public. We call the constellation of behaviors that constitute this concern **street crime**—crimes of violence, crimes against property, drugs, gangs, and the like. In this chapter we advance our sociological imagination as we employ the conceptual categories of *class* and *race/ethnicity* to analyze some key dimensions of the street crime problem. In the following chapters we will extend this analysis by unraveling the *gender* dimensions of crime and by examining other forms of criminality and victimization.

We begin by providing an overview of the economic context of urban street crime in the United States. We then consider the circumstances of racial and ethnic minority groups. We examine several sources of crime data and explore the question of whether people of color are differentially involved in crime and/or whether they are differentially selected for arrest by law enforcement officials. Finally, we situate our analysis of urban street gangs in the context of a broader theory of adolescent subcultures and the problem of law-violating behavior among middle-class youths.

■ The Economic Context of Urban Street Crime

Capitalist countries like the United States are marked by class inequality in the economic, educational, and cultural resources necessary, as we say in the Declaration of Independence, for "life, liberty, and the pursuit of happiness." Capitalism is an economic system based on the principle of private rather than public ownership of the major means of economic production (see Chapter 1). In this system a numerical minority of the population reaps a disproportionate amount of economic gain and consequent social privilege and political power, which some say is deserved and others say is not. Nevertheless, capitalism has shown itself to be a dynamic system capable of adapting to new and changing conditions.

Alvin Gouldner observed that the social order cannot "be understood without making the concerns of economics focal and problematic, . . . without clarifying and focusing on the problem of [economic] scarcity" (1970:95). Indeed, much macrosocial criminological theory (e.g., social disorganization, strain, and conflict theory) is in one way or another concerned with the relationship between class inequality and street crime. In this chapter we explore this relationship further by examining how transformations in the economy have affected patterns of street crime in the United States.

Over the past century, changing patterns of economic production have dramatically changed the American landscape. In earlier years, manufacturing plants were built in and around downtown factory districts that were adjacent to working-class neighborhoods. This pattern of urban land use promoted labor solidarity and union-organizing efforts (Gordon 1978). Over time, however, the larger capitalist corporations began to move their manufacturing plants to outlying suburbs, where taxes were lower, land was cheaper, and the quality of life was more pristine, precipitating a depletion of the economic base of the central or inner cities. As these companies grew, they were able to separate their production operations from their administrative, marketing, and product-development functions, which were "moved to office buildings in downtown business districts with access to financial services and contacts with other firms." Gradually, vibrant "industrial sites surrounded by working-class neighborhoods [were transformed into] downtown businesses adjacent to emptying manufacturing areas and deteriorating working-class districts" (Robinson 1993:298–299). More recently, even the nonmanufacturing corporate functions have been relocating to suburbia.

The transformation of the urban scene was also influenced by the massive migration of (largely rural) African Americans from the South to the North and the West Coast. After the Civil War, southern blacks had remained a source of cheap farm labor for white plantation owners. But such economic exploitation, along with adverse crop conditions, an abundant labor supply, and the mechanization of agriculture (to say nothing of white racial violence), encouraged African Americans to look elsewhere in their search for the American dream. During World War I, northern employers actively encouraged black migration to meet the demands of the war economy and to ease the labor shortage, which had been worsened by the curtailment of European immigrant labor. At other times, however, African Americans constituted a surplus labor supply that was used by employers to suppress white workers' wages and replace white workers who went on strike (Palen 1997; Robinson 1993).

Black migration tapered off during the depression era of the 1930s but accelerated during World War II and continued through the 1960s. While about half of African Americans still live in the South, they are one of the most urbanized segments of the U.S. population and are especially concentrated in large metropolitan areas (Palen 1997).

Over the years, capitalists also sought a more favorable business climate by shifting economic production away from the core cities of the northeastern and north-central regions of the United States to the southern and western states, where labor unions were weaker and wage scales were lower (Wallace & Humphries 1993). At the same time, the federal government's highway construction and home-lending programs favored suburban growth, which was motivated as well by "white flight" from people of color. Financial lending institutions practiced redlining and rarely invested in the inner city, contributing further to the depreciation of neighborhoods and property values (Brady 1983; Skogan 1986; see Chapter 6). Don Wallace and Drew Humphries (1993) attribute rising urban crime rates, in part, to these trends. In their research, they found that "central city hardship"—an index of several measures of socioeconomic disadvantage of central cities relative to their outlying suburban areas—was positively related to rates of several violent and property crimes. Similarly, other studies have found that the degree of suburbanization in a metropolitan area is associated with higher rates of central city crime (Farley 1987; Shihadeh & Ousey 1996). To be sure, crime exists in the suburbs as well as in urban areas, and among suburban communities crime rates vary with class composition and with opportunities to commit crime (e.g., large shopping centers and malls). Nevertheless, the street crime problem remains more acute in the depleted urban centers (Palen 1997).

According to Steven Margolin and Judith Schor (1990), the 1950s and 1960s were the golden age of postwar capitalism, when economic growth—and the G.I. Bill—created unprecedented prosperity for many people in the United States. However, capitalism has been marked by periodic swings in the **business cycle** (rises and falls in economic activity), some short-term, some long-term (Gordon et al. 1982). Over the long term, periods of economic growth eventually exhaust themselves due to factors such as the overproduction and underconsumption of products, outdated technologies, and diminishing supplies of skilled labor. A period of economic stagnation or decline then ensues, and businesses seek alternative strategies for growth. A phase of exploration and innovation typically follows, involving the "development and deployment of new production technologies and new social strategies for organizing the labor process" (Carlson & Michalowski 1997:214). These processes bring workers into or displace them from the productive process.

In the 1970s, unemployment, income inequality, and inflation increased, reducing the standard of living for a sizable portion of the U.S. population (Braun 1997; Hagan 1994). Between 1979 and 1982 the Federal Reserve Board raised interest rates to limit the expansion of credit and slow economic growth. While inflation consequently declined, unemployment and business bankruptcies soared. In the early 1980s, the Reagan administration hoped to stimulate the economy by cutting federal income taxes, increasing military spending, and reducing social programs and corporate regulations. While the economic downturn soon forced President Reagan to support a tax increase to reduce the federal deficit, overall the tax system shifted more to the benefit of corporations and private investors. Corporations began to recoup profits by acquiring other companies, often by borrowing money (with tax-deductible interest) and by downsizing and relocating to lower-wage domestic and foreign labor markets. They also received low-cost government loans and subsidies (corporate welfare) to help them relocate abroad and to advertise their products in foreign countries. At the same time, unions were weakened (e.g., striking air-traffic controllers were replaced), union membership fell to a historic low, and workers were increasingly kept in line by the threat of job loss (Carlson & Michalowski 1997; Schwendinger & Schwendinger 1993).

These trends have continued and have been exacerbated in recent years. The average American worker has been laboring harder and for longer hours (Ivins & Dubose 2003; Phillips 2002). Throughout the 1990s the average work year in the United States expanded by 184 hours, with U.S. workers averaging 350 more hours of work per year than their European counterparts. Economic recovery has also been uneven, consistent with the dual or segmented nature of the economy (Bluestone & Harrison 1982; Hagan 1994). The core or **primary labor market** jobs consist of the more skilled, better-paying, and secure jobs that have been concentrated in the unionized manufacturing sector of the economy (e.g., auto, aircraft, steel, petroleum, rubber, electronics, chemicals). The periphery or **secondary labor market** jobs require less skill, pay less, and are less secure and often part-time. These latter include janitors, dishwashers, maids, laundry workers, migrant farm workers, and the like, who may be employed but remain marginal to the economy. During the golden age of capitalism, primary labor market jobs expanded but have since declined due to the deindustrialization of the economy. Technological changes (especially computerization) have created new opportunities for good-paying jobs, but these jobs require much more education than previous entry-level manufacturing ones. The expanded service economy, with low-paying jobs in the secondary sector, such as the fast food industry, has constituted the other major area of job growth. Overall, between 1973 and 2000, the real income of the bottom 90 percent of taxpayers *fell* by 7 percent, while the income (not including capital gains) of the top one percent *rose* by 148 percent, the top 0.1 percent by 343 percent, and the top 0.01 percent by 599 percent (Krugman 2004).

These structural or macro-level changes in the economy have impacted the micro-level of social life in neighborhoods across the country. They have particularly affected poor, urban minority communities that are now without the very jobs that had encouraged urban migration in the first place. Under these conditions street crime becomes part of the repertoire of economic activity of many people, along with governmental subsidies and temporary or part-time secondary labor market jobs (Hagedorn 1988; Wilson 1987). We will say more about this later in the chapter.

■ Unemployment and Crime

Several criminological theories—from macro-level social theories to the micro-level theory of rational choice—converge in the expectation that unemployment increases the level of street crime (henceforth referred to as the U-SC relationship). Certainly, a class-based explanation of crime would predict such a relationship. Yet in a review of the literature published in 1987, Theodore Chiricos reported on an apparent consensus of doubt among criminologists regarding the U-SC connection. Some studies had found a positive relationship, some a negative relationship, and some no relationship between unemployment and crime. Conservative critics of liberal crime prevention policies used these findings to dismiss programs that attempted to increase job opportunities among the disadvantaged (Wilson & Herrnstein 1985).

In his review of over sixty aggregate-level studies, Chiricos (1987) tried to explain the inconsistent findings. **Aggregate studies** refer to those that use macro-level geographical areas like cities, states, or nations, rather than individuals, as the unit of analysis. Chiricos noted that property crimes (especially burglary and larceny) in these studies were more likely than violent crimes to be positively related to unemployment. A positive U-SC relationship was also more likely in studies that used data at lower levels of aggregation; that is, a positive U-SC relationship was more likely in studies that examined varying rates of unemployment and crime within a single city (intracity data) than in those that compared multiple cities or metropolitan areas (intercity/metropolitan data) or that used longitudinal national data. Chiricos reasoned that intracity data may be more sensitive to the social context or "milieu effects" of unemployment in a particular area; in other words, high unemployment in "a particular neighborhood or section of a city or county . . . creates a climate of hopelessness or anomie with [criminogenic] consequences even for those not directly unemployed (e.g., teenagers or others not in the labor force)" (p. 95). Thus Herman Schwendinger and Julia Schwendinger (1993) argue that government investments in crime prevention employment programs would help not only individuals directly involved in the programs but others in the community as well.

Another problem with U-SC research is that the official government measure of unemployment includes only those individuals who are considered temporarily unemployed and who continue to look for work. It therefore excludes those who are more or less permanently (or structurally) unemployed. The 1970s was a period of economic hardship marked by rising **structural unemployment**, where unemployment became a long-term rather than transitory state, and where those living at the margins of the economy increasingly lost faith in the possibility of advancement. According to Susan Carlson and Raymond Michalowski, "During periods of structural unemployment, a larger proportion of those who will lose jobs will be unable to reenter the labor force, or will do so at wages and under working conditions considerably less attractive than in the jobs they lost. Similarly, a larger share of young people hoping to enter the workforce for the first time will meet with failure or will find only dead-end 'hamburger' jobs" (1997:217).

Both Chiricos (1987) and Carlson and Michalowski (1997) found a positive relationship between unemployment and crime in the 1970s. In the post-1970s period, however, this relationship was weak, perhaps because the official unemployment rate had became increasingly disconnected from the plight of the structurally unemployed, who were most likely to engage in street crime. At the same time, other studies found that prison incarceration rates increased with rising unemployment and declining labor force participation. Researchers postulate that during times of economic hardship the criminal justice system is used to control the structurally marginalized "surplus population" (Chiricos & Delone 1992; Hochstetler & Shover 1997; Michalowski & Carlson 1999).

Still another issue that complicates the U-SC relationship is the possible countervailing effect of unemployment: it may increase the incentive or motivation for crime but also decrease the opportunity for crime. The latter is an expectation of routine activities theory, for when unemployment rises there are fewer economic goods (suitable targets) available to be stolen and more unemployed people at home to protect their property (capable guardians) (Cantor & Land 1975; see Chapter 4). Studies attempting to evaluate this countervailing effect, like the U-SC research as a whole, have been inconsistent (Kleck & Chiricos 2002). On the other hand, research that examined the effects of both unemployment and deterrence variables (i.e., the certainty and severity of punishment) found that the former had as much (or more) impact than the latter on lowering the rate of crime (Chiricos 1987). In addition, studies show that prison inmates are more likely than the general population to be unemployed prior to incarceration, that unemployment prior to incarceration is a strong predictor of recidivism following release, and that ex-convicts who find employment have lower recidivism rates (Conklin 2003).

Terence Thornberry and R. L. Christenson (1984) were among the first to point out that the U-SC relationship may be reciprocal or mutually reinforcing. In a longitudinal study of nearly 1,000 males born in Philadelphia in 1945, they found that unemployment was an immediate or short-term stimulus to increased criminal activity, but that crime over the long term also increased the likelihood of unemployment. John Hagan (1993) adds that involvement in early-life delinquency may actually precede unemployment in people's lives. Involvement in crime, especially for poor urban youths, embeds individuals in networks of criminal associations (including gangs) and at the same time distances them from networks of "job contacts that initiate and sustain legitimate occupational careers" (p. 469). This makes it increasingly difficult for youths to outgrow their youthful ties, and it eliminates possibilities for employment even before they become apparent. Unemployment, in turn, becomes a significant problem for accomplishing the transition to adulthood, making it more likely that earlier illegal commitments will be sustained. Hagan's own self-report survey research and a number of ethnographies of the urban poor support this hypothesis (Anderson 1999; Moore 1991; Padilla 1992; Sullivan 1989). Moreover, Elliot Currie (1985) notes that it is not just employment but also the *quality* of work that affects the rate of street crime. People's commitment to the conventional social order is, in part, influenced by the degree to which their work provides them with dignity, appreciation from others, and a sense of meaningful participation in their community (see Uggen 1999).

Clearly, the structural changes in the economy that we have been discussing, including the problem of unemployment, have had an especially deleterious impact on the lives of the urban poor, a phenomenon that entails that intersection of class, race, and ethnicity. We will explore this issue further shortly, but first we briefly consider the problem of homelessness and crime.

▓ *Homelessness and Crime*

In the past, the homeless population in the United States consisted primarily of unemployed, alcoholic men over fifty years of age. The homeless were less visible than they are today, living mainly in "skid-row areas of large cities or hobo villages beside train tracks" (Newman 2000:356). Nowadays the homeless population is more diverse and is more visible on the streets and in parks, train and bus stations, and abandoned buildings all over the country. About 46 percent are single men, 14 percent are single women, 36.5 percent are families (usually mothers) with children, and 3.5 percent are children living on their own.

Most researchers place the number of homeless at 300,000–500,000, with another 4–7 million who "are so poor they could be pushed into . . . [homelessness] by an economic downturn" (Palen 1997:193–194). About a quarter of the homeless actually have part-time or full-time jobs but are unable to accumulate enough money for rent. About 15 percent of the homeless are mentally ill, persons who in the past might have been hospitalized (Glaser 1997; Snow et al. 1986).

The decline in affordable low-income housing has been a major factor

in the rise of homelessness in the United States. During the 1980s and 1990s cities experienced dramatic reductions in single-room occupancy hotels, rooming houses, and the like. In addition, about "half a million units of low-income housing were lost to condominium conversion, abandonment, arson, and demolition," and federal housing subsidies for low-income people were cut by about 70 percent (Newman 2000:357; Palen 1997).

Homeless people, like the poor more generally, suffer more health problems than the general population and die at an earlier age (Newman 2000). They also experience higher rates of criminal victimization, with the nonwhite homeless having higher rates of victimization than the white homeless (Coston 1992; Fitzpatrick et al. 1993). However, the homeless also commit crimes themselves, stealing and prostituting to survive and often to support drug or alcohol addictions. One study of the southern California beach community of Santa Monica found that the homeless were responsible for about half of the serious felonies in that city (Melekian 1990). And since the homeless commit crimes against other homeless people, even homeless shelters are ridden with theft and violence, as well as drugs.

Homeless youths in particular are preyed upon by their adult counterparts, who quite literally attempt to take the clothes off their backs. One boy describes his experience in a shelter this way: "I was just a kid. . . . They were pushing me around. . . . They asked me to take my clothes off, they wanted to steal my clothes. Like they were four against me" (Hagan & McCarthy 1997:45). Another boy recalls:

> I fell asleep . . . and . . . in the middle of the night . . . I wake up and there's two guys at my bed. . . . One guy's trying to yank my boots off, and the other guy's undoing my pants. . . . Another night . . . I saw a guy get his face cut open, because he refused to give another a cigarette. They like cut him from here right down, with the knife . . . and that's when I said, . . . 'I'm out of here.'" (pp. 45–46)

Of course, homelessness itself may be the "ultimate state of victimization" for people of all ages (Fitzpatrick et al. 1993:366).

In a study of homeless youths in Toronto and Vancouver, Canada, Bill McCarthy and colleagues (2002) found that some homeless youth manage to form fictive "street families" that provide mutual support and protection that minimizes their victimization from predatory violence. As one youth remarked, "A street family . . . [is] basically a group friends, but it's more. . . . Some friends . . . you can't count on them, but like a street family you can count on. If you get in trouble they'll be there to help you" (p. 848). Another youth recalled, "My street family gave me more support on the streets and stuff; people loving and caring for you . . . being there for you. It feels better . . . than just being . . . alone when you don't know what to do" (p. 845). And according to another, "The difference between a street sister or brother and an average person is . . . you know they are solid, that they're not going to rat, they are not going to steal from you. . . . Being solid is if somebody walks up to a group of us and picks on one person . . . your street brother or sister is going to stand up for that person" (p. 850).

■ Racial/Ethnic Status and Street Crime

A **minority group** can be conceptualized as a group whose members are singled out by the dominant group (or groups) in a society for unequal or discriminatory treatment. In this section we are primarily concerned with the racial and ethnic minorities whose class position and disadvantaged social status increase their likelihood of involvement in street crime and/or contact with the criminal justice system.

Race, as we have noted, should be understood as a social construction rather than as a biological phenomenon, and distinct groups, if they ever did exist, no longer exist today due to interracial mixing (see Chapter 1). Furthermore, racial classification schemes are often unable to accommodate many people who think of themselves as biracial or multiracial. These schemes also collapse some groups that are quite culturally distinct (e.g., Chinese, Japanese, Korean, Vietnamese, and Filipino). The term "ethnicity," typically referring to cultural distinctions among groups with different national/cultural origins, is ambiguous as well. The category of Hispanic or Latino, for example, masks important distinctions between persons from Mexico, Puerto Rico, Cuba, and other Spanish-speaking countries.

Previously we observed that criminal justice data tend not to reflect the racial and ethnic diversity of the United States. Most data are categorized only in terms of white and black, with Hispanics often included as white. And criminal justice officials may be poorly trained about race and ethnic classifications and may make decisions based on stereotypes. Moreover, researchers analyzing this data have at times failed to acknowledge the social and political nature of such categories and have advanced explanations of crime that reflect racist assumptions about the biological inferiority of some groups of people. Such work ranges from the formulations of century-old criminologists like Cesare Lombroso to the more recent work on IQ and criminality by Richard Herrnstein and Charles Murray (see Chapter 3). Nevertheless, we still need to understand how "some crimes . . . come to be associated . . . directly or indirectly" with the categories of race and ethnicity (Holdaway 1997:396).

■ *The Color of Crime Data:*
Patterns of Offending and Victimization

The racial composition of arrests. In Chapter 2 we discussed the *Uniform Crime Reports (UCR)*, the most widely used source of official data on crime, as well as the two other methods of counting crime and criminals: victimization surveys and self-report surveys. You will recall that the *UCR* make a distinction between Index crimes (or Part I offenses) and non-Index crimes (or Part II offenses). Because Index crimes have been regarded as indicators of the general crime problem, and more data have been collected on these than other measures of crime, criminologists and the media that disseminate this information to the public have given more attention to these offenses.

The *UCR* provide national arrest data for four racial groups, categorized as white, black, American Indian/Alaskan Native, and Asian/Pacific Islander. Previously we presented race-specific (Index crime) arrest rates for these groups (see Table 2.5). (These rates were calculated by dividing the number of arrests for individuals in each group by the number of persons in that group.) Blacks had the highest arrest rates for both violent and property crimes, followed by American Indians/Alaskan Natives, whites, and Asians/Pacific Islanders, respectively. We also noted that these rates could be interpreted as representing "differential criminal involvement" and/or "differential likelihood of selection." In other words, we asked whether higher arrest rates reflect a group's greater involvement in *these types of crimes,* its greater vulnerability to being apprehended by the police, or both.

Table 7.1 breaks down (or disaggregates) the arrest data for Index and non-Index crimes for 2002 according to the percentage of arrests for each crime accounted for by each of the four racial groups. Ignoring for a moment the limitations of these data, a few conclusions can be drawn. American Indians/Alaskan Natives and Asians/Pacific Islanders constitute only a small proportion of arrests. This is not surprising, since these two groups constitute just 1 percent and 4 percent of the U.S. population, respectively. The relatively small percentage of American Indian/Alaskan Native and Asian/Pacific Islander arrests makes any meaningful observations based on these data problematic, other than suggesting that Asian/Pacific Islanders are generally *underrepresented* in arrests in comparison to their percentage in the population. (The percentage of American Indian/Alaskan Native arrests is comparable to their percentage in the population.) This leaves us with the white and black arrests to examine.

The percentage of white arrests (which collapses data for Hispanic and non-Hispanic whites) ranges from 48 to 77 percent for Index crimes and from 27 to 88 percent for non-Index crimes. Whites constitute about 82 percent of the U.S. population (69 percent non-Hispanic and 13 percent Hispanic). Examination of Table 7.1 shows that whites are *underrepresented* in arrests for all the Part I offenses. Among Part II offenses, the percentage of arrests for whites approximates or exceeds 82 percent only for drinking-related offenses: drunkenness (84 percent), liquor laws (88 percent), and driving under the influence (88 percent). Moreover, since other sources of data suggest that Hispanics have higher arrest rates than non-Hispanic whites for some crimes, particularly homicide, the underrepresentation of non-Hispanic whites is probably greater than suggested by these statistics (Martinez 1996; Mann 1993; Moore 1991; Padilla 1992). On the other hand, African Americans, who constitute about 13 percent of the U.S. population, constitute 21 to 54 percent of arrests for Index crimes and 9 to 68 percent of arrests for non-Index crimes. African Americans are thus *overrepresented* in arrests for all the Part I and nearly all the Part II offenses, including drug abuse violations, one of the most controversial areas of law enforcement.

Another way of looking at these arrest data is to examine the types of

Table 7.1 Racial Distribution of Arrests (2002)

	White	Black	American Indian or Alaskan Native	Asian or Pacific Islander
		Percentage Distribution[a]		
Percentage of population	82	13	1	4
Index crimes/Part I offenses				
Homicide[b]	48	50	1	1
Forcible rape	63	34	1	1
Robbery	44	54	1	1
Aggravated assault	63	34	1	1
Burglary	70	28	1	1
Larceny-theft	68	29	1	2
Motor vehicle theft	60	37	1	2
Arson	77	21	1	1
Non-Index crimes/Part II offenses				
Other assaults	66	31	1	1
Forgery and counterfeiting	69	29	1	1
Fraud	68	31	1	1
Embezzlement	68	30	< 1	2
Stolen property[b]	59	39	1	1
Vandalism	76	22	1	1
Weapons[b]	62	36	1	1
Prostitution and commercialized vice	57	40	1	2
Sex offenses[b]	74	23	1	1
Drug abuse violations	66	32	1	1
Gambling	27	68	1	4
Offenses against family and children	68	29	1	2
Driving under the influence	88	10	2	1
Liquor laws	88	9	2	1
Drunkenness	84	13	2	1
Disorderly conduct	67	31	2	1
Vagrancy	62	35	2	1
All other offenses (except traffic)	67	30	1	1
Suspicion	54	41	1	4
Curfew and loitering	69	29	1	1
Runaways	76	18	1	4

Sources: FBI 2003, tab. 43; U.S. Department of Commerce 2002, tab. 14.
Notes: a. Percentages may not add up to 100 due to rounding.
b. Homicide = murder and nonnegligent manslaughter. Sex offenses = all except forcible rape and prostitution. Stolen property = buying, receiving, possessing, etc. Weapons = carrying, possessing, etc.

crimes that each racial group commits most often. The more serious Index crimes constitute only 15 percent of all white arrests, 20 percent of black arrests, 14 percent of American Indian/Alaskan Native arrests, and 21 percent of Asian/Pacific Islander arrests. Table 7.2 rank-orders the types of

Table 7.2 Rank-Order of Most Common Arrests (2002)[a]

White	Black
1. Driving under the influence	1. Drug abuse violations
2. Drug abuse violations	2. Other assaults
3. Other assaults	3. Larceny-theft[b]
4. Larceny-theft[b]	4. Disorderly conduct
5. Liquor laws	5. Aggravated assault[b]
6. Drunkenness	6. Driving under the influence
7. Disorderly conduct	7. Fraud
8. Aggravated assault[b]	8. Burglary[b]
9. Fraud	9. Drunkenness
10. Burglary[b]	10. Vandalism

American Indian/Alaskan Native	Asian/Pacific Islander
1. Driving under the influence	1. Larceny-theft[b]
2. Other assaults	2. Other assaults
3. Liquor laws	3. Driving under the influence
4. Larceny-theft[b]	4. Drug abuse violations
5. Drunkenness	5. Liquor laws
6. Disorderly conduct	6. Runaways
7. Drug abuse violations	7. Aggravated assault[b]
8. Aggravated assault[b]	8. Disorderly conduct
9. Vandalism	9. Burglary[b]
10. Burglary[b]	10. Vandalism

Source: FBI 2003, tab. 43.
Notes: a. 1 = highest, 10 = lowest. Arrests do not include crimes listed as "all other offenses (except traffic)," a catchall category reflecting state and local laws not listed in the *UCR*.
b. Index crime.

crimes for which the four groups were arrested most often. Note that members of all groups tend to be arrested for similar crimes, that within each group's "arrest portfolio . . . the proportions of each type of crime do not vary substantially" (Mann 1993:45). Whites, for instance, share nine of the ten arrest categories with blacks and American Indians/Alaskan Natives, and eight of the ten categories with Asians/Pacific Islanders. Nevertheless, the overrepresentation of African Americans in these arrest data needs to be explained. Although a class analysis of street crime (which we will explore further) suggests reasons for expecting some differential involvement of poor, urban minorities, there is evidence that supports a differential selection interpretation of arrest disparities as well. And ultimately, analyses of racial arrest data must confront the question of whether such disparities necessarily imply discrimination (Walker et al. 2004).

We will explore the question of police bias in more depth in Chapter 11. For now we note that there is mixed evidence on this score, making generalizations difficult. Some research has found that race does matter, but there are countervailing factors that complicate the picture. For example, studies have shown that African Americans are more likely to be arrested on the basis of weak evidence and "in 'on-view' situations rather than with an [arrest] warrant" (Walker et al. 2004:110). Officers are also more likely to invoke their power to arrest when the victim is white and especially when the victim is white and the suspect is black (Bynum et al. 1982; Smith et al. 1984). On the other hand, since most crime is *intraracial,* committed by offenders against victims of the same group (see below), this may lead to fewer black arrests because police may be less likely to respond to crimes involving black victims and complainants than to crimes involving white victims and complainants. In addition, research suggests that African Americans are more distrustful of the police and may be less likely to provide witness testimony that might effectuate an arrest. Thus, in a study of over 335,000 arrests contained in the National Incident-Based Reporting System (see Chapter 2), Stewart D'Alessio and Lisa Stolzenberg (2003) found that blacks were actually *less likely* than whites to be arrested following incidents of robbery and assault, and that race played no role in the likelihood of arrest for forcible rape. Furthermore, some research has found that police bias against African Americans is minimal when controlling for offense seriousness and prior record of the offender (see Barkan 2001; Berger 1996).

Robert Sampson (1986) offers insight into the differential involvement versus selection issue from a class perspective. According to Sampson, police do patrol lower-class communities (which are often disproportionately populated by minority groups) more intensely than they patrol higher-status communities. He argues, however, that the bias in policing is more ecological, dependent on neighborhood context, than it is directed at individuals per se. In other words, given an encounter with the police, a person of one racial group may be no more or less likely to be arrested, but individuals differ in the chance that their offenses will be detected in the first place. Moreover, lower-class communities have a more active street life, largely because residents have less access to private space. "Since the regulation of public places is a central task of policing, . . . people in [these] . . . areas are subject to greater surveillance" (p. 878). Ultimately these processes translate into a greater likelihood of lower-class (including racial and ethnic minority) individuals accumulating a prior record of offending, if even for only minor crimes (Chambliss 1994). Thus research that finds that prior record predicts likelihood of subsequent arrest ignores the possibility that earlier ecological biases may affect later arrest outcomes regardless of whether discrimination is present in these later cases.

In addition, police are more likely to invoke their power to arrest when the suspect is disrespectful, and African Americans are more likely to respond in ways that are perceived this way (Black 1980). But it is also likely that black suspects' reactions stem from the hostile treatment and shakedowns they not uncommonly receive from police. As Coramae Richey Mann notes, people of color "may be stopped for questioning in sections of cities where they are not often seen, or for driving a car which seems beyond their means or is assumed by the police to be of doubtful legal possession; [indeed] minorities are often hassled simply for having a conversation on the street" (1993:138). This pattern of law enforcement has been referred to as "racial profiling," a problem we will examine in more detail later in the book.

Other research suggests that the degree of law enforcement discrimination is related to the size and consequent threat of the minority population. Dale Dannefer and Russell Schutt (1982) analyzed police and juvenile court records in six counties and found that racial bias (more severe dispositions independent of offense seriousness and prior record) was greater in areas marked by a higher concentration of minorities. They argue that law enforcement may have greater fear of residents "getting out of their place" as the presence of a minority group increases (p. 1115).

Steven Brandl and colleagues' time-series analysis (1995) of the city of Milwaukee between 1934 and 1987 also sheds light on this issue. Brandl and colleagues disaggregated data on police force size and examined the effect of the racial composition (percentage black) of the city over time on patrol, detective, and civilian police employment. Controlling for the level of crime, they found that racial composition was positively related to total police force size and to patrol officer size, but not to detective or civilian employment. They concluded that "the results are consistent with the view that racial conflict promotes increases in the size of the unit most directly responsible for controlling those groups which threaten the interests of the powerful" (pp. 559–560).

In a study of ninety cities, however, Pamela Jackson and Leo Carroll (1981) found that a community's allocation of police resources (as measured by per-capita police expenditures) exhibited a *curvilinear* relationship to the size of its minority population, irrespective of the level of crime. In other words, the degree of police resources increased with the size of a minority group until that group reached numerical dominance, at which point the resources declined. Jackson and Carroll argue that as African Americans become the dominant group in a city, they translate their numbers into political power in ways that direct expenditures away from police control. In a subsequent study, Jackson (1985) drew similar conclusions from an analysis of cities with varying proportions of Latinos (see also Kane 2003).

Victimization surveys. In Chapter 2 we presented data from the *National Crime Victimization Survey (NCVS)* that indicated that African Americans and Hispanics experienced higher rates of victimization from both property and violent crimes. We also noted that the data on victims' perceptions of the race of offenders were fairly consistent with the data from the *UCR*.

The *NCVS* includes data on the perceived race of the offender in both single-offender and multiple-offender victimizations for violent crimes (Pastore & Maguire 2002). (Single offenders accounted for 80 percent of all violent victimizations and multiple offenders accounted for 20 percent.) The data indicate that 64 percent of *single-offender* victimizations were committed by offenders perceived to be white and about 24 percent were committed by offenders perceived to be black; 41 percent of *multiple-offender* victimizations were committed by persons perceived to be white and 27 percent were committed by persons perceived to be black. While these *NCVS* data show that African Americans are more likely to be violent-crime offenders than would be expected by chance (they constitute about 13 percent of the population), overall they accounted for a smaller proportion of violent-crime victimizations than violent-crime arrests.

Victimization data also indicate that most crimes of violence are intraracial. Combining single-offender and multiple-offender victimizations, 67 percent of whites were victimized by offenders perceived to be white, while 78 percent of blacks were victimized by offenders perceived to be black (U.S. Department of Justice 1997). It is true, nevertheless, that black offenders were more likely than white offenders to cross racial lines. In other words, black offenders were more likely to victimize whites than white offenders were to victimize blacks. For single-offender victimizations, 17 percent of whites were victimized by persons perceived to be black, while 12 percent of blacks were victimized by persons perceived to be white; for multiple-offender victimizations, 24 percent of whites were victimized by persons perceived to be black, while 7 percent of blacks were victimized by persons perceived to be white. Some criminologists attribute this disparity to the relative sizes of the black and white populations. Since there are significantly more whites in the population than blacks, motivated black offenders have a greater chance of interacting with potential white victims than motivated white offenders have of interacting with potential black victims (O'Brien 1987).

Finally, Samuel Walker and colleagues offer a word of caution regarding *NCVS* data on African American offenders, which they believe may be inflated: "Victim memory is subject to decay over time and to 'retroactive reconstruction' to fit the popular conception of a criminal offender. If a victim believes that the 'typical criminal' is African American, this opinion may influence his or her perception of the race of the offender" (2004:45).

Self-report surveys. In Chapter 2 we discussed some of the ways in which self-report surveys have addressed the issue of race and crime. Initial research lent support to the discrimination hypothesis, as self-report delinquency surveys failed to confirm the black-white disparities found in the official *UCR* data. Attempts at reconciling the self-report and official findings focused on distinguishing the seriousness and frequency of delinquent conduct. One *National Youth Survey (NYS)* study did confirm race differences (i.e., higher rates for African Americans) for some of the more serious and high-frequency offenders, but the *NYS* results were inconsistent over the years (Elliott & Ageton 1980; Elliott & Huizinga 1983; Huizinga & Elliott 1987). (More consistent results were found for class differences.)

Overall, the racial and ethnic disparities found in self-report studies have been less pronounced than those found in official statistics. Recent national surveys of white, black, and Hispanic high school students, for example, show negligible racial/ethnic differences for a variety of violent acts and property crimes—such as getting into serious fights, hurting someone badly, stealing from stores, taking others' belongings, and vandalism—although for some delinquencies blacks were more likely to be high-frequency offenders, and students of color felt less safe on school property (Pastore & Maguire 2000, 2002). On the other hand, some criminologists express reservations about self-report studies conducted with students, since they exclude truants, dropouts, and incarcerated youths from the interview sample (Hagan & McCarthy 1997; Inciardi et al. 1993).

Self-report data also indicate that nonwhites do not generally use alcohol and other drugs more often than whites. In fact, the evidence indicates that whites use most substances more often than people of color. For example, the National Household Survey on Drug Abuse, conducted by the U.S. Department of Health and Human Services, asked over 25,000 persons twelve years of age or older about their consumption patterns (Maguire & Pastore 2001). The survey found that a higher proportion of whites than blacks and Hispanics said they had "ever used" alcohol, had used it "within the last year," and had used it "within the last 30 days" (see Table 7.3). Whites were also the most likely to report having "ever used" marijuana, although the proportion of blacks who reported using marijuana "within the last year" and "within the last 30 days" was slightly higher than the proportions for whites and Hispanics who reported such use.

In general, whites were more likely to have used cocaine, hallucinogens, inhalants, stimulants, and tranquilizers. Although African Americans were more likely than whites and Hispanics to have used crack cocaine and heroin, the proportion of any group reporting such use was small. These findings call into question the "war on drugs," which has resulted in the disproportionate arrest and incarceration of people of color (see Chapter 1). In order to put this bias against racial and ethnic minorities into historical perspective, we turn now to a consideration of drug prohibition.

Table 7.3 Self-Reported Drug Use by Race and Ethnicity (1998)

	Percentage Who Used		
	White	Black	Hispanic
Alcohol			
ever used	85.2	71.7	70.8
used within last year	67.8	50.4	58.5
used within last 30 days	55.3	39.8	45.4
Marijuana			
ever used	35.5	30.2	23.2
used within last year	8.4	10.6	8.2
used within last 30 days	5.0	6.6	4.5
Cocaine (includes crack)			
ever used	11.4	8.5	8.9
used within last year	1.7	1.9	2.3
used within last 30 days	0.7	1.3	1.3
Crack cocaine			
ever used	1.8	4.2	1.9
used within last year	0.3	1.3	0.7
used within last 30 days	0.1	0.9	0.3
Hallucinogens			
ever used	11.5	4.8	5.3
used within last year	1.8	0.4	1.6
used within last 30 days	0.8	0.2	0.7
Inhalants			
ever used	6.6	2.2	4.1
used within last year	1.0	0.3	0.9
used within last 30 days	0.3	0.2	0.4
Stimulants			
ever used	5.0	2.9	2.6
used within last year	0.7	0.6	0.8
used within last 30 days	0.3	0.2	0.4
Tranquilizers			
ever used	3.9	2.9	2.4
used within last year	1.0	0.6	0.1
used within last 30 days	0.3	0.1	0.3
Heroin[a]			
ever used	1.0	1.9	0.9
used within last year	0.1	0.2	0.1

Source: Maguire & Pastore 2001, tabs. 3.97–3.101.
Note: a. Data on heroin use within last 30 days are not available.

■ *Drug Prohibition: A Design for Discrimination*

A century ago there were relatively few laws on the books that prohibited the use of drugs in the United States. Cough elixirs with morphine (an opium derivative) were sold over the counter or ordered by mail from Sears Roebuck. Marijuana was used for migraine headaches, asthma, and other maladies, and sold in both fluid extracts and in cigarette form. Physicians used cocaine as a local anesthetic and as a treatment for fatigue and morphine addiction, and it was once the official remedy of the Hay Fever Association. Even Bordeaux wines, Coca-Cola soft drinks, liquors, cigarettes, tablets, ointments, and sprays contained cocaine. Doctors often prescribed opium to white, middle-aged women from the middle or upper class, the typical users of the time, to alleviate gynecological and nervous "disorders." And because it was thought to enhance an individual's physical and mental performance, employers also gave it to workers to increase productivity, and hence, employers' profits (Brecher 1972; Kennedy 2003).

A detailed account of how this state of affairs changed is beyond the scope of this chapter. The constellation of factors that influenced drug prohibition include such diverse issues as international treaties, the development of the medical profession, and law enforcement's interest in expanding its jurisdictional domain (Musto 1987; Waterston 1993). Here we will focus on the well-documented historical connection between drug prohibition and racial/ethnic hostilities in the United States.

Opium, the first drug to be regulated in the United States, was used primarily by the Chinese in the nineteenth century. Although the first large wave of Chinese immigrants was composed predominantly of more affluent Chinese, they were succeeded by laborers who worked in the mining industry and built the railroads in the West. By 1875 racism, **xenophobia** (fear of strangers or foreigners), and concern that lower-paid Chinese workers would displace whites led to ordinances prohibiting opium dens and smoking in San Francisco. Similar ordinances were passed the next year in Virginia City, Nevada. A major impetus for such laws was the belief that opium smoking enhanced workers' productivity, thereby placing nonsmoking whites at a disadvantage in the labor market. Federal legislation attempting to control Chinese drug use was also enacted. In 1887 the U.S. government outlawed the importation of opium *by the Chinese,* even though it remained legal for other groups to import the drug for smoking until 1909. Fear of Chinese immigrants and racial hostility culminated two years later in the passage of the Chinese Exclusion Act, which prohibited immigration of additional Chinese into the country (Helmer 1975; Musto 1987; Regoli & Hewitt 1997).

Cocaine was included with opiates in the Harrison Act of 1914, which regulated the possession and use of narcotics. Cocaine use, which was associated with African Americans, inspired racial fears in whites. Although poverty-stricken blacks used cocaine for relief from bronchial disease and tuberculosis, they did not use it to a greater extent than whites. In fact, it is likely that African Americans experienced lower rates of addiction because they were less likely to receive medical care and doctors' prescriptions for drugs (Helmer 1975; Kennedy 2003). Nevertheless, the media of those times promoted the myth of blacks' proclivity to drug-induced criminality.

In 1903, for example, an article in the *New York Tribune* claimed that "many of the horrible crimes committed in the Southern States by the colored people can be traced directly to the cocaine habit," and in 1914 the *Literary Digest* asserted that "most of the attacks upon white women of the South are a direct result of a cocaine-crazed Negro brain" (cited in Regoli & Hewitt 1997:379–380). Fear of cocaine and its ability to create superhuman strength among African Americans was also, according to David Musto (1987), the chief reason southern police switched from .32-caliber to .38-caliber pistols. Although relatively few people were incarcerated for drug violations as a result of the Harrison Act compared to subsequent antidrug legislation, the act was disproportionately applied to African Americans. By the end of the 1920s, African Americans, who constituted just 9 percent of the population, constituted 23 percent of all incarcerated drug offenders (Kennedy 2003).

Marijuana, a drug originally associated with Mexican immigrants in the Southwest, did not come under the control of the Federal Bureau of Narcotics (FBN) until the late 1930s, although many places had statutes outlawing its use by the mid-1920s. The Great Depression, which adversely affected employment opportunities, exacerbated the country's fear of Mexican workers who, like the Chinese, worked for lower wages than whites. Employers in agriculture and other industries supported the anti-Mexican campaign because Mexicans had been successfully organizing unions and strikes. Also fueling the concern about marijuana was the generally accepted notion that violence and sexual promiscuity accompanied its use (see Chapter 1). The FBN, headed by Harry Anslinger, began an aggressive campaign to have marijuana added to the list of controlled substances under its jurisdiction. Finally, in 1937 the Marijuana Tax Act (MTA) was passed, giving the FBN greatly expanded powers. By 1938, the first full year after the legislation went into effect, one of every four federal drug convictions involved a violation of the MTA. Violations of marijuana laws also expedited the deportation of Mexican workers back to their home country (Helmer 1975; Musto 1987; Regoli & Hewitt 1997).

Concern about cocaine use among African Americans resurfaced in the 1980s when media attention focused on crack cocaine (Chiricos 1996). Crack, a less expensive form of cocaine consumed primarily by low-income offenders, was frequently portrayed as an instantly addicting substance that incited violence among users. In the midst of a "moral panic," Congress passed the Anti–Drug Abuse Acts of 1986 and 1988, which specified mandatory prison terms for federal drug offenders (the length of time depending on the amount of the drug) and made penalties for crack cocaine 100 times greater than for comparable amounts of powder cocaine. For instance, a first-time offender convicted in federal court for possession of *five grams* of crack (about the weight of two pennies and providing fifteen

to twenty-five "hits") would now receive a mandatory minimum sentence of five years in prison. The street value of five grams of crack is about $400 dollars. In contrast, an offender would need to possess *500 grams* of powder cocaine valued at about $10,000 to receive the same sentence (Wallace 1993).

This federal policy, along with those that have been applied at the state level, has disproportionately impacted African Americans. Between 1980 and the early 1990s, for instance, the proportion of drug-possession arrests that was constituted by African Americans increased from 21 percent to about 35 percent, and the proportion of drug possession arrests for *juveniles* that was constituted by black youths increased from 13 percent to about 40 percent (Mauer 1999). In 1980 the drug arrest rate for white youths was actually higher than for nonwhite youths. As a result of the intensified policy of drug prohibition, the situation was reversed (Blumstein 1993; Tollet & Close 1991). Insofar as drug offenses have constituted the largest component of the rising prison population in the United States, U.S. drug policy must be viewed as discriminatory in effect, if not also in intent (Bush-Baskette 1998; Tonry 1995; see Chapters 1 and 12).

The state of Illinois was singled out in a study by Human Rights Watch for having the highest ratio of black to white inmates serving prison sentences for drug offenses (*Daily Jefferson County Union* 2000). These data have been interpreted as stemming, in part, from the Safe School Zone Act (SSZA), which was passed in that state in 1985. The SSZA mandated that youths as young as fifteen who sold drugs within 1,000 feet of a school had to be tried as adults. Three years later, safe zones were expanded to include public housing projects, thus increasing the likelihood that black, inner-city drug offenders would receive harsher prison sentences (Building Blocks for Youth 2002; Karp 2000).

Explaining Minority Involvement in Street Crime

The urban underclass. The historical and contemporary evidence of discrimination in drug policy is compelling. But minority involvement in street crime still requires explanation, and much evidence exists that suggests that this involvement can be explained from a class perspective. Clifford Shaw and Henry McKay (1942), for example, found that the ecological association between crime and adverse socioeconomic conditions in the city of Chicago persisted over the first three decades of the twentieth century, regardless of the race or ethnic group residing in the area (see Chapter 4). In a follow-up study, Robert Bursik and Jim Webb (1982) documented a similar pattern in Chicago through the 1940s. During this time crime rates remained fairly stable. Since the 1950s, however, racial/ethnic turnover has been accompanied by greater destabilization of these areas and increased rates of crime.

William Julius Wilson (1987) attributes this destabilization in Chicago and other urban areas to the general decline in entry-level manufacturing jobs as well as the movement of these jobs from the cities to the suburbs. These trends have deprived African American residents of the job opportunities enjoyed by earlier arrivals. Wilson argues that the structural correlates of crime and economic disadvantage—including poverty, joblessness, and family instability—are not race specific; crime rates can be expected to vary with such community conditions irrespective of racial composition (Krivo & Peterson 1996; Sampson & Wilson 1995; Wilson 1987). But what Wilson wants us to understand is how these conditions have come to be concentrated in certain African American communities in the United States.

Wilson's work (1987) addresses a profound paradox that has developed since the mid–twentieth century: conditions for some minorities, especially some African Americans, have deteriorated at a time when civil rights and antidiscrimination laws have expanded (see Cose 1999b). According to Wilson, the civil rights movement opened up opportunities for educated and middle-class African Americans to advance, but left behind the less educated and those with few job skills. Furthermore, Gary LaFree and Kriss Drass (1996) add, while expanded educational opportunities may have improved the prospects for graduates, they may have lowered the prospects for nongraduates. An increasingly educated work force may produce an educational inflation effect whereby "jobs are increasingly filled by those with more advanced credentials" and less educated workers are replaced with more educated ones (p. 617).

Wilson's thesis is consistent with research on the relationship between income inequality and crime, which finds that African American crime rates (over time and between geographical areas) are more highly associated with *intraracial* (within-group) inequality than with *interracial* (between-group) inequality (Harer & Steffensmeier 1992; LaFree & Drass 1996). In other words, it is inequality among African Americans rather than inequality between blacks and whites that is associated with the most variation in crime rates. Similarly, Ramiro Martinez (1996) found that intra-Latino inequality, not Anglo-Latino inequality, was related to rates of Latino homicide.

Expectations of racial and ethnic minority involvement in crime are consistent with strain theory, which postulates that the absence of economic opportunities will produce the greatest pressure for crime among disadvantaged groups. And the importance of within-group measures of inequality makes particular sense in light of strain theory's proposition about relative deprivation. Also, **reference group theory** predicts that members of a group will be more likely to look internally rather than externally for standards of comparison. "People assess how well, or badly, they are faring economically not by comparing themselves with the population as a whole, but with particular reference groups with whom they share some status attribute" (Harer & Steffensmeier 1992:1036; Merton & Rossi 1968).

Furthermore, according to Wilson (1987), as both middle-class blacks and working-class whites migrated to the suburbs, the inner city was depleted not only of financial resources but of social resources as well: positive role models who reinforce conventional values, provide networks of informal social control, and offer support for schools, churches, recreation, and other community organizations (Bursik & Grasmick 1993). Remaining are fewer male and female "old heads" who are respected for their wisdom about avoiding crime and staying out of trouble. Left to fill the void is a growing informal economy of off-the-books enterprises (e.g., unlicensed cabs, house cleaning, home and car repair), welfare dependency, and crime (e.g., drugs, stolen goods, prostitution, gangs) (Anderson 1999; Pattillo 1998; Robinson 1993).

While Wilson generally aligns himself with the liberal political movement, he has criticized liberals for failing to acknowledge the "social dislocations" that have become part of the "ghetto underclass" (1991:1). Male unemployment and imprisonment have reduced the number of reliable marriage partners, and female-headed households and out-of-wedlock births have risen. The increase in single-parent families has occurred in the larger society as well, but it is more pronounced among the poor (Brooks-Gunn et al. 1993; Krivo & Peterson 1996; Sampson & Wilson 1995). Although it is not surprising that a single mother in poverty has difficulty providing "her children with the social and material support needed for them to succeed," it is important not to misconstrue Wilson's position as a "decline in family values" argument (Neuman 1996:707). Wilson views these social dislocations not as a cause but as a *consequence* of structural changes in the economy that, in his view, have been exacerbated by the "blaming the poor" rhetoric of some conservative politicians and the failure (or absence) of government policies vis-à-vis the inner city.

Wilson (1987) also argues that there are **concentration effects** to these socioeconomic conditions that create and sustain a condition of social isolation. Patterns of residential segregation associated with expanded suburban housing markets and government-constructed public housing projects have geographically concentrated the minority poor (Hagan 1994; Krivo & Peterson 1996; Massey 1990). Freeways have divided and isolated core sectors of heavily populated cities, further separating residents from centers of employment. Minority workers also experience employer discrimination and lack familiarity with the cultural norms of the white-dominated workplace. Deficits in workplace experience accumulate over the life course and the resultant social disadvantages are passed on to the next generation (Anderson 1999; Cancio et al. 1996; Hagan 1993; Kasinitz & Rosenberg 1996; Tienda & Stier 1996).

Moreover, persistent residential segregation by race means that the black middle class is exposed to more criminogenic influences than the white middle class (Logan & Stults 1999). Black, middle-class neighborhoods are more likely than white, middle-class neighborhoods "to be nestled between areas that are less economically stable and have higher crime rates" (Pattillo 1998:751). As Sampson and Wilson note, "In not one city over 100,000 in the United States do blacks live in ecological equality with whites. . . . The 'worst' urban contexts in which whites reside are considerably better than the average context of black communities" (1995:42). It is important to reiterate, however, that Wilson's insightful analysis of racial inequality is not meant to suggest that the problems of the urban poor are the fault of the people who live in the inner city or that residents prefer to live under such conditions. Rather, Wilson urges us to recognize that crime prevention efforts that do not address the intersection of race and class are inevitably bound to fail.

Beyond the subculture of violence. An alternative approach to explaining racial and ethnic minority involvement in crime focuses specifically on the problem of violence. Marvin Wolfgang and Franco Ferracuti (1967) have advanced a **subculture of violence** theory based on the proposition that a subculture exists in certain segments of society (e.g., lower-class minority groups) that contains elements of mainstream (i.e., white middle-class) culture but that is more supportive of the use of physical force in everyday social interactions. This acceptance of force increases the probability of violent confrontations in response to jostles, insults, threats, or displays of weapons. Avoidance of violence by group members is more difficult, for it can lead to rejection by one's peers and loss of self-esteem.

Aggregate-level research testing this proposition has typically analyzed the relationship between the proportion of a given population that is nonwhite (e.g., percentage black or Latino) and rates of homicide. These studies, however, provide no direct measure of subcultural values, and some find that any nonwhite-homicide connection disappears when socioeconomic factors are taken into account (Kposowa & Breault 1993; Parker 1989; Williams 1984).

Aggregate research has also tested the proposition that this subculture of violence is more pronounced in some regions of the United States. Studies have found that the South (followed by the West) has the highest rate of homicide (Huff-Corzine et al. 1986; Nelsen et al. 1994). Interestingly, southern whites have especially high homicide rates. In addition, survey evidence indicates that in some defensive or retaliatory situations (e.g., in response to someone breaking into one's house, to someone seen beating a woman, and to someone seen beating a child after the child had accidentally damaged another's car), whites are more willing to use violence than blacks (Ellison 1991; Shoemaker & Williams 1987). Lynn Curtis (1975) adds that individuals throughout all sectors of society are influenced by multiple value systems. Mainstream cultural media, for instance, often glamorize violence, and physical prowess and toughness, sexual conquest, shrewdness and manipulativeness, and thrill-seeking and risk-taking behaviors are all part of the "subterranean values" of conventional culture (Matza & Sykes 1961). In any case, the United States clearly is a very violent nation. It has the highest homicide rate among industrial democracies, and even without the homicides committed by African Americans, the U.S. rate would still be a statistical outlier (Zimring & Hawkins 1997).

Sampson and Wilson (1995) approach the issue of crime and cultural (or subcultural) values somewhat differently than Wolfgang and Ferracuti. In their view, cultural influences exist but "vary systematically with structural features of the urban environment. . . . Community contexts . . . shape . . . [the] cognitive landscapes or ecologically constructed norms . . . regarding appropriate standards and expectations of conduct. That is, in structurally disorganized slum communities . . . a system of values emerges in which crime, disorder, and drug use are less than fervently condemned and hence expected as part of everyday life" (pp. 41, 50). It is true that there are voices in these communities that denounce these practices, but according to Sampson and Wilson these voices are being heard less often than in the past.

In his ethnographic research in Philadelphia, Elijah Anderson (1994, 1999) describes an oppositional street culture or **code of the street** that characterizes the inner-city, African American community (see Chapter 4). Even the most conscientious and concerned parents, he notes, feel it's important to encourage their children to be "streetwise," to learn how to handle themselves on the street. The heart of the street code is "respect"— being treated with proper deference. Even a fleeting or awkward glance, or eye contact that lingers too long, can be taken as an sign of disrespect or "dissing." Anderson argues that this code is a cultural adaptation to residents' lack of faith in the ability of the criminal justice system to offer them protection without discrimination. Under these circumstances, residents take on the responsibility of self-protection (see Kubrin & Weitzer 2003). Children witnessing disputes in the street see that "might makes right": "In almost every case the victor is the person who physically won the altercation, and this person often enjoys the esteem and respect of onlookers" (Anderson 1994:86). Under these conditions, humility or "turning the other cheek" is no virtue and can in fact be dangerous. Failure to respond to the intimidation or dissing of another encourages further violation.

Ruth Horowitz (1987) found a similar code of personal honor in a Chicano community in Chicago. Here "honor revolves around a man's ability to command deference in interpersonal relations . . . [and avoid] any aspersions on his masculinity" (p. 440). Gang youths and nongang youths differ in that the former "seek out and initiate challenges to another's honor as one way of publicly asserting . . . and enhancing their reputation," whereas the latter only defend their honor upon provocation (p. 441). In the culture of the gang, considerable value is placed on acquiring a reputation (or "rep") for oneself and the gang, and younger Chicano gang members "want to match or outdo the reputation of their predecessors" (Moore 1991:60). These youths take pride in being *"loco"* (crazy) or *"muy loco"* (very crazy) and in describing themselves as violent.

William Harvey (1986) suggests that the minority experience of powerlessness, alienation, frustration, and anger has coalesced in what he describes as a **subculture of exasperation**. Unable to vent their hostility toward whites or those in power, minorities channel their aggression in exhibitions of toughness against those they interact with on a daily basis. As Nathan McCall once thought, "I can't do much to keep whites from dissin' me, but I damn sure can keep black folks from doing it" (1994:55). Occasionally, however, an opportunity to put whites in their place presented itself. McCall recounts a time when he and his friends attacked an innocent white youth:

> The fellas and I were hanging out on our corner . . . when [a] white boy . . . came pedaling a bicycle casually through the neighborhood. . . . We all took off after him and knocked him off the bike. . . . We stomped . . . and kicked him . . . in the head and face and watched the blood gush from his mouth. I kicked him in the stomach and nuts. . . . With each blow delivered, I . . . remembered some recent racial slight: THIS is for all the times you followed me round in stores. . . . THIS is for the times you treated me like a nigger. . . . THIS is for G.P.—General Principle—just 'cause you white. . . . We walked away, laughing, boasting, competing for bragging rights about who'd done the most damage. . . . We called it "gettin' some get-back," securing revenge for all the shit they'd heaped on blacks all these years. (pp. 3–4)

Charles Silberman (1978) adds that the depletion of positive role models in the black community has made it difficult for young African Americans to learn how to control such rage. Moreover, contemporary popular media such as gangster rap reinforce and romanticize the value placed on rebellion and opposition to mainstream culture (Kitwana 2002; McCall 1997).

Alvin Poussaint (1983) sees elements of self-hatred in black-on-black crime, which is the leading cause of death among young African American males and females (Messerschmidt 1997). According to Poussaint, some African Americans are still psychologically scarred, still bear a legacy of internalizing the negative image imposed on them by their oppressors (see Chapter 1). Offenders and victims in black-on-black crime often share a low self-image and low threshold for frustration. Recall how Sanyika Shakur said he "had little respect for life when practically all my life I had seen people assaulted, maimed, and blown away . . . and no one seemed to care" (1993:102). McCall (1994) points out how this attitude pervaded his relationships with black women, which were marked by violence and sexual exploitation. Exploiting a black woman "was another way for a guy to show the other fellas how cold and hard he was. It wasn't until I became an adult that . . . I realized that we thought we loved sisters but we actually hated them. We hated them because they were black and we were black and, on some level much deeper than we realized, we hated . . . ourselves" (p. 50).

Finally, Wilson (1991) sees another consequence of the "cognitive landscape" of the urban poor: individuals' perceptions of self-efficacy and their ability to exercise personal agency to improve their lives over the long term are often undermined (see Chapter 1):

> People may seriously doubt that they can do or accomplish what is expected, or they may feel confident of their abilities but nonetheless give up trying because they believe that their efforts will ultimately be futile due to an environment that is unresponsive, discriminatory, or punitive. . . . Such beliefs affect the level of challenge that is pursued, the amount of effort expended in a given venture, and the degree of perseverance when confronting difficulties. (p. 11)

Nevertheless, children of color growing up poor do not face completely homogeneous life chances. In his research, Anderson (1999) found that residents distinguished between what they described as "decent" and "street" families, two orientations that often existed simultaneously within the same extended family network. The so-called decent families are composed mainly of the working poor and "tend to be better off financially than their street-oriented neighbors" (1994:83). Parents in these families socialize their children to accept mainstream values of hard work, self-reliance, respect for authority, and self-improvement through education. They tend toward strict child-rearing practices and encourage their children to "walk a straight moral line" and to be on guard against trouble that might come their way. On the other hand, parents from so-called street families lack effective parenting skills and socialize their children to accept the code of the street. Their lives are often disorganized and complicated by problems with drugs or alcohol or other self-destructive behaviors. Children are left to fend for themselves and "come up hard" on the street.

According to Anderson, the overwhelming majority of inner-city families "try to approximate the decent-family model" (1994:83). Children from these families, however, interact daily with children from the street and "have a chance to go either way" (p. 86). They realize they must choose a direction. The choice they make will depend largely on how fully they have already been socialized by their parents. On the other hand, children from street families rarely absorb the values of decent families. When they do, the positive influence almost always comes from nonfamily settings—such as church, youth groups, or school—where they have the opportunity to become involved with caring adult mentors (Williams & Kornblum 1985).

But the streets can be alluring for youths of all class backgrounds. Patrice Gaines (1993) grew up in a middle-class, African American family. In her youth she was powerfully attracted to the "bad boyz" who daringly defied the law, carrying guns and earning their money through robbery, theft, and drugs:

Their behavior was an aphrodisiac. When you're a black child who believes she has no control over her life, you create your own definition of freedom. These men exuded freedom. They controlled their lives, working when they wanted to and at what they chose to work at. . . . I wanted the power I thought they possessed, and before long, I reached for it much as . . . [they] did. . . . It was adventure—making up your own rules and knowing how to live the "street life." (pp. 5–7)

■ Adolescent Subcultures and Law-Violating Youth Groups

"Juvenile delinquency" is a term that is often used to describe the dimension of the crime problem associated with the behavior of young people. Juvenile gangs have been at the forefront of this concern. But although most youthful law violations are committed in groups, not all of these groups can be considered "gangs" (Erickson & Jensen 1977; Stafford 1984).

Malcolm Klein has defined a gang as consisting of youths who consider themselves to be a distinct group (usually one with a group name), who are perceived as a distinct group by others in the community, and who have "been involved in a sufficient number of delinquent incidents to call forth a consistent negative response from neighborhood residents and/or law enforcement agencies" (1971:13). The third element of Klein's definition—a consistent negative response from the community—would exclude as gangs many groups of delinquent youths who have avoided societal labeling. In his study "The Saints and Roughnecks," for example, William Chambliss (1973) found that the lower-class Roughnecks were more likely to elicit a negative community reaction than the middle-class Saints, even though the Saints were extensively involved in illegal activities (see Chapter 1). Walter Miller (1980) suggests that **law-violating youth group** may be a more appropriate term than "gang" for most delinquent groups. Other criminologists argue that the phenomenon of youth-group law violation should be addressed in terms of a broader theory of **adolescent subcultures** (Berger 1996; Schwendinger & Schwendinger 1985; Wooden & Blazak 2001).

Historically, the origins of modern adolescent subcultures can be traced to the rapid industrialization and urbanization experienced by capitalist societies in the late nineteenth century. After World War II these subcultures began to take on increasingly distinct characteristics. Currently, in the age of mass media (e.g., music, MTV, movies), these subcultures can exist as "geographically diffuse social movement[s]" of youths who do not require face-to-face interaction to maintain a common set of argot (slang), attitudes, beliefs, interests, and physical appearances (Campbell & Muncer 1989:272). Nevertheless, the most essential elements of adolescent subcultures still emerge in local interactional settings (Corsaro & Eder 1990; England 1967).

In advanced capitalist societies such as the United States, adolescents are differentiated from adults, and for years they are more or less segregated in educational institutions. In many respects, schools have replaced neighborhoods as the primary physical sites for the formation of adolescent subcultures. Even school-age youths who do not attend classes regularly generally go to school to meet their friends and to hang out with others. The segregation of youths in schools increases the frequency and intensity of interaction among peers, who turn to one another for social approval and personal validation (Brotherton 1994; Schwartz & Merten 1967).

According to the Schwendingers (1985), adolescent subcultures reflect the class backgrounds of youths yet are relatively independent of class status. Like economic classes, networks of adolescent groups are stratified in terms of status and prestige. The higher-status groups tend to recruit from the middle and upper classes, while the lower-status groups recruit from the lower and working classes. As Gary Schwartz and Don Merten observe, the "dominant values institutionalized in the status system of the . . . high school are those held by the majority of the upper-middle-class segment of [the] youthful population" (1967:461). However, youths often disagree about the relative worth or status of different groups, and regardless of class position, personal attributes such as athletic ability, physical attractiveness, personality, and interpersonal skills may allow movement up or down the status hierarchy of peer relations (Berger 1996).

The Schwendingers (1985) refer to two of the most enduring general types of adolescent subcultures as **streetcorner** and **socialite youths**. Streetcorner youths recruit from the lower strata of the adolescent population. These are the groups, like Chambliss's Roughnecks (1973), that are more likely to be perceived and labeled as bad or delinquent kids. They are at a competitive disadvantage, economically and culturally, when they begin formal schooling, and their position relative to more privileged youths often deteriorates further as times goes on. Moreover, unlike low-achieving affluent youths, streetcorner youths do not have the family resources to provide them with the extra tutoring, counseling, cultural experiences (e.g., travel), and the like that might help them recover from initial academic setbacks. Nor do they have the financial backing of their families that would allow them a second chance in life by financing their way through college after a mediocre educational career.

The socialite youths, on the other hand, are akin to Chambliss's Saints (1973). They are generally the elite group of adolescents who are for the most part college-bound regardless of academic achievement. These youths are better able to finance the material commodities necessary for full participation in adolescent subcultural activities (e.g., fashionable clothes, entertainment, alcohol/drugs, cars). While they may be less involved than streetcorner youths in more serious crimes, they are as (or more) involved in "vehicle violations, vandalism, drinking, gambling, petty theft, truancy, sexual promiscuity, and other garden varieties" of delinquency (Schwendinger & Schwendinger 1985:56). When their law violations are discovered by authorities, they are more likely to be "treated as 'pranks,' lapses of judgment, or expressions of 'bad taste'" and are typically ignored or covered up (p. 54). Hagan (1991) characterizes this group as a party sub-culture that is only "playing" at crime. Although socialite youths are less likely to get into trouble with the law, when they do they are better able than their streetcorner counterparts to finance attorney fees to help them avoid any serious consequences for their actions.

Members of youth subcultures refer to each other by various names or metaphors that serve as shorthand linguistic devices that enable them to communicate with one another about the characteristics and relative status of different groups. The particular group names are always in flux. While some are specific to certain localities, others are shared nationwide. In ear-lier decades, streetcorner youths were often called *greasers, hoods,* and *eses* (slang for "hey, man"). In later eras, they've been dubbed *burnouts, dirtballs, punkers, stoners,* and *homies,* for instance, or they've been refer-enced by their street gang names. Socialite youths were previously called *socialites* or *socs,* while *jocks* and *preppies* are more common today (Berger 1996; Schwendinger & Schwendinger 1985; Wooden & Blazak 2001).

▒ *Middle-Class Delinquency: Renegade Kids and Suburban Outlaws*

Self-report surveys have found variables derived from social learning theo-ry (e.g., peer-group influences) and social control theory (e.g., parent-child bonds) helpful in explaining middle-class delinquency (see Chapter 4). Few delinquency studies, however, have really taken us into the world of the white, middle-class, suburban teenager. Wayne Wooden and Randy Blazak's book *Renegade Kids, Suburban Outlaws: From Youth Culture to Delinquency* (2001), is a refreshing exception (also see Gaines 1990; Hersch 1998). Much of the data for Wooden and Blazak's book were derived from interviews with youths living in the suburbs of Los Angeles in the late 1980s and first half of the 1990s. According to Wooden and Blazak, the delinquencies of these youths are motivated in large part by boredom and alienation from conventional society. Crime is a form of risk-taking rebellion against what youths perceive as the tranquil mediocrity of con-temporary life. There is excitement to be found in testing the limits, in chal-lenging authority and getting away with it. But while most youths get their kicks in mildly delinquent ways, some progress into more serious forms of thievery and violence.

For the most part Wooden and Blazak characterize the **renegade kids** as authority-rejecting identity-seekers who are generally harmless to others. Many, however, abuse drugs and some engage in other self-destructive behaviors such as cutting or burning themselves or even suicide. The **suburban outlaws**, on the other hand, are those youths whose rebellion takes the form of more serious theft, property damage, and violence to others.

Punkers are a main focus of Wooden and Blazak's portrayal of renegade kids. Punkers are known for their defiant appearance. Skidd Marx, a seventeen-year-old male punker, sported "black hair spiked . . . with three separate 1-foot tails in back. . . . [He wore] eye makeup, a black leather jacket studded with spikes, a white T-shirt with a punk band logo, . . . black Levis rolled up high, and black Converse high tops . . . [and had] four hanging earrings in each ear and a loop pierced into his right nostril" (p. 36). When asked what "punk" meant to him, Skidd replied that it meant "doing your own thing" and getting "past what people look like on the outside" (p. 36). Some punkers claimed that the punk identity actually helped them move beyond previous involvement with drugs and alcohol.

Wooden and Blazak note that the suburban mall has become a common meeting place for youths, including punkers who are called "mall rats." Mall merchants have complained about punkers who shoplift and who scare away and accost customers. Such complaints notwithstanding, most punkers probably do not engage in such activities. It is more likely that most of the serious mall crime is committed by other offenders attracted to the suitable targets that shopping centers afford.

Wooden and Blazak's research also examines the delinquencies of higher-status renegade youths. The activities of one group of jocks, the *Spur Posse,* received national media exposure in 1993. The Spur Posse consisted of a group of twenty to thirty top high school athletes at one suburban school. These youths were preoccupied with "hooking up" (having sex) with as many girls as possible. They competed with each other to see who could "score" with the most girls, and they often took turns having sex with the same ones. The boys boasted of their conquests but considered the girls "sluts" (see Tanenbaum 2000). Eight of the Spur Posse were "arrested on charges of lewd conduct, unlawful intercourse, and rape allegedly involving seven girls from 10 to 16 years of age" (p. 58). They were also charged with burglary, assault, and intimidation of witnesses.

Taggers constitute one of the suburban outlaw groups studied by Wooden and Blazak. Taggers mimic the graffiti-writing "crews" that were first observed among lower-class youths (Williams & Kornblum 1985). Tagging offers its participants an exiting adrenaline rush, and some of the more extended "pieces" can be quite artistic. Nevertheless, the marking of school grounds and property as well as "overhead freeway signs, walls, . . . buses and trains, . . . traffic signs, bridges, and street poles" is perceived by most members of the community as vandalism, pure and simple, as sheer destruction of property (Wooden & Blazak 2001:120).

Wooden and Blazak attribute suburban tagging, in part, to the cultural diffusion of inner-city (especially African American) street culture: "The popularity of becoming part of the tagger scene . . . stem[s] from suburban white youths' interest in gangsta rap. . . . Enjoying hip-hop music and 'getting down' becomes, for these white 'home boys,' their form of replicating inner-city, black ghetto 'chic'" (p. 122). In addition, Wooden and Blazak suggest, suburban tagging is a response to the movement of inner-city gangs into suburbia:

> Rather than merely mimicking . . . these urban youths, suburban tagger crews are forming to compete or oppose them. In effect, the taggers have reversed the direction of gang diffusion from the inner-city outward. In other words, the tagger's movement patterns—and night runs—frequently are from suburban areas along freeways back toward the inner-city, leaving their marks or pieces . . . to indicate their presence and influence along the way. (pp. 122–123)

It is as if taggers are saying, "We will not be overlooked. We will not be trampled on." But most taggers want no trouble with inner-city gangs. As one youth explained, "We are afraid of gangs. . . . All we want is to be able to write on walls. . . . However, if a crew does write over a name of a gang, they must arm themselves. This is when taggers become violent. Some gangs now require 'payoffs' for taggers to move through their areas" (p. 124).

Unlike taggers, the *skinhead* suburban outlaws studied by Wooden and Blazak tended to embrace violence and attack minority groups, including racial/ethnic groups, immigrants, Jews, and gays. Skinheads can be recognized by their shaved or close-cropped hair, green flight jackets, suspenders, heavy jeans rolled up over industrial boots, and white power and/or Nazi regalia, although not all skinheads look this way today. Racist skinheads are aligned ideologically with the adult neo-Nazi movement, even to the extent of taking orders from such groups as the White Aryan Resistance and Aryan Brotherhood (see Chapter 10). They are critical if not hostile to the U.S. government, which they believe promotes the interests of nonwhites over the interest of whites. But not all skinheads are racist, or if they are, some "try to stay clear of overt racial violence" (p. 134). These skinheads are more survivalist in nature, being concerned with their future survival in the event of a nuclear holocaust or natural disaster. There are even antiracist skinhead groups with racially mixed membership that have been formed in reaction to the racist groups.

Stoner gangs, known for their extensive drug and alcohol abuse, are among the most violent suburban outlaw groups. They are also active in property crimes like armed robbery, burglary, and auto theft. Wooden and Blazak found that these youths are the most likely to have been physically (and sexually) abused, rather than merely neglected, by their parents. They describe these groups as cultlike, with a shared interest in heavy metal music and attire (e.g., metal-spiked wrist cuffs, collars and belts, and sacrilegious or anti-Christian items). Some stoner youths also engage in satanic rituals, including animal sacrifices. However, not all youths interested in satanism are hard-core criminals. Some merely like to "practice" satanic rituals and magic, smoke marijuana, and listen to heavy metal with a small group of friends in order to provoke or upset their parents.

■ Urban Street Gangs

Participation in law-violating youth groups—whether or not these groups are called gangs—is a common experience for young people of all class and racial/ethnic backgrounds. Nevertheless, urban street gangs have arguably drawn more media and public attention than those of the suburban variety. But like the suburban groups, inner-city gangs can be understood, in the Schwendingers' terms (1985), as streetcorner groups that are part of the broader adolescent subcultural phenomenon. As C. Ronald Huff notes, "It is important to acknowledge that it is normal and healthy for adolescents to want to be with their peers . . . and gangs represent an extreme manifestation of that age-typical emphasis on being together and belonging to something" (1993:6). In William Sanders's opinion (1994), however, it is the violence that distinguishes gangs from other adolescent groups.

Frederick Thrasher's classic study (1927) of Chicago youth gangs of an earlier era offers a convenient point of departure for a consideration of contemporary urban gangs. (Thrasher was part of the social disorganization school of thought discussed in Chapter 4.) Youth gang members in the 1920s were largely the children of economically disadvantaged, white European immigrants—primarily Irish, Italians, and Poles, but also Germans, Jews, Slavs, and Swedes. Most gang members started out in thievery, which was engaged in as much for sport as for economic gain. Gangs that formed more or less spontaneously as ordinary streetcorner groups were consolidated through rivalry and strife. As Jerome Skolnick observes, "Thrasher traced the rise of gangs to . . . the disintegration of family life, schools, and religion, . . . [the lack of] wholesome alternatives, . . . [and] the corruption and indifference of local politicians. The employment opportunities available to these [youths] usually involved monotonous jobs with low wages that could scarcely compete with the rewards of the gang or with the fun of bonding and stealing" (1992:111).

In many respects, Skolnick adds, contemporary gangs have not changed in fundamental ways. Youths still join gangs for fun and recreation, to enhance their ability to make money, for physical protection, and for a sense of belonging to a community or alternative family (Sanchez Jankowski 1991). In some Chicano barrios of Los Angeles, "children, parents, and even grandparents have belonged to the same gang [for decades]. Although the adults fear and disapprove of the violence of today's gangs, they take pride in the tradition of gang membership" and expect the younger generation to preserve and uphold the neighborhood gang name (Skolnick 1992:114). More generally, gangs (whatever their race or ethnic background) are often tolerated in their communities because gang youths are not social outsiders among residents; they are sons and daughters, grandchildren, nieces and nephews, the neighbors' kids. The majority of their time is not spent in law-violating activities, and their behavior is appropriate in most social situations (Horowitz 1987; Shelden et al. 2001; Venkatesh 1997).

In his urban ethnography, Mercer Sullivan (1989) studied three neighborhoods in Brooklyn, New York, in the early 1980s: Projectville was a largely African American community, Hamilton Park was predominately white, and La Barriada was largely a mixture of Hispanics and whites. Projectville had the highest rate of poverty (52 percent living under the poverty level), followed by La Barriada (43 percent), and Hamilton Park (12 percent). Projectville also had the highest overall crime rate, and Hamilton Park the lowest, while La Barriada had the highest rate of violent crime.

In all three neighborhoods, nevertheless, Sullivan found that male youths progressed through a series of life stages that influenced their involvement in and commitment to crime. During the early to mid-teen years, youths from the same neighborhood began hanging out together in loosely knit groups and participating in turf fights with youths from surrounding areas. They also stole items like radios, bicycles, and clothes, primarily for use rather than for sale on the open market; and when they did sell stolen property they had no idea of its actual market value. Importantly, however, these early-life forays into crime prepared them for more serious later-life criminality. Engaging in theft helped them revise their conception of "property rights . . . [as] no longer fixed but . . . [as] something over which [they] could exert control" (Robinson 1993:317). And from fighting they learned how to acquire and use weapons in violent crimes.

By the middle teenage years, the youths had acquired more experience in crime. They were now physically stronger and had a greater desire to consume commodities.

[They also] learned more about the value of stolen items and about the networks for converting them to cash; they were better able to weigh the risks and benefits between types of crime, as well as between crime and legitimate employment. The motivation for crime now became economic, a means of support rather than an occasional excursion to vary the day-to-day boredom of just hanging out . . . and as a youth took on crime as his main source of income, he dropped out of street fighting. (Robinson 1993:317)

Along the way, opportunities for legitimate employment, when available, reduced the incentive to engage in crime. The Hamilton Park white youths in particular had somewhat greater access to networks of legitimate employment and were thus the most likely to opt out of crime. Overall, Sullivan (1989) found that by their late teens most youths chose to desist from crime because escalating criminality increased their risk of apprehension. For example, the housing projects where the Projectville African American youths lived afforded limited opportunities for profitable theft. When these youths began committing robberies and purse snatchings outside of their own neighborhoods, they increased their exposure and hence their chances of getting caught. Some who became disillusioned with violent theft, however, became attracted to drug sales instead.

Felix Padilla (1992), in his ethnography of Puerto Rican gangs in Chicago, reports that youths often began their involvement in the drug trade as "runners" or "mules," but they soon realized that the distributors made most of the profits. Sullivan (1989) found that it was fairly easy for Brooklyn youths to obtain drugs on consignment until they acquired enough capital to stake themselves out. But even though a competent drug dealer could earn between $500 and $1,000 a week in the early 1980s, the life chances of these youths remained for the most part dismal. As one youth remarked, "I'm a good businessman. . . . I know how to buy and sell. But I've been ripped off, cut, and arrested. Now, I'm on probation and I won't get off so easy next time. But how am I gonna get a job now? . . . I can't go up to somebody and say, 'Listen, I know how to buy and sell. . . . I've been buying and selling for years'" (p. 175).

Gang members today are on the average older and have fewer opportunities to mature out of the gang than they did in Thrasher's day (Skolnick 1992). Hence some graduate to organized crime. Huff defines an **organized crime group** as a mostly adult collectivity that has a more "defined leadership and organizational structure" than a youth gang and that is "frequently and deliberately involved in illegal activities directed toward economic gain, primarily through the provision of illegal goods and services" (1993:4–5; see Chapter 6).

Observers of the gang scene report that as early as the late 1960s and early 1970s, gangs in some large metropolitan areas, most notably in

Chicago and New York, were beginning to be transformed "from territorially oriented younger members to commercially oriented older (19 plus) members" (Robinson 1993:312). Some African American and Latino groups, for instance, began to muscle in on the territory previously controlled by Italian American crime organizations (see Box 4.1). Needless to say, this transition of control has not always been peaceful.

Ironically, since the 1970s, incarceration of gang members has facilitated gang organization by bringing together a captive population of similarly situated offenders who can be easily recruited into larger, more powerful organizations (Balkan et al. 1980; Jacobs 1977; Irwin 1980). For example, Jeff Fort, a leader of Chicago's *Black P. Stone Nation,* formed the *El Rukns* while he was imprisoned in 1978. According to Cyril Robinson:

> Soon after his release, [Fort] met with representatives of the Italian syndicate having vice interests in El Rukn territory. Reputedly, the Italian group ordered Fort to keep hands off. After burning down the mob restaurant where the warnings were given, Fort, in turn, ordered the syndicate out of El Rukn territory. . . . By 1981, the El Rukns were investing their drug profits in real estate and other legitimate businesses and were employing pharmacists, doctors, accountants, and lawyers. Satellite clubs or alliances were [also] formed in other parts of the country. (1993:313)

Sanders (1994) studied gangs in San Diego, California, through the 1980s. He found that African American gangs were more likely to sell (but less likely to use) drugs than their Chicano counterparts. Sanders did not find San Diego gangs to be particularly well organized; gang cohesiveness was rooted more in "the strengths of neighborhood . . . solidarity and loyalty" than in a formally structured organization (p. 145). However, Martin Sanchez Jankowski (1991)—who studied thirty-seven gangs in Boston, Los Angeles, and New York—argues that most gangs that are in a mature stage of development have identifiable leadership positions and established codes of conduct. Moreover, Jankowski and others have concluded that by the late 1980s gang organizations of a variety of racial and ethnic backgrounds had become more entrepreneurial in nature, shifting away from turf fighting toward more "systematic involvement in drug distribution" (Padilla 1992; Taylor 1990; Venkatesh 1997:84).

Research also suggests that Asian American gangs are among the most highly entrepreneurial gangs in the country. Chinese gangs in particular, which can be found primarily in Boston, Los Angeles, New York, and San Francisco (as well as Toronto and Vancouver), have a well-defined hierarchical structure, are well-connected with adult crime groups and fraternal organizations, and have invested in legitimate businesses (Chin 1990; Shelden et al. 2001).

In interviews conducted by Skolnick and colleagues (1993), African

American gang members from Los Angeles indicated that perceived economic benefit has increasingly become the primary reason for joining gangs. Skolnick and colleagues attribute the change in Los Angeles, in part, to the expanded cocaine importation that has dramatically decreased the wholesale cost of the drug. Prospective gang members are now evaluated in terms of their ability to sell drugs. The gang provides members with access to and control of drug markets within the gang's territory, shared information about the drug market (e.g., sellers, prices, out-of-town markets), protection from competitors and the police, as well as cash, loans, and "fronting" of drugs, weapons, clothes, and cars.

While African American gangs in Los Angeles appear to have first emerged in the 1950s, the infamous supergangs or gang "nations"—the *Crips* and the *Bloods*—did not emerge until the late 1960s (Bing 1991; Klein et al. 1991). These gangs are said to be "deep," consisting of a large number of sets or factions. In 1991 Léon Bing reported the existence of fifty-six Crip sets and forty-three Blood sets. In 1993 Skolnick and colleagues reported that Crip or Blood crack-cocaine operations could be found in twenty-two states and at least twenty-eight cities in regions all over the country. Gang members indicated that around 1986 they began traveling extensively to expand their drug business. This expansion was motivated, in part, by pressure from police crackdowns in Los Angeles, saturation of the Los Angeles drug market, and higher prices that could be charged in out-of-town markets. Other observers, however, believe that large-scale drug operations are still generally conducted by "individuals and small groups acting on their own rather than for the gang" (Reiner 1992:72; Shelden et al. 2001).

In his San Diego study, Sanders (1994) found that African American gangs (including Crip and Blood sets) extended their activities over a broad territory, while Chicano gangs were more confined to the barrio and lacked allegiances outside their community. On the other hand, Joan Moore and colleagues characterized Los Angeles Chicano gangs as having a "widespread pattern of non-resident gang membership" and documented several ways in which such nonresident membership developed (1983:182). Sometimes gang membership was extended to relatives who lived outside the neighborhood. At times, families of gang members moved, but youths maintained affiliation with their original gang. Gangs also formed fighting alliances with gangs in other areas, or factions split apart and affiliated with other groups. Nonresident youths sometimes sought to join a gang because of its activities or reputation. Occasionally the borders of a barrio may have been unclear, leaving some members living in disputed areas, or freeway construction may have altered the community ecology, dividing a previously contiguous neighborhood.

In the Chicago area, both African American and Latino (primarily

Puerto Rican) gangs have grouped around the larger *People* and *Folks* gang nations or organizations (Bensinger 1984; Padilla 1992). These Chicago gangs can be traced to the late 1950s and early 1960s. Like the Crips and Bloods, People and Folks claim membership in multiple cities. John Hagedorn (1988), for instance, documented the emergence of People and Folks sets in Milwaukee, Wisconsin, around 1980.

Gangs now appear to be forming in smaller cities, towns, and even rural areas (Skolnick et al. 1993; Takata & Zevitz 1990). In a study of rural/small-town gang origins in southeastern Wisconsin, Linda Stoneall (1997) offers several hypotheses for the diffusion of youth gangs. Whereas Hagedorn (1988) traced the rise of gangs in Milwaukee (a city of about 650,000) to the deindustrialization and persistent racial segregation of that city, Stoneall suggests that economic development in smaller communities increases the size and diversity of the population in ways that can facilitate gang activity. As families of gang members move, often to escape the problems of large gang cities, youths bring with them gang experience and connections. Or at times youths with gang ties are dispersed through foster-home placements. Stoneall also suggests, like Skolnick and colleagues (1993), that gangs members are reaching out to new areas to expand their drug markets. In addition, school busing has contributed both to the diffusion of gangs and to a pattern of nonresident gang membership (Hagedorn 1988). At the same time, Stoneall argues, much of the apparent gang activity in small communities may simply be due to cultural diffusion and youth fads: the media exposes nongang youths to the broader gang subculture, and local peer groups transmit neighboring gang names, symbols, and styles that are emulated by youths. Adolescents who refer to themselves by the same gang name may not actually be in the same gang, or may not be in a gang at all; they may be a group of ordinary law-violating peers who are merely playing at being a gang.

The diffusion of gangs from urban to rural areas has also been noted in research on Native American youths. According to Ada Peco Melton:

> [A] 1994 Bureau of Indian Affairs (BIA) Law Enforcement Division Survey of 75 tribal and BIA law-enforcement officers in 31 states . . . identified 181 gangs active on or near Indian country. . . . The largest Indian tribe, the Navajo Nation, has reported the existence of more than 28 gangs in 13 of its tribal communities. . . . The infiltration of gangs appears similar to the migration of gangs from large metropolitan cities like East Los Angeles into such cities as Albuquerque [New Mexico] and Phoenix [Arizona]. . . . It is suspected that some of the gang organizing is being initiated by Indian teenagers who have returned to the reservation, village, or pueblo after being raised in a city. (2002:166)

While analysts continue to debate the distinction between gangs and other law-violating youth groups, it is clear that in some communities gangs have become "a recognized, albeit internally contradictory, community institution, performing a range of 'positive functions' while simultaneously engaging in behavior that has disrupted community social life" (Venkatesh 1997:107). In his ethnography of the Saints, an African American Chicago street gang, Sudhir Venkatesh (1997) reported that the gang has been channeling some of its drug profits to the resident population in order to integrate itself into the social fabric of the Blackstone housing project in which it is based. (The Saints studied by Venkatesh are not the same group as the Saints studied by Chambliss.) The gang has distributed groceries and clothing, lent residents money (both interest-free and at exorbitant rates), paid the bail bond for jailed residents, replaced playground equipment, encouraged younger gang members to attend school, and offered protection from other gangs and criminal predators. The residents, in turn, have provided the Saints cover, withholding information from the police and refusing "to allow police to enter their apartments without search warrants" (p. 95). As one resident, a prominent leader on a tenant council, remarked:

> [We] stopped cooperating with police a long time ago, 'cause [the police] harass us so much and they don't do a damn thing anyway. At least the gangs is giving us something, so lot of us prefers to help them 'cause we can *always* go to them and tell them to stop the shooting. Police don't do anything for us and they can't stop no shooting anyway. . . . [The Saints] is the one providing security around here. . . . We all niggers anyway when it come down to it. (p. 95)

Some residents admit that [the Saints] "make our lives miserable, but if we piss them off, police ain't gonna come 'round here and help us out. And, shit, I gotta tell you, that most of the time it's nice, 'cause they make sure I don't get robbed up in here, they walk through the buildings like . . . police never did that!" (p. 103). Another put it this way: "We have to listen to [the Saints], 'cause when the police leave, [Saints members] are the ones who'll let you know if shootings gonna start up again, you know, they'll tell you if it's safe to go outside at night, or if you can go up north [to Roaches territory] or if you should just stay in the building" (p. 103). In the words of one Saint gang member, "We [want] to be part of the community, help our community, 'cause we're here to stay" (p. 108).

8

Gender and Crime

Margo was just twelve years old when she was raped by her mother's lover:

> My mother and this . . . horny Dominican motherfucker . . . started to have
> a thing behind my stepfather's back. . . . I knew about sex and all of that,
> although I had never had sex. . . . One day I was upstairs doing my home-
> work and he comes into my room and tells me he wants to talk. . . . Well
> the next thing I know he's taking my blouse off. . . . I don't know why I
> didn't scream . . . but I just sat there. (Williams & Kornblum 1985:64)

As the man began to remove Margo's panties, she remembered hearing
about men who killed children they had molested, and she started to panic.
The other thing she couldn't get out in her mind was "how big he was. . . . I
was hurting so bad, I was so sore. I felt, my god, what did he do to me? . . .
I never told my mother anything for two years. And when I did . . . she
slapped me. She thought I was lying. . . . She was in love with this . . .
fucker . . . [and] didn't believe her own daughter" (pp. 64–65).

This traumatic experience in Margo's life profoundly shaped her attitudes toward men and her sense of trust in human relationships more generally. Indeed, child sexual abuse is common in the background of girls and
women who become involved in prostitution and other forms of crime
(Chesney-Lind & Shelden 2004; Boyer & James 1982; Widom & Ames
1994). Abused girls often learn to associate sex with manipulation and
come to view themselves as salable commodities. And in Harlem, New
York, where Margo grew up, there were few opportunities or positive role
models available to young African American women.

By the time she was fifteen years old, Margo was engaging in casual
prostitution, starting out "with offers of $100 or more for an hour or two"
(p. 66). At first she declined, "but then decided to stop being such a fool"
and started to accept money, gifts, and trips:

> If a guy approached me and said I was beautiful and asked how much would it cost him to have me, . . . if he looked well dressed and clean I would say $200, $300, $400. . . . Some liked it enough to pay high prices. . . . The sexual acts were sexual acts. But if they brought on a smile, a kiss or hug the morning after, it was worthwhile. I felt not only wanted but needed. At the same time, a lot of lonely hearts were warmed. Call it what you will, I see my actions in a benevolent light. I enjoyed the money, spending highly, indulging in things I wouldn't normally have. . . . I hate straight hours, time clocks and suspicious bosses. . . . The risk is the thrill. . . . If [what I do] bothers others, that's their problem. . . . When it comes to money you will find very few . . . to help you make it. (pp. 65–66, 68–69)

We hear the feistiness in Margo's voice as she defends the choices she's made and tries to put the best possible spin on them. Her feistiness, however, does not completely mask her sad undertone. We sense her loneliness, her neediness, her difficulty distinguishing exploitation and affection. For Margo, as for many others, the tremendous sense of powerlessness and vulnerability experienced at the hands of sexual abuse creates an immense need to feel in control, to convince herself she is in control, in spite of the danger that may be associated with **sex work**, a range of illegal and legal acts that include prostitution as well as stripping, performing sex acts on stage, and being photographed or filmed for pornographic pictures or movies (Zatz 1997).

Margo constructed a type of femininity that simultaneously confirmed and challenged conventional femininity. It was conventional in its emphasis on being attractive and seductive to men and on servicing their sexual needs; it was nonconventional in its rejection of domesticity and legitimate work as the primary signifiers of identity and in its approval of extramarital, pecuniary, and impersonal sex (Messerschmidt 1997). Nevertheless, the story of most women involved in prostitution, drugs, and/or other crime is a grim one indeed. (Most prostitutes do not make the kind of money Margo said she made, and many are homeless.) Not only do female offenders face the burden of gender oppression, but many share with their male counterparts the burdens of disadvantaged class and minority status, living lives of "powerlessness as members of the urban underclass" (Chesney-Lind et al. 1996:200).

In this chapter we take our sociological imagination into the world of crime as gendered action. Gender, like class and race/ethnicity, shapes the social world in which we live and enables and constrains the choices we make and the actions we take in our lives. Our emphasis here is on understanding how patterns of criminality are gendered. We examine both male and female criminality, with particular attention to female offenders. In the next chapter we focus on the problem of violence against women. We recognize, however, that women and girls (like Margo) do not always fit neatly into the categories of offender or victim/survivor, and our treatment of these topics reflects this overlap, these blurred boundaries.

■ Doing Gender

Traditional gender roles, as we noted earlier, are rooted in structural arrangements of inequality (see Chapters 1 and 5). Along with the changes that have occurred in society over the last three decades, conventional patterns persist. Although schools, for example, may be less likely than in the past to emphasize traditional feminine roles for girls, and girls are often encouraged to engage in physical activities and to participate in organized athletics, gender differences in children's informal playground behaviors are still apparent. Boys are still more likely to participate in team sports in the central play areas, while girls are more likely to play hopscotch or jump rope in smaller groups (Thorne 1993). Also, peer bonding among boys tends to focus on the transgression of public rules and on teasing or insulting routines consisting of disparaging remarks about one another's clothes, appearance, mothers, and so forth (Corsaro & Eder 1990). Males who lack such verbal skills or who have "thin skins" may increasingly become targets of ridicule and even physical attack. Friendships among girls, on the other hand, are more likely to involve mutual self-disclosure and discussions about intimate relationships (Giordano et al. 1986; Thorne & Luria 1986). Nevertheless, girls continue to use cosmetics, provocative clothing, and boyfriends to challenge parental authority; some "use sexuality as a proxy for independence, . . . ironically reinforc[ing] their status as sexual objects seeking male approval—ultimately ratifying their status as the subordinate sex" (Chesney-Lind & Shelden 2004:37; Pettiway 1997).

To some extent, however, such generalizations both minimize the variability *within* gender categories and exaggerate the differences *between* them. They also fail to acknowledge the ways in which people actively challenge or oppose conventional gender scripts to construct alternative masculinities and femininities. Gender is not a fixed or static trait but an ongoing social accomplishment that is constructed in relation to how others interpret our actions. Men and women, boys and girls, are continually **doing gender**, that is, "configur[ing] and orchestrat[ing] their actions in relation to how they might be interpreted by others in the particular social context in which they occur" (Messerschmidt 1993, 1997:4; West & Zimmerman 1987). Doing gender corroborates through social interaction one's social identification as male or female. And since the social circumstances and social situations we encounter differ, there are different ways of doing femininity and masculinity.

Joyce Canaan (1991), for instance, discovered different ways of doing masculinity among young, white, working-class men in Great Britain. One man, Andrew, explains how fighting corroborates one's masculinity: "Boys want to fight in a way to look good to girls. It's a manly thing. . . . The girl's there, someone's causing trouble, you ain't just gonna laugh it off. . . . [The girls] think, 'What's he doing? He's a bit of a wanker, ay he?' Whereas if you stand up and have a go . . . you try and impress them" (p. 119).

Andrew sees fighting as manly, as a way to demonstrate to the young women how tough or "hard" he is. He is motivated to fight not just to show off but because he fears that he'll be considered "soft" ("a bit of a wanker") if he doesn't. According to Canaan, the term *wanker* refers to one who masturbates. The use of wanker as a put-down thus suggests that these young men consider "only those who have sex with a woman" to be "real men." Moreover, they "link hardness with heterosexuality" when they consider "those who have sex without a woman and without penetration . . . not 'real men'" (p. 119).

Another way to do masculinity is evident in Steve and Neil's response to Canaan's question: "Don't people think you're a wanker if you don't fight?"

> S: Nay.
> N: A mate'll respect you if you walk away from drunkenness.
> S: If anyone comes up to you and says, "Do you want a fight?" you say, "Fuck off." If they doe (don't), you just beat them up. You give them a chance to walk away. Say, "I don't want to fight, alright? I doe want no trouble, just gu away like." You'm still standing your ground, you'm standing there saying, "Gu way." (p. 116)

Steve and Neil suggest that a man can be hard without acting hard. He can gain respect (even when drunk) by standing his ground, fighting only when there's no way not to. "Standing his ground" does not imply walking away: "By preventing a fight he shows that he can 'manfully' control himself without flying off the handle." A man's decision to reject another's invitation to fight allows him to redefine the situation. If the other accedes to this redefinition, the man "effectively demonstrates that he is the more powerful of the two. In so doing he shows that he is not only powerful when fighting, but that he, more than others, determines when he will and will not fight" (p. 116).

Canaan's interviews demonstrate that masculinities (like femininities) are not static—not finished products—but are continually constructed and reconstructed in social situations. James Messerschmidt (1993) points out, for example, that white, middle-class boys who engage in **accommodating masculinity** (relatively submissive, adaptive behaviors) during school

Box 8.1   Small-Town School Shootings

In April 1999, Eric Harris and Dylan Klebold went on a shooting rampage at Columbine High School in Littleton, Colorado, killing twelve students and a teacher and then taking their own lives. This was but one chapter in a series of mass shootings in the 1990s that occurred in small-town suburban and rural communities. Although school-related homicides overall have declined since 1992, there were over twenty school incidents in which more than one person was killed (*Wisconsin State Journal* 1999a, 1999b; Wooden & Blazak 2001).

Inner-city schools still experience more violence than schools in suburban and rural areas, but it's the small-town shootings that attract the bulk of attention (Cowley 1998; Lawrence 1998). With each new incident, similar claims of disbelief emerge from the small-town residents: "How could it happen *here*?" "This isn't the inner city!" "We're not that kind of people." The consistency of these remarks prompted Patricia Williams to wonder why young African Americans are so readily feared, while young white boys like Harris and Klebold seem "so shrouded in presumptions of . . . innocence . . . [even] after professing their love for Hitler, declaring their hatred for . . . [minorities] on a public Web site, . . . downloading instructions for making bombs, accumulating ingredients, assembling them under the protectively indifferent gaze . . . of the parents and neighbors, stockpiling guns and ammunition, . . . [and] procuring hand grenades and flak jackets" (1999a:9). Like the probation officers who were supervising Harris and Klebold after the youths had burgled a car, describing them as intelligent boys with lots of promise, classmates and teachers continued to insist that the two were "good boys."

All of these small-town school shooters have been white adolescent males with access to firearms for whom violence was a transcending experience, one that made them feel omnipotent. As Luke Woodham—the sixteen-year-old who shot nine students (two fatally) and also killed his mother in Pearl, Mississippi, in 1997—said, "Murder is not weak and slow-witted, murder is gutsy and daring. . . . I killed because people like me are mistreated every day" (Cowley 1998:25). James Gilligan attributes this attitude to "the patriarchal code of honor and shame [that] generates and obligates male violence" (cited in Steinem 1999:47). However, Gloria Steinem concludes that just as we are now beginning "to raise our daughters more like our sons—more like whole people—we must begin to raise our sons more like our daughters—that is, to value empathy . . . [and] to measure success by other people's welfare as well as [our] own" (1999:47).

hours may do masculinity differently after school, meeting friends to drink, carouse, or engage in vandalism. Moreover, while one's expression of masculinity or femininity is "always individual and personal," specific forms of masculinity and femininity "are available, encouraged and permitted, depending upon one's social situation, class, race, and sexual orientation" (1995:173).

Although there are different ways of doing masculinity and femininity, there are also culturally idealized forms of masculinity and femininity, what R. W. Connell (1987) calls **hegemonic masculinity** (traditional, dominant masculinity) and **emphasized femininity** (traditional, subordinate femininity). In other words, not all forms of masculinity and femininity are equally revered or privileged in the culture as a whole. Hegemonic masculinity in Western industrialized societies is achieved through work in the paid labor market and the subordinate treatment of women and girls; it is aggressive, controlling, and sexually driven—heterosexual and heterosexist. (**Heterosexism** is the belief in the inherent superiority of heterosexuality and its entitlement to a privileged social position vis-à-vis homosexuality/bisexuality.) Hegemonic masculinity subordinates other masculinities. It attempts to negate them, to prevent them from "gaining cultural definition and recognition as alternatives [by] confining them to ghettos, to privacy, to unconsciousness" (p. 186). Emphasized femininity, in turn, complements hegemonic masculinity. It is a femininity that "is defined around compliance with . . . subordination [to men] and is oriented to accommodating the interests and desires of men." Other types of femininity "are defined centrally by strategies of resistance or forms of noncompliance . . . [or] by complex strategic combinations of compliance, resistance, and co-operation" (p. 183).

In this chapter we will examine how crime is a resource for "doing gender" and how gender is a resource for "doing crime." We will see how gender intersects with class, race/ethnicity, and other social experiences in specific situational contexts to produce a range of criminal actions, some of which sustain and some of which reconfigure or undermine traditional notions of gender.

■ Gendered Patterns of Criminality: An Overview

▨ The Gender Composition of Arrests

Gender norms and expectations are reflected in statistical patterns of crime. Table 8.1 presents *Uniform Crime Reports (UCR)* data on the gender composition of arrests for both Index and non-Index crimes (Part I and Part II offenses) for 2002. With three exceptions, males constitute a clear majority of arrests for all crimes. Females constitute a majority of arrests for runaways (60 percent) and prostitution/commercialized vice (66 percent), and male and female arrests are comparable for embezzlement.

Girls are more likely than boys to experience family-related problems that lead them to run away from home. David Finkelhor and Larry Baron

Table 8.1　Gender Composition of Arrests (2002)

	Percentage Distribution	
	Male	Female
Index crimes/Part I offenses		
Homicide[a]	89	11
Forcible rape	99	1
Robbery	90	10
Aggravated assault	80	20
Burglary	87	13
Larceny-theft	63	37
Motor vehicle theft	83	17
Arson	85	15
Non-Index crimes/Part II offenses		
Other assaults	76	24
Forgery and counterfeiting	60	40
Fraud	55	45
Embezzlement	50	50
Stolen property[a]	82	18
Vandalism	83	17
Weapons[a]	92	8
Prostitution and commercialized vice	34	66
Sex offenses[a]	92	8
Drug abuse violations	82	18
Gambling	90	10
Offenses against family and children	75	25
Driving under the influence	83	17
Liquor laws	75	25
Drunkenness	86	14
Disorderly conduct	76	24
Vagrancy	82	18
All other offenses (except traffic)	78	22
Suspicion	80	20
Curfew and loitering	69	31
Runaways	40	60

Source: FBI 2003, tab. 42.
Note: a. Homicide = murder and nonnegligent manslaughter. Sex offenses = except forcible rape and prostitution. Stolen property = buying, receiving, and possessing. Weapons = carrying, possessing, etc.

(1986) estimate that about 70 percent of child sexual abuse victims are girls, and that the abuse of girls starts earlier, lasts longer, and is more likely to be perpetrated by family members. In addition, research indicates that a higher percentage of female than male runaways have been sexually abused (Janus et al. 1987). While self-report studies suggest that boys are as likely as girls to run away, parents are less tolerant of their daughters' transgressions and more likely to report them to authorities (Canter 1982; Cernkovich & Giordano 1979a; Chesney-Lind & Shelden 2004). In any event, that runaways often turn to prostitution as a means of survival on the streets is documented by studies that show that a majority of street prostitutes have been sexually abused as juveniles. Research also finds that child sexual abuse victims are more likely to be arrested for prostitution than nonsexually abused youths, even if the latter were physically abused or neglected (Silbert & Pines 1981; Widom & Ames 1994).

Prostitution would appear to be the quintessential female crime, given society's tendency to view women as sex objects and men's greater propensity to seek out impersonal sex. In terms of sheer numbers, however, men may have greater involvement in prostitution than women. Criminal laws in most of the United States make it a crime to be either a prostitute or a customer. Although the law is less likely to be enforced against customers, there are undoubtedly several male clients, or "johns," for every female prostitute. There is also a thriving business of male prostitution serving a primarily male clientele (Calhoun 1992; Luckenbill 1986; West & de Villiers 1993). Moreover, males dominate the ranks of pimps, those who live off the earnings of a prostitute and "act as her agent and/or companion" (Beirne & Messerschmidt 1995:204). And both males and females are involved in illegal procuring (encouraging or forcing others into prostitution) and in running brothels or controlling premises used for prostitution.

Following running away and prostitution, females are most likely to be arrested for the nonviolent property crimes of larceny-theft (37 percent), forgery and counterfeiting (40 percent), fraud (45 percent), and embezzlement (50 percent). Shoplifting is the type of larceny-theft that females are most likely to commit. Although a couple of studies found that the majority of apprehended shoplifters were female (Robin 1963; Sanders 1981), self-report research indicates that females are somewhat less likely to shoplift than males and that they shoplift fewer and less costly items (Belknap 2001; Chesney-Lind & Shelden 2004; Morris 1987). Perhaps store owners, considering females more prone to this crime, are more likely to scrutinize female shoppers.

Some criminologists see a connection between females' involvement in shoplifting and their role as consumers (Campbell 1991). Females spend more time shopping as a pastime than males do, and they seem especially vulnerable to advertising campaigns that encourage consumption of personal products such as cosmetics, jewelry, and clothes. There is also a consumer dimension in women's involvement in forgery and fraud, as in the case of passing bad checks, check forgery, and credit card fraud. And women, the primary recipients of governmental welfare, constitute the bulk of offenders in welfare fraud (Datesman & Scarpitti 1980).

Women who embezzle from their employers tend to steal smaller amounts than men do. One study found that 70 percent of those who embezzled over $1,000 were male, while over 80 percent of those who embezzled less than $150 were female (Franklin 1979). A study of bank embezzlers found that 60 percent of convicted women were bank tellers, compared to 14 percent of convicted men (Daly 1989). These women were more likely to steal cash from the till, while men were more likely to manipulate financial documents and to work in conjunction with others. And although both male and female embezzlers have reported a variety of motives for their crimes, women have been more likely to mention family need and men more likely to note problems such as gambling losses or living beyond their means (Cressey 1953; Zietz 1981). Women have also been less likely to engage in corporate law violations not recorded in the *UCR*. One study found that males committed 98 percent of Securities and Exchange Commission violations, 99.5 percent of antitrust violations, and 95 percent of bribery violations (Daly 1989). Clearly, women have not had the same opportunities to commit higher-level white-collar crimes. The current patterns reflect women's and men's different positions within the gender division of labor.

◼ Has Female Criminality Increased?

In 1975 Freda Adler advanced a thesis about the emancipated female criminal in her book *Sisters in Crime: The Rise of the New Female Offender*:

> The phenomenon of female criminality is but one wave in . . . [the] rising tide of female assertiveness—a wave which has not yet crested and may even be seeking its level uncomfortably close to the high-water mark set by male[s]. . . . [Females are now] robbing banks single-handedly, committing assorted armed robberies, muggings, loan-sharking operations, extortions, murders, and a wide variety of other aggressive violence-oriented crimes. (pp. 1, 14)

Adler offered a **masculinity-liberation theory** of female criminality to explain this purported trend. According to Adler, medical and technological advances have freed women from unwanted pregnancies and lightened the burden of housework, and the ideology of women's liberation has masculinized female behavior, engendering an "imitative male machismo competitiveness" (p. 98). Gender norms for males and females have begun to converge, and females have been striving for equality in both the world of legitimate work and the world of crime.

Initial evaluations of Adler's claims questioned the accuracy of the view that female criminality had, in fact, increased. At the time of her study, the most significant increases in female crime had occurred for the nonviolent property offenses (larceny-theft, forgery, fraud, embezzlement) that were consistent with traditional gender patterns. These increases could be explained, critics noted, in terms of the rising divorce rate, increased number of female heads of household, general structural problems in the economy, and increased opportunities for crime afforded by the expansion of self-service retail outlets, consumer credit, and governmental welfare (Simon 1975; Steffensmeier 1978; Steffensmeier & Cobb 1981).

Data from Table 8.2 show that between 1965 and 1975 the percentage of females arrested for violent Index Crimes remained essentially the same (about 10 percent), while the percentage arrested for property crimes increased from about 14 percent to 22 percent. Since then the percent of female arrests for violent crimes has increased to 17 percent and for property crimes to 31 percent. While these data belie Adler's expectations of gender convergence, they are increases nonetheless and need to be explained.

Some criminologists have attributed these trends to changing societal reactions and increased official labeling of female offenders. The changing position of women in society, media attention to the new "liberated" female criminal, and concern with equality and abolition of gender discrimination may have led law enforcement authorities to take females more seriously than in the past (Belknap 2001; Berger 1996; Merlo 1995). According to this view, females are now less likely to be the beneficiaries of official chivalry. To the extent that such chivalry still exists, however, it appears to exist only for suspects who display a more feminine, passive demeanor and who have committed less serious crimes. One study found that older and white female suspects were less likely to be arrested than younger, black, or hostile suspects (Visher 1983).

Other researchers have attributed changing arrest rates, in part, to legal reforms that decriminalized juvenile **status offenses** in various states. Status offenses designate crimes for which juveniles (but not adults) may

Table 8.2   Gender Composition of Index Crime Arrests (1965–2002)

Year	Total Index Crimes		Violent Index Crimes		Property Index Crimes	
	Percent Male	Percent Female	Percent Male	Percent Female	Percent Male	Percent Female
1965	86.6	13.4	89.8	10.2	85.8	14.2
1970	83.1	16.9	90.4	9.6	81.3	18.7
1975	80.2	19.8	89.5	10.5	77.9	22.1
1980	80.5	19.5	89.7	10.3	78.3	21.7
1985	78.6	21.4	89.1	10.9	76.0	24.0
1990	78.1	21.9	88.7	11.3	74.7	25.3
1995	76.1	23.9	85.1	14.9	72.7	27.3
2000	73.3	26.7	82.7	17.3	69.6	30.4
2002	72.9	27.1	82.6	17.4	69.3	30.7

Sources: FBI 1966, tab. 23; 1971, tab. 30; 1976, tab. 38; 1981, tab. 34; 1986, tab. 37; 1991, tab. 37; 1996, tab. 42; 2001, tab. 42; 2003, tab. 42.

be charged. Historically these have included not only running away, truancy, and curfew violations, but more vague transgressions such as "incorrigibility," "habitual disobedience," and "immoral behavior" (see Box 11.2). Decriminalization meant that juveniles could not be detained for very long or locked up for such charges. As a result, some jurisdictions began to reclassify some status offenders as criminals to enable greater control of these youths. For instance, runaway girls who had broken into parents' homes to obtain food and clothing were now being charged with burglary, or youths previously charged with "uncontrollable behavior" were charged with violent crimes (Curran 1984; Mahoney & Fenster 1982). In addition, increased attention to domestic violence has led to more "simple assault" or "battery" charges in family fights. Meda Chesney-Lind and Randall Shelden (2004) report cases where authorities have even advised parents who wanted to prevent their daughters from running away to physically stand in their way. If the girl then ran into the parent or pushed the parent aside, the parent could have the daughter arrested.

However much labeling has played a role in the changing gender arrest patterns, research has found a greater narrowing (though not a convergence) in female-male arrests for juveniles than for adults. Moreover, self-report surveys, which are not contaminated by the labeling process, indicate fewer and smaller gender differences than the arrest data. Here gender differences are most apparent for the more serious property and violent offenses, which are more frequently committed by males. A similar proportion of boys and girls commit less serious crimes, although males offend more frequently and have longer delinquent careers than females (Berger 1996; Chesney-Lind & Shelden 2004).

The Masculinity-Liberation Hypothesis

As we have seen, the empirical foundation of Adler's claims (1975) about the new female offender has been questioned. In addition, research has not generally supported the proposition that female offenders have become masculinized or proponents of feminist ideology. Survey studies that examined the relationship between self-reported delinquency and several stereotypical masculine personality or gender traits (e.g., aggressiveness, competitiveness, leadership, ambition) have yielded mixed or inconsistent results, and males have been found to be more delinquent than females regardless of gender orientation (Belknap 2001; Berger 1996; Chesney-Lind & Shelden 2004). Peggy Giordano and Stephen Cernkovich (1979) found no relationship between self-reported female delinquency and "liberated" attitudes toward family and occupational roles (e.g., whether women should have to do all the housework or stay at home and take care of the family, whether women should receive equal pay as men for equal work or be able to work in nontraditional occupations). Similarly, Josephine Figueria-

McDonough (1984) reported that profeminist attitudes were unrelated to delinquency among female high school youths, although they were positively associated with higher grades and more ambitious career goals. Giordano and Cernkovich (1979) even found traditional beliefs about male-female personality traits and interpersonal relationships (e.g., men are more logical than women, a guy likes a girl to look up to him, girls can't trust other girls with their boyfriends) to be associated with higher rates of female delinquency. These studies are consistent with research on adult female offenders who have been found to hold traditional beliefs about motherhood and women's dependency on men and to reject or be indifferent to the women's movement (Glick & Neto 1977; Miller 1986; Ogle et al. 1995).

At the same time, Giordano and Cernkovich (1979) did find that delinquent girls expressed nontraditional attitudes about what actions they considered appropriate, acceptable, or possible for girls. For example, delinquent girls were more likely than nondelinquents to agree with the statements: *"I just want to get in on a piece of the action—Gotta do what I gotta do to get ahead in this world"* and *"I think sometimes, if a guy can do it, why can't I?"* They were also more likely to think they had as much right as a guy to swear and to go into a bar alone.

While delinquent girls in the study said they were most likely to get into trouble when they were with a mixed group of boys and girls, they were not involved in these groups in passive ways, as mere accomplices to males. Most girls disagreed with the statement: *"It's usually the guys' idea and I just go along for the ride."* One girl even remarked, "While dudes are generally in on it some way, the girls are as much or more into it as they are" (p. 475). In fact, many girls indicated that they were most likely to get into trouble when they were alone or with a group of other girls. Giordano and Cernkovich concluded that contemporary females face a complex, multidimensional, and often contradictory set of behavioral scripts that specify what is "likely, possible, unlikely and impossible" for them to do, and that they are capable of simultaneously identifying with both traditional and nontraditional gender norms and expectations (p. 469).

■ Intersections of Gender, Race/Ethnicity, Class, and Crime

The female population is not an undifferentiated group. It is important, therefore, to examine the gender-crime relationship with regard to race/ethnicity and class. The *UCR* does not include data on class (see Chapter 2). Neither does it cross-classify gender and race/ethnicity. However, Darrell Steffensmeier and Emilie Andersen Allen were able to collect black and white gender-specific arrest data from Pennsylvania, which they describe as "a diversified and demographically heterogeneous state" (1988:56).

They found that within the same racial group, female rates were consistently lower than male rates. But female rates were often higher than male rates for different subgroups of the population. For instance, the black female rate was higher than the white male rate for crimes against persons, the urban female rate approximated or exceeded the rural male rate for minor property offenses, and the younger female rate was higher than the older male rate for both serious and minor property crimes.

In addition, self-report delinquency research found that black females were more likely than white females to commit aggravated assault, robbery, auto theft, and thefts of $50 or more, although their rates for burglary were virtually the same (Hindelang et al. 1981). Black female youths were also as likely as white male youths to commit aggravated assault and robbery. Other self-report research reported nonwhite females more likely to commit crimes against persons (e.g., attacking someone with fists, using a weapon to attack someone, participating in a gang fight), but white females were more likely to hit their parents and be involved in using and selling drugs, illegal drinking, and status offenses (Cernkovich & Giordano 1979a). Rates of self-reported offenses among black and white females tended to converge, however, as the girls grew older (Ageton 1983).

Data from the *National Crime Victimization Survey* on the perceived sex of the offender reveal similar patterns. In general, female rates of offending were lower than male rates, constituting about 17 percent of single-offender violent crimes, for example (U.S. Department of Justice 1997). Black males exhibited the highest rates, followed by white males, black females, and white females. But among juvenile offenders (twelve to seventeen years of age), black female rates were comparable to male rates for some crimes (Hindelang 1981; Laub & McDermott 1985).

Gendered patterns of crime also vary with class background. For instance, lower-class urban females self-reported more violent crime than their female counterparts in other groups or settings (Ageton 1983; Hill & Crawford 1990). In a study of female homicides in six large cities (Atlanta, Baltimore, Chicago, Houston, Los Angeles, New York), Coramae Richey Mann (1996) found that over three-fourths of the women arrested for murder were African American. These women also tended to be unemployed mothers who had not completed high school. Thus Sally Simpson argues that "race and class combine to produce uniquely situated populations of females (e.g., underclass black females) who . . . appear to have unique patterns of criminality . . . when compared with their gender and racial counterparts" (1991:115).

▪ Girls in Urban Gangs

In her research on girls in gangs, Anne Campbell (1987, 1991) interviewed lower-class minority youths in New York City. One cannot listen to these young women's accounts without questioning the adequacy of conventional gender explanations that emphasize the differences between females and males. The traditional assumption that males are more violent than females does not necessarily hold among these youths (Messerschmidt 1997; Simpson 1991). As one girl explained: "Round here you have to know how to fight. I'm glad I got a reputation. That way nobody will start with me. . . . They're going to come out losing. Like all of us. . . . We're crazy. Nobody wants to fight us. . . . They say, 'No, man. That girl might stab me or cut my face'" (Campbell 1987:462–463).

Chesney-Lind and Shelden (2004) suggest that the moderate increases in female violence may be attributed, in part, to increased involvement of girls in gang-related offenses, even though females generally remain less involved in gangs than males. Overall, the self-reported delinquency of female gang members is lower than that of male gang members but higher than that of nongang males (Esbensen & Huizinga 1993; Esbensen & Winfree 1998; Fagan 1990; Miller & Brunson 2000). In a study of gang membership among eighth-grade students in eleven cities, Dana Peterson and colleagues (2001) found that 10 percent of gang members were involved in *all male* gangs and 37 percent of gang members were involved in *majority male* gangs, while only 2 percent of gang members were involved in *all female* gangs and 3 percent in *majority female* gangs. (*Majority male* and *majority female* gangs were defined as those having at least two-thirds of the members as male or female, respectively.) Nearly half of gang members were involved in "gender balanced" gangs. Peterson and colleagues also found that gender patterns of gang offending varied according to the gender composition of the gangs: males reported higher rates of delinquency than females in gender-balanced gangs, both males and females in gender-balanced gangs reported higher rates of delinquency than males and females in all-male or all-female gangs and in majority-male or majority-female gangs, and males and females in majority-male gangs reported comparable rates of delinquency.

Messerschmidt (1997) views the gang milieu as an environment in which girls experiment with and reconfigure the boundaries of traditional femininity. Traditional (emphasized) femininity is the culturally dominant ideal that is associated primarily with middle-class, white, heterosexual women and that is organized around "the display of sociability rather than technical competence, fragility in mating scenes, compliance with men's desire for titillation and ego-stroking . . . [and] acceptance of marriage and child care" (Connell 1987:187). According to Messerschmidt, when gang girls act tough and are violent they are not "doing masculinity" but constructing an **oppositional femininity** that challenges the notion of femininity as a trait entirely distinct from masculinity.

Giordano and Cernkovich (1979) observe that gang girls are capable of identifying with and participating in aspects of both traditional and nontraditional gender roles. Elements of traditionalism still permeate the gang milieu. Girls, for example, are most often involved in gangs as girlfriends of male gang members or as "little sister" subgroups or female auxiliaries that take their name from the male gang (e.g., Latin Kings and Queens) (Shelden et al. 2001). One New York City gang girl told Campbell (1991) that when the boys were not around, they could do what they wanted. When the guys were there, however, they were "not allowed" to do as they pleased (p. 244). Similarly, a Los Angeles Chicana told John Quicker, "If it wasn't for [the boys] we wouldn't be around 'cause the guys started [the gang]. . . . The girls never start the gang; the guys do. And the girls that like them or back them up started it with their permission" (1983:101).

In her study of Chicano gangs in Los Angeles, Joan Moore found that the boys often treated the girls as possessions, "like a piece of ass." As one boy remarked, "It's just there . . . when you want a *chapete* (fuck). . . . The guys treat them like shit. . . . Just to have a partner for the time. . . . And then when they want something you know, get it—wham bam. . . . We used to . . . throw a *linea* (lining up to have sex with a girl), you know what I mean" (1991:54–55). Similarly, in her study of African American gangs in Fort Wayne, Indiana, Deborah Burris-Kitchen (1995) found that girls had difficulty getting the respect they felt they deserved. As one young woman said, "Guys around here don't respect women much. I think it is because of all the rap music bashin' women. I listen to some of this music calling women bitches and ho's and it upsets me. I think the guys around here think sex is all we're good for" (p. 104).

Other females noted a double standard: "Most women get respect if they sellin' drugs, but not if they using. It's ok for guys to use, but not us" (Burris-Kitchen 1995:104). And although gang males express pride over female members' willingness to fight, they are sometimes uncomfortable with or ambivalent about female aggression. One of Quicker's respondents explained, "I've asked my boyfriend and they all come up with the same answer. 'I don't think a girl should be in . . . the fights.' . . . They say it's right for a guy, but it's not right for girls. . . . That's what they all say, yet they are happy to have their own girls. They're proud. They say our girls do this, our girls are bad. . . . [So] I don't know what they're talking about" (1983:12).

Gang girls—largely lower-class, minority youths—have few opportunities to make it in mainstream society. They come from families where they have often experienced physical and sexual abuse, from families that are frequently "held together by their mothers who are subsisting on welfare. Most have dropped out of school and have no marketable skills" (Joe & Chesney-Lind 1995:413). The gang represents an alternative family, a social support system that buffers the dismal future that awaits them. But gang girls also recognize that they must negotiate a gender-stratified street environment dominated by males. As one said, "Females who are soft won't make it. . . . Someone think you weak, they goin' take from ya'. Even if you female you got to be willing to shoot" (Burris-Kitchen 1995:93). Campbell (1993) notes that gang girls know what it is like to be victimized:

> They know that, to survive, force must be met with more than unspoken anger or frustrated tears. Less physically strong and more sexually vulnerable than boys, they find that the best line of defense is not attack but the threat of attack. The key to this is the development of a reputation for violence, which will ward off opponents. There is nothing so effective as being in a street gang to keep the message blaring out: "Don't mess with me—I'm a crazy woman." (p. 133)

Females who are unwilling or unable to fight are thus viewed disparagingly. As one girl said, "Tramps. All they think about is screwing. . . . They don't fight. They don't go to rumbles with their guys. . . . They're a bunch of punks" (Campbell 1987:463). Another girl remarked, "You can belong as long as you can back up your shit and don't rat on your homegirls or back away [from a fight. You have to be] able to hold up the hood" (Harris 1988:109).

Although not equal in power, auxiliary female gangs are not mere appendages of male gangs. Girls in gangs have their own leaders and make most of their routine decisions without the boys (Bowker & Klein 1983; Giordano 1978). They take pride in their claims of autonomy and reject "any suggestion that they could be duped or conned by males" (Campbell 1987:460). In a study of San Francisco gangs, David Lauderback and colleagues (1992) found that African American females were less likely than Latinas to be affiliated with male groups. One African American gang, the Potrero Hill Posse, started out as a mixed-gender group, with girls selling drugs for their boyfriends. Eventually, however, the females disaffiliated themselves from the males and formed a gang of their own. Members are now required to be adept at either selling drugs (crack) or shoplifting.

Moore (1991) found that female gangs were not as closely bound to the barrio as male gangs and that girls often partied with boys from other gangs. Boys, however, were more likely to date girls who were not in gangs, expressing preference for those girls they perceived as more likely to fulfill traditional gender roles in the future. As one boy said, "You know that they are going to be good. You know they going to take care of business and . . . be a good housewife" (p. 75).

Some girls clearly rejected the traditionalism of male constructions of gender. "Not *me*," said one of Moore's informants, "they didn't treat me like that. They think we're possessions, but we're not. No way, I pick my own boyfriends. . . . You don't tell *me* who to be with" (p. 55). Similarly, some members of the Vice Queens, an African American gang in Chicago, constructed a nontraditional oppositional femininity by unabashedly placing themselves at the boys' disposal, openly encouraging them to fondle them and have sex with them. Although the boys viewed the girls as mere sex objects, the girls gained status among their female peers by "being able to keep four or five boys 'on the string' without any boys knowing of the others, but at the same time, avoiding sexual relationships with too many boys at one time" (Fishman 1988:21). Peggy Orenstein suggests, however, that such girls have simply learned to derive whatever pleasure they can from their subordinate and exploitative position vis-à-vis boys and have "recast mistreatment as excitement" (1994:209).

Gini Sikes (1997) interviewed Latina gang girls in San Antonio, Texas. She learned that "trains" (sex with a number of gang males in succession) were an option to "jump ins" (physical beatings by gang members) in gang initiation rituals. (Trains were not an option for male initiates.) The girls did not view the trains as rape but considered them "the coward's way in— after all, gang logic goes, all the girl does is lie down and spread her legs" (p. 110). Sikes found that most girls chose the "jump in" option.

Nevertheless, Campbell (1987) observes that serial monogamy, not promiscuity, is the norm for most gang girls and that girls who have sex outside of a steady relationship are often condemned. Gang girls may even avoid associating with "'loose' girls whose reputation might contaminate them by association" (p. 452). But once they are involved in a relationship, boys often attempt to exert control over their girlfriends' public appearance and behavior, not allowing them to wear shorts or low-cut blouses, to get "high," or to flirt with other guys. Males, on the other hand, reserve their prerogative to have other relationships. Masculinity norms make it difficult for boys to turn down an opportunity for sex, as this would be considered tantamount to an admission of homosexuality. Girls also accept this view of masculinity and blame other girls for "putting it in his face." In this way, romantic disputes between girls and boys are settled between girls. Nevertheless, the girls' main objective is not so much to "hold on to their man" as to gain other girls' respect (Campbell 1991; Horowitz 1983; Sikes 1997).

Occasionally gang girls fight to defend territorial turf and gain recognition for their group. However, much of their fighting occurs in response to competition over boyfriends, assessments of beauty (who is "the cutest"), and negative gossip regarding one's reputation or that of a family member—their mother especially. Fighting among girls is generally less lethal than among boys, since it usually involves fists or knives rather than guns. But gun use among females does appear to be increasing (Anderson 1994; Campbell 1993; Harris 1988).

Gang girls who fight or who are willing to use violence are not rejecting femininity but are constructing an alternative femininity that combines traditional and nontraditional gender traits. Although participation in a street fight involves physical aggression against rival gang members, it is also defined as an act of *caring* for one's gang and the "hood." Thus "what is usually considered atypical feminine behavior outside this situation is, in fact, *normalized* within the social context of interneighborhood conflict; girl-gang violence in this situation is . . . permitted and . . . encouraged . . . by *both* boys and girls as appropriate feminine behavior" (Messerschmidt 1997:82). Hence, doing femininity—"bad girl" femininity—can mean doing violence. Yet girls also play many of the more traditional feminine roles within the gang: child care, cooking, and preparing food and drink for parties. In addition, gang girls are very fussy about their physical appearance—their hair, makeup, wearing the right brand-name clothing—and they are disparaging of their peers who look drab or slovenly. Outside of the gang milieu they are unambiguously feminine. Campbell says that gang girls' concern "with their appearance [and] their pride in their ability to attract men . . . left me in no doubt that they enjoyed being women. They didn't want to be like men and, indeed, would have been outraged at such a suggestion" (1993:113; Vigil 1988).

At the same time, gang girls are often uninformed or misinformed about birth control, and rarely do they or their partners use it. Instead, they view pregnancy as an occupational hazard of sorts. Many of them get pregnant within a year after becoming sexually active, which may begin at or even before puberty. Becoming a mother does not require leaving the gang, and it offers girls an alternative source of status. Motherhood is valued, provided that the mother accepts responsibility for her child's welfare. The ability to care for children, however, often depends on parental or grandparental support and on the (diminishing) availability of governmental welfare. Abortion is generally condemned for the first pregnancy but is increasingly accepted after that. Wholehearted support for abortion, which might jeopardize their reputations as mothers, is uncommon (Campbell 1987; Miller 1986; Moore & Hagedorn 1996; Williams & Kornblum 1985).

In their research in Milwaukee, Wisconsin, Joan Moore and John Hagedorn (1996) found that Latina girls had higher hopes of getting married than their African American counterparts. Forty-three percent of Latina gang members and 75 percent of African Americans agreed with the statement, *"I'd rather raise my kids by myself,"* and 29 percent of the Latinas and none of the African Americans agreed that *"All a woman needs to straighten out her life is to find a good man"* (pp. 216–217). Male gang members, however, rarely marry the mothers of their children or contribute financially to their support, although they do take pride in their ability to father children, considering it a public demonstration of their masculinity. As one Potrero Hill gang member explained, speaking of her child's father,

"They just get you pregnant and . . . go on about their business with some-body else" (Lauderback et al. 1992:69). Moore and Hagedorn (1996) note that Latinas have been subjected to more traditional gender expectations than African American women, who for generations have been forced to assume independent economic and familial roles. Yet Philippe Bourgois, in his study of a New York Puerto Rican community, says that one of the problems facing inner-city communities today is the increasing number of mothers who are following "the paths of fathers in seeking independent lives in the underground economy or in substance abuse . . . [leaving no one] to cushion the fragmentation of the family unit" (1995:276; see Chapter 2).

■ Gender and Street Robbery

Crime data indicate that robbery is among the most gender-differentiated crimes, one of the quintessential male offenses (Miller 1998). Robbery, like other forms of male violence, provides a resource for accomplishing or doing masculinity when alternative means are unavailable. Messerschmidt (1993) argues that the dominant or hegemonic form of masculinity in socie-ty is defined not only in terms of men's power and social privilege vis-à-vis women, but also through men's ability to exercise authority and control over other men in the paid-labor market. Thus owners and managers have more power than workers, while workers have more power than the unem-ployed. Men who are without resources to construct a "breadwinner/good provider" form of masculinity may use crime as a suitable substitute.

In Chapter 7 we described the culture of respect and personal honor that lies at the heart of the "code of the street" and how males often respond vehemently to "dissing" in order to avoid any aspersions on their masculin-ity. Similarly, men who commit robbery are attempting to project a particu-lar image of masculinity to other men. Robbery is not only a means of acquiring money or property. It is also a means of establishing a position of dominance, of gaining "*an angle of moral superiority* over the intended victim" (J. Katz 1988:169; Messerschmidt 1993). Jody Miller notes that "men accomplish street robberies in a strikingly uniform [way] . . . using physical violence and/or a gun placed on or at close proximity to the victim in a confrontational manner" (1998:47). As one robber explained, when you "have the gun to his head, can't do nothing but respect that" (p. 48). Another said, "I don't even have to say nothing half the time. When they see that pistol, they know what time it is." While men sometimes rob women, these are deviations from the norm: "Male robbers . . . clearly view the act of robbery as a masculine accomplishment in which men compete with other men for money and status." Masculinity is not accomplished by robbing women, as women "are not viewed as real players . . . [on] the streets" (p. 50).

About half of all robberies are committed in groups, and males often feel compelled to commit robberies in order to impress other males (Miethe & McKorkle 1998). As one youth recalled, "My stepbrother had gave me a .22 automatic. He told me to walk over behind [this dude] and put the gun to his head and tell him to give me all his stuff. That's what I did" (Miller 1998:47). Another noted, "Someone pushed me to take up the challenge. He told me I wasn't capable of doing armed robbery. I said give me the gun. I'm going to do it" (Gabor et al. 1987:63).

Robbery also represents an **oppositional masculinity** insofar as it provides one with "fast money," allowing one to reject legitimate work in favor of a life of leisure that becomes the defining feature of one's identity (Messerschmidt 1997; Shover & Honaker 1992). And the conspicuous display of the fruits of this labor (e.g., fashionable clothing and jewelry, plenty of drugs and alcohol) projects an image not just of someone who possesses

valued commodities but of someone who possesses "things that may require defending" (Anderson 1994:88).

Miller (1998) notes that women and men of similar racial and class background do robbery differently. She interviewed thirty-seven active street robbers: fourteen women and twenty-three men, nearly all African American, from an underclass neighborhood in St. Louis. She found that women most commonly robbed other women because they were easier targets than men, and that women robbers were far less likely to use guns when robbing women. Although women-on-women robberies were most often committed with female accomplices, they were sometimes committed alone. Women rarely had male accomplices when robbing other women. Occasionally, female victims would defy the stereotype and resist the robbery. For instance, one women recalls an incident where she and a female accomplice confronted a woman following a basketball game:

> She was walking to her car. I was, shit . . . , let's get her motherfucking purse. . . . So I walked up to her and I pulled out the knife. I said "up that purse." And she looked at me. I said, "shit, do you think I'm playing?" . . . She was like "shit, you ain't getting my purse. Do what you got to do." I was like "shit, you must be thinking I'm playing." So I took the knife, stabbed her a couple of times on the shoulder, stabbed her on the arm and snatched the purse. . . . She just ran, "help, help." (p. 52)

Although women's robbery of men almost always involved guns, and often (but not always) male accomplices, Miller found that women sometimes capitalized on their sexuality to catch male victims off guard. In these cases they presented themselves as sexually available to the male targets, at times even drinking and partying first, making sure to consume less alcohol and drugs than the men. Ironically, it was men's assumption that they could take advantage of women that made them vulnerable. A woman robber recounts the time she went with a man to a hotel room:

> He was . . . drunk. . . . [and] didn't have on no clothes. . . . He was like, "shit, . . . ain't you gonna get undressed?" I was like "shit, yeah, hold up" and I went in my purse and I pulled out the gun. He was like "damn, what's up with you gal?" I was like, "shit, I want your jewelry and all the money you got." He was like . . . "bitch you crazy. I ain't giving you my shit." I said, "do you think I'm playing nigger? You don't think I'll shoot your motherfucking ass?" He was like . . . "you ain't gonna shoot me." So then I . . . fired the thing but I didn't fire at him. . . . I snatched his shit . . . [and] ran out the door. (p. 56)

Miller found that some women involved in prostitution also robbed their clients in a practice known as "viccing." One woman said she preferred to rob white men because "they be so paranoid they just want to get away. . . . [And] if you are sucking a man's dick and you pull a knife on them, they not gonna too much argue with you" (p. 55). Los Angeles gang girls interviewed by Sikes (1997) had a similar modus operandi. They would stake out card clubs, racetracks, and casinos looking for men to rob. "The one thing you look for when you choose the man," said one homegirl, "is a wedding ring—a big one. You want to know that he got money and you definitely want someone who's married. Married man's not gonna press charges." One girl would get the man to invite her back to his motel room. When the lights went out, homegirl-accomplices would burst in with guns. "If a man's half-naked with three girls and a gun on him, he's gonna give it up" (p. 84).

▧ Gender and the Drug Trade

Traditional gender arrangements continue to be apparent in the world of organized adult crime. Men in criminal organizations prefer to "work, associate, and do business with other men" (Steffensmeier 1983:1013). They do not want to take orders from women; they believe that women should take orders from men. Some researchers, however, have noted a change in women's roles in U.S. urban drug markets, with women playing a greater role in the crack-cocaine markets of the late 1980s and early 1990s than in the heroin markets of the 1960s and 1970s (Bourgois 1989; Merlo 1995; Mieczkowski 1994). In a study of New York City, Jeffrey Fagan concluded that "the size and seemingly frantic activity of the current drug markets has made possible for women new ways to participate in street networks. Their involvement in drug selling at high income levels defies the gendered norms and roles of the past, where drug dealing was an incidental income source often mediated by domestic partnerships" (1994:210).

Lisa Maher and Kathleen Daly note that the crack-cocaine market was once characterized as an "unregulated market of freelancers engaged in individual entrepreneurial activity," but as soon as the demand for crack was established, freelancing was "superceded by a more structured system of distribution" (1996:471). In their New York City ethnography of drug users between 1989 and 1992, they found evidence that women's subordinate role in the drug trade has persisted. Their research revealed a hierarchical distribution system of drug-business *owners* who employed several *crew bosses, lieutenants,* or *managers* who, in turn, were responsible for organizing and delivering supplies, collecting revenues, and hiring, firing, and paying lower-level street dealers and those who acted as *enforcers, look-outs, runners, holders, steerers,* and *touts* (persistent solicitors). According to one estimate, this New York crack-cocaine network employed about 150,000 people (Williams 1992).

In the course of their fieldwork, Maher and Daly (1996) interviewed over 200 women drug users and found not one who had filled the role of business owner and only one who had worked in a managerial capacity. They also conducted more extensive interviews with a subgroup of forty-five women (twenty Latinas, sixteen blacks, and nine whites), all of whom were regular users of smokable cocaine or crack, and over two-thirds of whom had used heroin at one time. Over 90 percent of these women were homeless, and 80 percent were mothers, although few of their children were living with them during the three-year study period. Over 40 percent had tested positive or believed they were positive for HIV. Compared to Fagan's sample (1994), a greater proportion were Latina (rather than African American), were homeless, and had neither completed high school nor had legitimate work experience.

These women most commonly performed the role of steerer or tout (42 percent). At times some would be given jobs as street-level dealers, but this was largely to fill temporary (though recurring) labor shortages caused by police arrest of male dealers. During the study period, however, only 27 percent of the women were involved in selling or distributing drugs. Only three of them ran "shooting galleries" (places where people gathered to use drugs), and even these galleries were under the control of or operated by a man or group of men.

About a third of the women in Maher and Daly's study "copped" drugs for others, typically white men. As one said, "They'd be . . . people very important, white people like lawyer[s], doctors that come and get off, you'd be surprised" (p. 480). Male dealers liked this arrangement because it protected them from undercover police officers. But few men were attracted to this role because it was considered a low-status activity. Male customers from outside the neighborhood were more likely to trust women (particularly white women) than men to purchase drugs for them. This trust, however, was often misplaced: "The combination of naive, inexperienced 'white boyz' and experienced 'street smart' women produced opportunities for additional income by, for instance, simply taking the 'cop' money" and returning to the client claiming that she had been "ripped off" (p. 481). Sometimes the women did not steal the money outright, but simply charged more than the drug cost. Sometimes they took some of the drug for themselves or adulterated it with cheaper ingredients.

A few of the women sold drug paraphernalia such as crack pipes, stems, or syringes ("works"). Men who sold "sealed" (new) works were more likely to have suppliers, most often contacts at local hospitals. Women were more likely to sell "used works," which they usually procured from diabetic family members or friends. Others would collect used works strewn around the neighborhood and exchange them for new ones through a needle exchange program. Sometimes men from outside the area, reluctant to carry drug paraphernalia, would give the women a "hit" of crack in exchange for use of their stem. Women who rented their stems in this way savored the accumulated residue, which they periodically scraped out and smoked.

Maher and Daly argue that the drug market is not an "equal opportunity employer" and that prostitution remains the only consistent option open to women surviving on the streets. During the course of their research, Maher and Richard Curtis (1992) spent a day hanging out with Bay, a twenty-six-year-old African American woman, as she "hustled" for cash and crack. Bay was having trouble getting sex work because she was seven months pregnant. As Maher and Curtis note, "Watching her panhandle change whenever she could, con a junkie out of a stolen bedspread for $1 and re-sell it for $2, get free condoms from health workers and sell them to girls on the stroll, and, finally, try for over an hour to pick up a date, we were left with the indelible impression that, in the absence of sex work, it was difficult, if not impossible, for women to 'get paid' in this neighbourhood" (p. 223).

Some studies have found that women involved in "prostitution prior to crack use tended to engage in prostitution substantially more frequently after becoming involved with crack" (Fagan 1994; Johnson et al. 1995:281). However, researchers have also observed that spread of crack use has flooded the market with *novice* sex workers needing money for drugs. This has caused a shift in the nature of prostitution from intercourse to fellatio and from indoors to outdoors (cars, alleys, parks, vacant lots), thus deflating the going rate for sexual transactions (Maher & Curtis 1992). One woman describes the current situation this way: "Women who do crack . . . [will] do anything for five dollars, and it hurts the girls that are out there. . . . [A] guy will come to me and say, 'I'll give you five dollars for a blow job.' . . . Or, 'Do you accept food stamps?' or 'Can I pay you later?'" (Pettiway 1997:90). Some women have even been exchanging sex directly for drugs. As one woman admits, "I've exchanged sex for drugs. . . . This guy that I know, he's a dealer and he wanted some head. So he gave me an eight-ball [3.5 grams of coke] . . . and I gave him a blow job. Other times, guys done gave me like four bags, three bags, and I done gave them a blow job. . . . That's what I mainly do is give blow jobs. . . . I don't really fuck a lot" (p. 16).

The heightened competition for "dates" has intensified the hostility between sex workers and increased the social isolation they experience. Candy, who has worked the streets for seventeen years, says, "These girls out here are just for the drug and theirself—no friendship, everyone's out to cut everyone's throat. . . . [Before] we were friends and we'd help one another out. . . . We'd stick together, . . . do a favour, call somebody up, go get a bag of dope. . . . These people don't know how to be ho's" (Maher & Curtis 1992:233–234). As cash and drugs become harder to get, sometimes the "ho's" even "vic" (rob) each other as well as their dates. And when they "be thirsty (needing drugs), . . . they ain't got no time to judge" the character of a date and increasingly end up with "rougher and nastier" men who vic them or beat them up (pp. 240, 243). Hence the streets have become more violent places to work. Clearly, Maher and Curtis conclude, "the advent of crack cocaine can in no way be seen as 'emancipatory' for women drug users" (p. 249).

Nevertheless, Maher and Daly (1996) do think there are race and ethnic differences in the gender stratification of drug markets, with Latinas playing more marginal roles than African American women. Recall that Fagan's sample (1994), consisting of more African American women, uncovered more highly placed female drug dealers. Other studies show that Latinas are less likely than their African American counterparts to be involved in dealing, particularly in ways that allow them independence from men (Lauderback et al. 1992; Moore & Mata 1981; Taylor 1993). It appears that women who deviate from traditional gender norms are less tolerated in Latino communities than in African American ones.

■ *Women in Prostitution*

Prostitution, which is illegal in most parts of the United States, can be defined as the provision of "nonmarital sexual services for material gain" (Goldstein 1979:33). It is, as we noted earlier, part of the broader phenomenon of "sex work," which includes both illegal and legal activities. The concept of sex work is useful in that it helps us to recognize certain commonalities in the experiences of different kinds of sex workers. In this section we will focus on females providing sexual services to male customers, although service providers as well as customers can be female or male.

In Leon Pettiway's study (1997) of drug-addicted, inner-city hustlers, he describes the lives of women who prostitute, sell drugs, shoplift, and perform various kinds of theft and fraud. Some of these women had left home to escape abusive and cruel treatment. For others "the seduction of the fast life, inducements from friends, and environments ridden with drugs and crime were in large measure responsible for their entry into the world" of street hustling (pp. xxvii–xxviii). Margaret, who started turning tricks "for survival," said that prostitution wasn't foreign to her before she got into it (p. 15):

> I knew my sisters was doing it. . . . Men always was hitting on me and it just came natural. . . . Wasn't nothing that . . . a woman don't already know. Except for when you call yourself a professional. Then you have to learn how to suck . . . real good and stuff like that. How to make them hurry up and reach a climax. . . . How to encourage them . . . [with] all that . . . talking. . . . "Fuck me" or . . . "All this big dick." . . . I never did like that. Moaning and groaning and all. . . . I picked up these rules by just being around. . . . I learnt . . . how to put the rubber on without them

knowing, how to go in their pocket [for their money] without them feeling. (pp. 10, 16, 40–41)

For Margaret and others like her sex work is not really about pleasing customers but about acquiring money and drugs. Charlie (Charlene) says there's no sexual attraction when she's tricking. It's "purely business." She lights a cigarette and tells the customer, "When the cigarette is burnt down, your time's up. If you want more time, that's more money. If you want to touch me, that's even more money" (p. 81). And Margaret, recognizing the drop in the going rate for oral sex, is equally blunt:

> When I turn tricks . . . I'm gonna give you two or three minutes and if you can't get it in that . . . time, sorry. . . . Before, I was aiming to please . . . 'cause the money was [better]. But now . . . it don't make me no difference whether they come or not. . . . I ain't making love. . . . They be . . . saying, ". . . you gotta play with my [titties]" "I ain't gotta play with your titties. . . . I'm sucking your dick. That's all I gotta do." (p. 44)

For Tracy, turning tricks in the projects where she lives seems easier and safer than going downtown to shoplift. However, she doesn't believe one can "earn an honest living and do drugs too" (p. 192). Likewise Charlie says, "I wish I hadn't prostituted. . . . It's degrading. . . . It's something I don't want to do, but it's something that my addictions make me do" (p. 95). Drug-addicted women who prostitute have a more difficult time than nonaddicted women maintaining their own standards about whom they will or will not service. If a guy "don't want to use no rubber," Margaret laments, "it be hard . . . to walk away [when he's] got ten . . . or five dollars in his pocket. . . . You want that money so bad" (p. 18).

Women, in addition to working the streets, often work in massage parlors and brothels as well as in bars and hotels. Those who prostitute in bars often double as waitresses, barmaids, or strippers. **Call girls**, considered the elite of the business, work for hotels or escort services or out of their own homes, servicing for the most part a higher class of clientele. According to Debra Satz (1995), call girls can earn $30,000 to $100,00 per year. This, the most lucrative type of prostitution, allows women "an unusual degree of independence, far greater than most other forms of work," and greater control over when and with whom they have sex (p. 68). Call girls are often paid not just for sexual services but for companionship as well. They may be taken to dinner, to the theater, even on trips.

Priscilla Alexander of the National Task Force on Prostitution (NTFP) believes that women's pathways into and responses to prostitution vary. As she writes:

> Some prostitution is forced, and forced prostitution is clearly rape combined with kidnapping and perhaps brainwashing. At the other end of the spectrum [however] are women who make a clear decision to work as prostitutes, a few because they enjoy sex and have no qualms about enjoying sex as work. Most women who work as prostitutes . . . do so out of economic motives. . . . Some get to like the work as they become skilled at it. Others hate it from the beginning to the end. And still others like some aspects of the job while hating parts of it. (1987:16)

In addition, some women prostitute occasionally or sporadically, some consistently for short periods, some for many years (Potterat et al. 1990).

Sunny Carter (1987) worked for five years as a call girl to pay medical expenses and provide the best life she could for a gravely ill son given only a few years to live. She screened her clients, refused to deal with men who held her in low regard, and says that she met many men "whose company [she] enjoyed [and] . . . who enriched [her] life . . . [and] pocketbook" (p. 164). "Peggy Morgan" (1987) uses a pseudonym when she describes her work as a stripper who also hustles drinks in the bar and gives men hand jobs for "tips" between dance sets. The customers Morgan serves "run the gamut":

> The best of them come in . . . knowing what they want—to get off—and what we want—money—and can pull the transaction off smoothly, making pleasant conversation and treating us with respect. . . . They get a willing ear to listen to them, or in the case of hand jobs, a witness to the potency of their pricks, a reassurance that they are still powerful, real men. But the macho, insecure types need more. . . . Not only do we have to work at getting them off and making them feel good, but we have to put up with their clumsy, grubby hands pawing our bodies—*and* pretend to enjoy it. It's not that these customers really want to please a woman. . . . [They see her as] . . . someone beneath them [and] . . . want to feel power over [her]. (p. 22)

Although Morgan had to get used to giving hand jobs (she threw up the first time) and doesn't like being fondled, she doesn't feel as though she's being violated because "it's not sexual, it's *work*" (p. 25). When she compares it to her alternatives—minimum-wage jobs or assembly-line drudgery—"putting up with the groping hands of a few drunk men looks pretty good" (p. 24). Besides, Morgan has experienced condescension and sexual harassment on "square jobs." At least here she makes a livable wage. As she says, "Nobody . . . enjoys being pawed, poked, [and] prodded . . . by men we wouldn't [normally] give the time of day. . . . [But] the bottom line in this business is money" (pp. 24–25).

Like the place Morgan worked, most strip clubs are darker and dingier than the high-end ones featured in popular movies. These clubs have sticky floors and crowds that "make crude demands." A woman unwilling to provide "hands-on treatment" won't walk away with much money. If she works in a club "where lap or 'private' dances are available" and she just wants to do stage performances, the stage fee *she* pays the owner and the tips she's expected to leave for deejays, bartenders, and managers can leave her in debt for the evening (Frey 2002:28). Private dances can yield "$20 for five minutes of work," which can quickly add up over the night, but as dancing has become less stigmatized, men increasingly want "more body, more tongue, more tit, and especially more pussy," says dancer Elisabeth Eaves (p. 30). Clearly the line between prostitution and other kinds of sex work is blurring.

According to Kathleen Barry (1995), women employ a variety of protective strategies in order to cope with prostitution. For example, *distancing* strategies help them "separate their sense of themselves, . . . their . . . personal identity, . . . from the act of prostitution" (p. 30). They often adopt a new name to protect their real self from the implications of prostituting. They might not tell family and friends what they're doing, move from the old neighborhood, even cut off all contact. Distancing is clearly evident in Judy Helfand's account (1987) of doing sex work. Needing money as well as assurance about her sexual attractiveness, Helfand took a job as a topless dancer. In spite of her fear that her parents would discover this, she liked the sense of power and independence the job gave her. However, she kept to herself, didn't make friends with coworkers, and disdained "the poor jerks who patronized the place" (p. 100). "I worked in sleazy places with people I had no respect for," she says. "With few exceptions I felt superior to all around me. This is how I protected myself from the shame and guilt of offering myself visually to men" (p. 102).

Women also consciously and intentionally *disengage*—try to switch off their feelings, to dissociate themselves from the act of prostitution. As Judy Edelstein, who works in a massage parlor providing sexual services as well as massages, observes, "When they touch my breasts, I tell myself they're not really touching me" (1987:63). And when Charlie was repulsed at the thought of turning her first trick, a friend told her to just "get high" before she went out (Pettiway 1997). Women also try to establish limits for their customers, "limits to the ways their bodies, their very selves, can be used" (Barry 1995:32). They may refuse to use their own bed, for example, to kiss, or to have sexual intercourse. They may insist on condoms, not just to protect themselves from disease, but to construct a barrier that demarcates the self. But how do you wall off the self, keep the barriers in place? Elisabeth Eaves found that for some sex workers, "honest decisions about boundaries and sexuality were impossible because they . . . both [became] subservient to cash" (quoted in Frey 2002:30). Edelstein tried to forget about her work when she went home, but the images intruded—images of guys' hands all over her, strangers sucking on her breasts. "Sometimes I wonder," she says, "how I can let the men do that. I wonder what there is left for me" (1987:63). She couldn't even make love with her partner without visualizing the customer's face.

What makes matters worse is that even though she is trying to disengage, customers expect a prostitute to act as if she *is* engaged, emotionally and sexually. Remember how Margaret resented having to "moan and groan," having to pretend to be excited at the sight of "all that big dick." "Performing" may require pretending to make love to the customer or pretending to get into his fantasy, no matter how bizarre or degrading. But trying not to feel (not "to be there") while one is simultaneously performing can become almost automatic. How, then, does one prevent this self-protective response from spilling over into her *real* love life? At times she can't disengage *enough* to protect her self during the prostitution sex. At times she can't *stop* disengaging or performing when she wants to, when she's with her partner. Her sense of feeling anchored or grounded is disrupted. Thus Barry believes (1995) that prostitution is an assault on the self: "Sex is an integral dimension of the human being. . . . When it is treated as a thing to be taken, the [self] is rendered into a thing, an objectification" (pp. 33–34). Human dignity is undermined; the self is violated.

Barry's portrait of prostitution is powerful and compassionate. Yet her analysis, in spite of its concern about the harms of prostitution, has caused some sex workers to bristle. For instance, Debi Sundahl, who works as a stripper, says, "Like many oppressed minorities, we [sex workers] have suffered under the assumption that we must be protected from ourselves. We know better than anyone what is . . . and what is not healthy about our work" (1987:179–180). For Debi, it is the struggle to resist internalizing society's negative stereotypes of sex workers—stereotypes that "leave little room for self-respect"—that is so stressful and disheartening. And Helfand, who "chose to pursue the highest paying, least demanding job" she knew of, asserts, "It makes me angry when [some] feminists lump all sex . . . workers into a pile of poor, exploited . . . victims without minds of their own. . . . Having a presence and physical body which men found sexually attractive was important to my self-esteem. Having men pay to get turned on by me was an affirmation of my sexual power." Helfand admits, however, that "what I never saw was that in basing my sense of worth on men's desire, I was far from developing a true sense of worth based on self love" (1987:101).

Than-Dam Truong (1990) believes that "sexual labor," as she calls it, should be destigmatized and considered comparable to other kinds of bodily labor. She notes that in different historical and political contexts, sexual labor has taken a number of forms (e.g., wet nursing, sperm donation, surrogate childbearing, commercial sex) in pursuit of the sustenance of life, procreation, and bodily pleasure. Similarly, Lillian Robinson (1996) suggests that the now common, neutral term "sex work" has made it easier to talk about prostitution, stripping, and the like without moralizing. Being a prostitute or a porn film actress, for example, can now "stand in opposition not to being a 'good girl,' but rather to being a chambermaid [or] grocery bagger," with the focus centering on issues such as working conditions and wages. Nevertheless, Robinson says, "It's a far cry from acknowledging that sex work is often the only work or the best work a woman can get to concluding that it is not a form of exploitation" (p. 184).

Although prostitution is sometimes portrayed as a victimless crime, prostitutes are often victimized. For instance, interviews with women entering Portland, Oregon's Council for Prostitution Alternatives (CPA) indicate that 84 percent of these women reported having been assaulted and 78 percent reported having been raped while working as prostitutes (CPA 1994). Similarly, in a survey of 200 San Francisco Bay area prostitutes, two-thirds said they had been beaten by customers many times and 70 percent reported that customers had raped them or forced sexual acts not agreed to (Silbert 1982). In addition, two-thirds claimed they were beaten regularly by their pimps. Pimps often "disciplined" their women for not bringing home enough money, for not obeying them, for trying to leave, or just to let them know who was boss. Unfortunately, prostitutes who are abused, whether by pimps, customers, or even police, find it virtually impossible to

get help because they often lack the resources to do so and because they are vulnerable to arrest (Barry 1995; Miller et al. 1993).

Bernard Cohen (1980) distinguishes between a "pimp" and a "man." Both live off the earnings of a prostitute, but a prostitute works *for* a pimp and *with* a man. The "man" is usually a husband or lover who watches over and protects "his woman" and supervises her work. The "pimp" is an agent and/or companion of several women. He tends to act more as a general manager of the women, since he is often not on the scene. In her Milwaukee study, Eleanor Miller (1986) found a continuum of managerial types rather than a clear-cut man-pimp dichotomy, with most men falling in the intermediate range:

> [Yet] women . . . rarely referred to a current manager as "my pimp." He was always . . . "my man." For the female at least, the personal side of the relationship far outweighed the business side in importance. . . . In fact, one of the most common reasons for a "woman" to leave a "man" was when some occurrence made it obvious that the relationship, from his point of view, was entirely for business purposes. On such occasions, women would say, "He wasn't nothin' but a pimp." (p. 39)

Barry (1995) describes how pimps looking to recruit a girl or woman target those who appear lonely, naive, and rebellious. If they're fleeing abusive homes or marriages, chances are they have little money and few job skills: "Suddenly he appears, he is friendly, . . . offers to buy her a meal, and . . . gives her a place to spend the night. She hears compliments for the first time in ages, as well as promises that he will buy her new clothes, . . . have her hair done, . . . make [her his] 'foxy lady'" (pp. 204–205). If she seems to be the daring and rebellious type, the pimp may come right out and offer her a proposal. He'll tell her he's a "businessman" and they could be "partners." She'll be his "woman." He'll give her "some schooling" and turn her out on the street. Her pockets will be "filled with money." If she seems scared or prudish, he'll make "his play for her as a lover," make her feel important, establish a sexual relationship. Then he'll insist she prove her love for him by prostituting herself. He'll tell her they need money and "if you love me, you'll do anything for me" (p. 206). If that doesn't work, he'll demonstrate his power and reduce her defenses with a beating or sexual assault. This is what she'll get, he tells her, "if you don't do what I tell you" (p. 208).

Once she's started tricking, pimps often undermine the woman's self-esteem through verbal abuse: "You're nothing but a goddamn whore, . . . you're worthless, . . . you're trash" (pp. 200, 207). She's lucky to have him, she thinks. Melinda, a former prostitute who eventually got free of her pimp, says that through verbal abuse and beatings her pimp put so much fear in her that she was "afraid to leave him. Yet by that time I was so much in love with him it really didn't matter. . . . When he put his arms around me . . . , when he told me he loved me I believed everything would work out all right" (p. 200).

Unfortunately, law enforcement does not help women escape from prostitution. Rather, as Eleanor Miller and colleagues observe, it tends "to strain, if not sever, [the woman's] social connection to her children and the other kin who might be militating against a life of prostitution, and to heighten her feelings of low self-esteem, depression, and hopelessness." Moreover, if she is "dependent on alcohol or other drugs and is not incarcerated for any length of time (which is usually the case), her arrest and the possible . . . consequences (e.g., loss of custody . . .) may motivate her to retreat even further into alcohol and drug use and to 'turn tricks'" to support her habit (1993:314). Arrest may also strengthen the woman's dependence on her pimp, as he may be the only one available to make arrangements for child care, bail, or legal representation (Alexander 1987).

Because penalizing prostitutes represents a costly and ineffective revolving-door approach that "ostracizes prostitutes and renders unlikely their voluntary movement into rehabilitation" or their willingness to report the abusiveness of their pimps, some have argued for the decriminalization or legalization of prostitution (Davis 1993:3). The NTFP and COYOTE (Call Off Your Old Tired Ethics) believe that prostitution is legitimate service work that adults should have the right to choose to do and that therefore all aspects of voluntary adult prostitution, "including relationships between prostitutes and third-party managers" (e.g., pimps and procurers), should be legal (COYOTE 1987:290). Nickie Roberts also favors the elimination of laws against prostitution because, as she says:

> The laws turn the government into the . . . biggest pimp through fines . . . women have to go out and earn. . . . [The laws] institutionalize and reinforce the whore stigma, which encourages rape and violence against prostitutes and . . . other women thought to behave like hustlers. The laws [also] . . . make it illegal for women to work together for safety's sake (two or more women constitute a brothel), effectively forcing women into the streets, where they must work alone and at great personal risk. (1994:44–45)

Others suggest a legalization approach similar to the one already in place in about a dozen counties in Nevada as well as in some cities and countries around the world. Here government regulations attempt to confine and control prostitution by mandating the number, size, and location of brothels permitted as well as the number of hours they can operate and the number of prostitutes they can employ. Prostitutes in Nevada brothels must have weekly medical exams and they usually are fingerprinted and required to carry identification cards. Their activities away from the property are significantly restricted, that is, when they "are allowed to go into town, which places they are allowed to frequent, and with whom they can talk" (Meier & Geis 1997; Miller et al. 1993:309).

Customers and brothel owners clearly benefit from this type of system, as do the city, county, and state governments that profit from the taxes levied and the licensing fees collected. Critics, on the other hand, note that the regulations put the government in control of nearly every aspect of a prostitute's life. Moreover, pimps are not eliminated but are provided with legal cover, and children are less protected from adult exploitation and the distorted sense of self that results from a culture that treats women as sex objects (Davis 1993). Internationally, legal regulation has even facilitated the trafficking of Asian females to Germany, the country that "has boasted that its system is the model for regulation of prostitution" (Barry 1995:228).

Another approach would decriminalize prostitution for both prostitutes and customers but "prohibit pimping, procuring, and trafficking . . . [as well as] third-party involvement in brothels and prostitution hotels" (Barry 1995:236). Proponents of this strategy favor vigorous efforts to prosecute pimps, as pimps often force females into prostitution or prevent them from leaving it. At the same time, this approach would prevent governments from legitimizing prostitution by regulating it (Miller et al. 1993).

Barry (1995) prefers an approach that would decriminalize prostitution for prostitutes but maintain its illegality for customers, pimps, procurers, and so forth. As long as the law allows men to buy women's bodies, she argues, you're not going to eliminate prostitution. And if you believe prostitution is harmful for women, then the law should be aimed at its elimination, without simultaneously turning prostitutes into criminals. Barry believes that most women would leave prostitution if they could, and what would enable them to do so is a comprehensive program of social services coupled with law enforcement against those who profit from the sale of women's bodies. Ideally such a program would include economic aid, job retraining, help finding housing and employment, counseling, medical assistance, and support and protection for leaving pimps. A program in Malmo, Sweden, has been providing such an array of services along with a media campaign that publicizes the available support networks and emphasizes that women are, in fact, leaving prostitution. This project has led to dramatic reductions in the number of women involved in prostitution.

While efforts to help women leave prostitution are important, Leah Platt (2001) believes that the so-called oldest profession will probably always exist and that public policy should focus on reducing the exploitative conditions under which prostitutes work. The "often mundane reality of illicit prostitution," Platt writes, is that it is "a job without overtime pay, health insurance, or sick leave—and usually without the recourse against

Box 8.2 Prostitution in International Context

All over the world women's entrance into prostitution is marked by deceit, coercion, and the pressures of "dire economic circumstances that make true consent impossible" (Monto 1998:507). Many prostitutes begin as sexually active teens who receive little financial or emotional support from their parents and drift into deviance (Davis 1993). Some are drawn by the lure of adventure and easy money. Some respond to advertisements by phony employment agencies or dance companies for exciting jobs overseas, but find that when they arrive at their destination the anticipated jobs are not available and they have to pay the organization back for expenses incurred. The jobs they are offered to help them get out of debt are jobs in bars with duties that they soon learn "extend far beyond being a hostess and serving drinks" (Barry 1979:90). Some of the women answering ads know they will be engaging in sex work but don't anticipate the slaverylike conditions they eventually find themselves in. In some cases women are placed into prostitution more directly through kidnapping and force. Mail-order-bride businesses also engage in a disguised form of trafficking in women, as would-be brides who do not "work out to the customers' satisfaction" are at times turned over to prostitution (Barry 1995:155). In poverty-stricken rural areas, some females are sold into prostitution by their parents or tricked with promises of marriage or employment. Some are coerced or recruited to service specialized markets: soldiers, sailors, businessmen, or immigrant laborers. In times of war, rape survivors, who are often considered disgraced by their families and communities, are especially vulnerable to networks of pimps and criminal organizations, as are refugees and other socially displaced females.

In recent years, global economic development has been accompanied by what Kathleen Barry describes as the "industrialization" and "widespread global diffusion" of prostitution. Prostitution, pornography, and other sex services are now major commodities in an increasing number of countries. Although prostitution remains illegal in many places, the laws often remain unenforced and a multitude of sex services that are sanctioned by law have emerged. Eros centers, escort services, sex holidays, telephone sex lines, and Internet solicitation represent some of the newer businesses. These ever-expanding "sex industries buy women's sexual exchange at a higher rate than most women can earn" in other jobs available to them (1995:52; Davis 1993). As multitudes of females enter prostitution under conditions that cannot technically be characterized as "forced" (i.e., physically coerced), prostitution is becoming normalized—increasingly seen and accepted as a personal occupational choice. At least twenty-five companies that arrange sex tours overseas operate in the United States alone (Budhos 1997). Some countries now even identify sex tourism as "an official, planned source of national income." And the growth of multinational conglomerates that specialize "in 'packages of sexual services' have transformed entire villages in Southeast Asia into prostitution-tourism centers" for businessmen and military personnel (Kirschenbaum 1991:13).

the abuses of one's employer, which can include being required to have sex without a condom and being forced to turn tricks . . . to work off crushing debts" to placement agencies or traffickers. These conditions should not be accepted as "hazards of the trade" or circumstances that women "bring upon themselves" but rather as "abuses of human rights and labor standards." Platt advocates a "middle ground" position that "supports a woman's right to control over her own body, as well as a prostitute's volition as an economic actor, without valorizing sex work as a liberating profession" (pp. 11–12).

◼ Women as "Fetal Abusers"

The image of a little African American baby lying "in a hospital incubator, some dozen tubes protruding from his nostrils, head, and limbs," is blazoned across the billboard. "'He couldn't take the hit,' the accompanying caption warns. 'If you're pregnant, don't take drugs'" (Gomez 1997:1). In the latter half of the 1980s, heart-wrenching pictures of pitiful drug-exposed infants began to peer out at us from magazines, TV screens, and billboards, beseeching us to "just say no" to drugs. The media coined the phrase "crack mothers" to refer to women who used crack or cocaine during pregnancy, presumably dooming their offspring, their "crack babies," to a lifetime of suffering and inferiority. While these claims, it turns out, have not been substantiated by scientific research (Lutiger et al. 1991), the media images of crack mothers were suffused with "the hyperbole associated with crack, addiction, race and its ties to the underclass, inner-city poverty, and welfare" (Humphries 1998:57). Demonized by the media, crack mothers became "threatening symbols of everything that was wrong with America" (p. 45).

In response, a wave of legislators, health professionals, police, social workers, reporters, and religious leaders "rushed forward to 'do something' to stem the tide" of drug-exposed babies (Gomez 1997:4). Fourteen separate hearings were held by eight different congressional committees between 1987 and 1991 to confront the problem of prenatal drug exposure. Some public hospitals initiated policies of universal drug testing for women giving birth; some began testing newborns. The Medical University of South Carolina went so far as to test some pregnant women without their consent and to turn those testing positive over to police for the purpose of criminal prosecution, a practice that was overturned by the U.S. Supreme Court in 2001 (Asseo 2001).

Due to the concern about "crack babies," women's custody rights were curbed and terminated throughout the country (Farr 1995; Gomez 1997). When prenatal drug exposure was suspected, social workers removed infants from a mother's custody, creating a population of "boarder babies" left to languish in hospitals for up to six months awaiting foster-home placements. In some cases "a single blood test on a pregnant woman or a newborn . . . [was] sufficient to label [the] woman a drug abuser," even though a positive test can only indicate that a drug has been introduced within the past twenty-four to seventy-two hours (Hubbard 1995:134). Frequency of drug use or substantive information about a mother's or child's impairment cannot be determined by one test alone.

In addition, pregnant women who used illegal drugs were prosecuted for delivering a controlled substance to a child (via the umbilical cord) and for child abuse, neglect, or endangerment (Farr 1995). An Illinois woman was charged with involuntary manslaughter when her newborn daughter, who was found to have cocaine in her urine, died two days after birth. Pregnant women who used alcohol also came under fire, as they were "placed under court orders not to drink" (Pollitt 1998:279).

Prosecutions of pregnant drug users for fetal harm have usually been unsuccessful, however. Appellate courts in some states have found that "women who take drugs during pregnancy cannot be prosecuted for endangering their fetuses, due to the absence of laws specifically identifying such behavior as a crime" (Farr 1995:236). In some cases, laws intended to protect *children* from abuse, neglect, or endangerment have been defined as inapplicable when fetal harm was alleged because the state's law did not explicitly recognize the personhood of a *fetus* (Sink 1998). On the other hand, the South Carolina Supreme Court has ruled that "a viable fetus—one able to live outside the uterus—is a child under law." The court stated that it was "absurd to recognize the viable fetus as a person for purposes of homicide laws and wrongful-death statutes but not for purposes of statutes proscribing child abuse" (Carelli 1998:4A). And in Wisconsin, legislation dubbed the "cocaine mom bill" was signed into law in 1998, specifically extending certain child abuse protections to fetuses. The law allows pregnant women who abuse drugs or alcohol to be confined in hospitals or drug treatment centers in order to protect fetuses from further drug exposure (*Daily Jefferson County Union* 1998).

Efforts to define the use of illegal drugs or alcohol during pregnancy as "fetal abuse" have been controversial. Is it appropriate to criminalize drug use during pregnancy and prosecute offenders? Should it be legal to exert controls over pregnant women to prevent them from using drugs? Public opinion has been divided. Some argue that since the government has a legal obligation to protect children from parents who abuse or endanger them, it should have a similar obligation to protect the fetus even if parents object. After all, drug-exposed infants may suffer, may be born with limited physical or mental abilities. They may require special treatment or hospitalization or become wards of the state, costing health care facilities and taxpayers huge sums of money. Who would dispute that the protection of future generations is an important goal?

Some argue, however, that criminalization of a mother's behavior during pregnancy is not the best means to this end. The threat of arrest, prosecution, and incarceration would deter pregnant women from seeking prenatal care, which is especially important as "pregnancies of drug-addicted women who get prenatal care result in healthier outcomes than do those in which there is no such care" (Farr 1995:241). In addition, forcing women to withdraw from drugs risks severe shock to their bodies and can be even more endangering to the fetus than continued drug use (Pollitt 1998). And drugs such as methadone, which are often given to treat drug addiction, are equally if not more harmful to the fetus than the illegal drug. Some studies even suggest that except for "heavy alcohol use, drug use during pregnancy has few if any long-term effects on children" (Weitz 1996:141).

Katha Pollitt (1998) argues that many women continue using drugs during pregnancy because they are unable to gain access to treatment programs due to long waiting periods or to restrictions that prevent enrollment during pregnancy. Entering a treatment program often means leaving the children one already has uncared for or turning them over to relatives, friends, or foster care. The potential risks associated with these options are unacceptable to some mothers and seem greater than the risks associated with fetal exposure. The possible, perhaps likely, stigmatization of one's children is another issue mothers consider.

Women who use cocaine during pregnancy—especially those likely to be tested for drugs or identified as addicts—are also likely to suffer from a host of other problems, and it is difficult to sort out the effects of these problems from the effects of prenatal drug exposure. These women have more nutritional deficiencies and poverty-related health concerns, receive less prenatal care, "bear and rear their kids in conditions of more profound deprivation, and are more persistently exposed to violence than other women" (Greider 1995:54–55). Attributing negative outcomes to children of drug-using mothers based solely or primarily on prenatal drug exposure ignores the impact of these many factors on women's and children's lives.

Clearly some mothers (some drug-using, some not) will be found to be unfit parents. However, Pollitt believes that a determination of unfitness should be made on the basis of a careful evaluation, not "on the presumption that even a single use of drugs during pregnancy renders a mother ipso facto . . . unfit" (1998:279). She notes that concern about crack babies has *not* developed as part of a comprehensive national campaign "to help women have wanted, healthy pregnancies and healthy babies." Judges send "pregnant addicts to jail, but they don't order drug treatment programs to accept them, or [order] Medicaid, which pays for heroin treatment, to cover crack addiction—let alone order . . . obstetricians to take uninsured women as patients, or the federal government to fund fully the Women, Infants, and Children supplemental feeding program" (p. 280). Ruth Hubbard adds that if the government wants to protect developing fetuses, the best "way to do that is to make it possible for pregnant women—and women in general—to have access to proper housing, food, jobs, a decent living environment, and good prenatal care" (1995:133). And we just can't assume a better home can be found for these children. People willing and able to adopt drug-exposed infants are in short supply. One study of boarder babies in New York City hospitals, for example, found that most were eventually sent home to their birth families. And of those who remained wards of the state, nearly a third "still didn't have a permanent home by the time they were three years old" (Greider 1995:56).

▨ *Women Who Kill*

According to criminological research, the patterns of men's and women's homicide differ. To begin with, males are more likely than females to both murder and be murdered. Males constitute about 90 percent of those arrested for murder and nearly 80 percent of murder victims. Most male-perpetrated homicides are *intragender,* committed against other males, while most female-perpetrated homicides are *intergender.* Thus both sexes are more likely to kill males than females, although males murder about twice as many females as females murder males (Benekos 1995).

A higher proportion of the homicides committed by women involves the murder of family members and intimate partners (Browne 1997; Browne & Williams 1993). For instance, mothers are more likely than fathers to be the perpetrators of **filicide**, the killing of one's children. Researchers attribute this to mothers' traditional role as primary caregivers and to the greater burdens children impose on mothers than on fathers (Benekos 1995; Gelles 1987; Ogle et al. 1995). Single mothers in particular often feel socially isolated and experience severe financial strains. In one study, single women who had delivered only 12 percent of the babies in the sample were responsible for over half of the maternal filicides (Daly & Wilson 1988). In another study, states with proportionately more female-headed single-parent families and higher levels of gender inequality were found to have higher filicide rates for children under five years of age (Baron 1993).

After the 1972 U.S. Supreme Court decision in *Roe v. Wade* that legalized abortion in the United States, **neonaticide**, the killing of newborns within hours of birth, declined (Lester 1992). Philip Resnick, who coined the term "neonaticide" in 1970, estimates that in the United States today there are approximately 250 cases a year (cited in Hoffman 1997). Accurate data are hard to come by, however, since it's likely that many discarded neonates are never discovered (Crittenden & Craig 1990). Most neonaticides are committed by women who are young and single and in severe denial of their pregnancies. They think: Maybe I'm just getting fat. Maybe my period is late. Maybe I'll miscarry or my boyfriend will come back. Maybe he'll want us to get married. That this state of denial knows no boundaries of class or race was made painfully clear in 1996 when the dead newborn son of white, upper-middle-class college students Amy Grossberg and Brian Peterson was found discarded in a dumpster. Grossberg had contemplated abortion, but like so many other young women, she "took her time—she wasn't sure, couldn't decide, was too ashamed, thought it would go away" (Hoffman 1997:5). According to Resnick, the desperate denial of pregnancy mentally protects the woman from bonding with the fetus. The fetus isn't a baby to her; it's "a foreign body, . . . an object to get rid of" (cited in Hoffman 1997:4). When the woman finds herself giving birth in some motel or restroom, squatting over a toilet or in a tub, the baby's cries shatter her defenses and a frantic effort to conceal the evidence all too often follows.

Many maternal infanticides are chalked up to a psychological imbalance linked to female hormones: postpartum depression or the more extreme postpartum psychosis (see Chapter 3). According to physician Donna Stewart, however, "Women who commit infanticide run a wide spectrum, from those in denial, who were concealing their pregnancy and . . . its consequence, to highly impulsive women who, in a fit of rage, shake their baby to death, to manic-depressive women, to those who are suffering from classical depression who wind up killing their babies and themselves." Stewart encourages us "to broaden our categories, [to] recognize the individuality of women" and the diversity of their experiences and circumstances. Only then will we be able to tailor prevention strategies appropriately (cited in Pearson 1997:79).

Exhaustion psychosis due to sleep deprivation has been considered by some to be more likely than hormonal change to cause aggression against children. This is a condition that can effect anyone who goes without sleep for lengthy stretches. The state of extreme exhaustion can leave one highly emotional, edgy, disoriented, even delusional. As Patricia Pearson observes, "When sleep deprivation combines with the constant demands of a baby, a lack of support, and insecurity or resentment about parenting, a normally well-balanced person can come perilously close to violence" (1997:81). And it's not only biological mothers who sometimes feel they're losing their grip with reality. Fathers and adoptive mothers experience postpartum exhaustion psychosis as well.

We should also remember that pregnancy and transition to motherhood are stressful for *all* women as they come to terms with changes in body image, their responsibilities, their relationships with husbands/partners and parents, and even society's perception of their role as mother. The **myth of motherhood**, the idealized view that mothers are always content and children are "nothing but joy" inevitably comes head to head with reality.

Most mothers are taken aback by "the hard, selfless, exhausting and isolating work involved in looking after a child" (Morris & Wilczynski 1994:209). Moreover, the traditional assumption that mothers instinctively know how to care for children can lead to a sense of failure when mothers experience difficulty doing what is supposed to come naturally. Jealousy, fear of losing one's identity, and even hostility toward the new baby are common in the course of adjustment (Oakley 1986; Robinson & Stewart 1986).

An analysis of data on 474 filicides in Britain from 1982 to 1989 led Allison Morris and Ania Wilczynski to conclude that "the unpalatable truth [is] that 'normal' women can kill their children when they are confronted by social and economic circumstances which are severe enough." They warn that the widespread tendency to define maternal "filicide as pathological diverts attention from the social conditions which are conducive to its occurrence: poverty, inordinate childcare responsibilities, social isolation, lack of support, the myths surrounding motherhood and cultural standards of 'good' (i.e., perfect) mothers" (1994:215).

Nevertheless, when women kill, the person they are most likely to kill is not a child but an intimate partner—a spouse, cohabitant, or lover. In Mann's six-city study (1996), for example, "domestic relationship" homicides constituted nearly 50 percent of the female-perpetrated homicides, while filicides constituted just over 10 percent. Overall, women perpetrate nearly 40 percent of all partner homicides but less than 10 percent of non-partner incidents (Browne 1997; Browne & Williams 1989).

While male partners are more likely to kill females after long periods of *inflicting* physical, sexual, and emotional abuse, females partners are more likely to kill males after *enduring* long periods of such abuse and after exhausting other alternatives that might extricate them from the relationship (Browne 1987; Dobash et al. 1992). Thus one study found that states that had fewer resources for battered women (e.g., shelters and other services) had higher rates of female-perpetrated homicides against male partners than states that had more resources (Browne & Williams 1989). And contrary "to the common assumption that women kill partners while they are sleeping or otherwise incapacitated," most of these domestic homicides occurred *during* an assault perpetrated by the man when the woman believed that she or her child might be seriously hurt or killed (Browne 1997:64; Jurik & Winn 1990; Maguigan 1991).

Angela Browne (1987) compared two groups of women who had both been involved in abusive domestic relationships: one group consisted of women who had murdered their partners and one group consisted of women who had not. She found that the women who killed their partners had been assaulted more often and had sustained more frequent and severe injuries. They also had been forced to endure more rape and other forced sexual activities. In addition, the men they killed were more likely to have abused alcohol or drugs and to have threatened to kill them.

Russell Dobash and colleagues (1992) argue that men and women who murder their partners tend not to have similar motives and intentions. Whereas women are much more likely to kill their partner in self-defense, men are more likely to kill in response to the partner's infidelity, to hunt down and kill partners who've left them, to kill partners as part of planned murder-suicides, and to stage **familicidal** massacres, killing the children as well as the partner.

Although women who kill are also less likely than their male counterparts to have a prior record of offending, Mann (1996) found that over half of the women in her study had prior arrest records and more than a third had prior arrests for violent crimes (see Faith 1993; Maguigan 1991). Even among those who killed domestic partners, 30 percent had a prior arrest for violent crime. Mann believes that these findings run counter to the image of women as passive victims of domestic violence. The women in her study, however, were most likely to be unemployed African American mothers with less than a high school education. According to Robbin Ogle and colleagues, chronic stress experienced by the underclass can lead to "unfocused explosions of angry aggression" against the most visible targets in one's social milieu (1995:175). And as we noted earlier, females with these backgrounds often defy gender stereotypes. Growing up in communities where so many women head households and so many experience abuse from the men in their lives, girls learn "there's no feminine currency in being frail" (Pearson 1997:28). In Mann's sample, in fact, nearly 60 percent who killed domestic partners defined their motive as self-defense.

When it comes to "serial murderers," most people think of male offenders such as Jack the Ripper, Ted Bundy, or Jeffrey Dahmer. In Eric Hickey's study (1991) of over 200 serial murderers (those who killed at least three people over a period of time), less than a fifth were women. Nevertheless, gender differences in serial murder occur more in modus operandi than in motive, that is, more in "the how" than in "the why" (Pearson 1997; Skrapec 1994). Serial murders by women rarely involve sexual assault, and they tend to be less visibly violent. On the other hand, the male and female motive for serial murder is similar: "a need for a sense of self as actor; a need for power that has generally arisen out of a formative history in which the individual as a child experienced him- or herself as powerless" (Skrapec 1994:244). Such experiences can "lead to a simmering yet pervasive rage" that, if left unresolved, can erupt into violence. Men predominate as serial killers because they are more likely to feel entitled to express their rage outwardly. Outward expression of rage has traditionally been less socially acceptable for women, who have tended to turn their anger inward, becoming depressed or self-destructive.

Female serial murderers have often been stereotyped as "black widows" who kill a series of husbands, children, or other relatives, or as "angels of death" who kill patients in their care (Skrapec 1994). Although there are proportionately more "black widows" among female serial murderers than "black widowers" among male serial murderers, women's crimes are more diverse than these stereotypes suggest. Belea Keeney and Kathleen Heide (1994) studied fourteen female serial murderers who are known to have killed sixty-two people (and suspected to have killed at least eighty-eight). Most of their victims were relatives, and 20 percent were acquaintances or strangers. Forty-three percent of the victims were in the offender's custodial care, and 57 percent were poisoned, 29 percent smothered, and 11 percent shot. Half of the murderers had "affective goals" (i.e., their motivation was exclusively interior or emotional) and half had "instrumental goals" (i.e., they killed for monetary or other gain).

Male serial killers are often given sinister nicknames such as *Jack the Ripper, The Night Stalker,* or *The Boston Strangler,* while their female counterparts are dubbed *Old Shoe Box Annie, Giggling Grandma, Beautiful Blonde Killer,* and the like, nicknames that tend to make light of their crimes, to be comical, patronizing, or sexually suggestive (Fox & Levin 1993; Hickey 1991). The names for the females dovetail with cultural stereotypes about women as unaggressive, as the gentle sex, sparking amusement or curiosity about female murderers rather than apprehension or dread. Women also tend to be "place-specific killers" who "don't prowl" (Pearson 1997:153; Rossmo 1994). They often confine their action to one home, one boardinghouse, or one hospital, selecting victims who enter their "comfort zone" by chance or design. Because they're usually "trappers" and not "stalkers," female serial killers don't arouse the anxiety we feel about the shadowy unknown. Nicknames like *Giggling Grandma* mask the horror of being preyed upon by people you know, trust, perhaps even love. And it's not just suffering or terminally-ill patients who are killed by "angels of death." It's also babies and adults "in little immediate health risk or discomfort" (Skrapec 1994:253).

To be sure, females represent only a small proportion of known serial murderers, who in turn represent only a small proportion of murderers in general. However, Candice Skrapec believes that we've been too complacent about female killers and that many homicides "remain unsolved, without viable suspects, because the offender was falsely assumed to be male" (1994:265). In Hickey's study (1991), the female murderers went undiscovered for longer periods of time and ended up averaging a larger number of victims than their male counterparts. Deaths that eventually get attributed to females often don't initially trigger suspicion of foul play. They occur right under our noses, seem ordinary, unexceptional: an old lady dies at home in her sleep, an intensive-care patient has cardiac arrest, an indigent man disappears from a boarding house, and so forth.

It wasn't until the death of the ninth child in the Tinning household that the police got involved. Although Marybeth Tinning's first child succumbed to illness, all the rest had deaths consistent with suffocation. Marybeth was initially praised as a real trooper as she whisked one child after another to the hospital for emergency care. Sometimes the rescue was successful. The child would be saved and sent home—for a time. The pattern became oddly familiar: the inevitable relapse, another frantic attempt at resuscitation. Eventually Marybeth, lavished with sympathy, would return from the hospital with yet another little body to bury. But as the death count rose, so did the suspicion. The grieving mother was unmasked and ultimately convicted (Skrapec 1994).

It is now believed that Marybeth Tinning had a condition known as **Munchausen Syndrome by Proxy** (MSP), whereby a person deliberately inflicts injuries on a child in a desperate bid for attention from doctors, family, and community (Pearson 1997). (Baron Munchausen was an eighteenth-century literary figure known for telling "tall tales" about the exploits of his true-to-life counterpart.) Persons with MSP usually "only go so far" with each injury, and the child is snatched from the jaws of death again and again. Ten to thirty percent of MSP victims eventually receive a fatal injury, however. And although accurate tallies elude us, some experts believe that MSP is "far from rare and . . . frequently missed," with perhaps as many as 500 new cases each year in the United States (Schreier & Libow 1993:38). MSP is thought to be mostly "the province of women who find themselves in maternal" or nurturing roles—biological or adoptive mothers, baby-sitters, caretakers, nurses, doctor's wives. "They have an expert grasp of medicine and a keen sense of medicine's power," which allows them to elicit symptoms, stage rescues, toss the unsuspecting "with stunning cruelty into constant states of peril" (Pearson 1997:94).

The death certificates of several of the Tinning children listed **sudden infant death syndrome** (SIDS) as the cause of death. The label "SIDS" was coined to describe those cases where a child was found unexpectedly dead but was believed to have died from an unknown natural cause. SIDS has become somewhat of a catchall explanation, however, one that is at times applied indiscriminately. And because natural death is very hard to distinguish from death due to suffocation, many infanticides are believed to go undetected. One study of crib deaths in Chicago found that over 20 percent "were related to suspected child abuse and neglect" (Christoffel et al. 1985:880). Of the 6,000 to 8,000 cases of SIDS reported annually in the United States, 10 to 20 percent are thought to involve accidental or deliberate suffocation (Emery & Newlands 1991; Reece 1993). As one Texas coroner said, "The only way you can prove [smothering] is to show a pattern of behavior" (quoted in Pearson 1997:109). But herein lies the rub. In 1972 an article in *Pediatrics* magazine claimed that multiple deaths in a single family were likely to have a genetic or inheritable component (Steinschneider 1972). This influential report effectively quelled the suspicions of coroners and doctors when they discovered several infant deaths in a single family. Twenty-two years after publication, however, the woman who served as the case study for the report admitted she had smothered all five of her children (Pearson 1997).

Clearly, when one looks at the arrest data for violent crimes, one is compelled to conclude that the extent to which women do violence (and get caught at it) is proportionately small. For men, doing violence can be a way to "do masculinity." But women's expression of aggression is also shaped by gender norms (which themselves vary by class, race, etc.), and many females learn to "do femininity" by turning their anger against themselves, becoming depressed or self-destructive, or by expressing aggression indirectly. Studies have shown, for instance, that as girls hone verbal and social skills, many abandon physical aggression for verbal and indirect tactics— gossiping, name-calling, bullying, excluding others from groups, setting others up for punishment or turning people against them (Frey & Hoppe-Graff 1994; Bjorkqvist et al. 1992). However, Patricia Pearson reminds us that although men may be more likely to "flamboyantly display force to promote and defend status in the public realm," women are not incapable of using "their own aggressive strategies to defend, maintain, and control their intimate relations, not just to 'defend their cubs,'" but as Marybeth Tinning did, "to defend their aspirations, their identity, and their place on the stage" (1997:20).

9

Sexual Violence

In her book *Pornography: Men Possessing Women,* feminist writer Andrea Dworkin relates this true account:

> She was 13 . . . [and] at a Girl Scout camp in northern Wisconsin. She went for a long walk in the woods alone during the day. She had long blond hair. She saw three hunters reading magazines, talking, joking. One looked up and said: "There's a live one." She thought they meant a deer. She ducked and started to run away. They meant her. They chased her, caught her, dragged her back to where they were camped. The magazines were pornography of women she physically resembled: blond, childlike. They called her names from the pornography: Little Godiva, Golden Girl, also bitch and slut. They threatened to kill her. They made her undress. It was November and cold. One held a rifle to her head; another beat her breasts with his rifle. All three raped her—penile penetration into the vagina. The third one couldn't get hard at first so he demanded a blow job. She didn't know what that was. The third man forced his penis into her mouth; one of the others cocked the trigger on his rifle. She was told she had better do it right. She tried. When they were done with her they kicked her: they kicked her naked body and they kicked leaves and pine needles on her. . . . "They told me that if I wanted more, that I could come back the next day." (1989:xviii–xix)

This story is but one of many that were told at public hearings of the Minneapolis City Council in 1983, testimonies of harm from sexual violence that implicate pornography in that harm. In this chapter we use our sociological imagination to explore the problem of sexual violence against women and children. We first introduce the notion of the continuum of sexual violence and note the common character of experiences that range from nonviolent sexual intimidation to acts of severe brutality. We also take a critical look at the role pornography plays in maintaining a cultural climate that sanctions such violence. We then examine in detail the problems of rape and sexual assault, child sexual abuse, and women battering.

■ The Problem of Sexual Violence

▒ *The Sexual Violence Continuum*

Liz Kelly (1987) advanced the concept of the **continuum of sexual violence** to help us understand that all sexual violations—from flashing or obscene phone calls to the more extreme forms of rape, battery, or even sexual murder—have a common character in that all entail use of abuse, coercion, or force to control and instill fear in women. Deborah Cameron and Elizabeth Frazer add that too many men seem to "need and feel entitled to . . . unrestricted sexual access to women, even—sometimes especially—against women's will," and that sexual violations "collectively function as a threat to women's autonomy" by limiting their freedom of action and undermining their self-esteem (1987:164). As Susan Brownmiller writes about rape, "A world without rapists would be a world in which women moved freely without fear of men. That *some* men rape provides sufficient threat to keep all women in a state of intimidation, forever conscious of the knowledge that the biological tool . . . may turn to weapon with a swiftness borne of harmful intent" (1975:209). Furthermore, since men's sexuality is often presumed to be naturally aggressive, women's fear of sexual violence seems inevitable. And to make matters worse, society then places responsibility on *women* to monitor their behavior so they won't be violated. If they are, they may be blamed for their victimization or find that their suffering is "trivialized, questioned, or ignored" (Cameron & Frazer 1987:164).

Cameron and Frazer help us see the *functional* similarity of violations ranging from nonviolent sexual intimidation to violent acts. They argue that both flashing and rape, for example, are acts that men do "to reassure themselves of their power and potency; both include, as a crucial factor in that reassurance, the fear and humiliation of the female victims" (p. 164). Acts of nonviolent sexual intimidation—the common, everyday verbal, visual, and physical intrusions—"serve to remind women and girls that they are at risk and vulnerable to male aggression just because they are female" (Sheffield 1989:483–484).

Suzanne Berne had a familiar experience that illustrates this notion. She was walking in her neighborhood one winter afternoon when someone called out to her. She turned to see a man with his pants open, exposing himself. She describes her reaction:

> I [wasn't] afraid, not exactly. But I [was] alone. Sometimes for a woman, this amounts to the same thing. . . . It could have been much worse. I wasn't raped, after all, as someone pointed out later. Only slightly violated. All I got was a small reminder that the world isn't as pleasant and safe as it sometimes appears to be. . . . [That man] is now part of my life; he is my reminder. He lives on that street every time I walk by. . . . He "flashed" me. . . . It [was] a flash, a sudden exposure—of weakness, of

aloneness. A woman remembers these moments because the exposure is hers. Ask any woman, and she will tell you exactly where she was . . . when it happened to her. Because it has happened to her.

Berne points out that a particularly insidious aspect of these sorts of intrusions—the "indecent exposure, . . . the construction worker's whistle, the obscene caller's mumbled requests"—is that the man's pleasure depends on the woman's witness. He needs her reaction for his thrill. "What happened to me," notes Berne, does not generally "happen to men. Men are not forced into this sort of collusion" (1991:10–11).

In a study designed to document the prevalence of sexual violence, Melanie Randall and Lori Haskell (1995) interviewed a random sample of 420 women living in Toronto, Canada. The interviews, which typically took about two hours to complete, were conducted face-to-face in private settings of the respondents' own choosing—mostly their own homes. The inquiries about violence were part of a larger discussion of women's safety. The findings document "the devastating 'normalcy' and pervasive presence of sexual violence in women's lives" (pp. 26–27).

Nearly all of the women (98 percent) in the Randall-Haskell study reported personally experiencing some form of sexual violation at some time in their lives: "sexually threatening, intrusive, or assaultive . . . experiences [that] ranged from being followed or chased on the street to receiving an obscene phone call, to being sexually harassed at work, to being sexually assaulted and/or raped in childhood or adulthood, to being physically and/or sexually assaulted in an intimate relationship." Over 40 percent of the women "reported at least one experience of incestuous and/or extrafamilial sexual abuse" before age sixteen, two-thirds reported at least one instance of sexual assault (from unwanted sexual touching of breasts or genitals to forced sexual intercourse) when they were sixteen years or older, and 40 percent reported completed rape in the sixteen-plus age range (p. 14).

Randall and Haskell argue that it is not "an exaggeration to say that part of the experience of being female . . . typically involves directly experiencing some form of sexual intrusion or violence and/or living with the . . . threat of it" (p. 9). In fact, Kelly (1987) found in her research that many women experienced sexual interaction not as a clearly "either/or" phenomena, that is, as *either* consensual *or* forced, but on a continuum moving from choice to pressure to coercion to force. Similarly, Jennifer Dunn's interviews with college sorority women led her to conclude that forcible interaction might be best characterized "as falling along an interpretive continuum ranging from perceptions of violation as relatively non-violent and unobtrusive to more explicitly threatening and dangerous definitions. . . . What connects meaning conferral along this continuum is the *undesired* character of the interaction from the perspective of the unwilling actor" (1999:441–442). We will explore this notion further later in this chapter.

Victimization surveys conducted in the United States also document the common experience of sexual violence. Studies, for instance, have found that anywhere from 18 to 44 percent of women have experienced attempted or completed rape at some time in their lives, and 12 to 24 percent have experienced completed rape (Belknap 2001; Koss 1988; Russell 1984; Tjaden & Thoennes 1998a). These surveys have varied in their methodology: some have involved in-depth, face-to-face interviews using empathic interviewers, while others have relied on impersonal telephone calls that asked a few sexually explicit "yes/no" questions to identify victims. Studies using the latter method tend to find lower rates of victimization.

One advantage of the Randall and Haskell (1995) study, besides its in-depth interview methodology, is that it provides us with data on a variety of violations that constitute the sexual violence continuum. Also important is its recognition that we cannot truly "understand the role that sexual violence plays in women's lives [if we focus] only on its specific manifestations, independent of one another." The study examined patterns of victimization and revictimization and documented that for many women sexual intrusion and violence are "ongoing dimensions of their life" (pp. 16–17). Over a quarter of the respondents, for example, reported experiencing sexual abuse/assault in *both* childhood and adulthood, and about one in ten experienced not only childhood sexual abuse *and* adult sexual assault *but also* physical assault in an intimate relationship.

■ The Gendered Politics of Sexual Murder

Sexual murder, the most extreme form of sexual violence, is the killing of another that provides an erotic thrill for the assailant. The gendered politics of sexual murder entails the terrorization of women who are not directly its victims but who live in fear of becoming victims. According to Jane Caputi (1989), the threat of sexual murder is analogous to the historical threat of lynching on blacks; it functions to keep women "in their place."

Sex murderers (also called lust killers) are almost exclusively male, and their victims are usually female. Although sexual murder is sometimes narrowly defined as murder following rape or sexual assault, this definition is flawed as some offenders are **necrophiliacs** (those who have an erotic interest in corpses) rather than rapists, and some are sexually aroused by the mutilation of victim's genitals or by the killing itself. Cameron and Frazer argue that "rape and sexual assault are neither necessary nor sufficient to make a murder 'sexual.' What is important is the eroticization of the act of killing in and for itself." Hence they define sexual murder as "all cases where the killer was motivated by sadistic sexual impulses—'the lust to kill'" (1987:18).

Further Exploration

Box 9.1 Stalking

Generally speaking, **stalking** refers to "the willful, repeated, and malicious following, harassing, or threatening of another person" (Melton 2000:248). Although stalking is not a new phenomenon, it was not conceptualized as a social problem until 1989, when an obsessed fan shot and killed Rebecca Shaeffer, a TV actress he had repeatedly tried to contact. Prior to this event, what came to be termed "stalking" was referred to as "obsession," "sexual harassment," or "psychological rape," and it was portrayed as uncomfortable and annoying rather than as dangerous and violent. The Shaeffer murder, however, became linked to other events, such as the repeated following of Jodie Foster by John Hinckley (see Chapter 3) and the following and stabbing of actress Theresa Saldana, generating a public concern about "celebrity staking." This concern played a major role in the passage of an antistalking law in California in 1990. Other states quickly followed suit, and the National Institute of Justice (NIJ) developed a model antistalking code for the states to use when drafting statutes (Emerson et al. 1998; Lowney & Best 1995).

As advocates of battered women made connections between stalking and the harassment and violence women often experience when they attempt to leave abusive partners, "the link between domestic violence and stalking was quickly recognized" (Melton 2000:248). Stalking became identified as a more serious social problem and was reframed from a *celebrity* issue to a *women's* issue (Lowney & Best 1995).

Research indicates that those who are stalked are most often "the current or former spouses or intimate partners of their stalkers" (Melton 2000:248). In these circumstances, stalking arises "out of efforts to maintain or to recreate a close relationship that has been terminated or that one party sought to terminate" (Emerson et al. 1998:295). Here the parties are or have been "intimately linked," often "exes," or are sometimes acquaintances who have been dating. In other circumstances, stalking involves "one-sided attempts to create close, usually romantic relationships" where none existed before. Included here would be (1) *unacquainted stalking,* where the person pursued is a stranger initially encountered in a semipublic or public place, (2) *pseudoacquainted* stalking, where the victim is a celebrity or public figure whom the pursuer has come to feel connected or emotionally attached to, and (3) *semiacquainted* stalking, where the victim is pursued by someone with whom he or she had contact in the past or by someone he or she has minimal present contact (e.g., a coworker in a larger firm).

Robert Emerson and colleagues term all of the above circumstances *relational stalking,* since they all "entail unilateral pursuit linked to some admiring or romantic interest in, or implied or specific assertions of

continues

Box 9.1   continued

rights to, a continuing, close or intimate relationship with another."
Relational stalking can be distinguished from *revenge stalking*, where
there are "no romantic or relational claims" but where the stalker seems
to believe that he or she has been maltreated and is "focused on intimidating the victim and perhaps on extracting . . . payback" (1998:295–296).
Psychiatrists, plastic surgeons, judges, and instructors are particularly
likely to be targeted by revenge stalkers.

Although all fifty states and the District of Columbia have passed
antistalking laws, the legal definitions of stalking differ considerably
from place to place. Most statutes require that stalking not be an isolated
event, while some specify a minimum number of acts (usually two) that
must take place. Some statutes specify particular acts such as surveillance, laying-in-waiting, vandalism, nonconsensual communication, and
telephone harassment. Some also consider threats against the victims'
immediate family as stalking (Tjaden & Thoennes 1998b).

Using a definition of stalking that closely resembles the NIJ model
code, the National Violence Against Women survey defined stalking as "a
course of conduct directed at a specific person that involves repeated
[i.e., on two or more occasions] visual or physical proximity, nonconsensual communication, or verbal, written or implied threats, or a combination thereof, that would cause a reasonable person [a high level of] fear."
The survey found that 8 percent of women and 2 percent of men in the
United States had been stalked at some time in their life, the majority by
people the victim already knew. The survey also found "a strong link
between stalking and other forms of violence [assault and rape] in intimate relationships" (Tjaden & Thoennes 1998b:2–3).

Caputi characterizes sexual murder as a form of "patriarchal terrorism"
(1989:438). Like other types of violence against women, sexual murder
"expresses not purely individual anger and frustration but a collective, culturally sanctioned **misogyny**"—the hatred or disdain of women—that is
important to the maintenance of men's collective power. Sexual murder,
note Cameron and Frazer, is "male violence taken to its logical extreme. . . .
Death is the ultimate negation of autonomy," and the mutilation of breasts
and genitals common in sexual murder "is the ultimate violation of the
female sex and body" (1987:164–165).

Between 1975 and 1980 Peter Sutcliffe, dubbed the Yorkshire Ripper,
roamed the North of England. He killed thirteen women (mostly prostitutes) before he was caught. Several more survived attempts on their lives.
While the Ripper was loose, the atmosphere was heavy with fear and
rumors circulated wildly about "what the killer did" (Cameron & Frazer

1987:x): Who was this shadow figure "who slipped into murder as gently and gradually as a child slips into a swimming pool at the shallow end, . . . this quiet man . . . who stole up behind women in the dark, smashed in their skulls with blows from a ball-headed hammer, then pulled up their skirts and blouses and carefully inflicted dozens of wounds with a specially sharpened hammer?" (Wilson 1984:19). After he was caught, Sutcliffe explained that he was "just cleaning up [the] streets" (Cameron & Frazer 1987:123). As to why he mutilated his victims' breasts and genitals, "It's just something that comes over me," he said (p. 1).

When Cameron and Frazer describe the Yorkshire Ripper's "reign of terror," we understand the meaning of "sexual terrorism," the power of fear to clip women's wings:

> Any man could have been the killer. . . . The whole weight of the culture colluded in the terror that affected women's existence in the North of England: the police who insisted we stay off streets, the commentators who so callously devalued the lives of prostitutes, the football crowds who chanted [e.g., Ripper eleven, police nil] and made jokes about the Ripper, those men, who under cover of protecting frightened women found a golden opportunity to threaten and assault us. (p. 165)

It is easy to fathom women's fear of a killer on the loose. It is disturbing, however, to contemplate how this fear is heightened by the chanting and the jokes, by the tendency to mythologize gruesome killers. The nickname "Yorkshire Ripper" was no coincidence. It resurrected the collective memory of panic surrounding the reign of nineteenth-century London's knife-wielding Jack the Ripper, a killer/mutilator who to this day has not been identified—nor forgotten. In fact, the 1988 centennial anniversary of Jack's crimes "was celebrated by multiple retellings of the Ripper legend." Ripper paraphernalia appeared—buttons, T-shirts, a computer game, even cocktails. *Jack the Ripper* (a made-for-TV movie), *Jack's Back* (an exploitation thriller), and "scores of new books on the master killer" were released (Caputi 1989:445).

Ted Bundy, another mythologized sex murderer, was convicted in the United States in 1979 of killing three women, though he was suspected of killing as many as fifty. When he escaped from jail while awaiting trial for murder in Aspen, Colorado, he quickly became a folk hero there (Larson 1980). T-shirts emblazoned "Ted Bundy is a One Night Stand" appeared. A radio station featured a Ted Bundy request hour, offering songs like "Ain't No Way to Treat a Lady." A restaurant hawked a "Bundyburger," which was actually nothing but a plain roll: "Open it and see the meat has fled," the sign explained (Caputi 1989:446). Are these simply examples of comic relief? Inventive ways to make a buck? Or do they reflect something more insidious? It's tempting to dismiss them as lighthearted, but what does it say about our culture that it's so easy to trivialize and eroticize a serial sex murderer?

Caputi (1987) observes that Bundy's victims, who were all young white women, were portrayed in the mainstream press as respectable and attractive. But when serial murder victims are not perceived as respectable (e.g., they are prostitutes, runaways, drug addicts, street women) and/or they are women of color, the media as well as public officials tend to discount the seriousness of the crime. As the prosecutor said at the trial of the Yorkshire Ripper, "Some of the victims were prostitutes, but perhaps the saddest part of this case is that some were not" (quoted in Holloway 1981:39). Moreover, when the victims are devalued, the police are more likely to delay notifying the public that a serial murderer is on the loose.

Shortly before his execution, Bundy claimed that he had been obsessed with pornography since his youth and that it had "inspired him to act out his torture and murder fantasies" (Caputi 1989:447). Although that was not the first time he had acknowledged his "thrill of reading about the abuse of female images," Bundy's claim was both ridiculed and scorned in the mainstream press, written off as a convenient excuse for his actions and a last-minute bid for absolution (Michaud & Aynesworth 1983:117). Some commentators seemed even "more angry at [Bundy's] aspersions on pornography than at his crimes" (Caputi 1989:448). However, what got lost in the clutter of these vehement dismissals was the fact that the truth was not necessarily an either/or, that Bundy could be both attempting to neutralize or diminish his responsibility for his compulsions and speaking honestly about influences that fueled his spiraling loss of self-control.

The Hillside Strangler, responsible for a series of sex murders in Los Angeles in 1977 and 1978, actually turned out to be co-murderers Kenneth Bianchi and Angelo Buono, who are both now serving life sentences. One of Bianchi's victims was named Cindy Lee Hudspeth. *Hustler* magazine presented a semiregular feature titled "Ads We'd Like to See," which parodied advertising. The hypothetical ad in the August 1980 issue, modeled after the well-known format for Dewers Scotch, was for "Doer's Lite Label." It starred none other than Kenneth Bianchi:

Kenneth Bianchi
Occupation: Hillside Strangler
Latest Accomplishment: Cindy Lee Hudspeth, 20
Quote: "You gotta treat 'em rough."
After knocking off a couple of bimbos, the Hillside Strangler likes to kick back and relax with Doer's Lite Label. (cited in Caputi 1987:53)

In this ad, violence is trivialized—it's good for a chuckle or two. A sex killer is presented as "a doer," a man of accomplishment. In an *it's just a joke so you can't really criticize kind-of-way,* the magazine affirmed its "collusion with sexual torture and murder" (p. 54).

But *Hustler* wasn't done milking the Hillside stranglings. In its March 1984 issue, the magazine offered "Free Beaver Hunt Caps" to all those who submitted nude photographs of themselves. Illustrations accompanying the offer showed both of the Hillside Stranglers wearing the caps. Underneath Bianchi's picture was the caption: "Ken Bianchi says, 'I was a real eager Beaver Hunter, but with this cap I could have caught some more.'" The caption under Buono's picture read: "Angelo Buono says, 'These caps are neat! I bet if I wore one, the girls would be dying to meet me'" (p. 54).

Note that this was from a magazine considered tame enough to be on display at your corner convenience store. The less accessible the fare (although the Internet has increased accessibility overall), the less likely the misogyny will have a humorous gloss, be in cartoon form, be passed off as art. Images that eroticize *real* sexual violence, even murder, will stare you in the face. For those who think, "But that's not sex, that's violence," remember that *everything* in pornography is sex to someone (Dworkin & MacKinnon 1988). It's someone's fantasy, someone's turn-on, perhaps someone's only way to get turned on. Some become progressively desensitized—find that over time they need the images to be more explicit, more extreme, more violent, more *real* to get aroused. For some, images cease to be enough. They feel compelled to act the fantasies out—in real life, on real people. Sometimes, like when Bianchi and Buono took photographs of the women they had tortured and killed, "the pornographic imperative comes full circle" (Caputi 1987:164).

■ The Problem of Pornography

By the mid-1970s many feminists had concluded that the problem of violence against women and children required a more direct confrontation with the cultural images that promote the climate that sustains and fosters such crimes. As Laura Lederer explained, "We noted the inconsistency in allowing (and even encouraging) women and young girls to be set up as sexual objects and willing victims in all forms of mass media, while at the same time protesting the victimization of females in real life. We began to make the connections between media violence to women and real-life violence to them, to recognize the threat which pornography poses to our lives" (1980:16–17).

We recognize that the kinds of sexual imagery people have in mind when they use the term "pornography" varies considerably. We find it useful, however, to distinguish between **erotica** and **pornography**. According to Gloria Steinem, erotica involves images or depictions of "mutually pleasurable sexual expression" between consenting subjects "who have enough power to be there by positive choice" (1980:37). Pornography, on the other hand, treats the body as an object to be controlled or dominated. It is "material that combines sex and/or the exposure of genitals with abuse or degradation in a manner that appears to endorse, condone, or encourage" the abuse or degradation. Sexual behavior that is *abusive* "ranges from [the] derogatory, demeaning, contemptuous, or damaging to [the] brutal, cruel, exploitative, painful, or violent. *Degrading* sexual behavior refers to sexual conduct that is humiliating, insulting, [or] disrespectful" (Russell 1993:2–3).

Some researchers argue that pornography is a *symptom* not a *cause* of attitudes that promote sexual violence (Baron & Straus 1989; Schwartz & DeKeseredy 1997). To be sure, pornography does not cause violence "in the way a virus causes disease, gravity causes objects to fall or a bell caused Pavlov's famous dogs to salivate" (Cameron & Frazer 1993:371). Individuals who engage in sexual violence are neither "impelled by instinct . . . [nor] responding unthinkingly or involuntarily" to pornographic stimuli. Rather, they interpret and "impose meaning on the stimuli" and then act in accordance with this meaning (pp. 368, 370).

Nevertheless, pornography can play an important role in shaping some forms of sexual desire and not others. As such, Catharine MacKinnon is among those who consider it central to the "cycle of abuse" of women and children. She believes that "as long as pornography exists as it does now, women and children will be used and abused to make it, as they are now. And it will be used to abuse them, as it is now" (1986:47). Although many people assume that women in pornographic pictures or films are willing participants who make good money, this is, as it is with women who prostitute, not necessarily the case. Many women and children are pressured or coerced by boyfriends, husbands, fathers, or pimps to pose or perform for pornography. They're often told to smile, to act like they like what's going on. Even when explicit force is not involved, "the compulsion of poverty, of drugs, of the street, of foreclosed alternatives, of fear of retribution for noncooperation can be enforcement enough" (p. 42).

Another common assumption is that images of harm or abuse that are frequently portrayed in pornography are produced by convincing makeup, trick photography, or actors who are "just acting." But photographs and videos are also made of *real* rapes, child molestations and beatings, even torture. And since a child is not considered legally capable of consenting to sex, each and every example of pornography involving adult-child sexual interaction is "a document of the sexual abuse of the child who was required for its production" (Kelly 1993:116; MacKinnon 1986).

As Dworkin says, "Pornography happens. . . . It happens to women [and children], in real life" (1997:126). Take Linda "Lovelace," for example, star of *Deep Throat,* the 1972 "porn movie that made porn movies chic" (Steinem 1993:23). Linda was taught by her husband, Chuck Traynor, to relax her throat muscles like a sword swallower so that she could receive the plunge of a man's fully erect penis without choking. Traynor held Linda captive and forced her to service men sexually, to endure public humiliation at parties as men lined up to experience her "deep throat." He coerced her to make porn films—even a sex film with a dog—and successfully hunted her down after the first three of her four escape attempts.

The women and children in pornography, however, are only its initial victims, for pornography is also used to force others to act it out. Many women, for instance, were taken to see *Deep Throat* by boyfriends, husbands, or pimps to learn "what a woman could do to please a man if she really wanted to" (Steinem 1993:24). (After the movie's release some hospitals even reported an increase in the number of women brought in dead from suffocation due to rape of the throat.) Recall also the fair-haired thirteen-year-old forced by the hunters to perform like Little Godiva and the Golden Girl. Then there's Katherine Brady, whose father began to molest her when she was eight years old, using pornography as a teaching tool, as a way to instruct her about sex, about what he wanted her to do for him: "When he showed me the pictures, he would describe the acts in detail: 'This is fellatio,' 'this is [how] you do . . . intercourse,' and so forth" (Russell 1993b:43).

Or take the case of "Ms. M," whose husband read her excerpts from pornography about bondage, anal intercourse, group sex, and wife swapping, and who pressured her to act them out. Sometimes he even invited friends to come to bed with them after she was already asleep. They had incredible arguments. She wanted to be a good wife, but she was repulsed by these things. He told her if she loved him she would do them. In order to prevent the group sex, which she found especially humiliating, she agreed to act out the bondage and other scenarios in private. He read the pornography "like a textbook"—how to tie the knots, how to bind her so she couldn't escape (p. 55). She had to dress up like the women in the magazine, to act out the scenes precisely.

Of course, many women who perform for pornography and many who read or watch it are not coerced to do so. Indeed, some feminists accuse their antipornography counterparts of overemphasizing the extent to which women are victimized by pornography. They insist that women can be autonomous agents of their own sexuality and that they can negotiate the risks and dangers of this power-laden terrain for their own purposes (Burstyn 1985; Snitow et al. 1983; Vance 1984). But antipornography feminists do not deny women's agency or their right to be assertive sexual actors. They don't suggest that pornography turns all men into rapists. And they don't condemn anyone who ever picked up a men's magazine, rented an X-rated video, or viewed pornography on the Internet. However, MacKinnon argues that the "fact that some people like pornography [or willingly get involved with it] does not mean that it does not hurt other[s]" (1986:49). In fact, there is considerable research from a wide range of sources—testimonials, interviews, media experiments, and surveys—that provides grounds for concern (Russell 1988).

Much of the experimental research on the effect of pornography on men has emphasized the study of sexually violent or aggressive pornography in laboratory settings, and there are of course differences among men in the way they respond to experimental exposure. The research on laboratory aggression, sexual arousal, and attitudinal change indicates that men who are already *predisposed* to sexual aggression—that is, those who report they would be likely to rape if they thought they would not be caught

or punished, those who are more sexually aroused by depictions of rape than by depictions of consensual sex, or those who harbor relatively high levels of anger toward women—are influenced by experimental exposure to a greater degree than are men who are not so predisposed. Nevertheless, most experimental male subjects are less aroused by rape scenes when female victims are portrayed as abhorring sexual assault than when female victims are portrayed as becoming involuntarily aroused. In general, experimental exposure to the latter type of pornography increases men's aggression against women in laboratory settings, their belief in the rape myths that justify sexual violence, their rape fantasies, their insensitivity to rape victims and the trauma of rape, and their self-reported possibility of committing rape. These findings are not surprising, given that in sexually violent pornography it is common for women who are depicted as initially resistant if not terrified of rape to become "sexually aroused to the point of cooperation" and eventually to become physically gratified in spite of their embarrassment or shame (Scully & Marolla 1985:253). Be that as it may, even the viewing of *nonviolent* pornography is associated with less sympathy toward rape victims and more trivialization of rape. Neil Malamuth, one of the leading researchers in the field, has concluded that the experimental evidence strongly supports the view that at least some pornography contributes "to a cultural climate that is more accepting of aggression against women" (1985:405; Allen et al. 1995; Berger et al. 1991; Donnerstein et al. 1987; Malamuth & Donnerstein 1984; see Chapter 2).

Although some analysts discount laboratory experiments because of their artificiality (Durham 1986), others note the evidence of harm that is contained in the testimony of victims and in the pictures of abuse themselves (MacKinnon 1986). In addition, survey research documents that many women have had negative experiences with pornography. In several studies, for example, women were asked, *"Have you ever been upset by anyone trying to get you to do what they had seen in pornographic pictures, movies, or books?"* About a tenth to a quarter admitted they had been (Harmon & Check 1989; Russell 1982; Senn 1993; Stock 1995). Furthermore, survey research with men shows that pornography can: "(a) be an important factor in shaping a male-dominant view of sexuality, (b) contribute to a user's difficulty in separating sexual fantasy and reality, (c) be used to initiate victims and break down their resistance to sexual activity, and (d) provide a training manual for abusers" (Jensen 1995:33). This research finds that pornography is often "an important factor in . . . what men come to see as acceptable, exciting, or necessary sex" (p. 51). Although one cannot conclude, of course, that all pornography users engage in abusive behavior, the research does suggest that "for some sex abusers, pornography is an integral part of their abuse" (p. 35).

Clinical evidence provided by professionals (e.g., therapists and district attorneys) who work with victims or with self-reported and convicted sex offenders also implicates pornography. Cheryl Champion, for instance, estimates that about 40 percent of clinical sex offender cases involve perpetrators who use pornography, typically in a very compulsive and obsessive manner, "for masturbation, fantasy contemplation, and actual acting out of their scenarios" (1986:24). Ray Wyre, who has worked with a wide range of sex offenders since the mid-1970s, notes that sex offenders often use pornography "to justify and legitimate what they do" (1992:236). According to Wyre, pornography can create and reinforce rape and child-abuse fantasies that "push men further along [a] continuum of sexual mistreatment of women and children," from inappropriate sexual gestures and conduct to horrendous crimes (p. 246).

Wyre is among a number of scholars and practitioners who encourage us to take concerns about pornography seriously. Many people are reluctant to do so, however, as they falsely assume that one who is critical of pornography must be prudish, anti-sex, or anti-male. Of course most of us don't go down the slippery slope Wyre observed, and pornographic imagery was clearly not the only factor in the downward slide of the sex offenders he worked with. But we are all shaped by our culture. We can all be drawn in, be affected by the media's messages about sex and gender. And it is not just women who bear the consequences of all this; it is men as well, for male socialization sets men up to be manipulated by pornography.

Cynthia Cockburn believes that "our culture cruelly constrains [men] in varying degrees to be the bearers of a gender identity that deforms and harms them as much as it damages women" (1988:316–317). Boys are pushed to behave more independently at an earlier age than girls, taught that they must always be in charge and able to control things, "conditioned to believe that they must be successful . . . and that success can only be achieved through competition and struggle," primarily with other males (Baker 1992:127). According to Peter Baker:

> In order to cope with the harsh masculine world into which they are thrust, boys learn not to trust their subjective feelings, . . . not to express their emotions, . . . [and to] remain cool and composed. . . . [As men they] are forced to give up . . . intimacy and closeness with each other. Despite the privileges [of being male], . . . the impact of . . . these messages about masculinity leaves men feeling bad about themselves and disconnected both from their inner selves and from other men and women. (1992:127–128)

No wonder, says Baker, many men become "unable to communicate how they really feel," perhaps even unaware of what it is they are feeling. No wonder they "attach such disproportionate importance to the sexual act," often the only means they have to feel close and intimate (p. 128). No wonder they find pornography so attractive. With it they "can retreat into a simple world where they are effortlessly in command," where there's no pressure to be romantic or expressive, no worries about one's desirability or manliness, no fear of criticism or rejection (p. 133).

David Steinberg characterizes pornography as a vehicle that helps men "fantasize sexual situations that soothe [their] wounds." Its cornerstone is:

> Images of women who are openly desirous of sex, who look out at us from the page with all the yearning we know so well yet so rarely receive. . . . Images of women hungry for sex with us, possessed by desire for us. . . . Receptive women who greet our sexual desire not with fear or loathing but with appreciation, even gratitude. And glamorous women whose mere bestowal of sexual attention mythically proves our sexual worth.

Steinberg notes, however, that the same fantasies that "may be soothing in the moment . . . often contribute to bad feelings about ourselves over time" (1990:56). As Harry Brod explains:

> The necessary corollary to pornography's myth of female perpetual availability is its myth of male perpetual readiness. Just as the former fuels male [anger] when real-life women fail to perform to pornographic standards, so do men's failures to similarly perform fuel male insecurities. Furthermore, . . . relating to one's body as a performance machine produces a split consciousness wherein part of one's attention is watching the machine, looking for flaws in its performance, even while one is supposedly immersed in . . . sensual pleasure. This produces a self-distancing self-consciousness which mechanizes sex and reduces pleasure.

Moreover, Brod observes, looking "to sex for fulfillment of nonsexual emotional needs, . . . [leaves men] disappointed and frustrated" (1995:395–396).

Michael Kimmel adds that pornography can also impoverish men's "sexual imaginations even in the guise of expanding our repertoires" (1990:318). Some men become dependent on it for arousal. Some become so desensitized that they need more and more explicit or degrading or violent imagery for the same turn-on. Some, as Wyre (1992) discovered, come to find that the fantasies and images are no longer enough. They feel compelled to act them out; and "the more bizarre the fantasies are, the less likely they will have a consenting partner to comply with what they want to do" (p. 243).

Current U.S. Supreme Court rulings have made it difficult to reduce the harm associated with some types of pornography. While the Court has ruled that *child* pornography may be banned, it has ruled that *adult* pornography is protected by the First Amendment. There are legitimate reasons to oppose governmental censorship of adult pornography. But there is also a need to keep children from being exposed and to prevent people from being violated in its making, as well as for educational interventions that teach people to recognize and critically evaluate material that endorses sexual violence (Berger et al. 1991; Lederer & Delgado 1995).

In addition, acts of conscientious objection by citizens may also be in order. In 1990, for instance, a ten-year-old boy walking home from school in Norman, Oklahoma, was brutally attacked by a man who stabbed his right eye (so severely that it had to be surgically removed) and slashed his genitals. Earlier that day the December issue of *Hustler* magazine had appeared on the racks in town with a cover feature that offered the following advice: "If you were going to gouge out an eye, do it slowly, taking care not to damage the optic nerve. Then you can leave the eyeball hanging on his cheek, still functioning. His brain will still receive the visual information, but he will be unable to . . . close his eyelids as, for example, you mutilate his genitals" (Parfrey 1990:1). The *Kansas City Star* reported that the boy had been assaulted in a way that had been "spelled out in bold type" in *Hustler.* The day after the attack, police officers in Norman "contacted all merchants in the area who sold the issue," expressing concern about the "inappropriateness" of the article and advising them "to read the magazine and decide for themselves whether to sell it or throw it away" (Montgomery 1990:C1). Most of the merchants voluntarily removed the issue (Russell 1993b).

It is not just pornography, however, but also mainstream media that trivialize or eroticize violence against women and children. The "Battered Chic" advertisement trend introduced in the 1980s, for instance, featured models who looked roughed up and bruised, wearing torn or tattered clothing. Fashion layouts continue to routinely exhibit models with frightened expressions, models looking over their shoulders at shadowy figures or running from danger. And these are not ads for locks or security devices. They are ads for glamour enhancers like lipstick and hair color. A pantyhose ad presents a woman buried in the sand from the waist *up,* her rear end exposed and her legs provocatively displayed in silky hose and high heels while an ominous crustacean inches its way toward her incapacitated body. A jeans ad provides what appears to be before-and-after shots of rape: a young woman slung over a man's shoulder being carried off to a garage, then hanging out of a car, disheveled, her blouse open. With images like these permeating the culture, it's no wonder violence often seems downright sexy.

Pornography, advertisements, and the media in general are also implicated in the sexual exploitation of children. As Ellen Bass observes, we are continually bombarded with cultural images that blur "the distinction between woman and girl-child" and that desensitize us to, even encourage, the sexual use of girls (1983:38). Little girls, for example, are often made up to look years older with cosmetics, provocative outfits, and sophisticated hairdos, while adult women are posed seductively sporting pigtails and skimpy girlish clothes, sucking lollipops or holding teddy bears. These images, says Bass, "confuse adult women with children . . . [and] vulnerability with sexual invitation" (p. 42).

■ Rape and Sexual Assault

Rape has traditionally been understood as the deviant act of a sick individual. Feminists have advanced an alternative perspective that views rape as "an extension or exaggeration of conventional sexual relations" and power differentials between women and men, as neither "an aberration nor a particularly unusual occurrence" (Jackson 1978:27, 29). According to this view, rape is not a biological inevitability but a form of socially conditioned sexual aggression that stems from traditional gender socialization and sexual learning (Berger et al. 1986). Support for this position is provided by cross-cultural studies that find some societies "rape prone" and some relatively "rape free." The societies with higher rates of rape are those characterized by greater male dominance, gender-role rigidity, and glorification of warfare (McConahay & McConahay 1977; Sanday 1981).

Sexual Scripts and Rape Myths

James Messerschmidt observes that while sexuality has become "a domain of extensive exploration and pleasure for women, . . . it remains simultaneously a site where gendered oppression may occur" (1993:76; see Chapter 1). Stevi Jackson (1978) argues that traditional **sexual scripts** have been a major source of the problem. In our society, sexual interactions have traditionally been scripted for an active, aggressive male, the one who seduces, and a passive female, the one who is seduced. The male's role has been to initiate and direct the sexual encounter, the female's role to acquiesce or refuse. She has been socialized to be modest and cautious, to assess the man's desire for a meaningful relationship. Since he knows that she may not want to jeopardize his respect by seeming too eager, however, he often ignores her resistance, presuming it's not indicative of her true feelings and desires. Besides, he may consider failure "to establish dominance over the woman, to make her please him," a threat to his masculinity (p. 31).

Women are raped in all kinds of situations and by all types of assailants—in their home and on the street, by strangers and by nonstrangers. But with sexual scripts like these, it is easy to see why **acquaintance rape**— rape involving an assailant the victim knows or is familiar with—is far more common than stranger rape. (Studies have found that over 80 percent of rape victims previously knew their assailants [Koss et al. 1987; Randall & Haskell 1995; Tjaden & Thoennes 1998a].) It is also easy to see how misunderstanding and conflict can occur in romantic or sexual interactions as each party attempts to negotiate the definition of the situation.

Recall that symbolic interactionism is the sociological perspective that is concerned with the meaning of social action to individuals (see Chapter 4). Symbolic interactionists point out that the very same experience can mean different things to different people. Thus in sexual interactions men are sometimes surprised when women interpret their advances as overly aggressive, inappropriate, even exploitative—"as foreplay to rape rather than as affection" (Weis & Borges 1973:89). Absence of consent can only be communicated clearly when the woman resists "beyond what is normally expected of women who want intercourse but wish to maintain a 'moral' appearance"—or who at least want to avoid being labeled a "slut" (p. 92). But how can the woman know what amount of resistance would be normally expected? Might that not vary from man to man or peer group to peer group? And what if she's sexually inexperienced? This is even trickier to negotiate nowadays as young women have increasingly rejected the traditional double standard and claimed their right to sexual desire, and as cultural icons from Madonna to Brittany Spears have mainstreamed the "hot babe" image.

All this is complicated by the culturally available **rape myths** that contain techniques of neutralization or rationalizations that justify rape (see Chapter 4). There is the common presumption, for instance, that a man has urgent sexual needs that prevent him from controlling his behavior and leave him "totally at the mercy of his desires . . . [once his] sexual response has been set in motion" (Jackson 1978:31). This myth places responsibility for limiting sexual activity in the woman's hands. It allows the man to rationalize ignoring her protests, to deny responsibility for forging ahead. She must be careful not to get him too aroused for she may be unable "to control the powerful forces she has unleashed" (p. 31). One convicted rapist likened a man's body to "a coke bottle—shake it up, put your thumb over the opening and feel the tension" (Scully & Marolla 1984:535).

Other rape myths (e.g., women secretly want to be raped, women eventually relax and enjoy rape) allow a man to deny that he injured the woman: "I didn't hurt her. I just gave her a good screw." There are even rape myths (e.g., women are tempting seductresses who invite sexual encounters) that allow men to deny that the woman is a victim at all. Here the man acknowledges that he did rape but justifies his actions on the grounds that the woman deserved what she got. (Sexually assertive women who deviate from traditional scripts are especially likely to be viewed as responsible for provoking the man to rape.) Sometimes it's not even what a man considers to be a woman's provocation that leads him to define her as a legitimate victim. Sometimes it's her perceived aloofness. "Women are damned both ways—they seem to be looking for it or they are too good for it, they are touchable or they are untouchable. Either way they are candidates for rape" (Medea & Thompson 1974:5).

Jackson (1978) points out that rapists do not invent these myths that diminish their responsibility or present their behavior as normal or acceptable. They adopt them from the larger culture, from the same scripts that structure the sexual interactions of the average couple on a date. Not only are these rationalizations used to justify conduct after the fact, but they also can motivate behavior by allowing one to "absolv[e] himself of guilt in advance" (p. 30). Believing that one's masculinity is culturally validated by sexual conquests helps as well.

So how can a woman get the man to take her resistance seriously—to recognize that "no" means "no," not "maybe" or "in a little while"? She's been socialized to be nurturing and self-sacrificing, to protect others' feelings, to bolster the male ego, to please and be pleasing. She's supposed to control the pace of the proceedings and to do so gently. Mild protestations may be effective with some, but probably not with a determined man with a shaken "coke bottle."

Moreover, it's not only men who have been socialized to ignore and deny the validity of women's feelings. Women have also been taught to question their own feelings and perceptions. Thus, once a woman has allowed an intimate encounter to advance beyond a preliminary stage, not only may the man assume she has committed to going "all the way," but the woman may believe she has relinquished her right to withdraw consent too (Foa 1977).

As the man continues to persist, the woman may also be too confused and embarrassed to know what to do next. Because her efforts to assert herself haven't been effective, she may simply stop resisting. Acquiescence may indeed seem preferable to the risk of bodily injury or the "humiliation of a lost fight." Perhaps she'll resign herself to what's going to happen, tell herself it'll be over soon, try to put her mind elsewhere. Perhaps she'll attempt to convince herself he isn't using her, that he's just swept away by her charm. Perhaps she'll try to redefine his aggression as romantic or as "hot sex," for eroticizing male dominance sure "beats feeling forced" (MacKinnon 1983:650). In the end, the man may misread her acquiescence as consent, assume his seduction techniques were effective after all. Perhaps "his conviction that women will consent if only he tries hard enough" will be reinforced, and it will be even more difficult for the next woman who tries to tell him "no" (Jackson 1978:32).

MacKinnon (1983) suggests that the whole notion of "consent" becomes problematic when male initiative and dominance comprise the normative pattern of sexual interaction and when men are socialized not to be too concerned about what women want. As we've seen, under these conditions it's difficult for women to assess how much resistance is necessary to convince men that they haven't granted consent or that they've withdrawn it. MacKinnon believes that true consent is absent under these conditions, and the fact that the man may not have used physical force doesn't guarantee that the woman had freely agreed to sex. He may fail to distinguish acquiescence and consent, and so may she. She may consider it rape, or she may be confused by the fact that she stopped resisting and *not* define the encounter as rape, even though she experienced it as unwanted and nonconsensual.

That many men and women have experienced coercive sexual encounters they didn't define as rape was documented by Mary Koss (1988) in an in-depth survey of over 6,100 college students across the United States. Koss found that "only 27 percent of the women whose experience met legal definitions of rape actually labeled themselves as rape victims," and 88 percent of the men who reported engaging in actions "that met legal definitions of rape . . . [insisted] that their behavior was definitely not rape" (pp. 16, 19).

Research also indicates that there are racial/ethnic differences in women's definitions of rape. Linda Williams and Karen Holmes (1981), for example, found that white women, in comparison to Latinas and African Americans, had a broader definition of what constitutes rape. White women were more likely to define rape as sexual intercourse without the woman's consent (rather than as sexual intercourse that was physically forced) and less likely to consider the woman's behavior or reputation, or her relationship with the offender, as relevant to whether a "real rape" had occurred. Monica Williams, director of a Los Angeles rape crisis program, suggests why African American women may have a narrower view of rape:

> I think our image has always been of strong and persevering and you can take it all, and it doesn't make a difference. . . . I started to notice that most of the women who were assaulted, that it wasn't a priority for them, that they couldn't see that they were hurting. . . . Usually their first concern was their children, or their home or their husband, or how'm I going to make ends meet. (quoted in Matthews 1989:525–526)

The legacy of racism also impacts African American women's response to rape. According to Angela Davis, "This country's history of ubiquitous racism in law enforcement," including its use of "the myth of the black rapist" to justify lynchings, has made many black women understandably reluctant to become involved in antirape activism as they fear it "might well lead to further repressive assaults on their families and communities" (1990:43–44). Marcia Ann Gillespie adds that African American women have "for the good of the race . . . routinely been expected to put our men first, no matter what. . . . When a woman steps forward and dares to . . . speak about and hold black men accountable for . . . rape, . . . [she] risks becoming a pariah." Gillespie urges black women to "redefine what is good for the race" by insisting that women's lives matter also (1993:80–81).

■ Rape Law and Its Reform

The common rape scenario that we've been describing is often written off as a "he said/she said" situation. But in a culture where sex has traditionally been scripted for an active male and a passive female, and where it is expected that men may have to be pushy to get what they want, it can be hard to tell the difference between sex and sexual assault. So when a man believes a woman has fabricated charges of rape "after the fact," it may be that her declaration of nonconsent contradicts his experience of the interaction. Moreover, since the law defines the criminality of the act in terms of the *accused's* criminal intent, it becomes difficult to define the act legally as a crime if the man believed that the woman's resistance was not all that genuine (MacKinnon 1983).

According to MacKinnon, the way the law does distinguish between sex and sexual assault is "by adjudicating the level of acceptable force starting just above the level set by what is seen as normal male sexual behavior . . . [not] at the victim's . . . point of violation" (1983:649). Thus the law, argues MacKinnon, adopts the male's perspective:

> [While] many women are raped by men who know the meaning of their acts to women and proceed anyway, . . . women are also violated . . . by men who have no idea of the meaning of their acts to women. To them, it is sex. Therefore, to the law it is sex. . . . The distance between most sexual violations . . . and the legally perfect rape measures the imposition of someone else's definition upon women's experiences. Rape, from women's point of view, is not prohibited, it is regulated. (pp. 651–653)

Feminists like MacKinnon have worked to reform the legal system to make it more responsive to and supportive of women, and feminists have been the driving force behind rape reform legislation. In the past, rape law contained special corroboration rules (not required for other violent crimes) that mandated that prosecutors produce evidence to verify a victim's testimony, for it was assumed that women would deliberately lie about rape in order "to explain premarital intercourse, infidelity, pregnancy, or disease, or to retaliate against an ex-lover or some other man" (Spohn & Horney 1992:24). Prosecutors were also required to demonstrate that a woman had tried to resist her assailant to a degree beyond what was expected of other violent crime victims. Judges gave jurors special cautionary instructions to warn them that rape was a charge that was easily made but difficult for the defendant to disprove, even if he was innocent.

Evidence of a woman's prior sexual history was admissible to impeach her testimony or to show that she had consented to intercourse, for it was assumed that "chastity was a character trait" and that women with premarital or extramarital sexual experiences were more likely to have agreed to sexual relations with the accused (p. 25). And spouses were granted immunity from prosecution on the assumption that when a woman married she

---

Further Exploration

Box 9.2   Marital Rape

Marital rape, the sexual assault of a woman by her husband, is estimated to occur in 9 to 14 percent of marriages in the United States (Bergen 1996; Russell 1982). David Finkelhor and Kersti Yllo argue that although many people consider forced sex in marriage to be a petty conflict, "unpleasant, but not particularly serious," this stereotype masks how abusive and traumatizing marital rape really is (1985:13–14).

Finkelhor and Yllo conducted in-depth interviews with women who had experienced forced sex with current or previous partners (marital or cohabiting). The assaults described were frightening and sometimes "brutal events that usually occurred in the context of an exploitative and destructive relationship" (p. 18). The sexual abuse was often "only peripherally about sex. More often it was about humiliation, degradation, anger, and resentment." The incidents left the women psychologically traumatized, sometimes even physically disabled. For most of the women, rape was "a chronic and constant threat, not an isolated problem" (p. 23). Oftentimes the sex that was forced was not vaginal intercourse but oral or anal sex, rape with objects, or other sexual humiliations— being forced to have sex with husband's friends or in front of others, to submit to gang rape, or to be photographed tied up or with objects in their vaginas. Some assaults even involved sadistic acts aimed at injuring the genitals—biting or burning them, or in one instance, ripping a woman's vagina in an attempt to pull it out.

About half of the women Finkelhor and Yllo interviewed were also battered by their partners. For these women, "entrapment and terror [were] part and parcel of their lives . . . [and] the sexual abuse was [often] a continuation of the beatings" (pp. 22–23). Marital rape, however, is emotionally devastating even when it does not involve additional violence. When the person who assaults you is someone you love and trust, the pain, humiliation, and betrayal is especially intense. If women are able to leave these abusive relationships, the passage of time helps the vividness of their anger wane, but for most women the emotional impact endures for years—even decades. An "inability to trust men, an aversion to intimacy and sex, and a lingering, acute fear of being assaulted again" is often the legacy they are left struggling to overcome (p. 18).

implicitly and irrevocably consented to the sexual advances of her husband (Berger et al. 1988).

Since the mid-1970s, however, states have generally reformed their rape laws to eliminate or modify some or all of these practices. One reform redefined the crime of rape as sexual assault, sexual battery, and the like in order to emphasize the idea that rape is a violent crime and not a crime of uncontrollable sexual passion. Such semantic changes were intended to divert attention from questions about consent, for assault is, "by definition, something to which the victim does not consent" (Bienen 1980:192). Redefining rape as sexual assault also broadened the definition of the crime beyond vaginal-penile intercourse to include oral and anal penetration, sexual penetration with objects, and in some statutes, touching of intimate body parts. Other reforms redefined the crime in gender-neutral terms to protect victims from female offenders and to protect male victims, and some removed or modified the spousal exemption (Berger et al. 1988; Spohn & Horney 1992).

Another set of reforms attempted to eliminate evidentiary rules that made it more difficult to convict offenders. Special corroboration and proof-of-resistance requirements, as well as cautionary jury instructions, were abolished. Reform statutes also introduced **rape shield laws** that limit admissibility of evidence regarding the complainant's prior sexual history. Less restrictive rape shield laws allow admission of evidence of prior sexual conduct after judicial determination of its relevance; more restrictive laws create a general prohibition of such information but allow specific exceptions—for instance, evidence of previous sexual contact between the complainant and defendant. The more restrictive statutes have been criticized for not sufficiently accommodating the defendant's right to present relevant evidence, the less restrictive for providing inadequate protection of the complainant's right to privacy (Berger et al. 1988; Spohn & Horney 1992).

Studies of the impact of rape law reform indicate that many criminal justice officials continue to operate on the basis of traditional assumptions about rape and fail to consistently comply with the statutes. Decisions regarding rape/sexual assault are still subject to much discretion, and the reforms do not necessarily affect the informal operations of the criminal justice system. For example, evidentiary reforms involving the victim's prior sexual history have been aimed at trial procedures, although most cases are handled informally through pretrial plea bargaining (if they go that far). At trial, requirements for closed hearings to determine relevancy of the complainant's prior sexual history are often not held, and this information is often admitted as evidence. Indices of closeness (e.g., dating, cohabiting, marriage) or of prior social interaction (e.g., the woman was acquainted with the accused or had agreed to interact socially with him) are still used by defendants to persuade judges and juries that they believed the woman had consented (Berger et al. 1994; Spohn & Horney 1992).

▪ *Personal Resistance Strategies*

In addition to law reform, the feminist movement has spawned a number of victim service and prevention efforts, including rape crisis centers, hot lines, improved public lighting, nighttime safety transit systems, and rape-avoidance and self-defense training. Self-defense training has been particularly controversial because it has challenged the conventional advice given to women, which encouraged them not to resist if attacked but to submit to rape in order to avoid further harm (Hazelwood & Harpole 1986; Storaska 1975). At most, this advice recommended pleading or reasoning with the assailant. Feminists, on the other hand, have generally encouraged women to fight back (Bart & O'Brien 1985; Delacoste & Newman 1981; Searles & Berger 1995).

Many studies now indicate that immediate active resistance (e.g., yelling, fighting, running away) and especially the use of multiple-resistance strategies reduce the likelihood that an attempted rape will be completed. Pleading and arguing seem to be less effective unless used in combination with other verbal strategies such as yelling and calling for help (Searles & Berger 1995).

The research is less clear regarding the question of whether resistance increases the likelihood of additional injury (i.e., injury beyond the rape itself). Joan McDermott (1979) found that resisters received greater additional injury than nonresisters, although most of these injuries were of a relatively nonserious nature (e.g., bruises, cuts, scratches). Moreover, women who resisted were much less likely to have rape completed. Other data indicate that the connection between resistance and additional injury may be related to the type of resistance employed. William Sanders (1980) reported that those who "struggled" (e.g., attempted to push the attacker away) were more likely than those who fought (e.g., hit, bit, kicked) or those who ran away to incur additional serious injury. Gary Kleck and Susan Sayles (1990) found that weaponless forceful resistance was associated with increased injury, but that this resistance was more likely to *follow* rather than *precede* the injury. They note that some advice-givers counsel nonresistance because a small proportion of "rapists are indeed incited to further violence by victim resistance." However, they conclude:

> The flaw in this reasoning is that it depends on an unstated, but false, premise that nonresistance does not entail any risks of its own. . . . Advice to not resist depends on the belief that the nonresisting rape victim trades off an increased likelihood of rape completion for a reduced likelihood of injury. Such a trade-off makes sense only if one assumes the additional

injury is in some sense a more serious harm . . . than the completion of the rape itself. (p. 160)

We do not think it is appropriate for anyone to give blanket advice to women about what they *should* do if attacked, as if all attack situations are the same, or to criticize what a woman *did* or *did not* do in a stressful and frightening situation. Nevertheless, teaching women and girls psychological and physical self-defense skills, and nurturing in them a strong sense of self-worth, both broadens the range of options they will have and increases the likelihood they will possess the self-confidence and presence of mind to evaluate their options and act in a way that is in their best interests. Regrettably, as Patricia Rozee and colleagues observe, remedies to sexual violence "aimed primarily at behavioral change among women place an unwarranted responsibility on individual women for their own safety. To live a life free of the fear of sexual assault ought to be a right afforded to us by the society in which we live" (1991:351).

■ The Sexual Abuse of Children

According to Ellen Bass (1983), whenever a child is used sexually by an adult, whether or not there is physical force or even the threat of it, coercion is involved. "There can be no equality of power, understanding, or freedom in sex between adults and children. Children are dependent upon adults: first for their survival; then for affection, attention, and an understanding of what the world in which they live is all about" (pp. 26–27). Because a child is not capable of giving informed consent to sex, sexual interaction with a child is by definition abuse, an illegal act everywhere in the United States. (We will discuss the issue of *adolescents* as sexual subjects later.)

Issues of legality aside, a child's lack of resistance should not be assumed to indicate willing participation. A child may submit without resistance for many reasons. She (or he) doesn't want to hurt the perpetrator's feelings. She's been taught to be kind and polite, to obey adults. This may be someone she loves, someone she believes loves her, someone she's learned to trust. She needs and wants attention and affection, and this seems to be the only form in which it is presented. She fears that if she resists, she will be punished or hurt—or someone else will be. She fears that if she resists, the person will say it was her idea or that she liked it and she'll get in trouble. She doesn't know what sex is, doesn't understand that this kind of touch is inappropriate. The perpetrator tells her it's okay, that everyone does this, shows her pictures of other children engaging in these acts—children who are smiling, children who look happy. The perpetrator says he (or she) knows what's best, tells her he's teaching her: "She is taken by surprise and has no idea what to do; . . . she thinks she has no choice" (p. 27).

■ The Frequency and Experience of Abuse

Child sexual abuse is distressingly common. Studies provide varying estimates of its prevalence, however, due to divergent research samples and definitions of abuse. Underreporting is also a serious problem. David Knudsen reviewed numerous studies and estimated that "at least 30 percent of girls and 20 percent of boys experience some form of sexual abuse" (1992:112). As we have seen, Randall and Haskell (1995) found even higher percentages of abuse among the women they interviewed, and over a quarter of the women who reported abuse said they were abused before age eight. A national U.S. sample of both genders found that 98 percent of girls and 83 percent of boys who are victimized are abused by men (Finkelhor et al. 1990).

Child sexual abuse varies widely from fleeting encounters to intense incestuous relations. Overall, girls are more likely than boys to be abused by family members, and they tend to experience their first abuse at a younger age (Nelson & Oliver 1998). The duration of abuse also tends to be longer for girls than for boys. Although girls and boys appear equally likely to experience sibling incest, girls are much more likely to experience incestuous abuse by parents. Andrea Nelson and Pamela Oliver (1998) describe incestuous abuse of boys as relatively rare yet traumatic and usually at the hands of men. Boys' contacts are most commonly with unrelated adults with whom they are acquainted. Nevertheless, some clinicians consider mother-son incest to be very underreported as opposed to very rare (Lawson 1993).

The abuse of children by members of the Catholic clergy and other religious officials has been known for some time, but the scandal did not generate much media attention until recently (Lavoie 2003; Zoll 2004a, 2004b). A study conducted by the John Jay College of Criminal Justice in conjunction with the U.S. Roman Catholic church found that over 10,600 abuse claims involving 4 percent of the U.S. clergy have been made since 1950. Researchers were able to substantiate about 63 percent of these claims, although about 30 percent could not be investigated because the clergymen had died. As much as $1 billion has been paid out by U.S. Catholic churches to settle these abuse claims. In 2003 the Boston Archdiocese alone agreed to pay $85 million to over 500 people who claimed they were sexually abused by priests, and at least 325 priests were removed from their positions or forced to resign. Since most of the allegations made public have involved priests and teenage boys, a leading Vatican official asserted that gay men should not be ordained as priests and that those already ordained should be removed from the clergy. This comment led the president of a national gay Catholic group to retort, "This is nothing more than a vicious, transparent attempt to shift the blame in an effort to deny institutional culpability in the scandal. . . . This [abuse] is about violence against children and abuse of power. It has nothing to do with sexual orientation" (quoted in Freiberg 2002:29). In fact, the Catholic Church has for centuries turned "a blind eye to the sexual exploits of priests regardless of their sexual orientation" (Dahir 2002:32). A. W. Richard Sipe, a psychotherapist and former monk who has studied clergy sexuality for over four decades, concludes that "gay priests respect their vows of celibacy in the same proportion as straight priests" (Feiberg 2002:29). Moreover, as Sipe observes, sexual orientation is hard to categorize since many priests are psychosexually immature and "haven't really sorted out their sexuality" (quoted on p. 30).

Regardless, the most common form of child sexual abuse overall involves the abuse of a girl by an older male. Bass describes how the experience can shape a child's view of herself and her world:

> When a man sexually uses a child, he is giving that child a strong message about her world: He is telling her that she is important because of her sexuality, that [sex is what] men want . . . from girls, . . . that relationships are insufficient without sex. He is telling her that she can use her sexuality as a way to get the attention and affection she genuinely needs, that sex is a tool. When he tells her not to tell, she learns there is something about sex that is shameful and bad; and that she, because she is a part of it, is shameful and bad. . . . She learns that the world is . . . not to be trusted, that even those entrusted with her care will betray her; that she will betray herself. (1983:27)

The sense of betrayal is especially intense when the abuser is a family member. For instance, in the most commonly reported type of incest, *father-daughter* incest (including incest between stepfathers and stepdaughters), "the father, in effect, forces the daughter to pay with her body for affection and care that should be freely given" (Herman 1981:4). This gross misuse of power shatters the protective bond that should exist between parent and child.

A child who must live with the abuser is a child who is trapped in a harmful environment, one who must somehow "find a way to preserve a sense of trust in people who are untrustworthy, safety in a situation that is unsafe, control in a situation that is terrifyingly unpredictable, [and] power in a situation of helplessness" (Herman 1992:96). This is quite a formidable task for anyone, let alone for one with an undeveloped system of psychological defenses. Adaptation to such a climate requires constant alertness. Abused children tend to become "minutely attuned" to the abuser's state of mind, often developing "extraordinary abilities to scan for warning signs of attack." When they perceive a threat, they almost reflexively try to protect themselves by avoiding the abuser (becoming as inconspicuous as possible, hiding, even running away) or by placating the abuser with demonstrations of obedience, by "trying to be good" (pp. 99–100).

These desperate efforts are never completely successful, however, and the child must live with the knowledge that the most powerful adult in her intimate life is a threat to her and that other adults who should be protecting her are not. According to Judith Herman (1992), the child experiences this lack of protection as a sign of indifference at best, as complicit betrayal at worst: "From the child's point of view, the parent disarmed by secrecy should have known; if she cared enough, she would have found out. The parent disarmed by intimidation should have intervened; if she cared enough, she would have fought. The child feels that she has been abandoned to her fate, and this abandonment is often resented more keenly than the abuse itself" (p. 100).

To avoid utter despair, the abused child desperately seeks to preserve faith in her parents and a sense of attachment to them. She resorts to a variety of psychological defenses as she struggles to construct an account of her fate that will absolve one or both parents of responsibility and blame. Sometimes she "tries to keep the abuse a secret from herself." She uses denial, suppression of thoughts, and dissociative states to wall the abuse off "from conscious awareness and memory," so she can believe that "it did not really happen." Or else she "minimize[s], rationalize[s], and excuse[s]," so that whatever did happen was not really abuse." In either case, notes Herman, when she cannot alter or escape "the unbearable reality in fact," she resorts to altering it "in her mind." Although these alterations of consciousness are sometimes deliberate, they often become automatic, feel involuntary and alien. When the abuse is prolonged as well as early and severe, some children even "form separated personality fragments [or alters] with their own names, psychological functions, and sequestered memories." These alters (sometimes called multiple personalities) enable the child "to cope resourcefully with the abuse while keeping both the abuse and the coping strategies outside of ordinary awareness" (pp. 102–103).

Reality, however, can't always be avoided by dissociation. So at times the child attempts to make sense of the abuse by blaming herself. This not only serves to justify the abuse but also enables the child "to preserve a sense of meaning, hope, and power. If she is bad, then her parents are good. If she is bad, then she can try to be good." If she tries hard enough, maybe her parents will forgive her and start treating her with kindness and concern. Unfortunately, her belief in her innate badness is likely to be reinforced by parental blame, by her own understandable rage or aggressive response to mistreatment, by her "participation in forbidden sexual activity," and by any "enforced complicity in crimes against others"—for example, if she was silent about another child being abused (pp. 103–104).

■ The Abuse of Boys

Most studies of adult-child sex ask respondents about "unwanted" or "abusive" experiences. However, Nelson and Oliver (1998) maintain that adolescents can sometimes be "sexual subjects" with adults, not just sexual objects or victims. Conceptualizing consent/coercion as a continuum rather than as an either/or phenomenon, Nelson and Oliver chose to avoid "abuse language" when they asked over 900 Wisconsin undergraduates the following screening question: *"When you were 15 years or younger, did you experience sexual contact with an adult?"* (Adults were defined as 18 years or older.)

Among the cases where there was at least a four-year gap between the child and adult, Nelson and Oliver found that 98 percent of girls' contacts were with men and 69 percent of boys' contacts were with women. (This percentage of woman-boy contacts is higher than is usually found in studies that use abuse language.) Adult-girl contacts were more common than adult-boy contacts, and girls' experiences were much more likely than boys' to be repeated and incestuous. Although *both boys and girls* usually defined their contacts with *men* as coercive and harmful, *boys* often defined their contacts with *women* as consensual and not harmful. What was crucial for most respondents was "whether the adult 'asked' or persuaded the child into sexual activity rather than 'taking,' unilaterally initiating sexual activity without trying to gain the child's cooperation" (p. 568). Generally speaking, women were more likely to "ask," men to "take." But even when manipulated and dominated by a woman, boys over age ten tended to report feeling that "their sense of masculine potency had been enhanced in the encounter" (p. 573). In spite of the fact that U.S. laws increasingly define sexual abuse in gender-neutral terms, Nelson and Oliver conclude:

> The constructions of masculine and feminine are so strong as to make it impossible for sexual contact between women and boys to have the same social meaning . . . as contact between men and girls. Dominance in woman-boy contacts is less straightforward than in man-girl contacts. [And] the sexual exploitation of a boy by a woman may not be experienced by the boy or seen by others as status-reducing victimization, but rather as status-enhancing "sex with a woman." (p. 560)

Although it is important to note that most of the woman-boy contacts reported in this study involved *adolescent* males and relatively *young* women (under twenty-two years), some of the males who had defined their woman-boy contacts as not harmful did reveal some confusion and tension as they attempted to evaluate whether they had been *less* masculine because

---

Further Exploration

Box 9.3   Rape of Adult Men

Because rape is often misconstrued as a crime that is sexually motivated, it is common for people to presume that men are rarely raped. The National Violence Against Women survey, however, indicates that about 92,700 adult men are raped each year in the United States, primarily by other men, and that about 3 percent of men have experienced attempted or completed rape at some point in their life (Tjaden & Thoennes 1998a). Just as fear of homophobic response silences boys who have been sexually abused, it also silences men who have been raped, regardless of sexual orientation. Knowing that heterosexual victims might not want to be presumed gay and that gay victims might not want to be outed, offenders often try to get their victims to ejaculate in order to discourage them from reporting the crime. That strategy is often effective, for although one can have an involuntary sexual response during a coerced encounter, ejaculation often confuses the victim and makes him feel complicitous. Responses of others frequently compound the problem. Police often ask, "Did you come?" and friends want to know how you could "let something like this happen?" (Pelka 1995:251).

Another misperception about rape is the assumption that a man who rapes another man must be gay or bisexual. But rape is often a way to exert control, to confirm one's "own power by disempowering others" (p. 251). Overcoming another man—rather than a woman or a child—and perhaps forcing an undesired sexual response, can make a man, regardless of his sexual orientation, feel especially powerful. Likewise, being victimized, being taken and used, can make a man feel like a traitor to his gender, since he no longer fits our culture's "definition of masculinity, as one empowered, one always in control." Rape survivor Fred Belka encourages other male survivors to challenge this "specious definition" by breaking their silence (p. 256).

---

they had been subordinate and dominated or *more* masculine because they had exhibited virility at an early age. Some of the respondents may have been attempting to put the best possible face on incidents that they experienced with some ambivalence if not outright distress.

Mike Lew (1990) argues that woman-boy sexual activity is rarely treated as abusive and that boys who attempt to talk about their pain or confusion often find that their experience is ignored, denied, trivialized, or even romanticized—written off as initiation into manhood or "scoring." Males, after all, are expected to be sexual aggressors, to be "strong enough to protect themselves against unwanted attention from . . . the 'weaker sex.'" Hence they may try to redefine their experiences so that they better fit the perceptions of others, even to the extent of joking or bragging about them.

A society that confuses sexual abuse with sex places the boy "in a powerful double bind. If he enjoyed the experience, then it wasn't abusive. If he didn't, he must be homosexual." Moreover, since it's shameful for a male "to admit not having enjoyed any form of sex with a woman," the victim is expected to enjoy his victimization (p. 58). And if the perpetrator is male, the boy is often presumed likely to become gay, if not thought likely to be so already. So in addition to dealing with the experience of exploitation, survivors often find themselves confronting societal homophobia. If they define themselves as heterosexual (or haven't yet thought much about sexual orientation), they may wonder, "Does this *mean* I'm gay?" If they define themselves as gay, they may wonder, "Is this *why* I'm gay?" or "Did this happen to me *because* I'm gay?" (p. 55). Girls exploited by women may struggle with these questions as well.

▪ Women and Abuse

While studies indicate that 80 to 95 percent of reported child abuse *cases* are committed by males, estimates of the proportion of *abusers* who are female range from 1 to 20 percent, with most at about 10 percent. Although female offenders participate in abuse that has been initiated by someone else, usually a male partner whom they want to please or are afraid to displease, many act alone. Compared to male offenders, it appears that the duration of abuse is less for female offenders and the number of victims per offender is lower. Female offenders are also more likely to know their victims and less likely to use violence during the abuse (Jennings 1994).

Unfortunately, our recognition of female abusers has been seriously impeded by stereotypic gender assumptions—women are the gentle sex, women aren't sexually aggressive, mothers are naturally nurturing, and so forth. But women's traditional role as caregivers provides them with not only considerable opportunity to abuse but also considerable ability to hide their crimes, since many child care activities are performed in private. In addition, mothers more frequently engage in the kinds of sexual activities that are less likely to be reported, such as fondling or caressing children sexually or keeping their children tied to them emotionally with implied promises of sexual gratification. A mother's sleeping with a child is also more common and less likely to raise eyebrows than a father's (Justice & Justice 1979).

Sometimes a female survivor ends up in a relationship where her daughter is being incestuously abused. Although this occurrence may be "simply a function of the great numbers of women and children who are victims of sexual abuse," it is not uncommon for this mother to be blamed for the inappropriate behavior of her mate (Conte 1986:117). She is assumed to "unconsciously replicate the abusive pattern" through her choice of a partner and her relationship to her daughter. Her lack of awareness of her daughter's abuse is said "to serve the denial she maintains about her own painful childhood experiences" (Green 1996:326). Herman acknowledges that some survivors (like some parents without abusive pasts) fail to protect their children, but she also notes that survivors "are often able to mobilize caring and protective capacities [for the sake of their children] that they have never been able to extend to themselves" (1992:114). In any event, the mother's past history cannot be considered a cause of her partner's present abuse.

The restigmatization of mothers who are survivors goes hand-in-hand with the misdirection of blame toward all mothers who live in families with father-daughter incest. Mothers deemed "incapable of intimacy" have been said to produce "rejected, emotionally needy daughter[s]" who are "vulnerable target[s] for the advances of sexually needy father[s]" (Green 1996:326). Mothers judged to have "immature dependency needs" have been criticized for "unconsciously delegating" their sexual responsibilities to their daughters. In addition, mothers have been said to harbor "masochistic need[s] to be . . . martyr[s]," to "unconsciously sanction . . . incest behavior to promote [their] own sense of superiority," even to fail to realize that "young girls are unsafe in their own homes with their own relatives without an adult female to protect them" (pp. 324–325; Russell 1986:384). One way or another, father-daughter incest has often been passed off "as a family problem that is the result of the selfish and irresponsible behavior of a dysfunctional mother" (Jacobs 1990:502).

We are not suggesting that mothers never miss clues of abuse, never dismiss suspicions by telling themselves that "he'd never do something like that" or "I'm just being paranoid." Of course we wish that mothers were sometimes more perceptive, more trusting of their own instincts, more courageous in taking difficult steps to guarantee their children's safety. We must remember, however, that mothers are not the perpetrators in father-daughter incest. As Ellen Bass and Laura Davis observe, "Regardless of how inadequate a mother may have been, no behavior on her part is license for any man to sexually abuse a child" (1988:125). It makes little sense to invest so much energy in misdirected blame that only serves the interests of the abuser and that deflects our energies from more useful strategies. And it's not only daughters who suffer in father-daughter incest. Mothers do, too, although the deep trauma they experience is often discounted. So when we hold a mother responsible for the criminal acts of the father, we are in essence blaming a victim (James & MacKinnon 1990; Russell 1986). In most cases "immediate intervention aimed at supporting mothers and helping them to believe, empathize with, and offer consistent emotional support and protection to their children may be the most effective way of reducing the child's emotional stress and disruption" (Everson et al. 1989:206).

▨   *Adult Survivors of Abuse*

Herman (1992) notes that the sense of inner badness felt by survivors of child sexual abuse is hard to shed even as an adult, though it's frequently camouflaged by a woman's persistent efforts to be good at whatever she undertakes. She'll likely have difficulty fully crediting herself for her achievements, since she often perceives her "performing self" as false and inauthentic and nurses the belief that those who praise her don't know her "secret and true self." When a survivor is successful at salvaging a more positive identity from the shards of an abusive childhood, "it often involves the extremes of self-sacrifice" wherein victimization is elevated to martyrdom (p. 106).

Many survivors are also dogged by chronic anxiety and depression that initially developed in childhood in response to the repeated traumas. Some find that their dissociative defenses occasionally go too far, producing not the desired feeling of detachment (which helps to brunt some of the pain), but "a sense of complete disconnection from others and disintegration of the self" (p. 108). Many learn as children that they can most effectively end this disconnected state by "a major jolt to the body," by deliberately inflicting injury on themselves, for instance. The physical pain (which is often not felt at first) seems "preferable to the emotional pain it replaces," and the self-abuse continues "until it produces a powerful feeling of calm and relief." This behavior may well continue in adulthood and is sometimes mistaken for attempted suicide. Many who practice it, however, "consider it a form of self-preservation" since it "relieve[s] unbearable emotional pain." Other self-destructive "soothing mechanisms" that survivors sometimes resort to in an attempt to alter intolerable affective states include "purging and vomiting, compulsive sexual behavior, compulsive risk-taking or exposure to danger, and the use of psychoactive drugs" (p. 109).

Herman also found that survivors frequently fall into a pattern of intimate relationships that are intense yet unstable. They hunger for love and nurturance but are fearful of exploitation or abandonment, of the "vulnerability that is inherent in sustained intimacy" (Briere 1992:67). Survivors often have unrealistic expectations of a partner, and their "old tapes" of abuse and betrayal make it easy for them to overreact, to become anxious, depressed, or rageful in response to what are inevitable and ordinary interpersonal conflicts.

In addition, childhood sexual abuse survivors are at substantial risk of further victimization as adults. In fact, the risk of rape, sexual harassment, or battering is approximately doubled for survivors (Russell 1986). Many factors make it difficult for a survivor to protect herself in intimate relationships. Since her capacity for empathy has developed in a context where the feelings of the abuser have taken precedence, she's highly attuned to the wishes of others and highly practiced in more or less automatic conformity to them (Jacobs 1994). Her diminished self-esteem undercuts her faith in her own judgment. Her reliance on dissociative defenses leads her "to ignore or minimize social cues that would ordinarily alert [one] to danger" (Herman 1992:112). And her longing to be cared about and cared for make it hard for her to set appropriate boundaries with others. As "R.C." acknowledged, "I approached each man from a place of need. I gave my 'self' in return for love" (Bass & Thornton 1983:103). In fact, observes Bass, sexual abuse teaches children "that they have no rights to their bodies" (1983:45).

Some people assume that survivors who are revictimized "ask for" abuse. Herman (1992), however, believes that this judgment misunderstands the complexity of the survivor experience. For some survivors, she writes, "The idea of saying no to the emotional demands of a parent, spouse, lover, or authority figure may be practically inconceivable." Even the more assertive often "passively experience repeated abuse as a dreaded but unavoidable fate . . . , [one that they accept] as the inevitable price of a relationship" (p. 112).

Sometimes a survivor may feel compelled "to relive the dangerous situation [in hopes of making] it come out right," of understanding or getting beyond the abuse (Herman 1992:111). "Lara," for example, who was repeatedly sodomized by her grandfather when she was a child, learned to switch off her feelings during the abuse. Now as an adult, Lara can't *feel* the love she has for people she's close to and she resents her grandfather "for taking away [her] capacity for emotion" (Russell 1995:90). She explains why she sometimes initiates sodomy with a lover in spite of the fact that she finds it painful: "In replaying my past . . . I think I'm trying to get back to the feelings I had when I was little so that I can somehow reclaim something that I lost because of the abuse." Lara describes herself as promiscuous and says that "the only time I feel at all is when I'm making love" (p. 91).

Although some survivors, like Lara, have trouble feeling emotion, others have trouble feeling sexual. They are unable to experience sexual pleasure, feel numb during sex, or have trouble "staying in" their body. For some, sexual interactions produce a general sense of terror or trigger flashbacks to the abuse (Bass & Davis 1988). Thus it is not uncommon for survivors to become either "sexually withdrawn" or "indiscriminately sexually active" (Klein & Chao 1995:72). But what seem to be opposite poles aren't necessarily so. As Lara says, "Being promiscuous doesn't mean you're loving sex to bits" (Russell 1995:90).

When sexual abuse has been paired with affection, a survivor often comes to see sex as the means to attention and love. Lara's grandfather, for instance, would stroke her hair, cuddle and kiss her, give her the kind of physical affection her parents never did. He was always telling her how special she was, and when he raped and sodomized her, he'd say, "I'm only doing this because I love you so much" (p. 80). This cruel exploitation of a child's need for approval was a highly effective means of control. As Lara says, "I came to feel I was so special to him because he abused me." Although Lara now understands intellectually that her grandfather was the perpetrator, she acknowledges, like so many survivors, that "the real me inside thinks it was my fault. . . . I have a feeling of guilt, of being naughty. It must have been something about me . . . that made my grandfather rape and abuse me" (p. 92). The legacy of the abuse for Lara is her feeling that she deserves to be hurt and her inability to shake some very self-destructive habits.

Dworkin and MacKinnon (1988) estimate that 65 to 75 percent of women in prostitution are survivors of child sexual abuse. Other researchers suggest that being "used sexually at an early age in a way that produces guilt, shame, and loss of self-esteem . . . [is] likely to lessen one's resistance to viewing oneself as a salable commodity" (James & Meyerding 1977:41). Lara, who has had several extramarital affairs, considers herself a whore and admits she probably would have worked as a prostitute had she not gotten married. "Being good in bed has always been my identity," she says, "because that's what I've known for longer than I've known anything else. . . . I've been trained to be a whore." Not only did Lara's grandfather instruct her from the age of four in sexual acts, he made her sit with her legs spread and pose seductively like the women in the pornography he showed her. Posing provocatively is automatic for her now. "It's like being a circus animal," she says. "If you train them hard enough, they'll remember what they have to do" (Russell 1995:87).

After Lara's grandfather abused her, he would give her sweets or presents. Over time she realized she had something he wanted and that she could manipulate him into giving her more in return. Being able to manipulate him made her feel proud and gave her a sense of power in a very powerless situation. But this sense of power had a price. When she thinks about it today, she feels as if her grandfather *bought* her, and she feels very cheap indeed. Nevertheless, Lara continues to expect men to give her gifts as payment for sex, though she acknowledges that this shows that she still feels used when she has sex. And the sense of power she gets from "trying to be the best lay in town," from making men obsess over her, can't begin to compensate for feeling used, for feeling like "absolute shit" (pp. 95–96).

Many practicing prostitutes describe a sense of power similar to that which Lara described. According to Diana Russell, however, "Such transient emotional 'power' does not . . . enable them to redress the exploitative imbalance of actual power relations in prostitution" (1995:96). A prostitute with an abusive past "may place her need for affection above the abuse" her pimp dishes out. Physical contact with another human being is, after all, a form of needed recognition, one that "breaks the agonizing loneliness" (Barry 1979:102). It's not that she desires or seeks out abuse, but, like the tricks he makes her turn, it's the price she pays for his attention and affection. It's not that she finds prostitution sexually liberating. It's that for so long she's been treated like a throwaway, someone to be used and abused, so that's the only perception of herself and her body she has.

Finally, although it is widely believed that one generation's sexually victimized children become the next generation's victimizers, Douglas Pryor (1996) argues that the relationship between being the victim of child sexual abuse and subsequent involvement in child molestation or rape is far from conclusive. Studies of identified sex offenders do find such a relationship, and **pedophiles** who sexually abuse boys are especially likely to have a history of childhood sexual trauma (Herman 1988). Pedophiles are "individuals whose maturation has not developed to enable effective adult relationships" and who thus have strong preferences for children (Knudsen 1992:116). Nevertheless, the majority of child abuse victims do not become perpetrators. As Herman observes, "Survivors of childhood abuse are far more likely to be victimized or to harm themselves than to victimize other people. . . . Trauma appears to amplify the common gender stereotypes: men with histories of childhood abuse are more likely to take out their aggressions on others, while women are more likely to be victimized by others or to injure themselves" (1992:113).

■ The Battering of Women

Research has found that about one in four women has been physically assaulted by an intimate partner at some time in her life (Randall & Haskell 1995; Tjaden & Thoennes 1998a). Confronting this violence, undermining it, is an uphill battle in a culture that normalizes, even eroticizes, violence. A *Hustler* magazine photo titled "Battered Wives," for example, portrayed a home kitchen where a man in a chef's hat and apron had just pulled a naked woman out of a large mixing bowl. There he stood, holding the woman by the neck with a pair of tongs, her body dripping with gooey batter. The caption read:

> This photo shows why it's no wonder that wife-beating has become one of society's stickiest problems! But today's liberated women should have expected this kind of response when they decided that men should do more of the domestic chores like cooking. Still, there's absolutely no excuse for doing something this bad. Now he's going to have to beat her just to smooth out all those lumps. (cited in Russell 1993a:41)

The eroticization of violence permeates not just pornographic magazines, but also advertising, song lyrics, music videos, movies, comic books, video games, and the like—virtually all forms of entertainment. Even Alex Comfort, a physician no less, tells us in his updated bestseller *The New Joy of Sex: The Gourmet Guide to Lovemaking for the Nineties,* that while "normal resentments" often build up between two people who live together, violent sex "tends to discharge them" (1991:98–99).

When violence is normalized, it is common to write off abuse or even murder as a "crime of passion." In 1989, New York City police officer Felix Key dragged Jean Singleton into the street, riddled her body with bullets, then killed himself as well. Singleton had been attempting to end their relationship because Key was extremely overprotective and jealous. The police department had previously disciplined Key for holding another woman at gunpoint and threatening her. Nevertheless, the department's official spokesperson refrained from using the word *murder,* describing "the killings as 'a lover's quarrel between the two of them'" (Jones 1994:125). And the front page headline of the *New York Post* read: "Tragedy of a Love Sick Cop"—language that practically invites us to sympathize with the murderer.

■ The Experience of Battering

According to Ann Jones, the fusion of violence with love and sex gives an aggressive man "an excuse for assault: 'I did it because I love you so much'" (1994:121–122). And it gives a victimized woman an explanation that can snare her in understanding, compassion, and forgiveness, often keeping her stuck in the relationship hoping against hope to work things out. Although Lisa Bianco had divorced her battering husband, Al Matheney, that didn't stop him from breaking into her house to beat and rape her. Matheney explained to Bianco that he was doing it because he loved her. Bianco wanted him prosecuted because, as she said, "If I don't do something, it's just going to happen again" (Jones 1994:43). Matheney was convicted of assault, although the rape charge was dropped after a probation consultant told the court that the two "very possibly could have been having a wonderful social affair with sex involved." At the sentencing hearing, Matheney's attorney explained to the judge, "Mr. Matheney . . . could never let go of this woman. . . . Just to call it love would be wrong. Although I'm sure that's what Al perceives it as. I perceive it as an obsession. A love obsession" (p. 119). Two years later Al Matheney, released on furlough, clubbed Lisa Bianco twenty times with a stolen shotgun, busting "the gun into three pieces and smashing [her] head to bits" (p. 44). Why did he do it? "Because he still loved her" (p. 119).

If abuse or even murder can be "love gone wrong," characterizing an

assault as sexually motivated opens the door to dismissing it as "rough sex" that somehow got out of hand. Even when force is clearly involved, it is sometimes said that "*they* got 'carried away' with sex" (Jones 1994:115). If the victim can't be discredited on the witness stand, can't be convincingly portrayed as "that kind of woman," perhaps the jury can be made to feel sorry for the poor sex-obsessed fellow. As Dworkin reports:

> On the same day the police who beat Rodney King were acquitted in Simi Valley, a white husband who had raped, beaten, and tortured his wife, also white, was acquitted for marital rape in South Carolina. He had kept her tied to a bed for hours, her mouth gagged with adhesive tape. He video-taped a half hour of her ordeal, during which he cut her breasts with a knife. The jur[ors] . . . saw the videotape. Asked why they acquitted, they said he needed help. . . . There were no riots afterward. (1997:49)

Abuse is not only disguised by the "language of love" but by the label *domestic violence,* a euphemism that keeps us dispassionately distant from the "repugnant spectacle" of human suffering (Jones 1994:81, 106). Advocates for battered women seeking funding for their services originally used this term to avoid offending men who controlled the distribution of funds. So effective was the label at hiding the reality of woman battering that when congressional legislation titled the Domestic Violence Act was proposed in 1978 to fund services for battered women, it was mistaken by many to be legislation aimed at combating political terrorism in the United States.

We prefer the term **battering**, which David Adams defines as "controlling behavior that serves to create and maintain an imbalance of power" between the batterer and the person battered (1988). Adams argues that a violent act is "any act that causes the victim to do something she does not want to do, prevents her from doing something she wants to do, or causes her to be afraid." Adams believes that violence does not have to "involve physical contact with the victim," since the intimidation of such things as "punching walls, verbal threats, and psychological abuse" can have the same effect. Psychological abuse, "behavior that directly undermines the self-determination or self-esteem" of the victim, is especially powerful when paired with physical violence because "covert controls" are reminders of the potential for additional violence. Swearing, shouting, sulking, or spewing accusations are particularly frightening and effective when "'reinforced' by periodic or even occasional violence" (pp. 191–192).

Jones suggests that "battering is not a series of isolated blow-ups. It is a *process of deliberate intimidation intended to coerce the victim to do the will of the victimizer. . . .* The batterer is not just losing his temper, not just suffering from stress, not just manifesting 'insecurity' or a spontaneous reaction 'provoked' by something the victim did. . . . These are excuses for violence," excuses that are effective at convincing the woman to give him another chance (1994:88–89). He's not a bad man, she tells herself. He didn't mean it. He wasn't himself. But of course he *was* himself. He wasn't out of control. He was "exercising control."

Adams argues that treatment programs that focus on reducing the batterer's stress or improving his interpersonal skills tend to minimize the central power and control dimensions of battering, for how a man copes with stress and conflict "depends as much on the gender and status of the person(s) with whom he is interacting as it does on his social skill level." A man who is abusive at home is often quite capable of being attentive, straightforward, and conciliatory if he thinks it is in his best interests to be so—with police officers, neighbors, or his boss and coworkers, for instance. That the man is "selectively abusive" indicates that he has "an established set of control skills" (1988:190–191). When he's abusive at home, writes Jones, he's "at work on his own agenda, which is to train 'his' woman to be what he wants her to be, and only what he wants her to be, all the time" (1994:89).

Although battering husbands are often traditionalists who believe in male superiority and men's right to head the family (Pagelow 1984), Linda Gordon's historical research on eighty years of family violence in Boston found that batterers were "not ideologues defending the dominance of their sex. . . . [They were men who] were using violence to increase their control over particular women, defending real material benefits." The "sense of entitlement" these men had "was so strong it was experienced as a need"

(1988:286–287). Then, as now, disappointment of their expectations (a hot meal, a cold beer, a tidy house, an ironed shirt, well-behaved kids, sex *now*) meant punishment—lessons the little lady had better learn *once and for all.*

But even the apologies the batterer may make when he thinks his punishment "got out of hand" or "went too far" are designed to control. He pleads: I'm sorry. I didn't mean to hit you so hard. You just get me so mad. I'm sorry. I didn't mean those things I said—it was just the booze talking. You know I love you. I'm sorry. I just had such a bad day. I didn't mean to hurt you. Why did you make me do that? Don't you know I'm *trying* to control my temper. I'm sorry. I just can't take it when you dress like that and men look you up and down. You're *my* woman after all. Who do they think they are? Who do *you* think you are? I'm sorry. You know I love you. Why can't you just do what I say? I'm sorry. I'll *try* not to get so angry. You know I can't live without you. Although the apologies are often intermingled with blame or denial, the professed remorse and promise of reform can be seductive indeed. Dubbed by psychologists as the **honeymoon phase**, these periods of supposed repentance can lull women into letting their guard down (Walker 1979). Although women often mistake these periods for love, they "are not respites from battering, as they appear, but part of the coercive process, pressuring women to forgive and forget, to minimize and deny, to *submit,* and thus to appear complicitous" (Jones 1994:93).

Many women who are in abusive relationships do not consider themselves battered women. The label "battered woman" conjures up an image of a helpless victim beaten down by more or less constant physical assaults. Women who have endured abuse appreciate the incredible vigilance, courage, and self-discipline it takes to survive day after day, and they often see themselves as strong women who somehow manage to cope. Living in an atmosphere of persistent threat, with violence both capricious and inevitable, a woman hems herself in. She "may give up bits and pieces of herself: her preferences, her opinions, her voice, her friends, her job, her freedom of movement, her sexual autonomy. She may learn to lie, or at least to keep the truth to herself. She may learn to say that sex was good when it wasn't, or that she's sorry when she's not. Unable ever to give the 'right' answer, she may retreat into silence" (Jones 1994:94). Her apparent passivity is often mistaken for submission, even masochism, but she doesn't give in. She lies low—at first while she attempts to make some sense of what's happening, then while she tries one thing after another to get him to change. Finally, when she realizes nothing she does to appease him will stop the abuse, she lies low while she contemplates leaving, checks out her options, perhaps—with tremendous determination and at enormous risk—squirrels away a dollar here, a dollar there for that "ticket to freedom."

Although such women are often stereotyped as passive, dependent, indecisive, ineffectual, helpless, and masochistic, Dworkin thinks that most of us have no idea "how brave [battered] women are—the ones who have stayed until now and the ones who have escaped, both the living and the dead" (1997:44). Battered women already live lives heavy with criticism and blame, and then they receive more when we ask with more than a hint of disdain: Why does she stay with the bum? Why doesn't she *just leave*? No wonder her sense of isolation grows.

When women do leave or when they announce that they're going to, men's attempts to control, punish, or even destroy them are likely to escalate, sometimes with lethal consequences (Stanko 1997). "If I can't have her, no one will" is a common sentiment among batterers. In fact, "more battered women are killed after they leave than before" (Dworkin 1997:43). If guilt, shame, love, pity, poverty, tattered self-esteem, sense of duty, family pressure, religious obligation, the specter of homelessness, the questions that ring in her ears (What will the kids do without a dad? What will *he* do without me? . . .) don't keep her stuck, *fear* often will.

In 1989 Nicole Brown Simpson asked the police to arrest her husband, O.J. Simpson. It was the *ninth* time the police had been called, but the first time he was arrested. How many beatings do women have to endure "per phone call to the police" before the violence is taken seriously?, Dworkin (1997) asks. Nicole's divorce was finalized in 1992. Yet even though she had escaped her marriage, she had not escaped the task of negotiating her safety, as O.J. continued to intimidate, threaten, stalk, and assault her. What O.J. called his "desire for reconciliation" was for Nicole pure hell. This is commonly part of the torment of "escape" for a battered woman: "Freedom is near but [the abuser] will not let [her] have it" (pp. 43–44).

A few months before Nicole was murdered, she told her mother, "I'm scared. . . . I go to the gas station, he's there. I go to the Payless Shoe Store, . . . he's there. I'm driving, and he's behind me" (quoted in Dworkin 1997:45). Nicole told her sister Denise, among others, that she expected O.J. to kill her and get away with it. Much of the evidence of her fear and despair, however, was called "hearsay" and excluded from her ex-husband's criminal trial. Nicole did what many abused women do—she tried to leave a trail. She kept a diary in which she carefully recorded descriptions of numerous physical assaults. And five days before that June 1994 night, when Nicole and her friend Ronald Goldman were brutally and repeatedly stabbed—Nicole's throat was slashed so deeply that she was almost decapitated—she phoned a battered women's shelter, terrified that O.J. was going to kill her. The jury was never informed of this call nor allowed to hear excepts from her diary. Why? Because Nicole could not be cross-examined. All told, most of the evidence of stalking and beating—from 1977 to May 1994—was excluded.

What else could Nicole have done? Killed O.J.? Since most battered women who kill go to prison, that's a risky proposition for any woman, let alone for one who takes a hero's life (Jones 1994). Besides, Nicole had two young children she would have wanted to see grow up. The average sentence for a woman who kills her mate is fifteen to twenty years (Gibbs 1993). (For a man it's two to six.) Couldn't Nicole have taken her children and gone into hiding? Even if she was willing to leave her home, her family and friends, all that was familiar, could she possibly have prevailed? Dworkin (1997) thinks not. With O.J.'s wealth and power, he would have hired investigators to hunt her down and "a dream team of lawyers . . . [to take] her children from her." Knowing that "she couldn't prevail . . . [Nicole] did what the therapists said: be firm, draw a line. . . . He could come to the recital but not sit with her or go to dinner with her family. . . . She did what most battered women do: kept up the appearance of normality" and waited for him to make his next move (p. 49).

About a year after Nicole and Ron were killed, a housekeeper at the home of another football celebrity dialed 911 in Missouri City, Texas. Felicia Moon fled in a car "in fear of her life," and her husband, Warren Moon, took off in hot pursuit. When Felicia returned to the house, she explained to the police that Warren "had strangled her to the point where she 'saw black.'" Felicia allowed "the police to take pictures of her scratches and . . . bruises," but she indicated that she "did not want to press charges . . . at that time" (Hill 1997:172). Moon was arrested nevertheless. At his trial Felicia testified that she had initiated "the violence by throwing a candleholder" and that the housekeeper had mistaken Warren's efforts "to calm her for aggression" (p. 174). The photographed scratches, she said, could have been from her own fingernails. Moon was found not guilty.

As a black woman married to a famous black man, Felicia was confronted with a special dilemma, a dilemma that invariably impacted on her decision to cast herself as the aggressor. Felicia had to save her husband's reputation "not only for himself but for the entire African American community." Warren Moon was a positive role model for African Americans, and Felicia "ultimately decided that the loss of her reputation would be less damaging to her standing in the community than would be her disloyalty to a black male hero" (p. 178). Black men have had a long history of suffering from white people's injustice, and her acknowledgment of intraracial battery would win Felicia no points from African Americans. As Joyce King, a black woman who directs a battered women's shelter in Boston, said, "Those of us who want to have a dialogue about [battery] are frozen out. When I try to talk to black women about the problem, they tell me that we have to be careful what we say and how we say it . . . because of how black men are treated in society. . . . Race is more important than gender" (quoted in Hill 1997:183). Thus, after the Moon trial, one juror commented that Felicia's "injuries were typical of those found in any marriage," a sad commentary on Felicia's sacrifice and on the public's ease at trivializing abuse (quoted on p. 186).

▪ *Partner Abuse in Gay and Lesbian Relationships*

It is not just partners in heterosexual relationships who experience the problem of battering. Research indicates that the rate of violence in gay and lesbian relationships is comparable to the rate in heterosexual ones. And as in heterosexual relationships, once violence occurs it tends to recur and to escalate in severity over time (Brand & Kidd 1986; Island & Letellier 1991; Renzetti 1992).

In addition to the kinds of physical, psychological, and sexual abuse we have described as part and parcel of battery, Barbara Hart (1986) maintains that there is an additional kind of coercion that is available to gay and lesbian batterers: **homophobic control**. Homophobic control of partners is possible because our society is homophobic and because gays and lesbians sometimes internalize the antigay prejudice they grow up with (see Chapters 5 and 10). Examples of homophobic control include threatening to tell the victim's family, friends, or employer that he or she is gay or lesbian; informing the partner that he or she "has no options because the homophobic world will not help" them; insisting that they deserve to be abused because of their sexual orientation; and telling a lesbian partner that no one will believe she has been battered because lesbians just aren't violent (p. 189).

One common but false assumption that many people make is that it is relatively easy for gays and lesbians to break up since they are not legally married. However, the deep emotional attachments and strong personal commitments that gays and lesbians develop make it difficult for them to leave abusive partners. They may also share a home and jointly own property that they stand to lose, and their financial loss may not be recoverable through legal action. Turning to relatives for financial or emotional support is often difficult or impossible if they are uncomfortable coming out to them or if they already have strained or severed relationships due to conflicts over their sexual orientation. They may not feel welcome at shelters or services designed for heterosexual women, and they may not reside in an area where the relatively few programs created specifically for gays or lesbians exist. The gay or lesbian community might also be quite limited where they live, and they may know few if any others who are "out." Thus they may consider their current partner their only source of support or their only possible lover. And if a gay man's battering partner has AIDS, he may feel incredibly guilty leaving him. If *he* is the one with AIDS, he may be highly dependent on his abuser for physical assistance and financial support (Hammond 1986; Letellier 1996; Renzetti 1996).

Pam Elliott (1996) argues that partner abuse is a power issue. Some people, she believes, will abuse their partners if "given the opportunity to get away with [it] . . . because they hunger for control over some part of their lives." Just as "some heterosexual men abuse their partners because they can get away with it in our sexist society, . . . some lesbians and gay men abuse their partners because they can get away with it in our homophobic society" (pp. 3–4).

Unfortunately, the power dynamic in gay and lesbian partner abuse is not always recognized. When survivors of abuse seek help, counselors, shelter volunteers, and police officers often wrongly assume that since both persons are the same sex, the situation is one of *mutual* battering. According to Connie Burk, the executive director of the Seattle-based Advocates for Abused and Battered Lesbians, when officers can't figure out who the abuser is, it's not uncommon for the abused partner to be arrested if "they're bigger or more butch" (quoted in Friess 1999:294). And it's not just ignorance or homophobic attitudes that impede justice. In some states, laws against battering do not even cover same-sex, nonrelated cohabitants (Wallace 1999). Given these additional hurdles, it's not surprising that gays and lesbians are generally less likely than heterosexuals to report partner abuse to the police.

▪ Dealing with Battering

Earlier we noted the controversy and inconclusive findings surrounding the policy of mandatory arrest of women batterers: whether the policy effectively sends a message that abuse won't be tolerated or whether it makes matters worse by making some offenders more angry and hostile toward their accusers (see Chapter 2). Nonintervention is clearly no solution, however, for the batterer will not stop on his (or her) own. Law enforcement must be part of the remedy, for some abusers who are determined to hurt their partners may be "deterred by nothing except confinement" (Stanko 1997:634).

Nevertheless, even with laws against battering on the books in every state, getting them applied when a man attacks his wife rather than his employer or neighbor—his fellow man—has been an uphill battle. Police officers, reluctant to look behind the curtain of privacy that has traditionally shielded family matters from public scrutiny, have hesitated to arrest when men continued to claim their ancient privilege to "chastise" their wives; and prosecutors and judges, afraid of breaking up families, have sat on their hands (see Chapter 1). Often, as Jones points out:

> Each branch of the criminal justice system . . . evades its duty by blaming
> another branch. Police say there's no point in making arrests when prose-
> cutors won't prosecute, and prosecutors in turn say they can't prosecute

when (a) police don't arrest, or (b) judges won't sentence anyway. Judges say that women waste the court's time. Blaming the victim allows everyone . . . to pass the buck; and buckpassing conveniently enables individuals within the system to acknowledge a problem without doing anything about it. They'd like to help, but . . . what can they do? . . . Why doesn't she just leave? (1994:145)

It is important to stop the pejorative stereotyping of battered women and recognize that it's not the woman but the battering partner—and the society that condones and encourages his behavior—that is the problem. Research is showing that "batterers vary in their ability to desist, in their techniques of control, in their patterns of dangerousness, and ultimately, in their lethality." This work promises to help efforts "to maximize the options for women seeking respite, escape, and refuge" from violence (Stanko 1997:630). If paired with legal sanctions against battering, counseling (especially if begun early) may be effective in interrupting some abusers' battering. Those most likely to respond to counseling are **sporadic batterers**, those "who are in the first or initial stages of violence progression and who are neither generally violent nor serious alcohol or drug abusers with a lengthy record of criminal and deviant conduct" (Ellis & DeKeseredy 1997:597). Not all counseling approaches are effective, however, as some "collude with batterers by not making their violence the primary issue or by implicitly legitimizing men's excuses for violence" (Adams 1988:177).

Adams advocates a **profeminist counseling** model that "provide[s] basic education to batterers about caretaking and communication skills . . . [but that] sees it as just as essential to challenge the sexist expectations and controlling behaviors that often inhibit men's motivation to learn and apply such skills consistently in a noncontrolling manner" (p. 192). Profeminist programs for batterers, which commonly utilize counseling groups for men, initially focus primarily on the protection of the men's partners. Men are expected to make "safety plans" in which they commit to "respecting the woman's fears and stated limits about the relationship, fully complying with restraining and vacate orders, eliminating drug or alcohol use if it has accompanied violent behavior, and ceasing any pressure or intimidation tactics intended to change his partner's plans or to deny her contact with others" (pp. 192–193). The batterer's program—or the local battered women's program if one exists—also contacts the man's partner to inform her of legal protection options and emergency shelter, support, and advocacy services.

Profeminist programs directly confront the ways batterers try to share or deny responsibility for their violence (e.g., by claiming loss of control or by blaming their partners, drugs or alcohol, or stress). They also identify and challenge more subtle kinds of abuse that the batterer will often try to use in place of physical violence. When the man has shown a "willingness to abstain from violent and controlling behaviors," greater attention is focused on the feelings, attitudes, and expectations that accompany abuse. Efforts are made to interrupt the underlying intent to devalue, denigrate, and dismiss (rather than understand) the partner. This process is essential since devaluation, which creates and strengthens negative stereotypes and attitudes, "often serves as an ideological justification for violence" (p. 194).

The profeminist counseling model is an encouraging development in antibattery efforts, but more should be done. Police, prosecutors, and judges need to take violence in the home more seriously. Improved and expanded services for battered women are in order: shelters in every town that welcome all comers regardless of sexual orientation, "medical services, legal services, social services, child care, child support, affordable housing, convenient public transportation, a decent job free of sexual harassment, a living wage" (Jones 1994:204). Similar interventions are needed to ameliorate other kinds of sexual violence. Social and economic changes that strengthen women's position in society in general and in the family in particular would lessen women's vulnerability and bolster their ability to protect themselves and their children.

10

Political and
Governmental Crime

On May 16, 1942, Gordon Kiyoshi Hirabayashi, an undergraduate student at the University of Washington, met with Federal Bureau of Investigation (FBI) special agent Francis Marion at the Seattle FBI office. "Five days earlier, [Hirabayashi] had defied a military order that required 'all persons of Japanese ancestry' to register for evacuation to the state fairground at Puyallup, south of Seattle . . . [where] Army troops herded them into cattle stalls and tents." From there they were "shipped to 'relocation centers' in desolate areas of desert or swampland, from California to Arkansas" (Irons 1988:39). Over 120,000 people were forced to endure what can only be described as concentration camp conditions, living under armed guard in tarpaper barracks. The internment of Japanese Americans was a response to Japan's attack on Pearl Harbor in December 1941. But the last camp did not close for more than a year after Japan surrendered to the United States in September 1945. And although the United States was at war with Germany and Italy as well, no such measures were taken against German Americans or Italian Americans.

Hirabayashi presented Agent Marion with a neatly typed four-page document titled "Why I refused to register for evacuation." Hirabayashi, who was a Quaker, explained that his opposition to the internment derived from his Christian principles. The evacuation order, he wrote, "forces thousands of energetic, law-abiding individuals to exist in a miserable psychological, and a horrible physical, atmosphere" (cited in Irons 1988:40). A majority of the evacuees were, like Hirabayashi, native-born citizens whose rights had been denied without due process of law. "If I were to register and cooperate under those circumstances," he said, "I would be giving helpless consent to the denial of practically all of the things which give me incentive to live. . . . I consider it my duty to maintain the democratic standards for which this nation lives" (pp. 39–40).

Hirabayashi was placed in the King County jail, where he awaited trial for five months. There it was learned that he had also violated military curfew orders that were in effect before the evacuation had begun. In October he went to trial both for refusing to evacuate and for violating the curfew. During the trial, Judge Lloyd Black described the Japanese as an "unbelievably treacherous and wholly ruthless" people and sentenced Hirabayashi to two concurrent terms of three months in jail (quoted on p. 42).

Four decades after Pearl Harbor, Japanese Americans organized a redress movement and persuaded the U.S. Congress to investigate what had occurred. The Commission on Wartime Relocation and Internment of Civilians concluded that the internment had *not* been "justified by military necessity" and had resulted from "race prejudice, war hysteria and a failure of political leadership" (cited on p. 47). Hirabayashi was vindicated in court as well, as were others. In 1987 the Ninth Circuit Court of Appeals vacated his two convictions. And by 1999 the U.S. government had paid some $1.6 billion in restitution to over 82,000 people of Japanese descent who were interned during the war (*Wisconsin State Journal* 1999c).

The Hirabayashi case illustrates the political nature of some types of crime. Hirabayashi, convinced of the truth and justification of his own beliefs, acted on his convictions and found himself in violation of the law. If one abandons a legalistic definition of crime, however, one is forced to conclude that the crime of the U.S. government was far greater than any crime Hirabayashi committed.

You will recall that conflict theory views crime as a contested terrain involving competing groups that struggle to assert or acquire economic and political power (see Chapters 1 and 5). Crime emerges as the norms, values, or interests of one group come into conflict with those of another. Throughout history various disenfranchised groups have engaged in violent and nonviolent civil disobedience as a means of political rebellion. In turn, groups in power have sought to suppress such resistance and have even violated their own laws (or the laws of other nations) as they commit "crimes of repression" (Quinney 1977). Government officials have engaged in illegal activities to advance their own interests or the perceived interests of the country and/or to maintain conditions favorable to capitalist profit-making at home and abroad. Thus government crime typically involves people *with* power acting upon people *without* power (Barkan 2001).

In this chapter we will use our sociological imagination to explore a range of political and governmental crimes. **Political crime**, according to Frank Hagan, is crime "committed for ideological purposes. Rather than being motivated by private greed or passion, the offenders believe they are following a higher conscience or morality that supersedes present society and law" (1997:2). Such crime can be committed against the government or by the government itself, and it can embroil innocent bystanders in political disputes. Political crime can also involve governmental officials who abuse their political power for economic and/or political gain. Often it entails attempts to cover up wrongdoings or perceptions of wrongdoings. Many a political career has been made and broken by crimes large and small, by secrets concealed and revealed, by lies told and untold.

■ Crime and Political Rebellion

The criminal has on numerous occasions throughout history been cast in the image of a hero (Quinney 1970). The Robin Hood legend of medieval times is a classic example of a thief who purportedly stole from the rich to give to the poor. Robin Hood was idolized as a rebel against a tyrannical social order. In the "Wild West" days of the United States, outlaws such as Frank and Jesse James were romanticized as well, as were depression-era bank robbers of the 1930s such as John Dillinger, Bonnie and Clyde, and Pretty Boy Floyd. At times, such offenders enjoyed the silent approval, perhaps even the protection, of the impoverished masses. In a quintessential Woody Guthrie folksong, Guthrie tells the tale of poor Oklahoma farmers who fed and temporarily housed Pretty Boy Floyd. In return, Floyd expressed his gratitude by leaving the farmers a large sum of money for their mortgage payments. In this folksong cum social commentary, the bandit's crimes, unlike the crimes of the rich, never drove a poor family from its home. To Friedrich Engels (1845), however, such criminality was but the crudest form of rebellion, for "criminals, by their thefts, could protest against the existing order only as individuals." Although many "doubtless sympathized privately with those who broke the law," crime never became "the universal expression of the workers' . . . discontent" (cited in Greenberg 1993:50). Moreover, if criminals stole from the rich, it was not because they were champions of the poor but because the rich simply had more to steal (Hobsbawm 1959).

Collective Rebellion in U.S. History

Compared to individual criminality, collective action, even in the form of mobs (disorderly crowds), riots, and violent insurrections, is a more potent form of "crime as rebellion": "Great shifts in the arrangement of power have ordinarily produced—and have often depended on—exceptional movements of collective violence" (Tilly 1989:62). The United States, for example, only acquired independence as a nation through revolutionary violence. And even after this country was founded, collective rebellions continued to play a significant role in its history.

Rebellions of U.S. farmers were prominent in the latter part of the eighteenth century. Many farmers, finding it difficult to make ends meet, were forced into deeper and deeper debt. They began protesting the foreclosure of farms and the jailing of debtors. Some took up arms. In a rebellion that left eleven men dead and countless others injured, Daniel Shays led an armed group of farmers in several skirmishes with the Massachusetts militia until his forces were subdued in the winter of 1787. After being sentenced to death, Shays escaped to Vermont and was later pardoned (Parenti 1983; Jensen 2002).

Nat Turner, an African American slave and preacher, led the most famous slave rebellion in U.S. history. In 1831, Turner, who believed that God wanted him to free the slaves, led a group of over sixty Virginian slaves in the massacre of about sixty whites, including the family of Turner's owner. Turner and about twenty others in his group were hanged, and Virginian whites retaliated and killed about one hundred nonparticipating slaves (Oates 1983).

The unrelenting threat of white mob violence, as well as organized racial violence (e.g., the Ku Klux Klan), has constantly loomed over African Americans both during and after slavery (see Chapter 2). African Americans accused of crimes or simply deemed "out of place" were victims of ceremonial mutilation-lynchings. And there were even many urban race riots in the nineteeth and early twentieth centuries where whites rioted against blacks (Feldberg 1980; Waskow 1967). In the East St. Louis riot of 1917, for instance, white rioters stopped streetcars, and "Negroes, without regard to age or sex, were pulled off and stoned, clubbed, and kicked. . . . Mob leaders calmly shot and killed Negroes who were lying in blood in the street. As the victims were placed in an ambulance, the crowds cheered and applauded" (Kerner Commission 1968:21).

One of the most well-known rebellions in U.S. labor history was the Haymarket riot of 1886. Several hundred workers gathered peacefully in Haymarket Square in Chicago to protest the police killing of six striking workers at an industrial plant the previous day. When about 200 police arrived at the scene against the orders of the Chicago mayor, an unidentified person hurled a bomb at the police, killing one officer and wounding several others. (Some believe the bomb-thrower was a provocateur attempting to instigate violence to discredit the workers.) A riot broke out and the police fired randomly into the crowd. By the end of the day, eight officers and a number of workers were dead. Eight labor leaders were charged with aiding the unknown bomb-thrower. Seven were sentenced to death and one to prison. Four of these men were hanged, one committed suicide, and the remaining three were pardoned in 1893 (Brecher 1980; Lens 1973).

It is interesting to note how mob action in preindustrial European cities of the late eighteenth and early nineteenth centuries differed from the modern inner-city race riots of today. Mob action of earlier times tended to involve protests whereby the urban poor articulated their demands to the political elites, who often made concessions (e.g., controlling food prices and distributing work) in exchange for the people's support. According to

Eric Hobsbawm, the people who constituted the "classical mob" did not riot merely because they were angry or frustrated but because they "expected to achieve something" (1959:111). Authorities, in turn, recognized that the mob was in some sense a permanent entity to which they had to respond periodically (Rude 1964).

Twentieth-century urban riots in the United States, on the other hand, appear more spontaneous in nature, but they, too, have often garnered the sympathy of the poor, as we noted in our discussion of racial conflict in Chapter 5. Moreover, Frances Piven and Richard Cloward (1971) argue that the expansion of governmental welfare in the late 1960s was a direct response to the political pressure and social unrest generated by the urban African American community. At the same time, as we also noted earlier, the riots provoked a white backlash and a punitive response from the police.

In Chapter 5 we also discussed civil disobedience—the deliberate yet nonviolent public refusal to obey a law that one thinks is unjust—as a mode of rebellion. Throughout history, the practice of civil disobedience, often associated with India's Mahatma Ghandi, has been an effective means of achieving social change. Before the Civil War, antislavery abolitionists, for instance, encouraged violation of the Fugitive Slave Law, which prohibited aiding escaped slaves or interfering with efforts to return slaves to their owners. Abolitionists often made their homes available to slaves fleeing southern plantations, and they helped organize the **Underground Railroad**, an informal network that lent assistance to southern slaves escaping to the north.

In speeches and essays, abolitionists Sarah and Angelina Grimke elucidated the interconnections between the struggle against slavery and the struggle for women's rights (Lerner 1998). Their advocacy of civil disobedience inspired Henry David Thoreau's famous 1849 treatise on the subject. Thoreau urged citizens to break the law if the law "is of such a nature that it requires you to be the agent of injustice to another" (1969:35). Later, suffragist Susan B. Anthony committed a celebrated act of civil disobedience when she cast her vote in the presidential election of 1872, in violation of federal law that denied women the right to vote. At her trial the judge did not allow Anthony to speak in her defense and ordered the jury to find her guilty. When permitted a final word before receiving her sentence (a $100 fine), Anthony declared, "I shall earnestly and persistently continue to urge all women to the practical recognition of the old revolutionary maxim, 'Resistance to tyranny is obedience to God'" (cited in Barkan 2001:388).

Some eighty years later, as you will recall, Rosa Parks refused to move to the back of the bus, sparking a movement of civil disobedience that challenged segregation laws and forever changed the social fabric of the United

States (see Chapters 1 and 5). And in his 1963 "Letter from Birmingham Jail," Martin Luther King Jr. wrote that "one has a moral responsibility to disobey unjust laws" (1994:463). King's noble stance, however, did not stop the FBI from investigating him for subversive activities. According to a 1976 report of the Senate Select Committee on Intelligence, headed by Senator Frank Church, from late 1963 to King's death in 1968

> [Dr. King] . . . was the target of an intensive [FBI] campaign . . . to "neutralize" him as an effective civil rights leader. . . . The FBI gathered information about Dr. King's activities through an extensive surveillance program in order to obtain information about the "private activities of Dr. King and his advisors" to use to "completely discredit" them. . . . The FBI mailed Dr. King a tape recording made from microphones hidden in his hotel rooms which one agent testified was an attempt to destroy Dr. King's marriage. The tape recording was accompanied by a note which Dr. King and his advisors interpreted as threatening to release the tape unless Dr. King committed suicide. (cited in Church Committee 1978:161–162)

The note read, in part: "King, there is only one thing left for you to do. . . . You are done. There is no way out. . . . You better take it before your filthy, abnormal fraudulent self is bared to the nation" (cited in Garrow 1981:126). The Church Committee noted that not only was the FBI's surveillance program against King "vastly excessive in breath," but it was illegal (1978:162). The FBI is permitted by law to investigate persons suspected of crimes, but it is not allowed to investigate persons for the purpose of discrediting them as political leaders.

■ Terrorism

Terrorism may be defined as the use or threat of violence intended to accomplish a political objective, whether it is the maintenance of the status quo or radical social change. Terrorists often target innocent people, though they generally do so to affect a government's policies or to overthrow a government altogether. One of the objectives of terrorism is to provoke a government to overreact, to break its own rules about the acceptable use of force and thereby undermine its own credibility. In the process, terrorists hope to polarize society and bring "fence-sitters" over to their side. On the other hand, **state-sponsored terrorism**, or state terrorism, is undertaken by governments themselves to control their own citizens' behavior or to change political arrangements in other countries (Friedrichs 2004; Gorenberg 2004; Martin 2003; White 2003).

Outside of the United States, two of the most persistent terrorist campaigns have involved conflicts in Northern Ireland and the Middle East. The Irish Republican Army, for example, has used terrorist bombings in its attempt to gain independence from the British. Similarly, Islamic nationalist groups such as Hamas and the Palestinian Islamic Jihad have used terrorism in their struggle against Israel and their attempt to establish a state for the Palestinian people (Hagan 1997; Martin 2003; White 2003).

Since the 1970s, U.S. citizens overseas have been targets of terrorism resulting from conflicts abroad, but the 1993 bombing of the World Trade Center (WTC) in New York City demonstrated for the first time that terrorism could happen here, on our own soil. The explosion, which left six people dead and over a thousand injured, shattered our sense of security. The WTC bombing, part of a failed plot to bomb other targets as well, was the act of Islamic extremists working under the leadership of Shaikh Omar Abdul Rahman, a man with a checkered past. Rahman had been expelled from Egypt for being part of a conspiracy in the 1981 assassination of Egyptian president Anwar Sadat, who had entered into a landmark peace accord with Israel. Although Rahman was on the State Department's list of undesirables, he had been given a Central Intelligence Agency (CIA) visa to enter the country. Rahman had been working with the CIA, which had been financing and training Afghan rebels who were resisting the Soviet Union's military occupation of Afghanistan between 1979 and 1989. Apparently it never occurred to the CIA that Rahman might try to target the United States. Rahman received a life sentence for his role in the bombing conspiracy. The other conspirators were given sentences ranging from twenty-five years to life (Hagan 1997; White 2003).

At the time, few Americans had ever heard of Osama bin Laden or the terrorist organization **Al-Qaida** (meaning "The Base"). Bin Laden, an exiled Saudi Arabian millionaire who had also gone to Afghanistan to fight the Soviets, is suspected of financing the 1993 WTC bombing. He is also believed to be responsible for the August 1998 bombings of the U.S. embassies in Kenya and Tanzania (which killed 12 Americans and nearly 300 Africans), the October 2000 bombing of the U.S.S. *Cole* during its docking in a Yemen harbor (which killed 17 sailors), and the infamous September 11, 2001, attacks (which killed over 3,000 people) (Martin 2003; Sperry 2003; *Wisconsin State Journal* 2004).

Al-Qaida, formed in the chaotic aftermath of the Afghan anti-Soviet resistance, recruited "Afghan Arab" veterans who had fought against the Soviets, and who, at a minimum, were sheltered by the Taliban military regime, which took control of most of the country in the latter half of the 1990s. Although the U.S. government never recognized the Taliban as the legitimate government of Afghanistan, in the years prior to September 11, 2001, the U.S. State Department and some U.S. oil companies were courting and negotiating with representatives of the regime, hoping to ensure their cooperation in the development of oil and gas pipelines in the region that would link energy reserves in the Caspian Sea to markets throughout Asia (Brisard & Dasquie 2002; Martin 2003; Sperry 2003).

According to Gus Martin, Al-Qaida is a now a transnational terrorist movement, with members and supporters throughout the Muslim world, and has as its main goals the linking of disparate "Muslim extremist groups . . . into a loose pan-Islamic revolutionary network" and the removal of "non-Muslim (especially Western) influences from Islamic regions and countries." It has groups, or "cells," in many different countries and communicates with members "using modern technologies such as telefacsimiles, the Internet, cell phones, and e-mail. Most Al Qaeda cells are small and self-sustaining and . . . receive funding when activated for specific missions" (2003:234–235).

The very real threat posed by Al-Qaida has reinforced the stereotype many Americans have of terrorists as persons of Middle Eastern descent. Prior to September 11, 2001, however, the greatest terrorist threat facing the United States came not from forces abroad but from those indigenous to the United States. We now turn to a discussion of terrorism as a homegrown product, as we examine terrorism of both the political "left" and the political "right."

Left-wing domestic terrorism. Arguably the heyday of left-wing terrorism in the United States was the 1960s and early 1970s, when violent groups emerged from the legal protests and civil disobedience of the anti–Vietnam War and civil rights movements of that era. The Weather Underground Organization (WUO), for instance, announced in 1969: "Kids know that the lines are drawn; revolution is touching all of our lives. Tens of thousands have learned that protest and marches don't do it. Revolutionary violence is the only way" (cited in Evans 1983:255). The WUO sought to promote chaos through violence in order to catalyze social upheaval and topple the capitalist system. The WUO took credit for some nineteen bombings between 1970 and 1974. While it faded from the scene after that, some former members were involved in incidents as late as the 1980s (Hagan 1997; White 2003).

Some analysts consider the militant Black Panther Party (BPP), originally the Black Panther Party for Self-Defense, to have been a left-wing terrorist group (Hagan 1997; White 2003). Founded by Huey Newton and Bobby Seale in Oakland, California, in 1966, its membership grew to several thousand nationwide. Believing that the police often harassed and beat unarmed black citizens, the BPP urged African Americans to arm themselves, and BPP members patrolled the streets of Oakland in order to monitor and deter police misconduct. But confrontations and hostility between the BPP and police led to several shoot-outs. Although some members and spinoffs of the BPP (e.g., the Black Liberation Army, founded by Eldridge Cleaver) did advocate violence as a strategy of social change, others began to stress service to the African American community (e.g., free breakfast programs for children, free medical clinics, alternative schools). In 1973 Seale ran for mayor of Oakland. He lost the election, although he did garner a third of the votes (Hamilton 2002).

Nevertheless, the story of the BPP does raise questions about the conduct of law enforcement. An informant working for the FBI, for example, infiltrated a Chicago BPP chapter and agitated for commando-type tactics. He even purchased rifles and ammunition on FBI orders and with FBI funds, providing the grounds for a raid by the Chicago police in which two BPP leaders, Fred Hampton and Mark Clark, were killed. The police claimed there was a shoot-out, although they fired nearly 100 shots and the Panthers fired at most one. The Chicago raid was part of a concerted nationwide law enforcement campaign against the BPP. By the late 1960s over 760 members had been arrested, and in 1969 thirteen individuals were tried for a bombing conspiracy in New York City. The major witnesses for the prosecution were four undercover agents who had infiltrated the leadership of a local BPP chapter. While all the defendants were eventually acquitted, the government's campaign was successful in neutralizing the BPP by 1972 (Balkan et al. 1980; Barkan 2001; Wolfe 1973).

Since the 1970s the anti–nuclear power and environmental movements of the political left have used civil disobedience to promote their causes. In 1976 the Clamshell Alliance organized a sit-in of over 1,400 people at the nuclear construction site in Seabrook, New Hampshire. This demonstration is said to have launched the anti–nuclear power movement (Dwyer 1983). Over the years radical environmentalists have chained themselves to trees and logging equipment to prevent the destruction of forests, and some have even camped out in treetop perches "defying anyone to cut the tree down with them in it" (Gwartney 1998:61). Antitechnology environmentalist Theodore Kaczynski, however, was quite clearly a terrorist. Dubbed the Unabomber, Kaczynski killed three people and wounded twenty-three others during nearly two decades of activity that preceded his capture in 1996. In a 35,000-word manifesto that was published (under threat of violence by Kaczynski) in the *Washington Post* and *New York Times* in September 1995, Kaczynski wrote:

> The Industrial Revolution and its consequences have been a disaster for the human race. . . . They have destabilized society, have made life unfulfilling, have subjected human beings to indignities, have led to widespread psychological suffering . . . and have inflicted severe damage on the natural world. . . . The positive ideal that we propose is Nature . . . WILD nature: those aspects of the functioning of the Earth and its living things that are independent of human management and free of human

interference and control. . . . With regard to revolutionary strategy, the only points on which we absolutely insist are that the single overriding goal must be the elimination of modern technology. (cited in *U.S. News & World Report* 1996b:35)

Kaczynski was sentenced to life in prison for his crimes.

The environmental philosophy from which Kaczynski derived his worldview is sometimes referred to as **deep ecology**, the belief that human beings are simply "ordinary member[s] of the biological community, no more important than" any other living creature (Eagan 1996:3). **Ecoterrorism**, of which Kaczynski is arguably the most extreme case, is a movement of people who advocate the use of violence and the willful destruction of property in order to "terminate, prevent, or minimize human alteration to any part of the natural environment or its animal species" (Nilson & Burke 2002:1). Some ecoterrorist groups, which are composed primarily of individuals from middle-class backgrounds, formed as off-shoots of mainstream environmental groups like Greenpeace, which strongly disapprove of ecoterrorist tactics. The Sea Shepard Conservation Society, for instance, established by former Greenpeace members, has sunk several whaling ships and rammed about a dozen other vessels over the years.

Earth First!, another ecoterrorist group, was formed for the explicit purpose of sharpening the conflict between the mainstream and radical environmental movements. Although they also engage in acts of civil disobedience, Earth First!ers' favorite tactic is "monkeywrenching—sabotaging logging equipment by inserting spikes into trees to damage saws, or pouring foreign substances into the fuel tanks of logging equipment" (Nilson & Burke 2002:3).

Radicals in the left-wing "animal rights" movement have also been involved in what some consider to be ecoterrorism (Hagan 1997). Most animal rights groups have engaged in peaceful protests against the hunting of deer, the wearing of fur, and the maiming, torturing, and killing of animals in laboratory experiments that have little social significance (i.e., that test nonessential consumer items such as cosmetics and household cleaning products). However, some activists have vandalized laboratories, freed animals, and thrown red paint (symbolizing blood) on persons wearing fur coats. In 1997 members of the Animal Liberation Front (ALF) were responsible for the bombing of offices and feed trucks belonging to a Utah fur breeders' agricultural cooperative, causing about $1 million in property damage. The following year members of the Earth Liberation Front (ELF) set fire to three buildings and four chair lifts at a Vail, Colorado, ski resort, damaging property worth about $12 million. ELF admitted to "starting the fires on behalf of the lynx," which were believed to be in danger of losing their natural habitat due to the expansion of the resort (Nilson & Burke 2002:4).

In 2003, ELF also took credit for setting fire to twenty new Hummer vehicles worth about $50,000 apiece at a southern California dealership to protest what members perceived to be the wasteful extravagance of such "mastodons of the highway" (Madigan 2003:A3). This arson was but one of a series of vandalisms that caused damage to about fifty other vehicles in the area as well. ELF also claimed responsibility for a fire that destroyed 1,500 apartments that were being built at a construction site. The damages were estimated at $50 million.

Right-wing domestic terrorism. Outside of radical Islamic terrorism, many analysts believe that indigenous white-supremacist groups of the political right pose the most serious domestic terrorist threat to the United States. Few people acknowledged this threat until Timothy McVeigh detonated a rented truck filled with 4,800 pounds of explosives at the Alfred Murrah Federal Building in Oklahoma City on April 19, 1995. The bombing killed 191 men, women, and children, making it "the worst single terrorist incident ever committed" in the United States prior to September 11, 2001 (Hagan 1997:160).

McVeigh and his accomplice, Terry Nichols, were affiliated with the contemporary **militia movement**, a network of groups that reject the legitimacy of the U.S. government. Described as "paramilitary groups oriented toward 'survivalism,' outdoor skills, guerrilla training, and outright sedition," these groups vehemently oppose gun control and advocate the stockpiling of arms and supplies in preparation for a final showdown (Hoffman 1993:220). According to the Anti-Defamation League (ADL) (1997), militia groups can be found in at least forty states, with a membership as high as 15,000 nationwide.

Being a militia sympathizer or a member of a militia group does not make one a terrorist, however. Many join such groups "out of a sense of powerlessness . . . [and frustration] with the rapid pace of change in the modern world" (White 2003:228). They are people who've never quite made it, who sense that some vague and shifting "system" has let them down. For them, joining a militia group can make them feel important, can give them a place to ground their manhood (Faludi 1999). Although most militia members were appalled by the Oklahoma City bombing, the paramilitary rhetoric of the militia can nevertheless incite some to violence and spawn extremist sects. Small groups of armed members have broken off into separate cells without centralized leadership, feeling encouraged to act on their own in the interest of the cause, that is, resisting the intrusion of the federal government by whatever means necessary.

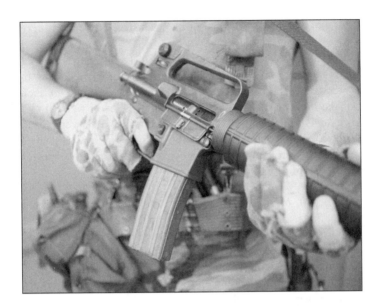

The boundaries of the militia movement blur into the domain of organized hate groups. McVeigh, for example, was influenced by *The Turner Diaries,* a right-wing novel written by William Pierce under the pen name Andrew Macdonald (1980). Pierce was the leader of the National Alliance (NA), one of the most well-organized and well-financed neo-Nazi groups in the United States (ADL 1997). The defining characteristic of Nazi ideology is its **anti-Semitism**—the hatred and discriminatory treatment of Jews—but neo-Nazis disdain other groups as well: racial and ethnic minorities, gays and lesbians, feminists, liberals, and people with disabilities. Through flyers, short-wave radio broadcasts, and the Internet, the NA voices its opposition to these groups. In *The Turner Diaries* a character named Earl Turner joins a violent revolutionary group that overthrows the Jewish-controlled ZOG (Zionist Occupied Government). In the book, ZOG has "outlawed gun ownership and invested human relations councils with police powers to force integration and **miscegenation** on the public" (Hamm 1993:50–51). ("Miscegenation" refers to the interbreeding or marriage between members of different racial groups.) Turner responded by leading an elite group of combatants called "The Order" in a series of terrorist attacks. The book describes the construction and detonation of bombs and endorses blowing up government buildings, power stations, fuel depots, industrial plants, missile silos, and synagogues, as well as assassinating government officials, liberal media figures, Jews, and other racial/ethnic minorities.

Although not all militia members are hate mongers, many are. Randy

Weaver, for instance, was a white separatist and follower of Christian Identity (CI), an anti-Semitic/racist movement derived from a nineteenth-century ideology known as Anglo-Israelism. CI preaches that white Europeans are the descendants of the lost tribes of Israel and that they have been chosen by God to lead the Aryan nations against the Satanic Jews and their allies. CI adherents believe in the inevitability of a global race war that only whites will survive. In 1992 Weaver sold an illegal firearm to undercover agents from the Bureau of Alcohol, Tobacco, and Firearms (BATF). He resisted arrest, fled, and holed up with his family in his mountain cabin near Ruby Ridge, Idaho. A federal marshal and Weaver's fourteen-year-old son were both killed in the shoot-out that ensued. The next day, before Weaver surrendered, a FBI sniper shot and killed Weaver's pregnant wife (Hagan 1997; Langer 1990; White 2003).

Ruby Ridge has become one of the battle cries of the militant right wing, as has the incident near Waco, Texas, involving David Koresh's Branch Davidian (BD) religious sect. In fact, Timothy McVeigh considered the Oklahoma bombing to be retaliation for what happened at Waco, and he planned the bombing to occur two years to the day following the FBI raid of the Waco BD compound (Hagan 1997). The Waco raid stemmed from federal authorities' concern about the huge stockpile of illegal weapons that Koresh was storing in the compound. As BATF agents attempted to serve a search warrant, they were met with a hail of gunfire that killed four agents and wounded several others. After a three-month standoff the FBI stormed the compound, not anticipating that Koresh and his followers would set a suicide-fire that would kill over seventy men, women, and children. Many people blame the FBI for its inability to resolve the incident without so many lives being lost. Moreover, for six years the FBI denied that its agents had fired any flammable material at the site, only to admit later that tear gas canisters containing pyrotechnic devices had been fired at an area *outside* the compound (Sniffen 1999). (These devices are not believed to have started the blaze that erupted several hours later.) At the time of the incident, the National Rifle Association bemoaned that "not too long ago, it was unthinkable for federal agents wearing Nazi bucket helmets and black storm trooper uniforms to attack law-abiding citizens. Not today" (cited in Russakoff & Kovaleski 1998:114). McVeigh took his revenge. Although Koresh "had nothing to do with the right-wing movement, he had the right formula: guns, a survivalist compound, and . . . messianic illusions" about saving the world from impending doom (White 2003:225). McVeigh received the death penalty and Nichols a life sentence for their crime.

Another movement of the political right, the antiabortion "pro-life" movement, has also been implicated in terrorism (Hagan 1997; White 2003). Pro-life advocates consider even legal acts of abortion to be murder. Most pro-life activism has involved civil disobedience, with arrests associated with Operation Rescue's campaign of picketing and blocking entrances to abortion clinics topping 40,000 by the early 1990s. The mainstream pro-life movement, however, has spawned an extremist fringe as well, and bombings and arsons have become a disconcerting part of the antiabortion campaign. "Pro-choice" abortion rights advocates and physicians have been stalked, harassed, and threatened with death. "Wanted" posters with doctors' names and addresses have even been posted on Internet websites, with names crossed off when doctors were killed (Dodge 1999). In one case, an antiabortion priest dubbed the murders "justifiable homicide" (quoted in Hagan 1997:103). In another, a clergyman blamed a new law against blocking clinic access for the violence of antiabortionists, who were now "being forced into" killing (quoted in Gegax & Clemetson 1998:34).

Militant antiabortion sentiments have also been expressed by the contemporary neo-Nazi movement. The telephone hotline of the White Aryan Resistance (WAR), an organization founded by former California Ku Klux Klan member Tom Metzger in 1983, once contained the following inflammatory message:

> Almost all abortion doctors are Jews. Abortion makes money for Jews. Almost all abortion nurses are lesbians. Jews will do anything for money; including the rape of innocent children followed by the ripping and tearing of the living child from the young mother's womb while still squirming. Jews must be punished for the holocaust and murder of white babies along with their perverted lesbian nurses who enjoy their jobs too much. (quoted in Hamm 1993:56–57)

■ Hate Crimes and Hate Groups

We have already noted the blurred boundaries between right-wing domestic terrorism and organized hate groups in the United States. **Hate crimes** are political crimes insofar as they involve attempts to preserve or assert the dominance of one group over another. Although history is replete with crimes that were motivated by hate, since the 1980s hate crimes have been increasingly perceived as a distinct category of criminality. Two well-publicized incidents in the 1980s stand out in the evolution of this perception. In 1984 Alan Berg, an outspoken Jewish radio talk show host in Denver, was machine-gunned down by white supremacists who called themselves "The Order" (after *The Turner Diaries*). Two years later, three black men were chased onto a highway by a mob of whites after the black men's car broke down in the Howard Beach area of New York City. One of the black men was killed by the oncoming traffic. WAR saluted the actions of the Howard Beach mob. More recently, in 1998, a middle-age black man, James Byrd, was severely beaten, chained to a truck by his ankles, and dragged to his death by three white men in Jasper, Texas, leaving a trail of blood a mile long. Police found a lighter bearing white supremacist symbols at the scene of the crime (Bureau of Justice Assistance [BJA] 1997; Hamm 1993; Van Boven & Gesalman 1998).

Throughout history members of dominant groups—primarily male members—have used violence and terror to draw social boundaries, exclude others, and sustain their dominance. Previously we noted that the dominant or hegemonic form of masculinity in society is defined not only in terms of men's power and social privilege vis-à-vis women but also through men's ability to exercise authority and control over *other men* (see Chapter 8). We saw how "white-supremacist masculinity" has been defined in terms of "subordinate African American masculinity" and how white violence against blacks has been a means by which whites have tried to preserve their dominance and bolster their masculine self-esteem (see Chapter 2). Such violence has also helped to distract economically marginal white men from their economic plight and to direct blame for their problems toward social minorities rather than toward more privileged white men or an inequitable social structure (Connell 1995; Lerner 1997).

Similarly, violence against gays has allowed some men to assert their masculinity by punishing those whom they perceive as "the betrayers of manhood" (Connell 1995:213). When society simultaneously puts a premium on males being masculine, devalues femininity, and "equates male homosexuality with femininity," the easiest and quickest way for males to demonstrate masculine status is to put down gays or accuse someone of being gay (Rotello 2002:72). The word "faggot," however, doesn't necessarily reference actual or perceived homosexuality; it is a label of utmost contempt for anyone who is deemed to be sissy, weak, or simply uncool. When thirteen-year-old (heterosexual) Aaron Vays moved from Russia to New York to pursue a career in figure skating, the boys on the hockey team told him that "only sissies, girls, communists, and fags figure-skated" (Wilchins 2002:72). It wasn't long before the teasing and taunting by schoolmates became tripping and punching. Eventually, Aaron was beaten so badly he had to be hospitalized.

Gloria Steinem (1999) observes that those who commit hate crimes assume that white, heterosexual males have a "natural right" to dominance and that it is appropriate—even manly—to exert this dominance through violence against others. The irony is that while this *group* of men is arguably the dominant group in society, many members feel powerless as *individuals*. They aspire to a level of dominance that they feel is expected but that they cannot achieve, and they lash out at others to compensate for their own feelings of inadequacy (Kimmel 2000).

Russell Henderson and Aaron ("Dopey") McKinney, high school dropouts who grew up hard and poor, were reviled for being "losers" in the status-obsessed college town of Laramie, Wyoming. Henderson, who had been battered by his mother's boyfriends, and McKinney, whose mother was known to lock him in the basement, were treated like wimps by everyone they knew. On one fateful night in 1998, Henderson and McKinney finished a pitcher of beer at a local bar and began groping in their pockets trying to come up with the $5.50 they owed. A small and graceful young man at the end of the bar offered to help. Matthew Sheppard, with his bleached hair, stylish clothes, and shiny shoes of patent leather, appeared to be making a masculine "pass" by offering to pay for their drinks (Minkowitz 1999).

Sheppard told Henderson and McKinney that he was gay, and the two boys played along, inviting Sheppard to come with them to McKinney's place so they could get to know each other better. But once inside McKinney's truck, McKinney pulled out a gun and smashed its butt into Sheppard's head. The boys laughed as they beat their victim again and again with gun and fists. As Sheppard pleaded for his life, they drove him out to a field, tied him to a fence, and left him to die.

The pistol-whipping death of Matthew Sheppard galvanized national outrage at hate crimes against gays and lesbians. The 1993 murder of Brandon Teena, memorialized in the 1999 film *Boys Don't Dry,* raised public consciousness about hate crimes against transgendered people as well (see Box 5.1). Brandon Teena, born Teena Brandon, had been living as a man. Two friends of a young woman he was sexually involved with "took him into a bathroom, forcibly revealed that he had female genitals, then beat and raped him" (Wilchins 2003:72). Several days later they returned to finish him off. Unfortunately, Teena's murder is not an isolated incident. According to E. F. Graff, "Once a month, someone transgendered is murdered, and those are just the documented cases" (2001:22).

Homophobia, as we noted earlier, refers to the fear of and disdain for anyone who is not heterosexual (see Chapter 5). According to Michael Kimmel, it entails "the fear that other men will unmask us, emasculate us, reveal to us and the world that we do not measure up, that we are not real men" (2000:13). Perhaps we don't seem man enough to be able to pay for our own pitcher of beer or man enough to be more appealing to a woman friend than a "man" with female genitals. And one does not have to be gay or lesbian or transgendered to be targeted for gender-related hate crimes. In 2001 an African American transit driver named Willie Houston and his fiancée were out on the town celebrating their engagement with friends. When they stopped at a public restroom, Houston's fiancée gave him her purse to hold while she went into the women's room. Meanwhile, Houston assisted a blind friend who wanted to use the men's room. When Houston entered the men's room with the male friend on one arm and the purse on the other, Lewis Davidson, who was in the bathroom at the time, became enraged and began to harass Houston. Wanting to avoid any further unpleasantness, Houston left the room. But Davidson went back to his car for a gun and returned to shoot and kill Houston in cold blood (Wilchins 2002).

Data on Hate Crimes

In 1990 the Hate Crime Statistics Act (HCSA) authorized the federal government to begin collecting hate crime data based on race, ethnicity, religion, and sexual orientation. This legislation was in large part the product of a political alliance that was formed among African American, Japanese American, Jewish, gay, and lesbian groups. In 1994 the Violent Crime Control and Law Enforcement Act added crimes based on disability to the HCSA list. Feminists argued that violence against women (e.g., rape, battering) should be counted as hate crime as well, but they were unable to convince legislators to include gender in the HCSA. Those who opposed the inclusion of gender believed that doing so would make the concept of hate crime too broad and cumbersome, since crimes against women are so pervasive in society (BJA 1997; Jacobs & Potter 1998; Jenness 1999; Levin & McDevitt 1999).

By 2002, forty-six states and the District of Columbia had passed laws covering hate crimes and were reporting data to the federal government. (Arkansas, Indiana, South Carolina, and Wyoming are the exceptions.) Some hate crime laws have entailed the creation of special categories of offenses while others have simply enhanced penalties for existing crimes. State hate crime laws dealing with race, ethnicity, and religious bias are more common than laws dealing with sexual orientation, disability, and gender. Hence some categories of hate crime are more likely than others to be included in national statistics (ADL 2003).

Joel Best argues that *hate crime* was an "umbrella term" developed by a diverse set of political activists "to establish a common cause" among them (1999:57). Although many crimes are motivated by one person's hatred of another, the distinguishing characteristic of hate crimes is the bias or prejudice that offenders hold toward members of another group. Often the purpose of the crime is not just to victimize an individual but to send a message to the entire group the victim represents. Thus hate crimes have a deleterious effect not just on selected individuals but on entire communities, "raising levels of fear, mistrust, and hostility between groups" (Martin 1995:305). And since membership in the targeted group is often *ascribed* (the quality that marks potential victims—their race or ethnicity, for example—cannot be changed), victims of hate crimes (and others like them) are left with a sense of vulnerability and a feeling that there is nothing they can do to prevent future incidents. From the offenders' perspective, the victims are indeed interchangeable, that is, anyone fitting the description can become a suitable target (Levin & McDevitt 1999).

Data collection on hate crimes suffers from the same limitations (e.g., victim underreporting) as the *Uniform Crime Reports* (BJA 1997; see Chapter 2). Immigrants, for instance, may fail to report victimization because they don't speak fluent English or because they come from cultures where victimization brings shame to the family name. Undocumented workers who are victimized may face deportation if they go to the police. And gay people often refrain from reporting because they fear negative repercussions (e.g., job loss, rejection by family and friends, hostile reactions from police and other criminal justice officials). In fact, several victimization surveys have found that most gays and lesbians have been victimized by hate crimes, although a large majority did not report their victimization to the police (Berrill 1992; Comstock 1991). One survey even found that 8 percent of antigay hate crimes were perpetrated by the police themselves. And in a 1988 Florida case involving the beating death of an Asian American gay man, the judge jokingly asked the prosecuting attorney, "That's a crime now, to beat up a homosexual?" When the prosecutor answered, "Yes, sir. And it's also a crime to kill them," the judge replied, "Times have really changed" (cited in Berrill & Herek 1992:294–295). Other judges have publicly described gays as "sick people," "flaming queens," and "volunteers for AIDS." And offenders (even in murder cases) have employed the so-called **homosexual panic defense** to assuage the seriousness of the charge against them, alleging that "the defendant's violent actions were committed in self-defense against the victims' unwelcome and aggressive sexual overtures or were part of an acute psychological panic resulting from those overtures" (p. 295).

Police investigating a report also have trouble determining whether the crime in question was, in fact, a hate crime, that is, whether it was motivated by bias rather than some other factor. The offender and victim may offer different accounts of what transpired, and expressions of bias that did not instigate the crime may emerge during or after the incident. It may also be difficult to know which of a victim's multiple statuses was the source of the bias motivation (e.g., race, religion, sexual orientation, gender). Unfortunately, few states provide training to law enforcement personnel that would enhance their ability to tease out these factors (ADL 2003; Martin 1995).

With these caveats in mind, Table 10.1 presents data on hate crime incidents by bias motivation for 2002. *Race* bias constituted the most common type (49 percent), with antiblack bias accounting for 68 percent of the race incidents. *Religious* bias constituted the second largest category (19 percent), with anti-Jewish bias accounting for 65 percent of the religious

Table 10.1   Hate Crime Incidents by Bias Motivation (2002)

	Incidents[a]	Percentage[b]
Race	3,642	48.8
Anti-black	2,486	33.3
Anti-white	719	9.6
Anti–Asian/Pacific Islander	217	2.9
Anti–American Indian/Alaskan Native	62	0.8
Anti–multiple races, groups	158	2.1
Religion	1,426	19.1
Anti-Jewish	931	12.5
Anti-Catholic	53	0.7
Anti-Islamic	155	2.1
Anti-Protestant	55	0.7
Anti–other religion	198	2.7
Anti–multiple religions, groups	31	0.4
Anti–atheism/agnosticism/etc.	3	< 0.1
Sexual orientation	1,244	16.7
Anti–male homosexual	825	11.1
Anti–female homosexual	172	2.3
Anti–other[c]	247	3.3
Ethnicity/National origin	1,102	14.8
Anti-Hispanic	480	6.4
Anti–other ethnicity/national origin	622	8.3
Disability	45	0.6
Anti-mental	25	0.3
Anti-physical	20	0.3
Total	7,462[d]	100.0

Source: FBI 2003, tab. 2.33.

Notes: a. An incident may include multiple offenses.

b. The subtotals for race and ethnicity/national origin do not total 48.8 percent and 14.8 percent, respectively, due to rounding.

c. Includes those listed as anti-homosexual, anti-heterosexual, and anti-bisexual.

d. There were three additional multibias incidents.

incidents. *Sexual orientation* bias was next, constituting 17 percent of hate crime incidents, with anti–male homosexual bias accounting for 66 percent of the sexual orientation incidents. *Ethnic* bias constituted 15 percent, with the miscellaneous category of non–Hispanic ethnicity/national origin bias accounting for 56 percent of these incidents. Finally, *disability* bias accounted for less than 1 percent of all incidents.

Among these hate crime incidents, intimidation (threatening words or conduct that place a person in reasonable fear of bodily harm) was the most commonly reported offense (33 percent), followed by vandalism and destruction of property (31 percent), simple assault (20 percent), and aggravated assault (11 percent). The remaining offenses were divided among several crimes against persons and property. Murder accounted for less than 1 percent of the reported offenses (FBI 2003).

◼ *Organized Hate Groups*

Although no more than 5 percent of hate crimes in the United States are committed by members of organized hate groups, there are about 700 hate groups that are active throughout the country today (Levin & McDevitt 1999; Southern Poverty Law Center [SPLC] 2003). The Ku Klux Klan (KKK), whose name derives from the Greek word *kuclos* (meaning "circle"), is perhaps the oldest hate group in the United States. Founded by a group of Confederate Army veterans in Tennessee after the Civil War, the KKK was a secret society of men who engaged in public demonstrations and overt intimidation to keep blacks and their white sympathizers (especially Jews) in their place. Known for their white robes and hoods and their cross-burning displays, KKK members also whipped, tortured, and even killed the people they opposed. Ted Gurr (1989) describes them as a "vigilante terrorist" group whose purpose is to defend the status quo or return society to the social arrangements of an earlier time.

By the 1920s KKK membership had grown to over 2 million, with chapters throughout the South and in a few nonsouthern states. The KKK was even successful in electing sympathizers to political office, but internal disputes and public criticism of its violent tactics weakened the organization and caused chapters to disband and membership to decline. In the 1960s the perceived threat of the civil rights movement rejuvenated the KKK, which carried out a number of terrorist attacks against civil rights activists. The FBI in turn made the KKK a law enforcement priority, and several members were convicted of crimes and sent to prison (Ingalls 2002; Martin 2003).

In the early 1970s KKK membership fell to about 5,000, and new leaders emerged with novel strategies to attract members. David Duke, for example, worked to improve the image of the "New Klan" by downplaying the violence, by appealing to whites who held mainstream conservative views (e.g., opposition to affirmative action, immigration, high taxes, and gun control), by accepting women into the organization, and by establishing youth groups. Membership rose to about 11,500 in the early 1980s. By the mid-1980s, however, internal squabbles and competition from a vast array of right-wing hate groups depleted the ranks to about 5,000 again (Hamm 1993).

The contemporary movement of right-wing hate groups has developed a perverse ideology that combines vitriolic hatred of racial/ethnic minorities, Jews, gays, and liberals with strident militarism and radical Christian fundamentalism. These groups are "linked together by an elaborate network of computer bulletin boards, cable access television, desktop publications, and telephone hotlines," and they are appealing not just to the traditional rural and middle-age constituency of the KKK but to a new generation of alienated youths as well (Hamm 1993:50; Martin 2003; White 2003).

Among the diverse hate groups of the political right, skinhead youth groups have received the most media attention. The skinhead movement originated in Great Britain in the early 1970s among angry, anti-immigrant, working-class youths united by white-power rock music with violent and racist lyrics. Clark Martell is credited with forming the first skinhead group in the United States. In 1979 this nineteen-year-old high school dropout received a four-year prison sentence for arson as a result of torching the house of a Latino family in Chicago. In prison he read Adolf Hitler's *Mein Kampf* (My Struggle), and upon his release he joined the Chicago-based American Nazi Party. Martell became interested in white-power rock and formed a group called Romantic Violence that was patterned after the British skinheads. Paraphrasing a passage from *Mein Kampf,* Martell declared: "Our heads are shaved for battle. Skinheads of America, like the dynamic skinheads in Europe, are working-class Aryan youth. We oppose the capitalist and communist scum that are destroying our Aryan race. The parasitic Jewish race is at the heart of our problem" (cited in Hamm 1993:39).

There is no single skinhead youth organization in the United States. Most are organized like other youth gangs, with local names that evolve over time (see Chapter 7). The Southern Poverty Law Center estimates their membership at about 3,500 to 4,000, with California, Florida, and the Midwest the sites of greatest activity (SPLC 1997). In his research, Mark Hamm (1993) found that not all skinhead youths shave their heads, and that most are drawn into the skinhead subculture through peer pressure and a common interest in heavy drinking. These youths are proud of their working-class heritage but are concerned about their prospects of obtaining or maintaining blue-collar employment. The vitriolic lyrics of white-power rock expose them to the ideology necessary to become "true believers." Jews and racial-ethnic minorities are portrayed in this music "as agents in a conspiracy to threaten the well-being of the average blue-collar worker." This message is conveyed with "such powerful emotion that youths . . . begin to link musical messages to their focal concerns about employment. Through almost daily exposure to songs such as 'Nigger, Nigger' and 'Race and Nation' . . . [they] are transformed into adherents of a bizarre form of Nazism" (p. 211). The music gives them a sense of participating in something larger than themselves. And, once drawn into the subculture, they are exposed to the underground literature and electronic network of groups like WAR. Most skinhead youths do not, however, end up joining adult organizations that share their ideology.

Currently the decentralization of hate groups in the United States makes detection, infiltration, and control difficult for law enforcement. Another impediment is that on the surface some of these groups emphasize mainstream conservative issues. But even when they don't openly advocate violence, these groups provide the ideological fervor that provokes some to action. Such individuals become even more dangerous when they believe they are on a mission from God. Christian Identity, a movement we noted earlier, is just one of several odd permutations of Christian belief that have emerged among the militant right-wing and that use "free-wheeling fundamentalism and violent passages of Christian scripture quoted out of context" to justify their cause (White 2003:228).

Finally, Hamm (1993) notes that in the modern electronic age, one can participate in the hate movement without even joining a group. WAR, for instance, is not really a membership organization at all. As Metzger explained in a WAR hotline message: "W.A.R. wears no uniform, carries no card, and takes no secret oaths; [it] doesn't require you to dress up and march around on a muddy field; [it] works the modern way, with thousands of friends doing their part on the job, behind the scenes, serving their race" (cited in Langer 1990:89). Over 2,000 hate sites can now be found on the Internet (Levin 2002; Sandberg 1999).

■ Governmental Crime and Presidential Scandals

William Marcy Tweed was a masterful local politician of the nineteenth century. "Boss Tweed," as he was known, led a powerful coalition of New York City Democrats. Tweed portrayed himself as a social reformer, establishing public parks programs and city construction/work projects and supporting (largely Irish) workers' right to strike and form unions. Tweed, however, also favored lower taxes. Although this agenda of social programs and tax cuts made him popular with voters, it produced a fiscal deficit. Tweed attempted to solve this problem by secretly selling short-term city bonds to raise money, but the plan went awry in the early 1870s as the bonds came due and there was no money to pay back investors. Investigation into this debacle revealed that Tweed and his associates (the Tweed Ring) had been exploiting their political power for financial gain—by selling office supplies to the city through a private printing company and padding the bill, and by paying phony city bills in order to receive kickbacks on the profits. Tweed's corrupt administration cost New Yorkers millions of dollars. He was sent to prison, where he died, leaving a legacy that still haunts us today. As he said, "New York politics were always dishonest—long before my time. . . . This population is too hopelessly split up into races and factions to govern it under universal suffrage, except by the bribery of patronage and corruption" (quoted in Douglas 1977:84).

In 1872, around the time Tweed went to prison, the nation learned of a scandal involving a construction/finance company called Credit Mobilier (CM), a subsidiary of the Union Pacific Railroad (UPR). Both CM and the UPR were essentially owned by the same individuals, and when the UPR was awarded a multimillion-dollar government contract to build a transcontinental railroad to the west, CM was given the job. CM submitted inflated bills to the UPR, and company officials pocketed millions of dollars. All this was made possible, in part, because Oak Ames was not only the director of the UPR but also a Republican member of the U.S. House of Representatives. Ames had secured the compliance of a number of key congressmen by selling them CM stock at far below market value and allowing them to finance their investment with expected future dividends they had not yet earned. A congressional investigation of the scandal did little more than censure (officially condemn) the participants, including Republican congressman James Garfield, who later became president, and two Republicans who served as vice president under President Ulysses Grant, Congressman Schuyler Colfax and Senator Henry Wilson (Dickenson 1977).

During the administration of President Warren Harding (1921–1923), Secretary of the Interior Albert Fall secretly leased U.S. Navy oil reserves in Elk Hills, California, and Teapot Dome, Wyoming, to private oil companies owned by Edward Doheny and Harry Sinclair, respectively. Fall received a $100,000 loan from Doheny and over $300,000 in cash, bonds, and livestock from Sinclair. In 1923 Fall resigned and joined Sinclair's business. The so-called Teapot Dome scandal was investigated for several years, and in 1929 Fall was convicted of bribery and sentenced to a year in prison. He was the first federal cabinet member ever sent to prison for a crime committed while in office (Dickenson 1977).

The political scandals involving Tweed, Credit Mobilier, and Teapot Dome all involved the criminal abuse of political power for economic gain. Such crimes continue to the present day. During the 1980s, for example, U.S. Navy undersecretary Melvyn Paisley was responsible for procuring weapons systems for the government that were worth hundreds of millions of dollars. Paisley sold classified information to defense firms competing for government business, granted contracts to firms that paid him bribes, and awarded a contract to a company that he co-owned. In a federal law enforcement operation called Operation Ill Wind, Paisley and a number of other government officials, corporate executives, and defense consultants were convicted of bribery, tax evasion, and fraud. Paisley received a four-year prison term. Around the same time, the Department of Housing and Urban Development (HUD) became a center of influence peddling and fraud, as HUD secretary Samuel Pierce and his aides steered lucrative government contracts to Republican Party benefactors and paid exorbitant consulting fees to Republican political insiders. Although Pierce himself was not prosecuted, a number of HUD officials were convicted in a scandal that cost taxpayers several billion dollars. More recently, in 1996, Democratic congressman Dan Rostenkowski, chair of the influential House Ways and Means Committee, was convicted of misappropriating several hundred thousand dollars of congressional funds for his own personal use during a corrupt political career that spanned three decades. He received a seventeen-month prison term (Friedrichs 2004; Rosoff et al. 2002; Simon 2002).

Governmental crime, however, can involve not only the abuse of political power for *economic* gain but also the abuse of political power for *political* gain. In the latter, crime is committed for the purpose of maintaining or advancing political influence and controlling or eliminating one's political opposition. We now turn to some notable instances of this type of criminality. All told, the events we describe have contributed to the government's declining **political legitimacy**. A legitimate political system is one that is generally accepted by the citizenry as representing its values and interests. A government forfeits this legitimacy when its leaders no longer enjoy that acceptance (Gerth & Mills 1946; Nye et al. 1997).

■ Watergate

The most famous burglary in the history of the United States took place on the morning of June 17, 1972. Five men dressed in business suits entered the headquarters of the Democratic National Committee at the Watergate hotel and office complex in Washington, D.C. They were there to check on malfunctioning electronic surveillance equipment they had planted on an earlier trip in order to spy on the Democratic Party. This time they were discovered by the night watchman, who called the police. The burglars, it turned out, were under the employ of President Richard Nixon's reelection campaign, the Committee for the Reelection of the President, dubbed CREEP. Nixon assured the U.S. public that the matter was under investigation by the proper authorities and that he knew nothing about what had transpired. Nixon did not anticipate, however, that two years later he would be forced to make public transcripts of tape-recorded White House conversations and admit that "portions of the tapes . . . are at variance with certain of my previous statements" (quoted in Miller 1974:29, *The Breaking of a President*).

Even prior to the discovery of the tapes, journalists investigating the burglary—especially Bob Woodward and Carl Bernstein of the *Washington Post*—had made headway unraveling the case. The press reported that a $25,000 check from Nixon's campaign fund had been deposited in the bank account of one of the Watergate burglars and that the White House had tried to involve the FBI and CIA in the concealment of evidence that linked CREEP officials to the crime. We also learned that Nixon aides had ordered a burglary of the office of Defense Department analyst Daniel Ellsberg's psychiatrist in an effort to discredit Ellsberg. In 1971 Ellsberg had leaked "The Pentagon Papers" to the press, revealing how government officials—both Republicans and Democrats—had deceived the public about the government's conduct in the controversial Vietnam War (Rosoff et al. 2002; Simon 2002).

The infamous tapes were not discovered until the Senate Select Committee on Presidential Campaign Activities had begun investigating the case in May 1973 and after White House presidential counsel John Dean had testified about the role he and others (including Nixon) played in a cover-up. Both the Senate committee and the special prosecutor who had been appointed by the Department of Justice asked Nixon to turn over the tapes. The president refused and the dispute moved through the courts. Eventually, in July 1974, the U.S. Supreme Court forced Nixon's hand. The excerpt from the tapes that proved most damaging at the time was of a conversation that took place just six days after the Watergate burglary between Nixon and his chief of staff, H. R. Haldeman. In this conversation Nixon said:

> Now, on the investigation, . . . the Democratic break-in thing, we're back in the problem area because the FBI is not under control . . . because they've been able to trace the money . . . through the bank sources. . . . And . . . it goes in some directions we don't want it to go. [Former attorney general and current CREEP chairman John] Mitchell came up with yesterday, and . . . John Dean analyzed very carefully . . . and . . . concurs now with Mitchell's recommendation that the only way to solve this . . . is for us to have [deputy CIA director Vernon] Walters call [acting FBI director L. Patrick] Gray and just say "Stay to hell out of this, . . . we don't want you to go any further on it." (quoted in Miller 1974:26)

After transcripts of the tapes were released, the House Judiciary recommended that Nixon be impeached for obstructing justice, abusing presidential powers, and illegally withholding evidence from Congress. Nixon saw the handwriting on the wall and reluctantly resigned on August 9, 1974. Vice President Gerald Ford became president, and he pardoned Nixon a month later for all federal crimes that Nixon *might* have committed and for which Nixon *might* have otherwise been prosecuted.

It is interesting to note that Ford had become vice president because his predecessor in that office, Spiro Agnew, had also been forced to resign. In 1973 federal officials began investigating charges that Agnew, as Baltimore County executive and governor of Maryland, had accepted bribes from contractors (e.g., highway construction companies) receiving government work. Apparently Agnew had continued to accept payments even while serving as vice president. Agnew pleaded "no contest" to charges of income tax evasion. He was fined $10,000 and sentenced to three years of unsupervised probation (Simon 2002).

While Agnew's crimes had nothing to do with Watergate, the **Watergate** scandal has come to refer not just to a single burglary but to a larger cluster of crimes and abuses of governmental power, including (but not limited to) other burglaries, illegal wiretapping, obstruction of justice, tax audits of political foes, false and defamatory stories disseminated about rival Democratic candidates, solicitation of campaign contributions in exchange for favors, and appropriation of campaign funds for private use (Rosoff et al. 2002). In the end, a number of White House and campaign aides served time in prison. G. Gordon Liddy, the former FBI agent who masterminded the Watergate burglary and who committed other illegal acts, served the longest sentence (fifty-two months). Liddy is currently a syndicated radio talk show host who proselytizes ultraconservative politics to his listening audience.

■ The Secret Government

In the Watergate tapes Nixon expresses concern that an investigation of his administration might disclose to the public "the whole Bay of Pigs thing . . . which would be very unfortunate . . . for [the] CIA and this country" (quoted in Miller 1974:27). It appears that the five Watergate burglars were former CIA operatives, four of them Cuban exiles who years earlier had been involved in a U.S. government-backed campaign to overthrow Cuban dictator Fidel Castro. In 1959 Castro had taken power after leading a successful revolution against his predecessor, dictator Fulgencio Batista. As Batista had been an ally of the United States, Castro turned to the Soviet Union for military and economic aid. Castro proceeded to nationalize U.S. businesses in Cuba, and the United States stopped buying Cuban sugar exports. (**Nationalization** refers to government ownership and control of industries and natural resources.) As vice president at that time, Nixon had been one of the main strategists behind a plan for about 1,400 CIA-trained Cuban exiles to invade the Bay of Pigs on the south coast of Cuba. When Nixon lost the 1960 presidential election to John Kennedy, the Kennedy administration inherited the anti-Cuban operation. The invasion took place in April 1961, about four months after Kennedy took office. But fearing that U.S. involvement would be made public, Kennedy withheld the air support he had promised, and the invaders were left defenseless and forced to surrender (Chambliss 1988; Moyers 1988).

The Bay of Pigs fiasco is perhaps the most well known of several anti-Castro operations. There were as many as two dozen assassination attempts on Castro's life, and in some of these the U.S. government sought the assistance of organized crime. Prominent figures in U.S. organized crime did not like Castro, because unlike Batista, Castro refused to allow them to do business in Cuba (Miller 1974; Simon 2002).

The Cuban affair was not the first or the last in a long line of similar ventures. The CIA, established by the National Security Act (NSA) of 1947, was a product of the Cold War with the Soviet Union, which began after World War II and lasted until the dissolution of that regime in 1991. Under the NSA, the CIA was permitted to gather intelligence information regarding perceived threats to the national security and to also engage in covert activities to oppose such threats. In 1953 the CIA backed a successful coup in Iran against the democratically elected government of Mohammed Mossadegh (Kinser 2003). The Iranians had decided to nationalize the oil industry, which was controlled by the British, and the United States was concerned that this policy did not bode well for U.S. oil interests in the region. A brutal dictatorship friendly to the United States was installed, until it was overthrown by an Islamic revolution led by Ayatollah Ruhollah Khomeini in 1979. The consequence of U.S. interference in the affairs of another country is aptly noted by Edwin Firmage: "You create in that state sufficient forces of unrest that . . . don't have stability. . . . And those . . . chickens come home to roost. . . . You create a nation who hates you enormously, who views you as a devil, . . . until you have embassies taken, hostages held. . . . Hatred simply doesn't . . . rest" (quoted in Moyers 1988:39).

In 1954 the CIA backed the overthrow of Jacob Arbenz, the democratically elected president of Guatemala. Arbenz had embarked on an ambitious reform program to redistribute land that was held by a small number of landowners to the impoverished peasantry. Some of that land was owned by the United Fruit Company, a U.S. corporation. In the late 1960s another U.S. corporation, International Telephone and Telegraph (ITT), funneled $13 million through the CIA to help block the election of Salvadore Allende. Allende had been campaigning to nationalize ITT's holdings. After Allende was elected in 1970, the U.S. government tried to destabilize the Chilean economy, withholding supplies necessary for Chilean industries, pressuring world financial institutions to deny Chile loans, and organizing an international boycott of Chilean products. The CIA supported military leaders who opposed Allende and encouraged them to assassinate General René Schneider, who disapproved of a planned coup. General Schneider was killed in 1970. Three years later the Allende government was overthrown, and Allende was killed as well. Some 45,000 pro-Allende Chileans were arrested, tortured, murdered, and/or exiled. A similar story has been repeated elsewhere in Latin America and other third world countries: military dictators backed by the U.S. government have ruled through fear, intimidation, and brutality; and government "death squads," some financed or trained by the CIA, have kidnapped, tortured, and murdered those who threatened their regime (Hitchens 2002; Kornbluh 2003; Moyers 1988; Simon 2002).

Some criminologists label such actions "state-sponsored terrorism" or "state terrorism" (Friedrichs 2004; Martin 2003). While these acts may be authorized under U.S. law, they may violate the laws of the nations where they are carried out. The United States, of course, has by no means been alone in its support of repressive, dictatorial regimes. Indeed, this has been the justification for U.S. intervention. We are told that we live in a danger-ous world and that our enemies are unscrupulous. As former president Herbert Hoover said in 1954: "Hitherto accepted norms of human conduct do not apply. . . . If the United States is to survive, long-standing American concepts of fair play must be reconsidered. . . . We must learn to subvert, sabotage and destroy our enemies by more clever, more sophisticated, more effective methods than those used against us" (quoted in Moyers 1988:42).

During the Cold War, the Soviet Union was considered to be our most dangerous enemy. That country, however, was not necessarily responsible for the governmental policies we opposed in places like Cuba, Iran, Guatemala, and Chile. But during the Cold War era everyone had to choose a side. You were either with the United States or with the Soviet Union. Nevertheless, the notion that we interfered with the national sovereignty of other nations in order to preserve democracy and human rights does not ring true.

We have Nixon to thank for opening our eyes to the "secret govern-ment," and the Church Committee, among others, for revealing what was really going on. As we have noted, those perceived to be enemies were not just external forces but those within our midst, not just militants like the Black Panthers but nonviolent activists like Martin Luther King. The FBI, under the leadership of J. Edgar Hoover from 1924 to 1972, engaged in so-called counterintelligence operations against members of the American Civil Liberties Union, the Socialist Workers Party, the Southern Christian Leadership Conference, and numerous other nonviolent groups and individ-uals, including some notable justices of the U.S. Supreme Court. The Church Committee concluded that the FBI investigated too many people and collected too much information for too long a time to justify any legiti-mate law enforcement objective. Moreover, unethical and illegal methods were used. These methods included the range of activities found in the Watergate affair, and more—illegal wiretapping and opening of citizens' mail, burglary, character assassination, dissemination of misinformation to the media, and agent provocateuring. **Agent provocateuring** involves undercover operatives who infiltrate organizations and try to encourage members to adopt violent tactics, which in turn are used to justify law enforcement against them. The CIA also conducted domestic operations, in violation of its 1947 charter, putting thousands of Americans under surveil-lance of one form of another (Charns 1992; Halperin et al. 1977; Marx 1981; Poveda 1990).

Bill Moyers notes that all this is made even "more chilling by the assassination of John Kennedy" (1988:44). The Warren Commission, appointed by President Lyndon Johnson and headed by U.S. Supreme Court justice Earl Warren, concluded in 1963 that assassin Lee Harvey Oswald acted alone. In 1979, however, a congressional investigation concluded that a conspiracy involving organized crime was likely responsible for the assassination. Some factions of organized crime hated the Kennedy administration, not only for its abandonment of the anti-Castro Bay of Pigs operation, but also for pursuing criminal prosecutions, particularly against Carlos Marcello, a New Orleans Mafia boss, and Jimmy Hoffa, the Teamsters Union president who had criminal ties (Hagan 1997; Simon 2002).

The CIA has also been embroiled in conspiracy theories regarding the Kennedy assassination. President Kennedy had incurred the wrath of CIA operatives who blamed him for the Bay of Pigs debacle. At times he even seemed to be an unreliable "cold warrior" in the escalating military campaign in Vietnam. A thorough investigation of the assassination might have revealed things about the secret government that were best left unknown. At a minimum it is clear that the Warren Commission did not investigate all leads. So suspicions linger and accusations "persist of a dark, unsolved conspiracy behind [Kennedy's] murder. You can dismiss them, as many of us do, but since we know now what our secret government planned for [others], the possibility remains: once we decide that anything goes, anything can come home to haunt us" (Moyers 1988:44; Scott 1993; Simon 2002).

■ The Iran-Contra Scandal

President Jimmy Carter was less supportive of the covert operations conducted by the CIA than were his predecessors (and successors). He appointed Admiral Stansfield Turner to direct the agency. When Turner reduced the agency's covert operation section from 1,200 to 400 agents, many in the CIA were quite obviously displeased (Chambliss 1988). They did not consider themselves dispensable. Better to have their old boss, George H. W. Bush, back at the helm. (Bush had served as CIA director for the one year prior to Carter's taking office in January of 1977.) The election of President Ronald Reagan and Vice President George Bush in November 1980 seemed like a dream come true to the CIA.

The most significant cluster of crimes that occurred during the Reagan administration became known as the **Iran-Contra** scandal. The two elements of this scandal—the Iran component and the Contra component—initially represented two independent foreign policy operations. Iran, you will recall, experienced an Islamic revolution that replaced the regime that had been installed and supported by the United States. In November 1979 pro-Khomeini forces seized the U.S. embassy in Tehran, taking over fifty U.S. hostages, who were not released until just after Reagan was inaugurated on January 20, 1981.

The hostage crisis had been a major problem for the Carter administration. Had Carter been able to pull an "October surprise" just before the election, he would have had a better chance of winning. Former Carter administration official Gary Sick (1991), among others, believes a deal may have been struck between the Reagan-Bush campaign and representatives of the Iranian government to delay the release of the hostages. There is evidence that William Casey, the Reagan-Bush campaign director who later headed the CIA, had met with Iranian arms dealers who had contacts in the Iranian government. It has also been alleged that the Reagan-Bush campaign had informants within the U.S. intelligence/military community who provided information about U.S. aircraft movements related to the hostage crisis. And it is believed that someone associated with the Reagan-Bush camp stole briefing papers from President Carter's reelection campaign before the October presidential debates. While such charges have never been proven, the history of our secret government makes such allegations entirely plausible to more than a few people knowledgeable about that era. If true, it "would be tantamount to treason" (Hagan 1997:74; Simon 2002).

During the early years of the Reagan administration, pro-Khomeini forces bombed U.S. (and French) embassies in the Middle East. Over 200 U.S. troops stationed in Beirut, Lebanon, were killed in their barracks during a suicide bombing. More hostages were taken, including William Buckley, the CIA's chief of station in Beirut. The U.S. government's official policy, the public was told, was not to negotiate with terrorists. It was also a violation of the U.S. Arms Export Control Act to sell arms to countries (like Iran) that supported terrorism. But negotiate with Iran we did. And selling arms (missiles and missile parts) to Iran we did, too, at first through Israel, but later directly. In the process, arms-merchant middlemen such as retired U.S. Air Force general Richard Secord and Iranian-born businessman Albert Hakim (now a U.S. citizen) grew rich. Following the arms sales, hostages were not always released. And when they were, more were taken. Perhaps the official policy of not negotiating with terrorists was the right stance after all. But there was money to be made, and the Reagan administration needed the money (Brinkley & Engelberg 1988).

This brings us to the Contra part of the Iran-Contra scandal. Like Iran, the Central American country of Nicaragua experienced a revolution in the late 1970s that the U.S. government opposed. Dictator Anastasio Somoza, an ally of the United States, was removed from power, and the Sandinista National Liberation Front took control of the government. The Sandinistas turned to Cuba and the Soviet Union for economic and military aid. The Reagan administration, which believed the Sandinistas were fomenting revolution elsewhere in Latin America, found this unacceptable.

The Contras, the armed Nicaraguan opponents of the Sandinista regime, did not have popular support in their country. They were essentially a creation of the CIA, which was now headed by Casey. Without the CIA and the money and training it supplied, there would have been no Contras. Although Reagan often compared the Contras to our "founding fathers," they included former military officers of the Somoza regime as well as men who condoned terrorism, accepted money from drug traffickers, and even trafficked in drugs themselves (Moyers 1988; Simon 2002).

In the aftermath of the Vietnam War, the U.S. public did not have the stomach for such a controversial foreign policy campaign, especially if it threatened to involve U.S. troops. And the CIA-Contra operation did not get good publicity: Nicaraguan harbors had been mined and oil facilities burned, and innocent people were being terrorized and killed. Excerpts of a CIA pamphlet on guerrilla warfare that the Contras had been reading were reported in the press: "It is possible to neutralize carefully selected and planned targets, such as court judges [and] security officials. . . . Professional criminals should be hired to [take] . . . demonstrators to a confrontation with the authorities to bring about uprisings and shootings that will . . . create a martyr" (Alpern 1984:30).

During the early 1980s, the U.S. Congress, which has constitutional power over governmental appropriations, vacillated in its support of the Contras, approving funds, taking them away, approving them again. But in a definitive legislative statement, the **Boland Amendment**, Congress proclaimed:

> During fiscal year 1985, no funds available to the Central Intelligence Agency, the Department of Defense, or any other agency or entity of the United States involved in intelligence activities may be obligated or expended for the purpose of which would have the effect of supporting, directly or indirectly, military or paramilitary operations in Nicaragua by any nation, group, organization, movement or individuals. (cited in Brinkley & Engelberg 1988:414)

President Reagan signed the Boland Amendment into law in October 1984, creating a perplexing problem for his administration: How would it maintain the Contras when it was *illegal* to do so? What followed was nothing short of an assault on the U.S. Constitution. As Senator John Kerry said, the administration was "willing to literally put the Constitution at risk because they believed somehow there was a higher order of things, that the ends do in fact justify . . . the means. That's the most . . . totalitarian doctrine I've ever heard of" (quoted in Moyers 1988:28).

The task of supporting the Contras was given to the National Security Council (NSC), a White House advisory board headed by Robert McFarland. According to McFarland, Reagan instructed him to find a way to keep the Contras' "body and soul together" (quoted in Brinkley & Engelberg 1988:12). McFarland assigned a U.S. Marine lieutenant colonel, Oliver North, the job of working out the details and being the White House liaison with the Contras. North and associates raised millions of dollars from private groups and individuals in the United States and from allies such as Saudi Arabia, Taiwan, and Brunei. Central American governments

Box 10.1 Drugs and the Secret Government

Over the years, officials of the U.S. government have cooperated with drug traffickers around the world when they perceived it to be in our country's foreign policy interests. During the Vietnam War era of the 1960s, for example, the Central Intelligence Agency (CIA) enlisted the support of General Vang Pao, a man who led an army of mercenary Meo tribespeople in Laos. General Pao was also the chief organizer of the Meo's primary cash-crop business—opium. His operation was one of the major sources of opium from the Golden Triangle region of Southeast Asia in Laos, Burma, and Thailand. The CIA even allowed Pao to operate a laboratory for the conversion of opium to heroin at its Long Cheng headquarters in northern Laos; and the CIA ran an airline, Air America, that was used to transport drugs. Some of the profits from the Southeast Asian drug network were laundered through the Nugan Hand Bank, an Australian institution that had a branch in Thailand. Several CIA officials, including former CIA director William Colby, had close associations with this bank, and Drug Enforcement Administration (DEA) agents reported that their investigations into this drug network were blocked by the CIA. Thus some observers attribute the increased supply of heroin that came into the United States during this era, at least in part, to the CIA's support (Chambliss 1988; McCoy 1972; Scott & Marshall 1991).

During the Iran-Contra conflict of the 1980s, the CIA lent similar support to Central and South American cocaine traffickers, who contributed to the large quantities of cocaine that were imported into the United States during that decade (Diamond 1996; Scott & Marshall 1991; Sharkey 1988). Even Oliver North is purported to have interfered with a DEA undercover investigation in Nicaragua. Moreover, Donald Gregg, Vice President Bush's national security adviser, ran Operation Black Eagle out of the vice president's office from 1983 to 1986. Gregg was a longtime Bush associate from Bush's day as director of the CIA. Operation Black Eagle involved an arrangement with then–Panamanian dictator Manuel Noriega to allow the use of Panamanian airfields and front companies for Contra operations. In turn, Gregg turned a blind eye when Noriega used Black Eagle cargo planes to smuggle drugs back into the United States. How ironic it is that this took place at a time when Bush was head of the Reagan administration's Task Force on Drugs. And it was not that Bush didn't know about Noriega's involvement in drugs; he was told about it by the U.S. ambassador to Panama. It is also ironic that when Noriega was indicted in 1990 for drug trafficking in the United States, the Bush administration had to send in U.S. troops to apprehend him. Noriega was captured, convicted, and sentenced to forty years in prison. In order to convict him, however, government prosecutors granted leniency to several other major drug dealers in exchange for their incriminating testimony against the Panamanian dictator (Cohn 1992; *Milwaukee Journal* 1988; Parry 1988; Simon 2002).

such as Costa Rica, El Salvador, Guatemala, and Honduras were pressured or cajoled (with a promise of military aid) to allow their countries to be used as bases for the Contra resupply operation. At the request of CIA director Casey, North worked with Secord and Hakim to create a private (profit-making) organization, which they dubbed "The Enterprise," to coordinate the operation. Senator Daniel Inouye described the Enterprise as "a shadowy government with its own air force, its own navy, its own fundraising mechanism, and the ability to pursue its own ideas of the national interest, free from all checks and balances and free from the law itself" (quoted in Moyers 1988:24). The link between the Iran and Contra initiatives was forged as profits from the Iranian arms sales were diverted through the Enterprise to the Contras. This became, according to North, "an attractive incentive" to continue to sell arms to Iran (quoted in Brinkley & Engelberg 1988:16). Moreover, Casey envisioned the Enterprise as a permanent "off-the-shelf" entity with the stand-alone capacity to conduct covert operations beyond the purview of Congress (p. 17).

The secrecy surrounding these operations began to crumble in October 1986, halfway through President Reagan's second term, when a Contra resupply plane linked to the CIA was shot down over Nicaragua. The story was covered worldwide. And in November a Lebanese magazine disclosed the arms sales to Iran. Reagan and other White House officials first denied the stories but soon decided they would have to cut their losses, concede that some improper conduct had occurred, and develop a cover story to protect the president. In the meantime, North and his secretary frantically destroyed as many incriminating documents and memoranda as possible. But they did not get everything.

The cover story cast North in the role of a renegade, a well-intentioned soldier who had gone too far. North, however, was not about to take all of the blame. When he was granted immunity to testify before the (televised) joint House and Senate hearing, which began in May 1987, he became a media sensation. He was "a defiant hero, an obedient soldier, a blameless scapegoat whose conduct had been dictated or approved by his superiors" (Rosoff et al. 2002:312). "This nation," North said, "cannot abide the communization of Central America. We cannot have Soviet bases on the mainland of this hemisphere" (quoted in Moyers 1988:28).

During the Watergate scandal, it had taken two years to develop evidence that linked Nixon to criminal activities. Just over two years after the Iran-Contra scandal broke, Reagan's term expired. It was only later that we learned the full extent of Reagan's complicity, but by then any question of impeachment was moot. Several members of the Enterprise and a number of Reagan administration officials, however, pled guilty or were convicted of crimes. (Casey, the man who probably knew the most about what had transpired, died in 1987.) The sentences overall were less severe than the sentences given to the Watergate defendants. All but one received only probation or fines. Admiral John Poindexter, who had succeeded McFarland as NSC adviser, received a six-month prison term, but his conviction was overturned on appeal. Like North, he had been granted immunity for his congressional testimony. Thus, said the U.S. Supreme Court, his right to a fair trial had been compromised. North had his three felony counts reversed on appeal as well. He pronounced himself "totally exonerated," became a highly paid luminary on the lecture circuit, and was Virginia's Republican nominee for the U.S. Senate in 1994. He lost the election and joined the ranks (along with Gordon Liddy) of ultraconservative talk-show hosts (Rosoff et al. 2002:314).

▓ *Iraqgate*

When the Iran-Contra story first broke, then–vice president George H. W. Bush claimed that he was out of the policymaking loop. Later he would say that he knew nothing of the details. Bush was in fact a major player in Iran-Contra, although the public did not realize this until after he became president in 1989. As vice president, Bush had spoken out in cabinet meetings in favor of both the Iran and Contra operations, and he had participated in discussions about potential illegalities. He had even helped arrange an apparent "quid pro quo" deal (something done in return for something else) with Honduran president Roberto Suazo Cordova, promising to deliver over $110 million in economic and military aid in exchange for support of the Contras (Hagan 1997; Moyers 1990b).

The evidence regarding Bush's involvement began to mount during the 1992 presidential campaign. It was not just Iran-Contra, however, that dogged the Bush administration. Between 1980 and 1988 Iran and Iraq had been at war with each other. This may explain why the Reagan-Bush administration wanted to supply Iran with arms. But the United States was supporting Iraq and its dictator, Saddam Hussein, as well, perhaps because we felt it was better to have these two countries fighting each other than causing problems for us. After the Iran-Iraq War was over, the Bush administration mistakenly calculated that Iraq was now the key to establishing stability in the Middle East, and the administration continued to provide Hussein military aid. When Hussein invaded Kuwait in August 1990, however, Bush felt compelled to take military action. Many gave Bush high marks for leading an international coalition in a decisive victory in the early-1991 Gulf War. Yet at the time few knew the full extent of Bush's prior support of Hussein.

The scandal dubbed **Iraqgate** did not surface until 1992, as Bush's reelection campaign was getting under way. The Atlanta branch of the Banca Nazionale del Lavoro (BNL), headquartered in Rome, had provided Hussein with several billion dollars in loans, guaranteed in part by the U.S.

government. The BNL claimed that the loans had been made for grain sales but that Hussein had deceived them and used the money to build up his military (including nuclear) capabilities. This was just a cover story. In reality the loans had been approved by the Bush administration with full knowledge of Hussein's intentions. The scheme, which was in violation of the U.S. Arms Export Control Act, had apparently been devised because the administration assumed that Congress would not support a policy of military aid to Iraq. It was Iran-Contra politics all over again (Friedman 1993; Hagan 1997; Simon 2002).

The Bush administration attempted to delay an official investigation of the BNL as well as an inquiry into an Iraqi firm that was skimming money from the (bogus) grain program. Administration officials (including the CIA) lied to Congress and submitted altered documents to conceal their activities. But the cover-up began to unravel, in large part due to the relentless reporting of conservative syndicated columnist William Safire (e.g., 1992a, 1992b). A month before the November election against Arkansas governor Bill Clinton, Bush appeared on *Larry King Live* and said he had been an innocent dupe. That was the best spin he could put on the affair.

Bush lost the election, but before leaving office he pardoned a number of individuals associated with the earlier Iran-Contra scandal. Congressional Democrats lost any motivation to pursue the defeated ex-president. Safire (1993) reported that the Clinton administration agreed to forego investigation of Iraqgate if Bush refrained from criticizing the new president during his first year in office. U.S. taxpayers were left to pay some $2 billion of Hussein's defaulted loans. This was, of course, not the end of the story of controversial U.S. actions toward Iraq.

■ Sex, Lies, and Real Estate

Before Clinton was elected president he had credibility problems of his own. During the 1992 campaign Clinton made several misleading (if not false) statements regarding his efforts to avoid military service during the Vietnam War, his smoking of marijuana while in college, his extramarital affair with Gennifer Flowers, and his dubious business associations with Arkansas "wheelers and dealers." These transgressions, the Bush campaign said, raised serious doubts about Clinton's honesty and moral character. Thus when choosing a president in 1992, the public was given a choice between "lies and damn lies."

Whitewater was perhaps the first Clinton scandal to be given a name. In the late 1970s Bill and Hillary Clinton became partners with James and Susan McDougal in a 230-acre Whitewater real estate development project that went bust. The McDougals were owners of the Madison Guaranty Savings and Loan in Arkansas. Madison Guaranty failed during the 1980s savings and loan debacle (see Chapter 6), leaving U.S. taxpayers with a $60 million bailout bill. The McDougals had engaged in several of the illegal financial schemes available to corrupt savings and loan operators, and after Clinton was elected president, they were convicted of several crimes. One scheme involved a fraudulent overvaluation of Madison Guaranty's real estate assets that was used by the McDougals to secure a $3 million government loan. Over a third of that money was lent to Jim Guy Tucker, Clinton's successor as governor of Arkansas, who used it to purchase a water and sewer utility. Susan McDougal served two years in prison for her crimes, James McDougal died in prison while serving a three-year term, and Tucker resigned from office and received four years probation and eighteen months' home detention (Coulter 1998; Stewart 1996; Woodward 1999).

If money from the McDougals' illegal transactions were used to repay Whitewater loans, the Clintons may have benefited indirectly. But according to James Stewart's account, "The Clintons had virtually nothing to do with Whitewater and were simply 'passive' investors" (1997:447). Their only wrongdoings pertaining specifically to Whitewater involved overvaluing assets on financial disclosure forms and overestimating losses on income tax returns. While these were relatively minor infractions, the story of the Clintons' financial activities during the 1980s hardly portrays them in a flattering light. They took advantage of whatever opportunities they had "to make easy money, even when that meant accepting favors or special treatment from people in businesses regulated by the state" (p. 445). The Clintons' behavior lent credence to accusations that they used their influence to thwart regulators investigating Madison Guaranty and to facilitate the McDougals' financial crimes.

The Clintons managed to dodge the Whitewater bullet. More troublesome, however, was their pattern of withholding information and making misleading statements. Before coming to Washington, D.C., for example, Hillary had worked for the Rose Law Firm (RLF) in Arkansas. The McDougals were among her clients. At first Hillary claimed that her legal work for the McDougals had been minimal, and she denied knowing anything about their crimes. RLF records revealed, however, that she had billed the McDougals for over a dozen meetings or conversations regarding questionable real estate transactions (Coulter 1998; Stewart 1996).

Throughout Clinton's presidency there were numerous occasions when his aides denied press reports or stonewalled official inquiries because they feared RLF records would be uncovered or other dubious activities would be revealed. In the so-called Travelgate scandal, staff members of the White House Travel Office were dismissed. Administration officials said they were ridding the office of corruption, but their plans to divert White House travel business to Clinton friends suggested another motive. In "Filegate," a White House aide was found collecting FBI files on hundreds of Republican Party officials in an effort that appeared aimed at finding information to discredit them. The aide was summarily dismissed. In "Fostergate," aides removed documents from the office of White House lawyer Vince Foster, a former RLF attorney, after he committed suicide. Someone obviously did not want these documents to be disclosed. The conservative press had a field day, circulating rumors that Foster (and others) had been murdered by assassins working on behalf of the Clintons (Conason & Lyons 2000; Stewart 1996; Woodward 1999).

Webster Hubbell, another former RLF lawyer, had been made an associate attorney general in the Clinton administration's Department of Justice. He was forced to resign in the face of a criminal indictment for income tax evasion and mail fraud related to his practice of overbilling clients at the RLF. Hubbell received a prison sentence of nearly two years, but during an eighteen-month period following his resignation he received $500,000 in consulting fees from various Clinton associates. One $100,000 fee was paid by a subsidiary of the Lippo Group, an Indonesia-based conglomerate that was accused of illegally funneling foreign campaign contributions to the Democratic National Committee. Mochtar and James Riady, who had controlling interest in the Lippo Group, had banking interests in Arkansas that dated back to the early 1980s. One of Lippo's clients was the People's Republic of China. Although Clinton said, "I don't believe you can find any evidence that I changed government policy because of a contribution," he did reverse his campaign stance against open trade relations with China and approved the sale of vital missile technology to that nation (quoted in Coulter 1998:241; Stewart 1996; Woodward 1999).

Each of these episodes, taken in isolation, might appear relatively insignificant. But taken as a whole, they begin to add up. Moreover, the Clintons' strategy of first brushing aside accusations, then promising full disclosure while simultaneously frustrating every inquiry, did not serve the president well. According to Stewart, "It would have been relatively easy, early on, to disclose everything and correct the record. But as time passed, the Clintons' drop-by-drop concessions gave credence to their critics and undermined their integrity" (1996:432).

In the long run, President Clinton's sexual misconduct caused him the most political damage. After losing a court challenge, Clinton was required to give a deposition in a sexual harassment lawsuit initiated against him by Paula Jones. In that deposition Clinton was asked about a sexual relationship he had had with a young White House intern, Monica Lewinsky. Under oath, in January 1998, Clinton denied the allegation and then told the U.S. public that he "did not have sexual relations with that woman." Seven months later, in the face of DNA evidence (traces of Clinton's sperm) found on Lewinsky's dress, the president admitted that he had not told the full truth about the Lewinsky affair. (He admitted that he received oral sex, which in his view did not constitute sexual relations.) Questions remained as to whether Clinton had committed perjury in the Jones deposition and in the subsequent testimony he gave before a grand jury, and as to whether he had encouraged Lewinsky to give false testimony as well.

In December 1998 a majority of the House of Representatives passed two articles of impeachment against the president (for perjury and obstruction of justice), making Clinton the first *elected* president ever to be impeached. (Andrew Johnson, who became president after the assassination of Abraham Lincoln in 1865, was the only other president to be impeached.) In February 1999, however, Clinton (like Johnson) was acquitted in the Senate, where the vote fell far short of the two-thirds majority needed to remove the president from office. Nevertheless, the Clinton presidency was severely damaged and Clinton's place in history indelibly tarnished.

The Degradation of Democracy

The scandals of the Clinton administration reinforced the public's cynicism about government, contributing further to the erosion of political legitimacy in the United States. Survey research over the past three decades documents a continued decline in voter turnout and people's confidence in government (Nye et al. 1997). Politicians are among the least-trusted professional groups in the nation (along with journalists and lawyers). Certainly, factors unrelated to political scandals (e.g., concern about taxation, growth in the federal government, antigovernment rhetoric) have contributed significantly to this trend, but few would deny that the events we've been describing in this chapter have helped weaken the social bonds that tie citizens to their political system.

The 2000 election. Then came the 2000 presidential election. During his drive to the presidency, George W. Bush—son of the former president and then governor of Texas—dodged accusations that he had used drugs during his youth (he acknowledged he had been a heavy drinker), and that he had received political favors to enroll in the National Guard to avoid serving in the Vietnam War and had not fulfilled all of his obligations to report for duty. After being defeated in the February New Hampshire primary by decorated war veteran Senator John McCain, Bush knew he had to win the South Carolina primary or his candidacy would be in serious jeopardy (Ackerman 2004; Corn 2003).

South Carolina Bush supporters, whom the Bush campaign claimed were acting on their own, started throwing mud, spreading vicious rumors about McCain. They said that McCain opposed health care legislation that would assist veterans. Not true. They made phone calls posing as pollsters and distributed leaflets, e-mails, and faxes saying that McCain had been brainwashed during his captivity as a prisoner-of-war in Vietnam, that he had fathered a child with a black prostitute, and that he had infected his wife with venereal disease and was responsible for her addiction to drugs. Bush never spoke out against these cruel smears made on his behalf, and he won the primary (Corn 2003).

The November 2000 election against Vice President Al Gore came down to the wire. Both candidates needed to take Florida to give them enough Electoral College votes (270) to win the election. (Each state has as many electoral votes as the total number of its senators and representatives in Congress; the District of Columbia has three votes.) Before the Florida vote came in, Gore was leading Bush by an electoral margin of 267 to 246. Florida has twenty-five electoral votes, and Gore needed only three more to reach the 270 majority that would have given him the presidency. But in a winner-take-all system, a Bush victory in Florida would give him a 271-to-267 victory (Corn 2003).

At 8:00 P.M. Eastern time, all the voting polls closed in Florida, except those in the western "panhandle" of the state, which remained open for another hour because that region was on Central time. The news media called the state, and the election, for Gore. Bush supporters complained that this early media pronouncement discouraged many voters in the ten heavily Republican districts in the panhandle from going to the polls. In a study based on voter turnout in previous elections, John Lott (2003) estimates that this early call for Gore suppressed Bush's vote total by 7,500 to 10,000.

Later that evening, however, the media retracted its call for Gore and pronounced Bush the winner. Although Gore had won the national popular vote by over half a million, the official Florida vote-count first placed Bush ahead by 1,784, just 0.03 percent of the 5.9 million ballots that were recorded. Under Florida law, if the vote margin is less than 0.05 percent, a mandatory recount is required. The initial recount was done inconsistently throughout the state—some of the counties did not actually recount the ballots but merely rechecked the math from election night tabulations—and it reduced Bush's official margin of victory to 327 (Corn 2003).

Besides the panhandle controversy, reports of problems with Florida ballots had been coming in throughout the day, problems that advantaged Bush over Gore. There was the case of the so-called butterfly ballot, which had candidates Bush and Gore on the left side and Reform Party candidate Pat Buchanan on the right. Evidence indicated that many (especially elderly) democratic voters found the ballot confusing, leading them to vote for Buchanan, or for both Buchanan and Gore, when they intended to vote for Gore. These "Democrats for Buchanan" ballots, which would have given Gore an estimated 6,000 to 9,000 additional votes, were forever lost to the vice president (Corn 2003; Dershowitz 2001; Palast 2003).

There were other sources of lost votes that also might have won the election for Gore. Thus the Gore campaign requested an additional *hand recount* in four heavily Democratic counties—Miami-Dade, Broward, Palm Beach, and Volusia—as it was permitted by law to do. It was at this point that the nation was introduced to the problem of antiquated punchcard ballots, which require voters to push a stylus through a perforated hole to dislodge a chad that might be left "hanging" or merely "dimpled." A punchcard system, which is less accurate than an optical-scan system, was used in about 60 percent of Florida precincts, including the four counties that were the target of the Gore recount request. Poor (particularly minority) residents were more likely to have voted with the antiquated technology and hence to have had their ballots discarded. These lost votes were referred to as "undervotes," in comparison to "overvotes," which included instances where a voter marked or punched a ballot and also specified the name of the *same* candidate in the space designated for "write-in" votes (Corn 2003; Dershowitz 2001; Lantigua 2001; Palast 2003).

Kathryn Harris, the Florida secretary of state, was in charge of the Division of Elections that supervised the election process. In spite of the obvious conflict of interest, Harris was also cochair of the Bush campaign in Florida, where George W. Bush's brother Jeb happened to be governor. As the hand recount was still ongoing, Harris predictably exercised her *discretionary* authority to bring the counting to an end within seven days of the election, as she was permitted (but not required) by law to do. Predictably as well, the Gore campaign filed a legal appeal to extend the recount deadline, while the Bush campaign appealed to stop it (Silverman 2002).

As both sides jockeyed for position in the courts, the Gore team received a favorable decision from the Florida Supreme Court, which ruled that a hand recount of the *undervotes* for the entire state should be undertaken. This statewide recount was begun, but it was soon stopped when the Florida court was reversed by the U.S. Supreme Court. In a slim five-to-four decision, the majority sided with the Bush team and decreed the election to be over. Thirty-six days after the initial ballots were cast, Harris certified that Bush had won by 537 votes.

Legal analyst Alan Dershowitz (2001), among others, has characterized the U.S. Supreme Court's decision in *Bush v. Gore* as a case of "supreme injustice." U.S. Supreme Court justices are nominated by the president (and confirmed by the Senate) and are chosen as much for their ideological predilections as their legal expertise. The composition of the 2000 Court clearly favored the Republicans, and many think its decision in *Bush v. Gore* was overtly political.

The basis of the Bush campaign's legal argument was that continuing the hand recount would violate the Fourteenth Amendment of the U.S.

Constitution, which says that a person may not be deprived of "the equal protection of the laws." In what was arguably a partisan interpretation of this clause, the Court ruled that continuing the recount would deprive Bush voters (but not Gore voters) of their right to equal protection. The majority reasoned that since the rules governing the hand recount varied from precinct to precinct—for example, whether or not both "hanging" chads and "dimpled" chads would be counted—the recount would be unfair to those voters whose ballots had been counted by machines before the recount had begun. But, as Dershowitz asks, wouldn't voters whose ballots were *not properly counted* by machines "suffer much more serious violations of their equal-protection rights" (p. 61)? Given the diversity of ballot designs and voting technologies that existed throughout the state (and indeed the entire country), the logical extension of the Court's ruling would have been to invalidate the entire presidential election. As Win McCormack suggests, the Court "speciously ignored the fact that the Florida ballots, prior to any recount, were *already* counted differently, and that the very purpose of recounting was to correct for this discrepancy" (2001:32).

Moreover, the Court's legal logic was inconsistent with the majority justices' own prior rulings. Previously, for instance, the majority of judges had ruled that claims about equal protection violations "should be able to identify with some degree of specificity the alleged victim" and also prove that the contested actions had a clear discriminatory purpose (Dershowitz 2001:77). The majority had also previously ruled that the Court's function is to establish legal precedents, not to declare unique dispositions. Yet in *Bush v. Gore,* the majority wrote: "Our consideration is limited to the present circumstances, for the problem of equal protection in election processes generally presents many complexities" (cited on p. 81). In other words, as Dershowitz pointedly notes, "In future election cases, don't try to hold the Court to what it said in this case, because it decided this case not on general principles applicable to all cases, but on a principle that has never before been recognized by any court and that will never again be recognized by this court" (p. 81).

A year after the election, a consortium of eight media organizations completed an unofficial hand recount of the Florida vote. The consortium concluded that if only the ballots of the four counties contested by Gore had been recounted, Bush would have won the election by about 225 to 400 votes (see Table 10.2). But if ballots for the entire state had been recounted Gore would have won by about 40 to 400 (CNN 2001; Corn 2001, 2003; Fessenden & Broder 2001).

In addition, there is a controversy over the way in which Florida election officials, under the supervision of Secretary of State Harris, tried to deny former convicted felons from voting in the election altogether. Most states deny felons serving time in prison or on parole the right to vote. All

Table 10.2   Florida Recount Vote, 2000 Presidential Election

	Estimated Margin of Victory if Additional Votes Had Been Counted[a]	
	Bush	Gore
Undervotes and overvotes		
Miami-Dade, Broward, Palm Beach, and Volusia Counties	> 225 to 400	
Entire state		> 40 to 400
Other votes		
Counting western-panhandle votes	> 7,500 to 10,000	
Counting butterfly and other confusing ballots[b]		> 6,000 to 12,000
Counting erroneously disqualified voters		> 30,000

Sources: CNN 2001; Corn 2001, 2003; Fessenden & Broder 2001; Lantigua 2001; Lott 2003; Palast 2003; Schechter 2002.

Notes: a. The numbers are highly provisional, but overall, the evidence suggests that were it not for procedural and ballot irregularities, Gore would have won the election.

b. Other ballot problems included the so-called caterpillar or broken ballot, which listed the names of candidates on more than one page of the ballot and, in at least one county, with preelection day instructions that told voters to vote for a candidate on each page.

but fourteen states, however, restore that right upon completion of sentence. Florida is one that does not. In 2000 there were an estimated 50,000 to over 100,000 former felons who had moved to Florida from other states with their voting rights intact. According to Florida court rulings, these individuals should have the right to vote in Florida elections. Nevertheless, the Governor's Office of Executive Clemency mailed these people a notice informing them that they were "required to make application for restoration of civil rights in the state of Florida," in other words, to ask Governor Bush for clemency in order to vote (cited in Palast 2003:40). Few of these individuals followed up on this "requirement"—a requirement that had been ruled null and void by the courts (Lantigua 2001; Uggen & Manza 2002).

As Florida election officials tried to purge their voter registration lists of people they deemed ineligible to vote, thousands of eligible voters were mistakenly removed. Take the case of the so-called former felons from Texas. ChoicePoint, a private firm with close Republican ties, was hired by the state of Florida to provide the names of Texas ex-felons who had moved to Florida. As it turned out, *none* of the approximately 8,000 people who were identified and consequently scrubbed from the voter list had actually been convicted of felonies—they had been convicted of misdemeanors. Under Harris's supervision, the state of Florida also hired Database Technologies (DBT) of Atlanta, since merged into ChoicePoint, to provide them with lists of ineligible voters who had moved to Florida from other states. As it turned out, the DBT lists contained an error rate of 15 percent.

And because African Americans experience higher rates of incarceration than other groups (see Chapter 12), the majority of people targeted by these purging efforts were black. Since African Americans vote overwhelmingly for Democratic candidates, these efforts significantly advantaged Bush (Lantigua 2001; Palast 2003).

Another problem that contributed to the skewed results involved the data criteria that were used to match people who appeared on the DBT/ChoicePoint ex-felon lists with the Florida voter lists. According to a vice president of ChoicePoint, Florida officials instructed the company to provide them with "more names than were actually verified as being a convicted felon" (quoted in Palast 2003:57). One way this was accomplished was to establish criteria that would identify a match even if only part of a name on the ex-felon list matched the name on the voting list. In one case, for example, Reverend Willie David Whiting, a black pastor living in Florida, was confused with Willie J. Whiting, a former felon from Texas, and hence the pastor was denied the opportunity to vote. Florida resident Johnny Jackson Jr. was matched with Texas ex-felon John Fitzgerald Jackson. David Butler of Florida was matched with Ohio ex-felon David Butler Jr. Randall Higgenbotham of Florida was matched with ex-felon Sean Higgenbotham, also of Florida. There were innumerable mistaken matches like these, as well as many misdemeanor offenders who were mistakenly identified as felons, as in the Texas ChoicePoint list. On top of all this, African American residents of Leon County "complained of a Florida Highway Patrol checkpoint on a road leading to a polling place . . . [that] amounted to harassment of black voters" (Lantigua 2001:17). If these types of problems had not occurred, Gore might have received more than 30,000 additional votes (Palast 2003).

Iraqgate, part 2. It was under this cloud of controversy that George W. Bush entered the White House. He had campaigned as a different kind of Republican, a "compassionate conservative," and once in office he demonstrated his compassion for future generations by instituting a tax cut that turned a multibillion-dollar national budget surplus into a massive debt that currently exceeds $7 trillion. In this tax program, the *top 1 percent* of income-earners will receive over *50 percent* of the benefits, while the *bottom 20 percent* will receive just *1 percent* (Citizens for Tax Justice 2002, 2003). And for those who favor radical deregulation of the economy, who do not want the government to serve as a check on corporate power, the Bush administration was a dream come true (Corn 2003; Ivins & Dubose 2003; Kennedy 2003).

The Bush administration also pursued national unilateralism in global affairs, withdrawing from international efforts to develop environmental and weapons disarmament treaties. And although the administration was successful in putting together an international coalition to topple the Taliban regime in Afghanistan after September 11, 2001, it decided to move forward without this cooperation (and in the face of international opposition) in a preemptive war against Saddam Hussein's Iraq, a war that was launched in March 2003.

The primary justification for this war was the administration's claim that Hussein was linked to Al-Qaida in the September 11 attacks *and* that he had a weapons of mass destruction (WMD) program—biological, chemical, and nuclear—that posed an imminent threat to the national security of the United States and the world. Before the war, however, high-ranking administration officials had received intelligence from the CIA informing them that such allegations could not be substantiated. At the time of this writing, no WMD have been found (Ackerman & Foer 2003; Ackerman & Judis 2003; Corn 2003).

Particular controversy arose over the president's January 2003 state-of-the-union speech, in which he told the world that "the British government has learned that Saddam Hussein recently sought significant quantities of uranium from Africa," suggesting that Iraq had reconstituted its nuclear weapons program (quoted in *New Republic* 2003:8). At the time, however, White House officials knew that this claim had been disputed by its own intelligence sources. Indeed, the CIA had previously dispatched former ambassador Joseph Wilson to Niger, the alleged source of the uranium, to investigate this claim. Wilson had concluded, as he later wrote in a scathing *New York Times* op-ed piece published in July 2003, that it had not taken him long to conclude "that the information was erroneous" and "that it was highly doubtful that any such transaction had ever taken place" (quoted in Kerr 2003:A9). Wilson also noted that Vice President Dick Cheney's office had been specifically informed of his findings by the CIA and that these findings had been discounted in order to legitimize the administration's efforts to skew intelligence so as to justify its desire for preemptive war.

Fuel was added to the fire when, a week after Wilson's op-ed piece was published, conservative political columnist Robert Novak reported that a Bush administration official had informed him that Valerie Plame, the wife of Ambassador Wilson, was a CIA operative. Novak's outing of Plame, who had worked undercover for three decades, destroyed her career and endangered her contacts overseas. While Novak's right to publish the information he received is protected by the First Amendment, the initial disclosure itself constitutes a felony crime that is punishable by up to ten years in prison. Wilson believes that the leak of his wife's name was intended to stifle complaints from knowledgeable persons inside the government who knew that the administration had misrepresented intelligence about the threat posed by Iraq. The Justice Department investigation into the source of this leak was still pending at the time of this writing (Beinart 2003; Hutcheson et al. 2003).

By the fall of 2003, as the war in Iraq was still ongoing and casualties on all sides were mounting, a CIA team of weapons inspectors led by David Kay reported that no WMD had been found in Iraq. One vial of ten-year-old botulinum was discovered in an Iraqi scientist's home, and this was touted by administration officials as verification of Iraq's biological weapons program. But this particular strain of botulinum, called *clostridium botulinum okra B,* is the type that is used in material marketed as Botox, for use as a medical treatment for muscle spasms and spasticity and as a cosmetic drug for wrinkles. This material can cause deadly food poisoning but is not very dangerous if inhaled. Moreover, Kay found no evidence that Iraq had succeeded in weaponizing this material (Drogin 2003; Lumpkin 2003).

Kay did find evidence, on the other hand, that Hussein had reconstituted Iraq's missile program, which would have enabled him to project missiles beyond the ninety-mile limit that had been imposed by United Nations (UN) resolutions, and that Hussein had never stopped trying to procure "raw materials, equipment, spare parts, and expertise overseas" for this program (Drogin 2003:26). This is an entirely different matter, however, than suggesting that Iraq had a WMD program in place that constituted an imminent threat requiring an immediate, preemptive war to stop it. Moreover, Kay found evidence that UN weapons inspections during the 1990s had had a significant impact on curtailing Hussein's weapons programs and that, at least for a while, more aggressive inspections might have been a suitable alternative to the controversial war that was waged by the United States.

The Bush administration's controversial actions take on more ominous significance in light of the history of the secret government in the United States that we've been discussing in this chapter. In February 2002, as John Judis reports, "the *New York Times* revealed that the Pentagon was launching a new Office of Strategic Influence to 'provide news items, possibly even false ones, to foreign media organizations.'" The brouhaha over this program of **strategic disinformation**—the intentional dissemination of false information for the purpose of achieving political goals—led the Pentagon to abandon the new office, although Secretary of Defense Donald Rumsfeld said, "You can have the name, but I'm gonna keep doing every single thing that needs to be done—and I have" (cited in Judis 2002:12). But, we have to ask, if the government planned a disinformation campaign for the foreign press, what did it have in mind for us?

We also know that the FBI has been working with local law enforcement agencies to develop profiles of antiwar activists throughout the country, collecting "extensive information on the tactics, training and organiza-tion" of the antiwar movement, and justifying this effort in the name of the war against terrorism. Civil rights organizations are worried about "a return to the well-documented abuses of the 1960s and 1970s" (Lichtblau 2003:A3). According to Anthony Romero, executive director of the American Civil Liberties Union, "The FBI is dangerously targeting Americans who are engaged in nothing more than lawful protest and dis-sent. The line between terrorism and legitimate civil disobedience is [being] blurred" (quoted on p. A3; see also Berlet & Scher 2003).

Meanwhile, dozens of U.S. energy and construction companies have been reaping billions of dollars in profits through government contracts to rebuild Iraq (Margasak 2003; Scherer 2003; Shorrock 2003). Some of these contracts were awarded without competitive bidding and include corpora-tions such as Halliburton that have close ties to the Bush-Cheney adminis-tration (see Chapter 6). Moreover, by the early part of 2004 Halliburton had been cited for *overcharging* the government (and hence the taxpayers) for services rendered by $83.3 million (Mayer 2004). Should the U.S. govern-ment go further and allow foreign investors to assume ownership of Iraqi economic assets (e.g., oil reserves), or should it appropriate Iraqi assets for its own purposes, such actions would be in violation of international law, which forbids an occupying "military power from plundering a defeated nation" (Greider 2003:5).

Finally, in the spring of 2004, reports of widespread abuse, even tor-ture, of Iraqi prisoners held by U.S. military personnel and private contrac-tors in the Abu Ghraib prison outside of Baghdad hit the news (Hersh 2004a, 2004b, 2004c). This shocking revelation has threatened to further undermine the legitimacy of the United States' military intervention in Iraq. Thus the story of presidential scandals and the debasement of democracy continues.

PART 3

Criminal Justice and the Search for Solutions

11

The Police and the Courts

In 1934, Mississippi sheriffs arrested three African Americans they suspected of murder. When one of the men denied the charges, the sheriffs hung him by a rope from the limb of a tree. The suspect continued to deny the charges after he was let down, so the sheriffs hung him from the tree again. When he still refused to confess, the sheriffs whipped him severely and told him they would continue to whip him until he confessed. He finally complied, as did the other two suspects, who were also whipped and pummeled. The three men were convicted and sentenced to death solely on the basis of their confessions. When they appealed their cases, the Mississippi Supreme Court upheld their convictions. The U.S. Supreme Court ruled in *Brown v. Mississippi* (1936), however, that confessions elicited by such obvious methods of brutality were inadmissible in court, and the defendants were cleared. Although *Brown v. Mississippi* was a landmark case, it was an easy one by any reasonable standard of justice (Skolnick & Fyfe 1993).

Nearly three decades later, Ernesto Miranda confessed to charges of kidnapping and rape after being interrogated and tricked by Arizona police, who told him he had been identified in a police lineup when in fact he had not been. Miranda, who had a history of psychological problems, had not been allowed to consult an attorney. It was this case that raised the issue of confessions extracted not through physical coercion but through psychological intimidation, when the accused is questioned in a police-dominated atmosphere, often for a long period of time without rest and without legal representation.

In *Miranda v. Arizona* (1966), the U.S. Supreme Court reversed Miranda's conviction, arguing that his Fifth Amendment right against self-incrimination and Sixth Amendment right to an attorney had been violated. The decision ushered in the now famous Miranda warning that must be given to a suspect once he or she is taken into police custody. The warning requires that before questioning suspects police must inform them that they have the right to remain silent and that any statement they make can and will be used against them in court. Police must also notify suspects that they have a right to an attorney prior to and during questioning, and if they are unable to afford an attorney, they have the right to have one appointed by the court. Finally, police must tell suspects that they may stop answering questions at any time.

The Miranda decision, along with other U.S. Supreme Court rulings, has drawn complaints from law-and-order advocates who believe that criminals are being granted so many rights that they are in effect being allowed to go free. Studies indicate, however, that few defendants have had their convictions reversed on the basis of a Miranda appeal. (Miranda himself was retried, without use of his confession, and convicted.) Moreover, the warning is required only for suspects "interrogated" after being taken into custody, not for individuals who are being "interviewed" during an investigation of a crime. And suspects are allowed to waive their Fifth and Sixth Amendment rights, as they often do (Guy & Huckabee 1988; Reid 1997; Skolnick & Fyfe 1993).

The legal decisions that constitute the law of criminal procedure in the United States are complex and many. Rather than review them here, we want to draw your attention to the competing objectives of law enforcement in a democratic society, to the tension between what Herbert Packer (1964) called the **crime control** and **due process models** of criminal justice. Under the crime control model, the repression of criminal conduct is the primary goal. Under the due process model, legal barriers are erected that make it more difficult to move the accused through the criminal justice system, thereby protecting individuals from arbitrary and abusive governmental authority. That due process protections sometimes work to the advantage of criminals is one price we pay for preserving our liberties. Many people feel that such liberties mean little if their safety is jeopardized. But consider the alternative if constitutional guarantees were abandoned. Few of us would want to live in a society that placed no limitations on governmental authority.

The criminal justice system consists of three broad areas: the police, courts, and corrections. This chapter will focus on the police and courts; Chapters 12 and 13 will focus on prisons and community corrections, respectively. In these chapters we will use our sociological imagination to examine the organizational processes that constitute the practice of criminal justice in the United States. We will consider how criminal justice personnel "do justice" through decisions and actions that are constrained—but not entirely dictated—by the formal properties of the legal system that defines their official mandate.

■ The Modern Police Force

In the United States the modern police force is a highly decentralized and fragmented system that consists of over 17,000 departments, mostly at the local level. Policing is primarily a civilian (i.e., nonmilitary) activity that is separated from the legislative and judicial branches of government. There is no national police force with general jurisdiction, although federal agencies like the Federal Bureau of Investigation (FBI) have jurisdiction over specifically identified federal crimes and over interstate crimes (Gaines & Cordner 1999).

▨ *Historical Background*

The modern police force in the United States evolved from the English system imported by the early American colonists. In medieval England during the eleventh century, local police functions were first carried out through an informal system of unpaid citizen volunteers and political appointees. Early English constables were responsible not only for ensuring law and order, but also for services such as garbage collection. The constables were assisted by night watchmen who patrolled the city ringing bells and assuring everyone that "all was well." By the nineteenth century, however, this informal system of policing could not keep pace with the growing problems of crime, social disorder (e.g., public drunkenness and riots), and poverty (e.g., vagrancy and beggary) that accompanied increasing industrialization and urbanization. In 1829 the first full-time, paid, centrally administered police force was established in London (Critchley 1972; Lundman 1980).

In colonial America, the constable/watch system resembled the informal English model. All males were expected to serve as members of the watch, which carried out both daytime and nighttime patrols. As nineteenth-century U.S. cities began to experience the problems of their English counterparts, a more formal police system emerged. Economic elites supported an expanded police apparatus to quell worker rebellions and clashes between immigrant ethnic groups. According to Sidney Harring (1993), the local police in northern cities were a major antistrike institution employed on behalf of corporations. At the earliest indication of a strike, police would patrol the area and try to prevent workers from "assembling and maintaining an effective picket line" (Harring & McMullin 1975:13). Similarly, in the southern United States the modern police evolved out of a system of citizen slave patrols that were responsible for preventing slave revolts and for retrieving runaway slaves. In 1837 the 100-member slave patrol in Charleston, South Carolina, was perhaps the largest police force in the entire country (Reichel 1999; Walker 1992).

Although the official capacity and legitimate authority to use force is central to the police role, firearms did not become standard equipment until late in the nineteenth century. Moreover, the early police did not command much respect from the public. As Samuel Walker observes, "Juvenile gangs made a sport of throwing rocks at the police or taunting them . . . [and people] who were arrested often fought back. . . . Officers responded by beating hostile citizens into submission . . . and excessive use of force [was] commonplace" (1992:9). In addition, police corruption was endemic to nineteenth-century policing. Failure to enforce laws allowed gambling, prostitution, drunkenness, and other vices to flourish. Pickpockets and other professional thieves were tolerated in return for goods or information. Payoffs to officers on the beat were shared with supervisors, and promotions within the department were bought by bribing superiors. In large cities the police were an integral part of the political machine that governed the city, and positions on the police department were often influenced by political connections.

Policing was an occupation that primarily attracted working-class men and, ironically, most officers were drawn from the very working-class population they were expected to control. Hence conflicting loyalties made them unreliable enforcers of capitalist rule during times of labor unrest. The potential for working-class solidarity was often neutralized, however, by recruitment of officers from a different immigrant ethnic group. And since police were paid at least twice the rate of ordinary workers, they were able to move into more comfortable neighborhoods, "fostering a class identification with the urban elites" (Institute for the Study of Labor and Economic Crisis 1982:27). Police uniforms and a military-style organization and discipline also served to distance the police from the public.

In the early twentieth century, the nature of policing underwent further reform. August Vollmer, a nationally recognized police chief, sought to professionalize police departments by recruiting officers of higher educational background, implementing standardized entrance exams, improving officer training, and using scientific technology in crime investigations (e.g., crime laboratories). Nevertheless, in 1931 the U.S. National Commission on Law Observance and Enforcement (known as the Wickersham Commission) found police forces around the country deficient in these areas. The commission also criticized police departments' frequent use of the "third degree," that is, use of physical coercion to gain information from suspects (Adler et al. 2000).

The Wickersham Commission provided further impetus to police reform, as did the image of the dedicated, morally irreproachable FBI agent that was fostered by longtime FBI director J. Edgar Hoover. By the 1960s "the professional model of the well-trained, highly disciplined, crime-fighting police force had taken hold across the nation" (Adler et al. 2000:110). In big-city police departments recruits were required to have a high school diploma and undergo psychological testing and background checks. Officer training was also improved, and the traditional foot patrol was replaced by patrol cars equipped with two-way radios, enabling a more rapid response to calls for assistance and allowing supervisors to remain in touch with those on the beat. But as departments began to implement more aggressive stop-and-search patrols, police-community relations became increasingly strained. African Americans in particular felt targeted by this police tactic as well as victimized by police brutality. Confrontations between police and citizens precipitated several race riots in the 1960s. Advocates of police reform called for remedial measures, including even higher educational requirements and better training for officers, the hiring of minority officers, greater attention to police-community relations, and more civilian (i.e., nonpolice) oversight over police misconduct.

■ Organizational Styles of Policing

The work of police is subject to a great deal of discretion. **Police discretion** may be defined as "the latitude or flexibility the officer has in deciding how an incident should be handled" (Fuller 1998:85). Discretion, however, is not entirely an individual matter, for it is significantly influenced by a department's **organizational style of policing**, that is, the philosophy and methods that govern its operation. In his book *Varieties of Police Behavior,* James Wilson (1968) identified three different organizational styles: the watchman, legalistic, and service styles.

Watchman-style departments emphasize the order maintenance function of policing. Order maintenance focuses on the informal handling of disputes and measures an officer's success by his or her ability to keep the peace on the beat rather than by the number of arrests made. Minor infractions are often ignored as long as order is maintained, and disorderly citizens are advised to leave the area or go home in order to avoid arrest. Officers are provided with little direct supervision and are encouraged to exercise their own judgment regarding when to enforce the law. Such leeway can be abused, however, if bribery or discrimination become the basis of discretionary decisionmaking.

In contrast, *legalistic-style* departments emphasize a by-the-book approach, whereby officers are expected to enforce the law against all violators. Officers are rewarded for the number of calls they handle and the number of arrests they make, and they are expected to be professional, impersonal, and hard-nosed. According to former Philadelphia and Los Angeles police chief Willie Williams (1996), this approach is often equated with a military style of policing. Individuals with a military penchant for following orders are recruited and trained to respond quickly to solve immediate problems. Their ability to envision how policing can be improved or performed differently is neither expected nor encouraged (Skolnick & Fyfe 1993).

Box 11.1   The Exclusionary Rule

The Fourth Amendment to the U.S. Constitution reads: "The right of the people to be secure in their persons, houses, papers, and effects, against unreasonable searches and seizures, shall not be violated, and no warrants shall issue, but upon probable cause, supported by oath or affirmation, and particularly describing the place to be searched, and the persons or things to be seized." In *Weeks v. United States* (1914), the U.S. Supreme Court ruled that evidence obtained by police in violation of this amendment can be excluded from court. Hence the **exclusionary rule** came into being. However, the Weeks decision applied only to federal cases, and it was not until *Mapp v. Ohio* (1961) that the Court decided that the rule applied to the states as well.

Some law-and-order advocates have criticized the exclusionary rule for allowing guilty suspects to be freed on the basis of a legal technicality. But research indicates that only about 1 to 2 percent of felony arrests are dismissed because of the rule, and these are primarily cases involving drugs, not violent crimes (Davies 1983; Walker 2001). In fact, the rule has led some police departments to improve officer training regarding "what they may and may not do in the area of search and seizure" (Reid 2003:419; Sachs 1982).

The exclusionary rule is a constantly evolving doctrine, however, and the Supreme Court has articulated several exceptions to it. For example, a warrantless search is permissible when the seized object is in *plain view,* and under the *public safety* exception a search may be conducted if police believe the public is in jeopardy. Under the *inevitable discovery* doctrine illegally seized evidence is admissible in court as long as the "police would have found it later by legal methods," and under the *good faith* exception such evidence is admissible if the officer who secured the evidence reasonably believed he or she was "acting in accordance with the law" (Reid 2003:419–420).

Police have also been given considerable latitude to search motor vehicles without a warrant. In a 1996 case, for instance, the Supreme Court unanimously upheld a stop and search in the District of Columbia in which two plainclothes officers in an unmarked vehicle followed two African American men who were driving a new Nissan Pathfinder in a "high drug area." Although the D.C. department prohibits plainclothes officers in unmarked vehicles from enforcing traffic ordinances unless the violation threatens public safety, the officers apparently stopped the Pathfinder for remaining too long at a stop sign. After searching the vehicle, drugs were found. The Court ruled that the seized evidence was admissible even in the absence of probable cause or reasonable suspicion (Cole 1999a).

Police may also conduct a search if the person consents to the search, and officers are not obligated to inform them that "they have the right to say no" (Cole 1999c:23). Wendy Kaminer reports that in Maryland police have been stopping African American motorists and asking them "with varying degrees of belligerency, to 'consent' to thorough searches of their cars. If [the motorists] decline, they are not free to leave; they are forced to wait on the side of the road for the arrival of drug dogs, who sniff and paw through their belongings and sometimes urinate in their cars" (1999:38). In addition, police may conduct sweeps of buses and trains that "exploit the fact that the traveler has nowhere to go," making it difficult to withhold cooperation (Cole 1999c:22).

Finally, *service-style* policing is common in communities with little serious crime, where officers have time to focus on other community needs, such as accident and drug prevention, youth mentoring, and recreational programming. Like watchman departments, service departments emphasize noncustodial methods of intervention: issuing warnings, mediating disputes, counseling, and making referrals to nonpolice agencies. Officers are encouraged to develop positive relationships with the community and to relate to citizens in a personal rather than aloof manner.

Wilson's observations (1968) serve as a useful point of departure for considering two highly significant trends in policing: the increasing militarization of the police and the growing concern with community relations.

Paramilitary policing. Peter Kraska and Victor Kappeler (1997) have documented the growth of what they call **paramilitary police units** (PPUs) in police departments throughout the United States. PPUs are notable for their use of advanced military equipment and technology such as submachine guns, semiautomatic and automatic shotguns, laser sights, nonlethal grenades (e.g., tear gas), battering rams, hydraulic door-jamb spreaders, explosives, and fortified tactical vehicles (e.g., tactical cruisers, military armored personnel carriers). PPU officers "wear black or urban camouflage 'battle dress' uniforms, lace-up combat boots, full body armor, Kelmar helmets, and sometimes goggles with 'ninja' style hoods" (p. 4).

Police administrators and personnel view PPUs as an elite officer core. Most of these units were first "formed in the late 1960s and early 1970s to respond to civil riots, terrorism, barricaded suspects, and hostage situations." Sometimes known as SWAT (special weapons and tactics) teams, PPUs today are involved in a range of high-risk activities that require "a squad of officers trained to be use-force-specialists" who have "an intensified operational focus on either the threatened or the actual use of collective force" (p. 4).

According to Kraska and Kappeler, contemporary PPUs do not merely react to preexisting emergencies but proactively seek out dangerous confrontations and at times even provoke an escalation of violence. For example, one PPU officer described how SWAT teams are used to saturate crime "hot spots" with officers who have, in his words, "bigger guns": "We send out two, two-to-four-men cars . . . [and] look for minor violations and do jump-outs, either on people on the street or automobiles. After we jump-out the second car provides periphery cover with an *ostentatious display of weaponry.* We're sending a clear message: if the shootings don't stop, we'll shoot someone" (p. 10).

PPUs are also being used to serve search warrants and arrest warrants, especially those requiring "no-knock" entries. Some drug raids even take place without warrants, which is apparently legal "if the police have reason to believe that waiting for a warrant would endanger lives or lead to the destruction of evidence" (p. 8). One former PPU member described a drug raid this way: "We did a crack-raid and got in a massive shoot-out in an apartment building. Shots were fired and we riddled a wall with bullets. An MP5 round will go through walls. When we went into the next apartment where the bullets were penetrating, we found a baby crib full of holes; thank god those people weren't home" (p. 9).

Nowadays PPUs are employed not just in the inner-city or large urban areas but in many smaller communities as well. In a national survey, Kraska and Kappeler found that nearly 80 percent of departments with at least 100 officers serving a jurisdiction of at least 50,000 people had PPUs; Kraska and Cubellis (1997) found that 65 percent of departments serving jurisdictions between 25,000 and 50,000 had PPUs. PPUs are also being used as the testing ground for military-style equipment that is being introduced into mainstream policing.

Kraska and Kappeler note that the growth of PPUs coincided with the popularization of the "war" metaphor of crime control in the 1980s (e.g., the war on drugs). If crime, as we are told, is a war, then police may be envisioned as an army that must gain control and maintain occupancy of an area by force. As one police chief explained, "It's going to come to the point that the only people that are going to be able to deal with . . . [the problem of crime] are highly trained tactical teams with proper equipment to go into a neighborhood and clear . . . and hold it" (1997:13).

Community policing. A seemingly contradictory approach to policing is known as **community policing** (CP), which has its origins in the late 1960s and early 1970s. Previously we described CP as a rather general term used to identify law enforcement strategies that put police in closer touch with the community (see Chapter 1). CP aims to promote trust between citizens and the police and to discourage the "us versus them" mentality that is especially prevalent among officers working in minority neighborhoods, where at times police seem unable to distinguish "between law-abiding residents and criminal suspects of the same color" (Williams 1996:224). Andrew Hacker observes that when most "white people hear the cry, 'the police are coming!' . . . it almost always means, 'help is on the way'" (1992:46). But African Americans experience the police quite differently:

> If you have been the victim of a crime, you cannot presume that the police will actually show up; or, if they do, that they will take much note of your losses or suffering. . . . If you are a teenager simply socializing with some friends, the police may order you to disperse and get off the streets. They may turn on a searchlight, order you against a wall. Then comes the command to spread your legs and empty out your pockets, and stand splayed there while they call in your identity over the radio. You may be a college student and sing in a church choir, but that will not overcome the police presumption that you have probably done something they can arrest you for. (p. 51)

Williams argues that CP means "changing the prevailing kick-butt-and-take-no-names policy of too many departments" and assigning officers to work *with* rather than *against* the community (1996:219). In CP, police officials meet regularly with residents, citizen advisory boards, and other community groups to seek input and to learn what the people want from their police. There is less reliance on patrol cars and greater use of foot patrols to provide opportunities for positive encounters, and officers are assigned to the same neighborhood for longer periods of time to enable relationships to develop with residents. As one CP officer in Chicago remarked, "Every day you go out there and you see people washing their cars or mowing their lawns or playing with the kids. If they see you and know you, they trust you." Before CP, one resident said, police "only saw the bad guys, not any of the good guys." Since CP, however, he's seen "a big difference" (Eig 1996:64).

CP replaces an incident-by-incident response to crime with one that seeks comprehensive solutions to community problems. It incorporates a watchman-style emphasis on the informal handling of disputes and a service-style emphasis on prevention and youth programming. Police are considered responsible not only for handling serious crime but also for quality-of-life issues such as noise complaints, graffiti, vagrancy, trash-filled alleys, and abandoned vehicles and buildings. Police, often the first public officials to encounter these problems, can refer them to other government agencies for remedial action. In fact, James Wilson and George Kelling (1996) argue that effective policing requires focusing on the little things that law enforcement often ignores. For instance, broken windows left unrepaired send a message that no one cares about the community, and untended property attracts vandals "out for fun or plunder," setting in motion a downward spiral of increasing disorder that emboldens more serious criminals (p. 202).

According to Gary Cordner, the evidence regarding the overall success of CP is mixed, though "a slight majority of the studies have detected crime decreases, providing reason for optimism" (1999:147). Effective CP, however, is contingent on a number of factors, including the adequacy of non-police follow-up to police referrals, the extent of community participation, the socioeconomic conditions of the community, and the particular type of CP that is being deployed (MacDonald 2002). Robert Taylor and colleagues note that "the police *cannot* be all things to all people. . . . [They] cannot be an isolated group . . . trying to address major social problems without the combined commitment and resources of the entire city" (1998:3).

Moreover, officers are often resistant to CP, viewing it as an abrogation of their role as crime-fighters. Police agencies remain for the most part "cloistered and inflexible. . . . [They] hire the same type of individuals . . . [and] train them the same way" they did before community policing became fashionable (Taylor et al. 1998:3). Police are often reluctant to relinquish their role as experts who possess a monopoly on the skills and knowledge necessary to deal with crime. At times they view CP as a public relations ploy, as a way to enhance their image rather than as a genuine attempt to respond to community concerns (Balkan et al. 1980; Boostrom & Henderson 1983). And even where CP exists, residents may remain unaware or unconvinced that the department has undertaken a serious change in orientation. As Jonathan Eig maintains, for CP to really work, "law-abiding residents must feel that there is a social movement afoot, that it's catching on, and that if they join it they might actually improve their neighborhoods. Criminals, in turn, have got to notice that police become much more effective when they have the eyes and ears of neighbors working for them" (1996:68).

Critics of CP believe it is naive to think that more police contact with residents will necessarily improve relationships. What it may do is increase opportunities for hostile interactions. When you give officers license to exercise discretion on their beats, you may be inviting them "to use force against people who threaten the tranquility of that neighborhood" (Anderson 1999:51). According to Kraska and Kappeler (1997), CP and PPU are not alternative but *complementary* policing strategies. In fact, a majority of the police commanders they interviewed believed that it will become increasingly necessary for PPUs to secure neighborhoods and clear them of their unruly elements before CP will even have a chance to work.

■ Police Culture and Doing Police Work

Despite the CP movement, the occupational culture of most police departments has remained fairly stable. According to Jerome Skolnick and James Fyfe (1993), two principal features of police work—danger and authority—combine to produce a distinctive outlook or **working personality** that guides the values, understandings, and behavior of officers, sometimes leading to admirable valor but sometimes leading to brutality or excessive use of force. As James Ahern notes, "The day the new recruit walks through the doors of the police academy he leaves society behind to enter a profession that does more than give him a job, it defines who he is. For all the years he remains . . . he will be a cop" (1972:3).

Although the job-related death rate for police officers is well below that of several other occupations (e.g., farming, construction, mining), police are constantly aware of the potential dangers they face (Bayley & Bittner 1999). Police role calls regularly conclude with the admonition "stay safe out there." As one officer said, "Most of the time this job is boring. . . . You just sit behind the wheel and go where they tell you. . . . But . . . you never forget that the next call you get or car you stop might be your last. . . . You know there's one hell of a lotta people out there who'd love to [knock] off a cop" (Van Maanen 1995:228–229). While officers are weary of colleagues who are hotheads or "hardchargers" (those who seek out and are overzealous in their willingness to rush into dangerous situations), most agree that police work requires courage and a willingness to take risks, that it is not for the fainthearted (Herbert 1998).

In addition, officers believe that both their safety and the effective performance of their job require that citizens respect their authority, for to some extent every stop, frisk, search, arrest, and handcuffing "involves an imposition of force on an essentially unwilling person, no matter how compliant" (Skolnick & Fyfe 1993:94). Suspects are not always compliant, however. Although shootings of officers are rare, police continually deal with "people who are willing to fight, struggle, hit, stab, spit, bite, tear, hurl, hide, and run. . . . All except the rawest rookie can show scars on their bodies from continual encounters with low-level violence" (Bayley & Bittner 1999:229). Hence police may at times decide to use force preemptively to establish control of a situation *before* it gets out of hand. In fact, one study found that nearly half of all incidents of police use of excessive force occurred in response to mere verbal defiance by a suspect (Reiss 1968).

Those who resist police demands for compliance can expect to receive some "payback." As the Los Angeles Police Department (LAPD) dispatcher who radioed for an ambulance following the police pummeling of Rodney King said, "They should know better than to run, they are going to pay a price when they do that" (Herbert 1998:359). King had taken police on a high-speed car chase after refusing to submit to a police stop. He was finally forced to the side of the road and ordered out of his vehicle. Four officers, two wielding metal nightsticks, administered dozens of blows while about ten other officers looked on. In another incident, one involving the injury of an LAPD officer, police intensified their surveillance of the community for several weeks, "looking for any pretense to make arrests . . . [in order] to reestablish a sense of police control over an unruly space" (p. 360).

The nature of police work also encourages officers to be suspicious, to be on guard for behavior that seems out of the ordinary. For example, a person wearing a coat on a warm day may be hiding a sawed-off shotgun or stolen goods, a dirty car with clean license plates (or vice versa) may indicate a stolen vehicle, or a white person in a black neighborhood may be attempting to buy drugs. Boundaries of neighborhoods are often heavily patrolled to prevent anyone from straying out of place, especially when it's lower-class or minority youths who are crossing over into higher-class or white areas. People out of place, police think, must be up to no good (Skolnick & Fyfe 1993; Werthman & Piliavin 1967).

Police suspiciousness often leads to the development of stereotypes that identify certain types of people as **symbolic assailants**, that is, "as persons whose gestures, language, or attire" trigger suspicion (Skolnick & Fyfe 1993:97). Unfortunately, as we have noted, minority racial status can mark one as a symbolic assailant (see Chapter 7). In 1995, for instance, Earl Graves Jr., an African American business executive, was exiting a commuter train in Manhattan, New York, when he was grabbed and frisked by two police officers. The officers were looking for a 5' 10" tall African American male suspect with a mustache. Graves, however, stood 6' 4" and had no mustache (Stout 1995).

In Los Angeles, Christopher Darden (1996), the African American prosecutor in the O.J. Simpson murder trial, learned of the racism in the LAPD when he went to work for the Special Investigation Division of the district attorney's office in 1988:

> Like any black person in L.A., I could feel the antagonism between African Americans and the police, but I didn't think a lot about it until it was my job to investigate and prosecute the police. . . . Most black men knew what it was like to be driving lawfully down some street when you caught the eye of a police officer, who spun around and pulled you over . . . looking for the pile of rock cocaine and the semiautomatic rifle that every black man obviously carries wherever he goes. . . . You knew what the real crime was: suspicion of being black. And there were other stories too: stories of people beaten, kicked, and knocked around by LAPD officers; stories of a police officer who planted so much evidence his colleagues called him Farmer; stories of cops who flat-out lied on the stand to get a conviction. There were even stories of racist cops, guys who collected Nazi paraphernalia and tossed around various racial epithets like gossip at a barbershop. (pp. 96–97)

No wonder it was not difficult for many (including the Simpson jurors) to believe that LAPD officer Mark Fuhrman might have planted the bloody glove that linked Simpson to the murder of Nicole Brown Simpson and Ronald Goldman (see Chapter 1). Fuhrman's racist attitudes and propensity to use excessive force were well known. Willie Williams, who served as LAPD police chief from 1992 to 1997, estimates that at the time there were about 200 to 300 officers like Fuhrman on the LAPD, "a small but significant number" (1996:262). He believes, however, that more was "being done in L.A. than ever before to screen out and evaluate police candidates, and to identify and deal with rogue cops. . . . Already I suspect they are less inclined to say certain things on the street or commit certain acts than the Mark Fuhrmans of the department were a decade or two ago" (p. 266).

▮ *Racial Profiling*

The experience of African Americans that is described by Darden has continued to receive media attention and has become known as "driving while black," or in Earl Graves's case, "walking while black" (Meeks 2000; Russell 2003). Also known as **racial profiling**, this practice entails police targeting of particular groups for more intrusive law enforcement because of their race, ethnicity, or national origin. Racial profiling has its roots in the more general practice of criminal profiling in which police officers use demographic traits of *known* offenders to identity *potential* offenders. Individuals who possess these traits then come under closer scrutiny because they fit the profile of someone who *might* commit a crime.

The 1992 case of Robert Wilkins, an African American attorney from Maryland, was significant in bringing the problem of racial profiling to the forefront of public attention. Wilkins was returning home from a family funeral in Chicago with his aunt, uncle, and cousin, Norman El-Amin. El-Amin was at the wheel of their rented Cadillac when they were stopped by a white state trooper for speeding on Interstate 68 in western Maryland. After El-Amin, with Wilkins's encouragement, refused the officer's request to search the car for contraband, the trooper called for a drug-sniffing police dog. Wilkins and his relatives were forced to stand on the side of the road in the rain while the dog searched for the nonexistent drugs. After no drugs were found, El-Amin was issued a $105 traffic ticket for speeding (Cole 1999b; Meeks 2000).

With the assistance of the American Civil Liberties Union (ACLU) of Maryland, Wilkins and his family sued the state of Maryland and in 1995 received a $95,600 settlement (including legal costs). As part of the settlement, the Maryland State Police (MSP) agreed to conduct a comprehensive investigation of driver stops on Interstates 68 and 95. The completed study disclosed that African American motorists were, in fact, disproportionately singled out for police stops and searches. Over 70 percent of the drivers stopped and searched by the MSP between 1995 and 1997 were black, even though blacks constituted just 17 percent of the motorists in the state, and even though blacks were no more likely than whites to have violated a traffic code or have illegal substances found in their vehicles (ACLU 1995; Lynch & Schuck 2003; Russell 2003).

By 2001, sixteen states had mandated the collection of race and ethnicity data on the drivers who were stopped by the state highway patrol, and twenty-three other states required such collection under specific circumstances (e.g., in cases where the driver was arrested or an officer used force to subdue the suspect). Some police officers, however, have tried to circumvent this requirement. In New Jersey, for example, 164 officers were cited by the New Jersey Attorney General's Office for regularly falsifying or concealing data so as to continue the practice of racial profiling without being reprimanded for it (Russell 2003).

Be that as it may, research suggests that nonwhite motorists are more likely to be stopped than whites. In a study of the New Jersey Turnpike, black drivers accounted for 35 percent of the stops, even though they constituted just 14 percent of all drivers and 15 percent of those who were speeding; and black and Hispanic drivers accounted for about 80 percent of the vehicles that were searched (Kocieniewski & Hanley 2000; Robinson 2000). In a survey of over a thousand stops on Interstate 95 in Florida conducted by the *Orlando Sentinel,* it was found that about 70 percent of those who were stopped were black or Hispanic, even though non-whites constituted about 5 percent of the motorists (Brazil & Berry 1992; Curtis 1992).

Nor, as we suggested earlier, is racial profiling confined to drivers. An investigation of "stop and frisk" practices in New York City in 1998 and 1999 found that over half of the pedestrians stopped by the police were black, a rate that is double the proportion of the New York population that is black. Moreover, nearly two-thirds of the pedestrians stopped by the special Street Crime Unit of the New York Police Department (NYPD) were black. And in precincts where blacks and Hispanics each constituted less than a tenth of the population, they were stopped 30 percent and 23 percent of the time, respectively (Spitzer 1999).

Proponents of racial profiling contend the practice is necessary for effective law enforcement, yet research questions the efficacy of this procedure. Of importance here is whether or not the stop leads to the discovery of contraband or a crime, the so-called hit rate. According to David Harris, "All the studies . . . [that] allow for the calculation of hit rates . . . show higher hit rates *not for blacks and Latinos, but for whites.* In other words, officers 'hit' less often when they use race or ethnic appearance to decide which persons seem suspicious enough to merit stops and searches than they do when they use suspicious behavior and not race as their way of selecting suspects" (2003:82, emphasis added).

▪ Minorities in Policing

In 1805, New Orleans became the first U.S. city to hire African Americans as police officers. "Free men of color," who were required to be supervised by white officers, were used to apprehend runaway slaves and to control the New Orleans slave population (Dulaney 1996). As late as the 1930s and 1940s, however, African Americans represented less than 1 percent of all officers in the country. It was not until the racial turmoil of the 1960s that sufficient political pressure was mounted to integrate police departments in the United States. The Equal Opportunity Act of 1972 made the Civil Rights Act of 1964 applicable to local police departments that had previously excluded people of color (and women) from patrol work and promotions in rank. By 2000 African Americans constituted about 12 percent of

all full-time police officers, and racial and ethnic minorities overall constituted less than 25 percent (Free 1996; Hickman & Reaves 2003).

Nevertheless, the majority of African American officers work in large-
city departments and in the South, where the percentage of the population
that is black is higher than the national average. Hence in these departments
African Americans remain underrepresented relative to the proportion of
the local labor pool they constitute. Data on other minority groups indicate
that they too are underrepresented in policing. And despite the presence of
some high-profile minority police chiefs, people of color remain underrepresented in the higher ranks (Free 1996).

Although one study of the NYPD found that over half of black officers
felt they were treated equally to whites (Leinen 1984), other research has
uncovered much discontent. African American officers, for example, have
reported being more closely supervised and more frequently sanctioned for
their mistakes. Common complaints include undeserved negative performance evaluations, fewer preferable assignments, less support from colleagues, and assignment only to minority neighborhoods (Fletcher 1995;
Free 1996; Johnson 1989). Studies have also found that people of color
(and women) were often segregated during roll calls and were unlikely to
socialize with white officers when off duty (Haarr 1997; Williams 1988). In
the LAPD, racial slurs during roll calls and patrol-car radio transmissions
were at one time commonplace, as were racist cartoons posted on locker-
room bulletin boards (Independent Commission on the LAPD 1991; Larsen
1991).

Furthermore, some research indicates that black *male* officers are more
likely than female officers (white or black) to be viewed as competent professionals by white male police. It seems that black men do not threaten the
masculine mystique of policing in the way that women police do. Black
women, however, who constitute over a third of women officers, are
viewed more negatively than white women officers by both white and black
male police. Black male officers sometimes appear even more hostile than
white male officers to black women police, in part because they compete
with black women for scarce affirmative action slots (Dulaney 1996;
Fletcher 1995; Martin 1994; Texeira 2002).

Many people have hoped that the quality of police, especially in minority neighborhoods, would be improved if people of color were to achieve
greater representation in the policing profession. Minority officers are less
likely than white officers to be viewed by minority residents as intruders,
and hence they may legitimate the presence of law enforcement in the community. Minority police also serve as role models for minority youths,
reminding them that legitimate employment opportunities are available to
them; and they help dispel the societal stereotype of criminals as people of

color, making it more difficult for prejudiced white officers to persist in making this stereotype an integral part of police culture. In addition, minority officers have been active in revising departmental policies aimed at minimizing police use of excessive force (Free 1996; Taylor Greene 1994).

Still, there are limits to the impact that minorities can have on policing, and numerous factors affect their influence. In places "where black officers are disliked by their (black) peers and shunned by racist colleagues, they have a minimal impact." In places "where they are respected and appreciated, they may make a difference. . . . [But] good rapport between black officers and citizens may not be able to overcome [the] socioeconomic factors that contribute" to crime (Taylor Greene 2003:207–208). And minority police are not, of course, confined to minority communities. Overall, there is little evidence that people of color actually do policing differently than whites. Black and white officers, for example, are about as likely to fire their weapons, use excessive force, and make arrests. It appears that the organizational style of a department is more important than race in accounting for officers' behavior (Black 1980; Fyfe 1981; Walker et al. 2004).

■ Doing Gender in Policing

Historically, women's involvement in policing overlapped with the job of social worker, so historians are uncertain about who was actually the first woman to be sworn in as an officer in the United States. Some credit Alice Stebbin Wells, who was sworn into the ranks of the LAPD in 1910, but others cite Lola Baldwin, who worked for the police department in Portland, Oregon, in 1905. In either case, for several decades thereafter there were very few women in policing, and those on the force tended to be assigned cases involving children and other women. Not until 1968, in the city of Indianapolis, was a woman assigned patrol duties (*History of Women in Policing* 2003; Martin & Jurik 1996).

In the 1970s, women benefited from the same civil rights and employment opportunity legislation as people of color. In addition, "the Crime Control Act of 1973 required police departments with 50 or more employees that received $25,000 or more in federal grants to implement equal employment programs for women or face withdrawal of funds" (Martin & Jurik 1996:53). Height and weight requirements for officers were lowered, and physical tests that emphasized upper-body strength were replaced by tests that assessed health and fitness. Still, in 2000 women accounted for little over 10 percent of all full-time officers in the United States (Hickman & Reaves 2003).

Susan Martin and Nancy Jurik observe that "few occupations . . . have resisted integration of women as vigorously as policing" (1996:63). Male officers believe that women officers undermine their "public image, citizen respect, social status, and group solidarity" (Gold 2000:160). Traditionally,

policing has been an occupation that men could use as a resource for demonstrating or "doing masculinity," for differentiating maleness from femaleness (see Chapter 8). Women's participation challenges male officers' belief that "real policing" is work that only "real men" can do. Thus women have often been assigned to desk duties and community relations and to cases involving rape and domestic violence. Women have also been more likely than men to be assigned to work the first shift, where writing speeding tickets, handling missing persons calls, and other light-duty work are common; and they've been more likely to be assigned to one-person patrol cars that minimize their contact with other officers. Veteran officers have been reluctant to work with women on patrol, have refused to teach them the skills they routinely impart to men, and have not responded quickly when women needed backup. Supervisors have often assigned women to work dangerous foot beats alone (while assigning men in pairs), given lower performance evaluations to women, and ignored sexual harassment and mistreatment of women by male colleagues. In addition, the "locker room" culture of police departments has traditionally been filled with crude talk about sex and women's bodies that female officers often find demeaning (Fletcher 1995; Haarr 1997; Morash & Haarr 1995; Texeira 2002).

In an extensive survey of women police officers in Texas, 77 percent of the respondents reported that they received "fair treatment" from other women officers, while only 57 percent reported that they received fair treatment from male officers (Taylor Greene & del Carmen 2002). Other research, however, indicated that negative attitudes toward women officers were strongest among older men who had entered policing in an earlier era of more traditional gender norms (Hayes 1998).

Most criminologists have concluded that female police officers are as capable as male officers. Some researchers found that women were less proficient than men in the use of firearms and that they made fewer arrests. But women received fewer citizen complaints and appeared more effective than men in using interpersonal skills to deescalate conflict situations without having to use force or make an arrest (Hale & Wyland 1999; Martin & Jurik 1996).

Women have adapted to the male-dominated environment of policing in different ways. Martin (1980) distinguishes between the *police*women and police*women* strategies. *Police*women try to gain acceptance from their male colleagues by acting like them, by adopting an aggressive or hard-nosed style. This strategy entails the risk of being rejected as unfeminine or of being labeled a "dyke" or "bitch." Police*women,* on the other hand, employ a more traditional feminine style by being reluctant to assert their authority or use force and by deferring to male partners when on patrol. This strategy encourages male officers to adopt a paternalistic or protective stance that reinforces their view that women are not cut out for real police work.

Increasingly, women officers have struck a balance between traditional femininity and masculinity by projecting an image of themselves as both team players and skilled professionals (Martin & Jurik 1996). They use humor to develop camaraderie with male colleagues and to thwart unwelcome sexual advances and harassment. Nevertheless, women officers do undermine the (often sexist) bonding rituals of all-male departments, and since the presence of women increases the frequency of sexual intimacy between officers, it intensifies the sexual competition between men. Although progress to date has been slow, some women have successfully climbed the police hierarchy. Currently there are about 150 women nationwide who serve as police chiefs (Karush 2003).

■ Police Corruption and Other Malfeasance

When Frank Serpico joined the NYPD in 1959, he had every intention of becoming a dedicated and loyal police officer. He soon learned, however, that the formal departmental regulations prohibiting corruption and bribery were in conflict with the informal norms of the NYPD culture. When he refused to accept his part of the "take," he was ostracized by his corrupt colleagues and forced to work alone. He was eventually shot and seriously injured during a drug raid, after his fellow officers failed to provide him with timely backup (Maas 1973).

Serpico became the most famous police whistle-blower in U.S. history, and his story led to the most well-known official inquiry into police corruption, the **Knapp Commission** (1972), headed by Judge Whitman Knapp. The Knapp Commission revealed extensive, routine payoffs among NYPD plainclothes officers involved in gambling and narcotics enforcement. Corruption among uniformed patrol officers was less lucrative but included payoffs from retail businessmen and construction-site operators in exchange for nonenforcement of city ordinances. Patrol officers also received money from traffic violators and prostitutes hoping to avoid legal sanction, from tow-truck operators who received business tips from officers investigating accidents, and from defendants trying to get their cases fixed. The commission found that higher-ranking officers and police officials were on the take as well (see Chambliss 1988).

The Knapp Commission distinguished between two general categories of corrupt officers: "grass-eaters" and "meat-eaters." The more numerous grass-eaters were less aggressive and accepted the smaller gratuities that happened to come their way. The meat-eaters, on the other hand, aggressively sought out ever-increasing opportunities for corrupt financial gain. Though fewer in number, their biweekly or monthly take yielded of thousands of dollars.

More recently, the **Mollen Commission** (1994), in its investigation of NYPD corruption, under the direction of Judge Milton Mollen, uncovered numerous instances of police offering protection to drug dealers, stealing drugs from dealers, and selling and using drugs. Much of this corruption was collaborative group activity, called "crew corruption" by the commission. The commission also identified a corrupt practice known as **testilying**, whereby officers give false testimony in court to cover up violations of due process law during the collection of evidence (see Box 11.1). One officer "who was working undercover for the . . . Commission said he feared that if he did not lie, the other cops would immediately suspect that he was working [for the commission] . . . because *real cops do lie*" (Dershowitz 1996:57). Similarly, an FBI investigation of New York state troopers between 1984 and 1992 found routine faking of fingerprint evidence, whereby police take a suspect's fingerprints from a police-station booking card or an object the suspect has touched, and then claim the fingerprints were found at the crime scene. Such practices are justified by even "honest" officers when they believe that the defendant really is guilty (see Barker & Carter 1999; Hunt & Manning 1991).

In the late 1990s, Los Angeles's Rampart area CRASH antigang unit thrust the LAPD into the news. (CRASH is an acronym for "Community Resources Against Street Hoodlums.") In the name of fighting a "war on gangs," these officers routinely planted evidence and perjured themselves to get convictions. They also stole and sold drugs, stole money, and engaged in unjustified beatings and even shootings of suspects. Nearly thirty officers were implicated in these actions and criminal charges were filed against some of them. The most well-known case involved officer Rafael Perez, who pled guilty to eight felony counts and cooperated in the investigation of others in exchange for a five-year prison term. Over 100 convictions stemming from the Rampart unit's arrests have been overturned and scores of lawsuits have been filed against the city of Los Angeles that will cost taxpayers millions of dollars (Gupta 2003; Rampart Independent Review Panel 2002).

Nationwide, according to former FBI director Louis Freeh, the FBI has "arrested police officers for corruption in every region of the nation, in large, medium-sized and small cities, towns, and villages; from the inner city precincts to rural sheriff's departments" (U.S. Department of Justice 1998). Between 1994 and 1997 alone, over 500 police officers were convicted of corruption. Most of these convictions involved illegal drugs.

The types of corrupt practices we've been discussing, though perpetrated by a minority of officers, persist because of the informal **code of silence** that the majority of police observe. Officers are understandably reluctant to inform on one another. As Jerome Skolnick and James Fyfe note, "It is not easy in any group to be identified as the rat, the squealer, the busybody, the one person who cannot be trusted. . . . Any member of any group who considers becoming a whistle-blower must know that however laudable one's motives, doing so will forever change one's own life and status in the group" (1993:111). The most practical path to follow is the one of least resistance: "stay out of trouble" and "don't make waves." Nobody's perfect, and drawing attention to another may expose one's own derelictions. Indeed, much of the "silent majority" is itself implicated in the kind of petty corruption that is commonplace among police. As former LAPD officer Joseph Wambaugh writes of one officer in his novel *The Choirboys:* He "had accepted a thousand packs of cigarettes and as many free meals in his time. And though he had bought enough clothing at wholesale prices to dress a dozen movie stars, he had never even considered taking a five dollar bill nor was one ever offered except once when he stopped a Chicago grocer in Los Angeles on vacation" (1975:65).

Moreover, there's always some outraged citizen who's going to file a complaint against you, or some reform-minded administrator who'll "come down on you for breaking some rules" (Van Maanen 1995:235). The most important thing is not to lose the support of one's colleagues, for an officer's very life depends on others' willingness to provide immediate and unquestioned backup. As one officer said, "I'll put up with a hell of a lot from guys working this sector. I don't care if they're on the take, mean or just don't do any more than they have to. . . . But if some sonfabitch isn't around on a help-the-officer call or shows up after everybody else in the city has already been there, I don't want him working around me" (p. 233).

Police sexual misconduct. Although police are politically a conservative lot, they do not necessarily uphold traditional "family" values. Studies indicate, for example, that at least half of married male police officers have had adulterous sexual relationships and about a third of officers have engaged in sexual activity while on duty (Baker 1985; Barker 1986). Moreover, there are many instances where officers have engaged in **police sexual misconduct** (PSM), that is, where they have abused their authority to seek sexual gratification.

Based on interviews with police officers and supervisors in five states, Allen Sapp (1986) identified several types of PSM. *Sexually motivated, nonsexual* contacts, for example, involve male officers who use their position of power to meet potential sexual partners (e.g., by making unwarranted traffic stops of female motorists or by making unnecessary "callbacks" to female crime victims). *Sexually voyeuristic* contacts involve attempts by male officers to view females in various stages of nudity (e.g., by patrolling areas where women are known to leave their drapes or blinds open while disrobing or by seeking out parked cars in areas known to be frequented by lovers). In one New York City case in 1996, a male officer tore a woman's T-shirt, exposing her breasts, in the course of arresting her for disorderly conduct. At the police station she was handcuffed to a holding cage for three hours, her breasts still exposed, while officers were permitted to observe and comment on her nudity and a male prisoner masturbated (Sontag & Barry 1997).

PSM also occurs when male officers make unnecessary body searches of female suspects and when they have sex with female offenders (including adolescent runaways, truants, and delinquents) in exchange for nonenforcement of the law. Sometimes male undercover officers have sex with prostitutes before making an arrest. As one officer said, "If the whore claims otherwise, no one believes her anyway since they think she is just trying to get her case tossed out." Finally, there are citizen-initiated contacts by police groupies who are "sexually attracted to the uniform, weapons, or power of the police officer" (Sapp 1986:91–92).

Kraska and Kappeler (1995) warn against dismissing the problem of PSM as one of women trading sexual favors or male officers passively confronting sexual opportunities they cannot resist, for much PSM entails the coercive abuse of power and outright force. In a study of PSM based on articles that appeared in *USA Today* and in records from Federal District Court, Kraska and Kappeler found that over half of PSM cases involved unnecessary strip searches of female suspects and nearly a third involved rape or sexual assault.

Police brutality and use of deadly force. Dramatic drops in New York City's violent crime rate in the 1990s have been attributed to, among other things, the use of computerized maps to identify crime "hot spots," improved police intelligence, and "zero-tolerance" policing that empha- sizes aggressive stop-and-search tactics and the arrest of minor law viola- tors (Anderson 1999; Greene 1999; see Chapter 2). At the same time, civil- ian complaints of harassment and brutality by NYPD officers have risen dramatically. In one of the most notorious cases, Abner Louima, a Haitian immigrant, was arrested for disorderly conduct. At the police station Louima was beaten and sodomized by NYPD officers with a toilet plunger, tearing a hole through his lower intestine and bruising his bladder.

Some use of physical force by police is necessary and inevitable. About 17 percent of adult arrests involve such force (beyond application of handcuffs), and these cases are most likely to occur when the suspect is resisting (Garner & Maxwell 1999). The most common injuries incurred by suspects are bruises, abrasions, and lacerations. "Officers are trained to use force progressively along a continuum," and official policy requires them to apply "the least amount of force necessary to accomplish their goals" (Adams 1999:5). **Police brutality** occurs when officers intentionally exceed their legal authority to use force. Research suggests that a minority of officers are responsible for the bulk of the brutality, although the code of silence often protects the offenders, allowing them to persist in their wrongdoing (Independent Commission on the LAPD 1991).

In a landmark study conducted in 1966, a team of researchers under the direction of Albert Reiss (1980) spent seven weeks observing patrol offi- cers' encounters with citizens (crime victims, witnesses, and suspects) in Boston, Chicago, and Washington, D.C. The observers found that just 1 percent of these encounters involved instances of excessive force. (Most likely the percentage would have been higher had the police not known they were being watched.) Excluding encounters with victims and witness- es, about 3 percent of encounters with *suspects* involved excessive force. Although these percentages appear low, they add up to a significant number of cases, making police brutality, according to Reiss, far from rare.

Police shootings of citizens constitute another dimension of police use of force. Fyfe (1982) distinguishes between **elective** and **nonelective shootings**. Elective shootings involve situations in which the officer shoots when the suspect poses little or no risk to the officer or others. Nonelective shootings involve situations where "the officer has little real choice but to shoot or to risk death or serious injury to himself or others" (p. 710). According to Fyfe (1988), nonelective shootings are more likely than elec- tive shootings to be influenced by factors *external* to the police, such as the type and amount of crime in a community and the proclivities of the crimi- nal population in that area. Elective shootings, on the other hand, are more likely to be influenced by *internal* factors, such as a department's formal policies and informal culture, the tactical training given to officers, and the nonlethal technologies that are available to subdue resisting suspects (e.g., electronic stun guns).

Shooting incidents, however, rarely fall clearly into one category or the other. As Hugh Barlow (1996) observes, an officer may in hindsight regard an encounter as closer to an elective shooting than he or she actually did at the time of the shooting itself. Moreover, "persons who later hear the 'facts' may interpret a situation differently from either the officer involved or any witness. . . . [This makes it] difficult . . . to construct a picture of an encounter that does justice to both the subjective interpretations of participants and the objective characteristics of the event" (p. 338). Fyfe (1988), who was formerly an NYPD lieutenant, notes that in his experience the more ambiguous shooting situations occurred when officers had been encouraged by supervisors and peers "to take charge of threatening situations quickly with as little assistance (and as little inconvenience to colleagues) as possible." In contrast, ambiguous shootings were less likely when officers were encouraged "to use caution, to take cover, and to search for nonlethal means of resolving potential violence" (p. 185).

Fyfe examined police shooting data from New York City (1971–1975), Philadelphia (1971–1975), and Chicago (1974–1978). In Philadelphia and Chicago, 21 and 25 percent of shooting incidents, respectively, involved citizens who were unarmed and made no threat or attempt to attack the police or other person. In New York, only 8.5 percent of shootings involved unarmed individuals. Fyfe observes that in New York the NYPD operated under a "defense of life only" policy that limited the use of deadly force. In Philadelphia and Chicago, on the other hand, "police were given relatively more freedom to use their guns in elective situations" (p. 186; see White 2001).

In 1985 the U.S. Supreme Court, in *Tennessee v. Garner,* restricted the type of police shootings that were constitutionally permissible. The case involved a Memphis police officer who had shot and killed Edward Garner, an unarmed, fifteen-year-old African American youth who had been fleeing from the police after breaking into an unoccupied residence. The shooting was consistent with the Memphis department's policy on the shooting of fleeing felons.

Data on Memphis police shootings showed that Memphis police officers were much more likely to shoot unarmed black suspects than unarmed white suspects (Fyfe 1988). The Court ruled, however, that Garner's rights had been violated not because of discrimination but because the shooting had violated his Fourth Amendment right against unreasonable seizure (see Box 11.1). According to the Court, police use of deadly force should be restricted to cases where "the officer has probable cause to believe that the suspect poses a significant threat of death or serious physical injury to the officer or others" (cited in Walker 1996:144). The Garner decision invalidated the police shooting guidelines of some departments in thirty-four states, although most large-city departments had already adopted the more restrictive policy on their own.

The issue of race remains one of the most salient issues concerning police shooting of suspects, as African Americans are disproportionately targeted in these incidents (Fyfe 1988). It is not white officers, however, but black officers who are *proportionately* more likely to be involved in both the on-duty and off-duty shootings of blacks. (Since there are more white officers, they account for more such shootings overall.) Fyfe attributes this pattern to the fact that black officers are more likely to work and live in neighborhoods where "their chances of encountering [dangerous] situations leading to shooting, justifiable or otherwise, [are] far greater" (p. 196). Fyfe also notes that in high-crime areas, police officers regardless of race are more likely to shoot preemptively at suspects who turn out to be unarmed. These officers, he observes, have greater reason to fear that any furtive movement by the suspect is life-threatening. Thus, Fyfe says, it is no surprise that internal departmental reviews give the benefit of the doubt to police who shoot suspects in neighborhoods perceived as dangerous.

At the same time, research has found higher rates of police shootings of suspects in cities with greater economic/racial inequality and higher percentages of black residents, regardless of the level of crime (Jacobs & O'Brien 1998; Sorensen et al. 1993). Such findings have often been interpreted in terms of Hubert Blalock's **power-threat theory** (1967) (sometimes referred to as minority group-threat theory): When dominant groups or public officials are threatened by a large racial underclass, they are more likely to tolerate, condone, and exercise force to maintain social order.

Although some criminologists believe that the problem of police brutality and shootings has diminished over the past few decades (Sherman 1986; Skolnick & Fyfe 1993), others point to the more than 2,000 civilian deaths in the 1990s that are indicative of an ongoing pattern of official abuse (Gupta 2004). The Rodney King beating, captured on videotape, led even President George H. W. Bush to remark, "How can I explain this to my grandchildren?" (quoted in Skolnick & Fyfe 1993:12). The King beating did not occur in Mississippi in 1934 but in Los Angeles in 1991. The Abner Louima beating occurred in New York in 1997. And in 1999 Amadou Diallo, an unarmed, African-immigrant street vendor, was killed by four NYPD officers who fired forty-one shots, hitting Diallo nineteen times. The officers, who were looking for a rape suspect, said they thought Diallo had a gun (De La Cruz 1999).

Police officers involved in brutality and use-of-deadly-force cases are rarely prosecuted and, if prosecuted, rarely convicted. One study in San Diego, California, for instance, found that not a single officer was prosecuted for any of the 190 civilian shootings that occurred from 1985 to 1990

(Petrillo 1990). In the King case, four officers were indicted but found not guilty of unlawful assault, although in a subsequent federal trial two were found guilty of violating King's civil rights and sentenced to thirty-month prison terms (Gibbs 1996). King also won a $3.8 million civil lawsuit against the city of Los Angeles. In the Louima case, one officer was convicted and sentenced to a lengthy prison term (CNN 2002). Three other officers had their convictions overturned on appeal, although Louima did receive a $8.7 million settlement from the city of New York. The four officers in the Diallo case were indicted but acquitted of all criminal charges, and the Diallo family was awarded $3 million (Feuer 2004; George 2000).

■ Prosecuting and Defending the Accused

After a suspect is arrested and taken into custody, the criminal justice process moves from the police to the criminal courts, where prosecutors, defense attorneys, judges, and jurors replace police officers as the leading players in a series of formal and informal deliberations that determine a defendant's fate. The criminal court system in the United States is a complex multitiered set of institutions that operate under state and federal law. The state system was adopted from the English system by the American colonists, and the federal system was established by the U.S. Congress (Adler et al. 2000). Courts in different jurisdictions function independently, and the precise processes vary from one place to another (see Box 11.2). However, there are a series of core stages or decision points that are roughly comparable throughout the United States.

■ Initial Screening

The prosecutor or district attorney is the primary gatekeeper of the court system, for he or she is assigned the task of determining the formal charge (if any) that will be filed against a defendant. The prosecutor usually makes this decision in consultation with the police but can decide independently to release a defendant. In a study of the seventy-five largest urban counties in the country, Gerard Rainville and Brian Reaves (2003) found that about a fourth of all felony arrests were dismissed at this stage in the process.

Technically, the prosecutor is supposed to file charges only when the case meets the standard of **probable cause**, that is, when there is a reasonable basis to believe that the defendant committed the crime. Many cases fail to meet this standard due to insufficient evidence or unreliable witnesses. Informally, the prosecutor also considers whether the case is serious enough to warrant utilization of scarce criminal justice resources, whether the defendant truly intended to commit the crime, and whether the defendant deserves to be held accountable for his or her actions. In addition, the prosecutor may take into account the defendant's prior offense record, age and health, and social standing in the community (Boland et al. 1992; Daudistel et al. 1979; Myers 2000).

Some research suggests that gender and racial/ethnic status influence prosecutors' charging decisions. In a study of Los Angeles, for example, Cassia Spohn and colleagues found that prosecutors' decisions to drop or lower charges revealed "a pattern of discrimination in favor of female defendants and against black and Hispanic defendants" (1987:183; see Daly 1994). In a study of a Midwestern city, Gary LaFree (1980) discovered that blacks accused of raping white women were given more serious charges than either blacks accused of raping black women or whites accused of raping white women. Similarly, Michael Radelet (1981) found that Florida defendants who murdered whites were more likely to be charged with first-degree murder than those who murdered blacks. In another Florida study, Radelet and Glenn Pierce (1985) examined cases of discrepancy between police and prosecutorial assessments of murders as either felony or nonfelony homicides. Felony homicides, or homicides that occur in the course of another felony crime (e.g., robbery), carry heavier penalties than nonfelony homicides. Radelet and Pierce found that a murder was most likely to be upgraded (from the initial police assessment) to a felony homicide, and least likely to be downgraded to a nonfelony homicide, when the defendant was black and the victim was white. And in an extensive review of the literature, Marvin Free (2002) concluded that prosecutors were consistently more likely to seek the death penalty in homicides involving white victims than in homicides involving black victims.

In the U.S. system of justice, the defendant is entitled to an **initial appearance** before a judge without unnecessary delay, usually within twenty-four hours following arrest. In minor cases (e.g., public drunkenness, loitering) the judge may in one condensed proceeding conduct a **summary trial** and issue a sentence. If the defendant cannot afford an attorney, the judge will assign a state-appointed attorney or public defender to the case. Only a third of federal felony defendants and 18 percent of state felony defendants are able to hire their own private counsel (DeFrances and Marika 2000; Harlow 2000).

In serious misdemeanor and felony cases, the judge also decides whether to keep the defendant confined in jail for pretrial detention or to release him or her on bail. (Judges usually follow prosecutors' bail recommendations.) The bail decision is of paramount importance, for defendants who are denied or unable to make bail are also more likely to be convicted and to receive prison terms (Reaves 1991; Williams 2003). Most defendants granted bail cannot afford it and have to pay a bail bondsperson or agency a 10–20 percent fee to front the entire amount. States that prohibit private bonding services may allow defendants to obtain bail by putting up a percentage or some noncash asset (e.g., real estate). Rainville and Reaves (2003) found that only about half of felony defendants who were required to post bail to secure release were able to do so. In addition, other research found that nonwhite defendants tended to be assigned higher levels of bail than white defendants, regardless of their prior record or the type of offense they committed. These different levels of bail were most heavily pronounced for drug offenses. And while nonwhite men and women were assigned similar bail amounts, white men were assigned higher bail than white women (Albonetti et al. 1989; Ewing & Houston 1991; Patterson & Lynch 1991).

Following the initial appearance, a judicial determination regarding probable cause may be made at a **preliminary hearing**, or "information" proceeding. This hearing "is not an inquiry aimed at determining the defendant's guilt or innocence . . . [but] at establishing . . . whether there is sufficient evidence for any reasonable and prudent person to believe a crime has been committed, and . . . [that] the defendant committed it" (Daudistel et al. 1979:178). It gives the prosecution and the defense attorney the opportunity to learn about each other's cases and to preserve the testimony of witnesses, who may later change their story. In some jurisdictions a **grand jury** may be used instead of a preliminary hearing. In grand jury proceedings the prosecutor presents evidence to a group of twelve to twenty-three citizens, who rarely reject the recommendation to indict, since defendants "may not even be allowed to present their version of the facts, much less to confront and cross-examine witnesses" (Myers 2000:450). After the preliminary hearing or grand jury decision the defendant appears before the court for **arraignment** and is asked to plead guilty, not guilty, or no contest. (A no contest plea is comparable to a guilty plea except that it cannot be used as an admission of guilt in a subsequent civil proceeding.)

■ *Negotiating Justice in an Adversary System*

Courts in the United States utilize an **adversary system** of criminal justice that puts prosecutors and defense attorneys in an oppositional relationship, with each side dedicated to presenting its best possible case. The trial court is the arena in which the adversary model operates in its purest form. However, in many jurisdictions over 90 percent of convictions are attained through informal **plea bargaining** negotiations, making the trial the exception rather than the rule (Largen & Brown 1997; Pastore & Maguire 2002). In plea bargaining the defendant agrees to plead guilty, waiving his or her Fifth Amendment right against self-incrimination. Since the prosecutor is handed a conviction on "a silver platter," he or she must offer something in return. The prosecutor may agree to lower the seriousness of the charge and consequently the sentence. Or in cases where multiple charges have been brought against the defendant, the prosecutor may agree to drop some of charges or to recommend to the judge that the sentences be served concurrently rather than consecutively.

Plea bargaining is a common practice because both the prosecuting and defense attorneys view themselves as better off with it than without it. Prosecutors are most likely to plea bargain when they have relatively weak cases that may not be provable "beyond a reasonable doubt" if the case goes to trial (Daudistel et al. 1979; Myers 2000). Certainty of conviction through plea bargaining often seems preferable to expending considerable time and resources in pursuit of an uncertain outcome. As one defense lawyer observed, "When a prosecutor has a dead-bang case he is likely to come up with an impossible offer like 30 to 50 years. When the case has a hole in it, however, the prosecutor may scale the offer all the way down to probation" (Heumann 1978:508).

Defendants plea-bargain for similar reasons. They risk losing at trial and receiving a harsher sentence, as prosecutors forced to go to trial generally ask for the maximum possible penalty in the event of conviction. Defendants also may want to get the ordeal over as soon as possible and avoid the publicity and higher attorney fees associated with a trial. Thus one of the defense attorney's most important functions is to get the best possible deal for his or her client when likelihood of acquittal is slim. And since defense attorneys typically believe that their clients are guilty of some charge, if not the current one, they will often induce them to cop a plea as a matter of course (Blumberg 1967; McIntyre 1987). They try to persuade their clients that the fee they are paying for legal representation will buy them a better deal, even though they may in fact get the same deal on their own. Defendants who benefit the most from plea bargaining (i.e., who actually get lower sentences than they would if they went to trial) are those who have committed less serious crimes and have a cleaner prior offense record (Myers 2000; Samaha 2000; Smith 1986).

Overloaded court dockets are another reason that plea bargaining is common. As one New York City prosecutor observed, "Our office keeps . . . [the] courtrooms busy trying five percent of the cases. If even 10 percent . . . end in a trial, the system would break down" (Zimring & Frase 1980:506–507). In *Santobello v. New York* (1971), the U.S. Supreme Court explicitly acknowledged that plea bargaining was essential to the management of overloaded courts and that when "properly administered . . . is to be encouraged" (cited in Reid 1997:507). The Court also held that prosecutors are obligated to keep the promises they make once an agreement is reached so that defendants' pleas are made voluntarily and with full knowledge of the consequences.

To some extent plea bargaining takes place in a legal marketplace of "going rates" where similarly situated people are routinely treated in a comparable fashion. Since both prosecutors and defense attorneys are interested in reducing the uncertainty and maximizing the efficiency of their work, they develop a common outlook regarding the disposition that is appropriate for particular kinds of cases (Daudistel et al. 1979; Heumann 1978; Myers 2000). Judges generally approve plea-bargaining agreements because they too have a stake in the smooth operation of the system. Nowadays it is not unusual for judges to order a continuance (postponement) on the first day of trial to encourage the attorneys to work out a deal. Some judges participate even more actively by supervising negotiations and by making bargaining recommendations themselves (Dawson 1992; Samaha 2000).

The Trial

Although few choose to exercise it, the Sixth Amendment gives defendants the right to a "speedy and public trial." Technically speaking, defendants are presumed innocent until proven guilty in a court of law, and prosecutors have the burden to prove their guilt beyond a reasonable doubt. Thus defendants do not need to prove their innocence. They need only to cast reasonable doubt on their guilt. These formal rules of the game serve to balance the informal presumption of guilt that is implicit in a prosecutor's decision to bring a case to trial in the first place.

The trial in an adversary system is not as much "a rational 'fact-finding' process aimed at discovering the 'truth'" as it is an impression-management process aimed at constructing a desired account of the alleged criminal event (Daudistel et al. 1979:236). Hence the prosecution and defense present (or ignore) the facts of a case in ways that support the conclusion they have already reached. For instance, they will call witnesses whose testimony is favorable to their point of view and will coach them regarding "what to say and what not to say in response to formal questioning" (p. 239). Each side attempts to undermine or damage the credibility of opposing witnesses, whether or not these witnesses are actually telling the truth. Each side makes objections to evidence or lines of questioning they consider damaging to their case, even if they expect the judge to overrule them. Judges play a key role in arbitrating the debate by ruling on objections and motions made by the attorneys, by deciding what evidence can and cannot be introduced, and by instructing the jury about the law governing the case.

Although few defense attorneys harbor illusions about the factual innocence of their clients, they believe it is their job to keep prosecutors honest, that is, to hold prosecutors to their legal obligation to prove guilt beyond a reasonable doubt (McIntyre 1987). As one defense attorney admits, "What I knew actually happened was not important. . . . What did matter was whether a version of the 'facts' could be presented that would . . . [cast]

doubt . . . [on my] client's guilt" (Subin 1993:31). But, critics say, it is one thing for a defense attorney to attack the prosecutor's case by pointing out its weaknesses; it is quite another thing to attack the case by advancing utter falsehoods. One defense attorney, for example, recalls how he humiliated a rape victim on the witness stand, making "her seem to be little more than a prostitute" (McIntyre 1987:141). This type of questioning is significantly different "from challenging *inaccurate* testimony," whether or not the client is innocent (Subin 1993:36).

Defense attorneys, however, believe that prosecutors are also known to behave disreputably. In fact, a study by the *Chicago Tribune* uncovered 381 defendants across the country who have "had their homicide convictions thrown out because prosecutors concealed evidence suggesting innocence or presented evidence they knew to be false" (Armstrong & Possley 1999:3A). Two-thirds of these defendants had been sentenced to death. Similarly, a two-year investigation by the *Pittsburg Post-Gazette* uncovered numerous instances of federal prosecutors "lying, hiding evidence, distorting the facts, engaging in cover-ups, paying for perjury and setting up innocent people in order to win indictments, guilty pleas and convictions." According to both newspapers, prosecutors were rarely punished for their misconduct. As one former prosecutor remarked, "It's a result-oriented process. . . . Whatever works is what's right" (*Wisconsin State Journal* 1998b:A2). More recently, a study by the Center for Public Integrity found that since 1970 appellate judges have "dismissed criminal charges, reversed convictions or reduced sentences" in more than 2,000 cases due to prosecutors who had "stretched, bent or broke rules" (Sniffen 2003:A3). Judges have cited 233 prosecutors for two or more cases of misconduct, although only two prosecutors have been disbarred for mishandling criminal cases.

Trial by jury. The Sixth Amendment provides defendants with the right to "an impartial jury," although the U.S. Supreme Court has ruled that this right need not apply to juveniles being processed in the juvenile justice system nor to adults if their conviction would result in a sentence of less than six months of incarceration. Moreover, according to the Court, the right to a jury requires neither a jury of twelve members (six-person juries are allowed in all but capital punishment cases) nor a unanimous jury verdict in noncapital cases (11–1, 10–2, and 9–3 verdicts have been upheld by the Court). Nevertheless, most jurisdictions maintain the tradition of twelve-member juries and unanimous verdicts for criminal trials (Neubauer 2001).

Defendants may choose either a bench trial (where the judge decides guilt or innocence) or a jury trial. Research indicates that judges and juries reach similar conclusions in about three-quarters of cases, but when there is disagreement juries are more likely to acquit (Kalven & Zeisel 1971). Judges do not have the authority to reverse a jury's verdict of acquittal, but they can reverse a verdict of guilty.

Potential jurors are randomly selected from various sources (e.g., telephone directories, voter and driver license registries, property tax lists). Some of these methods result in underrepresentation of low-income and minority residents, who are less likely to register to vote or own real estate. And since these groups are also more residentially mobile and less likely to have permanent addresses, they are less likely to receive jury summonses sent through the mail. Moreover, those with lower incomes are more likely to be excused from jury duty for reasons of economic hardship. Women are often granted exemptions for child care and family responsibilities (Benokraitis 1982; Fukurai et al. 1993; Grossman 1994; O'Reilly 1979).

The **voir dire** ("to speak the truth") is the next stage in the jury selection process. Here prospective jurors are questioned by the prosecutor and defense attorney under the supervision of the presiding judge. While the Sixth Amendment requires an impartial jury, the prosecutor and defense both prefer jurors who are predisposed to their side of the case. Sometimes they will even hire jury consultants to help them identify the demographic characteristics and attitudes of people who are more likely to convict or acquit. During the voir dire each side is allowed a limited number of **peremptory challenges**, enabling them to dismiss some jurors without explanation. Each side is also given an unlimited number of **challenges for cause** if they can demonstrate to the judge's satisfaction that a juror will be prejudicial in some way—for instance, if the juror knows the defendant, has been the victim of a crime that is similar to the one the defendant is accused of, or has already formulated an opinion on the case due to exposure to pretrial publicity (Samaha 2000).

Through the mid-1980s, prosecutors in some southern states disproportionately used their peremptory challenges to exclude African Americans

(Jost 1995). In *Batson v. Kentucky* (1986), however, the U.S. Supreme Court ruled that race was a constitutionally impermissible basis for excluding a prospective juror. Similarly, in *J.E.B. v. Alabama* (1994) the Court declared it was unconstitutional to exclude a prospective juror because of gender. On the other hand, in *Purkett v. Elem* (1995) the Court upheld a prosecutorial exclusion of an African American because "he had . . . shoulder length, curly, unkempt hair . . . [and] a mustache and . . . goatee-type beard" (cited in Reid 1997:434). The Court accepted the prosecution's argument that the exclusion based on physical appearance was "not a characteristic of a particular race." And in *Lockhart v. McCree* (1986) the Court ruled that in capital punishment cases jurors who oppose the death penalty can be disqualified from ruling on a defendant's guilt or innocence. This decision has disproportionately excluded blacks and women, since they are more likely than whites and men to oppose capital punishment (Bohm 1991; Currie & Pillick 1996).

Research on the effect of gender and race on jurors' decisions is somewhat mixed. In a review of studies of juror voting and gender, Cameron Currie and Aleta Pillick (1996) noted that few gender differences exist. Rape cases are the exception, with women more likely to convict. But in a review of studies of juror voting and race, Nancy King (1993) noted that blacks were more likely than whites to acquit, although both blacks and whites were more likely to acquit defendants of their own race than defendants of another race.

In his final summation in the O.J. Simpson criminal trial, defense attorney Johnnie Cochran beseeched the jury to acquit Simpson, arguing that he had been framed by the LAPD. Cochran told the jurors, nine of whom were African American, "There's something in your background . . . that helps you understand that this is wrong" (quoted in Darden 1996:369). The Simpson jury agreed, returning a unanimous verdict for acquittal. Although two white jurors and one Hispanic juror concurred in the decision, much of the white public viewed the verdict as biased by race (see Box 1.1).

Jury voting along racial lines is nothing new, although throughout most of our history it has been predominantly white jurors refusing to convict whites for committing crimes against blacks. In the last two decades, however, the most striking trend in jury verdicts has not been in the number of race-based acquittals but in the number of **hung juries** (Rosen 1997). Hung juries occur when unanimity is required but one or more jurors refuse to vote with the majority. The judge then declares a mistrial, and the prosecution must decide whether to seek a new trial. In recent years hung juries have occurred most often in cities with large minority populations during trials of black men. In these cases hung juries usually involve a single holdout (most often a black woman) who refuses to convict over the strenuous objections of fellow jurors, both black and white, for reasons that include mistrust of the police, concern about sending yet another black man to prison, or simply having difficulty "sitting in judgment of someone else" (p. 58). These holdouts see the defendants "as their nephews, their sons, . . . their brothers" (p. 62).

Former prosecutor Paul Butler (1997), who is African American, believes that black jurors should refuse to convict black defendants convicted of some nonviolent crimes. As he writes, "Black jurors ought to be thoughtful about who they send to prison. Murderers, rapists, robbers: absolutely yes, for the safety of the community. But when black people are prosecuted for drug offenses and other victimless crimes, I recommend . . . that jurors consider nullification—their legal power to ignore the written-down law in favor of a broader notion of justice" (p. 12).

Jury nullification enjoys a long history in the United States. It was used by the American colonists in their disputes with the British government, by northern juries to nullify fugitive slave laws, and by civil rights and antiwar activists during the political turmoil of the 1960s. U.S. courts have upheld jurors' right to disregard the facts of the case or the judge's instructions in order to vote their conscience. But the courts have not upheld jurors' right to be informed of the nullification doctrine (Bonsignore et al. 1994; Dershowitz 1996).

Nullification in political cases is nevertheless quite different from the cases resulting in mistrials in contemporary criminal courts (Rosen 1997). According to Judge Eric Holder, an African American who served on the Superior Court of the District of Columbia, "There are some folks who have been so seared by racism, who are so affected by what has happened to them because they are black, that, even if you're the most credible, upfront black man or woman in law enforcement, you're never going to be able to reach them" (quoted on p. 60). However, Jeffrey Rosen concludes that most jurors are "able to transcend their racially fraught experiences and . . . cast their votes on the basis of a scrupulous evaluation" of the evidence (1997:55). And research finds that about three-quarters of all felony trials result in a conviction (Maguire & Pastore 2001).

The problem of wrongful convictions. We have already discussed instances in which cases have been dismissed and convictions overturned due to police and prosecutorial misconduct. According to Joel Samaha, **wrongful convictions** arise in two ways: When (1) "convictions [are] obtained by illegal means, such as by forced confessions or unreasonable searches and seizures," and (2) "innocent people are convicted" (2000:358).

One case that recently came to light involved five young men (fourteen to sixteen years old) who were convicted of brutally raping and beating a woman who was jogging in New York City's Central Park in 1989. At the time, this case was quite racially charged, since the victim was white and the defendants were black. The heinousness of the crime led to a moral panic of sorts about so-called wilding youths roaming the city preying on innocent passersby (Maull 2002). In 2002, after the young men had completed prison terms of six to eleven and a half years, the convictions were overturned due to the confession and corroborative DNA testing of the real assailant, who was already serving a life sentence for the rape of three women and the rape and murder of a fourth. Authorities now believe that the confessions of the young men, upon which the convictions were based, were coerced by police. In such cases, suspects—especially frightened youths who are easily intimidated by aggressive law enforcement authorities—may think, "Even though I didn't do it, they're not going to believe me . . . [so] I may as well make a deal, make it easier on myself" (James Fox, quoted in Tanner 2002:A4).

Another source of wrongful convictions is eyewitness error. Various factors can influence a witness's perceptions of the crime and criminal: the amount of time the witness was exposed to the event, the distance between the observer and what was being observed, the amount of lighting around the crime scene, and postevent occurrences such as whether the witness was given leading information by the police. Racial stereotypes may also come into play and influence what witnesses of different racial groups "see" (e.g., all blacks look alike), especially when police lineups include only one person who resembles the alleged perpetrator. Police may also coach witnesses at lineups, and in cases that rely on informants, outright lying may occur (Huff et al. 1996).

Community pressure for arrest and conviction may also influence a "rush to judgment," and some law enforcement agencies may place too much emphasis on closing cases expeditiously and winning at all costs. Take, for example, the Dallas County District Attorney's Office, known for its high rate of wrongful convictions over the years. At one time it was common for prosecutors in this office to think: "Anyone can convict a guilty man; it takes a real prosecutor to convict an innocent one" (cited in Huff et al. 1996:43). Other problems include investigators who fail to follow alternative leads, the suppression of "exculpatory evidence even after [defense] motions for discovery have been made," and as we indicated earlier, police planting of evidence and perjury in court (p. 72).

The problem of wrongful convictions is particularly distressing in cases involving the death penalty, an issue we will explore in more detail in the next chapter. For now we simply note that researchers estimate that even if only 0.5 percent of convictions for *Index crimes* were to involve wrongful convictions, that would amount to nearly 10,000 persons a year (Huff et al. 1996). Moreover, racial disparities are apparent in both capital and noncapital cases, with African Americans constituting from 40 to 57 percent of the wrongfully convicted (Bedau & Radelet 1987; Scheck et al. 2000; Westervelt & Humphrey 2001).

■ Sentencing the Convicted

Sentencing of convicted offenders is a separate stage in the criminal justice process. In most jurisdictions the sentencing decision is the responsibility of the trial judge, although in some states the trial jury is allowed to determine or recommend sentences (Rottman et al. 1995). Usually a separate sentencing hearing is held, during which the prosecution and defense attorney argue for or against a particular sentence. At the hearing a probation officer also reports on the results of a **presentence investigation** (PSI) he or she has conducted. The PSI includes information about the offender's background and prior criminal offenses. The probation officer is then usually asked to make a sentencing recommendation, which is generally accepted by the judge. Some states also utilize **victim impact statements** (VIS), often incorporating them into the PSI report. VIS provide victims the opportunity to describe both the harm they have suffered and their views on the appropriate punishment (Adler et al. 2000; Rottman et al. 1995).

■ *Types of Sentences*

Outside of death penalty cases, the most basic sentencing decision involves the distinction between *probation* in the community and *incarceration* in a correctional facility (see Chapters 12 and 13). Overall, about 60 percent of adults under correctional supervision are on probation, as are about one-third of convicted felony offenders (Glaze 2003; Pastore & Maguire 2002). Offenders may also serve part of their sentence incarcerated and then part on community *parole*.

The length of the sentence offenders must serve is also decided at the sentencing hearing. For much of the twentieth century, most jurisdictions used some form of **indeterminate sentence**. Indeterminate sentences entail no specific time period or only a maximum (or a minimum and maximum) term. Offenders are periodically reviewed by correctional authorities (e.g., members of a parole board) who evaluate their behavior and readiness for release. The guiding correctional principle is **rehabilitation**, and the sentence is deemed completed only when the offender can demonstrate that he or she is sufficiently reformed, that is, when he or she is judged capable of becoming a law-abiding and productive member of society (Adler et al. 2000; Samaha 2000).

During the 1970s critics from both sides of the political spectrum took issue with indeterminate sentencing. The rehabilitation model, everyone agreed, was not working well, as the correctional system had been unable to deliver effective rehabilitative services and criminal justice officials had been unable to determine who was truly reformed (Lipton et al. 1975). Liberals argued that indeterminate sentencing fostered discriminatory treatment based on class and racial/ethnic status, and that uncertain release dates constituted a "cruel injustice to prisoners, suspending them in a nether world of uncertainty . . . [and] arbitrary decisions" (Adler et al. 2000:315; Greenberg & Humphries 1980). Conservatives, in turn, complained about dangerous offenders being released too early, and they called for sentencing reforms that would confine criminals for longer periods of time. They argued that **retribution**, not rehabilitation, should be the guiding philosophy of punishment. Also known as "just deserts," retribution entails sentences that are proportionate to the seriousness of the crime, not to the rehabilitative status of the criminal (von Hirsch 1976; Wilson 1975).

A **determinate sentence** refers to a term of punishment that is fixed at the outset, that is not dependent upon the behavior of offenders under correctional supervision. Increasingly state legislatures have been limiting judicial discretion by establishing systems of proportional punishments based on a retributive philosophy. Even where judges retain discretionary authority, they may be required to sentence the offender to a definite period of time. Many states have instituted a form of determinancy known as the **presumptive sentence**. Under this approach legislatures establish the penalty offenders are expected to receive for particular crimes but allow judges to shorten or lengthen these sentences if certain *mitigating* or *aggravating* conditions are present. For instance, a judge may shorten the sentence if the offender has shown remorse or offered the prosecution assistance in solving other crimes or apprehending other criminals. Conversely, a judge may lengthen the sentence if the offender has a prior criminal record, used a gun during the crime, or seriously injured the victim. Often legislatures will specify the mitigating and aggravating criteria that judges are permitted to consider (Samaha 2000).

A **mandatory sentence** is more restrictive than a presumptive sentence because it allows for no judicial discretion whatsoever. Nearly all state legislatures have established mandatory sentences for some crimes, such as murder, crimes involving guns, and some drug offenses. These provisions usually require the offender to serve a minimum period of incarceration, eliminating the possibility of probation (Adler et al. 2000; Samaha 2000).

In the federal system, the Sentencing Reform Act of 1984 authorized the U.S. Sentencing Commission to develop sentencing guidelines for federal crimes that were supposed to be "neutral as to race, sex, national origin, creed, and socioeconomic status" (cited in Heaney 1991:203). The commission established a formula whereby a score is given for a particular offense, and additional points are deleted or added for mitigating and aggravating factors: "Once the . . . score is computed, judges determine the sentence by consulting a sentencing table that converts scores into months to be served" (Senna & Siegel 1996:538). Some states have adopted similar schemes, which can be so complicated that they require a computer program to assist in the calculations (Adler et al. 2000).

Since the mid-1990s the federal government and over half the states have adopted mandatory "three strikes and you're out" sentences that require prison terms of twenty-five years to life for anyone convicted of a third felony (or in some states a second or fourth felony). Although touted by politicians as a way to protect the public from serious criminals, most of the three-strikes offenders have been sentenced for nonviolent crimes. A case in point is Jerry Dewayne Williams, a twenty-seven-year-old California man who was sentenced to twenty-five years to life for a third offense of stealing a pizza from a kid at a pizza parlor (Reid 1997; Shichor & Sechrest 1996).

Critics note that three-strikes policies have clogged already overcrowded courts, since defendants facing harsh sentences have little to lose by demanding a trial. Moreover, three-strikes penalties focus on the wrong age group of offenders, that is, on older offenders whose criminality is already declining. As Steven Barkan observes, "Criminality declines as people move out of their twenties and almost always halts by the time they reach their middle-age and elderly years" (2001:494). Nearly all three-strikes offenders would nevertheless remain in prison long after they stopped posing a threat to the public.

In California, judges have complained that the three-strikes mandate "basically castrates a judge" (quoted in Reid 1997:525). One judge refused to sentence forty-three-year-old Thomas Kiel Brown to life for stealing a $22 baseball cap from a store in a shopping mall. As he said, "No judge I know wants to let dangerous criminals loose. . . . But I'm sure the taxpayer doesn't want to spend more than $500,000 to put a petty thief in jail for stealing a cap." In 1996 the California Supreme Court dealt the state's statute a severe blow when it upheld a judge's decision not to impose a life sentence on Jesus Romero, a thirty-four-year-old who was convicted of possessing thirteen grams of cocaine. (Romero's prior convictions were for burglary and attempted burglary.) California law has traditionally given judges the power to disregard prior convictions when doing so seemed reasonable: "The California Supreme Court ruled that the state statute did not remove that traditional judicial power, and if it had done so, it would have violated the state constitution." Thus a California judge who believes that a mandatory sentence is not "in the furtherance of justice" is not required to impose it (Reid 1997:525).

In 2003, however, the U.S. Supreme Court rejected two defendants' claim that California's three-strikes provision violated the Eighth Amendment's prohibition against "cruel and unusual punishment." Gary Ewing and Leandro Andrade had received sentences of twenty-five years to life and fifty years, respectively (Mears 2003). Ewing's third offense involved stealing three $399 golf clubs from a Los Angeles country club, and Andrade's involved theft of $153 worth of videotapes from two Kmart stores. In a five-to-four decision, the Court ruled that the three-strikes law represented a "rational legislative judgement, entitled to deference," and that the Court would "not sit as a 'superlegislature' to second-guess these policy choices" (cited in Will 2003:74).

▨ Discrimination in Sentencing

Arguably one of the most persistent controversies in sentencing involves concerns about the discriminatory treatment of racial and ethnic minorities. Criminological research has shown that people of color often receive harsher criminal sentences than whites. Joan Petersilia and Susan Turner (1988), however, distinguish between *disparities* and *discrimination.* Disparities occur when legally relevant factors are applied but "have different results for different groups" (p. 92). Discrimination occurs when decisions are based on social status rather than on legitimate standards.

Most research has found that legally appropriate criteria such as offense seriousness and prior record account for the sentencing disparities that exist between people of color and whites (Barkan 2001; Myers 2000). However, offense seriousness and prior record may themselves be consequences of earlier discriminatory decisions made at the arrest and initial screening stages, and they may be consequences of previous sentencing decisions. Hence there may be little distinction between disparities and discrimination after all (Free 1997).

Furthermore, some evidence suggests that judges place more emphasis on offense seriousness and prior record when dealing with minority offenders (Miethe & Moore 1986; Nelson 1994; Welch et al. 1984). Other research suggests that in murder and rape or sexual assault cases offenders who victimize whites are given more severe sentences than those who victimize blacks, and black offenders who victimize whites are given the harshest penalties of all (LaFree 1989; Paternoster 1991; Spohn & Spears 1996; Walsh 1987). Moreover, in death penalty cases "the race of the victim is often more significant than the race of the offender, and may reflect not only the devalued status of black victims" but also the greater societal outrage at the victimization of members of the majority white group (Myers 2000:460).

Research has uncovered stronger evidence of discrimination against minorities convicted of less serious offenses than against minorities convicted of more serious ones (Spohn & Cederblom 1991; Unnever & Hembroff 1988). Cases of serious criminality call for more severe penalties for all offenders, regardless of minority status, leaving judges little room to exercise discretion based on legally suspect criteria. Similarly, research has shown greater discrimination in the probation versus incarceration decision (referred to as the in/out decision) than in the decision regarding sentence length for those incarcerated. Apparently, incarcerated offenders constitute a more homogeneous group of serious offenders who receive comparable treatment (Kramer & Steffensmeier 1993; Nelson 1994).

In addition, research suggests that discrimination is conditional, that is, dependent on other factors. For example, people of color are more likely to be incarcerated in the South and in areas with higher proportions of minority residents and higher unemployment rates (Bridges & Crutchfield 1988; Bridges et al. 1987; Chiricos & Crawford 1995). In these places, researchers argue, minorities are perceived by criminal justice officials to be a more volatile, socially disruptive, and potentially rebellious population. One "single-day" study of Georgia even found that *all* of the juvenile drug offenders in Georgia's correctional facilities were African American ("Single-Day Study" 1990).

The effect of race on sentencing is also contingent on *gender* and *age*. In an important study, Darrell Steffensmeier and colleagues (1998) examined the effects of race, gender, and age (controlling for offense severity and prior record) on the in/out and length-of-incarceration decision using data from nearly 139,000 cases in the state of Pennsylvania from 1989 to 1992. They found that males received more severe sentences than females, and that those aged twenty-one to twenty-nine years old received harsher penalties than those aged eighteen to twenty years and those aged thirty and older. (Those aged eighteen to twenty received harsher penalties than those aged thirty and older.) Significantly, blacks received more severe sentences than their white counterparts in each of their respective gender-age groups. Moreover, the sentencing inequities were the most pronounced for *black males aged twenty-one to twenty-nine*. (The one exception to this pattern was for white males aged fifty years and older, who received somewhat harsher sentences, perhaps due to the sentencing of older drug offenders involved in large-scale or upper-level drug trafficking.)

Steffensmeier and colleagues argue that race (i.e., young black male) has become a perceptual shorthand used by judges to make sentencing decisions that involve a high degree of uncertainty about "who is dangerous and who is not" (p. 767). Judges make assessments of offenders' past and future behavior that are consistent with societal stereotypes about various social groups. Judges view young black men, compared to other demographic groups, as more committed to street life, more dangerous, and less amenable to reform. They often assume that women are less blameworthy: they see them as playing minor roles in crime, as having more mental/health problems, or as victims of domestic abuse (see Bickle & Peterson 1991; Daly 1994; Daly & Bordt 1995). Judges assume that both

Further Exploration

Box 11.2   The Juvenile Justice System

In 1899 Illinois became the first state to establish a juvenile justice system that was independent from its adult criminal justice system. Today every state has separate court procedures and correctional facilities that handle juveniles (most often youths under seventeen or eighteen years). Typically these juvenile systems have legal jurisdiction over three categories of youths. *Delinquents* are juveniles who violate criminal laws for which adults could also be charged. *Status offenders* include those who commit acts for which adults could not be charged, for example, running away, truancy, curfew violations, and even vague transgressions such as "incorrigibility," "habitual disobedience," and "immoral behavior." Finally, *dependent* children are those who have been so neglected or abused that they need to become wards of the court.

The juvenile system is based on the premise that young people, due to immaturity, are less responsible and blameworthy for their conduct and hence should be granted consideration that might not be given to adults. Thus the juvenile system's official mission has been one of rehabilitation through the delivery of psychological and social services that are supposed to be in the "best interest" of the child. Originally the legal formalities of the adult system were viewed as undesirable. When a youth came before a juvenile court judge, the focus was not on the juvenile's guilt or innocence but rather on how the judge could make an informed assessment of the youth's life circumstances and formulate a course of treatment tailored to his or her particular needs. Hence testimony of any sort, regardless of its legal relevancy, was deemed germane, and attorneys were viewed as a hindrance to the process (Platt 1974; Ryerson 1978).

The absence of due process, however, led to much abuse. In 1964, for instance, fifteen-year-old Gerald Gault was arrested in Gila County, Arizona, for allegedly making an obscene phone call. Gault was already on probation for being in the company of another boy who had stolen a wallet. A juvenile court judge sentenced Gault to a juvenile correctional facility for up to six years, without allowing Gault to be represented by an attorney, to confront and cross-examine his accuser, or to be informed of his privilege against self-incrimination. The maximum penalty for an adult committing a similar offense in Arizona was a fine of $50 or a jail term of not more than two months. Gault and his parents appealed the case all the way to the U.S. Supreme Court, which ruled in 1967 that Gault's right to due process of law had been violated. The Court said that juveniles subject to institutional confinement were entitled to most (though not all) of the due process rights enjoyed by adults, including the right to counsel, the right to confront and cross-examine hostile witnesses, and the privilege against self-incrimination. But in a 1971 case, the Court ruled that juveniles did not have a constitutional right to a trial by

continues

Box 11.2 continued

jury, arguing that a jury was not necessary for a fair hearing or to fulfill the fact-finding function of the juvenile court (Binder et al. 1988).

The juvenile system has also been marred by some of the same discriminatory practices present in the adult system. Although the evidence is not entirely consistent, the tendency has been for minority and lower-class youths to be treated more severely than higher-status youths, and for females to be treated more leniently than males for serious crimes but more severely for status offenses. Overall, disparities in treatment between nonwhite/lower-class and white/higher-class offenders and between female and male offenders are more apparent at the early stages of juvenile court processing than at the latter stages (Bilchik 1999; Chesney-Lind & Shelden 2004; Engen et al. 2002; MacDonald & Chesney-Lind 2001).

In recent years, disillusionment with the rehabilitative ideal and the specter of serious juvenile offenders have led some states to lower the age at which the adult criminal court assumes jurisdiction for teenage defendants or to use a **waiver procedure** to transfer jurisdiction from the juvenile to the adult system. Most state legislatures specify an age at which youths can be transferred for particular crimes, though sometimes that decision is left to the discretion of the prosecutor. A study of the nation's seventy-five largest counties found that about two-thirds of transferred juveniles between 1990 and 1994 were charged with violent crimes, about two-thirds of those transferred were convicted, and about two-thirds of those convicted received prison or jail terms (Strom et al. 1998). However, in some states or counties a majority of transferred juveniles were nonviolent offenders—offenders who often received lighter penalties than they might have received had they remained in the juvenile system because in the adult system they were considered "lightweight" (Bishop et al. 1989; Howell 1996; Osbun & Rode 1984).

women and older men are more likely to have stable employment histories and responsibility for the care of dependents. Since judges view young black men, on the other hand, as lacking the social bonds that might insulate them from future criminality, they find less reason to give them a break. Judges also assume that incarcerating women (who might be pregnant) and older men poses greater child-welfare and health care costs to the corrections and social services systems. And they view young black men as better able than whites to "do time" and avoid being victimized in state prisons that are dominated by blacks (see Chapter 12). At the same time, Steffensmeier and colleagues attribute the relatively lighter sentences given to eighteen- to twenty-year-olds (as compared to twenty-one- to twenty-nine-year-olds) to judges' view of juveniles "as more impressionable and promising prospects for reform, and as more likely to experience victimization at the hands of [older] predatory inmates" (p. 779).

Many people have hoped that greater minority representation on the judiciary would minimize discriminatory sentencing practices. Susan Welch and colleagues (1988) found that white judges in "Metro City" (an unidentified northeastern city) issued more severe sentences to black offenders than to white offenders, while black judges issued comparable sentences to blacks and whites. Similarly, Malcolm Holmes and colleagues (1993) found that white judges in El Paso County, Texas, issued harsher penalties to Hispanic offenders than to white offenders, while Hispanic judges issued comparable penalties to these offenders.

On the other hand, Spohn (1990b) found that both black and white judges in Detroit sentenced black offenders more severely than white offenders. She suggests that most judges share common attitudes and that both black and white judges perceive black offenders as a greater threat. Since judges are selected from the "establishment center" of the legal profession and are socialized to the informal norms of the system, they tend to issue sentences that fall within the range of typical penalties for particular kinds of offenders (Holmes et al. 1993; Uhlman 1978:893). As one African American judge observes, "No matter how 'liberal' black judges may believe themselves to be, the law remains essentially a conservative doctrine, and those who practice it conform" (Wright 1973:22–23).

In another Detroit study, Spohn (1990a) found that in sexual assault cases black *female* judges issued longer sentences than black male judges. However, research has not found consistent differences overall in the sentencing practices of female and male judges, providing further evidence of homogeneity within the judiciary (Gruhl et al. 1981; Kritzer & Uhlman 1977).

Without a doubt, sentencing is a difficult decision that relies on a complex configuration of factors. Judges often make wise and warranted decisions that are based on legally appropriate criteria and reasonable evaluation of the offender's likelihood of reform. But all other things being equal, some offenders do appear to be treated more inequitably than others.

12

Punishment and Prisons

The "Friday circus" was about to begin. It had become weekly fare for the "entertainment-starved males" of the capital city of Kabul, Afghanistan. Thirty-thousand men and boys had come to the Olympic sports stadium to gawk and revel as a young woman named Sohaila received 100 lashes and two thieves had their right hands cut off. Sohaila, convicted of adultery for walking with a man who was not her relative, was lucky. She was single, so she was only to be flogged. "Had she been married, she would have been . . . stoned to death." The crowd cheered wildly as Sohaila was beaten but fell silent when the thieves were brought in. The air was crisp with tension as physicians wielding surgical scalpels severed the offenders' hands. The official overseeing the spectacle then triumphantly raised the amputated hands by their index fingers and warned onlookers that this was "the punishment for any of you caught stealing" (Goodwin 1998:26). The crowd was brought to its feet in celebration as the thieves were driven around the arena in a jeep. The year was 1998.

Such practices are, of course, prohibited in the United States. It is not unusual, however, to hear people make cavalier remarks about the need to resurrect such punishments here. Surely then, some argue, offenders would be deterred from crime. Thus when Michael Fay, an eighteen-year-old American living in Singapore, was sentenced in 1993 to six lashes with a rattan cane, four months in jail, and $2,200 in fines for vandalism ("egging" and spray-painting cars), many people considered his punishment well deserved. But caning is no mere slap on the wrist. Administered with full force by a martial arts expert, it causes severe pain, bleeding, and permanent scarring (Witt 1994).

Contemporary surveys indicate that a strong majority of the U.S. public believes that criminal punishments are not sufficiently severe, although this sentiment is stronger among men, whites, political conservatives, and religious fundamentalists (Barkan 2001; Pastore & Maguire 2002). Over

451

the last quarter century, however, we have not been weak-kneed in our resolve to punish criminals. Use of the death penalty has risen, sentences have gotten longer, and the number of people under correctional supervision has skyrocketed. In fact, the number of adults under correctional supervision increased from 1,840,421 in 1980 to 6,732,400 in 2002, a rise of 266 percent (see Table 12.1). The number of those who are incarcerated in jails or prisons has surpassed 2 million, an increase of 305 percent since 1980. The U.S. per capita prison population ranks with Russia's as the highest in the world. The state of California alone incarcerates more people than "France, Great Britain, Germany, Japan, Singapore, and the Netherlands combined" (Schlosser 1998:52).

The correctional system in the United States is a complex apparatus consisting of city and county jails, state and federal prisons, and community-based programs. **Jails** house individuals awaiting trial and those convicted of minor offenses who are generally serving not more than a year. State facilities contain about 90 percent of the prison population, but the bulk of offenders overall are on probation or parole (Harrison et al. 2003). **Probation** entails a period of community supervision in lieu of incarceration, while **parole** involves community supervision after release from confinement. **Community corrections** include a growing array of alternatives to incarceration that are drawing the attention of criminologists and criminal justice practitioners and policymakers.

In this chapter we use our sociological imagination to critically examine the system of punishment and incarceration in the United States, and in the next chapter we will look at community alternatives to prison. We will question whether current strategies for dealing with crime are charting the most effective course. In doing so, perhaps we will learn something about ourselves, for as Émile Durkheim observed, during times of public anxiety and uneasiness about the world, the collective urge to punish reinforces social solidarity by drawing us together in a "common posture of . . . [moral] indignation" (Erikson 1966:4; see Chapter 4). But, we must ask, is moral indignation the most appropriate sentiment upon which to build a

Table 12.1   Adults Under Correctional Supervision (1980 and 2002)

	1980	2002
Total population	1,840,421	6,732,400
Jail	182,288	665,475
Prison	319,598	1,367,856
Parole	220,438	753,141
Probation	1,118,097	3,995,165

Sources: Glaze 2003:1; Pastore & Maguire 1998, tab. 6.1.

system of punishment and corrections? Don't we have the responsibility to demand more of our political leaders who wage war against criminals, the nonviolent and violent alike, in spite of the inequities and injustices that this war has wrought (Cose 1999a)? We begin with a discussion of the death penalty, followed by a consideration of prisons.

■ The Death Penalty

Throughout most of our history the death penalty, or capital punishment, was considered "an appropriate and justifiable response to crime" (Smith 2000:621). Surveys indicate that two-thirds of the U.S. public continue to favor it for the crime of murder, although this proportion drops to just over half if respondents are given the option of choosing "life without the possibility of parole" (Pastore & Maguire 2002). Yet in spite of the public's support, the death penalty remains a controversial punishment.

Legal Lethality

In 1972 the U.S. Supreme Court, in *Furman v. Georgia,* ruled that the death penalty had been implemented arbitrarily and unfairly, and hence violated the Eighth Amendment prohibition against "cruel and unusual punishment." The penalty, the Court observed, had been administered disproportionately in the South and against the poor and people of color. Nevertheless, the Court stopped short of declaring capital punishment unconstitutional in principle; the problem, it held, was the manner in which it had been applied.

Use of the death penalty had already been on the decline since the 1930s, and in the years following *Furman* a temporary moratorium on capital punishment was imposed as cases worked their way through the courts. In decisions in 1976 and 1977, the Court clarified the conditions under which capital punishment may be imposed. States that wished to use the penalty needed to develop guidelines specifying *aggravating conditions* under which it applied (e.g., homicides committed in the course of another felony, homicides resulting in the death of more than one person, homicides against public officials, homicides involving especially brutal or heinous acts, homicides by an offender with a prior record of violence, homicides for pecuniary gain). Moreover, the Court held that capital punishment could not be mandatory, even if such aggravating circumstances were found. Judges and jurors had to be given the opportunity to consider *mitigating conditions* under which the offender's life could be spared. The Court also said that the penalty could not be imposed for rape, as had been done in the pre-Furman era (Bowers & Pierce 1980).

In 1977 Gary Gilmore of Utah became the first offender to be executed in the post-Furman period. The annual number of executions since then rose to a high of ninety-eight in 1999 but declined to sixty-five in 2003, a number that was still less than 40 percent of the annual average in the 1930s (Death Penalty Information Center [DPIC] 2003a). Southern states accounted for nearly 90 percent of the executions, with Texas, Oklahoma, and North Carolina accounting for over two-thirds. Currently, among the thirty-eight states that permit capital punishment, there are over 3,500 people on death row awaiting execution. Because of postconviction appeals, the average time between the imposition of a death sentence and the actual execution has been ten years and three months for those executed in the post-Furman period (Bonczar & Snell 2003). Moreover, it costs at least $2–3 million to process a capital punishment case from trial to execution—more than it costs to process a noncapital first-degree murder case and keep an offender in prison for the rest of his or her life: "Capital trials are more complex and time-consuming than other criminal trials at every stage in the legal process" (Costanzo 1997:62–63). The postconviction appeal stage is generally the most expensive part of all, and approximately 20 to 30 percent of appeals result in reversal of the conviction and/or sentence, a rate "many times higher than in noncapital cases" (Bohm 1998:453).

Death penalty cases are appealed on grounds of either due process violations or compelling new evidence of innocence. In one case involving the 1980 death of a sixteen-year-old white girl in Texas, the investigating police officer had told two janitors—one black and one white—that one of them would "hang" for the crime. The officer then turned to the black man, Clarence Lee Brandley, and said, "Since you're the nigger, you're elected" (Radelet et al. 1992:121). Brandley was indicted by an all-white grand jury and initially tried by an all-white trial jury. The first trial resulted in a hung jury, but a second trial resulted in conviction in 1981. Following the trial, misconduct by the police and prosecutor came to light when hair samples and photographs turned up missing. Although Brandley's first appeal was rejected in 1985, subsequent information from an informant and recanted testimony from a trial witness (the other janitor) shed further light on Brandley's innocence. He was granted a new trial in 1989, and nine months later the charges were dropped. All told, Brandley spent nine years on death row for a crime he did not commit. No law enforcement officials were ever reprimanded for their mishandling of the case (Parker et al. 2001).

In another case, in the state of Florida, Sonia Jacobs was released from death row after an appellate court concluded in 1990 that the prosecution had suppressed exculpatory evidence and that a prosecution witness (who turned out to be the real killer) had lied. Two years earlier, Jacobs's husband and codefendant, Jesse Tafero, had been executed after being "convicted and sentenced to death on exactly the same evidence" as Jacobs (Radelet & Bedau 1998:231).

Samuel Gross (1996) argues that mistaken convictions may be more common in capital murder cases than in other cases because police and prosecutors are under greater public pressure to apprehend the perpetrator as quickly as possible. This pressure may lead them to make hasty judgments, to use informants of questionable reliability, and to coerce suspects into confessions. The greater publicity given to such cases also provides jurors with information damaging to the defendant that might not be admissible in court. And since defendants in capital cases are most often poor, they do not have the resources to challenge a determined prosecutor successfully. Judges typically assign capital cases to inexperienced or mediocre defense attorneys. In Kentucky, for example, one-fourth of those on death row were represented by attorneys who were subsequently disbarred, suspended, or incarcerated (Kroll 1991). One trial in Alabama had to be postponed when the defense attorney arrived at court drunk; when the case resumed the next day the defendant was quickly sentenced to death. In four trials in Georgia the attorneys representing African American defendants used the term "nigger" to refer to their clients, all of whom were sentenced to death. And in Texas a defense attorney simply told the jury at the sentencing hearing, "You are an extremely intelligent jury. You've got that man's life in your hands. You can take it or not. That's all I have to say" (McCormick 1998:64). His client was executed.

Michael Radelet and colleagues (1992) found that 416 death penalty defendants in the twentieth century were wrongfully convicted, 23 of whom were executed. The Death Penalty Information Center (2003a, 2003b) reported that since 1973, 112 people have been released from death row due to posttrial findings of innocence. In 2000 Illinois governor George Ryan was so concerned about his state's record of wrongful convictions that he called for a moratorium on further executions and the establishment of a special panel to examine the death penalty. Upon leaving office in 2003, Ryan commuted the sentences of 167 prisoners who had received a death sentence in Illinois and granted an unconditional pardon to four others.

In spite of this history of wrongful convictions, state and federal officials continue to look for ways to limit the appeal process, for instance, by narrowing the time a defendant has to file an appeal and by restricting a defendant's ability to file additional appeals that raise claims not included in the original appeal. Limiting the process, however, will likely result in more wrongful executions (Bohm 1998).

In the Furman case a majority of justices on the Supreme Court were persuaded that the death penalty had been applied in a discriminatory manner. Fifteen years later, in *McCleskey v. Kemp* (1987), a more conservative group of justices had the opportunity to revisit the issue. Warren McCleskey had been sentenced to death in the state of Georgia for the murder of a white police officer. McCleskey appealed his case on the basis of statistical evidence that indicated that black offenders who murdered white victims had a higher probability of receiving a death sentence than defendants in cases with other racial patterns of offenders and victims. But a majority of justices were not persuaded that *statistical* evidence of racial disparity constituted a sufficient basis upon which to overturn McCleskey's sentence. The decision virtually "eliminated the federal courts as a forum for the consideration of statistically based claims of racial discrimination in capital sentencing" (Baldus & Woodworth 1998:409). Currently, over 40 percent of persons on death row are African American (Pastore & Maguire 2002).

Many people believe that if capital punishment is to be used, **lethal injection** constitutes the most humane method of inducing death. Most states now use lethal injection as the sole means of execution or allow the condemned person a choice between lethal injection and another method (i.e., electrocution, gas, hanging, or firing squad). Typically the lethal injection procedure entails strapping the person to a gurney and injecting him or her with a nonlethal chemical (sodium pentothal) to induce sleep and unconsciousness. The person is then administered pancuronium bromide, a muscle relaxant, and finally, potassium chloride, which induces cardiac arrest and permanently stops the heartbeat. Complications can arise, however, if the sodium pentothal is insufficient, the chemicals are administered out of sequence, or the executioners have difficulty locating a usable vein for the insertion of the catheter (Denno 1998).

Only one state (Nebraska) still uses electrocution as the sole method of capital punishment. The typical electric chair is capable of providing 2,640 volts and five amperes of electricity to the condemned person in two one-minute intervals. The procedure can cause severe burning of the flesh, even burning away of the ears, as well as intense muscle spasms and contractions, explosion of the penis, secretion of blood from the facial orifices, and vomiting, defecation, and urination. Needless to say, this method of death can be quite painful if the person does not lapse into unconsciousness immediately. Between 1979 and 1997 at least seventeen botched electrocutions occurred in the United States. In 1997, for example, before Florida changed its law to allow for lethal injection as well as electrocution, "Old Sparky," the state's seventy-four-year-old electric chair, caused flames up to a foot long to shoot out from Pedro Medina's covered head, filling the entire execution chamber with smoke (Carelli 1999; Denno 1998; Harrison & Beck 2003).

▣ *Gender and the Death Penalty*

Less than 2 percent of prisoners on death row are women (Pastore & Maguire 2002). The paucity of women receiving capital punishment reflects both their low representation among those convicted of murder and the fact that their homicides are more likely than men's to be domestic crimes and to lack premeditation (see Chapter 8). Women tend to be seen as less blameworthy for their crimes and more deserving of consideration (see Chapter 11). Moreover, society is generally "less willing to wreak horrible punishments" on women than on men: "When the ship is sinking, we put women in lifeboats first. When women enter the armed forces, they are kept away from the firing line. . . . We are uncomfortable with subjecting women to death or even danger" (Streib 1998:220).

The widely publicized lethal-injection execution of Karla Faye Tucker in Texas in February 1998 brought media attention to the issue of gender and the death penalty. Prior to the Tucker case, only one woman had been executed in the post-Furman era, and Texas had not executed a woman since 1863. (Prior to the March 1998 execution of serial murderer Judi Buenoano, Florida had not executed a woman since 1848 [Hancock 1998]. Buenoano had been found guilty of two murders: the arsenic poisoning of a husband in 1971 and the drowning of a paraplegic son she pushed out of a canoe in 1980. These deaths were only discovered to be murders after she was suspected of killing a fiancé in a car bombing in 1983 [Gillespie 2000].)

In spite of Tucker's conviction for the pickaxe murder of a man and woman in a 1983 robbery, she emerged as an appealing and sympathetic media figure, one who sparked "a worldwide debate over redemption and retribution" (O'Shea 1999:343). A born-again Christian who found God on death row, Tucker counseled fellow inmates and even married a prison minister. The Rutherford Institute, which usually limits its advocacy to cases of religious freedom and human rights, petitioned President Clinton to prevent the execution. Television evangelist Pat Robertson and even Pope John Paul II spoke on Tucker's behalf. While these supporters emphasized Tucker's religious conversion, they had never before made a plea on behalf of a condemned man who had converted to Christianity (Hancock 1998; Verhovek 1998). Nevertheless, Tucker acknowledged that there had been "people who have gone before the board who were just as committed to Christ as I am" but who were executed anyway. The "people" she referred to were men. "If you believe in the death penalty for one," she said, "you believe in it for everyone" (Pearson 1998:A19).

Tucker's appeal for clemency was denied. When asked about the "gender factor" in the case, a spokesperson for then-governor George W. Bush replied, "The gender of the murderer did not make any difference to the victim" (cited in Gillespie 2000:98). Neither did it make a difference to protestors carrying signs outside the prison while Tucker was strapped to the gurney, signs that read "Forget injection. Use a pickaxe" and "Axe and you shall receive" (pp. 98–99).

The fact that Tucker was white woman is also significant, for society's reluctance to execute women varies by the race of the offender. Nearly 40 percent of women executed from 1930 to 1967, for instance, were African American (Collins 1997). A study of women on death row in 1993 found African American and Latina offenders to be "overrepresented in the kinds of murders that . . . are at low risk of resulting in the death penalty" (Farr 1997:273). And of the women who were on death row at the time of Tucker's execution, over 40 percent were women of color (O'Shea 1999).

Like Tucker, Guinevere Garcia, an Illinois death row inmate, was critical of the system's chivalry. In 1996 Garcia asked that her execution proceed as scheduled. Although court hearings had determined that Garcia was mentally competent to consent to death by lethal injection, death penalty opponents lodged a petition to commute her sentence against her wishes, arguing that she had been "a battered woman and an abused child" (cited in O'Shea 1999:163). Garcia had been sentenced to death for killing her ex-husband, a crime she had committed four months after being released from a ten-year stint in prison for smothering her eleven-month-old daughter. "I killed George Garcia, and only I know why," she told the review board. "Do not generically label, package, and attempt to justify my actions as that of an abused woman." According to Patricia Pearson, "Garcia was contemplating her life in the face of her death and seeking some measure of redemption. By depicting her as a 'pitiable creature,' her supporters stole from her an elemental gesture of grace" (1997:60). Although Governor Jim Edgar had refused to stay the execution of the six men who had requested clemency since he had taken office, he ignored Garcia's plea to be allowed to die and commuted her sentence to life in prison. In 1997 Garcia slashed her wrist with a broken light bulb from her prison cell—an apparent, though unsuccessful, attempt to take her own life.

Juveniles and the Death Penalty

In 1642 a teenager named Thomas Graunger was executed for bestiality in Plymouth Colony, Massachusetts. Thus began the history of executing persons in the American colonies and later the United States for crimes committed while the offender was under eighteen years of age. Since the execution of Graunger, an estimated 365 individuals have been executed for crimes committed while they were juveniles. This constitutes just under 2 percent of all executions in the country since the beginning of the seventeenth century. In the post-Furman era, half of the twenty-two juveniles who have been put to death have been African American. Currently, there are about seventy-five prisoners (all male) who are awaiting execution for crimes they committed while they were sixteen or seventeen years of age (Cothern 2000; DPIC 2004a, 2004b).

Even those who favor the death penalty for adults may not consider it an appropriate punishment for juveniles (Moon et al. 2000). A case in point is the recent decision of Virginia jurors who rejected a death sentence for teenage sniper Lee Malvo, who was involved in a series of shootings in the Washington, D.C., area that killed ten people in 2002. In contrast, the jury that convicted John Muhammed, Malvo's forty-two-year-old accomplice, recommended the death sentence for him (Greenhouse 2004).

The relative sympathy some people feel toward juvenile offenders stems in part from the perception that mitigating circumstances—immaturity and/or psychological disturbance—may be factors in their crimes. In a study of ninety-one juveniles who had received a death sentence, for example, Dinah Robinson and Otis Stephens (1992) found that nearly a third suffered from psychological disturbances (e.g., depression, paranoia, self-mutilation), almost half came from dysfunctional families, and almost a third had low or borderline IQs.

In 1988 the U.S. Supreme Court vacated the death sentence of a youth who was fifteen years old at the time he committed a murder, declaring the execution to be a violation of the Eighth Amendment's prohibition against cruel and unusual punishment. A year later, however, the Court upheld death sentences for youths who were sixteen or seventeen years old when they committed their crimes. At the time of this writing, the Court had announced its attention to revisit the issue in the Missouri case of Christopher Simmons, who was seventeen years old when he killed a woman during a burglary in 1993. The Missouri Supreme Court had vacated Simmons's death sentence, but the state's attorney general wanted it reinstated and filed an appeal. Opponents of the death penalty hope that the U.S. Supreme Court will finally put an end to this practice. They are encouraged by the fact that in 2002 the Court ruled that executions of persons with mental retardation were unconstitutional. Four of the nine judges have expressed their clear opposition to the penalty for juveniles, but whether they will be able get a fifth vote to uphold the Missouri Supreme Court's decision remains to be seen (DPIC 2004c; Greenhouse 2004).

■ The Modern Penitentiary

▨ *Historical Background*

In colonial America over 160 offenses, from murder to disrespecting one's parents, were punishable by death. Corporal punishment, fines, and compensation to the victim or victim's family were the preferred penal responses, however. Wealthy offenders were more likely to be fined, while the poor were flogged. **Flogging** with a blunt instrument or whip was a public spectacle that directly involved the citizenry in the collective ritual of punishment, in the mobilization of moral sentiments that reinforces social solidarity. Although the practice of flogging waned over the years, it remained in use in the United States through the twentieth century and was not declared unconstitutional by a federal court until 1968 (Inciardi 2002; Rothman 1971; Shover & Inverarity 1995).

The collective ritual of the **pillory** was also used for corporal punishment in colonial times. Here the offender's head, hands, and feet were secured by a wooden frame. The violator was kept in public view and repeatedly whipped or pelted with rocks and eggs by passersby. It was not unusual for the offender's ears to be nailed to the pillory as well. Another device, the **brank**, was used to punish gossips, perjurers, liars, blasphemers, drunkards, and husband batterers. The brank, also called the "gossip's helm" or "dame's bridle," consisted of a cage that was secured around the head, with "a spike plate or flat dish of iron that was placed in the mouth over the tongue," causing severe pain if the offender tried to speak (Inciardi 1996:492).

Other colonial punishments included branding and use of dunking stools, duncecaps, and signs (e.g., "I am a fornicator"). The *scarlet letter,* for instance, "made famous by Nathaniel Hawthorne's novel of the same name, was used for a variety of offenses. The adulterous wife wore an *A,* cut from scarlet cloth and sewn to her upper garments. The blasphemer wore a *B,* the pauper a *P,* the thief a *T,* and the drunkard a *D*" (Inciardi 1996:492). In the 1990s this approach enjoyed renewed interest, as when persons convicted of drunk driving in Sarasota County, Florida, were required to put red stickers on the rear bumpers of their vehicles that read CONVICTED DUI (driving under the influence).

In the late eighteenth century the Quakers in Pennsylvania pioneered the use of prisons, an innovation that removed the public from direct participation in the collective ritual of punishment. Previously, jails had been used primarily to hold persons who were awaiting court action or who could not pay their debts. Now a separate wing of Philadelphia's Walnut Street Jail, the "penitentiary house," was used to confine convicted felons who were kept in solitary confinement. The Quakers viewed the penitentiary as a humane alternative to the cruelty and degradation of existing methods. Locked in isolation, offenders could "be made to contemplate the evil of their ways . . . [and] immerse themselves in self-reflection and penitence" (Barlow 1996:399; Clear & Cole 1994; Shover & Inverarity 1995).

In the early nineteenth century New York constructed the Auburn Prison, the first institution to use an architectural design that arranged cells in multiple tiers, with the entire facility surrounded by a fortresslike stone wall. Prisoners were confined in separate cells at night but allowed to eat and work together in small groups during the day. Solitary confinement was reserved for breaches of prison rules. The inmates, however, were required to maintain complete silence at all times. Hard work and a regimented life were to be the means to one's salvation. Whereas some earlier forms of punishment attempted to discipline the "body" through physical pain, these new methods sought to discipline the "mind" (Barlow 1996; Foucault 1979).

The Auburn approach eventually prevailed as the model for the modern penitentiary. Though considered more humane than earlier punishments, conditions in these institutions were deplorable. They were overcrowded, dirty and dilapidated, physically harsh, and notorious for failing to reform their inmates. Through the first half of the twentieth century, prisons in the United States were colloquially referred to as "Big Houses." Institutions like Alcatraz in California, Sing Sing in New York, and Stateville in Illinois became legendary as human warehouses. Guards ruled the Big Houses through the threat and use of force, and boredom terrorized the prisoners' souls (Johnson 2002; Rothman 1980).

Since the 1870s, however, prison reformers have often advocated a more rehabilitative penal philosophy. The National Prison Association proclaimed that the reformation of criminals required their moral regeneration, "not the infliction of vindictive suffering" (cited in Clear & Cole 1994:57). In 1876 the Elmira Reformatory in New York, under the leadership of Zebulon Brockway, promoted education as the key to successful rehabilitation. Elmira was designed for sixteen- to thirty-year-old, first-time offenders, who were placed in a school-like atmosphere and required to take courses in a variety of academic, vocational, and moral subjects. This approach was incorporated into the philosophy of juvenile "reform schools" as the juvenile justice system developed (see Box 11.2).

In the nineteenth century few women were incarcerated. Those who were were treated similarly to men. Gradually, separate women's quarters were created in men's institutions. Then, in the early 1870s, the first prison operated for and by women was established in Indianapolis. Reformers considered the fortresslike atmosphere characteristic of men's prisons to be inappropriate for women's institutions. These, they believed, should be organized instead around groups of cottages that housed twenty to fifty women in a homelike atmosphere. And inmates, they maintained, should be allowed private rooms rather than cells, be given the opportunity to decorate their quarters, and be taught domestic skills thought suitable to their feminine nature (e.g., ironing, laundry work, cooking) (Clear & Cole 1994; Pollock-Byrne 1990).

After World War I, psychological theories of criminality increasingly influenced modern conceptions of rehabilitation (see Chapter 3). In 1929 "rehabilitation as the primary purpose of incarceration became national policy." Diagnostic classification systems were developed to "differentiate inmates who were likely to benefit from [rehabilitation] from those who were not" and to guide programs of individualized treatment (Clear & Cole 1994:65–66). By the 1940s the modern "correctional" institution employing primarily group but also individual counseling along with vocational and educational training became the model penitentiary. Prison discipline was less intrusive, and inmates were allowed more personal amenities as well as recreational, visitation, and mail privileges. But in spite of all the well-intentioned rhetoric about rehabilitation, prison officials could not deliver on their promises, as genuine reform was overwhelmed by lack of know-how and by administrative and fiscal constraints. At best, prisoners were left on their own to undergo personal reform, a difficult task in institutions that were still quite grim and punitive (Johnson 2002).

From the early 1950s to the early 1970s, prisons in the United States experienced political turmoil that reflected the civil rights movement of the larger society. Prisoners frustrated with punitive prison practices protested nonviolently and rioted to pressure for reform. The most well-known riot of that era occurred in New York's Attica prison in 1971. Over 2,000 inmates took over the facility and held guards as hostages, demanding, among other things, improved diet and medical care, religious freedom (especially for black Muslims), education and rehabilitative programming, legal assistance, procedures for handling complaints, and access to the courts. Governor Nelson Rockefeller ordered state troopers to reclaim the institution by force and about forty people, both prisoners and guards, were killed (Adler et al. 2000; Balkan et al. 1980).

Attica and other prison protests and riots drew attention to the need for reform and ushered in a wave of civil rights lawsuits by prisoners. As a result, there is now more judicial scrutiny of prison conditions and of the behavior of prison personnel. At the same time, however, the 1970s witnessed the abandonment of the rehabilitative mandate of prisons in favor of a retributive philosophy (see Chapter 11). The penitentiary has primarily become a custodial institution where inmates are expected to "do their time" in proportion to the seriousness of their offenses.

The Incarceration Boom

Between 1930 and 1980, a period of five decades, the state and federal prison population in the United States increased by 144 percent. Between 1980 and 2002, just over two decades, it increased by 328 percent (see Table 12.1). In the late 1980s prison overcrowding resulted in court orders in about forty states to either expand facilities or restrict the size of prison populations. A decade later, both state and federal prisons were still operating at about 15 to 25 percent above capacity (Austin et al. 2001; Shichor 1997).

Criminological research shows that crime rates alone do not account for fluctuations in the size of the prison population over time. Several studies have found that prison admissions increase during times of higher unemployment, as incarceration is used to absorb and control the surplus supply of laborers who constitute a potentially rebellious population

(Chiricos & Delone 1992; Hochstetler & Shover 1997). Raymond Michalowski and Susan Carlson attributed rising state and federal prison admissions between 1980 and 1992 to the "growth of an urban underclass with declining access to income-replacing social welfare and public-job provision that began in the 1970s and accelerated throughout the 1980s" (1999:228).

Political factors also affect prison expansion. David Jacobs and Ronald Helms (1996) analyzed state and federal admissions between 1948 and 1989 and found that admission rates were positively associated with the strength of the Republican Party (as measured by the percentage of people who identified themselves as Republican in any given year) independent of the level of crime. They noted that the Republican Party, in comparison to the Democratic Party, has more consistently advanced a law-and-order agenda (see Chapter 1). Jacob and Helms also found that admission rates increased in the year following presidential elections. They argued that competition for votes caused incumbents from either party to enact severe penal policies during campaign years in order to appeal to the public's desire to crack down on crime.

David Greenberg and Valerie West's analysis (2001) of state imprisonment rates between 1971 and 1991 yielded results that support and extend previous research. They found that higher rates of imprisonment were associated with higher unemployment, a larger proportion of the population that was black, a conservative political culture, lower spending on welfare, and higher per capita state revenues. Greenberg and West also found that increased drug arrests during the 1980s impacted higher rates of imprisonment.

Other research supports the central role of the "war of drugs" on the incarceration boom (see Chapters 1, 5, and 7). In 2001, prisoners convicted of drug offenses constituted 55 percent of the federal prison population, up from 25 percent in 1980 (see Table 12.2). Over 20 percent of state prisoners were serving sentences for drug offenses, up from 7 percent in 1980, and many more had been convicted for crimes committed to get drug money. At the same time, the opportunities to receive drug treatment in prison have declined considerably (Austin et al. 2001; DiMascio 1997; Glaser 1997; Lock et al. 2002).

African Americans have been especially impacted by punitive penal policies. In 2000, African Americans, constituting just 13 percent of the U.S. population, constituted 45 percent of the prison population (see Table 12.3). And although males are much more likely than females to be incarcerated, both black males and black females are disproportionately more likely to be imprisoned than their white counterparts. African American women in particular have constituted one of the fastest-growing sectors of the prison population and currently constitute about half of all women who

Table 12.2   Number of Prisoners by Type of Offense (2001)

	State	Federal
Violent offenses	596,100	16,117
	(49.3%)	(11.3%)
Property offenses	233,000	10,664
	(19.3%)	(7.5%)
Drug offenses	246,100	78,501
	(20.4%)	(55.0%)
Public-order offenses[a]	129,900	36,443
	(10.7%)	(25.5%)
Other/unspecified[b]	3,600	1,041
	(0.3%)	(0.7%)
Total	1,208,700	142,766
	(100%)	(100%)

Source: Harrison & Beck 2003, tabs. 15, 18.

Notes: a. For state institutions this category includes weapons, drunk driving, court offenses, commercialized vice, morals and decency charges, liquor law violations, and other public-order offenses. For federal institutions it includes weapons, immigration, and other public-order offenses.

b. For state institutions this category includes juvenile offenses and unspecified felonies. For federal institutions it includes offenses not classifiable.

Table 12.3   Number of Prisoners by Race/Ethnicity and Gender (2000)

Race/Ethnicity	
White (non-Hispanic)	453,300
	(34.7%)
Black (non-Hispanic)	587,300
	(45.0%)
Hispanic	203,700
	(15.6%)
American Indian	13,240
	(1.0%)
Asian/Pacific Islander	9,670
	(0.7%)
Not reported	37,930
	(2.9%)
Gender	
Male	1,219,225
	(93.4%)
Female	86,028
	(6.6%)

Source: Stephan & Karberg 2003, tabs. 1, 4.

are incarcerated. These policies have had the unfortunate effect of further destabilizing some black communities by weakening family and community ties that might otherwise foster informal social controls (Austin et al. 2001; Bush-Baskette 1998; Maguire & Pastore 2001; Rose & Clear 1998).

Moreover, the incarceration boom has been extraordinarily expensive. It costs an average of $80,000 per inmate to construct a new maximum-security prison. And with financing costs (borrowed money) factored in, the total expenditure is two to three times the original investment. In addition, by the mid-1990s, operating costs of state and federal prisons approached $20 billion a year. And this figure does not include the hidden costs of expenses transferred to corrections departments from education, health, and other agencies. Money spent on prisons also diverts resources that might otherwise be devoted to crime prevention and general societal needs. Some states are now spending more money on corrections than on higher education (Austin et al. 2001; DiMascio 1997).

The irony of all this, as Franklin Zimring and Gordon Hawkins (1997) observe, is that expanded prison admissions have the greatest impact on less serious offenses, those offenses at the margin between meriting incarceration and meriting more lenient penal sanctions. In California, for example, the state with the largest prison population, "only 27 percent of the additional prison space added between 1980 and 1990 was used to increase the number of inmates who had been convicted of violent offenses" (p. 18). Nationwide the *proportion* of prisoners convicted of violent crimes has declined. Zimring and Hawkins are concerned that such penal policies, which narrow sentencing disparities between life-threatening and non-life-threatening offenses, diminish the deterrent effect of the law because offenders have less to lose by crossing the threshold of violence. Thus the incarceration boom, in their view, represents a misguided political response to the public's genuine concern about crime. Prison expansion provides little "bang for the buck" in protecting the public against the crimes that it fears most—crimes of violence.

■ Privatization of Prisons

In his January 1961 farewell address, President Dwight Eisenhower warned the American public to "guard against the acquisition of unwarranted influence, whether sought or unsought, by the military-industrial complex." Today, Eric Schlosser believes, the United States has "developed a **prison-industrial complex**—a set of bureaucratic, political, and economic interests that encourage increased spending on imprisonment, regardless of the actual need" (1998:54). Architectural and construction firms, investment bankers, and companies selling everything from security cameras to padded cells view this spending not as a burden on taxpayers but as an opportunity to profit.

The latest trend in corrections, the **privatization** of prisons, is a development that bears close scrutiny. Private companies, which serve over thirty states and the federal system, contract with the government to build and/or manage prisons. About 7 percent of adult prisoners are housed in private facilities, as are nearly 30 percent of juveniles who are being held in residential custody (Pastore & Maguire 2002; Stephan & Karberg 2003).

Privatization is touted as a way to save money, but research indicates that private prisons are not less costly to administer than public institutions. Moreover, private prisons are more likely to cut corners by reducing labor costs, which constitute 60 to 80 percent of prison operating budgets. Prison guards and correctional officers who work for private companies are paid less, receive fewer fringe benefits and less training, and have fewer opportunities for promotion than those who work for the government. On the other hand, top officials of private companies receive lucrative six-figure salaries, in addition to money earned from stock holdings in their firms (Pratt & Maahs 1999; Schlosser 1998; Shichor 1997).

Private prisons usually charge their customers, the taxpayers, a daily rate for each inmate. Like hotels, the companies have an incentive to keep their beds filled. Hence prisoners in private prisons are more likely than prisoners in government institutions to lose credits for "good time" that would lead to earlier release. In addition, "bed brokers" earn commissions for arranging to locate and transport prisoners from one state to another, county governments charge companies per-inmate licensing fees, and county sheriffs cut deals with companies that agree to build and operate new jails and share the profits with them (Bates 1998; Schlosser 1998).

The private shipping of prisoners from one state to another also poses considerable security risks, especially when untrained personnel are making the pickups and deliveries. It is not unusual for prisoners to spend a month on the road as transport vehicles visit dozens of states before arriving at their destination. This practice is even less regulated by the government than the interstate shipping of cattle.

There is also less accountability in the running of private prisons than in the running of government prisons. A training video from a correctional facility in Texas, operated by Capital Correctional Resources Inc., revealed correctional officers mistreating prisoners originally from Missouri—cursing, kicking, dragging, and zapping them with an electronic stun gun while they were lying on the floor. One of the officers had previously served prison time for beating a prisoner when he was employed at a Texas state prison. In a Kentucky correctional facility run by the U.S. Corrections Corporation, the company exploited unpaid prison labor for construction and renovation work not only on the prison but on several churches, a game-room business, a country club, and a private school as well. Company officials had business or personal interests in all of these projects.

In the world of privatization, falling crime rates, shorter prison terms, and community alternatives to prison are all bad for business. Hence private companies lobby state governments for policies that expand prison construction. One executive from the Corrections Corporation of America (CCA), the nation's largest private prison firm, likened profiting from prison to "selling cars, or real estate, or hamburgers." Another CAA executive remarked, in reference to a plan to build prisons in California "on spec" (i.e., without a contract to fill them), "If you build it in the right place, the prisoners will come" (quoted in Schlosser 1998:76).

■ Living and Working in Prison

Prisons are typically classified as maximum-, medium-, or minimum-security facilities, according to the amount of physical security that is available both within and on the perimeter of the institution. Prisoners are distributed into these prisons on the basis of the seriousness of their offense record and the perceived danger they pose to society. In all prisons, power is divided between the correctional staff and inmates. The staff maintain some semblance "of order as prisoners go through the formal routine of meals, counts, work, recreation, and [whatever] correctional programs" the prison may offer. However, "outside the formal schedule, on cell block tiers, in recreation areas, [and] on the yard," the prisoners are afforded a degree of self-rule that governs the institution as much as the official rules do (Johnson 2002:127).

■ The Society of Captives

In his classic book *The Society of Captives,* Gresham Sykes (1958) described prison life as a response to five types of deprivation or **pains of imprisonment**. According to Sykes, the most basic deprivation is the loss of liberty itself, which consists both of "confinement to the institution" and "confinement within the institution" (p. 65). Although this deprivation, like many others, induces more psychological than physical pain, it produces an intense boredom and loneliness that is more than most of us could bear. Second, prisoners are deprived of most goods and services enjoyed by citizens in the free society. While the public may at times complain about "country club prisons," most inmates lead a rather Spartan life, the "food to eat and roof over their heads" notwithstanding.

Deprivation of heterosexual contact is a third pain of imprisonment. Heterosexual deprivation leads some prisoners to become involved in homosexual acts they otherwise might not have engaged in, causes some to question their sexual orientation and/or gender identity, and exacerbates the problem of male-on-male rape. Fourth, inmates suffer a loss of autonomy as they are subjected "to a vast body of rules and commands which are designed to control [their] behavior in minute detail," from when to eat to when to take a shower (Sykes 1958:73). The fifth deprivation, the loss of physical security, is perhaps the greatest deprivation of all. Today, threats to one's security occur less at the hands of prison guards than at the hands of other prisoners. The contemporary prison, at least the maximum-security institution, is indeed a violent place. It bears no resemblance whatsoever to the therapeutic atmosphere envisioned by prison reformers of an earlier era (Brook 2004; Johnson 2002; Ross & Richards 2002).

Prisoners adapt to these pains of imprisonment, both individually and collectively, in a variety of ways. One adaptation entails the development of an **informal prison economy**, whereby prisoners barter for commodities such as extra and better food, clothing and personal grooming products, immersion coils for heating water and food, cigarettes, and illegal drugs and alcohol (including prison "home brew"). Some items may be purchased from the prison canteen or commissary with coupons earned from prison work or drawn on personal accounts. They may also be stolen from other inmates or prison facilities (e.g., kitchen, canteen, hospital), mailed by relatives and friends, or smuggled into the institution from the outside. There is also an informal economy of services, including sex, protection, and legal assistance. Typically, cigarettes are the medium of exchange. They have "a stable and well-known value, and come in denominations of singles, packs, and cartons" (Clear & Cole 1994:266). The demand for cigarettes remains high among prisoners, and even those who don't smoke keep cigarettes for bartering purposes. Besides, smoking cigarettes is part of the "tough guy" demeanor that helps minimize the chances of being victimized by other inmates (Ross & Richards 2002).

In addition, the prison experience requires adaptation to a **convict code** that governs relationships among prisoners and between prisoners and correctional staff. This code encourages prisoners to "do your own time" and "mind your own business." Inmates are advised to keep their distance from staff and above all not to squeal or inform on other inmates. They also learn to respond in kind to threats or assaults from other prisoners or risk becoming perennial targets for further victimization, including rape. As Jack Abbott (1981), a convict who gained notoriety for his book *In the Belly of the Beast,* writes, "When you walk across the yard or down the tier to your cell, you stand out like a sore thumb if you do not appear either callously unconcerned or cold and ready to kill. Many times you have to 'prey' on someone, or you will be 'preyed' on yourself" (p. 155; Bowker 1980; Ross & Richards 2002; Sykes 1958).

Convicts with a demonstrated capacity for violence often dominate today's prisons, especially state prisons. Most inmates, however, try to carve out their own private niches, insulating themselves from the violence. They spend as little time as possible in the mess hall, recreational areas, and prison yard; and they stay away from the informal economy. They stick to a few friends, if they can find them, and log long hours alone in their

cells. In a survey of 300 prisoners at a maximum-security institution in Tennessee, Richard McCorkle (1992) found that 40 percent of inmates said they avoided public areas and nearly 80 percent said they lived as loners. Vulnerable inmates rarely turn to staff for protection, for the convict code inevitably marks those who "snitch" as objects of derision and abuse. For some, voluntary segregation in protective custody (PC) is the only safe alternative. Prisoners opting for PC remain "confined to their cells for all but a small part of the day," even though such isolated living is difficult and often damaging to one's psychological well-being (Lockwood 1977:206).

Many prisoners find that they have more time than they have ever had before to read, which is one of the most constructive things they can do in the penitentiary. Some may try to earn their General Education Development (GED) certificates or even take college courses that are offered on site or through distance learning programs. Some join formal religious, cultural-identity, and self-help groups or clubs that are sponsored by the prison and that offer supervised space for meetings (Johnson 2002; McCall 1994; Ross & Richards 2002).

In the past few years we have heard a great deal about the need to build so-called **super-max prisons**. A survey by the National Institute of Corrections (1997) identified fifty-seven super-max prisons or super-max units within other institutions operating throughout the country. Sixteen of these facilities were in the state of Texas alone. Proponents of the super-max concept believe these facilities are necessary to control violent and seriously disruptive inmates. Prisoners are segregated and their movement and contact with other prisoners and correctional staff is restricted. They are required to spend twenty-three hours a day locked in cells that may be as small as eight by ten feet, and they are tightly monitored by sophisticated electronic surveillance and a higher guard-to-inmate ratio than is typical of ordinary prisons. Inmates are taken out one at a time for a shower or exercise in a private room. We actually know very little about the long-term consequences of this severe form of deprivation. We do know that some of these prisoners will spend years in these units before they are released and that in some cases they will reenter society without proper preparation and with inadequate supervision (Austin et al. 2001; Cullen & Sundt 2000).

Race/ethnicity and prison gangs. Racial and ethnic tensions are a significant feature of prison life. In an environment where the majority of prisoners are nonwhite, the power differentials of the outside society are reversed, making whites more vulnerable to victimization than other groups (Bowker 1980; Jacobs 1977; Johnson 2002). As one white, veteran convict observes:

> Most whites fuck up right away when they come into prison, because they try to be friendly. . . . If [a white] says hello or even nods to [the black convicts], then he's already doomed. . . . Half of them will think he is just being polite and treating them with respect, but the other half will know he is weak and afraid, because they know that a white man isn't even going to acknowledge them if he's been in prison before, because whites don't speak to [blacks] in prison. These [blacks] are going to move on that guy as soon as the [corrections officer] disappears. (Early 1992:419)

According to Robert Johnson, life in prison is strikingly similar to life in "our dangerous and yet highly differentiated urban slums," and many prisoners come from communities that are "as harsh and depriving as the prisons they wind up in!" (2002:54, 111). Thus in many respects the convict culture may be viewed not simply as an adaptation to the pains of imprisonment but as a continuation of the urban street culture that is imported into the prison from the outside. Consequently, whites (especially those of higher-class background) have greater difficulty adjusting to an institutional environment that is more incongruous with their prior experiences, and they are more likely than nonwhites to commit suicide (Hunt et al. 1993; Rodgers 1995).

Over the past few decades, prison gangs have become an increasingly significant feature of prison life. Gangs attract some of the most violent inmates and exert considerable control over the informal prison economy. Gangs have also been expanding their base of operations to the outside, with activities on the streets being dictated at times from behind bars. As we noted earlier, the incarceration experience has even facilitated gang organization by bringing together a captive population of similarly situated offenders who can be recruited into larger, more powerful organizations (see Chapter 7).

Prison gangs have been documented in most states and in the federal system. The American Correctional Association (1993) estimated that about 6 percent of the nation's prison population is involved in prison gangs, which are organized primarily along racial/ethnic lines (black, Latino, and white) and engage in both intra- and intergroup conflict. In the California prison system, for example, prison gangs can be traced to the emergence in the late 1950s of a Chicano gang, the Mexican Mafia. Two rival Chicano groups (La Nuestra Familia and the Texas Syndicate) also operate in California prisons. The Black Guerrilla Family has been for many years California's most well-known African American prison gang. And the Aryan Brotherhood, consisting of outlaw motorcycle and neo-Nazi convicts, is the most powerful white group and one of the most violent of all prison gangs (Balkan et al. 1980; Hunt et al. 1993; Ross & Richards 2002).

In a study of California prison gangs, Geoffrey Hunt and colleagues (1993) found that correctional officials responded to the prison gang problem by attempting to segregate gang members from the rest of the prison population. They also documented how a new generation of gangs emerged to fill the power vacuum that was created in the convict culture as members of the older gangs aged, dropped out, or went undercover. The Crips and Bloods, for instance, originally urban street gangs from Los Angeles, imported their rivalry into the prison system and abandoned the intragang disputes that often divided their members on the outside. As one convict observed, "When they are 'out there' they may fight amongst themselves. . . . But when they get to prison they are wise enough to know, we gotta join collectively to fend off everyone else." "Old school" prison gang members, on the other hand, complained that the younger generation did not accord them the respect they used to receive. From their point of view, the younger generation was "needlessly violent and erratic and not 'TBYAS'— thinking before you act and speak" (pp. 406–407).

Women in prison. Women's prisons are fewer in number than men's and more likely to be multiple-classification institutions, housing prisoners of various security risks in the same facility. Some states have no separate prisons for women and either confine them in a separate wing of a men's institution or transfer them to another state. Since the 1970s a number of states and the federal government have operated coeducational prisons, where female and male inmates sleep in separate units but are allowed varying degrees of contact during the day. Prison reformers hoped that coed prisons would normalize the incarceration experience and reduce prison violence; and overall, violence is lower in these facilities. But while sexual contact is prohibited, it occurs nevertheless, and some women do become pregnant. Women in coed prisons, however, are more likely than men to be sanctioned (e.g., lose "good time" or privileges) for violating the "no sexual contact" policy (Belknap 2001; Inciardi 2002; Maguire & Radosh 1999).

In many respects the inmate culture of women's prisons is similar to that of men's prisons. Women find ways to adapt to the pains of imprisonment, and they adhere to the convict code. Those who establish reputations for fighting and the ability to defend themselves physically achieve the highest status. At the same time, the gender norms of the larger society permeate the institution. Since women have less need to demonstrate toughness and physical prowess, women's prisons are comparatively less violent than men's. Women provide one another more interpersonal support and are more likely to develop emotional bonds with friends and sexual partners. In the male prison culture, male-on-male rape is accepted while consensual gay relationships are condemned. "The opposite is true in women's prisons; consensual lesbian relationships are more common and less taboo. The rape of women in prison by other prisoners is rare," although, as we will discuss shortly, the rape of women by prison administrators and guards "occurs far too commonly" (Belknap 2001:189–190; Clear & Cole 1994; Pearson 1997; Pollock-Byrne 1990).

In addition, prison gangs have yet to be reported in women's institutions, even though the number of younger inmates who have been members of street gangs has been increasing (see Chapter 8). And while male convicts join prison gangs, women in prison create "pseudofamilies." Racial/ethnic divisions are also less salient among female prisoners, who often form relationships that cut across those lines. Some white women, however, are able to gain advantage over others by appealing to guards for preferential treatment and assistance in settling disputes.

As with men, both preincarceration and incarceration factors influence women's feelings about and adaptations to prison. In a study of women in two California prisons, the California Institution for Women (CIW) and the Valley State Prison (VSP), Candace Kruttschnitt and colleagues (2000) found that many women have a history of abuse that makes them especially sensitive to mistreatment by correctional officers. As one woman remarked, "I was in an abusive relationship for lots of years and. . . . I feel sometimes that I'm still getting abuse. . . . There's a lot of males, mostly male [guards]. . . . They have this attitude where [they] know they have full control over us. . . . When I lived with an abusive man, you know, full control. And these men have that same attitude" (p. 702). At the same time, Kruttschnitt and colleagues found that features of the institutional environment influenced women's responses. In the CIW, which had a more rehabilitative orientation, women expressed more positive views about other prisoners and correctional staff. In the VSP, which had a more custodial orientation and strict disciplinary regimen, women were more negative about their experiences. The familylike relationships among inmates often noted in research on women's prisons were absent. As one woman said, "You don't have a friend here. . . . There's no closeness. . . . I don't have anyone I hang around with" (p. 704).

Although female prisoners are less likely than their male counterparts to be violent, they are more likely to be sanctioned for minor rule infractions. In a study of Texas prisons, for example, Dorothy McClellan (1994) found that women (but not men) were cited for "drying their underwear, talking while waiting in lines, displaying too many family photographs, and failing to eat all of the food on their plates" (Belknap 2001:164). Trafficking or contraband violations included lighting another woman's cigarettes, sharing shampoo in the shower, borrowing someone's comb, and possessing an extra pillowcase or bra. Criminologists have observed that "women's prison policies and supervision treat women like children" (p. 165). And when regulations are "oppressively petty . . . they wind women up to levels of teeth-grating irritability," causing conflicts to "flare with the frequency of brush fires" (Pearson 1997:210, 220).

Women in prison are also more likely than men to be sexually harassed and assaulted by correctional officers. According to a report by Amnesty International USA (1999), "Male prison staff routinely conduct strip and pat searches, scrutinize women in showers, and monitor female inmates by video." And in a 1990 lawsuit filed by fourteen prisoners in Iowa, women described a practice known as "four pointing," where they were stripped naked with "their hands and feet tied to the four posts of a cot in a spread-eagle position and left . . . for several hours" for all passersby to see (Maguire & Radosh 1999:351). The lawsuit was settled out of court after prison officials agreed to discontinue the practice.

One of the most famous incidents of prison rape involved the 1970s case of Joan Little in North Carolina. Little, a black women serving a seven- to ten-year sentence for theft and receiving stolen property, was sexually attacked by a white male guard. Little fought back, and the guard was killed after falling on the ice pick he was using to assault her. Little's indictment for first degree murder prompted a public outcry, and she was later acquitted. More recently, Amnesty International USA (1999) documented the ongoing problem of sexual extortion and assault against women prisoners by male correctional officers who threatened to withhold basic needs and privileges (e.g., food, showers, family visitations) if women did not provide sexual favors. Women who were raped were threatened with sanctions if they reported being violated (Belknap 2001).

In addition, female prisoners are more likely than male prisoners to experience emotional distress as absent parents. They are more likely to have been single heads of households with dependent children, with about two-thirds having preschool or school-age children (Owen & Bloom 1995). Because only about a quarter of incarcerated mothers have dependent children who are being cared for by fathers, children of incarcerated mothers are more likely than children of incarcerated fathers to be living in foster care and to be separated from siblings (Snyder-Joy & Carlo 1998). (About 90 percent of incarcerated fathers have children living with mothers.) And mothers in prison are more likely than fathers in prison to have their parental rights terminated. As a result, mothers suffer greater levels of stress, depression, guilt, and feelings of inadequacy (Baunach 1985; Browne 1989; Clark 1995; Hagan & Coleman 2001).

Correctional officials are beginning to recognize the importance of maintaining ties between incarcerated mothers and their children. As one prison reformer observes, "If you want healthy mothers and healthy children, if you want to break the cycle of crime, you have to let mothers and their children spend time together" (Harris 1997:53). Thus in some states children are allowed to meet with their mothers in playrooms or nurseries at any time. In some cases transportation is provided and children are even permitted to stay overnight. A program called Girl Scouts Beyond Bars has been established in several states. This program arranges for girls to meet regularly with their mothers to work on projects and engage in structured play activities (Moses 1995). At the Bedford Hills Correctional Facility in New York, children spend weekends with their mothers and an entire week during the summer. Mothers also make audiotapes of stories that are mailed to their children, enabling the children to hear their mothers' voices whenever they wish (Lord 1995).

Issues surrounding pregnancy also pose significant problems for women in prison. Research suggests that from 5 to 10 percent of incarcerated women are pregnant, and as many as a quarter are either pregnant or had given birth in the previous year (Belknap 2001). A few programs have begun to address this concern, allowing for month-long furloughs before and after birth, or allowing women who give birth while confined to keep their babies for a period of time or even for the entire length of sentence. Yet less than half of women's prisons provide prenatal care, only 15 percent provide adequate nutrition for mothers-to-be, and slightly more than 10 percent offer postnatal counseling (Wooldredge & Masters 1993). Some women prisoners have even been forced to give birth with their legs shackled to bedposts, restricting their movement in a way that endangers their health and the health of their newborns (Amnesty International USA 1999; Baunach 1985; Maguire & Radosh 1999).

Health care and HIV/AIDS in prison. In the United States prisoners have a constitutional right to medical care. The quality of that care, however, leaves much to be desired, especially since rates of HIV (human immunodeficiency virus), AIDS (acquired immunodeficiency syndrome), and other infectious diseases among prisoners are much higher than among the general population (Petersilia 2003a). As Jeffrey Ross and Stephen Richards (2002) note, if you get sick in prison, "pray it is nothing serious, as the medical services are limited and substandard":

> Prisoners suffering from chronic or acute illness will find medical staff to be few, overburdened, and even if they care to help, prevented from doing so by a prison healthcare system that is under-funded, bureaucratic, and severely limited in the services and medical procedures authorized. . . . If you need surgery, expensive medication, or sophisticated medical protocols, you need to have family and friends to pressure prison administrators. A life-threatening illness (e.g., cancer, heart attack, or stroke) will require outside intervention, possibly a lawsuit or a letter or phone call from a powerful politician, to get you transferred to a civilian hospital. Many prisons now have geriatric cellblocks filled with elderly prisoners, many of them in wheelchairs, on respirators, or in beds hooked up to machines or intravenous tubes. . . . Some prison systems allow elderly prisoners, or younger convicts diagnosed to die in a few months, to apply for compassionate release . . . to go home and die in the company of . . . loved ones. . . . [But] few prisoners ever make it out the door before they pass away, as the application process may taken many months to officially approve. (p. 101)

HIV and AIDS are especially serious problems in prison. Researchers estimate that as many as a quarter of the people living with HIV/AIDS in the United States have spent some time in the correctional system, although most HIV-positive inmates were infected before entering prison (AIDS Action 2001; Braithwaite & Arriola 2003). Although the majority of prison HIV/AIDS cases involve men (since there are more men in prison than women), the HIV/AIDS rate is proportionately higher among women. African American women in particular have the highest rates of HIV/AIDS as well as tuberculosis, cancer, and sexually transmitted diseases (Collins 1997; Hammett et al. 1999).

In 1985, 16 percent of the fifty-one state and federal prison systems in the United States had policies requiring all prisoners with HIV to be housed in separate units, and 75 percent required separation of prisoners with AIDS. By the late 1990s, however, only 4 percent of the systems required separate housing for HIV-infected inmates, and only 6 percent required separate housing for AIDS. A third of the systems made decisions regarding placement of HIV-infected inmates on a case-by-case basis, and nearly 60 percent did so when placing prisoners with AIDS. Moreover, there is considerable variation within prison systems in the treatment of those with HIV/AIDS, and many of these prisoners are denied equal access to prison jobs, education, and other programs. Because the primary methods of contracting HIV/AIDS involve sexual contact or intravenous drug use, the availability of condoms and clean needles could reduce the spread of disease. (Tattooing and body piercing is also a source of transmission.) But few prison systems have adopted condom distribution or other harm-reduction strategies (e.g., furnishing clean needles or bleach for disinfecting used needles). About a third of inmate deaths each year result from AIDS-related diseases, and when infected prisoners are released from prison without treatment, communities are at greater risk of escalating health problems (Abramsky 2002; Braithwaite & Arriola 2003; Cauchon 1995; Hammett et al. 1999; Oliverio 1990).

■ *Convict Labor and Prison Industries*

Prisoners in the United States "have always worked, and making them work [has been] seen as a way to accomplish numerous correctional objectives" (Clear & Cole 1994:362). Their work has been viewed as a form of punishment, as a means of rehabilitation, as an escape from idleness, and as a source of profit for the institution or government.

In the nineteenth century, prisons leased prisoners to private companies that used the workers to make products that were sold on the open market. In the South, following the Civil War, this system amounted to nothing less than legalized slavery, as African Americans constituted over 95 percent of prisoners in southern states (Free 1996; Shelden 1982). As one South Carolina official observed, "After the emancipation of the colored people, whose idea of freedom from bondage was freedom from work and license to pillage, we had to establish means for their control" (quoted in Sellin 1976:158). Private companies ran their own forced-labor camps where prisoners were beaten by their overseers and forced to work from daylight to dusk, at times in "black and noxious mud . . . almost to their waists" (Sellin 1976:150). In one Georgia camp sixty-one men were required to sleep in a nine-by-seventeen-foot room. Needless to say, the mortality rate among workers was high. In fact, over half of the prisoners in South Carolina camps during the late 1870s died (DuBois 1904).

In other instances prison officials allowed private companies to come into the institution and organize production inside the prison walls. Or prisons would simply contract to make the goods for the companies, with the companies providing only the raw materials. Some prisons even operated their own businesses and sold their products on the open market. But in the late nineteenth and early twentieth centuries, both private companies and organized labor began lobbying to limit unfair competition from prison industries that operated with minimal labor costs. In the 1930s and 1940s, the U.S. Congress and the states banned interstate commerce in prison-made goods. Laws were also passed that required prisons to sell products only to other state agencies, rather than on the open market, and that limited the number of prisoners who could be employed and the kinds of goods that could be produced (Clear & Cole 1994; Miller 1974, "At Hard Labor").

In the 1970s the federal government and the states began to reevaluate these restrictive policies. In 1979 Congress lifted its ban on interstate commerce in prison-made goods, provided that prisons met the conditions of the newly created Prison Industry Enhancement (PIE) certification program. This program, which is administered by the U.S. Department of Justice, allows prison-based joint ventures with private industry if prisoners are paid at local prevailing wage rates and other companies are not adversely affected by the arrangement. "Prevailing wage rates," however, allow for the deduction of incarceration costs and any training that is required, as well as social security, Medicare, victim compensation payments, and mandatory savings accounts. And work programs that produce goods for foreign export or for sale in intrastate commerce are not even covered by PIE standards (Miller 2000; Johnson 2002; Sexton 1995).

By the early 1990s PIE had certified over thirty correctional agencies to operate private-sector prison industries using convict labor for a diverse range of enterprises, including "data entry and information processing, electronic component assembly, garment manufacturing, contract packaging, metal fabrication, telemarketing, and . . . travel reservations" (Sexton 1995:3). Companies that have utilized prison labor to manufacture products or delivery services, or that have sold products made by inmates, include Nike, Dell, Microsoft, Honda, Konica, TWA, Best Western Hotels, McDonald's, Eddie Bauer, Target, J.C. Penny, and Kmart (Miller 2000).

Nevertheless, most prison work entails routine manual jobs that do not provide inmates with marketable employment skills. Only a minority of prisoners are actually involved in the manufacturing of goods. Others work in farming, forestry, ranching, and road construction and maintenance, and most simply perform menial tasks that are necessary for the functioning of the prison itself—mopping floors, laundering, cooking and cleaning in the kitchen, cutting grass, shoveling snow, and so forth. Wage rates in prison may range from as little as twelve cents an hour for mopping floors to as much as a seven dollars an hour for the most desirable PIE jobs, with most inmates earning less than a dollar an hour (Leonhardt 2000; Miller 2000; Ross & Richards 2002).

Clearly, some prison work opportunities are better than others. According to Johnson, the Federal Prison Industries program, established in 1934, "has met with consistent and continuing success" and is at the heart of the relatively better living conditions found in some federal prisons. Under its trade name, UNICOR, its "goal is not to maximize profits . . . [but] to maximize employment and training of prisoners." Evaluation studies of UNICOR and the vocational training that is available in the federal system found that participants "were less likely to violate prison rules" than a control group of nonparticipants, and they were "more likely to be rated as autonomous and responsible by [prison] officials." Upon release, these prisoners, both male and female, "made better adjustments than other inmates" (2002:304). They were more likely to find jobs and to get better-paying jobs, and their rates of recidivism were lower (Gaes et al. 1999; Saylor & Gaes 1994).

In the 1990s, controversy arose over the reemergence of the **chain gang**, a practice that had been discontinued for about three decades. In chain gangs, prisoners are shackled together at the ankle and made to work long hours on roads and in fields. Public opinion about chain gangs had soured after the release of *I Am a Fugitive from a Chain Gang,* a 1930s film about an innocent man who was cruelly treated by his prison overseers. But in 1995 three states—Arizona, Alabama, and Florida—resurrected this practice. In Phoenix, Arizona, for instance, women in ankle chains and orange jumpsuits can be found pulling weeds and picking up trash on city streets. While some passersby delight in the spectacle of chain gangs, others decry its use as a means of humiliating and degrading prisoners. In Alabama the Southern Poverty Law Center brought a lawsuit challenging that state's use of chain gangs as cruel and unusual punishment. The state agreed to stop shackling prisoners to each other, although it continues to use work crews of prisoners who have their own legs chained together (Brehm 2003; Pearson 1996).

■ *The Work of Correctional Officers*

In many respects, issues pertaining to the work of correctional officers (COs) parallel those of police. In Chapter 11 we discussed the difference between military and community styles of policing. In corrections there is a similar distinction between *custodial* and *human service* styles of correctional work.

Custodial-oriented officers place utmost priority on maintaining order within the institution. Unfortunately, research indicates that all too many COs are rather brutal custodians of our nation's prisons, seeking "order at any price," and using violence—both their own and that of their convict

allies—as "one of the tools of their trade" (Johnson 2002:201). Although these COs are a statistical minority, they are tolerated by other COs and even viewed as role models. Many COs equate authority with toughness and dominance and will put on a hard-nosed facade to appease their more aggressive colleagues (Toch & Klofas 1982).

So-called goon squad officers are those who epitomize the willingness to use force. They are the "physically powerful officers who 'enjoy a good fight' and . . . are called upon to rush to any area of the prison where it is felt that muscle power will restore the status quo" (Bowker 1980:102). They "are the men who 'get the job done' without recourse to such unmanly considerations as tact or persuasion" (Johnson 2002:216). Other COs maintain order simply by not interfering with the activities of prisoners who dominate the informal economy and convict culture and by not protecting weaker inmates who pose little threat to COs. As one CO said of the illicit drugs and sex in prison, "If I got in the middle of that shit, I would be crazy because I will either get seriously hurt or killed. It would be plain stupid" (Stojkovic 1990:225–226). Still other COs resort to petty abuses to gain leverage over prisoners. As one remarked:

> Guy wants to make a phone call? You can make him wait 10, 20 minutes. Guy wants some writing paper? Tell him you don't have any. Guy wants some matches? You can have a drawer full of matches, "I don't have any matches," you tell him. . . . And there's the ways that you can screw around with his property when he's not around. . . . One inmate . . . gave another officer a hard time. . . . This . . . inmate he loves plants. . . . And he had about . . . two dozen. . . . He woke up the next morning and every one of them plants was dead. . . . Say a guy works with . . . woodworking stuff. Just put [a] scratch in his furniture or something. He know[s] how it got there . . . why it was put there. But there's nothing he can do about it. . . . There's so many ways you can get these guys. (Kauffman 1988:66)

According to Johnson, COs are for the most part an "an alienated and . . . embittered lot" (2002:235). Surveys have found that about two-thirds are dissatisfied with their jobs (Cullen et al. 1989; Toch & Grant 1982). COs with a human service orientation, however, are more satisfied than others, for they find more meaning in their work. For them being a professional CO means caring about the prisoners. They "use their authority to help inmates cope with prison life . . . [and] they do the best they can with the resources at their disposal to make the prison a better place in which to live and work" (Johnson 2002:235). As one CO observed, "I often put myself in the inmate's position. If I was locked up and . . . my only contact with authorities would be the officer walking by, it would be frustrating if I couldn't get him to listen to the problem I have. There is nothing worse than being in need of something and not being able to supply it yourself and having the man who can supply it ignore you" (Jacobs & Retsky 1981:68).

Service-oriented COs help prisoners obtain basic goods and services within the institution. As one said, "If an inmate hasn't had a change of underwear in two weeks, you should care enough to get him a change of underwear. If he hasn't had a shower in a week, you should care enough to get him a shower" (Earley 1992:269). Some prisoners also need help dealing with the prison bureaucracy—setting up appointments with counselors, getting access to telephone calls and visitors, checking on the status of their prison bank account or their upcoming parole hearing, or getting their prescribed medication or proper work assignment. Perhaps the most important service function of all is providing for prisoners' physical security. According to one CO, "Security doesn't mean keep them from going over the wall. It means you try to make the guy feel . . . that he's not going to get killed or hurt . . . so an inmate can sit next to another inmate in the mess hall or auditorium and . . . [not] have to worry about something happening" (Lombardo 1988:293).

Criminologists have observed that the most common element in the testimonials of reformed prisoners is the self-respect that was fostered in them by caring COs: "This did not mean that the officers were unusually lenient, lax or permissive; it meant only that they treated the men with a personal interest and without pretension or condescension. . . . They were frank, fair and considerate" (Glaser 1969:92–93). Unfortunately, human service COs—who are perhaps the majority of prison guards—often feel they are violating an unofficial code that calls for a tough-minded custodial stance rather than a concerned effort to help prisoners (Johnson 2002). As one said, "I am almost ashamed to say it . . . [but] the key to being a good [CO] is having a caring attitude. Now that sounds to most staff here as being weak and not very macho. . . . It sounds like you are giving in to the inmate—or at least, that is how the staff interprets it . . . but it is not the same at all" (Earley 1992:269).

Minority and women COs. Issues pertaining to racial/ethnic minorities and women who work in corrections parallel those of minorities and women in policing. Minorities constitute less than a third of COs working in the adult system, with African Americans occupying over 70 percent of the minority positions. Less than 20 percent of COs are women, who are much more likely to work in women's prisons than in men's prisons. There are also fewer women who work in men's prisons than men who work in women's prisons; and women have fewer opportunities for advancement to supervisory positions in men's prisons than men have in women's prisons (Belknap 2001; Britton 1997; Pastore & Maguire 1998; Stephan & Karberg 2003).

Some white male COs, like their police counterparts, have resented the entrance of minorities and women into corrections. As one remarked:

> What will they think of next? They've lowered the standards so anybody can get in. First they brought in these minorities; some of them can hardly sign their name. Now we've got these women who can't even protect themselves. How do they expect to run a prison? Next thing you know, they'll be bringing kids in here to control the inmates. We might as well give the inmates the keys to the place and go home. (Zimmer 1986:59)

Apparently the prospect of women who are capable of doing correctional work is threatening to some male COs' sense of masculinity. As one female CO observed, "They can't go home and talk about how bad and mean they are and what a tough day they have had [if] some little chickie can do the same thing that he is doing" (Owen 1985:158).

While the evidence is mixed, some research suggests that minority and female COs are more likely than white male COs to favor a rehabilitative or human services approach to corrections (Johnson 2002; Van Voorhis et al. 1991; Whitehead & Lindquist 1989). Women in particular have been reported to have better communication skills and to be more effective at defusing inmate violence. Female COs even command more respect from male prisoners than male COs do, and the presence of women in male prisons helps normalize the prison environment (Kissell & Katsampes 1980; Owen 1985; Zimmer 1986). Research also indicates that female COs consider female prisoners to be more difficult to manage than males, "while for male [COs] the reverse is true, suggesting that each sex has less tolerance for . . . the power plays of its own gender" (Pearson 1997:220; Pollock-Byrne 1990).

Nancy Jurik (1985) found that COs' demographic characteristics had less impact on their attitudes toward prisoners and corrections than the organizational features of the workplace, however. Just as individual police officers conform to the organizational styles of their department, individual COs conform to the expectations of superiors who define the operational goals of their institution (e.g., custodial versus human services). Dana Britton (1997) found that the "organizational logic" of CO training programs emphasizes the physical skills perceived as necessary to deal with inmate violence. Training classes are filled with "war stories" of prison violence that often intimidate women and lead them to drop out. But the day-to-day reality of prison work, especially in women's prisons, tends to be quite different. COs consistently describe their job as more of a mental than a physical challenge. As one woman said, "They try to prepare you . . . for the physical part. But that's not what gets to you, it's the mental part. Playing the games with the inmates, they're constantly trying to figure out a way to get one over on you" (p. 804).

Sexual harassment is a particular concern for female COs. One woman observed that "on any given night, 10 or 11 guys will be jacking off—or sometimes they'll be lying there with their fly open like they don't notice. . . . They never do that in front of the men" (Britton 1997:805). Female COs, especially younger ones, are also prey to sexual harassment by male COs. Unfortunately, the occupational environment can offset or undermine the professional outlook and sense of mission CO recruits bring to the job, and some end up leaving this line of work (Jurik 1985; Martin & Jurik 1996).

13

Community Corrections
and Alternative Solutions

Eric Sterling, counsel to the U.S. House of Representatives Judiciary Committee from 1979 to 1989, recalls the political climate during which Congress passed the Anti–Drug Abuse Act of 1986. This act contained provisions for mandatory minimum sentences for federal drug offenders, with greater penalties for crack-cocaine offenders than for powder-cocaine offenders (see Chapter 5). Sterling now views his role in this legislation as "one of the greatest tragedies of my professional life" (quoted in Bikel 1999).

It was the summer of 1986. College basketball star Len Bias had just died of a cocaine overdose after being drafted and signed by the Boston Celtics. (Congressional officials were under the false impression that Bias had died from an overdose of crack rather than powder cocaine.) The leading congressional Democrat, Speaker of the House "Tip" O'Neill, was from Boston. During the July 4 congressional recess, O'Neill observed how much his constituents were "consumed with anger and dismay about Bias's death" (Sterling 1991:1). In the previous 1984 election, the Republicans had outmaneuvered the Democrats on the drug issue, successfully accusing them of being "soft on crime." O'Neill saw an opportunity for Democrats to gain some ground. As Sterling recalls:

> O'Neill knew that for Democrats to take credit for an anti-drug program in [the] November elections, the bill had to get out of both Houses of Congress by early October. That required action on the House floor by early September, which meant that committees had to finish their work before the August recess. Since the idea was born in early July, the law-writing committees had less than a month to develop the ideas . . . [and] write the bills. . . . One idea [that] was considered for the first time by the House Judiciary Committee four days before the recess . . . was . . . mandatory minimum sentences in drug cases. It was a type of penalty that had been removed from federal law in 1970 after extensive and careful

483

consideration. But in 1986, no hearings were held. . . . No experts on the relevant issues, no judges, no one from the Bureau of Prisons, or from any other office in the government, provided advice . . . before [the law] was rushed through the committee. . . . After bouncing back and forth between the Democratic controlled House and the Republican controlled Senate as each party jockeyed for political advantage, the Anti–Drug Abuse Act of 1986 . . . passed both houses a few weeks before the November election. (p. 1)

In the previous chapter we noted some unfortunate consequences of such knee-jerk crime policies, for example, an expanded prison population of nonviolent (especially African American) offenders who might be handled more judiciously through less expensive community correctional programs. In the world of crime politics, however, political expediency rather than rational deliberation often rules the day (Tonry 1999). In this book we have tried to provide a more thoughtful and informed foundation for considering solutions to the problem of crime. Although conventional law enforcement and imprisonment strategies are necessary elements of effective crime control, overreliance on these methods leads to neglect of alternatives that might have greater impact. In this concluding chapter we use our sociological imagination to explore some alternative measures that rely more on community interventions and preventative measures. We also consider proposals to establish a *more just social order* that many think is a prerequisite to *law and order* (see Chapter 5).

■ Community Corrections

Although a "get tough" retributive philosophy has dominated criminal justice policy in the United States since the 1970s, the majority of offenders under correctional supervision are serving all or part of their sentences in the community (see Table 12.1). Nevertheless, community corrections receives only a tenth of the monies that are spent on corrections overall. This problem is exacerbated by the fact that the United States is experiencing an unprecedented number of prisoners who are reentering society after serving time behind bars. This number is a direct outgrowth of the incarceration boom that we discussed in the previous chapter. Over 90 percent of all prisoners are eventually released. Thus the postincarceration population can be expected to grow in future years as more and more inmates complete their prison terms. The social costs of abandoning our commitment to rehabilitation have also concerned many criminologists. Funding for rehabilitation programs in state prisons, where most of the nation's prisoners are held, has been on the decline and currently constitutes a mere 1–5 percent of state prison budgets (Levrant et al. 1999; Petersilia 2003a, 2003b; Travis & Petersilia 2001).

If these problems are to be addressed, the relative paucity of resources for community corrections and rehabilitation programs inside and outside prison will need to be addressed. Fortunately, there is an emerging political consensus that we can longer afford to feed the prison-industrial complex. More and more people are starting to recognize that continuing our spending binge on prison expansion is not a cost-effective remedy to our nation's woes (Kuttner 2003b).

▪ *Probation: Conventional and Alternative Approaches*

Probation, a sentence of community supervision given in lieu of incarceration, is the most widely used correctional disposition. John Augustus, a wealthy nineteenth-century Boston shoemaker, is credited with developing this practice by personally providing bail and assistance to some 1,900 men and women. Augustus so impressed the Boston courts that the state of Massachusetts eventually endorsed the idea, becoming in 1880 the first state to employ probation officers statewide. By the 1950s every state had developed a probationary system of its own (Adler et al. 2000; Clear & Cole 1994).

Historically, probation has been regarded as a cost-effective alternative to prison, especially for nonviolent offenders, and as a means of reducing prison overcrowding. Although probation allows the offender to avoid the brutalizing experience of incarceration, as a stand-alone sentence it offers little in the way of rehabilitation. Nationally, the average caseload of adult probationers approaches 260, and it is not uncommon for caseloads to include several hundred offenders (Adler et al. 2000). In Los Angeles County "two thirds of the probationers are in caseloads of 1,000 and report only by mail, monthly" (Glaser 1997:22). One study found that nearly a quarter of adult felons and over a third of adult misdemeanants on probation had had no contact with their probation officer within the previous month (Bonczar 1997).

The conditions of probation require an offender to follow certain rules. Failure to comply may result in the revocation of probation and a subsequent jail or prison term. In addition to staying out of trouble and reporting periodically to a probation officer, probationers may be required to abstain from using alcohol, to undergo substance-abuse treatment and drug testing, to receive counseling, to refrain from using firearms, to reside in a supervised community "halfway house," to pay restitution to their victims, and/or to perform community service.

Research on the effectiveness of probation yields disparate results due to the varying conditions under which probation is implemented, the length of the probationary period being examined, the nature of the client population, and whether rehabilitative treatment is part of the program (Geerken & Hayes 1993; Gray et al. 2001). Also at issue is how the effectiveness of probation is measured. For instance, effectiveness may be defined broadly as nonviolation of any condition of probation or it may be defined more narrowly as avoidance of arrest, reconviction, or imprisonment. In general, national data indicate that about 60 percent of probationers successfully completed their probationary terms, although "successful completion" often occurred "even when serious, or numerous, technical violations" had been committed during the probationary period (Glaze 2003; Gray et al. 2001:539). About 14 percent of probationers were incarcerated due to a violation or conviction for a new offense. Nonetheless, research suggests that probationers had lower rates of recidivism than offenders with similar histories who had been released from prison and that probationers who received rehabilitative treatment did better than those who did not (Broome et al. 1996; Cohen 1995; Petersilia et al. 1985).

Intensive probation and home confinement. **Intensive probation supervision** (IPS) and **home confinement** (HC) offer two alternatives to conventional probation. Under IPS, probation officers work with significantly smaller caseloads, allowing for more frequent visitations with clients. The nature of IPS programs vary, with the best combining probationary supervision with other rehabilitative services (e.g., education and vocational training, individual and family counseling, substance abuse treatment). Many IPS programs, however, do little more than provide daily officer-client visits of ten minutes or less (Adler et al. 2000; Clear & Cole 1994).

Evaluations of IPS programs have been mixed. Some studies have found that the rates of probation violation were higher for IPS offenders than for those serving traditional probationary sentences. This higher rate was most likely due to the fact that more extensive supervision increases the likelihood that violations will be discovered. In any event, some research suggests that the recidivism rate of IPS offenders was lower than it was for offenders who were eventually released from prison and that this lower rate was produced at less cost (Adler et al. 2000; Barton & Butts 1990; Petersilia & Turner 1993; Reid 2003).

HC or house arrest requires offenders to serve all or part of their sentences within the confines of their homes. HC participants may also be allowed to leave their homes for certain activities, for example, to go to work or school, receive medical care, or attend religious services. Most HC programs employ some type of **electronic monitoring** (EM). EM ranges from something as simple as a telephone call verifying that the offender is home to a device that the participant wears that emits a continuous signal identifying his or her whereabouts. While research has failed to consistently demonstrate lower recidivism rates among HC/EM participants than among ordinary probationers with similar offense histories, many view it as

a positive development. It allows for the supervision of offenders at lower labor costs and "provides for community safety while allowing offenders to maintain and perhaps strengthen family ties and employment" (Adler et al. 2000; Reid 2003; Samaha 2000:382).

Critics of IPS and HC/EM are concerned that the government will abuse its supervisory authority and extend its high-tech monitoring to the general citizenry (Blomberg et al. 1993). They are also troubled about probation officers who have involved neighbors in the surveillance of offenders, creating a network of informants who end up spying on each other. At the same time, for wealthy offenders HC/EM may represent nothing more than being "grounded" in luxurious surroundings. For instance, in 1988 John Zaccaro Jr. (son of Geraldine Ferraro, the 1984 Democratic candidate for vice president) was convicted of a drug violation and sentenced to four months of confinement in his $1,500-a-month apartment complete with cable television, maid service, and YMCA privileges (Rackmill 1994). Despite their drawbacks, however, HC and EM do seem to be particularly appropriate sanctions for offenders with special needs, such as pregnant women, AIDS patients, the elderly and terminally ill, and the cognitively disabled (Lilly et al. 1993).

Shock programs and boot camps. **Shock probation** is a sentencing alternative that entails a probationary term that is granted following a brief period of confinement. It is designed to shock or scare offenders out of criminality by giving them a taste of incarceration. Similarly, **shock incarceration** (SI) is a military-style "boot camp" experience, usually lasting three to six months, that consists of intense physical activity (drills, exercise, and work), rigid discipline, and regimented daily routines. In many cases the U.S. Army and Marine Corps train correctional officers to serve as drill sergeants in these programs. The basic premise of SI is that offenders are in need of discipline and self-control. It is hoped that the program will serve as a crash course in character-building and personal responsibility that will help offenders change their ways (Adler et al. 2000).

Like other correctional strategies, evaluations of SI have been mixed. The most successful programs combine the boot camp experience with other rehabilitative interventions. Thus it is unclear that it is the military regimen per se that is responsible for lower recidivism among participants in successful SI programs (Bourque et al. 1996; MacKenzie et al. 1995; MacKenzie & Souryal 1995; McCorkle 1995). Furthermore, some criminologists are concerned that the intense physical and verbal tactics common to boot camps (e.g., belligerent drill sergeants barking orders and belittling participants) will reinforce an aggressive model of masculinity that underlies much criminal behavior (see Chapter 8). According to Merry Morash and Lila Rucker, the very notion that such tactics will "'train' people to act in a prosocial manner is fraught with contradiction. The idea rests on the assumption that forceful control is to be valued," while empathy toward others is not (1990:214).

Critics also point out that boot camps, many of which are privately run "with little or no oversight," can be overly harsh. At least a half dozen teenagers have died in boot camps in the past decade. Some youths have even reported that they were "punched, kicked and forced to eat dirt for minor infractions such as failing to stand up straight . . . [and that] they had bruised ribs from an exercise in which they were ordered to lie on their backs while counselors ran across their chests in boots" (Spencer 2001:28).

The inclusion of women in some boot camp programs raises additional concerns. Many female participants have previously been abused by men. For them, the military-style approach may be counterproductive. As one woman observed, "They get in your face and make you feel like dirt. . . . They grab you and push you around. . . . I have bruises on my arms. . . . For someone like me that's been physically and mentally abused that's all it reminds me of, being abused" (MacKenzie & Donaldson 1996:35). One thirteen-year-old boot camp offender said that the counselors, who liked to be called "sergeant," repeatedly called her a "whore" and "prostitute"

(Spencer 2001). On the other hand, some participants may find the program empowering. As one woman maintained, boot camp taught her to be more assertive, "to stand up for [her]self and . . . [not] take anybody's crap" (MacKenzie & Donaldson 1996:35).

■ *Parole and the Problem of Prisoner Reentry*

In contrast to probation, parole entails release into the community after an offender has served a portion of his or her sentence in confinement. In some states community correctional officers are assigned caseloads that include both probationers and parolees, while in other states parole is a specialized function. The conditions of parole are generally similar to those of probation, and parole may be revoked and the offender reincarcerated if he or she violates the rules. Overall, research indicates that about 45 percent of parolees successfully complied with the terms of their parole and about 40 percent were reincarcerated (Glaze 2003).

The practice of parole allows inmates to receive early release from prison for good behavior. But in the late 1980s the federal government eliminated parole for all new offenders, and many states followed suit, passing **truth-in-sentencing laws** that require inmates to complete all or most of their prison terms before being released from confinement (Seiter & Kadela 2003). Critics contend that denial of parole will increase prison overcrowding and remove inmates' incentive to cooperate while incarcerated. According to Joan Petersilia, it also means that an increasing number of prisoners will "max out" their sentences while incarcerated and will leave prison without any "obligation to report to a parole officer or abide by any other conditions of release" (2003a:3). In the late 1970s, less than 5 percent of prisoners served their full sentences prior to release; currently nearly 20 percent "max out." But even prisoners who don't serve their entire terms behind bars will find themselves receiving little help readjusting to society:

> If they live in a state that provides funds upon release (1/3rd of states do not), they will be given $25 to $200 gate money. Sometimes a list of rental apartments or shelters is provided, but the arrangements are generally left up to the offender to determine where to reside and how to pay for basic essentials during the first few months. Few prisons have transitional case managers to assist offenders, and the current process places the offender almost solely in charge of his or her own transition plan. (p. 4)

Moreover, few prisoners will find opportunities to "make good" when they return home. At the same time that rehabilitative services for inmates behind bars and after release were being reduced, the U.S. Congress and state legislatures were passing numerous "laws and regulations . . . restricting the kinds of jobs for which prisoners can be hired, easing the requirements for parental rights to be terminated, restricting their access to welfare benefits and public housing, disqualifying them from a host of job training programs, and limiting their right to vote" (p. 4).

While the public has supported such policies as a means of cracking down on crime, the abandonment of transition assistance and rehabilitative programming is shortsighted and will exacerbate the problems of communities to which prisoners return. Petersilia and Jeremy Travis advocate an alternative approach, one where correctional agencies would "create a seamless set of systems that span the boundaries of prison and community," with, for example, "linkages between in-prison job training and community-based employment and job training and between in-prison healthcare and community-based healthcare." Correctional agencies would also be "expected to link mental health services on both sides of the wall [and] to work with community-based domestic violence services when a prisoner with a history of spousal abuse is released" (Travis & Petersilia 2001:308).

In their review of prison reentry programs, Richard Seiter and Karen Kadela (2003) found favorable results from prison **work release** (or furlough) programs that allow inmates to work in the community for a few hours to a few days at a time. Prisoners who participated in work release, especially those who also received vocational training, had lower recidivism rates than those who did not. Seiter and Kadela also found that supervised community halfway houses helped ease the transition from prison to work.

The Texas Reintegration of Offenders (RIO) project is noteworthy for its focus on combining in-prison "life skills" training in a variety of areas (e.g., anger management, parenting skills, domestic violence awareness, personal health) with job-search workshops, placement services, and postrelease follow-up that helps offenders locate and maintain employment. Since the project began in 1985, participants have had lower recidivism rates than non-RIO offenders of similar racial/ethnic backgrounds and offense/incarceration histories (Finn 1998).

Drug rehabilitation, according to Seiter and Kadela (2003), is one of the most promising areas for correctional programming. Especially effective are programs based on social learning principles and utilizing guided group interaction or therapeutic community designs that rely upon the constructive influence of other recovering offenders (see Chapter 4). Lana Harrison (2001) advocates a phased-in **therapeutic continuum** that includes drug treatment in prison followed by both drug treatment and work release in a halfway house facility. Research on Delaware's therapeutic continuum program shows a relationship between length of time spent in the program and lower drug relapse and criminal recidivism rates (Inciardi et al. 1997). More generally, as discussed in Chapter 3, effective correctional interventions entail those that carefully match offenders' particular learning styles and psychological needs, enhance aggression management and stress management as well as academic and vocational skills, change antisocial attitudes and ways of thinking, foster familial bonds, modify peer associations and role models, and help access appropriate service agencies.

■ The Restorative Justice Movement

Over the past decade or two, another array of community corrections programs has been identified with the term **restorative justice**. According to Howard Zehr and Harry Mika, restorative justice involves a process by which all "parties with a stake in a particular offense come together to resolve collectively how to deal with [its] aftermath . . . and its implications for the future" (1998:54). Restorative justice is best understood in contrast to **adversarial justice**, which pits the accused against the accuser and hence encourages offenders "to deny, justify, or excuse their actions, thereby precluding the acceptance of responsibility" (Siegel 2003:272; see Chapter 11). Restorative justice is based on a *social* rather than a *legalistic* view of crime. Crime is defined as a conflict among the offender, victim(s), and others affected by the wrongdoing (e.g., family, school, community). "Fairness is assured, not by uniformity of outcomes, but through provision of necessary support and opportunities to all parties" (Zehr & Mika 1998:53). The goal is to empower people to resolve their own differences rather than relying on the state to do justice for them. Whereas adversarial justice aims to establish blame and administer punishment, restorative justice aims to establish obligations and promote healing.

In the distant past, as Andrew Karmen (2004) observes, victims were more involved in the response to law violation than they are today. In modern societies, the government has

> symbolically displaced the wounded person as the injured party, and the courts [have been] transformed from a forum to settle disputes between specific individuals into an arena for ritualized combat between representatives of the state and the accused. If the prosecution [succeeds], the state [inflicts] pain upon its vanquished opponent in order to teach them not to break the law again . . . and to make negative examples of them to serve as a warning to others. . . . Prisons . . . serve these purposes . . . [and] take troublemakers out of circulation to protect the public . . . and to force maladjusted persons to undergo compulsory treatment. (p. 342)

There is little in the process that benefits the victims of crime, outside of the satisfaction that offenders are being punished.

Karmen traces the rise of restorative justice to the emergence of the **victim rights movement** of the past few decades, which aims to give victims a greater role in the criminal justice process. Requiring the offender to make

restitution to the victim—or in its place, the community—is one way this can be done. Restitution, which is more common in the juvenile justice system than the adult system, is a sanction that requires the offender to compensate the crime victim and/or recompense the community through some form of monetary payment or service (e.g., working at a nursing home or hospital, performing grounds work at a city park, cleaning up graffiti). Typically, restitution is ordered as a condition of probation and is administered through a probation department (Schneider & Finkelstein 1998).

The purpose of restitution is not simply to punish law violators or compensate victims but to make offenders accountable to the *people they have harmed,* thereby erasing "one of the strongest defenses . . . to wrongdoing, [the] inability to empathize . . . with those who have suffered" (Binder et al. 1988:562). By requiring the sacrifice of time and convenience, the expenditure of effort, and the performance of meaningful tasks, it is hoped that offenders will acknowledge and understand their personal and social responsibilities: "By making fiscal atonement or contributing services, they can feel cleared of guilt, morally redeemed, and reaccepted into the fold" (Karmen 2004:295). As such, restitution is consistent with John Braithwaite's concept (1989) of "reintegrative shaming" (see Chapter 4). In reintegrative shaming, offenders receive social disapproval that is designed to invoke remorse. However, if they are remorseful and willing to right their wrongs, they are forgiven and welcomed back into the community.

Restitution orders do not always stipulate that victims are to be fully compensated for their financial losses, and much of the ordered restitution is never paid (Levrant et al. 1999). Nevertheless, some studies report high rates of completed payments as well as rates of recidivism that are equal to or somewhat lower than those of other sanctions (Glaser 1997; Langan & Cuniff 1992; Schneider 1986). The programs work best when care is taken to substantiate victim losses, construct appropriate repayment schedules, monitor offender compliance, and keep accurate accounts of monies earned and disbursed (Harland 1983). Effective programs must also help unemployed offenders locate jobs. Left on their own, most participants will not succeed. The jobs must pay well enough to provide for the offenders' own living expenses, with enough left over to make payments to victims. As Karmen notes:

> If a job pays wages [that are too] low, then the repayment cannot be completed within a reasonable period of time. If nearly all of the offender's earnings are confiscated and handed over to the victim, then commitment to the job and to repaying the debt is jeopardized. If the job is demeaning, then its therapeutic value as a first step in a new lifestyle built on productive employment is lost. If the job is temporary, only for the duration of the restitution obligation, then the risk of returning to . . . crime is heightened. (2004:300)

Some restitution programs are used in conjunction with **victim-offend-er mediation** (VOM), which brings offenders and victims together to work out a fair arrangement under the guidance of a trained mediator or coun-selor. Beyond restitution, VOM gives victims the opportunity to express their anger, indignation, anxieties, and fears, and to get answers to such lin-gering questions as "Why did you choose to attack me?" or "How did you gain entrance to my home?" or "How could I have avoided this?" Through this process victims may be helped to achieve some psychological closure to their experience. Offenders, in turn, are given the opportunity to accept responsibility for what they did, express genuine remorse, and agree to do as much as they can "to try to restore the victim to the condition he or she was in before the crime occurred" (Karmen 2004:347).

Research has found greater success in lowering the recidivism rates of juvenile offenders who participated in VOM than the rates of adult offend-ers who did so (Umbreit 1994). Juveniles have been more likely to com-plete restitution payments that were negotiated with victims than were "similar offenders ordered to make restitution by juvenile court judges who didn't directly involve victims or use mediation" (Karmen 2004:349). In general, however, offenders were more likely than victims to be satisfied with VOM conferences. Many victims have reported feeling even worse after the conferences: their hopes of achieving emotional closure were not realized and they felt pressured to forgive the offender when they were not "psychologically ready to do so" (Braithwaite & Daly 1998; Delgado 2000:762).

John Braithwaite and Kathleen Daly (1998) advocate the **community conference strategy** (CCS), based on the principle of reintegrative sham-ing, as a way to accomplish restorative justice. (CCS may be available in "neighborhood justice centers" [Karmen 2004].) CCS has been employed in New Zealand since 1989 as the preferred response to juvenile crime. CCS takes place after a warrant for an arrest is issued but before an actual arrest is made. The full power of the criminal justice system is invoked only as a last resort if a suitable victim-offender agreement cannot be worked out and successfully implemented.

In CCS both the victim and the offender are allowed to bring members of their immediate and extended families, as well as other significant others, into the mediation process. These "communities of care and con-cern" need not live in the area in which the victim and offender reside; they are simply people who genuinely care about the parties involved (Braithwaite & Daly 1998:156). This arrangement provides a supportive atmosphere in which victims are given voice in the shaming process and empowered to negotiate assurances that they "will be free from future pre-dation and harm." At the same time, the assemblage of "people who care about and respect the offender" helps foster and ensure his or her community reintegration (p. 155). These people are responsible for helping to supervise the offender and enforcing the agreements he or she has made. In this way "particular communities of citizens who care about particular people" try to devise unique solutions to problems in ways that seem fair and appropriate to all (p. 158).

Sharon Levrant and colleagues (1999) raise several concerns about the restorative justice movement. When programs like VOM or CSS are implemented in lieu of or before a trial, they may lack the due process safeguards that are available in the adversarial system. Evidence against the offender that would be inadmissible in court may be presented and used later at trial if an agreement between victim and offender cannot be worked out. Offenders may be pressured to participate under threat of harsher sanctions, and refusal to do so may be used against them in charging and sentencing decisions. In addition, research has yet to demonstrate that restorative justice programs have greater reformative impact on offenders than the vocational and therapeutic interventions we discussed earlier in this chapter.

Restorative justice seems to work best for less serious crimes and interpersonal conflicts that are not as likely to result in court action in the first place, and thus may have little impact on the workload of the criminal justice system. There is also scant evidence that citizen-volunteers, especially in socially disorganized neighborhoods, have the requisite abilities "to effectively mediate conflict between a potentially emotional victim and a resistant offender" (Levrant et al. 1999:12). And clearly it is white-collar offenders, with their greater resources (i.e., money and occupational skills), who are in the best position to negotiate, enforce, and fulfill acceptable agreements (Conners 2003; Delgado 2000).

Nevertheless, many criminologists believe that community correctional strategies that combine conventional rehabilitative treatment with restorative justice offer a promising alternative to the view that punishing offenders is "the only and best solution to crime," and programs implemented under the guise of restorative justice have been growing around the country (Levrant et al. 1999:23). The Minnesota Department of Corrections, for example, has a full-time restorative justice planner who is responsible for facilitating the development of restorative justice programs throughout the state (Sullivan et al. 1998). And the Vermont Department of Corrections has established reparative service boards of community volunteers who help develop an "agreement that requires the offender to (1) restore and make whole the victim(s) of his or her crime, (2) make amends to the community, (3) learn about the impact of the crime, and (4) learn ways to avoid reoffending" (Levrant et al. 1999:5; Walther & Perry 1997).

Increasingly, **drug courts** are becoming part of the restorative justice movement to develop community alternatives to prison. Drug courts were first established in 1989 in the city of Miami and were the brainchild of

Florida associate chief justice Herbert Klein. Drug courts operate on the principle that court-enforced treatment in the community is a viable alternative to both incarceration and voluntary treatment. According to Judge Perry Anderson, who presides over drug courts in the Boston area:

> The typical drug court combines substance-abuse treatment in the community, strict case management with direct judicial involvement, regular drug testing, and graduated incentives and sanctions based on performance in treatment. The ultimate reward is avoidance of a jail sentence or the expunging of criminal charges. The ultimate sanction is imprisonment. . . . Drug courts . . . offer a middle way between the war on drugs and the decriminalization of drugs. They protect public safety by providing strict, intense and coordinated supervision of participants . . . and in turning out a high percentage of graduates who are able to maintain their sobriety and obey the law. (2003:45, 48)

Thus far, research on the effectiveness of drug courts has been favorable, encouraging more and more jurisdictions to experiment with this alternative to incarceration (Adler et al. 2000).

■ In Search of Social Justice

The restorative justice movement is but one component of the peacemaking alternative to the war on crime that we introduced in Chapter 5. According to peacemaking criminologists, the elimination of crime will require the elimination of suffering more generally, and it will be necessary to establish a more *just social order* before we can establish *law and order.*

■ *Focus on Prevention*

Peacemaking solutions focus on the *prevention* rather than on the repression of crime. To be sure, any set of proposals to prevent crime will invariably fall short of the mark, either because we don't have the collective will to implement it or because the problem of crime is too complex and intractable, rooted in the very structure of society. Any serious effort to reduce crime (other than at the margins) would require dramatic social changes that would challenge the entrenched interests of those who benefit from current economic and political arrangements. Moreover, a certain level of crime, as Émile Durkheim observed, is normal and inevitable (see Chapter 4). Nevertheless, we firmly believe that more can be done to improve our situation, and that such improvement will require abandonment of the "war" mentality.

In many respects, the Chicago Area Project of the 1930s and the opportunity and community action programs of the 1960s (e.g., Mobilization for Youth) that we considered in Chapter 4 anticipated the comprehensive strategy that is currently required. Rather than review these earlier ventures, we will discuss what we believe to be essential ingredients of effective crime prevention.

Elliott Currie, among others, argues that "a commitment to full and decent employment remains the keystone of any successful anticrime policy" and that the government has an obligation to promote economic opportunities for those who need them (1985:263): "Employment not only reduces poverty, especially among the economic underclass . . . [but] also increases an individual's bond to society and sense of responsibility" (Barkan 2001:513). Research shows, however, that it is not simply employment but job *quality* (as measured by job satisfaction) that is important to the lowering of criminal recidivism, leaving us with the challenge of how to expand the number of quality job opportunities beyond the relatively few that are available to offenders today (Uggen 1999). Moreover, there is the dilemma of social *inequality* and the sense of relative deprivation that comes from living in an affluent society that dangles the enticements of materialism before everyone without being able to deliver the goods to all. Although some degree of inequality may be necessary to motivate individuals to work and achieve, too much inequality is criminogenic and destructive to the social fabric (see Chapters 4, 5, and 7).

As we have already suggested, there are people who benefit from this inequitable state of affairs. Any real remedy will have to go beyond vague calls for increasing opportunities. Left realists, for instance, have proposed using the tax system to create disincentives for corporations to close plants or relocate jobs to low-wage foreign countries. They also advocate the promotion of workplace democracy by including workers and community representatives on the boards of directors of large corporations. Such reforms might allow a broader range of people (not just corporate owners, managers, and shareholders) to benefit from our economy (see Chapter 5).

Efforts to address the social disorganization often found in inner-city areas are also required. We need to put an end to racially segregated and densely populated housing projects that concentrate poor minorities, socially isolating them from the middle class (of all races) and depriving them of the resources necessary for stable communities: strong families and positive role models that reinforce conventional values and provide networks of informal social control (see Chapters 4 and 7). Well-funded investments in family services and school programs are also part of the solution: prenatal and postnatal care for mothers and infants; training in parenting, child abuse/neglect prevention, and family therapy; quality preschools and child care; youth mentoring and recreation programs; smaller schools and class sizes; and education in conflict resolution and anger/stress management (Barkan 2001; Sherman et al. 1998; Williams & Kornblum 1985). A study by the RAND corporation found that in California investments in measures such as these yielded more crime reduction than comparable expenditures to enforce the state's three-strikes law (Greenwood et al. 1996).

The Omega Boys Club (OBC) is but one example of a successful program that could be expanded to reduce inner-city minority youths' attraction to crime. The OBC, founded in San Francisco in 1987, doesn't accept any government funding, relying instead on support from private foundations, trusts, civic groups, and private citizens. To attract new members, the OBC uses *Street Soldiers,* a radio call-in program that began in 1991 and that is now syndicated on about forty stations. It has also produced several television programs. The OBC is especially proud of the fact that over 160 ' of its members have gone on to college and over half of these have graduated college (Marshall & Wheeler 1996; www.street-soldiers.org).

The OBC relies primarily on peer-group counseling to deal with the anger, fear, and pain that inner-city youths often experience. Youths are instructed in African American history and culture and provided with college and job preparation skills. They are also challenged to avoid use of derogatory language (e.g., "nigger," "bitch") that demeans black men and women, themselves included. The OBC contrasts the rules for survival on the street with new rules for living that reflect the OBC philosophy. The street rules include: *"Gotta handle my business. Gotta do what I gotta do. Gotta get my money on. Gotta be down for my set. Gotta be down for my 'hood. Gotta get my respect. Gotta pack a gun to watch my back. Gotta pack a gun to watch my homie's back. Gotta be with my potna, right or wrong."* In contrast, the OBC philosophy says, *"Life is the most precious thing an individual will ever have. A friend will never lead a friend to danger. Change starts with oneself. Respect comes from within"* (Marshall & Wheeler 1996:130–131). There are currently over sixty projects around the country that have adopted the OBC approach (www.street-soldiers.org).

Any effort at crime prevention, be it a government-sponsored opportunity program or a private initiative like the OBC, ultimately confronts a broader culture that is conducive to crime. We previously discussed, for instance, research that examines the complexity of the relationship between media violence and crime (see Chapters 2 and 9). Franklin Zimring and Gordon Hawkins suggest that although criminologists "may lack the capacity to measure significant dimensions of the pervasive influence of mass media communications," the media may nevertheless "produce long-term citizen desensitization and value changes [as well as] a tolerance for violence that [may] interact with other . . . social conditions to elevate rates" of crime (1997:137). At the very least it makes sense for parents to monitor their children's media habits (including Internet use) to reduce unnecessary exposure to violence. Also important are efforts to encourage the development of more responsible programming.

In addition, the culture of economic consumerism needs to be challenged. As long as consumption remains a primary signifier of people's self-worth, no amount of economic opportunity or equality will be sufficient to satisfy the insatiable appetite for "things." As we noted earlier, in our society products are consumed not just for their practical function but also for what we think the product says about us. The satisfaction we gain, however, "is illusory, and it is supposed to be." Mass advertising has succeeded in blurring the boundary between real and symbolic needs and in orienting consumers to seek out "the latest version of the product whose difference lies only marginally in its substance but substantially in its image" (Barak & Henry 1999:164).

Neither can any credible crime prevention program ignore the powerful influence of *gender* (see Chapters 8 and 9). We must work to undermine the traditional gender socialization that encourages us to associate masculinity with power, superiority, and aggression. Media presentations that teach females as well as males to eroticize male dominance and female submission are especially important to critique and resist. And it is important that girls grow up knowing that they have every right to be treated with consideration, that it is not unfeminine, rude, or prudish to assert themselves or resist unwanted sexual advances. Boys should be given permission to express their feelings, to acknowledge hurt, fear, and vulnerability, for when we teach boys "to deny their own pain we inadvertently teach them to deny the pain of others" (Canada 1998:20). Efforts to support and expand social and economic policies that increase women's opportunities and reduce gender inequality are also necessary, for these will empower women to resist sexual exploitation and facilitate communication and mutual respect between women and men.

Moreover, we must recognize that male violence *against women* is related to the problem of male violence *against men*. As we previously observed, "children who grow up watching their mother being abused are more likely than other children to become delinquents and adult criminals *both* inside and outside the home" (DeKeseredy & Schwartz 1996:478–479; see Chapter 5). Thus it is important to expand the existing network of shelters and crisis services for battered women and survivors of rape. These safe havens of refuge and support "help protect . . . women from additional abuse . . . [and] reduce the likelihood that [their] children . . . will grow up in violent households" (Barkan 2001:516). We should also increase services for children who have grown up with abuse, such as summer camp programs that give children a respite from family conflict as well as "a safe place to express their fears," work on redirecting their anger, and learn what to do in emergencies (Dowling 1998:39). And both women and men need to muster the courage to confront acquaintances and friends who engage in sexist conversation, who make sexist jokes, and who perpetuate myths about woman abuse.

At the beginning of this chapter we acknowledged that conventional law enforcement and correctional strategies are necessary elements of effective crime control. We agree with those who favor community styles of policing as a means of improving the relationship between police and citizens and ensuring that the police have the eyes and ears of the community working *for* them rather than *against* them (see Chapter 11). Law enforcement personnel would benefit as well from expanded cultural sensitivity and diversity training, and greater representation of minorities and women in law enforcement would make the criminal justice system more representative of the population (Ogawa 1999).

Racial/ethnic disparities in punishments that are unrelated to the nature of one's offense should of course be eliminated. Mandatory sentencing practices (e.g., three-strikes laws) should be reevaluated and prisons should be used less often for nonviolent offenders. The war on drugs needs to be deescalated and reasonable gun regulations need to be enacted (see Chapter 5). Community correctional and restorative justice strategies that promote the reintegration of offenders offer reasonable alternatives to a costly and overcrowded prison system. The value of rehabilitation as a correctional philosophy needs reaffirmation, "both as an end in itself and as a means to the end of making society safer" (Cullen et al. 1999:201). In short, we need to be smarter about crime prevention and control, set some practical priorities (e.g., focus on violent crime), and not support overly punitive policies merely because they make us feel better, make us feel that we have drawn a line in the sand between the forces of good and the forces of evil.

■ The Problem of White-Collar Crime

The moral tone of a society, as we suggested before, is set by those at the top. Edward Ross observed long ago that "from [their] example and [their] excuses spreads a noxious influence that tarnishes the ideals of ingenuous youth on the threshold of active life" (1907/1977:31). White-collar crime, however, is not and has never been a principal focus of either conventional crime prevention or law enforcement. This situation must change; the problem of corporate accountability for wrongdoing needs to be addressed.

A reasonable first step in dealing with white-collar crime is to raise public awareness of it. The educational arena is one place where this could be done. But even criminal justice curricula do not always provide sufficient attention to white-collar crime. And while most business schools in the United States teach some business-ethics subject matter, studies find that "any improvements in students' ethical awareness or reasoning" as a result of these courses are short-lived. Clearly ethics courses that "promote values that put integrity and concern with the well-being of others ahead of personal or corporate enrichment and advantage" will not be effective if the rest of the business curriculum promotes "a mindset where attention to the bottom line trumps all other considerations" ((Friedrichs 2004:298–299); Mangan 2002).

Another proposal calls for corporations to develop organizational codes of ethics to encourage employees not simply to make decisions that benefit owners and stockholders but to make decisions that are consistent with a "broader social responsibility to promote society's well-being" (Friedrichs 2004:299). Most often, however, these codes are just "window-dressing" intended for public relations. As long as top management continues to send a message that "heads will roll" unless the company grows a certain percentage in the next year or makes a certain profit, then "you're going to have people shipping inferior goods, juggling the books, bribing when they have to, [and] trampling workers beneath them" (Wilkes 1989:24).

Ultimately, more criminal prosecution will likely be necessary to reduce corporate and other white-collar crime. In a nationwide survey of local prosecutors, Michael Benson and Francis Cullen (1998) found that corporate crime prosecutions were more likely to occur in communities with lower rates of violent street crime and with stronger and more diversified economies. They argue that when the public feels safe from street crime it is more likely to demand protection from other harms. In more prosperous communities there are also more resources available for white-collar prosecutions, and citizens feel less vulnerable to the job losses they think may follow. The public exhibits the strongest support for white-collar prosecutions of consumer fraud and environmental offenses. Nevertheless, research finds that major corporations are less likely than smaller companies to be prosecuted, as are higher-level executives compared to their subordinate managers (Cohen 1989; Friedrichs 2004).

The legal system has been rather forgiving of white-collar offenders, for when they are prosecuted and convicted they receive less serious penalties than other offenders. White-collar offenders are more likely to be fined or put on probation rather than be sent to prison, more likely to receive shorter terms when they are sent to prison, and more likely to obtain reversals of their convictions on appeal. The average fines imposed on corporations tend to be less than the amount of financial harm they cause. And companies responsible for the greatest amount of harm tend to pay fines at a much lower percentage of the harm they cause than companies that are responsible for more modest harm. Bank embezzlers and those who commit mail fraud or who defraud the government are among the white-collar offenders who receive the most serious penalties (Cohen 1989; Friedrichs 2004; Reiman 2004).

John Braithwaite and Gilbert Geis (1982) argue that sanctions for corporate crime should include provisions for publicizing wrongdoers and their misdeeds (e.g., in television spots), since corporations and their officers are genuinely afraid that such exposure will both damage their reputation and lower consumer demand for their products. Others advocate a system of corporate probation, whereby a company found guilty of a serious crime would be placed under the supervision of a probation officer/management specialist who has expertise in the field. Or public representatives with their own staffs could be added to corporate boards of directors to monitor the corporation and investigate complaints. Certainly, law-violating corporations should not be allowed to receive government contracts. These are but some of the measures criminologists have offered for dealing with corporate crime (Coleman 1998; DeKeseredy & Schwartz 1996; Friedrichs 2004).

■ *Winning the Peace*

The war on crime has brought us victor's justice. But it has not won the peace. As John Hagan and Juleigh Coleman observe, "All wars end with some level of vindictiveness, but at some point the vindictiveness threatens to destroy the peace the war was fought to achieve" (2001:365). It is time to search for another way.

We suffer no illusion that the problem of crime in our society can be "solved." We do retain hope, however, that progress can be made. As Nancy Wonders suggests:

> We can build bridges between diverse sectors of the population by forging an alliance between taxpayers tired of wasting money on prisons, parents fed up with the trade-off between education and incarceration, underrepresented racial and ethnic groups who are angry about the disproportionate impact of criminal justice policies on their communities, medical professionals who view drugs as a health problem rather than a criminal justice problem, and numerous other constituencies who have other good reasons to support change. (1999:125)

It will not be easy for such diverse groups to work together for change, "because so many of the differences [that divide] us have been made to matter, whether it is skin color, sex, social class, sexual orientation, or the style of the clothes we wear" (Wonders 1999:24). In the aftermath of September 11, 2001, we have been told that we must all stand together, united against the foreign enemies who want to destroy us, who want to ruin our cherished way of life. Desiree Taylor (2004) does not see the unity, however. To her, the United States feels like a country that is divided by people "who don't and perhaps won't take the time to really look at each other," who "live in separate worlds," who "can't feel each other's pains."

Taylor wonders what this country really stands for. "They tell us these are attacks on freedom and justice itself. But how is this possible when here at home justice, freedom, and the American Dream are denied to so many?" (p. 508).

We believe that what can bring many of us together is a commitment to an overarching philosophy of the "just society." We think the eminent philosopher John Rawls (1971) had it right when he called for a social order based on the principle of **distributive justice**. Distributive justice goes beyond the procedural or due process justice we expect of a fair legal system. It goes beyond the notion of personal liberty that is of course necessary for a free society. It goes beyond the illusion that an unfettered "free market" of economic production and consumption will necessarily produce desirable social outcomes. Distributive justice requires political institutions that attend to the problematic social landscape that is the consequence of market forces that leave too much misery and inequality in their wake. A just society, according to Rawls, should be arranged so as to bolster the life chances of those who are least advantaged. It is a society that strives for an economy that works *for people,* not a society that makes people work *for the economy.* The following passage from his book *A Theory of Justice* captures Rawls's vision of a just society:

> I assume that the basic structure [of society] is regulated by a just constitution that secures the liberties of equal citizenship. . . . Liberty of conscience and freedom of thought are taken for granted, and the fair value of political liberty is maintained. The political process is conducted . . . as a just procedure for choosing between governments and for enacting just legislation. I assume that there is fair (as opposed to formal) equality of opportunity. This means that . . . the government tries to ensure equal chances of education and culture for persons similarly endowed and motivated either by subsidizing private schools or by establishing a public school system. It also enforces and underwrites equality of opportunity in economic activities and in the free choice of occupation. This is achieved by policing the conduct of firms and private associations and by preventing the establishment of monopolistic restrictions and barriers to the more desirable positions. (p. 275)

Perhaps this is what Terry Williams and William Kornblum had in mind when they called for public policies that promote "continual opportunities for growth"—that supply the least advantaged with an ongoing "supply of diverse opportunities for entry into the economic and social mainstream" and that maximize the chances that no one will be left behind (1985:133). We understand that not everyone would support a political agenda that strives for such lofty goals, or if they did, that it would be easy to realize. But failure to try, we think, will only prove the adage: "We have met the enemy, and the enemy is us."

References

Abadinsky, H. 2003. *Organized Crime.* Belmont, CA: Wadsworth.

Abramsky, S. 2002. "The Shame of Prison Health." *Nation,* July 1:28–34.

Abbott, J. 1981. *In the Belly of the Beast.* New York: Vintage.

Ackerman, S. 2004. "AWOL." *New Republic,* Feb. 9:10–11.

Ackerman, S., and F. Foer. 2003. "The Radical." *New Republic,* Dec. 1–8:17–23.

Ackerman, S., and J. Judis. 2003. "The First Causality." *New Republic,* June 30:14–18, 23–25.

Adams, D. 1988. "Treatment Models for Men Who Batter." In K. Yllo and M. Bograd (eds.), *Feminist Perspectives on Wife Abuse.* Newbury Park, CA: Sage.

Adams, K. 1999. "What We Know About Police Use of Force." In *Use of Force by Police.* Washington, DC: U.S. Department of Justice.

Adler, F. 1975. *Sisters in Crime: The Rise of the New Female Offender.* New York: McGraw-Hill.

Adler, F., G. Mueller, and W. Laufer. 2000. *Criminal Justice: An Introduction.* NY: McGraw-Hill.

———. 2001. *Criminology.* New York: McGraw-Hill.

Adler, P., and P. Adler. 1983. "Shifts and Oscillations in Deviant Careers: The Case of Upper-Level Drug Dealers and Smugglers." *Social Problems* 31:195–207.

Ageton, S. 1983. "The Dynamics of Female Delinquency, 1976–1980." *Criminology* 21:555–584.

Agnew, R. 1985. "Social Control and Delinquency: A Longitudinal Test." *Criminology* 23:47–61.

———. 1992. "Foundation for a General Strain Theory of Crime and Delinquency." *Criminology* 30:47–87.

———. 1995. "Controlling Delinquency: Recommendations from General Strain Theory." In H. Barlow (ed.), *Crime and Public Policy.* Boulder, CO: Westview.

———. 2000. "Strain Theory and School Crime." In S. Simpson (ed.), *Of Crime and Criminality.* Thousand Oaks, CA: Sage.

———. 2001. *Juvenile Delinquency: Causes and Control.* Los Angeles: Roxbury.

Agnew, R., and H. White. 1992. "An Empirical Test of General Strain Theory." *Criminology* 30:475–499.

Ahern, J. 1972. *Police in Trouble.* New York: Hawthorn.

Aichorn, A. 1935. *Wayward Youth.* New York: Viking.

AIDS in Action. 2001. "Incarcerated Populations and HIV/AIDS." www.aidsaction.org.

Akers, R. 1985. *Deviant Behavior: A Social Learning Approach*. Belmont, CA: Wadsworth.

———. 1992. "Linking Sociology and Its Specialties: The Case of Criminology." *Social Forces* 71:1–16.

———. 1998. *Social Learning and Social Structure: A General Theory of Crime and Deviance*. Boston: Northeastern University.

———. 2000. *Criminological Theories: Introduction, Evaluation, Application*. Los Angeles: Roxbury.

Akers, R., M. Krohn, L. Lanza-Kaduce, and M. Radosevich. 1979. "Social Learning and Deviant Behavior: A Specific Test of a General Theory." *American Sociological Review* 44:636–655.

Albanese, J. 1985. *Organized Crime in America*. Cincinnati: Anderson.

Albrecht, S., B. Chadwick, and D. Alcorn. 1977. "Religiosity and Deviance: Application of an Attitude Behavior Contingent Consistency Model." *Journal for the Scientific Study of Religion* 16:263–274.

Albini, J. 1971. *The American Mafia: Genesis of a Legend*. New York: Appleton-Century-Crofts.

Albonetti, C., R. Hauser, J. Hagan, and I. Nagel. 1989. "Criminal Justice Decision Making as a Stratification Process: The Role of Race and Stratification Resources in Pretrial Release." *Journal of Quantitative Criminology* 5:57–82.

Alexander, P. 1987. "Prostitution: A Difficult Issue for Feminists." In F. Delacoste and P. Alexander (eds.), *Sex Work*. Pittsburgh: Cleis.

Allen, M., D. D'Alessio, and K. Brezgel. 1995. "A Meta-Analysis Summarizing the Effects of Pornography II." *Human Communication Research* 22:258–283.

Alpern, D. 1984. "A CIA Bombshell." *Newsweek*, Oct. 29:30.

American Civil Liberties Union (ACLU). 1995. "ACLU Announces Settlement of Lawsuit Over 'Racial Profile' Stops." Jan. 4, www.archive.aclu.org.

American Correctional Association (ACA). 1993. *Gangs in Correctional Facilities: A National Assessment*. Laurel, MD: ACA.

Amir, M. 1971. *Patterns in Forcible Rape*. Chicago: University of Chicago.

Amnesty International USA. 1999. "Amnesty International Report on Women in U.S. Prisons Documents Widespread Abuse." www.amnesty-usa.org.

Anderson, C. 2003. "Feds Release Patriot Act Information." *Wisconsin State Journal*, May 21:A3.

Anderson, D. 1995. *Crime and the Politics of Hysteria: How the Willie Horton Story Changed American Justice*. New York: Times Books.

———. 1997. "The Mystery of the Falling Crime Rate." *American Prospect*, May–June:49–55.

———. 1999. "Policing the Police." *American Prospect*, Jan.–Feb.:49–54.

Anderson, E. 1994. "The Code of the Streets." *Atlantic Monthly*, May:81–94.

———. 1999. *Code of the Street*. New York: Norton.

Anderson, L., and T. Calhoun. 1992. "Facilitative Aspects of Field Research with Deviant Street Populations." *Sociological Inquiry* 62:490–498.

Anderson, P. 2003. "Treatment with Teeth." *American Prospect*, Dec.:45–48.

Andrews, D., and J. Wormith. 1989. "Personality and Crime: Knowledge Destruction and Construction in Criminology." *Justice Quarterly* 6:289–309.

Andrews, D., et al. 1990. "Does Correctional Treatment Work? A Clinically Relevant and Psychologically Informed Meta-analysis." *Criminology* 28:369–404.

Anti-Defamation League (ADL). 1997. *1996 Audit of Anti-Semitic Incidents*. New York: ADL.

————. 2003. "Anti-Defamation League State Hate Crime Statutory Provisions." www.adl.org.

Armstrong, K., and M. Possley. 1999. "Study: Prosecutors Sacrifice Justice to Win." *Wisconsin State Journal,* Jan. 11:3A.

Armstrong, S. 2003. "Not My Daughter." *Ms.,* Summer:22–23.

Arrigo, B. 1999a. "Can Students Benefit from an Intensive Engagement with Postmodern Criminology?" In J. Fuller and E. Hickey (eds.), *Controversial Issues in Criminology.* Boston: Allyn and Bacon.

———— (ed.). 1999b. *Social Justice/Criminal Justice: The Maturation of Critical Theory in Law, Crime, and Deviance.* Belmont, CA: Wadsworth.

Asseo, L. 2001. "No Drug Tests for Pregnant Women." *Wisconsin State Journal,* Mar. 22:A3.

Attinger, J. 1989. "The Decline of New York." *Time,* Sept. 17:36–40, 44.

Austin, J., et al. 2001. "The Use of Incarceration in the United States." *Critical Criminology* 10:17–41.

Bachman, R., and L. Saltzman. 1995. *Violence Against Women: Estimates from the Redesigned Survey.* Washington, DC: U.S. Department of Justice.

Bai, M. 1999. "Can Pistols Get Smarter?" *Newsweek,* Aug. 2:41.

————. 2001. "A Gun Deal's Fatal Wound." *Newsweek,* Feb. 5:30–31.

Bailey, W. 1998. "Deterrence, Brutalization, and the Death Penalty: Another Examination of Oklahoma's Return to Capital Punishment." *Criminology* 36:711–733.

Baker, M. 1985. *Cops: Their Lives in Their Own Words.* New York: Fawcett.

Baker, P. 1992. "Maintaining Male Power: Why Heterosexual Men Use Pornography." In C. Itzin (ed.), *Pornography.* New York: Oxford University.

Baker, R. 2002. "What Are They Hiding?" *Nation,* Feb. 25:11–16.

Balbus, I. 1977. *The Dialectics of Legal Repression.* New York: Russell Sage.

Baldus, D., and G. Woodworth. 1998. "Race Discrimination and the Death Penalty: An Empirical and Legal Overview." In J. Acker et al. (eds.), *America's Experiment with Capital Punishment.* Durham, NC: Carolina Academic.

Balkan, S., R. Berger, and J. Schmidt. 1980. *Crime and Deviance in America: A Critical Approach.* Belmont, CA: Wadsworth.

Bandura, A. 1973. *Aggression: A Social Learning Analysis.* Englewood Cliffs, NJ: Prentice-Hall.

Barak, G., and S. Henry. 1999. "An Integrative-Constitutive Theory of Crime, Law, and Social Justice." In B. Arrigo (ed.), *Social Justice/Criminal Justice.* Belmont, CA: Wadsworth.

Barkan, S. 2001. *Criminology.* Upper Saddle River, NJ: Prentice-Hall.

Barkan, S., and L. Snowden. 2001. *Collective Violence.* Boston: Allyn and Bacon.

Barker, T. 1986. "An Empirical Study of Police Deviance Other Than Corruption." In T. Barker and D. Carter (eds.), *Police Deviance.* Cincinnati: Pilgrimage.

Barker, T., and D. Carter. 1999. "Fluffing Up the Evidence and Covering Your Ass: Some Conceptual Notes on Police Lying." In L. Gaines and G. Cordner (eds.), *Policing Perspectives.* Los Angeles: Roxbury.

Barlow, H. 1996. *Introduction to Criminology.* New York: HarperCollins.

Barlow, H., and D. Kauzlarich. 2002. *Introduction to Criminology.* Upper Saddle River, NJ: Prentice-Hall.

Barnett, H. 1993. "Crimes Against the Environment: Superfund Enforcement at Last." *Annals* 525:119–153.

Baron, L. 1993. "Gender Inequality and Child Homicide: A State-Level Analysis." In A. Wilson (ed.), *Homicide.* Cincinnati: Anderson.

Baron, L., and M. Straus. 1989. *Four Theories of Rape in American Society: A State-Level Analysis.* New Haven: Yale University.

Barrett, A. 1994. "Insider Trading." *Business Week,* Dec. 12:70.

Barry, K. 1979. *Female Sexual Slavery.* Englewood Cliffs, NJ: Prentice-Hall.

———. 1995. *The Prostitution of Sexuality.* New York: New York University.

Bart, P., and P. O'Brien. 1985. *Stopping Rape: Successful Survival Strategies.* New York: Pergamon.

Bartol, C., and A. Bartol. 1989. *Juvenile Delinquency.* Englewood Cliffs, NJ: Prentice-Hall.

Barton, W., and J. Butts. 1990. "Viable Options: Intensive Supervision Programs for Juvenile Delinquents." *Crime and Delinquency* 36:238–256.

Bass, E. 1983. "In the Truth Itself, There is Healing." In E. Bass and L. Thornton (eds.), *I Never Told Anyone.* New York: Harper and Row.

Bass, E., and L. Davis. 1988. *The Courage to Heal.* New York: Harper and Row.

Bass, E., and L. Thornton (eds.). 1983. *I Never Told Anyone.* New York: Harper and Row.

Bates, E. 1998. "Private Prisons." *Nation,* Jan. 5:11–18.

Baunach, P. 1985. *Mothers in Prison.* New Brunswick, NJ: Transaction.

Bayley, D., and E. Bittner. 1999. "Learning the Skills of Policing." In L. Gaines and G. Cordner (eds.), *Policing Perspectives.* Los Angeles: Roxbury.

Beccaria, C. 1764/1963. *On Crimes and Punishments.* Indianapolis: Bobbs-Merrill.

Becker, G. 1968. "Crime and Punishment: An Economic Approach." *Journal of Political Economy* 76:493–517.

Becker, H. 1963. *Outsiders: Studies in the Sociology of Deviance.* New York: Free Press.

Beckett, K. 1994. "Setting the Public Agenda: 'Street Crime' and Drug Use in American Politics." *Social Problems* 41:425–447.

Bedau, H., and M. Radelet. 1987. "Miscarriages of Justice in Potentially Capital Case." *Stanford Law Review* 40:21–179.

Beinart, P. 2002. "Eight Days." *New Republic,* Dec. 2–9:6.

———. 2003. "Theatre of the Absurd." *New Republic,* Oct. 13–20:6.

Beirne, P., and J. Messerschmidt. 1995. *Criminology.* Fort Worth: Harcourt Brace.

Belknap, J. 2001. *The Invisible Woman: Gender, Crime, and Justice.* Belmont, CA: Wadsworth.

Bellair, P. 1997. "Social Interaction and Community Crime: Examining the Importance of Neighbor Networks." *Criminology* 35:677–703.

Beneke, T. 1982. *Men on Rape.* New York: St. Martin's.

Benekos, P. 1995. "Women as Victims and Perpetrators of Murder." In A. Merlo and J. Polock (eds.), *Women, Law, and Social Control.* Boston: Allyn and Bacon.

Bennett, S., and P. Lavrakas. 1989. "Community-Based Crime Prevention: An Assessment of the Eisenhower Foundation's Neighborhood Program." *Crime and Delinquency* 35:345–364.

Bennett, T., and R. Wright. 1984. *Burglars on Burglary.* Aldershot, UK: Gower.

Benokraitis, N. 1982. "Racial Exclusion in Juries." *Journal of Applied Behavioral Science* 18:29–47.

Bensinger, G. 1984. "Chicago Youth Gangs: A New Old Problem." *Crime and Justice* 7:1–16.

Benson, M. 1985. "Denying the Guilty Mind: Accounting for Involvement in White-Collar Crime." *Criminology* 23:583–608.

Benson, M., and F. Cullen. 1998. *Combating Corporate Crime: Local Prosecutors at Work.* Boston: Northeastern University.

Bergen, R. 1996. *Wife Rape: Understanding the Response of Survivors and Service Providers.* Thousand Oaks, CA: Sage.

Berger, R. (ed.). 1996. *The Sociology of Juvenile Delinquency.* Belmont, CA: Wadsworth.

———. 2002. *Fathoming the Holocaust: A Social Problems Approach.* New York: Aldine de Gruyter.

Berger, R., W. Neuman, and P. Searles. 1994. "The Impact of Rape Law Reform: An Aggregate Analysis of Police Reports and Arrests." *Criminal Justice Review* 19:1–23.

Berger, R., P. Searles, and C. Cottle. 1991. *Feminism and Pornography.* Westport, CT: Praeger.

Berger, R., P. Searles, and W. Neuman. 1988. "The Dimensions of Rape Law Reform." *Law and Society Review* 22:329–357.

Berger, R., P. Searles, R. Salem, and B. Pierce. 1986. "Sexual Assault in a College Community." *Sociological Focus* 19:1–26.

Bergman, J., and J. Reynolds. 2002. "The Guns of Opa-Locka: How U.S. Dealers Arm the World." *Nation,* Dec. 2:19–22.

Berk, R., A. Campbell, R. Klap, and B. Western. 1992. "The Deterrent Effect of Arrest in Incidents of Domestic Violence: A Bayesian Analysis of Four Field Experiments." *American Sociological Review* 57:698–708.

Berlet, C., and A. Scher. 2003. "Political Profiling." *Amnesty Now,* Spring:20–23, 27.

Bernard, T. 1990. "Angry Aggression Among the 'Truly Disadvantaged.'" *Criminology* 28:73–96.

Berne, S. 1991. "'Excuse Me,' He Said." *New York Times Magazine,* June 30:10–11.

Berrill, K. 1992. "Anti-Gay Violence and Victimization in the United States: An Overview." In G. Herek and K. Berrill (eds.), *Hate Crimes.* Newbury Park, CA: Sage.

Berrill, K., and G. Herek. 1992. "Primary and Secondary Victimization in Anti-Gay Hate Crimes: Official Response and Public Policy." In G. Herek and K. Berrill (eds.), *Hate Crimes.* Newbury Park, CA: Sage.

Best, J. 1999. *Random Violence: How We Talk About New Crimes and New Victims.* Berkeley: University of California.

Betz, M. 1974. "Riots and Welfare: Are They Related?" *Social Problems* 21:345–355.

Bickle, G., and R. Peterson. 1991. "The Impact of Gender-Based Family Roles on Criminal Sentencing." *Social Problems* 38:372–394.

Bienen, L. 1980. "Rape III: National Developments in Rape Reform Legislation." *Women's Rights Law Reporter* 6:170–213.

Bikel, O. 1999. "Snitch." PBS documentary.

Bilchik, S. 1999. "Minorities in the Juvenile Justice System." *1999 National Report Series.* Washington, DC: U.S. Department of Justice.

Binder, A., G. Geis, and D. Bruce. 1988. *Juvenile Delinquency.* New York: Macmillan.

Bing, L. 1991. *Do or Die.* New York: HarperCollins.

Birsch, D., and J. Fielder (eds.). 1994. *The Ford Pinto Case: A Study in Applied Ethics, Business, and Technology.* Albany: State University of New York.

Bishop, D., C. Frazier, and J. Henretta. 1989. "Prosecutorial Waiver: Case Study of a Questionable Reform." *Crime and Delinquency* 35:179–201.

Bjorkqvist, K., K. Osterman, and A. Kaukiainen. 1992. "The Development of Direct and Indirect Aggressive Strategies in Males and Females." In K. Bjorkqvist and P. Niemela (eds.), *Of Mice and Women*. New York: Academic.

Black, D. 1970. "Production of Crime Rates." *American Sociological Review* 35:733–748.

———. 1980. *The Manners and Customs of the Police*. New York: Academic.

Black, D., and D. Nagin. 1998. "Do 'Right-to-Carry' Laws Deter Violent Crime?" *Journal of Legal Studies* 27:209–219.

Blalock, H. 1967. *Toward a Theory of Minority Group Relations*. New York: Wiley.

Blau, J., and P. Blau. 1982. "The Cost of Inequality: Metropolitan Structure and Violent Crime." *American Sociological Review* 47:114–129.

Block, A., and W. Chambliss. 1981. *Organizing Crime*. New York: Elsevier.

Blomberg, T., W. Bales, and K. Reed. 1993. "Intermediate Punishment: Redistributing or Extending Social Control?" *Crime, Law, and Social Change* 19:187–201.

Bluestone, B., and B. Harrison. 1982. *The Deindustrialization of America: Plant Closings, Community Abandonment, and the Dismantling of Basic Industry*. New York: Basic.

Blumberg, A. 1967. "The Practice of Law as a Confidence Game." *Law and Society Review* 1:15–39.

Blumstein, A. 1993. "Making Rationality Relevant." *Criminology* 31:1–16.

———. 2002. "Why Is Crime Falling—Or Is It?" In A. Blumstein et al. (eds.), *Perspectives on Crime and Justice*. Rockville, MD: National Institute of Justice.

Blumstein, A., and E. Graddy. 1982. "Prevalence and Recidivism in Index Arrests: A Feedback Model." *Law and Society Review* 16:265–290.

Blumstein, A., and J. Wallman (eds.). 2000. *The Crime Drop in America*. New York: Cambridge University.

Bogle, D. 1994. *Toms, Coons, Mulattos, Mammies, and Bucks: An Interpretive History of Blacks in American Films*. New York: Continuum.

Bohm, R. 1986. "Crime, Criminal, and Crime Control Policy Myths." *Justice Quarterly* 3:193–214.

———. 1991. "Race and the Death Penalty in the United States." In M. Lynch and E. Patterson (eds.), *Race and Criminal Justice*. Albany, NY: Harrow and Heston.

———. 1998. "The Economic Costs of Capital Punishment: Past, Present, and Future." In J. Acker et al. (eds.), *America's Experiment with Capital Punishment*. Durham, NC: Carolina Academic.

Boland, B., P. Mahanna, and R. Stones. 1992. *The Prosecution of Felony Arrests 1988*. Washington, DC: U.S. Department of Justice.

Bonczar, T. 1997. *Characteristics of Adults on Probation 1995*. Washington, DC: U.S. Department of Justice.

Bonczar, T., and T. Snell. 2003. *Capital Punishment, 2002*. Washington, DC: U.S. Department of Justice.

Bond-Maupin, L. 1998. "'That Wasn't Even Me They Showed': Women as Criminals on *America's Most Wanted*." *Violence Against Women* 4:30–44.

Bonger, W. 1916. *Criminality and Economic Conditions*. Boston: Little, Brown.

Bonnie, R. 1997. "Should the Insanity Defense Be Abolished?" In M. Katsh (ed.), *Taking Sides: Clashing Views on Controversial Legal Issues*. Guilford, CT: Dushkin.

Bonsignore, J., et al. (eds.). 1994. *Before the Law: An Introduction to the Legal Process*. Boston: Houghton Mifflin.

Boostrom, R., and J. Henderson. 1983. "Community Action and Crime Prevention: Some Unresolved Issues." *Crime and Social Justice* 19:24–30.

Bourgois, Philippe. 1989. "In Search of Horatio Alger: Culture and Ideology in the Crack Economy." *Contemporary Drug Problems* 16:619–649.

———. 1995. *In Search of Respect: Selling Crack in El Barrio.* Cambridge, UK: Cambridge University.

Bourque, B., M. Han, and S. Hill. 1996. *A National Survey of Aftercare Provisions for Boot Camp Graduates.* Washington, DC: National Institute of Justice.

Bowers, W., and G. Pierce. 1980. "Deterrence or Brutalization: What Is the Effect of Executions?" *Crime and Delinquency* 26:453–484.

Bowker, L. 1980. *Prison Victimization.* New York: Elsevier.

Bowker, L., and M. Klein. 1983. "The Etiology of Female Juvenile Delinquency and Gang Membership: A Test of Psychological and Social Structural Explanations." *Adolescence* 13:739–751.

Boyd, T. 1997. *Am I Black Enough for You? Popular Culture from the "Hood" and Beyond.* Bloomington: Indiana University.

Boyer, D., and J. James. 1982. "Easy Money: Adolescent Involvement in Prostitution." In S. Davidson (ed.), *Justice for Young Women.* Seattle: New Directions for Young Women.

Brady, J. 1983. "Arson, Urban Economy, and Organized Crime: The Case of Boston." *Social Problems* 31:1–27.

Braithwaite, J. 1989. *Crime, Shame, and Reintegration.* New York: Cambridge University.

Braithwaite, J., and K. Daly. 1998. "Masculinities, Violence, and Communitarian Control." In S. Miller (ed.), *Crime Control and Women.* Thousand Oaks, CA: Sage.

Braithwaite, J., and G. Geis. 1982. "On the Theory and Action for Corporate Crime Control." *Crime and Delinquency* 28:292–314.

Braithwaite, R., and K. Arriola. 2003. "Male Prisoners and HIV Prevention: A Call for Action Ignored." *American Journal of Public Health* 93:759–763.

Brand, P., and A. Kidd. 1986. "Frequency of Physical Aggression in Heterosexual and Female Homosexual Dyads." *Psychological Reports* 59:1307–1313.

Brandell, S. 1998. "FGM Roundup." *Ms.,* May–June:26.

Brandl, S., M. Chamblin, and J. Frank. 1995. "Aggregation Bias and the Capacity for Formal Crime Control: The Determinants of Total and Disaggregated Police Force Size in Milwaukee, 1934–1987." *Justice Quarterly* 12:543–562.

Braun, D. 1997. *The Rich Get Richer: The Rise of Income Inequality in the United States and the World.* Chicago: Nelson-Hall.

Bratton, W. 1998. *Turnaround: How America's Top Cop Reversed the Crime Epidemic.* New York: Random House.

Brazil, J., and S. Berry. 1992. "Color of Driver Is Key to Stops in I-95 Videos." *Orlando Sentinel,* Aug. 23:A1.

Brecher, E. 1972. *Licit and Illicit Drugs.* Boston: Little, Brown.

Brecher, J. 1980. *Strike!* Boston: South End.

Brehm, E. 2003. "Arizona Sheriff Introduces Female Chain Gang." Nov. 19, www.wsws.org.

Bridges, G., and R. Crutchfield. 1988. "Law, Social Standing, and Racial Disparities in Imprisonment." *Social Forces* 66:699–724.

Bridges G., R. Crutchfield, and E. Simpson. 1987. "Crime, Social Structure, and Criminal Punishment: White and Nonwhite Rates of Imprisonment." *Social Problems* 34:345–361.

Briere, J. 1992. *Child Abuse Trauma*. Newbury Park, CA: Sage.

Brinkley, J., and S. Engelberg (eds.). 1988. *Report of the Congressional Committees Investigating the Iran-Contra Affair*. New York: Random House.

Brisard, J., and G. Dasquie. 2002. *Forbidden Truth: U.S.-Taliban Secret Oil Diplomacy and the Failed Hunt for Bin Laden*. New York: Thunder's Mouth/Nation Books.

Britton, D. 1997. "Gender Organizational Logic: Policy and Practice in Men's and Women's Prisons." *Gender and Society* 11:796–818.

Brod, H. 1995. "Pornography and Alienation of Male Sexuality." In M. Kimmel and M. Messner (eds.), *Men's Lives*. Boston: Allyn and Bacon.

Broidy, L. 2001. "A Test of General Strain Theory." *Criminology* 39:9–35.

Broidy, L., and R. Agnew. 1997. "Gender and Crime: A General Strain Perspective." *Journal of Research in Crime and Delinquency* 34:275–306.

Brook, D. 2004. "The Problem of Prison Rape." *Legal Affairs,* Mar.–Apr.:24–29.

Brooks-Gunn, J., G. Duncan, P. Klebanov, and N. Sealand. 1993. "Do Neighborhoods Influence Child and Adolescent Development?" *American Journal of Sociology* 99:353–395.

Broome, K., et al. 1996. "Drug Treatment Process Indicators for Probationers and Prediction of Recidivism." *Journal of Substance Abuse Treatment* 13:487–491.

Brotherton, D. 1994. "Who Do You Claim? Gang Formations and Rivalry in an Inner City Public School." In *Perspectives on Social Problems,* vol. 6. Greenwich, CT: JAI.

Browne, A. 1987. *When Battered Women Kill*. New York: Macmillan.

———. 1997. "Violence in Marriage: Until Death Do Us Part?" In A. Cardarelli (ed.), *Violence Between Intimate Partners*. Boston: Allyn and Bacon.

Browne, A., and K. Williams. 1989. "Exploring the Effect of Resource Availability and the Likelihood of Female-Perpetrated Homicides." *Law and Society Review* 23:75–94.

———. 1993. "Gender, Intimacy, and Lethal Violence: Trends from 1976–1987." *Gender and Society* 7:78–98.

Browne, D. 1989. "Incarcerated Mothers and Parenting." *Journal of Family Violence* 4:211–221.

Browning, S., and L. Cao. 1992. "The Impact of Race on Criminal Justice Ideology." *Justice Quarterly* 9:685–701.

Brownmiller, S. 1975. *Against Our Will: Men, Women, and Rape*. New York: Simon and Schuster.

Brownstein, H. 1996. *The Rise and Fall of a Violent Crime Wave: Crack Cocaine and the Social Construction of a Crime Problem*. Guilderland, NY: Harrow and Heston.

Brownstein, R., and N. Easton. 1982. *Reagan's Ruling Class: Portraits of the President's Top One Hundred Officials*. New York: Pantheon.

Bryce, R. 2002. *Pipe Dreams: Greed, Ego, and the Death of Enron*. New York: Public Affairs.

Budhos, M. 1997. "Putting the Heat on Sex Tourism." *Ms.,* Mar.–Apr.:12–16.

Building Blocks for Youth. 2002. "Drugs and Disparity: The Racial Impact of Illinois' Practice of Transferring Drug Offenders to Adult Court." www.buildingblocksforyouth.org.

Bull, C. 2003. "Justice Served." *Advocate,* Aug. 19:35–38.

Bullard, R. (ed.). 1993. *Confronting Environmental Racism: Voices from the Grassroots*. Boston: South End.

Bullard, R., and B. Wright. 1989–1990. "Toxic Waste and the African American Community." *Urban League Review* 13:67–75.

Bureau of Justice Assistance (BJA). 1997. *A Policymaker's Guide to Hate Crimes.* Washington, DC: U.S. Government Printing Office.

Burkett, S., and D. Ward. 1993. "A Note on Perceptual Deterrence, Religiosity Based on Moral Condemnation, and Social Control." *Criminology* 31:119–134.

Burkett, S., and B. Warren. 1987. "Religiosity, Peer Associations, and Adolescent Marijuana Use: A Panel Study of Underlying Causal Structures." *Criminology* 25:109–134.

Burns, R., and J. Smith. 1999. "DNA: Fingerprint of the Future?" *ACJS Today* 18:1, 3–4.

Burris-Kitchen, D. 1995. *Sisters in the Hood.* Ph.D. diss., Western Michigan University.

Bursik, R. 1988. "Social Disorganization and Theories of Crime and Delinquency: Problems and Prospects." *Criminology* 26:519–551.

Bursik, R., and H. Grasmick. 1993. *Neighborhoods and Crime: The Dimensions of Effective Community Control.* New York: Lexington.

Bursik, R., J. Merten, and G. Schwartz. 1985. "Appropriate Age-Related Behaviors for Male and Female Adolescents: Adult Perceptions." *Youth and Society* 17:115–130.

Bursik, R., and J. Webb. 1982. "Community Change and Patterns of Delinquency." *American Journal of Sociology* 88:24–42.

Burstyn, V. (ed.). 1985. *Women Against Censorship.* Vancouver: Douglas and McIntyre.

Bush-Baskette, S. 1998. "The War on Drugs as a War Against Black Women." In S. Miller (ed.), *Crime Control and Women.* Thousand Oaks, CA: Sage.

Bussey, J. 2002. "Cheney, Halliburton Accused of Fraud." *Wisconsin State Journal,* July 11:A3.

Butler, P. 1997. "Brotherman: Reflections of a Reformed Prosecutor." In E. Cose (ed.), *The Darden Dilemma.* New York: HarperPerennial.

Butterfield, F. 1999. "Study Exposes Illegal Traffic in New Guns." *New York Times,* Feb. 21, www.nytimes.com.

Button, J. 1989. "The Outcomes of Contemporary Black Protest and Violence." In T. Gurr (ed.), *Violence in America.* Newbury Park, CA: Sage.

Bynum, T., G. Cordner, and J. Greene. 1982. "Victim and Offense Characteristics: Impact on Police Investigative Decision-Making." *Criminology* 20:301–318.

Calavita, K. 1983. "The Demise of the Occupational Safety and Health Administration: A Case Study in Symbolic Action." *Social Problems* 30:464–477.

Calavita, K., and H. Pontell. 1990. "Heads I Win, Tails You Lose: Deregulation, Crime, and Crisis in the Savings and Loan Industry." *Crime and Delinquency* 36:309–341.

———. 1993. "Savings and Loan Fraud as Organized Crime: Towards a Conceptual Typology of Corporate Illegality." *Criminology* 31:519–548.

Calhoun, C., and H. Hiller. 1988. "Coping With Insidious Injuries: The Case of Johns-Manville Corporation and Asbestos Exposure." *Social Problems* 35:162–181.

Calhoun, T. 1992. "Male Street Hustling: Introduction Processes and Stigma Containment." *Sociological Spectrum* 12:35–52.

Calsyn, D., D. Roszell, and E. Chaney. 1989. "Validation of MMPI Profile Subtypes Among Opioid Addicts Who Are Beginning Methadone Maintenance Treatments." *Journal of Clinical Psychology* 45:991–999.

Campbell, A. 1987. "Self Definition by Rejection: The Case of Gang Girls." *Social Problems* 34:451–466.

————. 1991. *The Girls in the Gang.* Cambridge, MA: Basil Blackwell.

————. 1993. *Men, Women, and Aggression.* New York: Basic.

Campbell, A., and S. Muncer. 1989. "Them and Us: A Comparison of the Cultural Context of American Gangs and British Subcultures." *Deviant Behavior* 10:271–288.

Cameron, D., and E. Frazer. 1987. *The Lust to Kill: A Feminist Investigation of Serial Murder.* New York: New York University.

————. 1993. "On the Question of Pornography and Sexual Violence: Moving Beyond Cause and Effect." In C. Itzin (ed.), *Pornography.* New York: Oxford University.

Canaan, J. 1991. "Is 'Doing Nothing' Just Boys' Play? Integrating Feminist and Cultural Studies Perspectives on Working-Class Young Men's Masculinity." In S. Franklin et al. (eds.), *Off-Centre.* London: HarperCollins.

Canada, G. 1998. "The Secret Life of Boys." *Hope,* Jan.–Feb.:16–20.

Cancio, A., T. Evans, and D. Maume. 1996. "Reconsidering the Declining Significance of Race: Racial Differences in Early Career Wages." *American Sociological Review* 61:541–556.

Canter, R. 1982. "Sex Differences in Self-Report Delinquency." *Criminology* 20:373–393.

Cantor, D., and K. Land. 1975. "Unemployment and Crime Rates in the Post–World War II United States: A Theoretical and Empirical Analysis." *American Sociological Review* 50:317–323.

Capaldi, D., P. Chamberlain, and G. Patterson. 1997. "Ineffective Discipline and Conduct Problems in Males: Association, Late Adolescent Outcomes, and Prevention." *Aggression and Violent Behavior* 2:343–353.

Caputi, J. 1987. *The Age of Sex Crime.* Bowling Green, OH: Bowling Green State University.

————. 1989. "The Sexual Politics of Murder." *Gender and Society* 3:437–456.

Carelli, R. 1998. "Cocaine Mother Cases Pose Legal Questions." *Wisconsin State Journal,* Apr. 18:4A.

————. 1999. "Court Has No Problem With Florida's Electric Chair." *Wisconsin State Journal,* Jan. 20:5A.

Carey, J. 1978. *Introduction to Criminology.* Englewood Cliffs, NJ: Prentice-Hall.

Carlson, S., and R. Michalowski. 1997. "Crime, Unemployment, and Social Structures of Accumulation: An Inquiry into Historical Contingency." *Justice Quarterly* 14:209–239.

Carpenter, C., B. Glassner, B. Johnson, and J. Loughlin. 1988. *Kids, Drugs, and Crime.* Lexington, MA: Lexington.

Carson, H. 1943. "The Psychopath and the Psychopathic." *Journal of Criminal Psychopathology* 4:522–527.

Carson, R. 2002. "Corporation." *World Book Encyclopedia.* Chicago: World Book.

Carter, D., and A. Bannister. 2002. "Computer-related Crime." In D. Shichor et al. (eds.), *Readings in White-Collar Crime.* Prospect Heights, IL: Waveland.

Carter, S. 1987. "A Most Useful Tool." In F. Delacoste and P. Alexander (eds.), *Sex Work.* Pittsburgh: Cleis.

Caspi, A., G. Elder, and E. Herbener. 1990. "Childhood Personality and the Prediction of Life-Course Patterns." In L. Robins and M. Rutter (eds.), *Straight and Devious Pathways from Childhood to Adulthood.* New York: Cambridge University.

Caspi, A., et al. 1994. "Are Some People Crime-Prone? Replications of the

Personality-Crime Relationship Across Countries, Genders, Races, and Methods." *Criminology* 32:163–195.

Cauchon, D. 1995. "AIDS in Prison: Locked Up and Locked Out." *USA Today,* Mar. 31:6.

Cernkovich, S., and P. Giordano. 1979a. "A Comparative Analysis of Female Delinquency." *Sociological Quarterly* 20:131–145.

———. 1979b. "Delinquency, Opportunity, and Gender." *Journal of Criminal Law and Criminology* 70:145–151.

———. 1987. "Family Relationships and Delinquency." *Criminology* 25:295–321.

Chaiken, J., and M. Chaiken. 1982. *Varieties of Criminal Behavior.* Santa Monica, CA: RAND.

Chalk, F., and F. Jonassohn (eds.). 1990. *The History and Sociology of Genocide.* New Haven: Yale University.

Chambliss, W. 1973. "The Saints and the Roughnecks." *Society* 11:341–355.

———. 1988. *On the Take: From Petty Crooks to Presidents.* Bloomington: Indiana University.

———. 1994. "Policing the Ghetto Underclass: The Politics of Law and Law Enforcement." *Social Problems* 41:177–194.

———. 1995. "Another Lost War: The Costs and Consequences of Drug Prohibition." *Social Justice* 22:101–124.

Chambliss, W., and R. Seidman. 1971. *Law, Order, and Power.* Reading, MA: Addison-Wesley.

Chamlin, M., and J. Cochran. 1997. "Social Altruism and Crime." *Criminology* 35:203–227.

Champion, C. 1986. "Clinical Perspectives on the Relationship Between Pornography and Sexual Violence." *Law and Inequality* 4:22–27.

Chancer, L. 1996. "O.J. Simpson and the Trial of the Century? Uncovering Paradoxes in Media Coverage." In G. Barak (ed.), *Representing O.J.* Guilderland, NY: Harrow and Heston.

Charns, A. 1992. *Cloak and Gavel: FBI Wiretaps, Bugs, Informers, and the Supreme Court.* Urbana: University of Illinois.

Chermak, S. 1994. "Body Count News: How Crime Is Presented in the News Media." *Justice Quarterly* 11:561–582.

Chesney-Lind, M. 1989. "Girl's Crime and Woman's Place: Toward a Feminist Model of Female Delinquency." *Crime and Delinquency* 35:5–29.

Chesney-Lind, M., and R. Shelden. 2004. *Girls, Delinquency, and Juvenile Justice.* Belmont, CA: Wadsworth.

Chesney-Lind, M., R. Shelden, and K. Joe. 1996. "Girls, Delinquency, and Gang Membership." In C. Huff (ed.), *Gangs in America.* Thousand Oaks, CA: Sage.

Chin, K. 1990. *Chinese Subculture and Criminality: Non-Traditional Crime Groups in America.* Westport, CT: Greenwood.

Chiricos, T. 1987. "Rates of Crime and Unemployment: An Analysis of Aggregate Research Evidence." *Social Problems* 34:187–212.

———. 1996. "Moral Panic as Ideology: Drugs, Violence, Race, and Punishment in America." In M. Lynch and E. Patterson (eds.), *Justice with Prejudice.* Guilderland, NY: Harrow and Heston.

Chiricos, T., and C. Crawford. 1995. "Race and Imprisonment: A Contextual Assessment of the Evidence." In D. Hawkins (ed.), *Ethnicity, Race, and Crime.* Albany: University of New York.

Chiricos, T., and M. Delone. 1992. "Labor Surplus and Punishment: A Review and Assessment of Theory and Evidence." *Social Problems* 39:421–446.

Chorover, S. 1973. "Big Brother and Psychotechnology." *Psychology Today,* Oct.:43–54.

Christoffel, K., E. Zieserl, and J. Chiarmonte. 1985. "Should Child Abuse and Neglect Be Considered When a Child Dies Unexpectedly?" *American Journal of Diseases of Children* 39:876–880.

Church Committee. 1978. "Report of the Senate Select Committee on Intelligence." In M. Ermann and R. Lundman (eds.), *Corporate and Governmental Deviance.* New York: Oxford University.

Citizens for Tax Justice. 2002. "Year-by-Year Analysis of the Bush Tax Cuts Shows Growing Tilt to the Very Rich." www.ctj.org.

———. 2003. "Bush Administration Pegs Its New Tax Cut Plan at $1.8 Trillion over Decade." www.ctj.org.

Clark, J. 1995. "The Impact of the Prison Environment on Mothers." *Prison Journal* 75:306–329.

Clarke, R. (ed.). 1992. *Situational Crime Prevention: Successful Case Studies.* New York: Harrow and Heston.

Clear, T., and G. Cole. 1994. *American Corrections.* Belmont, CA: Wadsworth.

Clinard, M. 1983. *Corporate Ethics and Crime: The Role of Middle Management.* Beverly Hills: Sage.

Clinard, M., and P. Yeager. 1980. *Corporate Crime.* New York: Free Press.

Cloward, R., and L. Ohlin. 1960. *Delinquency and Opportunity: A Theory of Delinquent Gangs.* New York: Free Press.

CNN. 2001. "Florida Recount Study: Bush Still Wins." www.cnn.com.

———. 2002. "Court Overturns Three Convictions in N.Y. Police Torture Case." Feb. 28, www.cnn.com.

Cochran, J., M. Chamlin, and M. Seth. 1994. "Deterrence or Brutalization? An Impact Assessment of Oklahoma's Return to Capital Punishment." *Criminology* 32:107–134.

Cochran, J., P. Wood, and B. Arneklev. 1994. "Is the Religiosity-Delinquency Relationship Spurious? A Test of Arousal and Social Control Theories." *Journal of Research in Crime and Delinquency* 31:92–123.

Cockburn, C. 1967. *"I Claud": The Autobiography of Claud Cockburn.* Harmondsworth, UK: Penguin.

Cockburn, C. 1988. "Masculinity, the Left, and Feminism." In R. Chapman and J. Rutherford (eds.), *Male Order.* London: Lawrence and Wishart.

Cohen, A. 1955. *Delinquent Boys: The Culture of the Gang.* New York: Free Press.

———. 1966. *Deviance and Control.* Englewood Cliffs, NJ: Prentice-Hall.

Cohen, B. 1980. *Deviant Street Networks: Prostitution in New York.* Lexington, MA: Lexington.

Cohen, L., and M. Felson. 1979. "Social Change and Crime Rate Trends: A Routine Activity Approach." *American Sociological Review* 44:588–608.

Cohen, L., and K. Land. 1987. "Age Structure and Crime: Symmetry Versus Asymmetry and the Projection of Crime Rates Through the 1990s." *American Sociological Review* 52:170–183.

Cohen, M. 1989. "Corporate Crime and Punishment: A Study of Social Harm and Sentencing Practices in the Federal Courts, 1984–1987." *American Criminal Law Review* 26:605–662.

Cohen, N. 1967. *Los Angeles Riot Study: Summary and Implications for Policy.* Los Angeles: Institute of Government and Public Affairs, University of California.

Cohen, P., and A. Sas. 1996. *Cannabis Use, A Stepping Stone to Other Drugs? The Case of Amsterdam.* Amsterdam, Netherlands: Center for Drug Research, University of Amsterdam. www.mir.drugtext.org.

Cohen, R. 1995. *Probation and Parole Violators in State Prison, 1991.* Washington, DC: U.S. Department of Justice.

Cohen, S. 1980. *Folk Devils and Moral Panics: The Creation of Mods and Rockers.* Oxford: Basil Blackwell.

Cohn, B. 1992. "Noriega: How the Feds Got Their Man." *Newsweek,* Apr. 20:37.

Cole, D. 1999a. *No Equal Justice: Race and Class in the American Criminal Justice System.* New York: Free Press.

———. 1999b. "Standing While Black." *Nation,* Jan. 4:24.

———. 1999c. "When the Reason Is Race." *Nation,* Mar. 15:22–24.

———. 2003. "Court Watching." *Nation,* July 21–28:3–5.

Coleman, J. 1998. *The Criminal Elite: Understanding White-Collar Crime.* New York: St. Martin's.

Collins, C. 1997. *The Imprisonment of African American Women.* Jefferson, NC: McFarland.

Comfort, A. 1991. *The New Joy of Sex: The Gourmet Guide to Lovemaking for the Nineties.* New York: Pocket.

Comstock, G. 1991. *Violence Against Lesbians and Gay Men.* New York: Columbia University.

Conason, J., and G. Lyons. 2000. *The Hunting of the President: The Ten-Year Campaign to Destroy Bill and Hillary Clinton.* New York: Thomas Dunne.

Connell, R. 1987. *Gender and Power: Society, the Person, and Sexual Politics.* Stanford, CA: Stanford University.

———. 1995. *Masculinities.* Berkeley: University of California.

Conklin, J. 2001. *Criminology.* Boston: Allyn and Bacon.

———. 2003. *Why Crime Rates Fell.* Boston: Allyn and Bacon.

Conners, R. 2003. "How 'Restorative' Is Restorative Justice? An Oppression Theory Critique." In M. Free (ed.), *Racial Issues in Criminal Justice.* Westport, CT: Praeger.

Conrad, P. (ed.). 1997. *The Sociology of Health and Illness.* New York: St. Martin's.

Conte, J. 1986. "Sexual Abuse in the Family: A Critical Analysis." *Journal of Psychotherapy and the Family* 2:113–126.

Cordner, G. 1999. "Elements of Community Policing." In L. Gaines and G. Cordner (eds.), *Policing Perspectives.* Los Angeles: Roxbury.

Corn, D. 2001. "Bush and Butterflies." *Nation,* Dec. 3:5–6.

———. 2003. *The Lies of George W. Bush: Mastering the Politics of Deception.* New York: Crown.

Corsaro, W., and D. Eder. 1990. "Children's Peer Culture." *Annual Review of Sociology* 16:197–200.

Cose, E. 1999a. "Casualties of the Drug War." *Newsweek,* Sept. 6:29.

———. 1999b. "The Good News About Black America." *Newsweek,* June 7:28–40.

Costanzo, M. 1997. *Just Revenge: Costs and Consequences of the Death Penalty.* New York: St. Martin's.

Coston, C. 1992. "The Influence of Race in Urban Homeless Females' Fear of Crime." *Justice Quarterly* 9:721–729.

Cothern, L. 2000. *Juveniles and the Death Penalty.* Washington, DC: Coordinating Council on Juvenile Justice and Delinquency Prevention.

Coulter, A. 1998. *High Crimes and Misdemeanors: The Case Against Bill Clinton.* Washington, DC: Regnery.

Council for Prostitution Alternatives (CPA). 1994. *Annual Report 1993–1994.* Portland, OR: CPA.

Court, J. 2003. "Identity Thieves." *Nation,* Nov. 3:8, 22.

Courtois, C. 1988. *Healing the Incest Wound: Adult Survivors in Therapy.* New York: Norton.

Coverman, S. 1983. "Gender, Domestic Labor Time, and Wage Inequality." *American Sociological Review* 49:487–493.

Cowley, G. 1991. "Video Vigilantes." *Newsweek,* July 22:42–45.

———. 1998. "Why Children Turn Violent." *Newsweek,* April 6:25.

COYOTE. 1987. "National Task Force on Prostitution." In F. Delacoste and P. Alexander (eds.), *Sex Work.* Pittsburgh: Cleis.

Cressey, D. 1953. *Other People's Money.* Glencoe, IL: Free Press.

———. 1969. *Theft of the Nation.* New York: Harper and Row.

———. 1972. *Criminal Organization: Its Elementary Forms.* New York: Harper and Row.

Critchley, T. 1972. *A History of Police in England and Wales.* Montclair, NJ: Patterson Smith.

Crittenden, P., and S. Craig. 1990. "Developmental Trends in the Nature of Child Homicide." *Journal of Interpersonal Violence* 5:202–216.

Crossette, B. 1995. "Female Genital Mutilation: A Reproductive Health Concern." Supplement to *Population Reports* 23, Oct.

Cruz, H. 2003. "In Scandal's Wake, Tips for Picking a Fund." *Wisconsin State Journal,* Nov. 23:C1, C4.

Cullen, F., and B. Applegate (eds.). 1997. *Offender Rehabilitation: Effective Treatment Intervention.* Aldershot, UK: Ashgate.

Cullen, F., P. Gendreau, G. Jarjoura, and J. Wright. 1997. "Crime and the Bell Curve: Lessons from Intelligent Criminology." *Crime and Delinquency* 43:387–411.

Cullen, F., B. Link, J. Cullen, and N. Wolfe. 1989. "How Satisfying Is Prison Work? A Comparative Occupational Approach." *Journal of Offender Counseling Services and Rehabilitation* 14:89–108.

Cullen, F., W. Maakestad, and G. Cavender. 1987. *Coporate Crime Under Attack: The Ford Pinto Case and Beyond.* Cincinnati: Anderson.

Cullen, F., and J. Sundt. 2000. "Imprisonment in the United States." In J. Sheley (ed.), *Criminology.* Belmont, CA: Wadsworth.

Cullen, F., J. Wright, and M. Chamblin. 1999. "Social Support and Social Reform: A Progressive Agenda." *Crime and Delinquency* 45:188–207.

Curran, D. 1984. "The Myth of the 'New' Female Delinquent." *Criminology* 30:386–399.

Currie, C., and A. Pillick. 1996. "Sex Discrimination in the Selection and Participation of Female Jurors: A Post-*J.E.B.* Analysis." *Judges' Journal* 35:2–6, 38–42.

Currie, E. 1985. *Confronting Crime: An American Challenge.* New York: Pantheon.

Curtis, H. 1992. "Statistics Show Pattern of Discrimination." *Orlando Sentinel,* August 23:A11.

Curtis, L. 1975. *Violence, Race, and Culture.* Lexington, MA: Lexington.

———. 1987. "The Retreat of Folly: Some Modest Replications of Inner-City Success." *Annals* 494:71–89.

D'Alessio, S., and L. Stolzenberg. 2003. "Race and the Probability of Arrest." *Social Forces* 81:1381–1397.

Dahir, M. 2002. "The Dangerous Lives of Gay Priests." *Advocate,* July 23:30–35.

Daily Jefferson County Union. 1998. "ACLU Considering 'Cocaine Mom' Lawsuit." June 17:A1.

———. 2000. "Blacks Target in Drug War." June 8:A15.

Dalgard, O., and E. Kringlen. 1976. "A Norwegian Twin Study of Criminality." *British Journal of Criminology* 23:711–741.

Dalton, K. 1961. "Menstruation and Crime." *British Medical Journal* 2:1752–1753.

Daly, K. 1989. "Gender and Varieties of White-Collar Crime." *Criminology* 27:769–793.

———. 1994. *Gender, Crime, and Punishment.* New Haven: Yale University.

Daly, K., and R. Bordt. 1995. "Sex Effects and Sentencing: A Review of the Statistical Literature." *Justice Quarterly* 12:143–177.

Daly, K., and M. Chesney-Lind. 1988. "Feminism and Criminology." *Justice Quarterly* 5:497–538.

Daly, K., and L. Maher (eds.). 1998. *Criminology at the Crossroads: Feminist Readings in Crime and Justice.* New York: Oxford University.

Daly, M. 1978. *Gyn/Ecology.* Boston: Beacon.

Daly, M. 2003. "Suits Cut Environmental Protections." *Wisconsin State Journal,* Apr. 19:A3.

Daly, M., and M. Wilson. 1988. *Homicide.* New York: Adline de Gruyter.

Dannefer, D., and R. Schutt. 1982. "Race and Juvenile Justice Processing in Court and Police Agencies." *American Journal of Sociology* 87:1113–1132.

Darden, C. 1996. *In Contempt.* New York: ReganBooks.

Datesman, S., and F. Scarpitti. 1980. "The Extent of Female Crime." In S. Datesman and F. Scarpitti (eds.), *Women, Crime, and Justice.* New York: Oxford University.

Datesman, S., F. Scarpitt, and R. Stephenson. 1975. "Female Delinquency: An Application of Self and Opportunity Theories." *Journal of Research in Crime and Delinquency* 12:107–123.

Daudistel, H., W. Sanders, and D. Luckenbill. 1979. *Criminal Justice: Situations and Decisions.* New York: Holt, Rinehart, and Winston.

Davies, T. 1983. "A Hard Look at What We Know (and Still Need to Learn) About the 'Costs' of the Exclusionary Rule." *American Bar Foundation Research Journal,* Summer:611–690.

Davis, A. 1990. *Women, Race, and Class.* New York: Vintage.

Davis, N. (ed.). 1993. *Prostitution: An International Handbook on Trends, Problems, and Policies.* Westport, CT: Greenwood.

Dawley, D. 1992. *A Nation of Lords: The Autobiography of the Vice Lords.* Prospect Heights, IL: Waveland.

Dawson, J. 1992. "Prosecutions in State Courts." *BJS Bulletin,* Mar.:1–9.

De La Cruz, D. 1999. "Police Charged with Murder." *Wisconsin State Journal,* Apr. 1:2A.

Death Penalty Information Center (DPIC). 2003a. "The Death Penalty in 2003: Year End Report." www.deathpenaltyinfo.org.

———. 2003b. "Innocence and the Death Penalty." www. deathpenaltyinfo.org.

———. 2004a. "Age Requirements for the Death Penalty." www.deathpenaltyinfo. org.

———. 2004b. "Juvenile Offenders on Death Row." www.deathpenaltyinfo.org.

———. 2004c. "Mental Retardation and the Death Penalty." www. deathpenaltyinfo.rog.

DeFrances, C. 2002. *Prosecutors in State Courts, 2001.* Washington, DC: U.S. Department of Justice.

DeFrances, C., and F. Marika. 2000. *Indigent Defense Services in Large Counties, 1999.* Washington, DC: U.S. Department of Justice.

DeKeseredy, W., and M. Schwartz. 1996. *Contemporary Criminology.* Belmont, CA: Wadsworth.

Delacoste, F., and F. Newman (eds.). 1981. *Fight Back: Feminist Resistance to Male Violence.* Minneapolis: Cleis.

Delgado, R. 2000. "Goodbye to Hammurabi: Analyzing the Atavistic Appeal of Restorative Justice." *Stanford Law Review* 52:751–775.

Denno, D. 1998. "Execution and the Forgotten Eighth Amendment." In J. Acker et al. (eds.), *America's Experiment with Capital Punishment.* Durham, NC: Carolina Academic.

DeParle, J. 1991. "Suffering in the Cities Persists as U.S. Fights Other Battles." *New York Times,* Jan. 27:15.

Derber, C. 1996. *The Wilding of America: How Greed and Violence Are Eroding Our Nation's Character.* New York: St. Martin's.

Dershowitz, A. 1996. *Reasonable Doubts: The O.J. Simpson Case and the Criminal Justice System.* New York: Simon and Schuster.

———. 2001. *Supreme Injustice: How the High Court Hijacked Election 2000.* New York: Oxford University.

Diamond, J. 1996. "Report Links CIA, Cocaine Boom." *Wisconsin State Journal,* Oct. 5:3A.

Diaz, T. 1999. *Making a Killing: The Business of Guns in America.* New York: New Press.

Dickenson, J. 1977. "How the Scandals of History Left Mud on the White House Steps." In J. Douglas and J. Johnson (eds.), *Official Deviance.* Philadelphia: Lippincott.

Dickey, C., and R. Nordland. 2000. "Big Tobacco's Next Legal War." *Newsweek,* July 31:36–39.

DiMascio, W. 1997. *Seeking Justice: Crime and Punishment in America.* New York: Edna McConnell Clark.

Dobash, R., et al. 1992. "The Myth of the Symmetrical Nature of Domestic Violence." *Social Problems* 39:71–91.

Dobkowski, M., and I. Wallimann (eds.). 1998. *The Coming Age of Scarcity: Preventing Mass Death and Genocide in the Twenty-First Century.* Syracuse: Syracuse University.

Dodge, L. 1999. "Abortion Foes Lose Suit Over Web Site." *Wisconsin State Journal,* Feb. 2:1A.

Donn, J. 2001. "Torrents of Tobacco Ads Strain Terms of Settlement." *Wisconsin State Journal,* Aug. 16:A5.

Donnerstein, E., D. Linz, and S. Penrod. 1987. *The Question of Pornography: Research Findings and Policy Implications.* New York: Free Press.

Douglas, J. 1977. "Major John Lindsay and the Revenge of Boss Tweed." In J. Douglas and J. Johnson (eds.), *Official Deviance.* Philadelphia: Lippincott.

Dowie, M. 1977. "Pinto Madness." *Mother Jones* 2:18–24, 28–32.

———. 1987. "The Dumping of Hazardous Products on Foreign Markets." In S. Hills (ed.), *Corporate Violence.* Totowa, NJ: Rowman and Littlefield.

Dowie, M., and C. Marshall. 1980. "The Bendectin Cover-Up." *Mother Jones* 5:43–56.

Dowling, C. 1998. "Violence Lessons." *Mother Jones,* July–Aug.:32–41.

Downes, B. 1968. "The Social Characteristics of Riot Cities: A Comparative Study." *Social Science Quarterly* 49:504–520.

Drogin, B. 2003. "Friendly Fire." *New Republic,* Oct. 27:23–27.

DuBois, W. (ed.). 1904. *Some Notes on Negro Crime, Particularly in Georgia.* Atlanta: Atlanta University.

Dugan, L. 2003. "Domestic Violence Legislation: Exploring Its Impact on the Likelihood of Domestic Violence, Police Involvement, and Arrest." *Criminology and Public Policy* 2:283–312.

Dugan, L., D. Nagin, and R. Rosenfeld. 2003. "Exposure Reduction or Retaliation? The Effects of Domestic Violence Resources on Intimate Partner Violence." *Law and Society Review* 37:169–198.

Dugdale, R. 1877. *The Jukes: A Study in Crime, Pauperism, Disease, and Heredity.* New York: Putnam.

Dugger, R. 2004. "How They Could Steal the Election This Time." *Nation,* Aug. 16/23:11–24.

Dulaney, M. 1996. *Black Police in America.* Bloomington: Indiana University.

Dunaway, R., F. Cullen, V. Burton, and T. Evans. 2000. "The Myth of Social Class and Crime Revisited: An Examination of Class and Criminality." *Criminology* 38:589–630.

Dunford, F., D. Huizinga, and D. Elliott. 1990. "Role of Arrest in Domestic Assault: The Omaha Police Experiment." *Criminology* 28:183–206.

Dunn, J. 1999. "What Love Has to Do with It: The Cultural Construction of Emotion and Sorority Women's Responses to Forcible Interaction." *Social Problems* 46:440–459.

Durham, A. 1986. "Pornography, Social Harm, and Legal Control." *Justice Quarterly* 3:95–102.

Durkheim, É. 1893/1964. *The Division of Labor in Society.* New York: Free Press.

———. 1897/1952. *Suicide.* New York: Free Press.

Dworkin, A. 1989. *Pornography: Men Possessing Women.* New York: Dutton.

———. 1997. *Life and Death.* New York: Free Press.

Dworkin, A., and C. MacKinnon. 1988. *Pornography and Civil Rights.* Minneapolis: Organizing Against Pornography.

Dwyer, L. 1983. "Structure and Strategy in the Antinuclear Movement." In J. Freeman (ed.), *Social Movements in the Sixties and Seventies.* New York: Longman.

Eagan, S. 1996. "From Spikes to Bombs: The Rise of Eco-Terrorism." *Studies in Conflict and Terrorism* 19:1–18.

Earley, P. 1992. *The Hot House: Life Inside Leavenworth.* New York: Bantam.

Ebert, R. 1986. *Robert Ebert's Movie Home Companion.* Kansas City, MO: Andrews, McMeel, and Parker.

Eck, J., and E. Maguire. 2000. "Have Changes in Policing Reduced Violent Crime? An Assessment of the Evidence." In A. Blumstein and J. Wallman (eds.), *The Crime Drop in America.* New York: Cambridge University.

The Economist. 1998. "On Prescription." Nov. 28:51–52.

Edelstein, J. 1987. "In the Massage Parlor." In F. Delacoste and P. Alexander (eds.), *Sex Work.* Pittsburgh: Cleis.

Ehrenreich, B., M. Dowie, and S. Minkin. 1979. "The Charge: Genocide; The Accused: The U.S. Government." *Mother Jones* 4:26–37.

Ehrenreich, B., and D. English. 1973. *Witches, Midwives, and Nurses.* Old Westbury, NY: Feminist Press.

Eig, J. 1996. "Eyes on the Street: Community Policing in Chicago." *American Prospect,* Nov.–Dec.:60–68.

Eigenberg, H. 1990. "The National Crime Survey and Rape: The Case of the Missing Question." *Justice Quarterly* 7:655–671.

"Eight Tray Gangster: The Making of a Crip." 1993. Discovery Channel documentary.

Einstader, W., and S. Henry. 1995. *Criminological Theory*. Fort Worth: Harcourt Brace.

Elias, R. 1986. *The Politics of Victimization*. New York: Oxford University.

Elias, T., and D. Schatzman. 1996. *The Simpson Trial in Black and White*. Los Angeles: General.

Elifson, K., D. Peterson, and C. Hadaway. 1983. "Religiosity and Delinquency: A Contextual Analysis." *Criminology* 21:505–527.

Elliott, D., and S. Ageton. 1980. "Reconciling Race and Class Differences in Self-Reported and Official Estimates of Delinquency." *American Sociological Review* 45:95–110.

Elliott, D., and D. Huizinga. 1983. "Social Class and Delinquent Behavior in a National Youth Panel." *Criminology* 21:149–177.

Elliott, P. 1996. "Shattering Illusions: Same-Sex Domestic Violence." In C. Renzetti and C. Miley (eds.), *Violence in Gay and Lesbian Domestic Relationships*. New York: Harrington Park.

Ellis, D., and W. DeKeseredy. 1997. "Rethinking Estrangement Interventions and Intimate Femicide." *Violence Against Women* 3:590–609.

Ellis, L., and A. Walsh. 1997. "Gene-Based Evolutionary Theories in Criminology." *Criminology* 35:229–276.

———. 2000. *Criminology: A Global Perspective*. Boston: Allyn and Bacon.

Ellison, C. 1991. "An Eye for an Eye? A Note on the Southern Subculture of Violence Thesis." *Social Forces* 69:1223–1239.

Emerson, R., K. Ferris, and C. Gardner. 1998. "On Being Stalked." *Social Problems* 45:289–314.

Emery, J., and M. Newlands. 1991. "Child Abuse and Cot Deaths." *Child Abuse and Neglect* 15:275–278.

Emirbayer, M., and A. Mische. 1998. "What Is Agency?" *American Journal of Sociology* 4:962–1023.

Empey, L., and M. Stafford. 1991. *American Delinquency*. Belmont, CA: Wadsworth.

Engen, R., S. Steen, and G. Bridges. 2002. "Racial Disparities in the Punishment of Youth: A Theoretical and Empirical Assessment of the Literature." *Social Problems* 49:194–220.

England, R. 1967. "A Theory of Middle Class Juvenile Delinquency." In E. Vaz (ed.), *Middle Class Juvenile Delinquency*. New York: Harper and Row.

Erickson, M., J. Gibbs, and G. Jensen. 1977. "The Deterrence Doctrine and the Perceived Certainty of Legal Punishment." *American Sociological Review* 42:305–317.

Erickson, M., and G. Jensen. 1977. "Delinquency Is Still Group Behavior." *Journal of Criminal Law and Criminology* 68:388–395.

Erikson, K. 1966. *Wayward Puritans: A Study in the Sociology of Deviance*. New York: Wiley.

Ermann, M., and W. Clements. 1984. "The Interfaith Center on Corporate Responsibility and Its Campaign Against Marketing Infant Formula in the Third World." *Social Problems* 32:185–196.

Esbensen, F., and D. Huizinga. 1993. "Gangs, Drugs, and Delinquency in a Survey of Urban Youth." *Criminology* 31:565–587.

Esbensen, F., and L. Winfree. 1998. "Race and Gender Differences Between Gang and Non-Gang Youth: Results from a Multi-Site Survey." *Justice Quarterly* 15:505–525.

Eschholz, S. 2003. "The Color of Prime-Time Justice: Racial Characteristics of Television Offenders and Victims." In M. Free (ed.), *Racial Issues in Criminal Justice*. Westport, CT: Praeger.

Estrich, S. 1987. *Real Rape*. Cambridge: Harvard University.

Evans, E. 1983. "The Use of Terrorism by American Social Movements." In J. Freeman (ed.), *Social Movements of the Sixties and Seventies*. New York: Longman.

Evans, T., F. Cullen, R. Dunaway, and V. Burton. 1995. "Religion and Crime Reexamined: The Impact of Religion, Secular Controls, and Social Ecology on Adult Criminality." *Criminology* 33:195–224.

Everson, M., et al. 1989. "Maternal Support Following Disclosure of Incest." *American Journal of Orthopsychiatry* 59:197–207.

Ewing, J., and B. Houston. 1991. "Some Judges Punish People Without Benefit of Trial." *Hartford Courant,* June 17:A1.

Eysenck, H. 1977. *Crime and Personality*. London: Routledge and Kegan Paul.

Fagan, J. 1990. "Social Processes of Delinquency and Drug Use Among Urban Gangs." In C. Huff (ed.), *Gangs in America*. Newbury Park, CA: Sage.

———. 1994. "Women and Drugs Revisited: Female Participation in the Cocaine Economy." *Journal of Drug Issues* 24:179–225.

Faith, K. 1993. *Unruly Women: The Politics of Confinement and Resistance*. Vancouver: Press Gang.

Faludi, S. 1999. "The Betrayal of the American Man." *Newsweek,* Sept. 13:48–50.

Farberman, H. 1975. "A Criminogenic Market Structure: The Automobile Industry." *Sociological Quarterly* 16:438–457.

Farley, J. 1987. "Suburbanization and Central-City Crime Rates: New Evidence and a Reinterpretation." *American Journal of Sociology* 93:688–700.

Farr, K. 1993. "The Five Sexes: Why Male and Female Are Not Enough." *Sciences* (Mar./Apr.):20–24.

———. 1995. "Fetal Abuse and the Criminalization of Behavior During Pregnancy." *Crime and Delinquency* 41:235–245.

———. 1997. "Aggravating and Differentiating Factors in the Cases of White and Minority Women on Death Row." *Crime and Delinquency* 43:260–278.

Fausto-Sterling, A. 2000. *Sexing the Body*. New York: Basic.

Federal Bureau of Investigation (FBI). 1966, 1971, 1976, 1981, 1986, 1991, 1996, 1998, 2003. *Uniform Crime Reports*. Washington, DC: U.S. Government Printing Office.

Feinberg, L. 1996. *Transgender Warrior*. Boston: Beacon.

Feldberg, M. 1980. *The Turbulent Era: Riot and Disorder in Jacksonian America*. New York: Oxford University.

Felson, M. 1998. *Crime and Everyday Life*. Thousand Oaks, CA: Pine Forge.

Ferraro, K. 1989. "Policing Woman Battering." *Social Problems* 36:61–74.

Ferraro, K. 1996. "Women's Fear of Victimization: Shadow of Sexual Assault?" *Social Forces* 75:667–690.

Ferrell, J. 1997. "Criminological Verstehen: Inside the Immediacy of Crime." *Justice Quarterly* 14:3–23.

Fessenden, R., and J. Broder. 2001. "Ballot Study Finds Court Didn't Give Bush Win." *Wisconsin State Journal,* Nov. 12:A1, A8.

Feuer, A. 2004. "New York Settles Lawsuit with Diallo Family for $3 Million." *New York Times,* Jan. 6, www.ny.times.com.

Figueira-McDonough, J. 1984. "Feminism and Delinquency: In Search of an Illusive Link." *British Journal of Criminology* 24:325–342.

Figueria-McDonough, J., W. Barton, and R. Sarri. 1981. "Normal Deviance: Gender Similarities in Adolescent Subcultures." In M. Warren (ed.), *Comparing Male and Female Offenders.* Beverly Hills: Sage.

Fineman, H. 1994. "The Virtuecrats." *Newsweek,* June 13:30–36.

———. 1999. "Under Fire." *Newsweek,* May 31:25–27.

Finkelhor, D., and L. Baron. 1986. "Risk Factors in Child Sexual Abuse." *Journal of Intepersonal Violence* 1:43–71.

Finkelor, D., G. Hotaling, I. Lewis, and C. Smith. 1990. "Sexual Abuse in a National Survey of Adult Men and Women: Prevalence, Characteristics, and Risk Factors." *Child Abuse and Neglect* 14:19–28.

Finkelor, D., and K. Yllo. 1985. *License to Rape: Sexual Abuse of Wives.* New York: Holt, Rinehart, and Winston.

Finn, P. 1998. *Texas' Project RIO.* Washington, DC: National Institute of Justice.

Fishbein, D. 1990. "Biological Perspectives in Criminology." *Criminology* 28:27–72.

Fisher, J. 1997. *Killer Among Us: Public Reactions to Serial Murder.* Westport, CT: Praeger.

Fishman, L. 1988. "The Vice Queens: An Ethnographic Study of Black Female Bang Behavior." Paper presented at the conference of the American Society of Criminology, Chicago.

Fishman, M. 1978. "Crime Waves as Ideology." *Social Problems* 25:531–543.

Fishman, M., and G. Cavender (eds.). 1998. *Entertaining Crime: Television Reality Programs.* New York: Aldine de Gruyter.

Fitzpatrick, K., M. La Gory, and F. Ritchey. 1993. "Criminal Victimization Among the Homeless." *Justice Quarterly* 10:353–368.

Fletcher, C. 1995. *Breaking and Entering: Women Cops Talk About Life in the Ultimate Men's Club.* New York: HarperCollins.

Foa, P. 1977. "What's Wrong with Rape?" In M. Vetterling-Braggin et al. (eds.), *Feminism and Philosophy.* Totowa, NJ: Littlefield, Adams.

Foote, D. 1999. "You Could Get Raped." *Newsweek,* Feb. 8:64–65.

Foucault, M. 1979. *Discipline and Punish: The Birth of the Prison.* New York: Vintage.

Fox, J., and J. Levin. 1993. "Female Serial Killers." In C. Colliver (ed.), *Female Criminality.* New York: Garland.

Frank, N. 1993. "Maiming and Killing: Occupational Health Crimes." *Annals* 525:107–118.

Franklin, A. 1979. "Criminality in the Work Place: A Comparison of Male and Female Offenders." In F. Adler and R. Simon (eds.), *The Criminality of Deviant Women.* Boston: Houghton Mifflin.

Frease, D. 1973. "Delinquency, Social Class, and the Schools." *Sociology and Social Research* 57:443–459.

Free, M. 1996. *African Americans and the Criminal Justice System.* New York: Garland.

———. 1997. "The Impact of Federal Sentencing Guidelines on African Americans." *Journal of Black Studies* 28:268–286.

———. 2002. "Race and Presentencing Decisions in the United States: A Summary and Critique of the Research." *Criminal Justice Review* 27:203–222.

Freeman, R. 1996. "Why Do So Many Young American Men Commit Crimes and What Might We Do About It?" *Journal of Economic Perspectives* 10:25–42.

Freiberg, P. 2002. "Mass Confusion." *Advocate,* Apr. 30:28–31.

Frey, C., and S. Hoppe-Graff. 1994. "Serious and Playful Aggression in Brazilian Girls and Boys." *Sex Roles* 30:249–269.

Frey, H. 2002. "The Naked Truth." *Nation,* Nov. 25:28, 30–32.

Friedlander, K. 1947. *The Psychoanalytic Approach to Juvenile Delinquency.* London: Routledge and Kegan Paul.

Friedman, A. 1993. *Spider's Web: The Secret History of How the White House Illegally Armed Iraq.* New York: Bantam.

Friedrichs, D. 1999. "Postmodernism, Postmodernity, and Postmodern Criminology." In J. Fuller and E. Hickey (eds.), *Controversial Issues in Criminology.* Boston: Allyn and Bacon.

———. 2004. *Trusted Criminals: White Collar Crime in Contemporary Society.* Belmont, CA: Wadsworth.

Friess, S. 1999. "Behind Closed Doors: Domestic Violence." In C. Albers (ed.), *Sociology of Families Readings.* Thousand Oaks, CA: Pine Forge.

Fukurai, H., E. Butler, and R. Krooth. 1993. *Race and the Jury: Racial Disenfranchisement and the Search for Justice.* New York: Plenum.

Fuller, J. 1998. *Criminal Justice: A Peacemaking Perspective.* Boston: Allyn and Bacon.

Fyfe, J. 1981. "Who Shoots? A Look at Officer Race and Police Shooting." *Journal of Police Science and Administration* 9:367–382.

———. 1982. "Blind Justice: Police Shootings in Memphis." *Journal of Criminal Law and Criminology* 73:707–722.

———. 1988. "Police Use of Deadly Force: Research and Reform." *Justice Quarterly* 5:165–205.

Gabor, T., et al. 1987. *Armed Robbery: Cops, Robbers, and Victims.* Springfield, IL: Charles Thomas.

Gaes, G., T. Flanagan, L. Motiuk, and L. Stewart. 1999. "Adult Correctional Treatment." In M. Tonry and J. Petersilia (eds.), *Prisons.* Chicago: University of Chicago.

Gaines, D. 1990. *Teenage Wasteland: Suburbia's Dead End Kids.* New York: HarperCollins.

Gaines, L., and G. Cordner (eds.). 1999. *Policing Perspectives.* Los Angeles: Roxbury.

Gaines, P. 1993. "Tough Boyz and Trouble." In M. Golden (ed.), *Wild Women Don't Wear No Blues.* New York: Anchor.

Gallagher, M., and D. Blankenhorn. 1997. "Family Feud." *American Prospect,* July–Aug.:12–16.

Garfinkel, S. 2000. "Privacy and the New Technology." *Nation,* Feb. 28:11–15.

Garner, J., and C. Maxwell. 1999. "Measuring the Amount of Force Used By and Against the Police in Six Jurisdictions." In *Use of Force by Police.* Washington, DC: U.S. Department of Justice.

Garrow, D. 1981. *The FBI and Martin Luther King Jr.* New York: Penguin.

Geerken, M., and J. Hayes. 1993. "Probation and Parole: Public Risk and the Future of Incarceration Alternatives." *Criminology* 31:549–564.

Gegax, T., and L. Clemetson. 1998. "The Abortion Wars Come Home." *Newsweek,* Nov. 9:34–35.

Geis, G. 1996. "The Heavy Electrical Equipment Antitrust Cases: Price-Fixing Techniques and Rationalizations." In M. Ermann and R. Lundman (eds.), *Corporate and Governmental Deviance.* New York: Oxford University.

Geis, G., and R. Meier (eds.). 1977. *White-Collar Crime.* New York: Free Press.

Gelles, R. 1987. *Family Violence*. Newbury Park, CA: Sage.

George, T. 2000. "N.Y. Verdict Stirs Up Emotions." *Wisconsin State Journal*, Feb. 26:2A.

Gerber, J., and J. Short 1986. "Publicity and Control of Corporate Behavior: The Case of Infant Formula." *Deviant Behavior* 7:195–216.

Gerth, H., and C. Mills (eds.). 1946. *From Max Weber: Essays in Sociology*. New York: Oxford University.

Gibbons, D. 1999. "Review Essay: Changing Lawbreakers—What Have We Learned Since the 1960s?" *Crime and Delinquency* 45:272–293.

Gibbs, J. 1996. *Race and Justice: Rodney King and O.J. Simpson in a House Divided*. San Francisco: Josey-Bass.

Gibbs, N. 1993. "Til Death Do Us Part." *Time*, Jan. 18:38–45.

Giddens, A. 1981. *The Constitution of Society: Outline of the Theory of Structuration*. Berkeley: University of California.

Gillespie, L. 2000. *Dancehall Ladies: Executed Women in the Twentieth Century*. Lanham, MD: University Press of America.

Gillespie, M. 1993. "What's Good for the Race." *Ms.*, Jan.–Feb.:80–81.

Ginzburg, R. 1988. *100 Years of Lynching*. Baltimore: Black Classic.

Gioia, D. 1996. "Why I Didn't Recognize Pinto Fire Hazards: How Organizational Scripts Channel Managers' Thoughts and Actions." In M. Ermann and R. Lundman (eds.), *Corporate and Governmental Deviance*. New York: Oxford University.

Giordano, P. 1978. "Girls, Guys, and Gangs: The Changing Social Context of Female Delinquency." *Journal of Criminal Law and Criminology* 69:126–132.

Giordano, P., and S. Cernkovich. 1979. "On Complicating the Relationship Between Liberation and Delinquency." *Social Problems* 26:467–481.

Giordano, P., S. Cernkovich, and D. Holland. 2003. "Changes in Friendship Relations Over the Life Course: Implications for the Distance from Crime." *Criminology* 41:293–327.

Giordano, P., S. Cernkovich, and M. Pugh. 1986. "Friendships and Delinquency." *American Journal of Sociology* 91:1170–1202.

Glaser, D. 1969. *The Effectiveness of a Prison and Parole System*. Indianapolis: Bobbs-Merrill.

———. 1997. *Profitable Penalties: How to Cut Both Crime Rates and Costs*. Thousand Oaks, CA: Pine Forge.

Glaser, D., and M. Zeigler. 1974. "The Use of the Death Penalty v. Outrage at Murder." *Crime and Delinquency* 20:333–338.

Glass, A. 1999. "Judge Finds Microsoft at Fault." *Wisconsin State Journal*, Nov. 6:1A, 4A.

Glaze, L. 2003. *Probation and Parole in the United States, 2002*. Washington, DC: U.S. Department of Justice.

Glick, R., and V. Neto. 1977. *National Survey of Women's Correctional Programs*. Washington, DC: U.S. Government Printing Office.

Glueck, S., and E. Glueck. 1950. *Unraveling Juvenile Delinquency*. New York: Commonwealth Fund.

———. 1968. *Delinquents and Nondelinquents in Perspective*. Cambridge: Harvard University.

Goddard, H. 1912. *The Kallikak Family: A Study in the Heredity of Feeblemindedness*. New York: Macmillan.

Godfrey, M., and V. Schiraldi. 1995. *How Homicide Rates Have Been Affected by California's Death Penalty*. San Francisco: Center on Juvenile and Criminal Justice.

Gold, M. 2000. "The Progress of Women in Policing." *Law and Order* 48:159–161.

Goldstein, J. 1986. *Aggression and Crimes of Violence*. New York: Oxford University.

Goldstein, J., et al. 1975. "Punitiveness in Response to Films Varying in Content: A Cross-National Field Study of Aggression." *European Journal of Social Psychology* 5:149–165.

Goldstein, P. 1979. *Prostitution and Drugs*. Lexington, MA: Heath.

Gomez, L. 1997. *Misconceiving Mothers*. Philadelphia: Temple University.

Goode, E. 1999. *Drugs in American Society*. New York: McGraw-Hill.

Goodwin, J. 1998. "Afghan Women Under the Taliban." *On the Issues,* Summer:26–31, 57–58.

Gordon, D. 1978. "Capitalist Development and the History of American Cities." In W. Tabb and L. Sawyers (eds.), *Marxism and the Metropolis*. New York: Oxford University.

Gordon, D., R. Edwards, and M. Reich. 1982. *Segmented Work, Divided Workers: The Historical Transformation of Labor in the United States*. New York: Cambridge University.

Gordon, D. 1994a. "Drugspeak and the Clinton Administration: A Lost Opportunity for Drug Policy Reform." *Social Justice* 21:30–37.

———. 1994b. *The Return of the Dangerous Classes: Drug Prohibition and Policy Politics*. New York: Norton.

Gordon, L. 1988. *Heroes of Their Own Lives: The Politics and History of Family Violence*. New York: Viking.

Gordon, M. 2002. "Investigator: Big Banks Helped Enron Hide True Financial State." *Wisconsin State Journal*, July 24:A4.

Gorenberg, G. 2004. "The Terror Trap." *American Prospect,* Jan.:13–15.

Goring, C. 1913. *The English Convict*. London: H.M.S.O.

Gottfredson, G. 1987. "Peer Group Interventions to Reduce the Risk of Delinquent Behavior: A Selective Review and a New Evaluation." *Criminology* 25:671–714.

Gottfredson, M., and T. Hirschi. 1990. *A General Theory of Crime*. Stanford, CA: Stanford University.

Gouldner, A. 1970. *The Coming Crises of Western Sociology*. New York: Avon.

Graff, E. 2001. "The M/F Boxes." *Nation*, Dec. 17:20–24.

———. 2003. "In the Bedroom." *American Prospect*, Spring:A22–23.

Grant Bowman, C. 1992. "The Arrest Experiments: A Feminist Critique." *Journal of Criminal Justice* 83:201–208.

Grasmick, H., R. Bursik, and B. Arneklev. 1993. "Reduction in Drunk Driving as a Response to Increased Threats of Shame, Embarrassment, and Legal Sanctions." *Criminology* 31:41–67.

Grasmick, H., R. Bursik, and J. Cochran. 1991. "Render Unto Caesar What Is Caesar's: Religiosity and Taxpayers' Inclinations to Cheat." *Sociological Quarterly* 32:251–266.

Gray, M. 1998. *Drug Crazy: How We Got Into This Mess and How We Can Get Out*. New York: Random House.

Gray, M., M. Fields, and S. Maxwell. 2001. "Examining Probation Violations: Who, What, and When." *Crime and Delinquency* 47:558–572.

Gray, W., and J. Scholz. 1993. "Does Regulatory Enforcement Work? A Panel Analysis of OSHA Enforcement." *Law and Society Review* 27: 177–213.

Green, J. 1996. "Mothers in 'Incest Families': A Critique of Blame and Its Destructive Sequels." *Violence Against Women* 2:322–348.

Greenberg, D. 1977. "Delinquency and the Age Structure of Society." *Contemporary Crises* 1:189–223.

——— (ed.). 1993. *Crime and Capitalism: Readings in Marxist Criminology.* Philadelphia: Temple University.

Greenberg, D., and D. Humphries. 1980. "The Dialectics of Crime Control." In D. Black (ed.), *Toward a General Theory of Control.* New York: Academic.

Greenberg, D., and V. West. 2001. "State Prison Populations and Their Growth, 1971–1999." *Criminology* 39:615–653.

Greene, J. 1999. "Zero Tolerance: A Case Study of Police Policies and Practices in New York City." *Crime and Delinquency* 45:171–187.

Greenhouse, L. 1999. "Court Says Cops Can't Take Media for Home Search." *Wisconsin State Journal,* May 25:2A.

———. 2004. "Court to Rule on Death Penalty Issue." *Wisconsin State Journal,* Jan. 27:A3.

Greenwood, P., et al. 1996. *Diverting Children From a Life of Crime: Measuring Costs and Benefits.* Santa Monica, CA: RAND.

Greider, K. 1995. "Crackpot Ideas." *Mother Jones,* July–Aug.:53–56.

Greider, W. 2001. "Enron's Rise and Fall." *Nation,* Dec. 24:5–6.

———. 2003. "Occupiers and the Law." *Nation,* Nov. 17:5–6.

Griffin, M. 1988. "The Legacy of Love Canal." *Sierra* 73:26–30.

Griffin, S. 1981. *Pornography and Silence: Culture's Revenge Against Nature.* New York: Harper and Row.

Gross, S. 1996. "The Risks of Death: Why Erroneous Convictions are Common in Capital Cases." *Buffalo Law Review* 44:469–500.

Grossman, J. 1994. "Women's Jury Service: Right of Citizenship or Privilege of Difference?" *Stanford Law Review* 46:1115–1160.

Gruhl, J., C. Spohn, and S. Welch. 1981. "Women as Policymakers: The Case of Trial Judges." *American Journal of Political Science* 25:308–322.

Grunwald, M. 2003. "Washed Away: Bush vs. the Missouri River." *New Republic,* Oct. 27:16–18.

Gupta, A. 2004. "Over 2,000 Police Killings in the U.S. in Past Decade." www.baltimore.indymedia.org.

Gurr, T. (ed.). 1989. *Violence in America: Protest, Rebellion, Reform.* Newbury Park, CA: Sage.

Gusfield, J. 1963. *Symbolic Crusade: Status Politics and the American Temperance Movement.* Urbana: University of Illinois.

Guy, K., and R. Huckabee. 1988. "Going Free on a Technicality: Another Look at the Effect of the Miranda Decision on the Criminal Justice Process." *Criminal Justice Research Bulletin* 4:2–3.

Gwartney, D. 1998. "The Moral High Ground." *Newsweek,* Apr. 10:61.

Haarr, R. 1997. "Patterns of Interaction in a Police Patrol Bureau: Race and Gender Barriers to Integration." *Justice Quarterly* 14:53–85.

Hacker, A. 1992. *Two Nations: Black and White, Separate, Hostile, Unequal.* New York: Ballantine.

Hadaway, C., P. Marier, and M. Chaves. 1993. "What the Polls Don't Show: A Closer Look at U.S. Church Attendance." *American Sociological Review* 58:741–752.

Hagan, F. 1997. *Political Crime: Ideology and Criminality.* Boston: Allyn and Bacon.

———. 1998. *Introduction to Criminology.* Chicago: Nelson-Hall.

Hagan, J. 1989. *Structural Criminology.* New Brunswick, NJ: Rutgers University.

——. 1991. "Destiny and Drift: The Risks and Rewards of Youth." *American Sociological Review* 56:567–582.

——. 1992. "The Poverty of a Classless Criminology." *Criminology* 30:1–20.

——. 1993. "The Social Embeddedness of Crime and Unemployment." *Criminology* 31:465–491.

——. 1994. *Crime and Disrepute*. Thousand Oaks, CA: Pine Forge.

Hagan, J., and C. Albonetti. 1982. "Race, Class, and the Perception of Criminal Injustice in America." *American Journal of Sociology* 88:329–355.

Hagan, J., and J. Coleman 2001. "Returning Captives of the American War on Drugs: Issues of Community and Family Reentry." *Crime and Delinquency* 47:352–367.

Hagan, J., and B. McCarthy. 1997. *Mean Streets: Youth Crime and Homelessness*. Cambridge, UK: Cambridge University.

Hagan, J., A. Gillis, and J. Simpson. 1985. "The Class Structure of Gender and Delinquency: Toward a Power-Control Theory of Common Delinquent Behavior." *American Journal of Sociology* 90:1151–1178.

Hagan, J., et al. 1998. "Subterranean Sources of Subcultural Delinquency Beyond the American Dream." *Criminology* 36:309–339.

Hagedorn, J. 1988. *People and Folks: Gangs, Crime, and the Underclass in a Rustbelt City*. Chicago: Lake View.

Hale, D., and S. Wyland. 1999. "Dragons and Dinosaurs: The Plight of Patrol Women." In L. Gaines and G. Cordner (eds.), *Policing Perspectives*. Los Angeles: Roxbury.

Halperin, M., J. Berman, R. Borosage, and C. Marwick. 1977. *The Lawless State: The Crimes of the U.S. Intelligence Agencies*. New York: Penguin.

Hamilton, R. 2002. "Black Panther Party." *World Book Encyclopedia*. Chicago: World Book.

Hamlin, J. 1988. "The Misplaced Role of Rational Choice in Neutralization Theory." *Criminology* 26:425–438.

Hamm, M. 1993. *American Skinheads: The Criminology and Control of Hate Crimes*. Westport, CT: Praeger.

Hammett, T., P. Harmon, and L. Maruschak. 1999. *HIV/AIDS, STD, and TB in Correctional Facilities*. Washington, DC: U.S. Department of Justice.

Hammond, N. 1986. "Lesbian Victims and the Reluctance to Identify Abuse." In K. Lobel (ed.), *Naming the Violence*. Seattle: Seal.

Hancock, L. 1998. "Tucker Case Revives Fight Over Death Row's Gender." *Wisconsin State Journal*, Feb. 1:7A.

Harer, M., and D. Steffensmeier. 1992. "The Differing Effects of Economic Inequality on Black and White Rates of Violence." *Social Forces* 70:1035–1054.

Harland, A. 1983. "One Hundred Years of Restitution: An International Review and Prospectus for Research." *Victimology* 8:190–202.

Harlow, C. 2000. *Defense Counsel in Criminal Cases*. Washington, DC: U.S. Department of Justice.

Harmon, P., and J. Check. 1989. *The Role of Pornography in Woman Abuse*. Toronto: La Marsh Research Programme on Violence and Conflict Resolution, York University.

Harring, S. 1993. "Policing a Class Society: The Expansion of the Urban Police in the Late Nineteenth and Early Twentieth Centuries." In D. Greenberg (ed.), *Crime and Capitalism*. Philadelphia: Temple University.

Harring, S., and L. McMullin. 1975. "The Buffalo Police, 1982–1900: Labor

Unrest, Political Power and the Creation of the Police Institution." *Crime and Social Justice* 8:5–14.

Harris, D. 2003. "The Reality of Racial Disparity in Criminal Justice: The Significance of Data Collection." *Law and Contemporary Problems* 66:71–98.

Harris, M. 1988. *Cholas: Latino Girls and Gangs*. New York: AMS Press.

Harris, M. 1997. "When Mothers Do Time." *Hope,* Sept.–Oct.:52–59.

Harrison, L. 2001. "The Revolving Prior Door for Drug-Involved Offenders: Challenges and Opportunities." *Crime and Delinquency* 47:462–484.

Harrison, P., M. Paige, and A. Beck. 2003. *Prisoners in 2002*. Washington, DC: U.S. Department of Justice.

Hart, B. 1996. "Preface." In K. Lobel (ed.), *Naming the Violence*. Seattle: Seal.

Hartjen, C. 1974. *Crime and Criminalization*. New York: Praeger.

Hartnagel, T., J. Teevan, and J. McIntrye. 1975. "Television Violence and Violent Behavior." *Social Forces* 54:341–351.

Harvey, W. 1986. "Homicide Among Young Black Adults: Life in the Subculture of Exasperation." In D. Hawkins (eds.), *Homicide Among Black Americans*. Lanham, MD: University Press of America.

Hathaway, S., and E. Monachesi. 1963. *Adolescent Personality and Behavior*. Minneapolis: Minnesota University.

Hay, D., et al. 1975. *Albion's Fatal Tree: Crime and Society in Eighteenth Century England*. London: Allen Lane.

Hayes, P. 1998. "Station House Society: Joking and Police Subculture." Paper presented at the conference of the Academy of Criminal Justice Sciences, Albuquerque, NM.

Hays, T. 1999. "Jury Puts Blame on Several Gun Companies." *Wisconsin State Journal,* Feb. 12:3A.

———. 2003. "NAACP's Gun Lawsuit Shot Down." *Wisconsin State Journal,* July 22:A3.

Hazelwood, R., and J. Harpold. 1986. "Rape: The Dangers of Providing Confrontational Advice." *FBI Law Enforcement Bulletin,* June:1–5.

Healy, W., and A. Bronner. 1936. *New Light on Delinquency and Its Treatment*. New Haven: Yale University.

Heaney, G. 1991. "The Reality of Guidelines Sentencing: No End to Disparity." *American Criminal Law Review* 28:161–232.

Heilprin, J. 2002. "Clean Air Regulations are Relaxed." *Wisconsin State Journal,* Nov. 23:A1, A7.

Heise, L. 1989. "Crimes of Gender." *World Watch,* Mar.–Apr.:12–21.

Helfand, J. 1987. "Silence Again." In F. Delacoste and P. Alexander (eds.), *Sex Work*. Pittsburgh: Cleis.

Helmer, J. 1975. *Drugs and Minority Oppression*. New York: Seabury.

Henry, S., and D. Milovanovic. 1994. "The Constitution of Constitutive Criminology: A Postmodern Approach to Criminological Theory." In D. Nelken (ed.), *The Futures of Criminology*. London: Sage.

———. 1996. *Constitutive Criminology: Beyond Postmodernism*. London: Sage.

Hepburn, J. 1978. "Race and the Decision to Arrest: An Analysis of Warrants Issued." *Journal of Research in Crime and Delinquency* 15:54–73.

Herbert, S. 1998. "Police Subculture Reconsidered." *Criminology* 36:343–369.

Herman, J. 1981. *Father-Daughter Incest*. Cambridge: Harvard University.

———. 1988. "Considering Sex Offenders: A Model of Addiction." *Signs* 13:695–674.

———. 1992. *Trauma and Recovery*. New York: Basic.

Herrnstein, R. 1995. "Criminogenic Traits." In J. Wilson and J. Petersilia (eds.), *Crime*. San Francisco: Institute for Contemporary Studies.

Herrnstein, R., and C. Murray. 1994. *The Bell Curve: Intelligence and Class Structure in American Life*. New York: Free Press.

Hersch, P. 1998. *A Tribe Apart: A Journey into the Heart of American Adolescence*. New York: Ballantine.

Hersh, S. 2004a. "Chain of Command." *New Yorker,* May 17:38–43.

———. 2004b. "The Gray Zone." *New Yorker,* May 24:38–44.

———. 2004c. "Torture at Abu Ghraib." *New Yorker,* May 10:42–47.

Heschel, A. 1962. *The Prophets*. Vol. 1. New York: Harper and Row.

Heumann, M. 1978. *Plea Bargaining: The Experience of Prosecutors, Judges, and Defense Attorneys*. Chicago: University of Chicago.

Hickey, E. 1991. *Serial Murderers and Their Victims*. Pacific Grove, CA: Brooks/Cole.

Hickman, M., and B. Reaves. 2003. *Local Police Departments 2000*. Washington, DC: Bureau of Justice Statistics.

Higgins, P., and S. Albrecht. 1977. "Hellfire and Delinquency Revisited." *Social Forces* 55:952–988.

Hill, A. 1997. "Moon's Paradox." In E. Cose (ed.), *The Darden Dilemma*. New York: HarperPerennial.

Hill, G., and E. Crawford. 1990. "Women, Race, and Crime." *Criminology* 28:601–626.

Hill, K. 1998. "Guarding Privacy Difficult in Information Age." *Wisconsin State Journal,* Dec. 27:Forum 11, 41.

Hindelang, M. 1981. "Variations in Sex-Race-Age-Specific Incidence Rates of Offending." *American Sociological Review* 46:461–474.

Hindelang, M., T. Hirschi, and J. Weis. 1978. "Correlates of Delinquency: The Illusion of Discrepancy Between Self-Report and Official Measures." *American Sociological Review* 44:995–1014.

———. 1981. *Measuring Delinquency.* Beverly Hills: Sage.

Hirschel, J., and I. Hutchison. 1992. "Female Spouse Abuse and the Police Response: The Charlotte, North Carolina, Experiment." *Journal of Criminal Law and Criminology* 83:73–119.

Hirschi, T. 1969. *The Causes of Delinquency*. Berkeley: University of California.

Hirschi, T., and M. Hindelang. 1977. "Intelligence and Delinquency: A Revisionist Critique." *American Sociological Review* 43:571–587.

Hirschi, T., and R. Stark. 1969. "Hellfire and Delinquency." *Social Problems* 17:202–213.

History of Women in Policing. 2003. www.womenandpolicing.org.

Hitchens, C. 2002. *The Trial of Henry Kissinger.* New York: Verso.

Hobsbawm, E. 1959. *Primitive Rebels: Studies in Archaic Forms of Social Movements in the Nineteenth and Twentieth Centuries*. New York: Norton.

Hochschild, A., and A. Machung. 2003. *The Second Shift*. New York: Penguin.

Hochstetler, A., and N. Shover. 1997. "Street Crime, Labor Surplus, and Criminal Punishment, 1980–1990." *Social Problems* 44:358–368.

Hoffman, B. 1993. "Terrorism in the United States: Recent Trends and Future Prospects." In B. Schechterman and M. Slann (eds.), *Violence and Terrorism*. Guilford, CT: Dushkin.

Hoffman, J., and F. Cerbone. 1999. "Stressful Life Events and Delinquency Escalation in Early Adolescence." *Criminology* 37:343–373.

Hoffman, M. 1997. "Fatal Denial? The Tragic Case of Amy Grossberg and Brian Peterson." *On the Issues* 6:3–5.

Hofstader, R. 1959. *Social Darwinism in American Social Thought.* Boston: Beacon.

Holdaway, S. 1997. "Some Recent Approaches to the Study of Race in Criminological Research." *British Journal of Criminology* 37:383–400.

Holland, J. 2000. "Health Groups Directly Link Media to Child Violence." *Wisconsin State Journal* July 7:1A, 3A.

Hollinger, R., and J. Clark. 1983. *Theft by Employees.* Lexington, MA: Lexington.

Holloway, W. 1981. "'I Just Wanted to Kill a Woman': The Ripper and Male Sexuality." *Feminist Review* 9:33–40.

Holmes, M., et al. 1993. "Judges' Ethnicity and Minority Sentencing: Evidence Concerning Hispanics." *Social Science Quarterly* 74:496–506.

Holmlund, C. 1994. "A Decade of Deadly Dolls: Hollywood and the Woman Killer." In H. Birch (ed.), *Moving Targets.* Berkeley: University of California.

Honey, M. 1995. "Pesticides: Nowhere to Hide." *Ms.,* July–Aug.:16–24.

Horney, J. 1978. "Menstrual Cycles and Criminal Responsibility." *Law and Human Behavior* 2:25–36.

Horney, J., D. Osgood, and I. Marshall. 1995. "Criminal Careers in the Short-Term: Intra-Individual Variability in Crime and Its Relation to Local Life Circumstances." *American Sociological Review* 60:655–673.

Horowitz, I. 1997. *Taking Lives: Genocide and State Power.* New Brunswick, NJ: Transaction.

Horowitz, R. 1983. *Honor and the American Dream.* New Brunswick, NJ: Rutgers University.

———. 1987. "Community Tolerance of Gang Violence." *Social Problems* 34:437–450.

Howell, J. 1996. "Juvenile Transfers to the Criminal Justice System: State of the Art." *Law and Policy* 18:17–60.

Hubbard, R. 1995. *Profitable Promises: Essays on Women, Science, and Health.* Monroe, MN: Common Courage.

Huesmann, R., and L. Eron (eds.). 1986. *Television and the Aggressive Child: A Cross-National Comparison.* Hillsdale, NJ: Lawrence Erlbaum.

Huff, C. 1993. "Gangs in the United States." In A. Goldstein and C. Huff (eds.), *The Gang Intervention Handbook.* Champaign, IL: Research Press.

Huff, C., A. Rattner, and E. Sagarin. 1996. *Convicted But Innocent: Wrongful Conviction and Public Policy.* Thousand Oaks, CA: Sage.

Huff-Corzine, L., J. Corzine, and D. Moore. 1986. "Southern Exposure: Deciphering the South's Influence on Homicide Rates." *Social Forces* 64:906–924.

Huizinga, D., and D. Elliott 1987. "Juvenile Offenders: Prevalence, Offender Incidence, and Arrest Rates by Race." *Crime and Delinquency* 33:206–233.

Humphries, D. 1998. "Crack Mothers at Six: Prime-Time News, Crack/Cocaine, and Women." *Violence Against Women* 4:45–61.

Hunt, G., S. Riegel, T. Morales, and D. Waldorf. 1993. "Changes in Prison Culture: Prison Gangs and the Case of the 'Pepsi Generation.'" *Social Problems* 40:398–409.

Hunt, J., and P. Manning. 1991. "The Social Context of Police Lying." *Symbolic Interaction* 14:51–70.

Hutcheson, R., S. McCaffrey, and J. Landay. 2003. "Justice Department Probing Leak of Name." *Wisconsin State Journal,* Oct. 1:A1, A7.

Hutchinson, E. 1996. *Beyond O.J.: Race, Sex, and Class Lessons for America.* Los Angeles: Middle Passage.

Ianni, F., and E. Reuss-Ianni (eds.). 1976. *The Crime Society: Organized Crime and Corruption in America.* New York: New American Library.

Inciardi, J. 1996/2002. *Criminal Justice.* Fort Worth: Harcourt.

Inciardi, J., R. Horowitz, and A. Pottieger. 1993. *Street Kids, Street Drugs, Street Crime: An Examination of Drug Use and Serious Delinquency in Miami.* Belmont, CA: Wadsworth.

Inciardi, J., et al. 1997. "An Effective Model of Prison-Based Treatment for Drug-Involved Offenders." *Journal of Drug Issues* 27:261–278.

Independent Commission on the Los Angeles Police Department (ICLAPD). 1991. *Report of the Independent Commission on the Los Angeles Police Department.* Los Angeles: ICLAPD.

Ingalls, R. 2002. "Ku Klux Klan." *World Book Encyclopedia.* Chicago: World Book.

Institute for the Study of Labor and Economic Crisis (ISLEC). 1982. *The Iron Fist and the Velvet Glove: An Analysis of the U.S. Police.* San Francisco: Synthesis.

International Criminal Tribunal for the Former Yugoslavia. 1999. "Fact Sheet." www.un.org.

Inverarity, J., P. Lauderdale, and B. Feld. 1983. *Law and Society: Sociological Perspectives on Criminal Law.* Boston: Little, Brown.

Ireland, D. 1998. "The Right Plays the Gay Card." *Nation,* Sept. 7:21–22, 24.

Irons, P. 1988. *The Courage of Their Convictions: Sixteen Americans Who Fought Their Way to the Supreme Court.* New York: Penguin.

Irwin, J. 1980. *Prisons in Turmoil.* Boston: Little, Brown.

Isikoff, M., and D. Klaidman. 2003. "Ashcroft's Campaign to Shore Up the Patriot Act." *Newsweek,* Aug. 26:6.

Island, D., and P. Letellier. 1991. *Men Who Beat the Men Who Love Them.* New York: Harrington Park.

Ivins, M., and L. Dubose. 2003. *Bushwhacked: Life in George W. Bush's America.* New York: Random House.

Jackson, B. 1988. *Honest Graft: Big Money and the American Political Process.* New York: Knopf.

———. 1990. "The Savings and Loan Crisis." CNN documentary.

Jackson, D. 2002. "Executive Robber Barons Have Left Scorched Earth in Their Wake." *Wisconsin State Journal,* Sept. 1:F3.

Jackson, P. 1985. "Ethnicity, Region, and Public Fiscal Commitment to Policing." *Justice Quarterly* 2:167–195.

Jackson, P., and L. Carroll. 1981. "Race and the War on Crime: The Sociopolitical Determinants of Municipal Police Expenditures in Ninety Non-Southern U.S. Cities." *American Sociological Review* 46:290–305.

Jackson, S. 1978. "The Social Context of Rape: Sexual Scripts and Motivation." *Women's Studies International Quarterly* 1:27–38.

Jacobs, D., and R. Helms. 1996. "Toward a Political Model of Incarceration: A Time-Series Examination of Multiple Explanations for Prison Admission Rates." *American Journal of Sociology* 102:323–357.

Jacobs, D., and R. O'Brien. 1998. "The Determinants of Deadly Force: A Structural Analysis of Police Violence." *American Journal of Sociology* 103:837–862.

Jacobs, D., and R. Wright. 1999. "Stick-Up, Street Culture, and Offender Motivation." *Criminology* 37:149–173.

Jacobs, J. 1977. *Stateville: The Penitentiary in Mass Society.* Chicago: University of Chicago.

Jacobs, J. 1990. "Reassessing Mother Blame in Incest." *Signs* 15:500–514.

Jacobs, J., and K. Potter. 1998. *Hate Crimes: Criminal Law and Identity Politics.* New York: Oxford University.

Jacobs, J., and H. Retsky. 1981. "Prison Guard." In R. Ross (ed.), *Prison Guard/Correctional Officers.* Canada: Butterworth.

Jacobs, P., M. Brunton, and M. Melville. 1965. "Aggressive Behavior, Mental Abnormality and the XYY Male." *Nature* 208:1351–1352.

James, J., and J. Meyerding. 1977. "Early Sexual Experiences as a Factor in Prostitution." *Archives of Sexual Behavior* 77:31–42.

James, K., and L. MacKinnon. 1990. "The 'Incestous Family' Revisited: A Critical Analysis of Family Therapy Myths." *Journal of Marital and Family Therapy* 16:71–88.

Jamieson, K. 1994. *The Organization of Corporate Crime: Dynamics of Antitrust Violation.* Thousand Oaks, CA: Sage.

Jang, S., and B. Johnson. 2001. "Neighborhood Disorder, Individual Religiosity, and Adolescent Use of Illicit Drugs: A Test of Multilevel Hypotheses." *Criminology* 39:109–141.

Jang, S., and T. Thornberry. 1998. "Self-Esteem, Delinquent Peers, and Delinquency: A Test of the Self-Enhancement Thesis." *American Sociological Review* 63:586–598.

Janofsky, M. 2003. "Man Who Shot Reagan Allowed to Visit Parents Unsupervised." *New York Times,* Dec. 18, www.nytimes.com.

Janus, M., A. McCormack, A. Burgess, and C. Hartman. 1987. *Adolescent Runaways: Causes and Consequences.* Lexington, MA: Lexington.

Jarvik, L. S., V. Klodin, and S. Matsuyama. 1984. "Human Aggression and the Extra Y Chromosome: Fact or Fantasy?" In I. Jacks and S. Cox (eds.), *Psychological Approaches to Crime and Its Correction.* Chicago: Nelson-Hall.

Jaspin, E., and S. Montgomery. 1998. "Review Uncovers Thousands of Unsafe Meat Shipments." *Wisconsin State Journal,* Jan. 18:7A.

Jeffery, C. 1978. "Criminology as Interdisciplinary Science." *Criminology* 16:149–170.

Jenkins, P. 1994. *Using Murder: The Social Construction of Serial Homicide.* New York: Aldine de Gruyer.

Jenness, V. 1999. "Managing Differences and Making Legislation: Social Movements and the Racialization, Sexualization, and Gendering of Federal Hate Crime Law in the U.S., 1985–1998." *Social Problems* 46:548–571.

Jennings, K. 1994. "Female Child Molesters: A Review of the Literature." In M. Elliott (ed.), *Female Sexual Abuse of Children.* New York: Guilford.

Jensen, G., and M. Erickson. 1979. "The Religious Factor and Delinquency: Another Look at the Hellfire Hypothesis." In R. Wuthnow (ed.), *The Religious Dimension.* New York: Academic.

Jensen, G., and M. Karpos. 1993. "Managing Rape: Exploratory Research on the Behavior of Rape Statistics." *Criminology* 31:363–385.

Jensen, M. 2002. "Shay's Rebellion." *World Book Encyclopedia.* Chicago: World Book.

Jensen, R. 1995. "Pornographic Lives." *Violence Against Women* 1:32–54.

Joe, K., and M. Chesney-Lind. 1995. "Just Every Mother's Angel: An Analysis of Gender and Ethnic Variations in Youth Gang Membership." *Gender and Society* 9:408–430.

Johnson, B., A. Golum, and J. Fagan. 1995. "Careers in Crack, Drug Use, Drug Distribution, and Nondrug Criminality." *Crime and Delinquency* 41:275–295.

Johnson, B., S. Jang, D. Larson, and S. Li. 2001. "Does Adolescent Religious Commitment Matter? A Reexamination of the Effects of Religiosity on Delinquency." *Journal of Research in Crime and Delinquency* 38:22–44.

Johnson, B., D. Larson, Spencer Li, and S. Jang. 2000. "Escaping from the Crime of Inner Cities: Church Attendance and Religious Salience Among Disadvantaged Youth." *Justice Quarterly* 17:377–391.

Johnson, L. 1989. "The Employed Black: The Dynamics of Work-Family Tension." *Review of Black Political Economy* 17:69–85.

Johnson, R. 2002. *Hard Time: Understanding and Reforming the Prison.* Belmont, CA: Wadsworth.

Johnston, L., P. O'Malley, and J. Bachman. 1986. *Drug Use Among High School Students, College Students, and Other Young Adults: National Trends Through 1985.* Rockville, MD: National Institute on Drug Abuse.

———. 1997. *National Survey Results on Drug Use from the Monitoring the Future Study, 1976–1996.* Washington, DC: U.S. Government Printing Office.

Jones, A. 1980. *Women Who Kill.* New York: Fawcett.

———. 1994. *Next Time She'll Be Dead.* Boston: Beacon.

Jones, J. 1986. *Labor of Love, Labor of Sorrow: Black Women, Work, and the Family from Slavery to the Present.* New York: Vintage.

Jost, K. 1995. "The Jury System: The Issues." *CQ Researcher* 5:995–998 ff.

Judis, J. 2002. "Strategic Disinformation." *American Prospect,* Sept.:12–13.

Jurik, N. 1985. "An Officer and a Lady: Organizational Barriers to Women Working as Correctional Officers in Men's Prisons." *Social Problems* 32:375–388.

Jurik, N., and R. Winn. 1990. "Gender and Homicide: A Comparison of Men and Women Who Kill." *Violence and Victims* 5:227–242.

Justice, B., and R. Justice. 1979. *The Broken Taboo: Sex in the Family.* New York: Human Science.

Kalven, H., and H. Zeisel. 1971. *The American Jury.* Boston: Little, Brown.

Kaminer, W. 1999. "Taking Liberties: The New Assault on Freedom." *American Prospect,* Jan.–Feb.:33–40.

Kandel, E., and S. Mednick. 1991. "Perinatal Complications Predict Violent Offending." *Criminology* 29:519–529.

Kane, R. 2003. "Social Control in the Metropolis: A Community-Level Examination of the Minority Group-Threat Hypothesis." *Justice Quarterly* 20:265–295.

Kaplan, H., S. Martin, and R. Johnson. 1986. "Self-Rejection and the Explanation of Deviance: Specification of the Structure Among Latent Constructs." *American Journal of Sociology* 92:384–411.

Kaplan, J. 1983. *The Hardest Drug: Heroin and Public Policy.* Chicago: University of Chicago.

Kappeler, V., M. Blumberg, and G. Potter. 2000. *The Mythology of Crime and Criminal Justice.* Propects Heights, IL: Waveland.

Karmen, A. 2004. *Crime Victims: An Introduction to Victimology.* Belmont, CA: Wadsworth.

Karp. 2. 2000. "State Drug Law Hits City, Teens, Minorities." *Chicago Reporter.* www.chicagoreporter.com.

Karush, S. 2003. "Awe-Struck Girl Now Police Chief." *Wisconsin State Journal,* Nov. 8:A3.

Kasinitz, P., and J. Rosenberg. 1996. "Missing the Connection: Social Isolation and Employment on the Brooklyn Waterfront." *Social Problems* 43:180–196.

Kassindja, F., and L. Bashir. 1998. *Do They Hear You When You Cry?* New York: Delacourte.

Katz, J. 1980. "The Social Movement Against White-Collar Crime." In E. Bittner and S. Messinger (eds.), *Criminology Review Yearbook.* Beverly Hills, CA: Sage.

———. 1988. *Seductions of Crime: Moral and Sensual Attractions in Doing Evil.* New York: Basic.

Katz, J., and W. Chambliss. 1995. "Biology and Crime." In J. Sheley (ed.), *Criminology.* Belmont, CA: Wadsworth.

Katz, S. 1988. "Quantity and Interpretation: Issues in the Comparative Historical Analysis of the Holocaust." *Holocaust and Genocide Studies* 4:127–148.

———. 1996. "The Uniqueness of the Holocaust: The Historical Dimension." In A. Rosenbaum (ed.), *Is the Holocaust Unique?* Boulder, CO: Westview.

Kauffman, K. 1988. *Prison Officers and Their World.* Cambridge: Harvard University.

Keeney, B., and K. Heider. 1994. "Gender Differences in Serial Murderers." *Journal of Interpersonal Violence* 9:383–398.

Kelly, D., and R. Balch. 1971. "Social Origins and School Failure." *Pacific Sociological Review* 14:413–430.

Kelly, L. 1987. "The Continuum of Sexual Violence." In J. Hanmer and M. Maynard (eds.), *Women, Violence, and Social Control.* Atlantic Highlands, NJ: Humanities International.

———. 1993. "Pornography and Child Abuse." In C. Itzin (eds.), *Pornography.* New York: Oxford University.

Kennedy, J. 2003. "Drugs Wars in Black and White." *Law and Contemporary Problems* 66:153–181.

Kennedy, R. 2003. "Crimes Against Nature." *Rolling Stone,* Dec. 13:180–194.

Kerner Commission. 1968. *Report of the National Advisory Commission on Civil Disorders.* New York: Bantam.

Kerr, J. 2003. "Envoy: Bush Manipulated Findings." *Wisconsin State Journal,* July 7:A9.

Kessler, S. 1998. *Lessons from the Intersexed.* New Brunswick, NJ: Rutgers University.

Killias, M., M. Aebi, and D. Ribeaud. 2000. "Learning Through Controlled Experiments: Community Service and Heroin Prescription in Switzerland." *Crime and Delinquency* 46:233–251.

Kilpatrick, D., and M. Himelein. 1986. "Male Crime Victims, the Most Victimized, Often Neglected." *National Organization for Victim Assistance Newsletter* 10:5–7.

Kim, R. 1999. "The Truth About Hate Crimes Law." *Nation,* July 12:16.

———. 2003. "Queer Cheer." *Nation,* July 21–28:5–6.

Kimmel, M. (ed.). 1990. *Men Confront Pornography.* New York: Crown.

———. 2000. "Masculinity as Homophobia." In E. Disch (ed.), *Reconstructing Gender.* Mountain View, CA: Mayfield.

Kimmelman, J. 2000. "Just a Needle-Stick Away." *Nation,* Nov. 27:17, 19–20, 22.

King, H., and W. Chambliss. 1984. *Harry King: A Professional Thief's Journey.* New York: Wiley.

King, M. 1994. "Letter from Birmingham Jail." In J. Bonsignore et al. (eds.), *Before the Law.* Boston: Houghton Mifflin.

King, N. 1993. "Postconviction Review of Jury Discrimination: Measuring the Effects of Juror Race on Jury Decisions." *Michigan Law Review* 92:63–130.

Kinser, S. 2003. *All the Shah's Men: An American Coup and the Roots of Middle Eastern Terror.* New York: Wiley.

Kiragu, K. 1995. "Female Genital Mutilation: A Reproductive Health Concern." *Population Reports Supplement* 41:25–30.

Kirschenbaum, G. 1991. "A Potential Landmark for Female Human Rights." *Ms.,* Sept.–Oct.:13.

Kissell, P., and P. Katsampes. 1980. "The Impact of Women Corrections Officers on the Functioning of Institutions Housing Male Inmates." *Journal of Offender Counseling Services and Rehabilitation* 4:213–231.

Kitsuse, J., and A. Cicourel. 1963. "A Note on the Uses of Official Statistics." *Social Problems* 11:131–139.

Kitwana, B. 2002. *The Hip Hop Generation: Young Blacks and the Crisis in African-American Culture.* New York: BasicCivitas.

Kleck, G. 1991. *Point Blank: Guns and Violence in America.* New York: Aldine de Gruyter.

Kleck, G., and T. Chiricos. 2002. "Unemployment and Property Crime: A Target-Specific Assessment of Opportunity and Motivation as Mediating Factors." *Criminology* 40:649–679.

Kleck, G., and M. Gertz. 1995. "Armed Resistance to Crime: The Prevalence and Nature of Self-Defense with a Gun." *Journal of Criminal Law and Criminology* 85:150–187.

Kleck, G., and S. Sayles. 1990. "Rape and Resistance." *Social Problems* 37:149–162.

Kleiman, M. 1998. "America's War on Marijuana." *Frontline.* www.pbs.org.

Klein, D. 1973. "The Etiology of Female Crime: A Review of the Literature." *Issues in Criminology* 8:3–30.

Klein, H., and B. Chao. 1995. "Sexual Abuse During Childhood and Adolescence as Predictors of HIV-Related Sexual Risk During Adulthood Among Female Sexual Partners of Injection Drug Users." *Violence Against Women* 1:55–76.

Klein, M. 1971. *Street Gangs and Street Workers.* Englewood Cliffs, NJ: Prentice-Hall.

Klein, M., C. Maxson, and L. Cunningham. 1991. "'Crack,' Street Gangs, and Violence." *Criminology* 29:623–650.

Kleinknecht, W. 1996. *The New Ethnic Mobs.* New York: Free Press.

Klofas, J., and R. Weisheit. 1987. "Guilty but Mentally Ill: Reform of the Insanity Defense in Illinois." *Justice Quarterly* 4:39–50.

Knapp Commission. 1972. *Knapp Commission Report on Police Corruption.* New York: Braziller.

Knudsen, D. 1992. *Child Maltreatment.* Dix Hills, NY: General Hall.

Kocieniewski, D., and R. Hanley. 2000. "Racial Profiling Routine, New Jersey Finds." *New York Times,* Nov. 27, www.nytimes.com.

Komisar, L. 2001. "After Dirty Air, Dirty Money." *Nation,* June 18:16–19.

Konopka, G. 1966. *The Adolescent Girl in Conflict.* Englewood Cliffs, NJ: Prentice-Hall.

Koren, G., H. Shear, K. Graham, and T. Einarson. 1989. "Bias Against the Null Hypothesis: The Reproductive Hazards of Cocaine." *Lancet* 8677:1440–1443.

Kornbluh, P. 2003. *The Pinochet File: A Declassified Dossier on Atrocity and Accountability.* New York: New Press.

Koss, M. 1988. "Hidden Rape: Sexual Aggression and Victimization in a National Sample of Students in Higher Education." In A. Burgess (ed.), *Rape and Sexual Assault II.* New York: Garland.

Koss, M., C. Gidycz, and N. Wisniewski. 1987. "The Scope of Rape: Incidence and

Prevalence of Sexual Aggression in a National Sample of Higher Education Students." *Journal of Consulting and Clinical Psychology* 55:162–170.

Kovandiz, T., and T. Marvell. 2003. "Right-to-Carry Concealed Handguns and Violent Crime: Crime Control Through Gun Decontrol." *Criminology and Public Policy* 2:363–396.

Kposowa, A., and K. Breault. 1993. "Reassessing the Structural Covariates of U.S. Homicide Rates: A County Level Study." *Sociology Focus* 26:27–46.

Krafka, C. 1985. *Sexually Explicit, Sexually Violent, and Violent Media: Effects of Multiple Naturalistic Exposures and Debriefing on Female Viewers.* Ph.D. diss., University of Wisconsin–Madison.

Kramer, J., and D. Steffensmeier. 1993. "Race and Imprisonment Decisions." *Sociological Quarterly* 34:357–376.

Kramer, R., and R. Michalowski. 1995. "The Iron Fist and the Velvet Tongue: Crime Control Policies in the Clinton Administration." *Social Justice* 22:87–100.

Krane, J. 2003. "Experts Worried about Power Grid Hackers." *Wisconsin State Journal,* Sept. 12:D10.

Kraska, P. 1990. "The Unmentionable Alternative: The Need for, and the Argument against, the Decriminalization of Drugs." In R. Weisheit (ed.), *Drugs, Crime, and the Criminal Justice System.* Cincinnati: Anderson.

Kraska, P., and L. Cubellis. 1997. "Militarizing Mayberry and Beyond: Making Sense of American Paramilitary Policing." *Justice Quarterly* 14:607–629.

Kraska, P., and V. Kappeler. 1995. "To Serve and Pursue: Exploring Police Sexual Violence Against Women." *Justice Quarterly* 12:85–111.

———. 1997. "Militarizing American Police: The Rise and Normalization of Paramilitary Units." *Social Problems* 44:1–18.

Krisberg, B. (ed.). 1978. *The Children of Ishmael: Critical Perspectives on Juvenile Justice.* Palo Alto, CA: Mayfield.

Kritzer, H., and T. Uhlman. 1977. "Sisterhood in the Courtroom: Sex of Judge and Defendant in Criminal Case Disposition." *Social Science Journal* 14:77–88.

Krivo, L., and R. Peterson. 1996. "Extremely Disadvantaged Neighborhoods and Urban Crime." *Social Forces* 75:619–650.

Krohn, M. 2000. "Sources of Criminality: Control and Deterrence Theories." In J. Sheley (ed.), *Criminology.* Belmont, CA: Wadsworth.

Krohn, M., and J. Massey. 1980. "Social Control and Delinquent Behavior: An Examination of the Elements of the Social Bond." *Sociological Quarterly* 21:529–543.

Kroll, M. 1991. *Chattahoochee Judicial District: Buckle of the Death Belt.* Washington, DC: DPIC.

Krugman, P. 2004. "The Death of Horatio Alger." *Nation,* Jan. 5:16–17.

Kruttschnitt, C. 1982. "Respectable Women and the Law." *Sociological Quarterly* 23:221–234.

Kruttschnitt, C., R. Gartner, and A. Miller. 2000. "Doing Her Own Time? Women's Responses to Prison in the Context of the Old and the New Penology." *Criminology* 3:681–717.

Kruttschnitt, C., J. McLeod, and M. Dornfeld. 1986. "Family Violence, Television Viewing Habits, and Other Adolescent Experiences Related to Violent Criminal Behavior." *Criminology* 24:235–266.

Kubrin, C., and R. Weitzer. 2003. "Retaliatory Homicide: Concentrated Disadvantage and Neighborhood Culture." *Social Problems* 50:157–180.

Kuper, L. 1990. "The United States Ratifies the Genocide Convention." In F. Chalk and K. Jonassohn (eds.), *The History and Sociology of Genocide.* New Haven: Yale University.

Kushner, T. 1998. "Matthew's Passion." *Nation,* Nov. 9:4–6.

Kuttner, R. 2003a. "The Great Crash, Part II." *American Prospect,* June:47–49.

———— (ed.). 2003b. "Prison Break: Special Report on Criminal Justice Reform." *American Prospect,* Dec.:33–56.

LaFree, G. 1980. "The Effect of Sexual Stratification by Race on Official Reactions to Rape." *American Sociological Review* 45:842–854.

————. 1989. *Rape and Criminal Justice: The Social Construction of Sexual Assault.* Belmont, CA: Wadsworth.

————. 1998. *Losing Legitimacy: Street Crime and Decline Social Institutions in America.* Boulder, CO: Westview.

LaFree, G., and K. Drass. 1996. "The Effect of Changes in Intraracial Income Inequality and Educational Attainment on Changes in Arrest Rates for African Americans and Whites, 1957 to 1990." *American Sociological Review* 61:614–634.

Lane, C. 1994. "The Tainted Sources of 'The Bell Curve.'" *New York Review of Books,* Dec. 1:14–19.

Langan, P., and M. Cuniff. 1992. *Recidivism of Felons on Probation, 1986–1989.* Washington, DC: U.S. Department of Justice.

Langer, E. 1990. "The American Neo-Nazi Movement Today." *Nation,* July 16:82–107.

Lantigua, J. 2001. "How the GOP Gamed the System in Florida." *Nation,* Apr. 30:11–17.

Laporte, S. 1998. "Download Your Local Sheriff." In M. Fisch (ed.), *Criminology 98/99.* New York: McGraw-Hill.

Largen, P., and J. Brown. 1997. *Felony Sentences in State Courts, 1994.* Washington, DC: U.S. Department of Justice.

Larsen, P. 1991. "Racism 'Widespread' in LAPD: Panel Cites Comments on Patrol-Car Computers." *San Bernardino Sun,* July 10:A1.

Larson, R. 1980. *Bundy: The Deliberate Stranger.* Englewood Cliffs, NJ: Prentice-Hall.

Laub, J., and M. McDermott. 1985. "An Analysis of Serious Crime by Young Black Women." *Criminology* 23:81–98.

Laub, J., and R. Sampson. 1993. "Turning Points in the Life Course: Why Change Matters to the Study of Crime." *Criminology* 31:301–325.

Lauderback, D., J. Hansen, and D. Waldorf. 1992. "Sisters Are Doin' It for Themselves: A Black Female Gang in San Francisco." *Gang Journal* 1:57–72.

Lavoie, D. 2003. "$85 Million Payout Goes to Sex Abuse Victims." *Wisconsin State Journal,* Sept. 10:A3.

Lawrence, R. 1998. *School Crime and Juvenile Justice.* New York: Oxford University.

Lawson, C. 1993. "Mother-Son Sexual Abuse: Rare or Underreported?" *Child Abuse and Neglect* 17:261–269.

Lea, J., and J. Young. 1984. *What Is to Be Done About Law and Order?* New York: Penguin.

Lederer, E. 2003. "War Crimes Tribunal Hires a Chief Prosecutor." *Wisconsin State Journal,* Apr. 22:A3.

Lederer, L. (ed.). 1980. *Take Back the Night: Women on Pornography.* New York: Morrow.

Lederer, L., and R. Delgado (eds.). 1995. *The Price We Pay: The Case Against*

Racist Speech, Hate Propaganda, and Pornography. New York: Hill and Wang.

Lee, M., and M. Ermann. 1999. "Pinto 'Madness' as a Flawed Landmark Narrative: An Organizational and Network Analysis." *Social Problems* 46:30–47.

Leinen, S. 1984. *Black Police, White Society.* New York: New York University.

Leland, J. 1998. "Savior of the Streets." *Newsweek,* June 1:20–25.

Lemert, C. 1997. *Postmodernism Is Not What You Think.* Malden, MA: Blackwell.

Lemert, E. 1951. *Social Pathology.* New York: McGraw-Hill.

Lens, S. 1973. *The Labor Wars: From the Molly Maquires to the Sitdowns.* New York: Doubleday.

Leonard, E. 1982. *Women, Crime, and Society: A Critique of Criminology Theory.* New York: Longman.

Leonard, W., and M. Weber. 1970. "Automakers and Dealers: A Study of Criminogenic Market Forces." *Law and Society Review* 4:407–424.

Leonhardt, D. 2000. "As Prison Labor Grows, So Does the Debate." *New York Times,* Mar. 19:A1.

Lerner, G. 1997. *Why History Matters.* New York: Oxford University.

———. 1998. *The Grimke Sisters from South Carolina: Pioneers for Women's Rights.* New York: Oxford University.

Lerner, M. 1996. *The Politics of Meaning.* Reading, MA: Addison-Wesley.

Lesieur, H., and J. Sheley. 1987. "Illegal Appended Enterprises: Selling the Lines." *Social Problems* 34:249–260.

Lester, D. 1992. "Roe v. Wade Was Followed by a Decrease in Neonatal Homicide." *Journal of American Medical Association* 207:3027.

Letellier, P. 1996. "Twin Epidemics: Domestic Violence and HIV Infection Among Gay and Bisexual Men." In C. Renzetti and C. Miley (eds.), *Violence in Gay and Lesbian Domestic Relationships.* New York: Harrington Park.

Levin, B. 2002. "Cyberhate: A Legal and Historical Analysis of Extremists' Use of Computer Networks in America." *American Behavioral Scientist* 45:958–988.

Levin, J., and J. McDevitt. 1993. *Hate Crimes: The Rising Tide of Bigotry and Bloodshed.* New York: Plenum.

———. 1999. "Hate Crimes." *Encyclopedia of Violence, Peace, and Conflict.* San Diego: Academic.

Levitt, S. 1999. "The Limited Role of Changing Age Structure in Explaining Aggregate Crime Rates." *Criminology* 37:581–597.

Levrant, S., F. Cullen, B. Fulton, and C. Thomas. 1999. "Reconsidering Restorative Justice: The Corruption of Benevolence Revisited?" *Crime and Delinquency* 45:3–27.

Lew, M. 1990. *Victims No Longer.* New York: Harper and Row.

Liazos, A. 1978. "Schools, Alienation, and Delinquency." *Crime and Delinquency* 24:355–3261.

Lichtblau, E. 2003. "Some Fear FBI Is Back to Hooverism." *Wisconsin State Journal,* Nov. 23:A3.

Lilly, J., R. Ball, G. Curry, and J. McMullen. 1993. "Electronic Monitoring of the Drunk Driver: A Seven-Year Study of the Home Confinement Alternative." *Crime and Delinquency* 42:491–516.

Lingren, R., and N. Taub. 1993. *The Law of Sex Discrimination.* Minneapolis: West.

Lipton, D. 1996. "Prison-Based Therapeutic Communities: Their Success with Drug-Abusing Offenders." *National Institute of Justice Journal,* Feb.:12–30.

Lipton, D., R. Martinson, and J. Wilks. 1975. *The Effectiveness of Correctional Treatment: A Survey of Treatment Evaluation Studies.* New York: Praeger.

Lock, E., J. Timberlake, and T. Arcury. 2002. "Battle Fatigue: Is Public Support Waning for 'War'-Centered Drug Control Strategies?" *Crime and Delinquency* 48:380–398.

Lockwood, D. 1977. "Living in Protection." In H. Toch (ed.), *Living in Prison*. New York: Free Press.

Logan, J., and B. Stults. 1999. "Racial Differences in Exposure to Crime: The City and Suburbs of Cleveland in 1990." *Criminology* 37:251–276.

Lombardo, L. 1988. "Alleviating Inmate Stress: Contributions from Correctional Officers." In R. Johnson and H. Toch (eds.), *The Pains of Imprisonment*. Prospect Heights, IL: Waveland.

Lombroso, C., and W. Ferrero. 1895. *The Female Offender*. London: T. Fisher Unwin.

Lorber, J. 1997a. "Female Genital Mutilation: A Women's Rights/Cultural Conflict." *SWS Network News* 14:5–6.

———. 1997b. "'Night to His Day': The Social Construction of Gender." In L. Richardson et al. (eds.), *Feminist Frontiers*. New York: McGraw-Hill.

Lord, E. 1995. "A Prison Superintendent's Perspective on Women in Prison." *Prison Journal* 75:257–269.

Lott, J. 1998. *More Guns, Less Crime: Understanding Crime and Gun Control Laws*. Chicago: University of Chicago.

———. 2003. "Let the Sunshine In." www.nationalreview.com.

Lott, J., and D. Mustard. 1997. "Crime, Deterrence, and Right-to-Carry Concealed Handguns." *Journal of Legal Studies* 26:1–68.

Lowney, K., and J. Best. 1995. "Stalking Strangers and Lovers: Changing Media Typifications of a New Crime Problem." In J. Best (ed.), *Typifying Contemporary Problems*. New York: Adline de Gruyter.

Luckenbill, D. 1986. "Deviant Career Mobility: The Case of Male Prostitutes." *Social Problems* 33:283–296.

Lumpkin, J. 2003. "Official Weapons Assertions Doubtful." *Wisconsin State Journal*, Oct. 5:A3.

Lundman, R. 1980. *Police and Policing*. New York: Holt, Rinehart, and Winston.

———. 2001. *Prevention and Control of Juvenile Delinquency*. New York: Oxford University.

Lutiger, B., K. Graham, T. Einarson, and G. Koren. 1991. "Relationship Between Gestational Cocaine Use and Pregnancy Outcome: A Meta-Analysis." *Teratology* 44:405–414.

Lynch, M. 1996. "Class, Race, Gender, and Criminology: Structured Choices and the Life Course." In M. Schwartz and D. Milovanovic (eds.), *Race, Gender, and Class in Criminology*. New York: Garland.

Lynch, M., and A. Schuck. 2003. "Picasso as Criminologist: The Abstract Art of Racial Profiling." In M. Free (ed.), *Racial Issues in Criminal Justice*. Westport, CT: Praeger.

Maas, P. 1973. *Serpico*. New York: Viking.

MacCoun, R., and P. Reuter. 1997. "Interpreting Dutch Cannabis Policy: Reasoning by Analogy in the Legalization Debate." *Science* 278:47–52.

MacDonald, A. 1980. *The Turner Diaries*. Arlington, VA: National Alliance.

MacDonald, J. 2002. "The Effectiveness of Community Policing in Reducing Urban Violence." *Crime and Delinquency* 48:592–618.

MacDonald, J., and M. Chesney-Lind. 2001. "Gender Bias and Juvenile Justice Revisited: A Multiyear Analysis." *Crime and Delinquency* 47:173–195.

MacKenzie, D., R. Brame, D. McDowall, and C. Souryal. 1995. "Boot Camp Prisons and Recidivism in Eight States." *Criminology* 33:327–357.

MacKenzie, D., and H. Donaldson. 1996. "Boot Camp for Women Offenders." *Criminal Justice Review* 21:21–43.

MacKenzie, D., and C. Souryal. 1995. "Inmates Attitude Change During Incarceration: A Comparison of Boot Camp with Traditional Prison." *Justice Quarterly* 112:325–353.

MacKinnon, C. 1983. "Feminism, Marxism, Method, and the State: Toward Feminist Jurisprudence." *Signs* 8:635–658.

———. 1986. "Pornography as Sex Discrimination." *Law and Inequality* 4:38–49.

Madigan, N. 2003. "Burning of Hummers a Message?" *Wisconsin State Journal*, Aug. 31:A3.

Madriz, E. 1997. "Images of Criminals and Victims: A Study of Women's Fear and Social Control." *Gender and Society* 11:342–356.

Maguigan, H. 1991. "Battered Women and Self-Defense: Myths and Misconceptions in Current Reform Proposals." *Pennsylvania Law Review* 140:379–486.

Maguin, E., and R. Loeber. 1996. "Academic Performance and Delinquency." In M. Tonry (ed.), *Crime and Justice*. Chicago: University of Chicago.

Maguire, B., and P. Radosh. 1999. *Introduction to Criminology*. Belmont, CA: West/Wadsworth.

Maguire, K., and A. Pastore. 1997, 1999, 2001. *Sourcebook of Criminal Justice Statistics*. Washington, DC: U.S. Department of Justice.

Maher, L., and R. Curtis. 1992. "Women on the Edge of Crime: Crack Cocaine and the Changing Contexts of Street-Level Sex Work in New York City." *Crime, Law, and Social Change* 18:221–258.

Maher, L., and K. Daly. 1996. "Women in the Street-Level Drug Economy: Continuity or Change?" *Criminology* 34:465–491.

Mahoney, A., and C. Fenster. 1982. "Female Delinquents in a Suburban Court." In N. Rafter and E. Stanko (eds.), *Judge, Lawyer, Victim, Thief*. Boston: Northeastern University.

Malamuth, N. 1985. "The Mass Media and Aggression Against Women: Research Findings and Prevention." In A. Burgess (eds.), *Rape and Sexual Assault*. New York: Garland.

Malamuth, N., and E. Donnerstein (eds.). 1984. *Pornography and Sexual Aggression*. New York: Academic.

Mangan, K. 2002. "The Ethics of Business Schools." *Chronicle of Higher Education*, Sept. 20:A14–A16.

Mann, C. 1993. *Unequal Justice: A Question of Color*. Bloomington: Indiana University.

———. 1996. *When Women Kill*. Albany: State University of New York.

Manning, P. 1999. "Semiotics and Justice: 'Justice,' Justice, and JUSTICE." In B. Arrigo (ed.), *Social Justice/Criminal Justice*. Belmont, CA: Wadsworth.

Margasak, L. 2003. "Halliburton Gets More Work in Iraq." *Wisconsin State Journal*, May 8:E1–E2.

Margolin, S., and J. Schor. 1990. *The End of the Golden Age*. Oxford: Clarendon.

Marris, P., and M. Rein. 1973. *Dilemmas of Social Reform*. Chicago: Aldine.

Marshall, J., and L. Wheeler. 1996. *Street Soldier*. New York: Delta.

Martin, G. 2003. *Understanding Terrorism: Challenges, Perspectives, and Issues*. Thousand Oaks, CA: Sage.

Martin, P., and R. Hummer. 1989. "Fraternities and Rape on Campus." *Gender and Society* 3:457–473.

Martin, S. 1980. *"Breaking and Entering": Policewomen on Patrol.* Berkeley: University of California.

———. 1994. "'Outsider Within' the Station House: The Impact of Race and Gender on Black Women Police." *Social Problems* 41:383–400.

———. 1995. "'A Cross-Burning Is Not Just an Arson': Police Social Construction of Hate Crimes in Baltimore." *Criminology* 33:303–326.

Martin, S., and N. Jurik. 1996. *Doing Justice, Doing Gender: Women in Law and Criminal Justice Occupations.* Thousand Oaks, CA: Sage.

Martinez, R. 1996. "Latinos and Lethal Violence: The Impact of Poverty and Inequality." *Social Problems* 43:131–146.

Martz, L. 1990. "A Dirty Drug Secret." *Newsweek,* Feb. 19:74, 77.

Marx, G. 1981. "Ironies of Social Control: Authorities as Contributors to Deviance Through Escalation, Non-Enforcement, and Covert Facilitation." *Social Problems* 28:221–246.

Massey, D. 1990. "American Apartheid: Segregation and the Making of the Underclass." *American Journal of Sociology* 96:329–357.

Masson, J. 1984. "Freud and the Seduction Theory." *Atlantic Monthly,* Feb.:33–60.

Matthews, N. 1989. "Surmounting a Legacy: The Expansion of Racial Diversity in a Local Anti-Rape Movement." *Gender and Society* 3:518–532.

Matthews, R., and J. Young (eds.). 1992. *Issues in Realist Criminology.* Beverly Hills: Sage.

Matza, D. 1964. *Delinquency and Drift.* New York: Wiley.

Matza, D., and G. Sykes. 1961. "Juvenile Delinquency and Subterranean Values." *American Sociological Review* 26:712–719.

Mauer, M. 1994. *Americans Behind Bars: The International Use of Incarceration, 1992–1993.* Washington, DC: Sentencing Project.

———. 1999. *Race to Incarcerate.* New York: New Press.

Mauer, M., and T. Huling. 1995. *Young Black Americans and the Criminal Justice System.* Washington, DC: Sentencing Project.

Maull, S. 2002. "Prosecutor Wants Convictions Tossed in Central Park Case." *Wisconsin State Journal,* Dec. 6:A1, A11.

Mayer, J. 2004. "Contract Sport." *New Yorker,* Feb. 16 and 23:80–91.

McBride, J. 1999. "Straw Buyers Funnel Guns from Dealers to Criminals." *Milwaukee Journal Sentinel,* May 16:A1, A14.

McCaffrey, S. 2003. "Detainees Faced Abuse." *Wisconsin State Journal,* June 3:A3.

McCaghy, C., Capron, and J. Jamison. 2003. *Deviant Behavior: Crime, Conflict, and Interest Groups.* Boston: Allyn and Bacon.

McCall, N. 1994. *Makes Me Wanna Holler: A Young Black Man in America.* New York: Vintage.

———. 1997. *What's Going On: Personal Essays.* New York: Random House.

McCarthy, B., J. Hagan, and M. Martin. 2002. "In and Out of Harm's Way: Violent Victimization and the Social Capital of Street Families." *Criminology* 40:831–865.

McClam, E. 2003a. "Defense: Everyone's Doing It." *Wisconsin State Journal,* Apr. 23:C10.

———. 2003b. "Judge Sets Date for Martha Stewart." *Wisconsin State Journal,* June 20:D10.

McCleary, R., B. Nienstedt, and J. Erven. 1982. "Uniform Crime Reports as

Organizational Outcomes: Three Time Series Experiments." *Social Problems* 29:361–372.

McClellan, D. 1994. "Disparity in the Discipline of Male and Female Inmates in Texas Prisons." *Women and Criminal Justice* 5:71–97.

McConahay S., and J. McConahay. 1977. "Sexual Permissiveness, Sex-Role Rigidity, and Violence Across Cultures." *Journal of Social Issues* 33:134–143.

McCorkle, R. 1992. "Personal Reactions to Violence in Prison." *Criminal Justice and Behavior* 19:160–173.

———. 1993. "Punish or Rehabilitate? Public Attitudes Toward Six Common Crimes." *Crime and Delinquency* 39:240–252.

———. 1995. "Correctional Boot Camps and Change in Attitude: Is All This Shouting Necessary?" *Justice Quarterly* 12:365–375.

McCorkle, R., and T. Miethe. 2002. *Panic: The Social Construction of the Street Gang Problem.* Upper Saddle River, NJ: Prentice-Hall.

McCormack, W. 2001. "Deconstructing the Election: Foucault, Derrida, and GOP Strategy." *Nation,* Mar. 26:25–34.

McCormick, A. 1977. "Rule Enforcement and Moral Indignation: Some Observations on the Effects of Criminal Antitrust Convictions upon Societal Reaction Processes." *Social Problems* 25:30–39.

McCormick, J. 1998. "The Wrongly Convicted." *Newsweek,* Nov. 9:64.

McCoy, A. 1972. *The Politics of Heroin in Southeast Asia.* New York: Harper and Row.

McDermott, J. 1979. *Rape Victimization in Twenty-six American Cities.* Washington, DC: U.S. Government Printing Office.

McDowall, D., C. Loftin, and B. Wiersema. 1995. "Easing Concealed Firearms Laws: Effects on Homicide in Three States." *Journal of Criminal Law and Criminology* 86:193–206.

McGahey, R. 1986. "Economic Conditions, Neighborhood Organization, and Urban Crime." In A. Reiss and M. Tonry (eds.), *Communities and Crime.* Chicago: University of Chicago.

McIntyre, L. 1987. *The Public Defender: The Practice of Law in the Shadows of Repute.* Chicago: University of Chicago.

Mead, G. 1934. *Mind, Self, and Society.* Chicago: University of Chicago.

Mears, B. 2003. "Supreme Court Upholds Long Sentences Under Three-Strikes-You're-Out Law." Mar. 5, www.cnn.com.

Medea, A., and K. Thompson. 1974. *Against Rape.* New York: Farrar, Straus, and Giroux.

Mednick, S., V. Pollock, and J. Volavka. 1982. "Biology and Violence." In M. Wolfgang and N. Weiner (eds.), *Criminal Violence.* Beverly Hills: Sage.

Meeks, K. 2000. *Driving While Black: Highways, Shopping Malls, Taxicabs, Sidewalks—How to Fight Back If You Are a Victim of Racial Profiling.* New York: Broadway.

Meier, R., and G. Geis. 1997. *Victimless Crime? Prostitution, Drugs, Homosexuality, Abortion.* Los Angeles: Roxbury.

Melekian, B. 1990. "Police and the Homeless." *FBI Law Enforcement Bulletin* 59:1–7.

Melton, A. 2002. "Traditional and Contemporary Tribal Justice." In C. Mann and M. Zatz (eds.), *Images of Color, Images of Crime.* Los Angeles, Roxbury.

Melton, H. 2000. "Stalking: A Review of the Literature and Direction for the Future." *Criminal Justice Review* 25:246–262.

Menard, S., and B. Morse. 1984. "A Structuralist Critique of the IQ-Delinquency

Hypothesis: Theory and Evidence." *American Journal of Sociology* 89:1347–1378.

Merlo, A. 1995. "Female Criminality in the 1990s." In A. Merlo and J. Pollock (eds.), *Women, Law, and Social Control*. Boston: Allyn and Bacon.

Merlo, A., and J. Pollock (eds.). 1995. *Women, Law, and Social Control*. Boston: Allyn and Bacon.

Merton, R. 1938. "Social Structure and Anomie." *American Sociological Review* 3:672–682.

———. 1964. "Anomie, Anomia, and Social Interaction." In M. Clinard (ed.), *Anomie and Deviant Behavior*. New York: Free Press.

———. 1968. *Social Theory and Social Structure*. New York: Free Press.

Merton, R., and A. Rossi. 1968. "Contributions to the Theory of Reference Group Behavior." In H. Hyman and E. Singer (eds.), *Readings in Reference Group Theory and Research*. New York: Free Press.

Messerschmidt, J. 1983. *The Trial of Leonard Peltier*. Boston: South End Press.

———. 1993. *Masculinities and Crime: Critique and Reconceptualization of Theory*. Lanham, MD: Rowman and Littlefield.

———. 1995. "From Patriarchy to Gender: Feminist Theory, Criminology, and the Challenge of Diversity." In N. Rafter and F. Heidensohn (eds.), *International Feminist Perspectives in Criminology*. Buckingham, UK: Open University.

———. 1997. *Crime as Structured Action: Gender, Race, Class, and Crime in the Making*. Thousand Oaks, CA: Sage.

Messner, S. 1986. "Television Violence and Violent Crime: An Aggregate Analysis." *Social Problems* 33:218–235.

———. 1989. "Economic Discrimination and Homicide Rates: Further Evidence on the Cost of Inequality." *American Sociological Review* 54:597–611.

Messner, S., and R. Rosenfeld. 2001. *Crime and the American Dream*. Belmont, CA: Wadsworth.

Michalowski, R. 1983. "Crime Control in the 1980s: A Progressive Agenda." *Crime and Social Justice* 19:13–23.

———. 1985. *Order, Law, and Crime*. New York: Random House.

Michalowski, R., and S. Carlson. 1999. "Unemployment, Imprisonment, and Social Structures of Accumulation: Historical Contingency in the Rusche-Kirchheimer Hypothesis." *Criminology* 37:217–248.

Michalowski, R., and R. Kramer. 1987. "The Space Between Laws: The Problem of Corporate Crime in a Transnational Context." *Social Problems* 34:34–53.

Michaud, S., and H. Aynesworth. 1983. *The Only Living Witness*. New York: Liden.

Miethe, T., and R. McCorkle 1998. *Crime Profiles: The Anatomy of Dangerous Persons, Places, and Situations*. Los Angeles: Roxbury.

Miethe, T., and C. Moore. 1986. "Racial Differences in Criminal Processing: The Consequences of Model Selection on Conclusions about Differential Treatment." *Sociological Quarterly* 27:217–237.

Mignon, S., and W. Holmes. 1995. "Police Response to Mandatory Arrest Laws." *Crime and Delinquency* 41:430–442.

Miller, E. 1986. *Street Woman: The Illegal Work of Underclass Women*. Philadelphia: Temple University.

Miller, E., K. Romenesko, and L. Wondolkowski. 1993. "The United States." In N. Davis (ed.), *Prostitution*. Westport, CT: Greenwood.

Miller, J. 1998. "Up It Up: Gender and the Accomplishment of Street Robbery." *Criminology* 36:37–65.

Miller, J., and R. Brunson. 2000. "Gender Dynamics in Youth Gangs: A Comparison of Males' and Females' Accounts." *Justice Quarterly* 17:419–448.

Miller, J., and D. Lynam. 2001. "Structural Models of Personality and Their Relation to Antisocial Behavior: A Meta-Analytic Review." *Criminology* 39:765–795.

Miller, K. 2000. "Prison Labor: Some Facts and Issues." www.kcd.com.

Miller, M. 1974. "At Hard Labor: Rediscovering the Nineteenth Century Prison." *Issues in Criminology* 9:91–114.

Miller, M. 1974. *The Breaking of a President.* Vol. 4. City of Industry, CA: Therapy Productions.

Miller, S. 1993. "Arrest Policies for Domestic Violence and Their Implications for Battered Women." In R. Muraskin and T. Alleman (eds.), *It's a Crime: Women and Justice.* Englewood Cliffs, NJ:Prentice-Hall.

Miller, W. 1973. "Ideology and Criminal Justice Policy: Some Current Issues." *Journal of Criminal Law and Criminology* 64:141–162.

———. 1980. "Gangs, Groups, and Serious Youth Crime." In D. Shichor and D. Kelly (eds.), *Critical Issues in Juvenile Delinquency.*" Lexington, MA: Lexington.

Mills, C. 1959. *The Sociological Imagination.* New York: Oxford University.

Milwaukee Journal. 1988. "Memo Hints Bush Knew Noriega Link." May 8:A11.

———. 1994a. "Clinton Vows to Fight Repeal of Crime Bill." Dec. 21:A3.

———. 1994b. "The Crime Bill." Aug. 26:A3.

Minkowitz, D. 1999. "Love and Hate in Laramie." *Nation,* July 12.

Minor, W. 1984. "Neutralization as a Hardening Process: Considerations in the Modeling of Change." *Social Forces* 62:995–1019.

Mintz, M. 1985. *At Any Cost: Corporate Greed, Women, and the Dalkon Shield.* New York: Pantheon.

Mieczkowski, T. 1994. "The Experiences of Women Who Sell Crack: Some Descriptive Data from the Detroit Crack Ethnography Project." *Journal of Drug Issues* 24:227–248.

Mokhiber, R. 1988. *Corporate Crime and Violence: Big Business and the Abuse of Public Trust.* San Francisco: Sierra Club.

Monahan, J., and H. Steadman. 1983. "Crime and Mental Disorder: An Epidemiological Approach." In M. Tonry and N. Morris (eds.), *Crime and Justice.* Chicago: University of Chicago.

Montgomery, R. 1990. "*Hustler* Article Blamed for Mutilation of Boy, 10." *Kansas City Star,* Nov. 2:C1.

Monto, M. 1998. "Holding Men Accountable for Prostitution." *Violence Against Women* 4:506–517.

Moon, M., J. Wright, F. Cullen, and J. Pealer. 2000. "Putting Kids to Death: Specifying Public Support for Juvenile Capital Punishment." *Justice Quarterly* 17:663–684.

Moore, A. 1997. "Intimate Violence: Does Socioeconomic Status Matter?" In A. Cardarelli (ed.), *Violence Between Intimate Partners.* Boston: Allyn and Bacon.

Moore, J. 1991. *Going Down to the Barrio.* Philadelphia: Temple University.

Moore, J., and J. Hagedorn. 1996. "What Happens to Girls in the Gang?" In C. Huff (ed.), *Gangs in America.* Thousand Oaks, CA: Sage.

Moore, J., and A. Mata. 1981. *Women and Heroin in Chicano Communities.* Los Angeles: Chicano Pinto Research Project.

Moore, J., D. Vigil, and R. Garcia. 1983. "Residence and Territoriality in Chicano Gangs." *Social Problems* 31:182–194.

Moore, M. 1995. "Public Health and Criminal Justice Approaches to Prevention." In M. Tonry and D. Farrington (eds.), *Building a Safer Society.* Chicago: University of Chicago.

Morash, M., and M. Chesney-Lind. 1991. "A Reformulation and Partial Test of the Power Control Theory of Delinquency." *Justice Quarterly* 8:347–377.

Morash, M., and R. Haarr. 1995. "Gender, Workplace Problems, and Stress in Policing." *Justice Quarterly* 12:113–140.

Morash, M., and L. Rucker. 1990. "A Critical Look at the Idea of Boot Camps as a Correctional Reform." *Crime and Delinquency* 36:204–222.

Morgan, P. 1987. "Living on the Edge." In F. Delacoste and P. Alexander (eds.), *Sex Work.* Pittsburgh: Cleis.

Morgan, R., and G. Steinem. 1983. "The International Crime of Genital Mutilation." In L. Richardson and V. Taylor (eds.), *Feminist Frontiers.* Reading, MA: Addison-Wesley.

Morganthau, T. 1986. "Kids and Cocaine." *Newsweek,* March 17:58–65.

Morris, A. 1987. *Women, Crime, and Criminal Justice.* Oxford: Blackwell.

Morris, A., and A. Wilczynski. 1994. "Rocking the Cradle." In H. Birch (ed.), *Moving Targets.* Berkeley: University of California.

Morris, N., and G. Hawkins. 1970. *The Honest Politician's Guide to Crime Control.* Chicago: University of Chicago.

Moses, M. 1995. *Keeping Incarcerated Mothers and Their Daughters Together: Girl Scouts Beyond Bars.* Washington, DC: U.S. Department of Justice.

Mosher, C., T. Miethe, and D. Phillips. 2002. *The Mismeasure of Crime.* Thousand Oaks, CA: Sage.

Moss, K. 1990. "Legal Issues: Drug Testing of Postpartum Women and Newborns as the Basis for Civil and Criminal Proceedings." *Clearinghouse Review* 23:1406–1414.

Moyers, B. 1988. *The Secret Government: The Constitution in Crisis.* Cabin John, MD: Seven Locks.

———. 1990a. "Global Dumping Ground." PBS documentary.

———. 1990b. "High Crimes and Misdemeanors." PBS documentary.

———. 1991. "Circle of Recovery." PBS documentary.

Ms. 2002. "Female Genital Mutilation: Flash Forward." Spring:44.

———. 2003. "Global." Summer:23.

Musolf, G. 1993. "Some Recent Directions in Symbolic Interactionism." In L. Reynolds, *Interactionism.* Dix Hills, NY: General Hall.

Musto, D. 1987. *The American Disease: Origins of Narcotic Control.* New York: Oxford University.

Myers, D. 1997. "Racial Rioting in the 1960s: An Event History Analysis of Local Conditions." *American Sociological Review* 62:94–112.

Myers, M. 2000. "The Social World of America's Courts." In J. Sheley (ed.), *Criminology.* Belmont, CA: Wadsworth.

Nadelmann, E. 1989. "Drug Prohibition in the United States: Costs, Consequences, and Alternatives." *Science* 245:939–947.

Nader, R. 1965. *Unsafe at Any Speed: The Designed-In Dangers of the American Automobile.* New York: Grossman.

Nanda, S. 2000. *Gender Diversity: Crosscultural Variations.* Prospect Heights, IL: Waveland.

Narayan, U. 1995. "The Discriminating Nature of Industrial Health-Hazard Policies and Some Implications for Third World Women Workers." In J. Callahan (ed.), *Reproduction, Ethics, and the Law.* Bloomington: Indiana University.

Nation. 2000. "Firestonewalling." Oct. 2:3–4.

National Institute of Corrections. 1997. *Supermax Housing: A Survey of Current Practice.* Washington, DC: U.S. Department of Justice.

Naughton, K. 2000. "Spinning Out of Control." *Newsweek,* Sept. 11:58.

Neergaard, L. 1998. "Critics Question If FDA Values Speed over Safety." *Wisconsin State Journal,* July 11:2A.

Nelsen, C., J. Corzine, and L. Huff-Corzine. 1994. "The Violent West Reexamined: A Research Note on Regional Homicide Rates." *Criminology* 32:149–161.

Nelson, A., and P. Oliver. 1998. "Gender and the Construction of Consent in Child-Adult Sexual Contact.' *Gender and Society* 12:554–577.

Nelson, J. 1994. "A Dollar or a Day: Sentencing Misdemeanants in New York State." *Journal of Criminal Justice* 31:183–201.

Neubauer, D. 2001. *America's Courts and the Criminal Justice System.* Belmont, CA: Wadsworth.

Neuman, W. 1996. "William Julius Wilson: Racism Is Not Sufficient." *Journal of American Studies* 28:699–717.

———. 1998. "Negotiated Meanings and State Transformation." *Social Problems* 45:315–335.

———. 2003. *Social Research Methods.* Boston: Allyn and Bacon.

Neuman, W., and R. Berger. 1988. "Competing Perspectives on Cross-National Crime: An Evaluation of Theory and Evidence." *Sociological Quarterly* 29:281–313.

New York Times. 2003. "Errors at FBI may be Issue in 3,000 Cases." Mar. 17:A18.

New Republic. 2000. "Sherman's March." Apr. 17–24:15.

———. 2003. "Sixteen Words." July 28–Aug. 4:8–9.

Newman, D. 2000/2002. *Sociology: Exploring the Architecture of Everyday Life.* Thousand Oaks, CA: Pine Forge.

Newman, G. 1993. "Batman and Justice: The True Story." *Humanity and Society* 17:261–274.

———. 1998. "Popular Culture and Violence: Decoding the Violence in Popular Movies." In F. Bailey and D. Hale (eds.), *Popular Culture, Crime, and Justice.* Belmont, CA: Wadsworth.

Newman, O. 1972. *Defensible Space: Crime Prevention Through Urban Design.* New York: Macmillan.

Newsweek. 1999. "A Painful Tradition." July 5:32–33.

Nichols, L. 1999. "White-Collar Cinema: Changing Representations of Upper-World Deviance in Popular Films." In *Perspectives on Social Problems,* vol. 11. Stamford, CT: JAI.

Nilson, C., and T. Burke. 2002. "Environmental Extremists and the Eco-Terrorism Movement." *ACJS Today,* Jan.–Feb.:1–6.

Noonan, J. 1994. "Virginian Liberators." In J. Bonsignore et al. (eds.), *Before the Law.* Boston: Houghton Mifflin.

Nordland, R., and J. Bartholet. 2001. "The Web's Dark Secret." *Newsweek,* Mar. 19:44–51.

Nye, J., P. Zelikow, and D. King (eds.). 1997. *Why People Don't Trust Government.* Cambridge: Harvard University.

Oakley, A. 1986. *From Here to Maternity: Becoming a Mother.* Harmondsworth, UK: Penguin.

Oates, S. 1983. *The Fires of Jubilee: Nat Turner's Fierce Rebellion.* New York: New American Library.

O'Brien, R. 1987. "The Interracial Nature of Violent Crimes: A Reexamination." *American Journal of Sociology* 92:817–835.

Office of National Drug Control Policy. 1989. *National Drug Control Strategy.* Washington, DC: U.S. Government Printing Office.

Ogawa, B. 1999. *Color of Justice: Culturally Sensitive Treatment of Minority Crime Victims.* Boston: Allyn and Bacon.

Ogle, R., D. Maier-Katkin, and T. Bernard. 1995. "A Theory of Homicidal Behavior Among Women." *Criminology* 33:173–193.

Oliver, M. 1994. "Portrayals of Crime, Race, and Aggression in 'Reality-Based' Police Shows: A Content Analysis." *Journal of Broadcasting and Electronic Media* 38:179–191.

Oliverio, J. 1990. "The Treatment of AIDS Behind the Walls of Correctional Facilities." *Social Justice* 17:113–125.

Orcutt, J. (ed.). 1983. *Analyzing Deviance.* Homewood, IL: Dorsey.

Orcutt, J., and J. Turner. 1993. "Shocking Numbers and Graphic Accounts: Quantified Images of Drug Problems in Print Media." *Social Problems* 40:190–212.

O'Reilly, J. 1979. "Jury Representation by Neighborhood." In R. Alvarez et al. (eds.), *Discrimination in Organizations.* San Francisco: Jossey-Bass.

Orenstein, P. 1994. *School Girls.* New York: Doubleday.

Osbun, L., and P. Rode. 1984. "Prosecuting Juveniles as Adults: The Quest for 'Objective' Decisions." *Criminology* 22:187–202.

O'Shea, K. 1999. *Women and the Death Penalty in the United States, 1900–1998.* Westport, CT: Praeger.

Owen, B. 1985. "Race and Gender Relations Among Prison Workers." *Crime and Delinquency* 31:147–159.

Owen, B., and B. Bloom. 1995. "Profiling Women Prisoners: Findings from National Surveys and a California Sample." *Prison Journal* 75:164–185.

Packer, H. 1964. "Two Models of the Criminal Process." *University of Pennsylvania Law Review* 113:1–68.

Padilla, F. 1992. *The Gang as an American Enterprise.* New Brunswick, NJ: Rutgers University.

Pagelow, M. 1984. *Family Violence.* New York: Praeger.

Pager, D. 2003. "The Mark of a Criminal Record." *American Journal of Sociology* 108:937–975.

Palast, G. 2003. *The Best Democracy Money Can Buy: The Truth About Corporate Cons, Globalization, and High-Finance Fraudsters.* New York: Plume.

Palen, J. 1997. *The Urban World.* New York: McGraw-Hill.

Parenti, M. 1983. *Democracy for the Few.* New York: St. Martin's.

Parfrey, A. 1990. "Mayhem Manuals." *Hustler,* Dec.:1–2, 56–58, 67–68.

Park, R., and E. Burgess. 1924. *Introduction to the Science of Sociology.* Chicago: University of Chicago.

Parker, K., M. Dewees, and M. Radelt. 2001. "Racial Bias and the Conviction of the Innocent." In S. Westervelt and J. Humphrey (eds.), *Wrongly Convicted.* New Brunswick, NJ: Rutgers University.

Parker, R. 1989. "Poverty, Subculture of Violence, and Type of Homicide." *Social Forces* 67:983–1007.

Parry, R. 1988. "Guns for Drugs?" *Newsweek,* May 23:22–23.

Parsons, T. 1951. *The Social System.* New York: Free Press.

Passas, N. 1990. "Anomie and Corporate Deviance." *Contemporary Crises* 14:157–178.

———. 1995. "The Mirror of Global Evils: A Review Essay on the BCCI Affair." *Justice Quarterly* 12:377–405.

Pastore, A., and K. Maguire 1998, 2000, 2002. *Sourcebook of Criminal Justice Statistics.* Washington, DC: U.S. Department of Justice.

Pate, A., and E. Hamilton. 1992. "Formal and Informal Deterrents to Domestic Violence: The Dade County Spouse Assault Experiment." *American Sociological Review* 57:691–697.

Paternoster, R. 1987. "The Deterrent Effect of the Perceived Certainty and Severity of Punishment: A Review of the Evidence and Issues." *Justice Quarterly* 4:173–217.

———. 1989. "Absolute and Restrictive Deterrence in a Panel of Youth: Explaining the Onset, Persistence/Desistance, and Frequency of Delinquent Offending." *Social Problems* 36:289–309.

———. 1991. *Capital Punishment in America.* New York: Lexington.

Paternoster, R., and L. Iovanni. 1989. "The Labeling Perspective and Delinquency: An Elaboration of the Theory and an Assessment of the Evidence." *Justice Quarterly* 6:359–394.

Paternoster, R., and P. Mazerolle. 1994. "General Strain Theory and Delinquency: A Replication and Extension." *Journal of Research in Crime and Delinquency* 31:235–263.

Paternoster, R., and R. Triplett. 1988. "Disaggregating Self-Reported Delinquency and Its Implications for Theory." *Criminology* 26:591–625.

Patterson, E., and M. Lynch. 1991. "Bias in Formalized Bail Procedures." In M. Lynch and E. Patterson (eds.), *Race and Criminal Justice.* Albany, NY: Harrow and Heston.

Patterson, R., and M. Stouthamer-Loeber. 1984. "The Correlation of Family Management Practices and Delinquency." *Child Development* 55:1299–1307.

Pattillo, M. 1998. "Sweet Mothers and Gangbangers: Managing Crime in a Black Middle-Class Neighborhood." *Social Forces* 76:747–774.

Pearson, F., D. Lipton, C. Cleland, and D. Yee. 2002. "The Effects of Behavioral/Cognitive Programs on Recidivism." *Crime and Delinquency* 48:476–496.

Pearson, M. 1996. "Alabama to Halt Use of Chain Gangs." *Denver Post,* June 21:A2.

Pearson, P. 1997. *When She Was Bad.* New York: Viking.

———. 1998. "Sex Discrimination on Death Row." *New York Times,* Jan. 13:A19.

Pelka, F. 1995. "Raped: A Male Survivor Breaks His Silence." In P. Searles and R. Berger (eds.), *Rape and Society.* Boulder, CO: Westview.

Peltier, L. 1989. "War Against the American Nation." In B. Schultz and R. Schultz (eds.), *It Did Happen Here.* Berkeley: University of California.

Pepinsky, H. 1999. "Peacemaking Primer." In B. Arrigo (ed.), *Social Justice/Criminal Justice.* Belmont, CA: Wadsworth.

Pepinsky, H., and R. Quinney (eds.). 1991. *Criminology as Peacemaking.* Bloomington: Indiana University.

Perry, S., and J. Dawson. 1985. *Nightmare: Women and the Dalkon Shield.* New York: Macmillan.

Petersilia, J. 2003a. "Prisoner Reentry and Criminological Knowledge." *Criminologist,* Mar.–Apr.:1–5.

———. 2003b. *When Prisoners Come Home: Parole and Prisoner Reentry.* New York: Oxford University.

Petersilia, J., et al. 1985. *Granting Felons Probation.* Santa Monica, CA: RAND.

Petersilia, J., and S. Turner. 1988. "Minorities in Prison: Discrimination or Disparity?" *Corrections Today* 50:92–94.

————. 1993. "Evaluating Intensive Supervision Probation/Parole: Results of a Nationwide Experiment." *National Institute of Justice Research in Brief,* May:1–10.

Peterson, D., J. Miller, and F. Esbensen. 2001. "The Impact of Sex Composition on Gangs and Gang Member Delinquency." *Criminology* 39:411–439.

Peterson, R., and W. Bailey. 1998. "Is Capital Punishment an Effective Deterrent to Murder? An Examination of Social Science Research." In J. Acker et al. (eds.), *America's Experiment with Capital Punishment.* Durham: NC: Carolina Academic.

Petrillo, L. 1990. "When a Cop Shoots, Who Takes a Close Look?" *San Diego Union,* Dec. 21:A1, 10.

Pettiway, L. 1997. *Workin' It: Women Living Through Drugs and Crime.* Philadelphia: Temple University.

Pfohl, S. 1985. *Images of Deviance and Social Control: A Sociological History.* New York: McGraw-Hill.

Pfost, D. 1987. "Reagan's Nicaraguan Policy: A Case Study of Political Deviance and Crime." *Crime and Social Justice* 27–28:66–87.

Phillips, H. 2002. "Judge OKs Microsoft Settlement." *Wisconsin State Journal,* Nov. 2:A1.

Phillips, K. 2002. *Wealth and Democracy: A Political History of the American Rich.* New York: Broadway.

Piliavan, I., R. Gartner, C. Thornton, and R. Matsueda. 1986. "Crime, Deterrence, and Rational Choice." *American Sociological Review* 51:101–119.

Piven, F., and R. Cloward. 1971. *Regulating the Poor: The Functions of Public Welfare.* New York: Vintage.

Pizzo, S., M. Fricker, and P. Muolo. 1989. *Inside Job: The Looting of America's Savings and Loans.* New York: McGraw-Hill.

Platt, A. 1974. "The Triumph of Benevolence: The Origins of the Juvenile Justice System in the United States." In R. Quinney (ed.), *Criminal Justice in America.* Boston: Little, Brown.

Platt, L. 2001. "Regulating the Global Brothel." *American Prospect,* July 2–16:10–14.

Polk, K., D. Frease, and F. Richmond. 1974. "Social Class, School Experience, and Delinquency." *Criminology* 12:84–96.

Pollitt, K. 1998. "'Fetal Rights': A New Assault on Feminism." In R. Weitz (ed.), *The Politics of Women's Bodies.* New York: Oxford University.

Pollock-Byrne, J. 1990. *Women, Prison, and Crime.* Pacific Grove, CA: Brooks/Cole.

Polsky, N. 1969. *Hustlers, Beats, and Others.* Garden City, NY: Anchor.

Porterfield, A. 1943. "Delinquency and Its Outcome in Court and College." *American Journal of Sociology* 49:199–208.

Potterat, J., D. Woodhouse, J. Muth, and S. Muth. 1990. "Estimating the Prevalence and Career Longevity of Prostitute Women." *Journal of Sex Research* 27:233–243.

Poussaint, A. 1983. "Black-on-Black Homicide: A Psychological-Political Perspective." *Victimology* 8:161–169.

Poveda, T. 1990. *Lawlessness and Reform: The FBI in Transition.* Belmont, CA: Brooks/Cole.

————. 1994a. "Clinton, Crime, and the Justice Department." *Social Justice* 21:73–84.

————. 1994b. *Rethinking White-Collar Crime.* Westport, CT: Greenwood.

Power, S. 2002. *"A Problem from Hell": America and the Age of Genocide*. New York: Basic.

Pratt, T., and J. Maahs. 1999. "Are Private Prisons More Cost-Effective Than Public Prisons? A Meta-Analysis of Evaluation Research Studies." *Crime and Delinquency* 45:358–371.

President's Commission on Law Enforcement and Administration of Justice (PCLEAJ). 1967. *The Challenge of Crime in a Free Society*. Washington, DC: U.S. Government Printing Office.

Pryor, D. 1996. *Unspeakable Acts: Why Men Seriously Abuse Children*. New York: New York University.

Quadagno, J., and C. Fobes. 1995. "The Welfare State and the Cultural Reproduction of Gender: Making Good Girls and Boys in the Job Corps." *Social Problems* 42:171–190.

Quay, H. 1983. "Crime Causation: Psychological Theories." In S. Kadish (ed.), *Encyclopedia of Crime and Justice*. New York: Free Press.

Quicker, J. 1983. *Homegirls: Characterizing Chicana Gangs*. San Pedro, CA: International Universities.

Quinney, R. 1970. *The Social Reality of Crime*. Boston: Little, Brown.

———. 1977. *Class, State and Crime: On the Theory and Practice of Criminal Justice*. New York: David McKay.

———. 1999. "The Prophetic Meaning of Justice." In B. Arrigo (ed.), *Social Justice/Criminal Justice*. Belmont, CA: Wadsworth.

———. 2000. "Socialist Humanism and the Problem of Crime: Thinking About Erich Fromm in the Development of Critical/Peacemaking Criminology." In K. Anderson and R. Quinney (eds.), *Erich Fromm and Critical Criminology*. Urbana-Champaign: University of Illinois Press.

Rackmill, S. 1994. "An Analysis of Home Confinement as a Sanction." *Federal Probation* 58:48–52.

Radelet, M. 1981. "Racial Characteristics and the Imposition of the Death Penalty." *American Sociological Review* 46:918–927.

Radelet, M., and H. Bedau. 1998. "The Execution of the Innocent." In J. Acker et al. (eds.), *America's Experiment with Capital Punishment*. Durham, NC: Carolina Academic.

Radelet, M., H. Bedau, and C. Putnam. 1992. *In Spite of Innocence: Erroneous Convictions in Capital Cases*. Boston: Northeastern University.

Radelet, M., and G. Pierce. 1985. "Race and Prosecutorial Discretion in Homicide Cases." *Law and Society Review* 19:587–621.

Rafter, N. 1992. "Criminal Anthropology in the United States." *Criminology* 30:525–545.

Rainville, G., and B. Reaves. 2003. *Felony Defendants in Large Urban Counties, 2000*. Washington, DC: U.S. Department of Justice.

Rampart Independent Review Panel. 2002. "The Los Angeles Police Department Rampart Division Scandal: Exposing Police Misconduct and Responding to It." In M. Ermann and R. Lundman (eds.), *Corporate and Governmental Deviance*. New York: Oxford University.

Rand, M., J. Lynch, and D. Cantor. 1997. *Criminal Victimization 1973–95*. Washington, DC: U.S. Department of Justice.

Randall, M., and L. Haskell. 1995. "Sexual Violence in Women's Lives: Findings from the Women's Safety Project, A Community Survey." *Violence Against Women* 1:6–31.

Rankin, J. 1980. "School Factors and Delinquency: Interaction by Age and Sex." *Sociology and Social Research* 64:420–434.

Rankin, J., and R. Kern. 1994. "Parental Attachments and Delinquency." *Criminology* 32:495–515.

Rashke, R. 1981. *The Killing of Karen Silkwood.* New York: Penguin.

Rawls, J. 1971. *A Theory of Justice.* Cambridge: Harvard University.

Reaves, B. 1991. *Pretrial Release of Felony Defendants 1988.* Washington, DC: U.S. Department of Justice.

Reckless, W. 1967. *The Crime Problem.* New York: Appleton-Century Crofts.

Reece, R. 1993. "Fatal Child Abuse and Sudden Infant Death Syndrome: A Critical Diagnostic Decision." *Pediatrics* 91:423–429.

Reed, I. 1991. "Tuning Out Network Bias." *New York Times,* Apr. 9:A11.

Reeves, J., and R. Campbell. 1994. *Cracked Coverage: Television News, the Anti-Cocaine Crusade, and the Reagan Legacy.* Durham, NC: Duke University.

Regoli, R., and J. Hewitt. 1997. *Delinquency in Society.* New York: McGraw-Hill.

Reichard, K. 1998. "Look at Me!" *Isthumus,* Aug. 7:35–36.

Reichel, P. 1999. "Southern Slave Patrols as a Transitional Police Type." In L. Gaines and G. Cordner (eds.), *Policing Perspectives.* Los Angeles: Roxbury.

Reid, S. 1997/2003. *Crime and Criminology.* New York: McGraw-Hill.

Reiman, J. 2004. *The Rich Get Richer and the Poor Get Prison: Ideology, Class, and Criminal Justice.* Boston: Allyn and Bacon.

Reinarman, C., and H. Levine. 1989. "The Crack Attack: Politics and Media in America's Latest Drug Scare." In J. Best (ed.), *Images of Issues.* New York: Aldine de Gruyter.

Reiner, I. 1992. *Gangs, Crime and Violence in Los Angeles.* Arlington, VA: National Youth Gang Information Center.

Reiss, A. 1951. "Delinquency as a Failure of Personal and Social Controls." *American Sociological Review* 26:720–732.

———. 1968. "Police Brutality: Answers to Key Questions." *Transaction* 5:10–19.

———. 1971. *The Police and the Public.* New Haven: Yale University.

———. 1980. "Police Brutality." In R. Lundman (ed.), *Police Behavior.* New York: Oxford University.

Relman, A., and M. Angell. 2002. "America's Other Drug Problem." *New Republic,* Dec. 16:27–41.

Renzetti, C. 1992. *Violent Betrayal: Partner Abuse in Lesbian Relationships.* Newbury Park, CA: Sage.

———. 1996. "The Poverty of Services for Battered Lesbians." In C. Renzetti and C. Miley (eds.), *Violence in Gay and Lesbian Domestic Partnerships.* New York: Harrington Park.

Resnick, S. 1993. "Fear Itself." *Utne Reader,* Mar.–Apr.:64–65.

Ressler, R., and T. Schachtman. 1992. *Whoever Fights Monsters.* New York: St. Martin's.

Reuter, P. 1995. "The Decline of the American Mafia." *Public Interest* 120:89–99.

Rhodes, A., and A. Reiss. 1970. "The 'Religious Factor'and Delinquent Behavior." *Journal of Research in Crime and Delinquency* 7:83–98.

Richardson, L., V. Taylor, and N. Whittier (eds.). 1997. *Feminist Frontiers.* New York: McGraw-Hill.

Riley, T. 1986. *The Price of a Life: One Woman's Death from Toxic Shock.* Bethesda, MD: Adler and Adler.

Roberts, J., and L. Stalans. 2000. *Public Opinion, Crime, and Criminal Justice.* Boulder, CO: Westview.

Roberts, N. 1994. "The Game's Up." *New Statesman and Society* 7, July 16:44–45.

Robin, C. 1963. "Patterns of Department Store Shoplifting." *Crime and Delinquency* 9:163–172.

Robinson, C. 1993. "The Production of Black Violence in Chicago." In D. Greenberg (ed.), *Crime and Capitalism*. Philadelphia: Temple University.

Robinson, D., and O. Stephens. 1992. "Patterns of Mitigating Factors in Juvenile Death Penalty Cases." *Criminal Law Bulletin* 28:246:275.

Robinson, G., and D. Stewart. 1986. "Postpartum Psychiatric Disorders." *Canadian Medical Assoc. Journal* 134:31–37.

Robinson, L. 1996. "Subject/Position." In N. Maglin and D. Perry (eds.), *"Bad Girls"/"Good Girls."* New Brunswick, NJ: Rutgers University.

Robinson, M. 2000. "The Construction and Reinforcement of Myths of Race and Crime." *Journal of Contemporary Criminal Justice* 16:133–156.

Rodgers, L. 1995. "Prison Suicide: Suggestions from Phenomenology." *Deviant Behavior* 6:113–126.

Roncek, D., and D. Gaggiani. 1985. "High Schools and Crime: A Replication." *Sociological Quarterly* 26:491–505.

Roncek, D., and A. LoBosco. 1983. "The Effect of High Schools on Crime in Their Neighborhood." *Social Science Quarterly* 64:589–613.

Rose, D., and T. Clear. 1998. "Incarceration, Social Capital, and Crime: Implications for Social Disorganization Theory." *Criminology* 36:441–479.

Rosen, J. 1997. "One Angry Woman." *New Yorker,* Feb. 24:54–63.

Rosenbaum, A. 1993. *Prosecuting Nazi War Criminals.* Boulder, CO: Westview.

Rosenbaum, D. 1988. "Community Crime Prevention: A Review and Synthesis of the Literature." *Justice Quarterly* 5:323–395.

Rosenbaum, J., and L. Prinsky. 1991. "The Presumption of Influence: Recent Responses to Popular Music Subcultures." *Crime and Delinquency* 37:528–535.

Rosenberg, D. 2003. "Love Canal's Long Shadow." *Newsweek,* Aug. 4:50–51.

Rosoff, S., H. Pontell, and R. Tillman. 2002. *Profit Without Honor: White-Collar Crime and the Looting of America.* Upper Saddle River, NJ: Prentice-Hall.

Ross, E. 1907/1977. "The Criminaloid." In G. Geis and R. Meier (eds.), *White-Collar Crime.* New York: Free Press.

Ross, J., and S. Richards. 2002. *Behind Bars: Surviving Prison.* Indianapolis: Alpha.

Rossmo, D. 1994. "Targeting Victims: Serial Killers and the Urban Environment." In T. O'Reilly-Fleming and S. Egger (eds.), *Serial and Mass Murder.* Toronto: University of Toronto.

Rotello, G. 2002. "Who's the Butchest of Them All?" *Advocate,* Apr. 30:72.

Rothman, D. 1971. *The Discovery of the Asylum.* Boston: Little, Brown.

———. 1980. *Conscience and Convenience: The Asylum and Its Alternatives in Progressive America.* Boston: Little, Brown.

Rottman, D., C. Flango, and R. Lockley. 1995. *State Court Organization 1993.* Washington, DC: U.S. Department of Justice.

Rowe, D. 1986. "Genetic and Environmental Components of Antisocial Behavior: A Study of 265 Twins." *Criminology* 24:513–532.

Rozee, P., P. Bateman, and T. Gilmore. 1991. "The Personal Perspective of Acquaintance Rape Prevention: A Three-Tier Approach." In A. Parrot and L. Bechhofer (eds.), *Acquaintance Rape.* New York: Wiley.

Rubenstein, R., and J. Roth. 1987. *Approaches to Auschwitz: The Holocaust and Its Legacy.* Atlanta: John Knox.

Rude, G. 1964. *The Crowd in History.* New York: Wiley.

Ruffins, P. 1988. "'Toxic Terrorism' Invades Third World Nations." *Black Enterprise* 19:31.

Russakoff D., and S. Kovaleski. 1998. "Two Angry Men." In B. Schechterman and M. Slann (eds.). *Violence and Terrorism.* New York: McGraw-Hill.

Russell, D. 1982. *Rape in Marriage.* New York: Macmillan.

———. 1984. *Sexual Exploitation: Rape, Child Sexual Abuse, and Workplace Harassment.* Beverly Hills: Sage.

———. 1986. *The Secret Trauma: Incest in the Lives of Girls and Women.* New York: Basic.

———. 1988. "Pornography and Rape: A Causal Model." *Political Psychology* 9:41–73.

———. 1993a. *Against Pornography: Evidence of Harm.* Berkeley, CA: Russell.

——— (ed.). 1993b. *Making Violence Sexy: Feminist Views on Pornography.* New York: Teachers College.

———. 1995. "The Making of a Whore." *Violence Against Women* 1:77–98.

Russell, K. 1998. *The Color of Crime: Racial Hoaxes, White Fear, Black Protectionism, Police Harassment, and Other Macroaggressions.* New York: New York University.

———. 2003. "'Driving While Black': Corollary Phenomena and Collateral Consequences." In M. Free (ed.), *Racial Issues in Criminal Justice.* Westport, CT: Praeger.

Ryan, P., and G. Rush (eds.). 1997. *Understanding Organized Crime in Global Perspective.* Thousand Oaks, CA: Sage.

Ryerson, E. 1978. *The Best-Laid Plans: America's Juvenile Court Experiment.* New York: Hill and Wang.

Sachs, S. 1982. "The Exclusionary Rule: A Prosecutor's Defense." *Criminal Justice Ethics* 1:31–32.

Safetyforum.com. 2003. "Chrysler Minivan Latch Failure Is a Safety Defect That Involves Children." www.safetyforum.com.

Safire, W. 1992a. "Democrats Slow to See Potential in Bush Cover-Up of Lavoro Scandal." *Milwaukee Journal,* April 4:A9.

———. 1992b. "Iraq Diverted Grain, Bush Admits." *Milwaukee Journal,* Oct. 9:A9.

———. 1993. "Iraqgate Giveaway." *New York Times,* May 20:A13.

Samaha, J. 2000. *Criminal Justice.* Belont, CA: Wadsworth.

Sampson, R. 1985. "Structural Sources of Variation in Race-Age-Specific Rates of Offending Across Major U.S. Cities." *Criminology* 23:647–673.

———. 1986. "Effects of Socioeconomic Context on Official Reaction to Delinquency." *American Sociological Review* 51:876–885.

———. 1987. "Urban Black Violence: The Effect of Male Joblessness and Family Disruption." *American Journal of Sociology* 93:348–382.

Sampson, R., and W. Groves. 1989. "Community Structure and Crime: Testing Social-Disorganization Theory." *American Journal of Sociology* 94:774–802.

Sampson, R., and J. Laub. 1990. "Crime and Deviance Over the Life Course: The Salience of Adult Social Bonds." *American Sociological Review* 55:609–627.

———. 1993. *Crime in the Making: Pathways and Turning Points Through Life.* Cambridge: Harvard University.

Sampson, R., and W. Wilson. 1995. "Race, Crime and Urban Inequality." In J. Hagan and R. Peterson (eds.), *Crime and Inequality.* Stanford, CA: Stanford University.

Sanday, P. 1981. "The Socio-Cultural Context of Rape: A Cross-Cultural Study." *Journal of Social Issues* 37:5–27.

———. 1990. *Fraternity Gang Rape.* New York: New York University.

Sandberg, J. 1999. "Spinning a Web of Hate." *Newsweek,* July 19:28–29.

Sanchez Jankowski, M. 1991. *Islands in the Street: Gangs and American Urban Society.* Berkeley: University of California.

Sanders, W. 1980. *Rape and Woman's Identity.* Beverly Hills: Sage.

———. 1981. *Juvenile Delinquency.* New York: Holt, Rinehart, and Winston.

———. 1983. *Criminology.* Reading, MA: Addison-Wesley.

———. 1994. *Gangbangs and Drive-Bys: Grounded Culture and Juvenile Gang Violence.* New York: Aldine de Gruyter.

Sapp, A. 1986. "Sexual Misconduct and Sexual Harassment by Police Officers." In T. Barker and D. Carter (eds.), *Police Deviance.* Cincinnati: Pilgrimage.

Satz, D. 1995. "Markets in Women's Sexual Labor." *Ethics* 106:63–85.

Saylor, W., and G. Gaes. 1994. "The Post-Release Employment Project: Prison Work has Measurable Effects on Post-Release Success." In P. Kratcoski (ed.), *Correctional Counseling and Treatment.* Prospect Heights, IL: Waveland.

Schaffner, L. 1999. *Teenage Runaways: Broken Hearts and "Bad Attitudes."* Binghamton, NY: Haworth.

Schapiro, M. 2002. "Big Tobacco: Uncovering the Industry's Multibillion-Dollar Global Smuggling Network." *Nation,* May 6:11–20.

Schechter, D. 2002. "Counting on Demoncracy." Globalvision Inc. documentary. www.CountingonDemoncracy.org.

Scheck, B., P. Neufield, and J. Dwyer. 2000. *Actual Innocence.* New York: Doubleday.

Scherer, M. 2003. "K Street on the Tigris." www.motherjones.com.

Schlosser, E. 1998. "The Prison-Industrial Complex." *Atlantic Monthly,* Dec.:51–77.

———. 1999. "The Politics of Pot: A Government in Denial." *Rolling Stone,* Mar. 4:47–52.

———. 2003. *Reefer Madness: Sex, Drugs, and Cheap Labor in the United States.* Boston: Houghton Mifflin.

Schlossman, S., et al. 1984. *Delinquency Prevention in South Chicago: A Fifty-Year Assessment of the Chicago Area Project.* Santa Monica, CA: RAND.

Schneider, A. 1986. "Restitution and Recidivism Rates of Juvenile Offenders: Results from Four Experimental Studies." *Criminology* 24:533–552.

Schneider, P., and M. Finkelstein (eds.). 1998. *RESTTA National Directory of Restitution and Community Service Programs.* Bethesda, MD: Pacific Institute for Research and Evaluation.

Schreier, H., and J. Libow. 1993. *Hurting for Love: Munchausen by Proxy Syndrome.* Guilford, CT: Guilford.

Schuessler, K., and D. Cressey. 1950. "Personality Characteristics of Criminals." *American Journal of Sociology* 43:476–484.

Schur, E. 1971. *Labeling Deviant Behavior.* New York: Harper and Row.

———. 1973. *Radical Non-Intervention: Rethinking the Delinquency Problem.* Englewood Cliffs, NJ: Prentice-Hall.

———. 1984. *Labeling Women Deviant: Gender, Stigma, and Social Control.* New York: Random House.

Schuyten, P. 1979. "Computers and Criminals." *New York Times,* Sept. 27:D2.

Schwartz, G., and D. Merten. 1967. "The Language of Adolescence: An Anthropological Approach to Youth Culture." *American Journal of Sociology* 72:453–468.

Schwartz, M., and W. DeKeseredy. 1997. *Sexual Assault on the College Campus: The Role of Male Peer Support.* Thousand Oaks, CA: Sage.

Schwartz, M., W. DeKeseredy, D. Tait, and S. Alvi. 2001. "Male Peer Support and a Feminist Routine Activities Theory: Understanding Sexual Assault on the College Campus." *Justice Quarterly* 18:623–649.

Schwartz, M., and D. Friedrichs. 1994. "Postmodern Thought and Criminological Discontent: New Metaphors for Understanding Violence." *Criminology* 32:281–295.

Schwartz, R., and J. Skolnick. 1962. "Two Studies of Legal Stigma." *Social Problems* 10:133–142.

Schwendinger, H., and J. Schwendinger. 1970. "Defenders of Order or Guardians of Human Rights?" *Issues in Criminology* 5:123–157.

———. 1974. *The Sociologists of the Chair: A Radical Analysis of the Formative Years of North American Sociology.* New York: Basic.

———. 1985. *Adolescent Subcultures and Delinquency.* New York: Praeger.

———. 1993. "Giving Crime Prevention Top Priority." *Crime and Delinquency* 39:425–446.

Schwendinger, J., and H. Schwendinger. 1983. *Rape and Inequality.* Beverly Hills: Sage.

Scott, P. 1993. *Deep Politics and the Death of JFK.* Berkeley: University of California.

Scott, P., and J. Marshall. 1991. *Cocaine Politics: Drugs, Armies, and the CIA in Central America.* Berkeley: University of California.

Scully, D., and J. Marolla. 1984. "Convicted Rapists' Vocabulary of Motives: Excuses and Justification." *Social Problems* 31:530–544.

———. 1985. "'Riding the Bull at Gilley's': Convicted Rapists Describe the Rewards of Rape." *Social Problems* 32:251–263.

Shorrock, T. 2003. "Big Bucks in Iraq." *Nation,* Nov. 10:5–6.

Searles, P., and R. Berger (eds.). 1995. *Rape and Society: Readings on the Problem of Sexual Assault.* Boulder, CO: Westview.

Segrave, J., and D. Hastad. 1985. "Evaluating Three Models of Delinquency Causation for Males and Females: Strain Theory, Subculture Theory, and Control Theory." *Sociological Focus* 18:1–17.

Seiter, R., and K. Kadela. 2003. "Prisoner Reentry: What Works, What Does Not, and What Is Promising." *Crime and Delinquency* 49:360–381.

Sellin, T. 1938. *Culture Conflict and Crime.* New York: Social Science Research Council.

———. 1976. *Slavery and the Penal System.* New York: Elsevier.

Senn, C. 1993. "The Research on Women and Pornography: The Many Faces." In D. Russell (ed.), *Making Violence Sexy.* New York: Teachers College.

Senna, J., and L. Siegel. 1996. *Introduction to Criminal Justice.* Minneapolis: West.

Setterberg, F., and L. Shavelson. 1993. *Toxic Nation: the Fight to Save Our Communities from Chemical Contamination.* New York: Wiley.

Sewell, W. 1992. "A Theory of Structure: Duality, Agency, and Transformation." *American Journal of Sociology* 98:1–29.

Sexton, G. 1995. *Work in American Prisons: Joint Ventures With the Private Sector.* Washington, DC: U.S. Department of Justice.

Shakur, S. 1993. *Monster: The Autobiography of an L.A. Gang Member.* New York: Penguin.

Shapiro, B. 1999. "Going for the Gunmakers." *Nation,* Feb. 22:5–6.

Sharkey, J. 1988. "The Contra-Drug Tradeoff." *Common Cause,* Sept.–Oct.:23–33.

Shaw, C., and H. McKay. 1942. *Juvenile Delinquency and Urban Areas.* Chicago: University of Chicago.

Shaw, C., F. Zorbaugh, H. McKay, and L. Cottrell. 1929. *Delinquency Areas.* Chicago: University of Chicago.

Sheffield, C. 1989. "The Invisible Intruder: Women's Experiences of Obscene Phone Calls." *Gender and Society* 3:483–488.

Shelden, R. 1982. *Criminal Justice in America: A Sociological Approach.* Boston: Little, Brown.

Shelden, R., S. Tracy, and W. Brown. 2001. *Youths Gangs in American Society.* Belmont, CA: Wadsworth.

Sheldon, W. 1949. *Varieties of Delinquent Youth.* New York: Harper and Row.

Sheley, J. 1985. *America's "Crime Problem."* Belmont, CA: Wadsworth.

Sherman, L. 1986. *Citizens Killed by Big City Police, 1970–1984.* Washington, DC: Crime Control Research Corp.

———. 1992. *Policing Domestic Violence: Experiments and Dilemmas.* New York: Free Press.

———. 2001. "Reducing Gun Violence: What Works, What Doesn't, What's Promising." In F. Zimring et al. (eds.), *Perspectives on Crime and Justice.* Rockville, MD: National Institute of Justice.

Sherman, L., and R. Berk. 1984. "Specific Deterrent Effects of Arrest for Domestic Assault." *American Sociological Review* 49:261–272.

Sherman, L., P. Gartin, and M. Buerger. 1989. "Hot Spots of Predatory Crime: Routine Activities and the Criminology of Place." *Criminology* 27:27–56.

Sherman, L., and D. Smith. 1992. "Crime, Punishment, and Stake in Conformity: Legal and Informal Control of Domestic Violence." *American Sociological Review* 57:680–690.

Sherman, L., et al. 1991. "From Initial Deterrence to Long-Term Escalation: Short-Custody Arrest for Poverty Ghetto Domestic Violence." *Criminology* 29:821–850.

———. 1998. *Preventing Crime: What Works, What Doesn't, What's Promising.* Washington, DC: U.S. Department of Justice.

Shichor, D. 1997. "Private Prisons in Perspective." In M. Schwartz and L. Travis (eds.), *Corrections.* Cincinnati: Anderson.

Shichor, D., and D. Sechrest (eds.). 1996. *Three Strikes and You're Out: Vengeance as Public Policy.* Thousand Oaks, CA: Sage.

Shihadeh, E., and G. Ousey. 1996. "Metropolitan Expansion and Black Social Dislocations: The Link Between Suburbanization and Center-City Crime." *Social Forces* 75:649–666.

Shoemaker, D. 1996. *Theories of Delinquency: An Examination of Explanations of Delinquent Behavior.* New York: Oxford University.

Shoemaker, D., and J. Williams. 1987. "The Subculture of Violence and Ethnicity." *Journal of Criminal Justice* 15:461–472.

Shorrock, T. 2003. "Big Bucks in Iraq." *Nation,* Nov. 10:5–6.

Shover, N., and D. Honaker. 1992. "The Socially Bounded Decision Making of Persistent Property Offenders." *Howard Journal of Criminal Justice* 31:276–293.

Shover, N., and J. Inverarity. 1995. "Adult Segregative Confinement." In J. Sheley (ed.), *Criminology.* Belmont, CA: Wadsworth.

Sick, G. 1991. *October Surprise: America's Hostages in Iran and the Election of Ronald Reagan.* New York: Times Books.

Siegel, L. 2003. *Criminology.* Belmont, CA: Wadsworth.

Siegel, L., B. Welsh, and J. Senna. 2003. *Juvenile Delinquency: Theory, Practice, and Law.* Belmont, CA: Wadsworth.

Sikes, G. 1997. *8 Ball Chicks: A Year in the Violent World of Girl Gangs.* New York: Anchor.

Silberman, C. 1978. *Criminal Violence, Criminal Justice.* New York: Random House.

Silbert, M. 1982. "Prostitution and Sexual Assault: Summary of Results." *International Journal of Biosocial Research* 3:69–71.

Silbert, M., and A. Pines. 1981. "Sexual Child Abuse as an Antecedent to Prostitution." *Child Abuse and Neglect* 5:407–411.

Silk, L., and D. Vogel. 1976. *Ethics and Profits: The Crisis of Confidence in American Business.* New York: Simon and Schuster.

Silver, A. 1974. "The Demand for Order in Civil Society." In R. Quinney (ed.), *Criminal Justice in America.* Boston: Little, Brown.

Silverman, F. 2002. "Who Counts? Election Reform in America." PBS documentary.

Simon, D. 2002. *Elite Deviance.* Boston: Allyn and Bacon.

Simon, R. 1975. *Women and Crime.* Lexington, MA: Heath.

Simons, R., et al. 2002. "A Test of Life-Course Explanations for Stability and Change in Antisocial Behavior from Adolescence to Young Adulthood." *Criminology* 40:401–434.

Simpson, C. 1993. *The Splendid Blonde Beast: Money, Law, and Genocide in the Twentieth Century.* New York: Grove.

Simpson, S. 1989. "Feminist Theory, Crime, and Justice." *Criminology* 27:605–631.

———. 1991. "Caste, Class, and Violent Crime: Explaining Difference in Female Offending." *Criminology* 29:115–135.

———. 1992. "Corporate-Crime Deterrence and Corporate-Crime Control Policies: Views from the Inside." In K. Schlegel and D. Weisburd (eds.), *White-Collar Crime Reconsidered.* Boston: Northeastern University.

Sinclair, U. 1906. *The Jungle.* New York: New American Library.

"Single-Day Study Finds All Blacks in State Youth Prisons." 1990. *Juvenile Justice Digest* 18:5–6.

Sink, L. 1998. "DA Seeks to Restrict 'Cocaine Mother.'" *Milwaukee Journal Sentinel,* April 7:A1.

Skinner, B. 1953. *Science and Human Behavior.* New York: Macmillan.

Skipper, J., and W. McWhorter. 1981. "A Rapist Gets Caught in the Act." In J. Skipper et al. (eds.), *Deviance: Voices from the Margins.* Belmont, CA: Wadsworth.

Skogan, W. 1986. "Fear of Crime and Neighborhood Change." In A. Reiss and M. Tonry (eds.), *Communities and Crime.* Chicago: University of Chicago.

Skolnick, J. 1992. "Gangs in the Post-Industrial Ghetto." *American Prospect,* Winter:109–120.

———. 1996. "Passions of Crime." *American Prospect,* Mar.–Apr.:89–95.

Skolnick, J., R. Bluthenthal, and T. Correl. 1993. "Gang Organization and Migration." In S. Cummings and D. Monti (eds.), *Gangs.* New York: State University of New York.

Skolnick, J., and J. Fyfe. 1993. *Above the Law: Police and the Excessive Use of Force.* New York: Free Press.

Skrapec, C. 1994. "The Female Serial Killer." In H. Birch (ed.), *Moving Targets.* Berkeley: University of California.

Slate, R. (ed.). 2003. Special Issue: "Mental Health and the Criminal Justice System." *Crime and Delinquency* 49(1).

Sloan, A. 2001. "Lights Out for Enron." *Newsweek*, Dec. 10:50–51.

———. 2002. "Lucky Timing Is Good (Big Time)." *Newsweek*, Mar. 18:43.

———. 2003. "Unfair Fight." *Newsweek*, Dec. 8:44–45.

Sloane, D., and R. Potvin. 1986. "Religion and Delinquency: Cutting Through the Maze." *Social Forces* 65:85–105.

Smith, D. 1986. "The Plea Bargaining Controversy." *Journal of Criminal Law and Criminology* 77:949–967.

Smith, D., C. Visher, and L. Davidson. 1984. "Equity and Discretionary Justice: The Influence of Race on Police Arrest Decisions." *Journal of Criminal Law and Criminology* 75:234–249.

Smith, D. 1976. "Some Things That May Be More Important to Understand About Organized Crime Than Cosa Nostra." In F. Ianni and E. Reuss-Ianni (eds.), *The Crime Society*. New York: American Library.

———. 1980. "Paragons, Pariahs, and Pirates: A Spectrum-Based Theory of Enterprise." *Crime and Delinquency* 26:358–386.

Smith, M. 2000. "Capital Punishment in America." In J. Sheley (ed.), *Criminology*. Belmont, CA: Wadsworth.

"Smoking Gun." 2003. www.organizedcrime.about.com.

Sniffen, M. 1999. "FBI May Have Used Flammables at Waco Standoff." *Wisconsin State Journal*, Aug. 26:A1.

———. 2003. "First Study on Prosecutorial Misconduct Released," *Wisconsin State Journal*, June 26:A3.

Snitow, A., C. Stansell, and S. Thompson (eds.). 1983. *Powers of Desire: The Politics of Sexuality*. New York: Monthly Review.

Snow, D., S. Baker, L. Anderson, and M. Martin. 1986. "The Myth of Pervasive Mental Illness Among the Homeless." *Social Problems* 33:407–423.

Snyder, J., and T. Carlo. 1998. "Parenting Through Prison Walls." In S. Miller (ed.), *Crime Control and Women*. Thousand Oaks, CA: Sage.

Sontag, D., and D. Barry. 1997. "Using Settlements to Measure Police Abuse." *New York Times*, Sept. 17, www.nytimes.com.

Sorensen, J., J. Marquart, and D. Brock. 1993. "Factors Related to Killings of Felons by Police Officers: A Test of the Community Violence and Conflict Hypotheses." *Justice Quarterly* 10:417–440.

Sorensen, J., A. Widmayer, and F. Scarpitti. 1994. "Examining the Criminal Justice and Criminological Paradigms: An Analysis of ACJS and ASC Members." *Journal of Criminal Justice Education* 5:149–166.

Southern Poverty Law Center (SPLC). 1997. "Skinhead Violence: Klanwatch Documents a Dramatic Increase in Activity by Young Racist Gangs." *Intelligence Report*, Winter. Montgomery, AL: SPLC.

———. 2003. "U.S. Map of Hate Groups." www.tolerance.org.

Spencer, J. 2001. "Tough Love, Teen Death." *Newsweek*, July 16:28.

Sperry, P. 2003. *Crude Politics: How Bush's Oil Cronies Hijacked the War on Terrorism*. Nashville: WND.

Spitzer, E. 1999. *The New York City Police Department's "Stop and Frisk" Practices*. New York: Civil Rights Bureau. www.oag.state.ny.us.

Spitzer, S. 1975. "Toward a Marxian Theory of Deviance." *Social Problems* 22:638–651.

Spohn, C. 1990a. "Decision Making in Sexual Assault Cases: Do Black and Female Judges Make a Difference?" *Women and Criminal Justice* 2:83–105.

———. 1990b. "The Sentencing Decisions of Black and White Judges: Expected and Unexpected Similarities." *Law and Society Review* 24:1197–1216.

Spohn, C., and J. Cederblom. 1991. "Race and Disparities in Sentencing: A Test of the Liberation Hypothesis." *Justice Quarterly* 8:305–327.

Spohn, C., J. Gruhl, and S. Welch. 1987. "The Impact of the Ethnicity and Gender of Defendants on the Decision to Reject or Dismiss Felony Charges." *Criminology* 25:175–191.

Spohn, C., and J. Horney. 1992. *Rape Law Reform: A Grassroots Revolution and Its Impact*. New York: Plenum.

Spohn, C., and J. Spears. 1996. "The Effect of Offender and Victim Characteristics on Sexual Assault Case Processing Decisions." *Justice Quarterly* 13:649–679.

Stafford, M. 1984. "Gang Delinquency." In R. Meier (ed.), *Major Forms of Crime.* Beverly Hills: Sage.

Stanko, E. 1997. "Should I Stay or Should I Go? Some Thoughts on the Variants of Intimate Violence." *Violence Against Women* 3:69–35.

Stannard, D. 1992. *American Holocaust: Columbus and the Conquest of the New World.* New York: Oxford University.

Stark, R. 1984. "Religion and Conformity: Reaffirming a Sociology of Religion." *Sociological Analysis* 45:273–282.

Steadman, G. 2002. *Survey of DNA Crime Laboratories, 2001.* Washington, DC: Bureau of Justice Statistics.

Steffensmeier, D. 1978. "Crime and the Contemporary Woman: An Analysis of Changing Levels of Female Property Crime, 1960–1975." *Social Forces* 58:1080–1108.

———. 1983. "Organization Properties and Sex-Segregation in the Underworld: Building a Sociological Theory of Sex Differences in Crime." *Social Forces* 61:1010–1032.

———. 1986. *The Fence: In the Shadow of Two Worlds.* Totowa, NJ: Rowman and Littlefield.

Steffensmeier, D., and E. Allen. 1988. "Sex Disparities in Arrests by Residence, Race, and Age: As Assessment of the Gender Convergence/Crime Hypothesis." *Justice Quarterly* 5:53–80.

Steffensmeier, D., E. Allen, M. Harer, and C. Streifel. 1989. "Age and the Distribution of Crime." *American Journal of Sociology* 94:803–831.

Steffensmeier, D., and M. Cobb. 1981. "Sex Differences in Urban Arrest Patterns, 1934–79." *Social Problems* 29:37–50.

Steffensmeier, D., C. Streifel, and M. Harer. 1987. "Relative Cohort Size and Youth Crime in the United States, 1953–1984." *American Sociological Review* 52:702–710.

Steffensmeier, D., J. Ulmer, and J. Kramer. 1998. "The Interaction of Race, Gender, and Age in Criminal Sentencing: The Punishment Cost of Being Young, Black, and Male." *Criminology* 36:763–797.

Stein, J. 2002. "The New Politics of Pot." *Time,* Nov. 4:56–66.

Steinberg, D. 1990. "The Roots of Pornography." In M. Kimmel (ed.), *Men Confront Pornography.* New York: Crown.

Steinem, G. 1980. "Erotica and Pornography: A Clear and Present Difference." In L. Lederer (ed.), *Take Back the Night.* New York: Morrow.

———. 1993. "The Real Linda Lovelace"" In D. Russell (ed.), *Making Violence Sexy.* New York: Teachers College.

———. 1999. "Supremacy Crimes." *Ms.*, Aug.–Sept.:44–47.

Steinschneider, A. 1972. "Prolonged Apnea and the Sudden Infant Death Syndrome: Clinical and Laboratory Observations." *Pediatrics* 50:646–654.

Stephan, J., and J. Karberg. 2003. *Census of State and Federal Correctional Facilities, 2000.* Washington, DC: Bureau of Justice Statistics.

Sterling, E. 1991. "Drug Laws and Snitching: A Primer." *Frontline.* www.pubs.org.

Stevens, D. 2003. *Applied Community Policing in the Twenty-First Century.* Boston: Allyn and Bacon.

Stevens, S. 1999. "Big Brother at Work." *Wisconsin State Journal,* Oct. 10:1B, 7B.

Stewart, J. 1991. *Den of Thieves.* New York: Simon and Schuster.

———. 1996. *Blood Sport: The President and His Adversaries.* New York: Simon and Schuster.

Stock, W. 1995. "The Effects of Pornography on Women." In L. Lederer and R. Delgado (eds.), *The Price We Pay.* New York: Hill and Wang.

Stojkovic, S. 1990. "Accounts of Prison Work: Corrections Officers' Portrayals of Their Work Worlds." In *Perspectives on Social Problems,* vol. 2. Greenwich, CT: JAI.

Stone, C. 1975. *Where the Law Ends: The Social Control of Corporate Behavior.* Prospect Heights, IL: Waveland.

Stoneall, L. 1997. "Rural Gang Origins: A Wisconsin Case Study." *Sociological Imagination* 34:45–58.

Storaska, F. 1975. *How to Say No to a Rapist and Survive.* New York: Warner.

Stout, D. 1995. "Black Businessman Ponders Ordeal as a Suspect." *New York Times,* May 9:B1.

Strasburger, V., and B. Wilson. 2002. *Children, Adolescents, and the Media.* Thousand Oaks, CA: Sage.

Streib, V. 1998. "Executing Women, Children, and the Retarded: Second Class Citizens in Capital Punishment." In J. Acker et al. (eds.), *America's Experiment with Capital Punishment.* Durham, NC: Carolina Academic.

Stretesky, P., and M. Lynch. 1999. "Corporate Environmental Violence and Racism." *Crime, Law and Social Change* 30:163–184.

Strom, K., S. Smith, and H. Synder. 1998. *Juvenile Felony Defendants in Criminal Courts.* Washington, DC: U.S. Department of Justice.

Subin, H. 1993. "The Criminal Lawyer's 'Different Mission': Reflections on the 'Right' to Present a False Case." In M. Katsh (ed.), *Taking Sides: Clashing Views on Controversial Legal Issues.* Guilford, CT: Dushkin.

Sullivan, C. 1997. "Societal Collusion and Culpability in Intimate Male Violence: The Impact of Community Response Toward Women with Abusive Partners." In A. Cardarelli (ed.), *Violence Between Intimate Partners.* Boston: Allyn and Bacon.

Sullivan, D., L. Tifft, and P. Cordella. 1998. "The Phenomenon of Restorative Justice." *Contemporary Justice Review* 1:7–20.

Sullivan, M. 1989. *Getting Paid: Youth Crime and Work in the Inner City.* Ithaca: Cornell University.

Sundahl, D. 1987. "Stripper." In F. Delacoste and P. Alexander (eds.), *Sex Work.* Pittsburgh: Cleis.

Surette, R. 1998. *Media, Crime, and Criminal Justice.* Belmont, CA: Wadsworth.

Sutherland, E. 1937. *The Professional Thief.* Chicago: University of Chicago.

———. 1947. *Principles of Criminology.* Philadelphia: Lippincott.

———. 1949. *White Collar Crime.* New York: Dryden.

———. 1983. *White Collar Crime: The Uncut Version.* New Haven: Yale University.

Swasy, A. 1993. *Soap Opera: The Inside Story of Procter & Gamble.* New York: Times Books.

Sweezy, P. 1953. *The Present as History.* New York: Monthly Review.

Sykes, G. 1958. *The Society of Captives: A Study of a Maximum Security Prison.* Princeton: Princeton University.

Sykes, G., and F. Cullen. 1992. *Criminology.* Fort Worth: Harcourt Brace Jovanovich.

Sykes, G., and D. Matza. 1957. "Techniques of Neutralization: A Theory of Delinquency." *American Sociological Review* 22:664–670.

Szasz, A. 1986a. "Corporations, Organized Crime, and the Disposal of Hazardous Waste: An Examination of the Making of a Criminogenic Regulatory Structure." *Criminology* 24:1–27.

———. 1986b. "The Process and Significance of Political Scandals: A Comparison of Watergate and the 'Sewergate' Episode at the Environmental Protection Agency." *Social Problems* 33:202–217.

Takata, S., and R. Zevitz. 1990. "Divergent Perceptions of Group Delinquency in a Midwestern Community: Racine's Gang Problem." *Youth and Society* 21:282–305.

Tanenbaum, L. 2000. *Slut! Growing Up Female with a Bad Reputation.* New York: HarperCollins.

Tanner, R. 2002. "False Confessions May be Frequent." *Wisconsin State Journal,* Dec. 7:A4.

———. 2003. "Forensic Scientists Under Scrutiny After Rash of Errors." *Wisconsin State Journal,* July 7:A3.

Tappan, P. 1947. "Who Is the Criminal?" *American Sociological Review* 12:96–102.

Task Force on Organized Crime. 1967. *Task Force Report: Organized Crime.* Washington, DC: U.S. Government Printing Office.

Tavris, C. 1992. *The Mismeasure of Woman.* New York: Simon and Schuster.

Taylor, C. 1990. *Dangerous Society.* East Lansing: Michigan State University.

———. 1993. *Girls, Gangs, Women, and Drugs.* East Lansing: Michigan State University.

Taylor, D. 2004 "How Safe Is America?" In P. Hill Collins (ed.), *Race, Class, and Gender.* Belmont, CA: Wadsworth.

Taylor, R., and J. Covington. 1988. "Neighborhood Changes in Ecology and Violence." *Criminology* 26:553–589.

Taylor, R., E. Fritsch, and T. Caeti. 1998. "Core Challenges Facing Community Policing: The Emperor *Still* Has No Clothes." *ACJS Today* 27:1, 3–5.

Taylor Greene, H. 1994. "Black Perspectives on Police Brutality." In A. Sulton (ed.), *African-American Perspectives on Crime Causation, Criminal Justice, and Crime Prevention.* Englewood, CO: Sulton.

———. 2003. "Do African American Police Make a Difference?" In M. Free (ed.), *Racial Issues in Criminal Justice.* Westport, CT: Praeger.

Taylor Greene, H., and A. del Carmen. 2002. "Female Police Officers in Texas: Perceptions of Colleagues and Stress." *Policing* 25:385–398.

Teixeira, R. 2002. "Is the Big-Business Era Over?" *American Prospect,* Aug. 26:12–13.

Tennenbaum, D. 1977. "Personality and Criminality: A Summary and Implications of the Literature." *Journal of Criminal Justice* 5:225–235.

Tewksbury, W. 1994. "The Ordeal as a Vehicle for Divine Intervention in Medieval

Europe." In J. Bonsignore et al. (eds.), *Before the Law.* Boston: Houghton Mifflin.

Texeira, M. 2002. "'Who Protects and Serves Me?' A Case Study of Sexual Harassment of African American Women in One U.S. Law Enforcement Agency." *Gender and Society* 16:524–545.

Theilgaard, A. 1984. "A Psychological Study of the Personalities of XYY- and XXY-Men." *Acta Psychiatrica Scandinavia* 69:1–133.

Thistlethwaite, A., J. Wooldredge, and D. Gibbs. 1998. "Severity of Dispositions and Domestic Violence Reduction." *Crime and Delinquency* 44:388–398.

Thomas, E. 2003. "The War Over Gay Marriage." *Newsweek,* July 7:39–44.

Thomas, K. 1998. "FGM Watch." *Ms., Mar.–Apr.:28.

Thomas, W. 1923. *The Unadjusted Girl.* New York: Harper and Row.

Thompson, C. 1998. "The Psycho-Femme Thriller: A Woman's Place." In *Perspectives on Social Problems,* vol. 10. Stamford, CT: JAI.

Thomson, E. 1997. "Deterrence Versus Brutalization: The Case of Arizona." *Homicide Studies* 1:110–128.

Thoreau, H. 1969. "Civil Disobedience." In H. Bedau (ed.), *Civil Disobedience.* New York: Pegasus.

Thornberry, T. 1987. "Toward an Interactional Theory of Delinquency." *Criminology* 25:863–891.

Thornberry, T., and R. Christenson. 1984. "Unemployment and Criminal Involvement: An Investigation of Reciprocal Causal Structures." *American Sociological Review* 49:398–411.

Thornberry, T., and M. Farnworth. 1982. "Social Correlates of Criminal Involvement: Further Evidence on the Relationship Between Social Status and Criminal Behavior." *American Sociological Review* 47:505–518.

Thorne, B. 1993. *Gender Play: Girls and Boys in School.* New Brunswick, NJ: Rutgers University.

Thorne, B., and Z. Luria. 1986. "Sexuality and Gender in Children's Daily Worlds." *Social Problems* 33:176–190.

Thottam, J. 2003. "Why They're Picking on Martha." *Time,* June 16:44–46.

Thrasher, F. 1927. *The Gang.* Chicago: University of Chicago.

Tienda, M., and H. Stier. 1996. "Generating Labor Market Inequality: Employment Opportunities and the Accumulation of Disadvantage." *Social Problems* 43:147–165.

Tierney, J. 1994. "Porn, the Low-Slung Engine of Progress." *New York Times,* Jan. 9, Section 1:18.

Tigges, L., I. Browne, and G. Green. 1998. "Social Isolation of the Urban Poor: Race, Class, and Neighborhood Effects on Social Resources." *Sociological Quarterly* 39:53–77.

Tilly, C. 1989. "Collective Violence in European Perspective." In T. Gurr (ed.), *Violence in America.* Newbury Park, CA: Sage.

Tittle, C., and R. Meier. 1990. "Specifying the SES/Delinquency Relationship." *Criminology* 28:271–299.

Tittle, C., W. Villemez, and D. Smith. 1978. "The Myth of Social Class and Criminality: An Empirical Assessment of the Empirical Evidence." *American Sociological Review* 43:643–656.

Tittle, C., and M. Welch. 1983. "Religiosity and Deviance: Toward a Contingency Theory of Constraining Effects." *Social Forces* 61:53–80.

Titunik, N. 1992. "When Worlds Collide." *Isthmus,* May 1–7:1, 8–9.

Tjaden, P., and N. Thoennes. 1998a. *Prevalence, Incidence, and Consequences of Violence Against Women.* Washington, DC: U.S. Department of Justice.

————. 1998b. *Stalking in America: Findings from the National Violence Against Women Survey.* Washington, DC: U.S. Department of Justice.

Toch, H., and J. Grant. 1982. *Reforming Human Services: Change Through Participation.* Beverly Hills: Sage.

Toch, H., and J. Klofas. 1982. "Alienation and Desire for Job Enrichment Among Corrections Officers." *Federal Probation* 46:35–44.

Toffler, B. 2003. *Final Accounting: Ambition, Greed, and the Fall of Arthur Andersen.* New York: Broadway.

Tollet, T., and B. Close. 1991. "The Overrepresentation of Blacks in Florida's Juvenile Justice System." In M. Lynch and E. Patterson (eds.), *Race and Criminal Justice.* Albany, NY: Harrow and Heston.

Tomlinson, T., and D. Sears. 1967. *Los Angeles Riot Study: Negro Attitudes Toward the Riot.* Los Angeles: Institute of Government and Public Affairs, University of California.

Tonry, M. 1995. *Malign Neglect: Race, Crime, and Punishment in America.* New York: Oxford University.

————. 1999. "Why Are U.S. Incarceration Rates So High?" *Crime and Delinquency* 1999:419–437.

Toobin, J. 1994. "An Incendiary Defense." *New Yorker,* July 11:56–59.

Tracy, P., M. Wolfgang, and R. Figlio. 1990. *Delinquency Careers in Two Birth Cohorts.* New York: Plenum.

Travis, J., and J. Petersilia. 2001. "Reentry Reconsidered: A New Look at an Old Question." *Crime and Delinquency* 47:291–313.

Tremblay, P., and C. Morselli. 2000. "Patterns of Criminal Achievement: Wilson and Abrahamse Revisited." *Criminology* 38:633–659.

Trojanowicz, R., M. Morash, and P. Schram. 2001. *Juvenile Delinquency: Concepts and Controls.* Englewood Cliffs, NJ: Prentice-Hall.

Truong, T. 1990. *Sex, Money, and Morality: Prostitution and Tourism in Southeast Asia.* London: Zed.

Tunnell, K. 1992. *Choosing Crime: The Criminal Calculus of Property Offenders.* Chicago: Nelson-Hall.

Turk, A. 1969. *Criminality and the Legal Order.* Chicago: Rand McNally.

————. 1975. "Prospects and Pitfalls for Radical Criminology." *Crime and Social Justice* 4:41–42.

Turman, K. 2001. *Understanding DNA Evidence: A Guide for Victim Services Providers.* Washington, DC: U.S. Department of Justice.

Turque, B., and F. Chideya. 1991. "The Exorcism of Gina." *Newsweek,* Apr. 15:62.

Tyler, G. (ed.). 1967. *Organized Crime in America.* Ann Arbor: University of Michigan.

Uggen, C. 1999. "Ex-Offenders and the Conformist Alternative: A Job Quality Model of Work and Crime." *Social Problems* 46:127–151.

Uggen, C., and J. Manza. 2002. "Democratic Contraction? The Political Consequences of Felon Disenfranchisement in the United States." *American Sociological Review* 67:777–803.

Uhlman, T. 1978. "Black Elite Decision Making: The Case of Trial Judges." *American Journal of Political Science* 22:884–895.

Umbreit, M. 1994. "Victim Empowerment Through Mediation: The Impact of Victim Offender Mediation in Four Cities." *Perspectives,* Summer:25–28.

Unnever, J., and L. Hembroff. 1988. "The Prediction of Racial/Ethnic Sentencing Disparities: An Expectation States Approach." *Journal of Research in Crime and Delinquency* 25:53–82.

U.S. Department of Commerce. 2002. *Statistical Abstract of the United States 2002.* Washington, DC: U.S. Government Printing Office.

U.S. Department of Justice. 1997. *Criminal Victimization in the United States 1994.* Washington, DC: Bureau of Justice Statistics.

———. 1998. "Press Release on Police Corruption." Washington, DC: FBI National Press Office, Jan.21, www.fbi.gov.

———. 2000. *Juvenile Justice.* Vol. 7, No. 1. Washington, DC: Office of Juvenile Justice and Delinquency Prevention.

U.S. News and World Report. 1996a. "A Marijuana Mecca Rethinks Its Drug Laws." Apr. 15:15.

———. 1996b. "The Unabomber's Worldview." Apr. 15:35.

Van Boven, S., and A. Gesalman. 1998. "A Fatal Ride in the Night." *Newsweek,* June 22:33.

Van Maanen, J. 1995. "Kinsmen in Repose: Occupational Perspectives of Patrolmen." In V. Kappeler (ed.), *The Police and Society.* Prospect Heights, IL: Waveland.

Van Voorhis, P., F. Cullen, B. Link, and N. Wolfe. 1991. "The Impact of Race and Gender on Correctional Officers' Orientation to the Integrated Environment." *Journal of Research on Crime and Delinquency* 28:472–500.

Vance, C. (ed.). 1984. *Pleasure and Danger: Exploring Female Sexuality.* Boston: Routledge and Kegan Paul.

Vandal, G. 1991. "'Bloody Caddo': White Violence Against Blacks in a Louisiana Parish, 1865–1876." *Journal of Social History* 25:373–388.

Vaughan, D. 1982. "Toward Understanding Unlawful Organizational Behavior." *Michigan Law Review* 80:1377–1402.

———. 1983. *Controlling Unlawful Organizational Behavior.* Chicago: University of Chicago.

Venkatesh, S. 1997. "The Social Organization of Street Gang Activity in an Urban Ghetto." *American Journal of Sociology* 103:82–111.

Verhovek, S. 1998. "Tucker Executed: Last-Minute Appeals Fail in Texas, Washington." *Wisconsin State Journal,* Feb. 4:1–3A.

Vigil, J. 1988. *Barrio Gangs.* Austin: University of Texas.

Vincentnathan, S. 1995. "Societal Reaction and Secondary Deviance in Culture and Society: The United States and Japan." In F. Adler and W. Laufer (eds.), *The Legacy of Anomie Theory.* New Brunswick, NJ: Transaction.

Visher, C. 1983. "Gender, Police Arrest Decisions, and Notions of Chivalry." *Criminology* 21:5–28.

Vizzard, W. 2000. *Shots in the Dark: The Policy, Politics, and Symbolism of Gun Control.* Lanham, MD: Rowman and Littlefield.

Vold, G., T. Bernard, and J. Snipes. 1998. *Theoretical Criminology.* New York: Oxford University.

von Hirsch, A. 1976. *Doing Justice: The Choice of Punishments.* New York: Hill and Wang.

Waegel, W. 1989. *Delinquency and Juvenile Control.* Englewood Cliffs, NJ: Prentice-Hall.

Waldo, G., and S. Dinitz. 1967. "Personality Attributes of the Criminal: An Analysis of Research Studies," *Journal of Research on Crime and Delinquency* 4:185–201.

Walker, J. 1996. "Police and Correctional Use of Force: Legal and Policy Standards and Implications." *Crime and Delinquency* 42:144–156.

Walker, L. 1979. *The Battered Woman.* New York: Harper and Row.

Walker, S. 1992. *The Police in America.* New York: McGraw-Hill.

————. 2001. *Sense and Nonsense About Crime: A Policy Guide*. Belmont, CA: Wadsworth.

Walker, S., C. Spohn, and M. Delone. 2004. *The Color of Justice: Race, Ethnicity, and Crime in America*. Belmont, CA: Wadsworth.

Wallace, D., and D. Humphries. 1993. "Urban Crime and Capitalist Accumulation, 1950–1971." In D. Greenberg (ed.), *Crime and Capitalism*. Philadelphia: Temple University.

Wallace, H. 1993. "Mandatory Minimums and the Betrayal of Sentencing Reform: A Legislative Dr. Jekyll and Mr. Hyde." *Federal Probation* 57:9–19.

Wallace, H. 1999. *Family Violence: Legal, Medical, and Social Perspectives*. Boston: Allyn and Bacon.

Walsh, A. 1987. "The Sexual Stratification Hypothesis and Sexual Assault in Light of the Changing Conceptions of Race." *Criminology* 25:153–173.

Walsh, D. 1980. *Break-Ins: Burglary from Private Houses*. London: Constable.

Walters, G. 1992. "A Meta-Analysis of the Gene-Crime Relationship." *Criminology* 30:595–613.

Walters, G., and T. White. 1989. "Heredity and Crime: Bad Genes or Bad Research?" *Criminology* 27:455–485.

Walther, L., and J. Perry. 1997. "The Vermont Reparative Probation Program." *ICCA Journal on Community Corrections* 8:26–34.

Wambaugh, J. 1975. *The Choirboys*. New York: Dell.

Warner, B. 1997. "Community Characteristics and the Recording of Crime: Police Recording of Citizens' Complaints of Burglary and Assault." *Justice Quarterly* 14:631–650.

Warr, M. 1998. "Life-Course Transitions and Desistance from Crime." *Criminology* 36:183–216.

————. 2000. "Public Perceptions of and Reactions to Crime." In J. Sheley (ed.), *Criminology*. Belmont, CA: Wadsworth.

Washington, W. 2002. "Child Porn Rise, Internet Linked." *Wisconsin State Journal*, Mar. 13:A5.

Waskow, A. 1967. *From Race Riot to Sit-In*. Garden City, NY: Doubleday.

Waterston, A. 1993. *Street Addicts in the Political Economy*. Philadelphia: Temple University.

Websdale, N. 1995. "An Ethnographic Assessment of the Policing of Domestic Violence in Rural Eastern Kentucky." *Social Justice* 22:102–122.

Webster, B., and M. McCampbell. 1992. "International Money Laundering: Research and Investigation Join Forces." *NIJ Research in Brief*, Sept.:1–8.

Weis, K., and S. Borges. 1973. "Victimology and Rape: The Case of the Legitimate Victim." *Issues in Criminology* 8:71–115.

Weiss, M. 1984. *Double Play: The San Francisco City Hall Killings*. Reading, MA: Addison-Wesley.

Weitz, R. 1996. *The Sociology of Health, Illness, and Health Care*. Belmont, CA: Wadsworth.

Welch, S., M. Combs, and J. Gruhl. 1988. "Do Black Judges Make a Difference?" *American Journal of Political Science* 32:126–136.

Welch, S., J. Gruhl, and C. Spohn. 1984. "Sentencing: The Influence of Alternative Measures of Prior Record." *Criminology* 22:215–277.

Welsh, B., and D. Farrington. 1999. "Value for Money? A Review of the Costs and Benefits of Situational Crime Prevention." *British Journal of Criminology* 39:345–369.

Werthman, C., and I. Piliavin. 1967. "Gang Members and the Police." In D. Bordua (ed.), *The Police*. New York: Wiley.

West, C. 1994. *Race Matters.* Boston: Beacon.

West, C., and D. Zimmerman. 1987. "Doing Gender." *Gender and Society* 1:125–151.

West, D., and B. de Villiers. 1993. *Male Prostitution.* New York: Harrington Park.

Westervelt, S., and J. Humphrey (eds.). 2001. *Wrongly Convicted: Perspectives on Failed Justice.* New Brunswick, NJ: Rutgers University.

Wheeler, S. 1992. "The Problem of White-Collar Motivation." In K. Schlegel and D. Weisburd (eds.), *White-Collar Crime Reconsidered.* Boston: Northeastern University.

Wheeler, S., and M. Rothman. 1982. "The Organization as Weapon in White Collar Crime." *Michigan Law Review* 80:1403–1426.

White, H., R. Pandina, and R. LaGrange. 1987. "Longitudinal Predictors of Serious Substance Use and Delinquency." *Criminology* 25:715–740.

White, J. 2003. *Terrorism: An Introduction.* Belmont, CA: Wadsworth.

White, M. 2001. "Controlling Police Decisions to Use Deadly Force: Reexamining the Importance of Administrative Policy." *Crime and Delinquency* 47:131–151.

Whitehead, J., and S. Lab. 1989. "A Meta-Analysis of Juvenile Correctional Treatment." *Journal of Research in Crime and Delinquency* 26:276–295.

Whitehead, J., and C. Lindquist. 1989. "Determinants of Correctional Officers' Professional Orientation." *Justice Quarterly* 6:69–87.

Widom, C. 1989. "Child Abuse, Neglect, and Violent Criminal Behavior." *Criminology* 27:251–271.

Widom, C., and M. Ames. 1984. "Criminal Consequences of Childhood Sexual Victimization." *Child Abuse and Neglect* 18:303–318.

Wilchins, R. 2002. "Teenage Terrorism." *Advocate,* Oct. 15:72.

———. 2003. "The Problem with 'Passing.'" *Advocate,* May 13:72.

Wilkes, P. 1989. "The Tough Job of Teaching Ethics." *New York Times,* Jan. 22:E1, 24.

Will, G. 2003. "Three Strikes and You're In." *Newsweek,* Mar. 17:74.

Williams, J. 1987. *Psychology of Women.* New York: Norton.

Williams, K. 1984. "Economic Sources of Homicide: Reestimating the Effects of Poverty and Inequality." *American Sociological Review* 49:283–289.

Williams, K., and R. Hawkins. 1986. "Perceptual Research on General Deterrence: A Critical Review." *Law and Society Review* 20:211–236.

Williams, L. 1988. "Police Officers Tell of Strains of Living as a 'Black in Blue.'" *New York Times,* Feb. 14:1, 26.

Williams, L., and K. Holmes. 1981. *The Second Assault: Rape and Public Attitudes.* Westport, CT: Greenwood.

Williams, M. 2003. "The Effects of Pretrial Detention on Imprisonment Decisions." *Criminal Justice Review* 28:299–316.

Williams, M. (ed.). 2003. *The Terrorist Attack on America.* Farmington Hills, MI: Greenhaven.

Williams, P. 1999a. "The Auguries of Innocence." *Nation,* May 24:9.

———. 1999b. "Smart Bombs." *Nation,* June 7:10.

Williams, T. 1992. *Crackhouse: Notes from the End of the Line.* New York: Addison-Wesley.

Williams, T., and W. Kornblum. 1985. *Growing Up Poor.* Lexington, MA: Lexington.

Williams, W. 1996. *Taking Back Our Streets: Fighting Crime in America.* New York: Scribner.

Wilson, C. 1984. "The Ripper Revealed." *Time Out,* Apr.:19–25.

Wilson, J. 1968. *Varieties of Police Behavior: The Management of Law and Order in Eight Communities.* Cambridge: Harvard University.

———. 1975. *Thinking About Crime.* New York: Basic.

Wilson, J., and R. Herrnstein. 1985. *Crime and Human Nature.* New York: Simon and Schuster.

Wilson, J., and G. Kelling. 1996. "Broken Windows: The Police and Neighborhood Safety." In G. Bridges et al. (eds.), *Criminal Justice.* Thousand Oaks, CA: Pine Forge.

Wilson, W. 1987. *The Truly Disadvantaged: The Inner City, the Underclass, and Public Policy.* Chicago: University of Chicago.

———. 1991. "Studying Inner-City Social Dislocations: The Challenge of Public Agenda Research." *American Sociological Review* 56:1–14.

Wisconsin State Journal. 1998a. "Illinois Organization Pleads Guilty to Fraud." July 17:2A.

———. 1998b. "Newspaper: Prosecutors Lie, Cheat with Impunity." Nov. 11:2A.

———. 1999a. "Assaults on U.S. Schools." Apr. 21:3A.

———. 1999b. "Shootings in U.S. Schools." May 21:2A.

———. 1999c. "Washington." May 20:2A.

———. 2002a. "Felons Not Hindered by Gun Laws." Jan. 17:A3.

———. 2002b. "Ford Settles Claims over Rollover Risks." Dec. 24:C9–10.

———. 2002c. "More Gays, Lesbians, Kicked Out of Military." Mar. 14:A3.

———. 2004. "Trade Center Toll Settles at 2,749." Jan. 24:A3.

Witt, K. 1994. "Many in U.S. Back Singapore's Plan to Flog American Youth." *New York Times,* Apr. 5:A4.

Wolfe, A. 1973. *The Seamy Side of Democracy: Repression in America.* New York: David McKay.

Wolfgang, M. 1972. "Cesare Lombroso." In H. Mannheim (ed.), *Pioneers in Criminology.* Montclair, NJ: Patterson Smith.

Wolfgang, M., and F. Ferracuti. 1967. *The Subculture of Violence.* London: Tavistock.

Wolfgang, M., R. Figlio, and T. Sellin. 1972. *Delinquency in a Birth Cohort.* Chicago: University of Chicago.

Wonders, N. 1999. "Postmodern Feminist Criminology and Social Justice." In B. Arrigo (ed.), *Social Justice/Criminal Justice.* Belmont, CA: Wadsworth.

Wood, P., W. Gove, J. Wilson, and J. Cochran. 1997. "Nonsocial Reinforcement and Habitual Criminal Conduct: An Extension of Learning Theory." *Criminology* 35:335–366.

Wooden, W., and R. Blazak. 2001. *Renegade Kids, Suburban Outlaws: From Youth Culture to Delinquency.* Belmont, CA: Wadsworth.

Woodward, B. 1999. *Shadow: Five Presidents and the Legacy of Watergate.* New York: Touchstone.

Woodward, K. 1998. "The New Holy War." *Newsweek,* June 1:26–29.

Wooldredge, J., and K. Masters. 1993. "Confronting Problems Faced by Pregnant Inmates in State Prisons." *Crime and Delinquency* 39:195–203.

Wozniak, J. 2002. "Toward a Theoretical Model of Peacemaking Criminology: An Essay in Honor of Richard Quinney." *Crime and Delinquency* 48:204–231.

Wriggens, J. 1995. "Rape, Racism, and the Law." In P. Searles and R. Berger (eds.), *Rape and Society.* Boulder, CO: Westview.

Wright, B. 1973. "A Black Broods on Black Judges." *Judicature* 57:22–25.

Wright, B., A. Caspi, T. Moffitt, R. Miech, and P. Silva. 1999. "Reconsidering the Relationship Between SES and Delinquency: Causation but Not Correlation." *Criminology* 37:175–194.

Wright, E., C. Costello, D. Hachen, and J. Sprague. 1982. "The American Class Structure." *American Sociological Review* 47:709–726.

Wright, J., and F. Cullen. 2001. "Parental Efficacy and Delinquent Behavior: Do Control and Support Matter?" *Criminology* 39:677–705.

Wright, J., and P. Rossi. 1986. *Armed and Considered Dangerous: A Survey of Felons and Their Firearms.* New York: Aldine de Gruyter.

Wright, J., and T. Vail. 2000. "The Guns-Crime Connection." In J. Sheley (ed.), *Criminology.* Belmont, CA: Wadsworth.

Wright, L. 1994. "One Drop of Blood." *New Yorker,* July 25:46–55.

Wright, R., and S. Decker. 1994. *Burglars on the Job: Street Life and Residential Break-Ins.* Boston: Northeastern University.

Wyre, R. 1992. "Pornography and Sexual Violence: Working With Sexual Offenders." In C. Itzin (ed.), *Pornography.* New York: Oxford University.

Yeager, P. 1987. "Structural Bias in Regulatory Law Enforcement: The Case of the U.S. Environmental Protection Agency." *Social Problems* 34:330–344.

Yochelson, S., and S. Samenow. 1976, 1977. *The Criminal Personality,* vols. 1–2. New York: Jason Aronson.

Zatz, M. 1987. "Chicano Youth Gangs and Crime: The Creation of a Moral Panic." *Contemporary Crises* 11:129–158.

Zatz, N. 1997. "Sex Work/Sex Act: Law, Labor, and Desire in Constructions of Prostitution." *Signs* 22:277–308.

Zehr, H., and H. Mika. 1998. "Fundamental Concepts of Restorative Justice." *Contemporary Justice Review* 1:47–55.

Zietz, D. 1981. *Women Who Embezzle or Defraud: A Study of Convicted Felons.* New York: Praeger.

Zillmann, D., J. Weaver, N. Mundorf, and C. Aust. 1986. "Effects of Opposite-Gender Companion's Affect to Horror on Distress, Delight, and Attraction." *Journal of Personality and Social Psychology* 51:586–594.

Zimmer, L. 1986. *Women Guarding Men.* Chicago: University of Chicago.

Zimring, F., and R. Frase. 1980. *The Criminal Justice System.* Boston: Little, Brown.

Zimring, F., and G. Hawkins. 1992. *The Search for Rational Drug Control.* Cambridge, UK: Cambridge University.

———. 1997. *Crime Is Not the Problem: Lethal Violence in America.* New York: Oxford University.

Zingraff, M., J. Leiter, K. Myers, and M. Johnson. 1993. "Child Maltreatment and Youthful Problem Behavior." *Criminology* 31:173–202.

Zoll, R. 2004a. "4% of Clerics Accused Since 1950." *Wisconsin State Journal*, Feb. 27:A3.

———. 2004b. "Priest-Abuse Claims Exceed Estimates." *Wisconsin State Journal*, Feb. 11:A1, A7.

Index

About the Book

Why is the composition of the prison population substantially different from that of the larger society? Why is corporate crime so neglected by the criminal justice system? What have been the results of the "war on drugs"? *Crime, Justice, and Society* explores these and other significant questions in a compelling introduction to criminology.

Highlighting issues of class, race, ethnicity, and gender, the authors present the study of crime and criminals in an accessible manner. While innovative, their book is organized as a core text for standard introductory criminology courses.

The many outstanding features of this new edition include:

- Strong theoretical coverage, enhanced by a new chapter on critical theory.
- Discussion of a comprehensive range of topics—from organized crime, street crime, and sexual violence to political crime, corporate fraud, and police profiling.
- Real-life examples, conveying the experiences of offenders, victims, and criminal justice personnel.
- An approach that facilitates critical thinking.

Ronald J. Berger is professor of sociology and coordinator of the Criminal Justice Program at the University of Wisconsin–Whitewater. He has published ten books, including *The Sociology of Juvenile Delinquency, Rape and Society* (with P. Searles), *Feminism and Pornography* (with P. Searles and C. Cottle), *Fathoming the Holocaust,* and *Storytelling Sociology* (with R. Quinney).

Marvin D. Free Jr. is professor of sociology at the University of Wisconsin–Whitewater. His previous books include *Racial Issues in*

Criminal Justice and *African Americans and the Criminal Justice System.*

Patricia Searles is professor of sociology and women's studies and chair of the Department of Sociology at the University of Wisconsin–Whitewater. Her previous books include *Rape and Society* (with R. Berger) and *Feminism and Pornography* (with R. Berger and C. Cottle).